Literacy Teaching and Learning
Current Issues and Trends

Zhihui Fang
University of Florida

PEARSON

Merrill
Prentice Hall

Upper Saddle River, New Jersey
Columbus, Ohio

Library of Congress Cataloging-in-Publication Data

Literacy teaching and learning: current issues and trends / Zhihui Fang, editor/author.
    p. cm.
    Includes bibliographical references.
    ISBN 0-13-118178-5
    1. Language arts. 2. Reading. I. Fang, Zhihui.
LB1576.L5594 2005
372.6—dc22   2004044912

Vice President and Executive Publisher: *Jeffery W. Johnston*
Senior Editor: *Linda Ashe Montgomery*
Editorial Assistant: *Laura J. Weaver*
Production Editor: *Linda Hillis Bayma*
Production Manager: *Susan Hannahs*
Production Coordinator: *Tempe Goodhue/nSight, Inc.*
Design Coordinator: *Diane C. Lorenzo*
Cover Designer: *Terry Rohrbach*
Cover image: *Corbis*
Director of Marketing: *Ann Castel Davis*
Marketing Manager: *Darcy Betts Prybella*
Marketing Coordinator: *Tyra Poole*

This book was set in Century Schoolbook by Laserwords Pvt. Ltd. It was printed and bound by Courier Kendallville, Inc. The cover was printed by The Lehigh Press, Inc.

Pearson Prentice Hall™ is a trademark of Pearson Education, Inc.
Pearson® is a registered trademark of Pearson plc
Prentice Hall® is a registered trademark of Pearson Education, Inc.
Merrill® is a registered trademark of Pearson Education, Inc.

Pearson Education Ltd.
Pearson Education Australia Pty. Limited
Pearson Education Singapore, Pte. Ltd.
Pearson Education North Asia Ltd.
Pearson Education Canada, Ltd
Pearson Educación de Mexico, S.A. de C.V.
Pearson Education-Japan
Pearson Education Malaysia, Pte. Ltd.

10 9 8 7 6 5 4 3 2 1
ISBN 0-13-118178-5

To my students and those who choose to enter the world's most challenging profession—teaching!

Preface

Literacy teaching and learning is a dynamic field that shapes and is shaped by social, cultural, political, economic, scientific, and technological developments. As new frontiers are explored, old territories are reexamined, new horizons arise, and fresh perspectives emerge. What was once a rather narrow discipline is now a vast landscape ripe for unprecedented interdisciplinary inquiries. This book offers a glimpse into this broad landscape by presenting major issues and trends in literacy education at the turn of the new millennium.

The 30 articles included in this text were carefully selected to provide a balanced, up-to-date perspective on major topics of current significance to literacy educators. They come from nearly 20 different journal and book sources published around the world in the past 15 years or so. They were written by noted scholars with diverse perspectives (e.g., psychological, sociocultural, constructivist, linguistic, critical), from a variety of academic disciplines (e.g., literacy education, educational psychology, special education, linguistics, English as a second language), and in different countries (e.g., the United States, Britain, Australia). These readings address a myriad of major topics that are of both theoretical and practical significance in literacy teaching and learning today. They reflect the complexity, diversity, fertility, and vitality of the field of literacy education.

Organization of Text

The book is divided into 10 sections. Each section contains an Introduction, 3 thematically related articles, a Study Guide, several Inquiry Projects, and Further Reading. The Introduction situates the Section readings within the broader context of contemporary literacy education and provides a summary for each of the articles. The Study Guide, which follows the readings, is designed to assist readers in digesting and thinking about major points presented in the articles. The Inquiry Projects are intended to further the readers' understanding of the articles by guiding them to investigate or apply key concepts, ideas, and issues. Further Readings lists current books and articles for more in-depth examination and exploration of each topic.

Intended Audience

In my past few years of teaching, I have had no trouble finding textbooks for beginning methods courses in reading and language arts. In fact, there are a plethora of such texts available. However, I had considerable difficulty locating a text that provides more in-depth and balanced discussion of key issues and trends in literacy education. While some may point to books such as *Theoretical Models and Processes of Reading, Handbook of Reading Research,* and *Handbook of Research on Teaching the English Language Arts,* my experience suggests that these texts are not accessible to most graduate or undergraduate students and are more appropriate for advanced doctoral students. *Literacy Teaching and Learning: Current Issues and Trends* is designed to fill the void that exists between introductory methods courses and advanced doctoral seminars. It is intended for preservice and in-service teachers, graduate students of reading/literacy education and related fields, as well as those enrolled in alternative certification programs. It can also be used for purposes of professional development training. The book is suitable for courses such as Trends and Issues in Reading/Literacy Education, Classroom Reading II, Foundations of Reading/Literacy Education, and Seminar in Reading/Literacy Education. It is also appropriate for more generic courses such as Teaching Reading/Literacy in Grades K–8. This book can stand on its own, but, depending on the time and focus of specific courses, it can also be supplemented with texts that are more oriented toward strategy, theory, or research.

Acknowledgments

I want to acknowledge my colleagues in the School of Teaching and Learning at the University of Florida and thank them for their friendship and support. In particular, I have benefited from many conversations with Richard Allington, Danling Fu, Linda Lamme, and Anne McGill-Franzen. Their words and work have expanded my scholarly horizons and enriched my thinking about current issues and trends in literacy education.

I also thank my mentors from Purdue University, who guided me through graduate school and who continue to support my growth as teacher and scholar. They are Margie Berns, Beverly Cox, Deborah Dillon, Charles Elster, Carol Hopkins, Jill May, Susan Nierstheimer, David O'Brien, and Maribeth Schmitt.

Linda Montgomery and her team at Merrill/ Prentice Hall deserve special recognition. It was in a meeting with Linda more than two years ago that the idea for this book was first mentioned. Without her commitment, vision, leadership, encouragement, and guidance, this book would not have come to fruition. Laura Weaver was patient, prompt, and resourceful whenever I needed assistance during the preparation of this manuscript. Becky Savage graciously agreed to assist me with the unenviable, but essential, task of obtaining permissions for the articles included in this volume. Linda Bayma was a tireless and creative problem solver in her role as production editor. In addition, I am indebted to Tempe Goodhue of nSight, Inc., for her very meticulous and professional work in shepherding the manuscript through production.

Finally, this book is dedicated to my former and current students at the University of Florida and to those who choose teaching, especially in trying times, as a career. I have learned a great deal from these courageously bright minds about real and significant issues that matter most to teachers and children. I am grateful to them for being the impetus for this book.

Contents

Understanding Literacy and Literacy Acquisition

INTRODUCTION

To be a teacher of literacy presumes at least an understanding of what literacy is and what literacy acquisition involves. The three articles in this opening section address this basic need. They explore current thinking and research that inform prevailing conceptions of literacy and major models of literacy instruction.

In the first article, Australian scholars Barbara Comber and Phil Cormack examine the protean nature of literacy and its implications for literacy teaching and learning. Drawing upon current sociological and anthropological research, Comber and Cormack argue that literacy is multiple and complex and that it is best viewed as socially and culturally constructed practices. They challenge us to move beyond the traditional conception that narrowly defines literacy as a universal set of isolated skills and processes to be mastered. The authors suggest that we need to look at how literacy is used in different settings and how it is taught, learned, and practiced in different communities. They assert that literacy and literacy teaching are never neutral because they are inextricably tied up with issues of power and ideology. They urge teachers to reflect on the potential impact of their practices on their students by always asking why particular texts and particular ways of thinking/talking/reading/writing/behaving are privileged in particular classrooms.

The second article, by American researcher Charles Perfetti, focuses on the nature of the reading acquisition process. It offers an alternative perspective to that of Comber and Cormack. While acknowledging the validity and importance of viewing reading as a socio-cultural phenomenon, Perfetti emphasizes that we should not forget about the contributions of research in the old-fashioned, positivist tradition. He suggests that substantial research about the cognitive processes that underlie

skilled reading and reading acquisition can inform reading education on some basic, highly contested issues such as the role of context in word recognition, whether learning to read is as natural as learning to speak, and which approach (analytic or holistic) better facilitates reading acquisition. Drawing on empirical cognitive research, the author concludes that:

- Skilled reading involves reading words rather than skipping them.
- Skilled readers use context to *interpret* words/sentences, whereas poor readers use it to *identify* words.
- Phonology mediates skilled readers' word identification.
- Learning to read involves learning to crack the code of written language.
- Phonemic awareness, while critical to early success in reading acquisition, must be developed in conjunction with word identification.

In short, scientific evidence from cognitive research appears to support a code-oriented approach to beginning reading instruction. This article is particularly relevant at the present time when federal and state mandates for instructional practices seem to be based primarily on the kind of "scientific evidence" presented in this article.

Finally, as our society becomes increasingly multilingual and multicultural, so does our student population. For many students, English is not the language spoken at home. It is thus imperative to better understand the characteristics and literacy needs of these English-language learners. How is the reading process of non-native English speakers similar to and different from that of native English speakers? What are the pedagogical implications of these similarities and differences? The third article, by American ESOL experts Suzanne Peregoy and Owen Boyle, addresses these and other related questions. Synthesizing research, theory, and practice in the field of second-language reading,

Peregoy and Boyle suggest that the process of reading English is essentially similar for native and non-native speakers in that both bring similar knowledge sources (e.g., background knowledge, decoding ability, language knowledge, genre knowledge, metacognitive skills) to bear upon the comprehension process. However, they differ in the extent of their English-language proficiency, background knowledge relevant to the text, and primary language literacy abilities and experiences. The authors also provide a brief overview of instructional strategies that address the special characteristics of English-language learners. They emphasize that more research is needed to better understand the nature and processes of literacy development within this diverse student population.

Looking Beyond 'Skills' and 'Processes': Literacy as Social and Cultural Practices in Classrooms

Barbara Comber and Phil Cormack
University of South Australia

Changing Theories About Literacy

Researchers in the past have usually perceived literacy as being something that individuals did in their heads. They tended to talk mostly about reading as an internal, psychological act. Many theories of reading were built on laboratory tests which assessed where the readers' eyes were directed as they read. Other studies developed theories of reading through analysing readers' answers (oral and written) to questions. Other researchers focused on errors in performance as a way into how people approached reading and writing. Some researchers interrupted people's reading and writing and asked them to think aloud about what they were doing—to provide an account of how they were doing what they were doing and why. Others interviewed competent writers (journalists and novelists for example) and tried to get them to explain how they did it.

Such studies were used to develop theories about what 'really' went on when readers read and writers wrote and the kinds of conditions, knowledge and help which might have assisted them in their learning. These studies were based on a view of the individual learner doing brain work, solving the literacy puzzle—somehow getting better through learning how to do ever more complex things with texts.

Researchers and teachers were frustrated by what these investigations told them. These studies didn't provide answers to questions such as why some children learned to read 'easily' and others didn't. They didn't explain why some cultural groups did better at school than others, nor did they explain the different uses to which different groups of people put literacy. In some societies for example only men learn to read and write. In some societies literacy is restricted to business uses, in others for religious purposes.

This need to look differently at literacy shifted literacy research out of the laboratory and away from set-up situations and tests. Researchers began to look at how literacy was used in different settings and how it was taught, learned and practised in different communities. Thus there was a move towards sociological investigations. The results of these studies have influenced much recent thinking about literacy teaching. Three issues arising from this research are discussed in this article. They can be summarised as:

- Literacy can be understood as socially and culturally constructed practices.
- Literate competence is about cultural display (what is seen as 'good work' or successful performance in a classroom or centre are culturally preferred ways of talking, listening and behaving).
- When children come to school or kindergarten, they have to work out what counts as literacy in that context.

Literacy as Socially and Culturally Constructed Practices

To say that literacy is socially constructed is to acknowledge that you are differently literate than your grandparents, that today's children and their children are and will be differently literate than their teachers. Literacy is not a set of unchanging and universal 'skills' or knowledge. What counts as literacy varies according to factors such as place, institution, purpose, period in history, culture, economic circumstance, and power relations. Margaret Meek explains how new technologies have changed the face of child literacy.

> Now even before they can read, four-year-olds can call up files on personal computers, play games and compose poems and tunes on them. (Meek, 1992, p. 226)

To say that literacy is socially constructed is to recognise that we use a multiplicity of literacies to get things done in our lives. It is to realise that girls and boys may do different things with books and in composing their own texts. But more than this it is to realise that none of this happens genetically, naturally or by accident. If boys read and write differently from girls we need to look at how this is taught and learned in our culture.

> … literacy is constructed by individuals and groups as part of everyday life. At the same time literacy also is constructive *of* everyday life. In literate societies it becomes a crucial element of one's cultural 'tool kit' (Bruner, 1991) for doing social relations, work, and for handling economically valuable and culturally significant information. But how much latitude and free play individuals and groups exercise … are influenced by the institutions, ideologies and interests operant in these societies. (Luke, 1993, p. 4)

Luke's point is that not only do people shape literacy to suit their needs, but that what counts as literacy in particular societies, institutions or communities also shapes what people can and can't do. Literacy is not neutral, but a technology through which people exercise power over one another. One way to illustrate this point is to look at a study of the history of literacy in western societies.

Literacy in Different Times and Places

We know the alphabet (a means of representing sounds in print) was invented by the Greeks around 600 BC. A popular view is that since that time there has been steady 'progress' in the development of literacies with milestones such as the invention of the printing press and computer technologies resulting in modern day sophisticated literacies of today's 'advanced' societies. Literacy has been connected with 'civilisation', 'progress', 'commerce' and, especially in recent times, with 'economic competitiveness'.

… not only do people shape literacy to suit their needs, but … what counts as literacy … also shapes what people can and can't do.

However Graff (1994) labels such claims for literacy as 'myths'. For example, he argues that there has been no direct link between levels of literacy and economic performance. In reviewing the history of literacy in the western world he states that:

> … major steps forward in trade, commerce, and even industry took place in some periods and places with remarkably low levels of literacy; conversely, higher levels of literacy have not been proved to be stimulants or springboards for 'modern' economic developments. (p. 158)

This is not to say that literacy won't make a difference in children's lives. Children who do not have the literacies which count may be denied access to important rights and opportunities in today's society.

However, there are no guarantees that come with literacy because many other factors, such as gender, race, ethnicity, geographic location, class, and socio-economic status, determine the opportunities people have to capitalise on what they learn in school.

History shows us that literacy has been taught and used selectively in different societies at different times. For example, in ancient Greece literacy was not taught to women; one of the most successful literacy campaigns ever (in Sweden in the 16th century) taught reading (for religious purposes of reading the bible) but not writing; and in modern times different societies and religions shape some sorts of literacy for some groups and other sorts of literacy, or none, for other groups (Luke, 1990). Even in places with 'universal' literacy programs, such as Australia today with compulsory schooling, different groups have quite different literate competencies. Some research suggests that girls and boys participate in different literacies (Martin, 1984; Gilbert and Rowe, 1989; Kamler, 1992; Christian-Smith, 1993). There are different outcomes for literacy for various social, cultural and economic groups. These differences have a social and economic impact on members of these groups.

> The history of literacy instruction would indicate that what is at stake here is which discourses, genres, contexts, subject positions and practices will be distributed to whom and by whom. Even predating the Greek alphabet, this history can be reread as one of the selective distribution of knowledge and competence to particular groups in the populace. (Luke, 1990, p. 86)

The historical and contemporary evidence is that the literacy people learn has a great deal to do with what gets taught to whom. This may seem like an obvious statement, but it is an explanation that has tended to be overlooked in theories about literacy learning that focus on internal cognitive skills. These decisions involve the political, economic, religious, technological, social and cultural forces at play at any one time. Literate practices are 'shaped' towards particular ends by those who exert influence over what gets taught as literacy. What forces might have been at play in the Swedish literacy campaign mentioned above?

In a complex post-industrial society, uses of text have exploded. The change from an agricultural and industrial economy to a service and information based economy, and the expansion of mass media have made print pervasive in the lives of people at all levels of society. Just 'getting by' today requires new kinds of literate competence. To be able to do more than get by—to have some choice and exercise power over these new kinds of texts—requires adaptability, specialised knowledge and the ability to look beyond the 'obvious' and critique texts. In broad terms, as our society has changed, so too has literacy and what it means to be 'literate'.

Indeed to say that 'literacy' and what it means to be 'literate' has changed, is too simplistic. Australia is increasingly a society of diverse groups and communities which use literacy in different ways for different purposes; they make it work for them. As well, groups and institutions use literacy to 'shape' people into desired ways of thinking and behaving. This applies to work groups, religious groups, geographic communities (see, for example, Heath, 1983) and educational institutions. Literacy is used in ways and for purposes that are unique to classrooms and preschools. It is also used to 'shape' students into particular ways of thinking and behaving.

What does it mean for teachers that there are many fast-changing literacies which are socially and culturally constructed? According to Luke (1993) the first implication is that teachers need wide-ranging and specialised literate competence themselves— we need to learn to use new forms of literacy such as word processing, the internet, visual and multimedia texts that the children we teach may access from a very early age. The second implication is that teachers need to find out about the many forms of literacy operating in their community and should not operate on assumptions about literacy and learning which are taken from their own experience of growing up.

> ... it is at once convenient and perilous to develop programs and approaches to teaching based on 'self-reproductive' assumptions: that is, assumptions which unquestioningly mirror and produce for the next generation aspects of our own childhoods and educations. These might include beliefs that how we learned literacy is best for all children; relatedly, that the values and attitudes we had towards literacy and book culture as children are the 'norm' against which we can judge and assess our students.... The danger here is that we will judge our students against these benchmarks, this despite the fact that in the 15 or 20 years that have lapsed, the student clienteles of schools, the life experience and cultural background of primary school students have changed in profound ways. These are different children from us. This is, in many substantive respects, a different, multimediated literate culture, a different job market and economy, and a different polycultural social environment. (Luke, 1993, p. 5)

We would add a third implication that teachers need to develop an awareness that what happens in their own classrooms and preschools in the name of literacy learning and teaching is also socially and culturally constructed. It is to this issue we now turn our attention.

Literacy and Discourse

One of the things that has been noticed by researchers who have looked at literacy in educational and other social contexts is that literacy is more than isolated 'skills' of reading and writing. They have had to invent new terms such as 'learning encounters', 'writing occasions', 'reading encounters', 'speech events' to describe the complexity of what they see. Implicit in these descriptions is the belief that the experiences from which children learn are social events or transactions, usually involving a great deal of talk, in which they must deal with a range of social and cultural demands which are interwoven with the production or comprehension of print. The term "literacy event" is now a commonly used label for situations where one or more people are engaged in an activity which involves print (Anderson, Teale and Estrada, 1980).

... literacy is more than isolated 'skills' of reading and writing.

Studies of literacy events have shown that different social situations demand the use of certain sorts of texts, in particular ways, using 'appropriate' language. More than this, there seem to be rules operating about who can read, write and speak and in what ways according to situation. Theorists have turned to the concept of 'discourse' to try to explain how and which kinds of language get used in different contexts. Some theorists broaden their definition of discourse from language to include ways of behaving and the values that people must appear to hold that go with that language. Gee (1990) uses an example of the 'biker bar' to explain how these go together to make up a discourse:

> Imagine that I park my motorcycle, enter my neighborhood 'biker bar', and say to my leather-jacketed and tattooed drinking buddy, as I sit down: 'May I have a match for my cigarette, please?' What I have said is perfectly grammatical English, but is 'wrong' nonetheless (unless I have used a heavily ironic tone of voice). It is not just *what* you say, but *how* you say it. In this bar, I haven't said it in the 'right way'. I should have said something like, 'Gotta match?' or 'Give me a light, would'ya?'
>
> Now imagine that I say the 'right' thing ('Gotta match?' or 'Give me a light, would'ya?'), but while saying it, I carefully wipe off the bar stool with a napkin to avoid getting my newly pressed designer jeans dirty. In this case, I've still got it wrong. In *this* bar, they just don't do that sort of thing. I have *said* the right thing, but my 'saying-doing' combination is nonetheless wrong. It's not just *what* you say or even just *how* you say it, it's also what you *are* and *do* while you say it. It's not enough to just say the right 'lines', one needs to get the whole 'role' right (like a role in a play or a movie). (p. xv)

People are usually unaware of the discourse of a situation because they are so familiar with the role they must play; it seems natural to act that way. However, if we are put into a new context—e.g. participating in a job interview for the first time, travelling into another culture—we find ourselves at a loss, not knowing what to do, or say, or even how to hold one's body. Some comedy (see, for example, Mr Bean) is based on the comedian acting 'out of discourse' in situations where the viewer/listener is very familiar with the unspoken rules that operate—situations such as listening to a sermon in church, waiting in line, or eating at a restaurant. In all situations, including those involving literacy, there are rules (usually unwritten) about what language can be used, how to behave, and the values one should hold. According to Gee a discourse can involve rules on how to act, talk, and write. He says that discourses:

> ... are always ways of displaying (through words, actions, values and beliefs) *membership* in a particular social group or social network (people who associate with each other around a common set of interests, goals and activities). (Gee, 1990, pp. 142–143)

A key discourse operating in children's lives is the discourse of the classroom and preschool, particularly in relation to learning literacy. Literacy events in classrooms and preschools such as listening to stories, shared book time, free writing/drawing time, have rules of discourse operating just as powerfully as those played out in the biker bar, church and restaurant. There are rules about what can be said, written and done, and how. There are rules about where the body should be ('eye contact', 'on the carpet', 'in your seat'); how the body should be held ('sit up straight', 'bottoms on floor'). There are also rules about the values/beliefs that are to be displayed ('be responsible', 'be independent'). For some children, these discourses are a long way from the discourses in their community, for other students there are similarities. (Gee makes the point that as a young urban professional, he would have less trouble and take less time to learn the discourse of a 'yuppie' bar than he would a 'biker bar'.) So much of being successful in a literacy event, then, is to do with being able to fit the discourse which involves much more than reading and writing 'skills'. In other words, being successful in the classroom is about displaying the sets of various words/actions/values/beliefs that 'count'. Hence literate practices come to shape identity in non-neutral ways. The good five year old listener must display eye contact, wait their turn, and sit up straight. These ways of behaving are not the only ways of listening and actually may require behaviours at odds with politeness norms in non-Western cultures.

Literate Competence in the Classroom and Preschool Is About Cultural Display

Children's performance is always judged in terms of how well they display their competence. A display of competence in an educational setting usually depends on an ability to say something or to listen in a certain way, even to hold the body a certain way (e.g. eye contact). Ways of talking, listening and acting are not the same in all cultures yet in a classroom only a narrow range is acceptable.

Literacy practices or the discourses that are a part of literacy events are not the same in all classrooms. What comes to count as literacy in a classroom depends on what texts are produced or interpreted, what kinds of talk go on around these texts, and what is assessed as 'good work'. Researchers currently are considering what kinds of literate performances (i.e. the things students must do, say in relation to texts) 'count' in the early years of schooling. In this section we consider how literacy is constructed by looking at transcripts from classroom interactions and by considering how teachers' views about their students have an impact on student performance in literacy.

In any literacy lesson things happen that tell students what literacy *is*. They include the kinds of talk that goes on (e.g. the questions asked, the topics discussed), the kinds of activity that go with print (e.g. reading individually, shared book, play activities involving 'print'), the texts that are used and, especially, what gets counted as 'good work'.

> ... students will be credited and credentialled differently according to how well they can match the formal academic literacy curriculum as taught and listened for by teachers. (Baker and Freebody, 1993, p. 280)

The following transcript from Baker and Freebody (1993) shows how teachers require particular kinds of literate knowledge and 'display'. Picture a class sitting in front of the blackboard where some sentences have been written. One of these sentences contains the word 'slobby'.

Teacher	Well, how would you find out where it says *slobby*?
Jane	You'd look at *slobby*.
Teacher	Well how would you do that?
S.	Oh.
S.	It's easy.
Jane	Find ... find the ... find the person, like Zak.
Teacher	Yes, that's one way, you could go and ask Zak, because he knows how to write *slobby*. But if Zak is busy, what else could you do?

Jane	Look on the board.
Teacher	Hmmm, where would we look … Christine? No, just stay there and tell me darling. Hmmm? There? Where?
Children	Next to the monster.
Teacher	But how would you know that says *slobby?*
C.	Because it has /s/
Teacher	So does this one
C.	I know that //
Teacher	/s/ so does this one
S.	'Cause, 'cause they know 'cause it's got a 'b', two 'b's over there
Zak	An a 'o'
Teacher	Oh, that's a good idea, Zak, yes you can look for some other sounds that you can hear *slo:obby* good boy.

Jane's interpretation of the question—"… how would you find out where it says 'slobby'?"—is different from what her teacher intended. The thinking behind the question is not obvious to this group of first grade children. Their suggested strategies, including asking a classmate who already knows how to write the word, are not the strategies the teacher is looking for. Yet in another context such as writing time, asking a peer may be exactly right. If children ask a peer expert at that time it may be considered 'resourceful'. When Christine offers to get out of her seat and physically locate the word she is asked to tell rather than show. She must use words rather than actions. Asking Zak, or physically locating the word on the blackboard, are unacceptable answers to the question: 'How would you find out where it says slobby?' In this lesson where the agenda is sounding out, specifically noting vowels, children are required to operate with decontextualised language use; to use language to describe linguistic processes, rather than use other social and physical solutions.

Although two other students point out features of the word, it is Zak (who can already read and write) whose contribution is praised and accepted as the best answer. What the teacher requires here is not necessarily direct reading performance but a particular social/cultural display. Students must take on the teacher's thinking behind the task which is not about reading 'slobby' but about displaying an acceptable version of the school learning process. Notice how much in this example that 'literacy' is tied up with physical movement in the class (or lack of movement in this case) and focuses on a 'talking about' ability. Literacy is much more than decoding in first grade—it is constantly being connected with issues such as how to sit, what questions to ask, what it is possible to say, to whom, and in what tone of voice.

Just as what goes on in 'reading' texts is socially and culturally constructed, so also is what gets written *into* texts. This extract reported by Luke (1993, p. 47) is taken from a lesson where a teacher is presenting 'modelled writing' (i.e. the teacher writes in front of the children and involves them in creating the text—a teaching technique recommended in 'process writing' approaches).

Teacher	Now when you write a story, Allison, there's something very important you gotta do. You gotta keep reading your story as you write it because you might miss a really important word. So I'm gonna read mine again [points to story script on paper]: 'A long time ago there lived a princess'. I think I can make it a bit better than that.
S1	A dragon too.
Teacher	No, no. No. What. How about: when you think about a princess, what do you think about?
S2	A prince…
Teacher	No
S2	A prince
Teacher	No, what do you think she'd look like?
S3	A…
Teacher	With long hair? What colour?
S3	Yellow, black … [chorus laughter]
Teacher	What about long, long golden hair.

Here students are told that stories can be made better, but how this is done is not explained. Why 'a prince' was not acceptable is not made clear. Finally the physical appearance of the Anglo-European princess, as signalled by her golden hair, is given pride of place. Here what is valued as a literate form is the fairy tale genre and what comes with that genre is a highly gendered, white world view. The children in this classroom, a significant proportion of whom are Aboriginal and Torres Straight Islanders, are inducted into a version of literacy with particular gender and race values built in. To be a successful writer is to take on a particular world view as demonstrated by the teacher.

It is not only teachers who have a say in how literacy is constructed in the classroom. What counts as literacy must be negotiated between the children themselves. Here Jameel stands in front of his K/1 class to read his writing (Dyson, 1993, p. 9) at sharing time.

Jameel	(reading) Sat on Cat. Sat on Hat. hat sat on Cat. CAt GoN. 911 for CAt. [Dyson's punctuation]
Mollie	It doesn't make any sense.
Jameel	What part of it doesn't make sense?
Peer	(unidentified) it makes sense to me. You can tell with his picture [of the cat on hat, the hat on cat, "the speeding guys," and the crying faces]
Mollie	It doesn't make sense.

Jameel	If your mother got hit wouldn't you call 911/ Wouldn't you call 911? Would you call 911? Would you call 911? [911 is the emergency services phone number in the USA]
Mollie	That's where it doesn't—
Edward G.	It makes sense!
Peer	Yeah!
Jameel	If a car was passin' by—and then you were by the house and then if a car was going past and then you got hit—I'm talking about the hat and the cat got hit.
Edward G.	G. It sounds like a poem.
Mollie	It doesn't make sense.

At this point their teacher sends them off to a side table to continue their discussion.

Mollie	Read that story.
Jameel	What don't make sense?
Mollie	Read it to me again.
Jameel	OK. You can read these words.
Mollie	No I can not. They're smashed together.
Jameel	(laughs) Don't you know [how to read]!?! (asked with mock amazement).

In sharing time peers play a role in deciding what counts as an appropriate display of literate competence. Mollie brings her expectations of what a narrative should do but Jameel resists her criticisms and her suggestions for changes. Mollie's literacy frames represent a match with the school world's universe. Jameel's do not. Here Jameel's writing represents an opportunity for performance—a social event. When Mollie won't read his story Jameel implies that she has the problem, that in fact she doesn't know 'how to read'. We see the child learner negotiating ways to be a student and a friend, finding out how certain displays of literate competence work socially and academically.

Because language use and literacies vary, students acquire different views of what counts as appropriate literacy performance. Classroom and preschool language performance and literacies may differ quite markedly from what children are required to produce at home and in their communities. Some students' home and community language and literacies fit the school literate discourse quite well. However, increasingly in our polycultural society, many students find major differences between community, home, school and preschool requirements. In short, some students must construct new identities, new discursive repertoires, in order to do well in educational settings.

'Individual Differences'

In early childhood education, there has been a strong philosophical emphasis on the *individual*. Success and failure in literacy tasks has tended to be explained using an 'individual differences' hypothesis. However this individual difference explanation tends to ignore

the wider social and cultural factors that are at play in student literate performance. It means that children who learn literate practices in their community that match school and preschool practices, are seen to possess individual 'ability'. On the other hand students who do not have these experiences in their communities have their failure to thrive in school literacy explained by individualised problems such as lack of ability or motivation. Other explanations place the blame for school failure with parents; cultural differences are read off as cultural deficits. Edelsky (1992) explains the consequences of such deficit ways of reading cultural differences.

> Some children come to school already 'privileged,' already knowing this way of using language. It isn't that if you're a non-standard speaker you can't ever acquire standard English. You can, but it's with considerable effort. So you're at a disadvantage because you spend more energy doing it, and in stressful times you forget more easily. As a result, schools often make it look as if the kids who already know the standard dialect are somehow smarter and deserve higher grades. But in reality they are getting higher grades because they rely on knowledge they already had before they ever entered the classroom door. So the political arrangements in the society at large affect whether kids are seen as smart or not. (p. 325)

Some students end up being punished for not having the very competences that schools are mandated to teach. Heath (1991) argues that teachers need to learn more about the variety of ways the language is used and learned in students' communities and use this information when designing literacy programs.

> We need to know more about alternative ways of learning and of using language in order to *add* these ways to those already valued in the classroom. The goal is *not* to use this knowledge about minorities' ways of using language and habits of learning to tailor classrooms to fit the daily habits of each minority group. Instead, schools must be able to incorporate some of these additional ways in order to facilitate learning about learning by *all* students. Moreover, studies that point out cross-cultural differences in behaviors fundamental to schooling—such as language use, habits of critical thinking, concepts of time and space, gender relations, and valuations of written information—should serve primarily as evidence that language and thought skills valued by the school do not come naturally with developmental growth. (p. 21)

Literacy Acquisition

Heath's point about developmental growth presents a real challenge to assumptions that there is a universal path of literacy development characterised by movement along a continuum with particular developmental markers—a view represented by Figure 1.

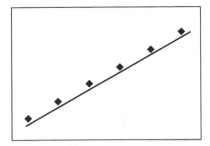

Figure 1   A continuum for universal literacy development.

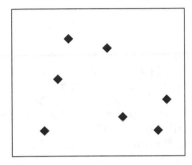

Figure 2   A scatter graph representation of literacy learning.

The view that literacy is socially and culturally constructed implies that students will learn what is shown to 'count' as literacy in certain settings and for particular purposes. Perhaps the acquisition of literate competences could be better represented by a 'scatter graph' rather than points on a single line where points are placed according to contexts and purposes in which the competence is developed (see Figure 2).

This view of learning recognises that schools must choose from many possibilities what is important to teach students. Curriculum documents and national policy statements have an impact on how such decisions are made. However, an invaluable resource is the teacher's knowledge of the language and literacy valued in students' communities.

Children Have to 'Read' the Educational Setting and the Teacher to Work Out What Counts as Literacy

Literacy is constructed differently in different classrooms. Early school literacy events such as shared book experience, modelled writing, hearing a child read, or reading to children, will look different in different settings depending why and how they are being used. Teachers may be unaware of difficulties students have in 'working out' the required literacy learning performances. What's required may seem 'obvious' and 'natural' to the teacher but may be alien and illogical to students. The following transcript analysis demonstrates how contexts are constructed during school literacy lessons and how these contexts require particular forms of literate behaviour from children. Students must learn to read the context in order to perform in ways that match the teachers' expectations.

Teaching literacy is a social and cultural practice.

This transcript and analysis in a kindergarten class is taken from Baker (1991, p. 104).

Teacher	Look for books, that's right. Alright the little boy's name is To:ony. Have a look at Tony in the first picture what he's doing.
S.	( )
Teacher	Elaine?
Elaine	Drawing on the blackboard.
Teacher	He's drawing on the blackboard but what's he drawing on the blackboard, Nina?
Nina	The day?
Teacher	Not the day! I can [think of something else Valerie.
V.	[his name
V.	His na:ame?
Teacher	He's writing his name. Let's all read it together put your finger at the top.
Teacher & *Students*	(unison, singsong) TONY IS WRITING HIS NAME
Teacher	Ah goodness me. The next one, what's Tony doing have a look at the picture don't look at the words, see if the picture tells you the story. Anna?

To make the 'right answer' children need to follow the teacher's reasoning (Baker & Freebody, 1993). They focus on making sense of the kind of response the teacher requires. The connection between what the teacher is asking the student to do and the literacy curriculum is not clear. Why does the teacher ask what Tony is 'drawing' when, in fact, he is writing? why must 'name' be sounded out as 'na:ame'? why does the teacher direct the children not to look at the words? Here the reader is not to use the words as clues, but must learn to read the pictures and the part of the pictures that the teacher sees as significant. Each picture is taken as a new puzzle to be solved: "... The next one ..." Children's actual competence with the book is not significant here—rather it is learning to read in this particular way with the teacher that is the focus of the activity. Elaine must wonder why her answer was not good enough and Nina why her answer was wrong. Students must work to identify what is required of them—what counts as literacy here.

Our point is not to suggest that what the teacher was doing was right or wrong, or good practice or bad. Rather, it is to highlight the work that students must do to work out what counts as good work or being a good student in *any* lesson; as Baker and Freebody put it, how they must display their literate competence. Students from groups whose ways of learning, relating to adults, and displaying competence are quite different from those preferred by the classroom culture may have extra difficulty working out what is required of them.

Considerations for Teachers

The central lesson from the issues discussed in this article is that there are no ways of teaching or learning literacy that are simple or 'natural'. Literacy teaching is not neutral. What teachers decide to do in their preschools and classrooms, what counts as good work have cultural, political and social implications for their students. Teaching literacy is a social and cultural practice. Therefore teachers have important intellectual work to do in learning how to examine the ways classroom and preschool literacies serve, or fail to serve, the children they teach. Teachers can consider:

- what kinds of texts are privileged in the classroom or preschool and whose identities (gender, race, social group) are given pride of place.
- what kinds of listening, speaking, reading, viewing and writing students are asked to do and what kind of use they can make of this in their lives now and in the future.
- what literate practices count as good work and how these relate to the literate and thinking practices students bring to school and preschool.

These questions arise from a recognition that there is no single 'right' way to teach literacy. All approaches to teaching literacy construct literacy in particular ways that have varying consequences for students. The good news for teachers is that, if literacy is 'constructed', then teachers can choose to change the construction of literacy in their setting—if they find it is not currently working for their students.

However, to do this, teachers need tools for considering the literacies produced in their teaching practice and the consequences for their students. Analysis of classroom discourse is one potentially productive path for finding out what our teaching works to do.

References

Anderson, A., Teale, H. and Estrada, E. (1980) 'Low income children's preschool literacy experiences: some naturalistic observations', *The quarterly newsletter of the laboratory of comparative human cognition,* Vol 3, pp. 59–65.

Baker, C. and Freebody, P. (1993) 'The crediting of literate competence in classroom talk', *The Australian journal of language and literacy,* 16:4, pp. 279–294.

Baker, C. (1991) 'Classroom literacy events', *Australian journal of reading,* 14:2, pp. 103–108.

Christian-Smith, L. (1993) 'Constituting and reconstituting desire: fiction, fantasy and femininity' in *Texts of desire: essays on fiction, femininity and schooling.* The Falmer Press, London.

Dyson, A. H. (1993) *Social worlds of children learning to write in an urban primary school.* New York: Teachers College Press.

Edelsky, C. (1992) 'A talk with Carole Edelsky about politics and literacy', *Language Arts,* 69:5, pp. 324–329.

Gee, J. (1990) *Social linguistics and literacies: Ideology in discourses.* The Falmer Press, London & Philadelphia.

Gilbert, P. with Rowe, K. (1989) *Gender, Literacy and the classroom.* Melbourne: Australian Reading Association.

Graff, Harvey (1994) 'The legacies of literacy', in Maybin, J. (ed) *Language and literacy in social practice.* Multilingual Matters, Adelaide, pp. 151–167.

Heath, Shirley Brice (1991) 'The sense of being literate: historical and cross-cultural features' in Barr, B., Kamil, M., Mosenthal, P. and Pearson, P. D. (eds) *Handbook of reading research: volume II.* Longman, New York, pp. 3–25.

Kamler, (1992 May) 'The social construction of free topic choice in the process writing classroom', *Australian journal of language and literacy,* 15:2, pp. 105–122.

Luke, Allan (1990) 'Producing the literate: from psychology to linguistics', in Christie, F. (ed) *Literacy in social process: papers from the Inaugural Australian Systemic Linguistics Conference,* Centre for Studies of Language Education, Darwin, pp. 83–95.

Luke, Allan (1993) 'The social construction of literacy in the primary school,' in Unsworth, L. (ed) *Literacy learning and teaching: Language as social practice in the primary school.* Macmillan, Melbourne, pp. 1–53.

Martin, J. R. (1984) *Factual writing: exploring and challenging social reality.* Deakin University Press, Geelong, Victoria.

Meek, M. (1992) 'Literacy: re-describing reading', in Kimberley, K., Meek, M. and Miller, J. (eds) *New readings: Contributions to an understanding of literacy.* A & C Black, London.

Cognitive Research Can Inform Reading Education

Charles A. Perfetti
University of Pittsburgh

The connection between research and practice is not a simple one of the first producing and the second consuming, especially in education.[1] There are obstacles to the use of good research in any field, and in reading education the obstacles are compounded. For one thing, research on reading abounds, promiscuously popping up in disciplines of all sorts and in publications of widely varying quality. That makes it difficult to distinguish what's both valid and useful from what's sterile, spurious, or both. Second, the problems of practice are more complex than the conclusions that come from research. When there is an incongruence between simple conclusions and complex realities, one may despair that the research is irrelevant.[2]

The title of my paper is a claim that there has been enough quality research to inform reading education on some basic issues. My concern is with good research of a particular kind: Research about the cognitive processes that underlie skilled reading and learning how to read. This is a narrow scope and must be (and has been) supplemented by good research on relevant social, cultural, and instructional aspects of the problem.

There are four clear contributions of cognitive research that deserve special attention. This attention is deserved for three reasons. First, in each case the evidence has accumulated in a reliable fashion. The conclusions do not rest on a single study or two, but on solid results from converging research. Second, in each case the results speak clearly to issues of reading instruction. Indeed in each case they imply that certain reading goals should be privileged over others. Finally, these four solid results span a range of school levels from skilled reading through middle-grade to beginning reading. They are as follows:

1. Skilled readers read words rather than skip them.
2. Less skilled readers do rely on context.
3. Skilled readers use phonology in reading.
4. Children learn to read successfully by learning how their writing system works.

Skilled Readers Read Words to Identify Them

The idea that context and readers' goals are important in reading is correct. The evidence shows that skilled readers adjust their reading goals, make inferences, use context, and monitor their comprehension. (See Yuill and Oakhill, 1991.) These higher order abilities and strategies are very important to skilled comprehension. It does not follow from these facts, however, that readers skip words when they read. The incorrect idea that skilled reading involves a strategy of sparse sampling of words coupled with a heavy use of context can be put to rest by clear evidence to the contrary. The evidence comes from studies that monitor what readers' eyes do when they read. From such studies have come the following picture: first, the eyes gain information useful for reading only when they are at rest, fixated on a specific small region of the text. When the eyes move, as they do in rapid saccades after each fixation, there is no information gained. Thus, the experience of reading is one that is smooth and free of interruptions; but the actual mechanics of reading involve alternations of stops (fixations) and movements, with only the fixations providing useful information.

Most important is the fact that readers' eyes fixate on most words on the page when they are reading for most purposes, from over 50% to nearly 80% depending on the reading purpose and the type of word. So-called content words—nouns, adjectives, verbs—are read more often than so-called function words—forms of *to be*, articles, prepositions. However, some of this difference appears to be due to differences in length of these different classes of words. The reader's ability to direct his or her eyes to a certain word is quite limited (Rayner and Pollatsek, 1989). And reading for gist can get by with fewer eye fixations than reading in order to answer questions (Just and Carpenter, 1987). But the general picture is clear: readers fixate on most of the content words on the page and their ability to answer comprehension questions is generally limited to text locations that they have actually fixated (Just, Carpenter and Masson, 1982).

Readers must read lots of words in order to read effectively.

There is no mystery as to why readers sample texts densely. It is a simple matter of retinal sensitivity. The eyes can make out the letters of a word only within a degree or two of central visual angle. The effect of this is to allow a window of reading that is confined to only 4–6 spaces to the right of the eye's fixation (Rayner and Pollatsek, 1989). That is enough to read a word, and sometimes the first couple of letters of the immediately following word. But it demonstrates the limits of peripheral vision in actual reading of words. Thus, readers must read lots of words in order to read effectively. The use of context is important, and one finds shorter fixation times on words that are more predictable (Ehrlich and Rayner, 1981). But this context effect does not extend to skipping words.

Less Skilled Readers Use Context

The use of context, to repeat the obvious, is important in reading. Both the context provided by the text itself and that provided by the reader's knowledge help the reader interpret words and sentences. Without the use of context, the reader would not be able to figure out the relevant meaning aspects of words—because most words have multiple general senses rather than specific meanings—nor to draw appropriate inferences—because such inferences depend on implicit information provided by other parts of the text or the reader's knowledge.

Skilled readers … use context to interpret words and sentences. … Less skilled readers … use context to identify words.

The importance of context has been widely appreciated. Less widely appreciated, but well established by research, are two equally important facts about context use. (1) Skilled readers do not use context much to identify words; they use context to *interpret* words and sentences. (2) Less skilled readers, by contrast, use context to identify words. These facts came to light in research some years ago by Stanovich and West (1981) and by Perfetti, Goldman, and Hogaboam (1979). The basic result in these studies was that differences between skilled and less skilled readers in the speed of word identification were large when words were presented in isolation, but were reduced when words were presented in context. Fuller theoretical accounts of these results are in Stanovich (1980, 1981) and Perfetti and Roth (1981).

These findings appeared counterintuitive to people who had become accustomed to thinking of context use as a characteristic of skilled readers and 'word calling' (word reading devoid of meaning) as characteristic of poor readers. Actually, the results are very sensible and easily understood: Skilled readers identify words too quickly on the basis of lexical processes for context to have much effect. Less skilled readers are slower in identifying words, because they lack basic word identification skill; thus they are able to benefit from the additional boost of context. Indeed, when the basic word identification speed of skilled readers is slowed down, context facilitates identification. The hallmark of skilled reading is fast *context-free* word identification. And rich *context-dependent* text understanding.

Skilled Readers Use Phonology

How skilled readers identify words is another question that has been answered by research, and again the research answer overturns some misconceptions. It is common to assume that reading for a skilled reader involves a visually based print-to-meaning process. The facts emerging from an intense 20 year period of word identification research are otherwise. Despite differing conclusions on the details of word identification, the research supports an important role for phonology. The disagreement concerns whether phonology mediates all written word identification: When phonology is observed is it 'pre-lexical' (mediating identification) or is it 'post-lexical' (resulting from identification)? This question has received slightly differing answers from well-conceived research. However, a penetrating analysis by Van Orden, Pennington, and Stone (1990) makes a good case in favour of a natural mediating role for phonology in word identification. Empirical results from Lukatela and Turvey (1990) and Perfetti, Bell and Delaney (1988), among many others, also have helped make the case that phonology plays a role in skilled readers' identification of words.

… phonology plays a role in skilled readers' identification of words.

There is also much research consistent with an alternative view on this question, that phonology mediates word identification only for low frequency words with regular spelling patterns (Paap and Noel, 1991; Seidenberg, Waters, Barnes and Tanenhaus, 1984). This alternative conclusion conforms with the conclusions of Dual Route Theory (Coltheart, 1978), which assumes that word identification takes place along the faster of two mechanisms, one that involves the conversion of letters to phonemes prior to word identification and one that 'looks up' the word based on its spelling.

Given these different conclusions concerning the details of word identification, it is important to get clear on the consensus that exists. On all accounts, the connections between written units—letters and strings of letters—and speech units (phonemes) are activated during word identification. The only question is how often this activation actually produces word identification. The consensus ranges from quite often (low frequency words) to very often (virtually all words). (See Berent and Perfetti (1995) for a model that reconciles these differences.) Importantly, this consensus extends to actual text reading as well. Although much of the research has used methods that focus on the reading of single words, research requiring the reading of texts also provides evidence for phonological processes (see Perfetti, Zhang and Berent (1992)).

Finally, another element of this consensus is that regardless of the details that bring about word identification, all accounts are consistent with the possibility that phonological information is commonly activated as part of word reading. That is, even when phonology does not 'mediate' identification, the phonological form of the word is retrieved as a product of the identification process. Especially interesting in this respect is recent evidence that this retrieval of phonological word forms may be universal across writing systems (Perfetti, Zhang and Berent, 1992; Perfetti and Zhang, 1995a).

Skill in reading involves reading words rather than skipping them, it involves context-free word reading skill, and it involves phonology.

The key to this conclusion is evidence on reading Chinese, which is usually (although not entirely accurately) believed to be a writing system based on a logographic principle; i.e., basic units in the writing system correspond to word meanings rather than to speech units. In fact it has been common to assume that reading Chinese is strictly a process of print-to-meaning, with no role for phonology. The research, however, reveals a different picture. In a series of studies using different word processing tasks, we have found that the phonological forms of written Chinese words are activated even when the subject is required to do only semantic processing (Perfetti and Zhang, 1995a). What we call the *word identification reflex*, the retrieval of a phonological word form as part of word identification, occurs in Chinese as well as English.

Thus far, I have reviewed evidence that points to characteristics of skilled reading. Skill in reading involves reading words rather than skipping them, it involves context-free word reading skill, and it involves

phonology. Context is used for higher level processes of meaning interpretation rather than for word identification. The final section addresses how this skill comes about. What is it that must be learned by a child in order to become a skilled reader?

Successful Readers Learn How Their Writing System Works

The central fact for learning to read is that a child must learn a writing system, specifically how the writing system encodes his or her language (see Perfetti and Zhang, 1995b). Learning to read is often defined in other terms, such as learning to 'get meaning from print'. This meaning-getting idea is not wrong; but it does not provide a specific learning problem. Whatever else learning to read is, it is a kind of learning. Children do not need to learn that language has meaning; they do not have to learn how to use context to figure out meanings. They are well practised in these things in the uses they have made of language before they come to school. What they need to learn is what is new for them as they encounter reading. The new thing to be learned is the writing system. How does the child's writing system work?

Writing systems differ just as languages do. However, while the child seems to implicitly (and biologically) know the principles of language design prior to acquiring spoken language (Pinker, 1984), there appears to be no parallel case to make for writing systems. As products of human invention, they vary in how they work. A child learning to read English, Italian, Hungarian, or Korean learns an alphabetic writing system, in which graphic units associate with phonemes; to learn to read Japanese Kana is to learn a syllabary system, in which graphic units correspond to syllables; to learn to read Arabic, Hebrew, or Persian is to learn a modified alphabetic system in which consonants are more reliably represented than are vowels. Finally, the case that most contrasts with English and other alphabetic orthographies is Chinese, which is usually said to be a logographic system; i.e., one in which the basic principle is morphological: The writing system provides units that correspond to meanings (morphemes) rather than to phonemes or syllables. This traditional story of Chinese is misleading, however, because there is actually a considerable amount of syllable-based phonology in the writing system (DeFrancis, 1989).

Whether the child will learn an alphabetic or logographic system, or no system at all, is a matter of cultural and national traditions. It is interesting that even the mere possibility of writing systems may not be part of the natural language endowment. The design of (spoken) languages may be universal, the design of writing systems appears not to be. Nevertheless, there is an important fact about writing systems that is easy to overlook, especially when Chinese is treated as if it were strictly a meaning-based system. All writing systems, even Chinese, make some reference to speech. No full writing system has ever evolved to be based only on a mapping of written units to meanings. The implications of this fact are important: Writing systems have developed to represent speech. The only differences among them are (1) which units of speech are represented in the basic units of the writing system (phonemes or syllables), and (2) to what extent a meaning-based principle exists to compete with the speech-based principle. (This amounts to the question of how reliably speech units are represented by units of the writing system.)

The Alphabetic Principle

Reading in an alphabetic orthography requires the child to learn the alphabetic principle one way or another. But the alphabetic principle is difficult, as indicated by the lateness and uniqueness of its discovery by the Phoenicians and Greeks. Its discovery (or invention) lagged far behind the writing systems that merely provided symbols for objects and meanings (Gelb, 1952). It should not be surprising then, as Gleitman and Rozin (1977) noted, that learners might have some trouble in 'replicating' this discovery.

Phonological Awareness

An obstacle for learners of the alphabetic principle is that young children are likely to have only dim awareness of the phonological structure of their language. Because phonemes, especially stop consonants, are abstractions over highly variable acoustic events, their status as discreet speech segments is not readily accessible. The child learning to read an alphabetic writing system needs to discover the alphabetic principle, but may lack at least half of what is needed. Letters must be associated with phonemes, but the child may not have an adequate representation of phonemes.[3]

This assumption that children have inadequate explicit representations of phonemes (phonemic 'awareness') has been well established. Earlier studies by Liberman, Shankweiler, Fischer, and Carter (1974) that found failure among 4 and 5 year old children in a tapping task—tap once with a stick for each sound in a short word—were followed by a number of studies that confirmed the general inability of many pre-literate children to demonstrate awareness of phonemes in various tasks. More important, studies began to show a relationship between phonemic awareness and

learning to read (Fox and Routh, 1976; Lundberg, Olofsson, and Wall, 1980; Stanovich, Cunningham, and Cramer, 1984; Tunmer, Herriman, and Nesdale, 1988). The literature demonstrating the details of this relationship has become substantial. (See Rieben and Perfetti (1991) and Brady and Shankweiler (1991) for collections of research.)

The question raised by the correlation between phonemic awareness and learning to read is whether the first is a necessary cause of the second. The evidence of training studies (Bradley and Bryant, 1983; Treiman and Baron, 1983; Vellutino and Scanlon, 1991) gives some support to the causality conclusion, as do longitudinal studies using cross-lag correlations (Mann, 1991; Perfetti, Beck, Bell, and Hughes, 1987). At least some phonological knowledge functionally mediates learning how to read in an alphabetic writing system.

Nevertheless, it seems clear that literacy itself is necessary for the development of a full blown phonemic awareness. Studies of adult illiterates (Morais, Cary, Alegria, and Bertelson, 1979; Morais, Bertelson, Cary, and Alegria, 1986) found that adults who had not learned to read were very weak in tasks requiring analysis of phonemic structure, although they do much better at syllable-level and rhyming tasks. Such results suggest the limited level of phonological awareness that can be developed outside of literacy contexts. Indeed, although there are many opportunities for oral language use to promote rhyming and syllabic ability, there is little outside of literacy contexts that can serve to draw attention to the existence of phonemes.

The consensus from the research is that the relationship between phonemic awareness and learning to read is not one-directional but reciprocal. Perfetti et al. (1987) found that, prior to instruction, a simple ability to synthesize phonemes into syllables predicted progress in first grade reading, whereas an ability to delete the initial or final phonemes from syllables did not; instead, the deletion performance, a more analytic ability, was initially predicted by progress in learning to read, and, as it developed with literacy gains, in turn, predicted further progress in reading. Such results strongly suggest that for the more analytic phonemic abilities there is a dynamic and reciprocal relationship, in which phonemic ability is first promoted through literacy acquisition and which then enables further gains in literacy.

… the relationship between phonemic awareness and learning to read is not one-directional but reciprocal.

It is important to be clear about the implications of the research on phonemic awareness. The fact that literacy affects phonemic awareness as well as vice versa does not negate the functional role of knowledge of phonemes in learning to read. It rather reflects the invisibility of phonemic structures, i.e., the fact that specific phonemes are not an ordinary nor salient part of the perceptual experience of hearing words. Moreover, this lack of visibility can be compounded in the reading situation, which requires the child to coordinate temporally represented phonemes with spatially represented print. Good literacy instruction makes phonemes more visible while it promotes their mapping to printed symbols. The fact that literacy and phonemic awareness can develop in tandem has implications for reading instruction. Rather than stressing phonological training in isolation, phonological training and word reading can be effectively linked together.

Conclusion: What About Comprehension?

I have argued that there are four well established and important classes of research results that can inform reading instruction. I appear, however, to have ignored comprehension. The reason is not a lack of clear research on comprehension. Indeed, models of text comprehension (Kintsch, 1988), studies of goal directed reading and inferences (Trabasso and van den Broek, 1985), studies of comprehension monitoring (Baker, 1979, 1985; Baker and Anderson, 1982)—to mention only a few of many—have contributed equally to understanding of reading processes. But these comprehension discoveries either have been well disseminated into educational thinking or have only the vaguest of implications or both. They deserve attention in a fuller account of reading, but not in a focused search for critical results.

What makes these four special is that (1) they converge on clear principles of reading pedagogy and (2) they appear to be underrepresented in the education of reading teachers. They do not, in my view, point to a particular method of teaching. Rather they point to general goals of reading education that can be met in a wide variety of ways. The central goal is that children should learn how their writing system works. This means, for alphabetic writing systems, making sure they learn the alphabetic principle, something that requires some attention to fostering students' phonemic awareness.

... children should learn how their writing system works.

The other basic facts I've stressed support the importance of this conclusion. There is no shortcut to reading words. Words are read more than skipped, and context doesn't alter this fact much. Besides, an emphasis on context is easily misplaced. Children learn to use context readily, even when they are not good at reading. Helping students develop text problem solving skills, e.g. using contexts to figure out interpretations, intentions, conclusions, etc., is a good idea. But getting good at word identification is an important goal in setting the stage for the successful use of such comprehension strategies.

Because it turns out that phonology is so pervasive in skilled word reading, it is counterproductive to think of phonology antagonistically. It is a central fact of ordinary word identification. Its use originates in a strong connection that is learned between the written forms of words and their pronunciations.

Finally, it is interesting to consider again the case of Chinese. As I noted, Chinese reading involves more phonology than previously assumed. Full writing systems build on speech, not on meanings only. Especially interesting is the fact that Chinese education acknowledges the value of alphabetic reading. Chinese students start out not with characters but with an alphabetic script (*pin yin*). There is systematic instruction over the first 8 weeks of school in letter-sound correspondences. A Chinese student masters the reading of this alphabetic script and then moves on to characters (which are first presented above *pin yin* spellings). The only purpose this *pin yin* stage serves is to help the student later learn to read his or her own script. In effect, Chinese students learn a system like English (but more regular) just to make their own system easier. This emphasis on letter-phoneme learning where it is not necessary is in striking contrast to its avoidance in the training of English language teachers. One would imagine that because the alphabetic principle is necessary rather than merely convenient in the reading of English, teaching it—in whatever manner—should be the prime goal of early reading instruction. Comprehension is not sacrificed by an intelligent approach to this goal.

Notes

1. See Glaser (1976, 1982) for an insightful analysis of how research and practice connect in education.
2. The problem, more often, however, is that there is an additional layer of analysis that must be done to implement recommendations from simple conclusions into practice. It is never quite clear who is to do this work in education. It is neither the job of teachers nor researchers. But the failure to get it done is no doubt one of the greatest obstacles to research-stimulated improvements in education.
3. The child also may have no advance knowledge about how a writing system might map phonological or even acoustic properties of the language. Rozin, Bressman, and Taft (1974), for example, found that many preschool children could not perform their *mow-motorcycle* test, which asked children which of two printed words corresponded to each of two spoken words, 'mow' and 'motorcycle'. Successful performance on this task requires not

awareness of phonemes, but merely the idea that acoustic length might correspond to visual length or number of letters. Lundberg and Torneus (1978) reported in Sweden, where reading instruction does not begin until eight, even six-year-old children performed inconsistently on the *mow-motorcycle* test.

References

Baker, L. (1979). Comprehension monitoring: Identifying and coping with text confusions. *Journal of Reading Behavior, 11*, 365–374.

Baker, L. (1985). Differences in the standards used by college students to evaluate their comprehension of expository prose. *Reading Research Quarterly, 20*, 297–313.

Baker, L., and Anderson, R. I. (1982). Effects of inconsistent information on text processing: Evidence for comprehension monitoring. *Reading Research Quarterly, 22*, 281–294.

Berent, I., and Perfetti, C. A. (1995). A rose is a REEZ: The two-cycles model of phonology assembly in reading English. *Psychological Review, 102*, 146–184.

Bradley, L., and Bryant, P. E. (1983). Categorizing sounds and learning to read—a causal connection. *Nature, 301*, 419–421.

Brady, S. A., and Shankweiler, D. (Eds.) (1991). *Phonological processes in literacy: A tribute to Isabelle Y. Liberman.* Hillsdale, NJ: Lawrence Erlbaum Associates.

Coltheart, M. (1978). Lexical access in simple reading tasks. In G. Underwood (Ed.), *Strategies of information processing* (pp. 151–216). New York: Academic Press.

Defrancis, J. (1989). *Visible speech: The diverse oneness of writing systems.* Honolulu: University of Hawaii.

Ehrlich, S. F., and Rayner, K. (1981). Contextual effects on word perception and eye movements during reading. *Journal of Verbal Learning and Verbal Behavior, 20*, 641–655.

Fox, B., and Routh, D. K. (1976). Phonemic analysis and synthesis as word-attack skills. *Journal of Educational Psychology, 68*, 70–74.

Gelb, I. J. (1952). *A study of writing.* Chicago: University of Chicago Press.

Glaser, R. (1976). Components of a psychology of instruction: Toward a science of design. *Review of Educational Research, 46*, 1–24.

Glaser, R. (1982). Instructional psychology: Past, present, and future. *American Psychologist, 37*, 292–305.

Gleitman, L. R., and Rozin, P. (1977). The structure and acquisition of reading I: Relations between orthographies and the structure of language. In A. S. Reber and D. L. Scarborough (Eds.), *Toward a psychology of reading: The proceedings of the CUNY conferences* (pp. 1–54). Hillsdale, NJ: Lawrence Erlbaum Associates (Distributed by Wiley).

Just, M. A., and Carpenter, P. A. (1987). *The psychology of reading and language comprehension.* Boston: Allyn and Bacon.

Just, M. A., Carpenter, P. A. and Masson, M. E. J. (1982). *What eye fixations tell us about speed reading and skimming* (eyelab tech report). Pittsburgh: Carnegie-Mellon University.

Kintsch, W. (1988). The role of knowledge in discourse processing: A construction-integration model. *Psychological Review, 95*, 163–182.

Liberman, I. Y., Shankweiler, D., Fischer, F. W. and Carter, B. (1974) Explicit syllable and phoneme segmentation in the young child. *Journal of Experimental Child Psychology, 18*, 201–212.

Lukatela, G., and Turvey, M. T. (1990). Automatic and prelexical computation of phonology in visual word identification. *European Journal of Cognitive Psychology, 2*, 325–344.

Lundberg, I., Olofsson, A., and Wall, S. (1980). Reading and spelling skills in the first school years predicted from phonemic awareness skills in kindergarten. *Scandinavian Journal of Psychology, 21*, 159–173.

Lundberg, I., and Torneus, M. (1978). Nonreaders' awareness of the basic relationship between spoken and written words. *Journal of Experimental Child Psychology, 25*, 404–412.

Mann, V. A. (1991). Phonological abilities: Effective predictors of future reading ability. In L. Rieben and C. A. Perfetti (Eds.), *Learning to read: Basic research and its implications* (pp. 121–133). Hillsdale, NJ: Lawrence Erlbaum Associates.

Morais, J., Bertelson, P., Cary, L., and Alegria, J. (1986). Literacy training and speech segmentation. *Cognition, 24*, 45–64.

Morais, J., Cary, L., Alegria, J., and Bertelson, P. (1979). Does awareness of speech as a sequence of phones arise spontaneously? *Cognition, 7*, 323–331.

Paap, K. R., and Noel, R. W. (1991). Dual-route models of print and sound: Still a good horse race. *Psychological Research, 53*, 13–24.

Perfetti, C. A., Beck, I., Bell, L., and Hughes, C. (1987). Phonemic knowledge and learning to read are reciprocal: A longitudinal study of first grade children. *Merrill-Palmer Quarterly, 33*, 283–319.

Perfetti, C. A., Bell, L., and Delaney, S. (1988). Automatic phonetic activation in silent word reading: Evidence from backward masking. *Journal of Memory and Language, 27*, 59–70.

Perfetti, C. A., Goldman, S. R., and Hogaboam, T. W. (1979). Reading skill and the identification of words in discourse context. *Memory and Cognition, 7*, 273–282.

Perfetti, C. A., and Roth, S. F. (1981). Some of the interactive processes in reading and their role in reading skill. In A. M. Lesgold and C. A. Perfetti (Eds.), *Interactive processes in reading* (pp. 269–297). Hillsdale, NJ: Lawrence Erlbaum Associates.

Perfetti, C. A., and Zhang, S. (1995a). Very early phonological activation in Chinese reading. *Journal of Experimental Psychology: Learning, Memory, and Cognition, 21*, 24–33.

Perfetti, C. A., and Zhang, S. (1996b). The universal word identification reflex. In D. L. Medin (Ed.), *The psychology of learning and motivation, Vol. 33* (pp. 159–189). San Diego: Academic Press.

Perfetti, C. A., Zhang, S., and Berent, J. (1992). Reading in English and Chinese: Evidence for a 'universal' phonological principle. In R. Frost and L. Katz (Eds.), *Orthography, phonology, morphology, and meaning* (pp. 227–248). Amsterdam: North-Holland.

Pinker. S. (1984). *Language learnability and language development.* Cambridge, MA: Harvard University Press.

Rayner. K. and Pollatsek, A. (1989). *The psychology of reading.* Englewood Cliffs, NJ: Prentice Hall.

Rieben, L., and Perfetti, C. A. (Eds.) (1991). *Learning to read: Basic research and its implications.* Hillsdale, NJ: Lawrence Erlbaum Associates.

Rozin, P., Bressman, B., and Taft, M. (1974). Do children understand the basic relationship between speech and writing? The Mow-Motorcycle test. *Journal of Reading Behavior, 6,* 327–334.

Seidenberg, M. S., Waters, G. S., Barnes, M. A., and Tanenhaus, M. K. (1984). When does irregular spelling or pronunciation influence word recognition? *Journal of Verbal Learning and Verbal Behavior, 23,* 383–404.

Stanovich, K. E. (1981). Attentional and automatic context effects in reading. In A. M. Lesgold and C. A. Perfetti (Eds.), *Interactive processes in reading* (pp. 241–267). Hillsdale, NJ: Lawrence Erlbaum Associates.

Stanovich, K. E. (1980). Toward an interactive-compensatory model of individual differences in the development of reading fluency. *Reading Research Quarterly, 16,* 32–71.

Stanovich, K. E. Cunningham, A. E., and Cramer, B. (1984). Assessing phonological awareness in kindergarten children: Issues of task comparability. *Journal of Experimental Child Psychology, 38,* 175–190.

Stanovich, K. E., and West, R. F. (1981). The effect of sentence context on on-going word recognition: Tests of a two-process theory. *Journal of Experimental Psychology: Human Perception and Performance, 7,* 658–672.

Trabasso, T., and Van den broek, P. (1985). Casual thinking and the representation of narrative events. *Journal of Memory and Language, 24,* 612–630.

Treiman, R., and Baron, J. (1983). Phonemic-analysis training helps children benefit from spelling-sound rules. *Memory and Cognition, 11,* 382–389.

Tunmer, W. E., Herriman, M. L., and Nesdale, A. R. (1988). Metalinguistic abilities and beginning reading. *Reading Research Quarterly, 23,* 134–158.

Van orden, G. C., Pennington, B., and Stone, G. (1990). Word identification in reading and the promise of sub-symbolic psycholinguistics. *Psychological Review, 97,* 488–522.

Vellutino, F. R., and Scanlon, D. M. (1991). The effects of instructional bias on word identification. In L. Rieben and C. A. Perfetti (Eds.), *Learning to read: Basic research and its implications* (pp. 189–203). Hillsdale, NJ: Lawrence Erlbaum Associates.

Yuill, N., and Oakhill, J. (1991). Children's problems in text comprehension: An experimental investigation. Cambridge: Cambridge University Press.

English Learners Reading English: What We Know, What We Need to Know

Suzanne F. Peregoy
San Francisco State University

Owen F. Boyle
San José State University

Of all school learning, success in literacy, especially reading, is certainly among the most important achievements for all students due to its key role in academic learning and consequent social and economic opportunities. In recent years, pressures to prepare a highly literate populace together with concerns over reading achievement have prompted federal and state leaders in the United States to focus attention on ways to teach reading more effectively. Debates over best teaching practices have fueled differences between whole language and phonics advocates.

The result is a highly vocal and polarized rhetoric that fails to capture the reality of today's classrooms: dedicated teachers combining experience, insight, and professional judgment to address the increasingly diverse and changing learning needs of their students. Often missing in the debate are the literacy needs of English learners, though as a group, they score among the lowest in reading achievement nationwide. Finding a place for English learners in the discussion of best practices is thus imperative.

The inadequacy of efforts to define simple guidelines for teaching English learners to read is not due to lack of concern on the part of researchers, educators, or politicians. Rather a combination of factors makes English learners' reading a conceptually difficult topic to encompass. Among these factors are the dynamic, evolving, and sometimes controversial state of reading research in general; a lack of consistent, generalizable research findings on second language reading processes and programs in particular; and the rapid growth and tremendous diversity among English learners themselves (Fitzgerald, 1995).

As we write this article, we enter the arena well aware of these obstacles. Nonetheless, we see this as an opportunity to synthesize research, theory, and practice in the field of second language reading. We begin by describing English reading processes among native and non-native English speakers. Then, using theory, experience, and research where available for support, we offer a set of recommendations for teaching English learners to read in English.

Diversity Among English Learners

The most salient feature of English learners as a group is their remarkable diversity. At the very least, these students vary in age, prior educational experiences, cultural heritage, socioeconomic status, country of origin, and levels of both primary language and English language development, including literacy development. Some are immigrants or children of immigrants and represent languages from every continent in the world. Others have roots in U.S. soil that go back for generations, maintaining languages as diverse as Spanish, Navajo, Chippewa, Cherokee, Choctaw, Apache, and Crow. Of course English learners also vary along personal lines, as do all students, in terms of their interests, desires, aptitudes, and potentials.

Just as English learners vary one from another, so do the classrooms and programs that serve them. While some classrooms serve English learners from the same primary language background, often Spanish, other classrooms may include students from over 10 different primary language backgrounds. Some students will receive literacy instruction in the primary language; many will not. Regardless of program type or classroom composition, tremendous diversity will be found in any classroom in terms of students' English proficiency, reading and writing ability, primary language literacy, and literacy practices in the home.

... the process of reading in English is essentially similar for all readers, ... native or non-native English speakers.

As daunting as the diversity among second language readers may be, one unifying factor in the equation is that the *process* of reading in English is essentially similar for all readers, whether they are native or non-native English speakers (Fitzgerald, 1995; Goodman & Goodman, 1978). This process involves decoding written symbols into the language they represent to arrive at meaning. What differ between native and non-native English readers are the cognitive-linguistic and experiential resources they bring to the reading task, especially in terms of those variables that relate directly to reading comprehension in English, i.e., (a) English language proficiency, (b) background knowledge related to the text, and (c) literacy abilities and experiences, if any, in the first language. We elaborate later on these three differences between native and non-native English readers, but first we briefly describe how native English speakers read in English in order to establish those elements of the reading process shared in common by native and non-native English readers.

Good Readers Reading in English

How do good readers read? That is, how do native English speakers who are also good readers make sense of a text written in English? First, good readers generally approach a text with a particular purpose in mind. They have enough experience with written language to know its various uses, and they put that understanding into practice when selecting a text to achieve their purpose.

Along with a purpose, good readers may bring at least some prior knowledge of the text topic. The more familiar the topic, the easier it will be for the reader to understand the text. That is, comprehension is affected by the extent to which the reader is familiar with the topics, objects, and events described in a text (Anderson, 1994). Good readers activate prior knowledge of the text topic by imagining what they know and do not know about the topic, predicting what the text will be about, and generating questions the text might answer.

Having set a purpose and activated prior knowledge, the good reader begins reading by visually processing the print from left to right, top to bottom of the page, given that we are talking about reading in English. Processing the print involves decoding the words on the page, i.e., producing a mental or verbal equivalent to access meaning. However, decoding word by word is insufficient, as evidenced by some students who accurately call out every word in a sentence without understanding the meaning.

As they are decoded, the words on the page must also be interpreted, initially in the context of the phrases and sentences of which they are a part, and subsequently across sentences and paragraphs as the larger meaning of the text is constructed. The comprehension process thus depends upon the reader's knowledge of the particular vocabulary and grammatical structures that comprise the sentences of the text and also upon the reader's familiarity with the way the text as a whole is structured.

As the good reader moves across sentences and paragraphs to construct the larger meaning of a text, familiarity with the genre and its text structure comes into play in the comprehension process, helping the reader anticipate and predict the direction and flow of ideas (Kintsch & Van Dijk, 1978). For example, a text that begins, "Once upon a time," signals the beginning of a fairy tale told with a narrative text structure.

Contrast that with a paragraph that begins, "Three key events led to California's rapid rise to statehood." This sentence signals an informational text that will probably be written with an enumeration text structure. Good readers are sufficiently familiar with a variety of genres and text structures to use this knowledge for predicting and confirming meaning across sentences, paragraphs, and passages that comprise a text.

As good readers move through the text, decoding and constructing meaning, they need to hold on to their ongoing textual interpretation in order to elaborate, modify, and further build upon it, thereby keeping their interpretation going and growing. Reading is thus a complex, cognitive-linguistic process that engages background knowledge and taxes both short- and long-term memory. It is also a process that takes place in a social context while serving as a social act of communication between the author and reader. In this interactive view, text comprehension is simultaneously driven by the reader's purpose, prior knowledge, and ongoing interpretation as these interact with decoding to achieve communication (Rumelhart, 1994).

What differ between native and non-native English readers are the cognitive-linguistic and experiential resources they bring to the reading task.

Finally, good readers are strategic readers, meaning they monitor their understanding as they read to check whether their interpretation makes sense and to make sure they are achieving their purpose (Brown, Campione, & Day, 1980). They employ fix-up strategies, such as rereading a confusing part, to assist themselves in comprehending a text and achieving their purpose for reading. In this sense, reading is an active process of constructing and confirming meaning, one that is both linear and sequential as well as recursive and selective in that good readers may preview the text, reread a sentence, or go back to a different section to double check their evolving interpretation.

We have briefly described how good readers set a purpose for reading and bring several knowledge resources to bear upon the comprehension process, among them: decoding ability, language knowledge, background knowledge, written genre knowledge, familiarity with text structures, and comprehension-monitoring abilities. Non-native English readers engage in a similar reading process, calling into play similar knowledge resources, with certain important differences that we focus on in the next sections: (a) English language proficiency, (b) background knowledge, and (c) literacy knowledge and experience in the primary language.

English Language Proficiency

English language proficiency stands out as the defining difference between native and non-native English speakers, even though English learners range along a broad continuum from non-English to fully English proficient. In this context, English language proficiency refers to an individual's general knowledge of English, including vocabulary, grammar, and discourse conventions, which may be called upon during any instance of oral or written language use (Canale & Swain, 1980; Peregoy & Boyle, 1991).

To the extent that a reader is limited in English language proficiency, the ability to make sense of a text written in English is likewise hindered. Even second language readers who are proficient in English have been found to read more slowly than native English speakers, attesting to the comprehension difficulties related to English language proficiency during reading (Fitzgerald, 1995). This fact calls into question the validity of standardized reading achievement test results for many English learners.

Background Knowledge: Text Content

Interestingly, the comprehension challenges imposed by limited English proficiency are alleviated when the text concerns content with which the second language reader is familiar. For example, in one study, Arab Muslim and Hispanic Catholic college students in the United States were given two passages to read, one with Muslim-oriented content and one with Catholic-oriented content (Carrell, 1987). For both groups, comprehension was better when reading the passage reflecting their own cultural tradition. In similar studies involving culturally familiar and culturally unfamiliar passages of similar linguistic difficulty, comprehension was higher for the culturally familiar text (Fitzgerald, 1995). In other words, familiarity with text content alleviated limitations associated with second language proficiency in text comprehension.

Background knowledge is a powerful variable for both native and non-native English readers. However,

it becomes doubly important in second language reading because it interacts with language proficiency during reading, alleviating the comprehension difficulties stemming from language proficiency limitations. Therefore, building background knowledge on a text topic through first-hand experiences such as science experiments, museum visits, and manipulatives can facilitate success in reading.

Background Knowledge: Text Structure

In addition to familiarity with text content, familiarity with text structure also facilitates reading comprehension (Carrell, 1987, 1992). Because text structure conventions can vary from one language to another, explicit instruction on English text structures is beneficial for English learners, especially those who are literate in their primary language. For example, knowing how a story plot or a cause/effect argument is structured can facilitate reading comprehension in those genres.

Text structure knowledge boosts comprehension by helping readers anticipate and predict the direction of a plot or argument, thereby facilitating attention to the larger meaning of the text. For example, familiarity with problem/solution text structure can assist the reader in anticipating, seeking, and finding the author's proposed solution to the problem posed. Similarly, calling students' attention to headings and subheadings used in content area texts provides them a strategy for previewing text content and creating potential questions to answer when reading.

Familiarity with English text structures results from extensive experience reading a variety of texts in English, especially when explicit discussion of text structure is provided to help students perceive these patterns and use them to understand text. All English learners can benefit from text structure instruction, especially those who are literate in the primary language, given that text structure conventions may vary across languages and cultures. By showing students the elements, organization, and sequencing that make up a "good essay," a "good story," or a "good argument" in English, teachers can immediately boost the quality of their students' reading and writing.

Assisting English learners with expository text structures is especially critical because content area texts become longer, more complex, and more conceptually dense from the third grade and up through high school and college. Text structure knowledge can help students grapple with these challenging texts, promoting reading comprehension and learning in science, social studies, and other content areas.

In summary, to the extent that the reader's background knowledge is reflected in a text, the text is easier to understand. Furthermore, background knowledge and language knowledge *interact* during second language reading, so that comprehension limitations can be overcome to some extent when the text topic is familiar. Knowledge of text structure conventions also enables readers to predict and confirm the meaning in a passage, enhancing comprehension. By tailoring instruction to students' English proficiency and building background knowledge for particular text content and structure, teachers significantly increase their students' chances for success in reading English.

Success in reading English is a valued outcome in itself, but it has the additional benefit of providing a useful source of linguistic input for English language development. Wide reading not only increases reading ability but also promotes English language development (Elley & Mangubhai, 1983). Furthermore, wide reading increases general background knowledge, which in turn facilitates comprehension when reading texts of all kinds, including content area texts.

Phonemic Awareness and Phonics

Thus far we have highlighted language knowledge and background knowledge as important aspects of the reading process. These factors can only be brought into play, however, if the reader has adequate knowledge of the writing system to access the language encoded in the text, a fact that holds equally true for both first and second language readers. In English and other languages that use alphabetic writing systems, speech sounds are represented by letters and letter sequences, reflecting the nature of the alphabetic principle. In order for beginning readers to make use of the alphabetic principle, they need to be able to (a) hear individual speech sounds in words, i.e., phonemic awareness; and (b) learn the symbols that represent those sounds, i.e., phonics or graphophonics. Without substantial knowledge of these sound/symbol correspondences, readers are deprived of a useful tool for recognizing unfamiliar words.

Phonics is not the only tool readers may use to unlock an unfamiliar word. Good readers also use context to help them predict a word that fits grammatically and makes sense in the context of the sentence and passage. Here again, we see language knowledge, background knowledge, and experience with written texts fueling word recognition, as a passage is read and comprehended. The essential question is not whether students should be taught sound/symbol correspondences but rather how these should be taught.

For English learners, there is very little research either on phonemic awareness (the ability to hear, isolate, and manipulate sounds in spoken words) or phonics instruction (instruction on sound/letter correspondences). However, because both phonemic awareness and phonics are language-based processes, and because English learners vary in their English language proficiency, English language proficiency must be taken into consideration in deciding how and when to emphasize phonemic awareness and phonics instruction, a topic we return to in our instructional recommendations at the end of this article.

Experience in the Primary Language

Another difference English learners bring to their reading is the quantity and kind of literacy knowledge and experience they have in their primary language, if any, a variable that ties in closely with the age of the student, prior educational experiences in the primary language, and the socioeconomic status and educational level of the parents. When a student begins English reading instruction solidly literate in the primary language, even in a language that uses a very different writing system from English such as Russian or Chinese, that student possesses funds of knowledge that go well beyond simply being able to read (Moll, 1994).

For example, students who are literate in their home language have some knowledge of the *functions* of print. While the purposes of literacy in the primary language may differ from those they are learning for English, students literate in their primary language have nonetheless experienced the value, utility, and perhaps pleasures of print. In terms of reading *per se*, they have exercised the process of making sense from print, and, depending on their reading abilities, they are more or less automatic at decoding and comprehending text in their primary language.

Education in the primary language … facilitates academic adjustment while providing a solid experiential base for literacy development in English.

In addition, students literate in the primary language are typically accustomed to the discipline and demands of school, whether educated in the United States or elsewhere. Education in the primary language thus facilitates academic adjustment while providing a solid experiential base for literacy development in English. The power of primary language literacy as a foundation for second language literacy provides the cornerstone for many bilingual education programs in the United States and worldwide.

Types of Writing Systems

When we make the claim that primary language literacy provides a good foundation for English literacy, we are suggesting that various aspects of reading and writing transfer across languages, including attitudes and expectations about print as well as the general process of decoding, interpreting the language, constructing meaning from text, and monitoring comprehension (Carrell, 1991; Pritchard, 1990; Tragar & Wong, 1984). At a more specific level, transfer of literacy ability from one language to another depends on the similarities and differences between their writing systems, including the unit of speech symbolized by each character.

For example, alphabetic writing systems, such as the three different ones used for English, Greek, and Russian, represent speech sounds or phonemes with letters or letter sequences. In contrast, in logographic writing systems, such as Chinese, each written character represents a meaning unit or morpheme; while in syllabic writing systems, such as kana in Japanese and Sequoyah's Cherokee syllabary, each written symbol represents a syllable.

In addition to differences in the unit of speech represented, directionality and spacing conventions differ across writing systems. For example, Hebrew reads from right to left whereas English and other European languages read from left to right. Chinese traditionally reads right to left. We suggest that specific differences among writing systems must be explicitly addressed when teaching English reading to students who are literate in their primary language. In order to do so, teachers need to learn about the writing systems their students use and the extent to which they are literate in them.

Writing Systems Similar to English

While providing substantial funds of knowledge upon which to base English literacy, the ability to read (and write) in another language thus poses the challenge of learning the similarities and differences between the ways English and the primary language are portrayed in print. To the extent that the writing systems are similar, positive transfer can occur in decoding.

Take Spanish and English, for example. In our experience (Peregoy, 1989; Peregoy & Boyle, 1991), certain features transfer readily such as the idea that speech sounds are represented by letters and letter sequences and the notion that print is read left-to-right and top-to-bottom. Specific letter-sound correspondences may transfer as well. For example, a native Spanish speaker who is proficient in reading Spanish will encounter a similar alphabet in English, with consonant letters representing similar sounds in the two languages. For example, the letters b, c, d, f, l, m, n, p, q, s, and t represents sounds that are similar enough in both English and Spanish that they may transfer readily to English reading for many students. Consequently, minimal phonics instruction is needed by many students for these consonants.

In contrast, the vowel letters look the same in Spanish and English but represent sounds very differently. Therefore English vowel sounds and their numerous, "unruly" spellings present a challenge to Spanish literate students learning to read English because the one-to-one correspondence between vowel letters and vowel sounds in Spanish does not hold true in English. Moreover, English has a plethora of vowel spellings that often include "silent letters." Consider the "long a" sound as spelled in the following words: *lake, weight, mail*. These spellings present a challenge to native and non-native English speakers alike. For Spanish literate students, explicit instruction on English vowel spelling patterns is often useful, preferably in the context of reading simple texts. At the same time, attention to text comprehension is essential, given that some students learn to decode English so well that they *appear* to be comprehending when in fact they are merely "word calling," i.e., pronouncing words without understanding the meaning.

Writing Systems Different from English

Clearly, some students may begin English reading instruction accustomed to a writing system that bears little or no resemblance to the one they must learn for English. For example, students who are literate in a logographic system such as Chinese are faced with learning the English convention of representing speech sounds instead of meaning units, and the practice of reading from left to right instead of right to left. These differences may require considerable concentration in the early stages of English reading acquisition as students develop an understanding of the alphabetic principle and begin to learn specific sound/symbol correspondences.

Early on, memorization of whole words and their meanings may prove useful for Chinese literate students, transferring a strategy they may have used to learn Chinese characters. Eventually, though, they need to grasp the alphabetic principle, attend to individual sounds in spoken English words (phonemic awareness), and associate those sounds with certain letters and letter sequences (phonics). As students learn to decode English, they also need to develop the English language knowledge that will allow them to access the meaning of the text, or their decoding will not lead to text comprehension.

In contrast to students with logographic literacy, some English learners may be literate in alphabetic writing systems that nonetheless use letters and print conventions that are very different from English, such as Arabic, Hebrew, and Thai. These students are apt to be well-versed in the alphabetic principle, which they acquired in the process of learning to read in the primary language, and that understanding should transfer easily to English reading. They are also more or less aware of various functions of print and have had considerable experience constructing meaning from text, another source of positive transfer. What will be new for these students are the specific letters and letter/sound correspondences used in English. To learn to read in English, they need to learn the specific conventions of how English is represented in print while at the same time developing English language proficiency to facilitate reading comprehension.

Students with Minimal Literacy Experience

It is important to note that some English learners may come to school at any age with minimal literacy experience or abilities in any language. Before selecting instructional interventions for non-literate students, teachers need to find out as much as possible about the student's non-literacy. For example, is it due to minimal or interrupted schooling resulting from family mobility or circumstances of immigration? Is it because the family stems from a background without a literate tradition? Or does the child have some sort of visual, auditory, or linguistic processing difficulty that hinders the reading process? Knowing the student's prior experiences helps teachers know where to start.

By and large, students without prior literacy experiences benefit from exposure to the many practical purposes that written language can serve in daily life (Hamayan, 1994). Daily modeling of reading and writing is needed in which meaning and purpose are palpably clear, such as read alouds using texts with reliable picture cues to convey meaning, making and using lists of classroom duties, and reading students' names from a word wall to take roll.

In a language and literacy rich environment, learners will begin to develop English language proficiency while simultaneously gaining a rudimentary sense of how print works, both in form and function. These experiences will also offer opportunities for students to grasp the essence of the alphabetic principle upon which the English writing system is based. From there, students can benefit from word identification strategy instruction, using stories, poems, and songs they already know well due to repeated exposures in which textual meaning and purpose are made clear.

A Note of Caution

We have described our view of the reading process of English learners as similar to that of native English speakers, with important differences stemming in particular from variations in English language proficiency, background knowledge, and prior literacy experiences. We based our discussion on current theory and research in reading, including second language reading. Throughout our discussion, we have suggested ways to facilitate English learners' reading success by addressing the particular resources and special needs they bring to the task.

We need to point out here certain critical issues regarding the research base in second language reading. First, most of the research on second language reading has been conducted with older learners in secondary school or college. This is particularly the case for research on background knowledge and language proficiency effects on reading comprehension. Relatively little research addresses elementary school-aged English learners, and when it does, it focuses on students who are already able to read connected text (e.g., Peregoy, 1989; Peregoy & Boyle, 1991).

Beginning English reading acquisition and instruction for English learners, especially among students who are not literate in the primary language, are virtually untouched topics in the research literature, creating a dilemma for those who seek a strong research base to validate instructional practices. Teaching practices for native English speakers cannot simply be applied whole cloth to English learners without modifications that consider, at the very least, students' English language proficiency and primary language literacy. Topics such as phonemic awareness, phonics, decoding, and effective approaches to beginning reading instruction are yet to be adequately researched for English learners.

In terms of phonemic awareness, in particular, research must address several important questions: (a) At what point in non-native English language development does phonemic awareness in English emerge? (b) How difficult is it for beginning English language learners to hear and manipulate speech sounds in English, and do these abilities vary based on the age of the learner? based on the student's primary language (e.g., Spanish vs. Turkish vs. Cantonese vs. Crow)? (c) Does primary language literacy in an alphabetic writing system facilitate phonemic awareness in English? What about primary language literacy in a logographic or syllabic writing system?

If English learners do not demonstrate phonemic awareness, what methods of reading instruction will best promote their English literacy development? Virtually no research addresses these issues.

Instructional Implications

Below we draw a number of instructional implications from our discussion of English learner reading. For our purposes here, we provide only a brief overview of instructional strategies. For more in-depth descriptions, see Boyle and Peregoy (1998), Peregoy and Boyle (1997) and Opitz (1998).

Learning About Students

Learning as much as possible about individual English learners is essential to planning effective literacy instruction, especially in the broad areas we have discussed in this article: English language proficiency, prior knowledge and life experiences, and literacy in the primary language. This kind of information makes it possible to validate students for what they *do know* and build from there.

Building learning activities upon familiar concepts, for example, not only facilitates literacy and content learning but also helps students feel more comfortable and confident at school. In addition to school records, if they exist, good initial sources of information include the students themselves, their families, and community organizations. It may also be helpful to talk with other teachers who have students from the same family. In addition, school personnel such as community liaisons and paraprofessionals may prove helpful in providing information about students.

English Language Proficiency

By definition, English learners are still learning English. Classroom instruction often consists of oral language interactions between teachers and students. When using English as the language of instruction, teachers need to use sheltering strategies to assure that students will be able to understand and participate successfully in learning activities. Pairing non-verbal cues (e.g., pictures, demonstrations, and gestures) with verbal instruction helps make lessons comprehensible for students. Paraphrasing and defining important vocabulary in context also aid comprehension. As lessons are made more comprehensible for students, instruction simultaneously promotes language acquisition and content learning. For second language learners, every lesson is a potential language learning opportunity, and must be structured as such (Peregoy & Boyle, 1999).

Sensitivity to the varied language development levels of English learners will determine how much sheltering is needed, how much time it will take for students to process instructional content, and by what means (e.g., oral, written, pictorial, dramatization) they will display their learning. The more experience teachers have working with English learners, the more knowledgeable they become in determining those aspects of English their students are apt to find difficult, including vocabulary; word order; verb forms to express past, present, and future; word formation elements such as prefixes, suffixes, and roots; and function words such as articles, prepositions, and conjunctions.

Beyond these linguistic elements, day-to-day observation allows teachers to gauge how well students use English to accomplish routine learning tasks and social interactions in ways that are appropriate to the classroom context. This knowledge helps teachers plan specific modifications in their own instructional language and guides them as they plan ways to prepare students for reading and understanding specific texts.

English learners who are beginning English reading instruction may be literate in the primary language due to education in another country or as a result of bilingual instruction in the United States. The benefits of primary language literacy are many, both as a foundation for English literacy and as a vehicle for developing full bilingualism and biliteracy. Although primary language reading instruction is beyond the scope of this article, suffice it to say that primary language development, including literacy, is a valuable educational goal for English learners themselves and for U.S. society as a whole (see Fillmore, this issue). Indeed without instruction in the primary language, oral and written skills are apt to deteriorate or become lost completely. Even so, many English learners find themselves learning oral and written English simultaneously, without the benefit of primary language instruction. The strategies for teaching English reading described below are applicable to English learners with or without primary language literacy abilities. The discussion assumes that English is the language of instruction.

Beginning Readers

When English learners are beginning to read in English, attention to meaning is paramount at every step of instruction. In addition to using sheltering strategies to help students understand the *lesson*, teachers need to help students understand the meaning and purpose of the *text*. Texts used for beginning reading instruction should be short, simple pieces such as poems, pattern books, songs, simple directions, or recipes. Student understanding of the meaning and purpose may be developed by reading the text aloud, pointing out and defining or dramatizing important content words, and using other sheltering strategies to help students understand the text. Repetition, perhaps with hand movements like those used in finger plays, is useful for this purpose and can be fun and enjoyable.

This phase of the lesson serves English language development and provides exposure to the forms and functions of print, creating a firm foundation for sight word recognition and subsequent instruction on specific sound/symbol correspondences and other word identification strategies. By using whole texts for which meaning has been developed, students learn the details of print in the context of reading for a purpose.

When English learners are beginning to read in English, attention to meaning is paramount at every step of instruction.

The above procedures apply for students of different ages. However, for older students care must be taken to assure that text content is age-appropriate. One way to do so is to base early reading instruction on student generated text, such as pattern poems, beginning "I like_____." Similarly, texts may be generated in class based on a particular learning experience, such as planting a garden, baking a casserole, or driving a car. The students provide the ideas, perhaps in one or two words, and the teacher writes the ideas down in conventional English sentences. These texts provide initial, meaningful encounters with print on which to base reading instruction.

To help teachers choose materials, many book lists are available on picture books with content appropriate for older students (e.g., Benedict, 1992) and on high interest, easy reading (e.g., Riechel, 1998; Rosow, 1996). (Searching the internet using keywords, *high interest low vocabulary*, yields a number of good resources including Libraries Unlimited at *http://www.lu.com/lu/*.) In addition to providing appropriate materials, it is important to learn about the student's primary language and whether the student is literate in it. If so, the teacher can validate the student for this accomplishment and anticipate areas of positive and/or negative transfer to reading in English.

Intermediate Readers

English language learners who can read connected text develop as readers by reading longer, more complex texts in a variety of genres. Teachers need to prepare students for any given text by focusing on specific aspects of its genre, vocabulary, grammar, content, and text structure that may be new to them. The strategies described below may be selected before, during, and after reading to facilitate reading comprehension in any genre, including stories, essays, or content area textbook selections.

Teachers need to prepare students for any given text by focusing on specific aspects of its genre, vocabulary, grammar, content, and text structure that may be new to them.

Before reading.   Students need to know their purpose for reading, and what they will be asked to do with the information after reading. Teachers therefore need to assess students' background knowledge pertinent to the text to be read and build background before students begin to read. It is often helpful to introduce important concepts/vocabulary through visuals, demonstrations, and graphic or pictorial organizers prior to reading. While doing so, teachers can informally assess the extent of their students' knowledge of the topic. Brainstorming and clustering about a topic in small groups is another to way to assess and build background information for students who are fairly fluent in English, provided sheltering strategies are used. Teachers may prepare students for unfamiliar text structures by presenting graphics that sketch the structure illustrated with two or three examples of actual text that follow the structure. Recipes and business letters are two easy text structures to display graphically, for example, while story maps offer a useful graphic representation of narrative structure.

Staying with a text.   To help students "get into" and stick with the text, the teacher may read a page or two aloud to the students, asking prediction questions to help them anticipate the direction of the piece. If the piece is especially difficult, the teacher may guide students through it by reading and discussing one paragraph at a time. Other strategies include pairing students to read to each other, with the teacher on hand to assist through rough spots. Additional strategies to help keep students on track during reading include student response logs and story maps or other graphic depictions of text meaning.

After reading.   Strategies used after reading serve to help students process the story or passage more deeply and to organize and remember the information. Some strategies include: mapping, dramatization, creating a mural, and writing a script for a play or a readers' theater. Any of these strategies may be used for in-depth literature study, content area reading, and theme-related projects.

Conclusion

In this article, we have discussed the special characteristics English learners bring to the task of reading and learning to read in their new language. We have pointed out the tremendous diversity among second language readers, illustrating the difficulties inherent in making simple generalizations concerning their reading acquisition and instruction. Using theory and research, we have presented a view of reading comprehension to illustrate similarities and differences in reading processes of English learners and native English speakers.

Throughout our discussion we have emphasized the need to consider English language proficiency, prior knowledge and experiences, and primary language literacy as important factors in English learner reading, variables that must be considered by teachers and researchers alike as they go about their work. Not only do we need to learn more about reading development among English learners of varying ages and backgrounds, we also need to learn more about the most effective instruction for particular groups of English learners. Specific programs and materials need to be developed and evaluated in terms of how well they meet the literacy development needs of particular groups of students. There is much to be done as teachers and researchers work together to expand the knowledge base for creating the best instruction for English learners and their literacy development.

References

Anderson, R. C. (1994). Role of reader's schemata in comprehension, learning and memory. In R. B. Ruddell, M. R. Ruddell & H. Singer (Eds.), *Theoretical models and processes of reading* (4th ed.; pp. 469–482). Newark, DE: International Reading Association.

Benedict, S. (1992). *Beyond words: Picture books for older readers and writers.* Portsmouth. NH: Heinemann.

Boyle, O., & Peregoy, S. (1998). Literacy scaffolds: Strategies for first- and second-language readers and writers. In M. Opitz (Ed.), *Literacy Instruction for culturally and linguistically diverse students* (pp. 150–157). Newark, DE: International Reading Association.

Brown, A., Campione, J. C., & Day, D. J. (1980). *Learning to learn: On training students to learn from texts* (Technical Report No. 189). Urbana: University of Illinois, Center for the Study of Reading.

Canale, M., & Swain, M. (1980). Theoretical bases of communicative approaches to second language teaching and testing. *Applied Linguistics, 1*(1), 1–47.

Carrell, P. L. (1987). Content and formal schemata in ESL reading. *TESOL Quarterly,* 21, 461–481.

Carrell, P. L. (1991). Second language reading: Reading ability or language proficiency? *Applied Linguistics, 12,* 159–179.

Carrell, P L. (1992). Awareness of text structure: Effects on recall. *Language Learning, 42,* 1–20.

Elley, W., & Mangubhai, F. (1983). The impact of reading on second language readers. *Reading Research Quarterly, 19,* 53–67.

Fitzgerald, J. (1995). English-as-a-second-language learners' cognitive reading processes: A review of research in the United States. *Review of Educational Research, 65,* 145–190.

Goodman, K., & Goodman, Y. (1978). *Reading of American students whose language is a stable rural dialect of English or a language other than English* (Final Report No. c-003-0087). Washington, DC: National Institute of Education.

Hamayan, E. (1994). Language development of low literacy children. In F. Genesee (Ed.), *Educating second language children: The whole child, the whole curriculum, the whole community* (pp. 278–300). Cambridge, UK: Cambridge University Press.

Kintsch, W., & Van Dijk, T. A. (1978). Toward a model of text comprehension and production. *Psychological Review, 85,* 363–394.

Moll, L. C. (1994). Literacy research in community and classrooms: A sociocultural approach. In R. B. Ruddell, M. R. Ruddell, & H. Singer (Eds.), *Theoretical models and processes of reading* (4th ed.; pp. 179–207). Newark, DE: International Reading Association.

Opitz, M. (1998). *Literacy instruction for culturally and linguistically diverse students.* Newark, DE: International Reading Association.

Peregoy, S. (1989, Spring). Relationships between second language oral proficiency and reading comprehension of bilingual students. *Journal of the National Association for Bilingual Education, 13,* 217–234.

Peregoy, S., & Boyle, O. (1991). Second language oral proficiency characteristics of low, intermediate and high second language readers. *Hispanic Journal of Behavioral Sciences, 13*(1), 35–47.

Peregoy, S., & Boyle, O. (1997). *Reading, writing, and learning in ESL: A resource book for k-12 teachers* (2nd ed.). New York: Longman.

Peregoy, S., & Boyle, O. (1999, Spring & Summer). Multiple embedded scaffolds: Support for English speakers in a two-way Spanish immersion kindergarten. *Bilingual Research Journal, 23*(2 & 3), 110–126.

Peregoy, S., & Boyle, O. (2000). *Reading, writing, and learning in ESL: A resource book for k-12 teachers* (3rd ed.). New York: Longman.

Pritchard, R. (1990, December). *Reading in Spanish and English: A comparative study of processing strategies.* Paper presented at the annual meeting of the National Reading Conference, Miami, FL.

Riechel, R. (1998). *Children's non-fiction for adult information needs: An annotated bibliography.* North Haven, CT: Linnet Professional Publications.

Rosow, L. (1996). *Light 'n lively reads for ESL, adult and teen readers: A thematic bibliography*. Englewood, CO: Libraries Unlimited.

Rumelhart, D. E. (1994). Toward an interactive model of reading. In R.B. Ruddell, M. R. Ruddell, & H. Singer (Eds.), *Theoretical models and processes of reading* (4th ed.; pp. 864–894). Newark, DE: International Reading Association.

Tragar, B., & Wong, B. K. (1984). The relationship between native and second language reading comprehension and second language oral ability. In C. Rivera (Ed.), *Placement procedures in bilingual education: Education and policy issues* (pp. 152–164). Clevedon, UK: Multilingual Matters.

STUDY GUIDE

1. How has literacy been conceptualized traditionally? How is it currently viewed? What prompts such a shift in perspective? (Comber & Cormack)
2. What is meant by "literacy as socially and culturally constructed practices"? What are the pedagogical implications of a socioculturally oriented view of literacy? (Comber & Cormack)
3. It has been suggested that literacy is a necessary instrument for social progress, cognitive development, and cultural and scientific advancement. Do you believe in this "literacy myth"? Why or why not? It has also been suggested that literacy is a tool of enslavement. Do you agree with this observation? Why or why not? (Comber & Cormack)
4. What is discourse? What is the relationship between literacy and discourse? How can literacy teachers design instruction and assessment that effectively accommodate the needs of all children who come to school with diverse discourses? (Comber & Cormack)
5. Citing Allan Luke, Comber and Cormack note that "not only do people shape literacy to suit their needs, but … what counts as literacy … also shapes what people can and can't do … Literacy is … a technology through which people exercise power over one another." Explain what these statements mean by giving specific examples from real life.
6. Does literacy development follow a linear or scatter plot trajectory? Why? (Comber & Cormack)
7. From a historical perspective, the standards of literacy have changed dramatically. What forces contribute to these changes? What implications do such changes have on the lives of ordinary people and for literacy teaching and learning? (Comber & Cormack)
8. What is the role of context in skilled and less skilled readers' print processing? (Perfetti)
9. Current instructional practices seem to encourage children to look for contextual cues while decoding words. Is this a sound teaching strategy? In other words, is this strategy based on "scientifically based reading research"? Explain your answer. (Perfetti)
10. What does learning to read involve? Is it as natural as learning to speak? Support your answer with research-based evidence. (Perfetti)
11. Do children best acquire reading skill in a holistic manner or through direct instruction that emphasizes attention to specific language components (e.g., phonemes, words)? Please cite research evidence to support your answer. (Perfetti)
12. How is the reading acquisition process in first and second languages similar? How is it different? What implications do these similarities and differences have for teaching English-language learners to read and write in English? (Peregoy & Boyle)
13. How does the nature of—and prior experience with—the writing system of English learners' native/primary languages influence their reading acquisition in English? (Peregoy & Boyle)
14. What are the roles of phonemic awareness and phonics in the reading acquisition of non-native speakers who are learning to read and write English? (Peregoy & Boyle)

INQUIRY PROJECTS

1. Interview your great-grandparents, grandparents, parents, and children about their conception of literacy, how they learned to read and write, what contributed to their literacy learning, and what uses literacy has had for them at various stages of their lives. Compare and contrast the definition, value, and use of literacy across different generations and professions.
2. Collect transcript samples of two or three literacy events in an elementary or middle grade classroom (e.g., shared reading, guided reading, book talk, writing conference). Analyze these transcripts to determine how power positioning and ideology/value/beliefs affect teacher/student participation and construction of meaning in these events.

3. The question of how to start children on the lifelong task of learning to read is, perhaps, the oldest and most controversial one in literacy education. For decades, while the paradigm has shifted and new terminology has been created, the fundamental disputes remain unresolved. Read Ken Goodman's *On Reading* (1996) and Marilyn Adams' *Beginning to Read* (1990) in parallel. Compare and contrast their views on beginning reading process and instruction. Discuss the ways in which your prior knowledge and experience influence your responses to the two texts.

4. Find two primary grade students with limited English proficiency from very different language and cultural backgrounds. Collect samples of their oral reading and writing. Compare and contrast the ways in which their native languages, background knowledge, and prior literacy experiences influence their oral reading and writing fluency.

FURTHER READING

Adams, M. J. (1990). *Beginning to read: Thinking and learning about print.* Cambridge, MA: MIT Press.

Bernhardt, E. (1991). *Reading development in a second language: Theoretical, empirical and classroom perspectives.* Norwood, NJ: Ablex.

Brandt, D. (2001). *Literacy in American lives.* Cambridge: Cambridge University Press.

Chall, J. (1996). *Learning to read: The great debate* (3rd Ed.) New York: Harcourt Brace.

Coles, G. (1998). *Reading lessons: The debate over literacy.* New York: Hill & Wang.

Fitzgerald, J. (1995). English as a second language learners' cognitive reading processes: A review of research in the United States. *Review of Educational Research, 65,* 145–190.

Gee, J. P. (1996). *Social linguistics and literacies: Ideology in discourses.* London: Falmer.

Goodman, K. (1996). *On reading.* Portsmouth, NH: Heinemann.

Hammond, J. (1990). Is learning to read the same as learning to speak? In F. Christie (Ed.), *Literacy for a changing world* (pp. 26–53). Melbourne, Australia: Australia Council for Educational Research.

Hasan, R. (1997). Literacy, everyday talk and society. In G. Williams & R. Hasan (Eds.), *Literacy in society* (pp. 377–424). New York: Longman.

Olson, D. R. (1994). *The world on paper: The conceptual and cognitive implications of writing and reading.* Cambridge, UK: Cambridge University Press.

Smith, F. (2003). *Unspeakable acts, unnatural practices: Flaws and fallacies in "scientific" reading instruction.* Portsmouth, NH: Heinemann.

Stanovich, K. (2000). *Progress in understanding reading: Scientific foundations and new frontiers.* New York: Guilford Press.

Street, B. (1984). *Literacy in theory and practice.* New York: Cambridge University Press.

Promoting Motivation and Engagement

INTRODUCTION

It is now widely recognized that motivation plays a critical role in children's literacy development and long-term achievement. Not surprisingly, developing engaged readers and writers remains one of the top concerns among practicing teachers. However, it is only recently that the topic has risen to the top of the research agenda among literacy scholars. How can teachers and parents individually and collaboratively establish contexts that promote the development of engaged readers/writers who are motivated, knowledgeable, skillful, strategic, goal-oriented, self-regulated, and socially interactive? Recent research, as encapsulated in the three articles in this section, provides some of the answers to this important question.

The first article, by Julianne Turner and Scott Paris, describes the influence of classroom contexts on young children's motivation for reading. Drawing on data gathered from observation of 12 first-grade classrooms, Turner and Paris argue that open-ended literacy tasks are more likely to increase student engagement in learning because they offer genuine choice, appropriate challenges, student control over learning, and opportunities for peer collaboration and meaning making. They suggest that motivation does not reside solely in the child, but is situated in the interaction between students and their literacy environments. They conclude that it is the actual daily tasks that teachers provide in their classrooms, rather than the type of reading program being followed, that have the utmost impact on student motivation for, and engagement in, literacy learning. Finally, the authors offer useful instructional strategies for fostering student motivation in the classroom.

In the second article, Roger Bruning and Christy Horn describe factors that are important for developing and maintaining students' motivation to write. They first discuss the complexity involved in the writing process and the unique challenges posed by writing. Next, drawing upon analysis of written discourse and relevant social-cognitive research, Bruning and Horn propose that four conditions are critical to fostering students' motivation for writing, namely, nurturing functional beliefs about writing, creating authentic writing goals and contexts, providing a supportive and constructive context for writing, and maintaining a positive emotional environment. They suggest that teachers' own conceptions of writing are key to establishing such conditions. The authors also offer research-based suggestions/ideas for establishing these conditions, as well as directions for future research in each area.

Shifting away from the classroom context to the home, Linda Baker discusses, in the third article, the role of parents in motivating struggling readers. She reviews the latest research about the influences of home environment (i.e., print experience, parents' perspectives on the nature and importance of literacy, and the affective quality of home literacy interactions) on children's reading motivation, concluding that supportive home environments foster children's motivation for reading and ultimately improve their reading achievement. She also offers a myriad of research-based suggestions to teachers for ways they can enlist parental support to help motivate struggling readers in the school and home contexts. The author endorses a more relaxed and flexible approach to home reading that provides children with enjoyable print experiences at home, rather than an approach that focuses on skills development, because the latter tends to undermine the affective quality of parent-child interaction and negatively impact the child's reading engagement. Baker maintains that factors such as choice, collaboration and risk-free environments are key to enhancing motivation not only in school, but at home as well.

How Literacy Tasks Influence Children's Motivation for Literacy

Julianne Turner
University of Notre Dame

Scott G. Paris
University of Michigan

It is 10:45 on Tuesday morning, time for first-grade literacy instruction. Mike's teacher has just completed a lesson on rhyming words and has distributed two worksheets to the children for practice in decoding. Mike glances at the first worksheet requiring him to use rhyming words to complete a sentence. He quickly decodes the word choices, *Jam, ham*, and *Sam*, and places them in the sentence blanks, *Sam put grape jam on his ham*. Then he moves on to a worksheet on short *u*. He begins by coloring and cutting. Fifteen minutes later, he is still laboriously decorating cups, tubs, and other objects on the sheet. When the teacher reminds the children that they have only 5 minutes left for morning work, he hurriedly matches several pictures to words on the worksheet and hands it in. Later, when asked what he was supposed to learn that morning, Mike replied, "vowels." When queried about why vowels were a good thing to learn, he shrugged his shoulders with an "I don't know."

Across the hall, the teacher is reading *Clifford's Birthday Party* (Bridwell, 1988) and discussing plans for celebrating his birthday in class. On easel paper, she lists various activities and labels each one as "reading," "writing," "planning," or "thinking." One of the activities, writing a story about Clifford, is required. But students may choose other activities that include writing invitations to Clifford's party, making a list of the needed preparations, designing and writing a birthday card for Clifford, following directions to make Clifford's cake, and reading and listening to other Clifford stories.

Lauren takes out paper to begin her story, thinks for a while, then asks Susan about her plans. Susan replies, "When Clifford goes swimming." Lauren suggests that it would be funny if he got everyone wet, then begins to write, saying the words as she writes them. Unable to spell a word, she walks to the easel where some Clifford books are displayed.

She copies the word and continues writing. Several minutes later, she asks if Megan knows how to spell *house*. Together they construct a phonetic approximation, *hos*. When she finishes, she reads her story to Megan, then makes two changes. When asked what she was supposed to learn from this activity, Lauren replied, "What Clifford does, and why he is funny." When pressed about why this might be a good thing, she answered, "I want to be an author when I grow up."

What distinguishes how Mike and Lauren approach, engage in, and understand their literacy activities? It is not ability; both are average readers. Nor is it experience, because both own books and have enjoyed them with their families. The biggest difference between these two children is their classroom literacy contexts, specifically the activities they complete during literacy instruction. Although both are progressing as readers and writers, they are developing different conceptions of literacy from their classroom tasks.

Mike understands that his instructional work is important and that he must do it accurately, neatly, and turn it in on time. He is pleased to get frequent stickers and gold stars on his papers and thinks he is a good reader. However, he is often bored by the rote nature of his work and completes it quickly with little thought.

Open-ended tasks ... provide appropriate challenges, ... choices, some student control over learning, opportunities to collaborate with others and to construct meaning through reading and writing.

Lauren, on the other hand, thinks about her work, plans, and discusses it with others. She visualizes how literacy will play a part in her future. She is effortful and she tries a variety of strategies as she works. She is seldom bored because her classroom offers choices that are challenging, meaningful, and related to her interests. Although Lauren wants the teacher to evaluate her work positively, she also strives to meet her own standards of quality.

In this article, we discuss how classroom tasks affect students' motivation for literacy. We propose that tasks influence students' affect, such as desire to read and write, understanding of the goals of literacy, and self-regulations as readers and writers. We illustrate our proposition with examples gathered during a study of motivation for literacy in 12 classrooms of 6-year-olds (6 integrated language-arts and 6 skills-based) (Turner, in press). The first author observed 84 children during literacy instruction over 5 days in each classroom. After observations, students were interviewed to determine their understanding of and value for literacy.

A variety of other data were gathered to provide as complete a picture of classroom instruction as possible. These included daily field notes, verbatim transcripts of literacy lessons, and descriptions of all the tasks the children completed. Literacy tasks were classified as *open* or *closed*. In open tasks, students were in control of both the products they created and the processes they employed. There was no one correct answer, nor was there a specified procedure to use. Open tasks required students to set goals, select and organize information, choose strategies, and assess the final results. For example, if students were composing, they decided what information about the topic interested them, how to organize it to create a theme, and what they wanted the final message to be. Because there were many "correct" answers to open tasks, students approached tasks as problems to solve rather than as exercises to complete.

Closed tasks were those in which either the product (e.g., there is one correct answer), the process (e.g., sound out the word), or both were specified. For example, in many worksheet activities, students were given cloze sentences and directed to fill in the blanks with selected vocabulary words. Closed tasks afforded students fewer opportunities to control their learning and explore their interests because these tasks did not permit students to make choices and decisions.

The major finding of the study was that the most reliable indicator of motivation was not the type of reading program that districts follow, but the actual daily tasks that teachers provided students in their classrooms. Tasks that provided opportunities for students to use reading and writing for authentic purposes (like reading trade books and composing), that conveyed the value of literacy for communication and enjoyment, and that allowed students to be actively involved in constructing meanings and metacognitions about literacy were most successful in motivating students.

Creating Contexts for Motivation

Why did open-ended tasks have such a powerful effect on students' engagement? We can summarize the influence of open tasks on students' motivation with six *C*s, an easy mnemonic to remember critical features of motivating tasks (e.g., Ames, 1992; Lepper & Hodell, 1989). First, open-ended tasks allow students to make personal *choices* among literacy activities. Second, these activities provide *challenge* for all students. Third, they allow students to take *control* over their own learning through planning, evaluation and self-monitoring. Fourth, they foster the sharing of expertise through *collaboration*. Fifth, open activities foster *constructive comprehension* or making meaning through reading and writing. Sixth, the *consequences* of open activities promote feelings of competence and efficacy. In the sections that follow, we describe how teachers can use these characteristics of open tasks as a guide for designing literacy activities that engage and support their students' learning.

Choice

Research has shown that choice is a powerful motivator. When students can choose tasks and texts they are interested in, they expend more effort learning and understanding the material (Schiefele, 1991). Similarly, when students are allowed to select the tasks that have personal value, they are more likely to use learning strategies like summarizing or backtracking rather than shortcuts like memorizing, copying, or guessing. Open-ended activities provide students with opportunities to mold tasks to interests and values, thus supporting their efforts to make meaning while engaging them affectively.

Students in the study who were allowed to choose among activities and who had options about how to organize and plan showed more personal responsibility for their literacy learning because the activities themselves required such behaviors. For example, when selecting texts, students decided what their interests were, whether they were of the appropriate level, and how the text supported their reading progress. Similarly, in writing, students selected an approach to the topic, organized information, and monitored their execution. How did teachers provide choices and how did those choices affect students' learning?

Providing choices during literacy instruction. In many of the classrooms observed, teachers structured the morning literacy time to encourage students to make personal choices. They wanted to demonstrate to students that literacy means pursuing personal aesthetic and informational goals. There are many ways that choices can be offered as part of the literacy curriculum. For example, students can select from a variety of tasks appropriate for their learning needs and interests. Interest can also be stimulated in reading and writing through the integration of literacy activities with science, art, and music, or in relation to classroom themes like chocolate, bears, or the March wind. For instance, in some classrooms students wrote and followed recipes for chocolate milkshakes and read, wrote, and listened to bear stories. These choices involved meaning making and learning goals, while capitalizing on individual interests and familiarity.

Another kind of choice that students can make is selecting their own texts for oral reading practice. Unlike traditional approaches in which all students read the same basal stories, students can be encouraged to think about choosing texts based on interest and level. Sometimes children may select texts in order to improve fluency or gain mastery, but at other times, they may select them for the pure enjoyment of the language. If children select inappropriate books, teachers can suggest more (or less) challenging texts. Then students take responsibility for evaluating texts to set new reading goals.

This approach to oral reading not only creates a greater interest in reading, it also encourages wider reading. Because children are expected to select books for free reading and reading with the teacher, they frequently browse in the classroom library. As a result, they become familiar with many books, and, as they exchange evaluations of books with their peers, they regularly discover new books. Compared to children whose daily reading experiences are confined to basal stories, these children have rich experiences in selecting, evaluating, and enjoying literature.

Another crucial element of choice is that it can encourage students to take personal responsibility for their tasks by setting goals and deciding how to reach those goals. For example, in one class, students read a text about the life cycle of the butterfly. The composition assignment was to use the text as a source of ideas. Students were expected to decide which ideas in the text interested them and how they wanted their final product to represent those ideas. Thus, students chose both process and product.

Liza, fascinated by the life cycle, composed this text: "I would fly away and find a mate. We will lay eggs and have children. It would start again so I would be a grandma and I will die and that would be my life. And then the little ones would be a mother and its mom will die and we will start over again."

Butterflies inspired Joanna to write an action story: "One day I pretended to be a butterfly. I jumped in. I hit my head on the ceiling. Then I landed on the couch. My brother tried, too, but he didn't land on the couch, but instead landed on the floor."

In contrast, in classrooms where teachers assigned identical topics for composition, students had limited opportunities to integrate their interests with the topics. Closed tasks denied students the chance to make decisions about organizing information and creating unique products. In one class, the teacher told the children to write about "what I did at the farm today." Instead of personal elaborations, many students' efforts were mechanical, like these compositions: "We went to the farm. We had some food" [Betty]. "I did not like the farm kos it is sikey (stinky). I liked it a little" [Andrew].

Allowing students to make choices encourages them to develop an interest in literacy, and it provides students an opportunity to plan and regulate their literacy learning.

Challenge

Some teachers, especially those in first grade, are justifiably wary of tasks that may overtax young students and cause frustration or failure. The solution is to assign tasks that children can master easily, thinking that such tasks will inspire confidence. However, we found that students showed scant enthusiasm for such literacy activities. The most motivated students were those who were engaged in moderately challenging tasks that led them to make new discoveries and to reorganize their understandings.

Moderately challenging tasks lead to positive feelings because they provide feedback to students about what they are learning and how they are progressing. If tasks are too easy, students become bored. If they are too difficult, students are likely to become frustrated. However, open tasks can be used to provide enough flexibility so that students can tackle a problem and use their competencies to solve it. In other words, open tasks allow all students to work at their fullest capacity by adjusting the goals and relative difficulty of the tasks.

Interviews with talented and successful people support the motivational value of moderately difficult tasks. When asked about their deep commitment to their work, chess masters, rock climbers, basketball players, musical composers, and surgeons report that the exhilaration of operating at one's optimum level is all the reward they need for their efforts (Csikszentmihalyi, 1990). The real compensation in such "peak" experiences is receiving accurate information about what they can do and how they can improve. Where do these experts acquire the information they use to improve? They cull it from their errors. Unlike many school children, they do not look upon their errors as failures, but as a way to diagnose what went wrong and how to improve (Clifford, 1991). As a result, the next time they engage in that activity, they adjust the challenge to skills so that they can continue to advance.

How can teachers accomplish such a feat? In the classrooms that successfully promoted challenge, teachers designed tasks that required reflection and planning and that could not be accomplished in a rote or automatic fashion. An additional feature of these tasks was that they could be accomplished in a variety of ways. Because solutions were not obvious, children drew on the resources they had and were developing. Thus challenging tasks tended to "pull" learning in a variety of ways. They prompted students to use more organizational and self-monitoring strategies, such as arranging the pieces of a game ahead of time; to use more and varied reading strategies, such as using title, picture, and sound-symbol cues simultaneously; and to persist longer at an activity.

Challenging tasks.   One example of a challenging task that all students can accomplish successfully is the text scramble. Teachers reproduce text from stories or nursery rhymes on oaktag, cutting the sentences into individual words. Students reconstruct the sentences in a meaningful way. The task requires students to design a plan; monitor for decoding, meaning, punctuation, and upper and lower case letters; attend to sequencing; and use rehearsal for text memory. The task is accessible to students at various developmental levels. Students can solve it using a variety of strategies (i.e., they can use meaning or punctuation clues or both), and there are several solutions (i.e., students can recreate the original sentences from the text or create sentences of their own). This task encourages persistence. Instead of giving up, asking for answers, or going on to a new activity, students use their errors diagnostically (Clifford, 1991).

Steve, a below-average reader, made more than 25 attempts to arrange the words in one sentence so that they made sense. He tried many arrangements, rereading and checking each time to determine if it "sounded right." He also used teacher hints ("What does a sentence start with?") to introduce new strategies. After Steve finally completed the task, the teacher congratulated him. Steve smiled proudly and then asked for another sentence to complete.

Most closed or rote tasks lack personal challenges. In tasks where children fill in words, match sounds with pictures, or underline key words, there is little need to use learning strategies or maintain concentration. Many students complete such tasks as if they are operating on "automatic pilot." The skills-focused tasks that provide the staple fare in their classrooms do not seem to provide students with opportunities for adjusting the tasks to make them personally challenging. As a consequence, meaning making, self-regulation, and pride in accomplishment suffer.

Control

A third feature of open-ended activities is that they provide students some control over their learning. A significant goal of literacy education is to support learners' independence and versatility as readers. When teachers and students share control, students learn to make crucial literacy decisions themselves.

Sharing control has consequences for motivation as well. When teachers completely control classroom tasks and processes, students are likely to perceive that they are being pressured to think or perform in a certain way. However, when teachers share control (e.g., invite children to sequence tasks, choose partners, or design a strategy), students interpret instruction as information they can use to learn and improve (Deci, Vallerand, Pelletier, & Ryan, 1991). For example, research has shown that children in shared-control classrooms reported more interest in their schoolwork and perceived themselves as more competent than those in teacher-controlled classrooms (Ryan & Grolnick, 1986).

Students want to see themselves as originators of plans and ideas, not as followers in a grand scheme they may not understand. Tasks and classroom structures that are overly controlling unwittingly undermine intrinsic motivation by removing the element of student participation, standard setting, and decision making. Shared control provides students with both the tools and the opportunities to take responsibility for their learning. They select strategies to reach their goals and protect their intentions by avoiding distractions (Corno, 1992). For example, one student clearly communicated her need to concentrate when she said, "Shut up, Jason, I am *trying* to work. Do you mind?"

Open tasks facilitate student control.   Because open tasks are more cognitively complex than closed tasks, they require students to think strategically and to monitor and evaluate their learning. When students are actively involved in controlling their learning, they feel greater ownership of their performance and achievement. Typical open tasks include trade book reading, composition, partner reading, and games or interactive activities in which students manipulate text to create meaning or solidify skills. For example, when students compose, they can use wall charts of vowel sounds and lists of favorite vocabulary that the class has generated as sources for spelling and ideas.

Another activity that promotes student control is sequencing sentence strips from a favorite story. Students paste the strips in sequence and then illustrate the accompanying text. In this activity, students have to plan how to accomplish the task. When Susan completed this task, she followed these steps. First, she drew on her memory of the text to sequence the strips in the appropriate order. Then she used text features to check her work (in the story, characters appeared in a logical order). Finally, she compared her version to the actual text which she got from the classroom library.

However, during closed tasks children have fewer opportunities to select, monitor, and evaluate their strategy use. These tasks mostly require automatized responses or repeated application of the same response as opposed to active strategy use. For example, one common task required students to decode two words and decide which one has a certain sound. In another typical closed task, students read a sentence and decided which of two words correctly completed the sentence.

Although the goal of using sound-symbol knowledge is an important one, the tasks used to meet this goal are very limiting. Children do not have to devise a plan or organize information. As a result, they have few opportunities to see how sound-symbol knowledge facilitates reading comprehension. Indeed, many closed tasks (such as those in some workbooks) are so repetitive that after several months of first-grade reading instruction students recognize the pattern and little thinking is required to accomplish them. Less active involvement in literacy activities leads to disempowerment and ultimately to disinterest for many students.

Interviews with children further illuminate how students use their problem-solving skills to gain control over tasks. In this study, when students engaged in open tasks were asked about the learning difficulties they had encountered and how they handled those difficulties, they were likely to respond by naming a specific difficulty, such as "I knew they had the same letter, but not the same sound" and by saying that they heightened their effort to solve the difficulty. By contrast, students who were engaged in mostly closed tasks were more vague about their problems, often saying that the words were hard or that they had trouble following directions. In addition, they often responded that when they had learning difficulties they "guessed" or "just did it."

The difference in the students' responses appears to indicate that those who spend time in open tasks are more self-directed and aware of how learning processes can be used, whereas those in closed tasks are more narrowly focused either on meeting the expectations of the teacher or on the task.

Collaboration

Although previous conceptions of teaching and learning emphasized the teacher's role in transmitting knowledge, more recent ideas have emphasized the social and interactional nature of learning. Some have described the desired relationship between teachers and students (as well as among students) as an apprenticeship in which a more able companion guides, supports, and challenges another's understanding (e.g., Newman & Schwager, 1993). In addition to cognitive benefits, social guidance and cooperation in classrooms are also fundamental to motivation.

Social interaction is motivational in several ways. First, peer comments and ideas can pique students' curiosity and spark further interest. Second, children's observations of their classmates' progress may increase their confidence in their own ability to succeed (Schunk, 1989). Third, research in cooperative learning has shown that working with others promotes student engagement in work and group consciousness (Slavin, 1987). Collaboration can increase both effort and persistence. Situations that encourage productive social interaction offer ways for students to develop competence and efficacy as readers and writers.

Modeling and coaching were two activities we observed in classrooms that supported student motivation. In many classrooms, mixed-ability groups worked together on related tasks. Children in these groups could observe that there were multiple ways of planning and executing tasks, and they could borrow strategies that seemed useful. At the same time, children could develop more refined understandings of tasks and procedures by observing others more expert than they (Collins, Brown, & Newman, 1989). For example, Shannon profited from the clues Kate provided when they were working on flash cards together. When Shannon mispronounced words, Kate read a sentence from the back of the card to provide context, asked questions like "Does this have an *s* in it?", and promoted with "What is the opposite of *slow*?"

In addition, students often adopted a coaching role, integrating cognitive and motivational strategies to support successful completion of tasks. For example, Anna, an able reader, shared the oral reading of a story with Matt, a less able reader. When Matt accidentally skipped a page, Anna reminded him, "That doesn't make sense yet; it happened later. Go back." When Matt stumbled on a word, Anna said, "Don't ask me for help. Try to sound it out." Matt dutifully (and successfully) did so.

Students in classrooms where collaboration was encouraged gave and received help routinely, but because tasks differed, the help rarely consisted of giving answers. For example, during a Bingo game, one child helped her peers by pronouncing, then spelling, bingo words. One of the players requested help, asking, "Is *listen* spelled *l-i-s-t-e-n*?" These activities supported learning, encouraged continued persistence and engagement, and helped students feel like competent readers and writers.

In classrooms where students completed mostly closed activities, children remained at their desks working on identical tasks. Although teachers did not actively discourage collaboration on seatwork (indeed, in some classrooms, desks were in work groups of four), there was a premium on quiet because teachers met with reading groups at that time. Also, students had fewer models. They worked at the same desks with the same peers day in and day out. The same was true in reading groups. In some classes, reading groups were formed by ability, so the models available were limited both in number and in expertise. Finally, because all children completed identical tasks, it appeared that children in classes doing closed activities regarded help seeking more as cheating than helping a peer learn. Thus, there were more behaviors like veiled glances at a neighbor's work as well as shielding papers from prying eyes. When students perceive situations as competitive, they focus less on effort and learning and more on appearing able or out-performing their peers (Ames, 1992).

Opportunities to learn from and with others.   Collaboration can be encouraged in several ways. First, in classrooms where students have a choice of tasks, they can select activities and join groups of children with the same interests at various centers around the classroom. Because most children complete several tasks during reading time, they have opportunities to work with many other children. Moreover, the students in the interest groups can be encouraged to help peers and to provide explanations of goals and processes. Additionally, when appropriate, teachers can redirect students' questions to a peer who has successfully completed a similar activity. Finally, students can be asked to demonstrate to peers or to explain an important understanding they have gained.

In one classroom where students frequently generated prediction questions about text, the teacher asked students to help her spell as she wrote the questions on the easel. As students spelled, she asked them to explain their thinking processes in selecting the letters for the words or where they had learned the words. Modeling how to request and give help and then providing opportunities for students to assist each other will encourage children to regard literacy as an opportunity for engagement and improvement rather than a search for the correct answer or a race to completion. Thus, open tasks in collaborative classrooms are more likely to foster intrinsic interest in learning through help seeking, help giving, and child discussions about ideas and strategies.

Constructing Meaning

Open and closed tasks offer students different opportunities to construct meaning. When they complete open tasks, students have more chances to construct meaning in text as well as to build a rationale for the meaningfulness of literacy activities.

Constructing meaning promotes motivation by assisting children in making sense of their learning—the tasks in which they engage and the strategies they employ (Paris & Byrnes, 1989). They use information gleaned from their daily tasks in literacy to construct purposes for reading and writing and how they may be entertaining, informational, and useful. If children find that literacy allows them to solve interesting problems, they will associate reading and writing with thinking, challenge, and personal growth. If, however, they associate literacy with completing exercises, they may interpret it simply as manipulating symbols or solving abstract puzzles (Resnick, 1987). Increasingly, national assessments like the National Assessment of Educational Progress (Mullis, Campbell, & Farstrup, 1993) suggest that many children continue to separate learning to read and write in school from out-of-school uses of reading and writing.

Children's responses to the interview question "What are you supposed to learn from your reading activity?" provides clear evidence of the effect of tasks on students' understanding of and appreciation for reading and writing. After completing open tasks, children frequently responded that they were learning new information (e.g., "About the life cycle of a butterfly" or "Where the wind goes") and monitoring their self-improvement ("So I can read second-grade books"). However, children who completed mostly closed tasks typically took a more limited view. They often responded that they were learning word parts (e.g., "short a") or that they "didn't know" what they were supposed to learn from their activities. Apparently their tasks did not provide enough information for them to set meaningful literacy goals.

Literacy tasks support the construction of meaning. How did teachers in this study promote students' motivation through meaning making? In one classroom, the children and teacher created thematic lists of favorite vocabulary words on large charts. There were color words, Halloween words, apple words, words about birds, and others. Sean used the charts to add some words to his personal word bank. However, in the process he had many opportunities to construct meaning. As he read the sentences on the "black" chart, he was aided by the context: "Blackberries are black. A scary bat is black. A bowling ball is black. A crayon can be black. A blackbird is black. The sky is black at night. A witch's hat is black. Watermelon seeds are black." Compared to the limited vocabulary and decontextualized sentences that most worksheets offer (e.g., "Can a goat float in a boat?"), this task provided opportunities to use meaning as an aid both in building a rich vocabulary and in learning to use many decoding strategies.

During free reading time in one classroom, two students retreated to the puppet theater to share a story. As they read, they spontaneously picked up puppets and began to act out the story. This task allowed students to use various ways to create meaning. Compared to the typical exercise of reading short paragraphs and answering comprehension questions, this open task supported students' creative responses to text and generated enthusiasm for personal and meaningful interpretations. However, tasks alone cannot facilitate meaning making. Students must have an understanding of how to approach literacy tasks if they are to solve them meaningfully. Therefore, instruction is an important factor in providing students tools to use in constructing meaning.

Instruction supports the construction of meaning. Teachers who are most successful in motivating their students introduce, model, and provide opportunities for students to use many reading strategies. In addition to teaching sound-symbol correspondences and the use of sentence context for decoding, they teach comprehension skills such as predicting, question-asking, relating stories to prior knowledge, and making inferences. For example, one teacher demonstrated how students could use a combination of strategies by covering up key words in a big book with self-sticking notes and asking students to use the context to predict the words and then use sound-symbol cues to confirm or revise.

Teachers can introduce both instructional and recreational texts by asking students what they know about the topic and asking them to predict what the author would say. When asked to predict what the text *Noisy Nora* (Wells, 1973) would be about, students suggested: "A little mouse that makes a lot of noise," "She gets in trouble for making things fall down," and "She is annoying." Before studying the text *A House Is a House for Me* (Hoberman, 1978), the teacher asked what kinds of houses creatures live in. Children's responses ranged from the conventional (e.g., cement, mansion, wood, apartment) to the imaginative (e.g., cave, tree house, mouse hole, gingerbread, cage). During reading, children delighted in discovering their contributions in print. After reading, children added to their original lists of dwellings.

In addition to teaching a variety of reading/thinking strategies, successful teachers foster metacognition about learning and reading. Reflectiveness can be encouraged by inviting students to plan and evaluate their learning. In this study, in classes where students engaged in many open tasks, students were guided to make and sequence choices and to evaluate their decisions.

Some teachers regularly conducted a discussion at the end of literacy activities in which students were invited to describe both more and less successful strategies and to help each other by making suggestions for "working smarter." One teacher emphasized the importance of self control for learning by helping her students maintain attention. Used judiciously, her brief question "Are you focused?" reminded students that they needed to redirect attention to stay in control of their learning. Other tactics, such as asking students "How do you know?" and requiring them to explain the process they use to complete an activity reminds students that they have a major role in deciding which information is useful and valuable.

Motivation does not reside solely in the child; rather it is in the interaction between students and their literacy environments.

In classrooms where strategy teaching is largely confined to decoding sound-symbol correspondences, there may be little emphasis on comprehension or on how strategies can be used in reading extended text. This approach to literacy instruction not only limits students' strategic repertoires, but it also restricts opportunities to use reading strategies in meaningful situations. Unless students have many chances to use reading strategies in authentic reading and writing, they may begin to doubt their usefulness and value.

Consequences

Open and closed tasks also have different consequences for students. Closed tasks direct attention to correct answers, often reported by numbers, red pencil, stars, or smiley faces. Children may be forced to judge their performance by the number of stars they receive, whether their paper was hung on the board, and how they compare to other students. In contrast, open tasks seldom have one correct answer, allowing students to focus on whether they achieved their purposes, whether they used good tactics, and whether they tried to do their best. Rather than stars or stickers, students can base their self-assessments on the effort they expended, their enjoyment, or the meaningfulness of the activity. The consequences of this latter focus are usually positive feelings about effort, ownership, achievement, and responsibility.

The motivational outcomes of literacy tasks influence how students interpret their roles in learning to read. Those interpretations can affect their desire to persist and to remain involved in literacy. Tasks affect the consequences of literacy in two ways.

First, open tasks support a constructive approach to failure (Clifford, 1991). If a task can be approached at an appropriate difficulty level, miscues or errors evoke a strategy orientation in which students interpret "failures" not as evidence of insufficient ability or effort but as temporary setbacks caused by less than optimal strategy use. In these situations, students adapt their strategies rather than give up. When students are moderately challenged, they are likely to show such positive responses to failure as increased persistence, more varied strategy use, greater task interest, and increased task performance.

Second, when students see tasks as controllable, they are more likely to take personal responsibility for them (Weiner, 1979). In addition, they have confidence that they can adjust their effort and strategy use appropriately. They do not interpret all situations in a similar manner, such as the student who says, "I'm not good at reading" or "I'll never figure this out." Instead, with open tasks and appropriate support from cognitive and metacognitive strategy instruction, students are able to maintain a belief in their ability to succeed as readers and writers.

In fact, students define failure differently in open and closed tasks. In closed tasks, if students cannot get the correct answer, they may become frustrated or discouraged because the one avenue to success is blocked. However, in open tasks, if one approach does not work, another can be tried. Errors are regarded as information about what one does or doesn't know or what one has or hasn't tried. In either case, this information can be used to adjust goals or strategies.

For example, when Steve was engaged in the text scramble, he ran into several obstacles. He had rearranged the sentence. "Then she felled some chairs" several ways. Each time, the word *some* was inappropriately placed. Finally, Steve revealed that he did not know that word. With some cues and strategy support, he decoded *some* and completed the sentence. Similarly, after he failed to use a teacher cue, "What does a sentence start with?", Steve asked what the difference between upper- and lowercase *t* was. In both cases, he used the information not as signals of his low ability, but as clues to help him reach a meaningful solution.

In summary, open-ended tasks are more likely to provide appropriate challenges, genuine choices, some

student control over learning, opportunities to collaborate with others and [opportunities] to construct meaning through reading and writing. These activities support student motivation through positive, affective consequences and by fostering students' determination, effort, and thoughtful engagement.

If students are to be motivated readers and writers, we must give them the tools and the reasons to read and write and allow them to discover the many paths to literacy.

The classroom observations and examples reported in this article suggest that motivation for literacy is not necessarily a quality that children bring to instruction. That is, motivation does not reside solely in the child; rather it is in the interaction between students and their literacy environments (Paris & Turner, 1994). This finding underscores the considerable role that instruction plays in influencing children's motivation for literacy. Because children come to know and understand literacy primarily through the activities in which they engage, literacy tasks have enormous potential to influence students' feelings and attitudes toward literacy as well as their use of learning strategies and self-regulation.

Teachers who foster motivation in literacy classrooms:

1. *Provide authentic choices and purposes for literacy.* They recast activities to emphasize the enjoyment and the informational values of literacy. Instead of referring to daily tasks as work, these teachers rename them by emphasizing their function, such as "Today we are going to plan for *Clifford's* birthday party by writing invitations, composing stories about what the party will be like, and making lists of guests."

2. *Allow students to modify tasks so the difficulty and interest levels are challenging.* They demonstrate to students the many ways that a task can be done. Students are given concrete examples of successful, but different, approaches to tasks. Students are taught to assess whether a task is too easy or difficult for them and how to adjust goals or strategies for appropriate difficulty. Such teachers point out how students have molded tasks to their interests and assign tasks that can be modified in many ways.

3. *Show students how they can control their learning.* They teach students how to evaluate what they know, and how to monitor and evaluate their learning. Reminders such as "Are you staying focused?" and "What's more important—that you made a mistake or what you learned?" guide students' inner speech so they can self-monitor.

4. *Encourage collaboration.* These teachers emphasize the positive aspects of help seeking and help giving. They design activities so that students have opportunities to work with many different peers. They teach students how to help each other by emphasizing the giving of clues, not answers. Some individual activities are recast as collaborative ones. For example, students work on flash cards together. One student gives hints, such as putting the word in context or giving a synonym or antonym. Similarly, individual reading is sometimes done in pairs.

5. *Emphasize strategies and metacognition for constructing meaning.* Students need a repertoire of strategies in order to respond flexibly in reading and writing situations. Extensive applications of comprehension (as well as decoding/encoding) strategies assist students in acquiring an understanding of what literacy is as well as how to use and understand it.

6. *Use the consequences of tasks to build responsibility, ownership, and self-regulation.* Group evaluation is a regular part of literacy instruction. Students are encouraged to share their successes and their failures. These teachers help students see that errorless learning is not learning at all. Real learning comes about through error, since errors provide information about needed improvement. Such teachers emphasize the value of effort and honing strategies. These tools equip students to attempt more and more challenging tasks.

Our purpose in this article was to share the motivational strategies of some expert teachers in literacy instruction. These teachers were successful in helping their students develop an interest in reading, in encouraging wide reading in the classroom and at home, and in instilling an intrinsic desire for learning and reading in many of their students. They did this by molding literacy instruction to the needs, interests, and skills of their students. If students are to be motivated readers and writers, we must give them the tools and the reasons to read and write and allow them to discover the many paths to literacy—paths that fit the diverse goals, purposes, interests, and social needs of children.

References

Ames, C. (1992). Classrooms: Goals, structures, and student motivation. *Journal of Educational Psychology, 84*, 261–271.

Bridwell, N. (1988). *Clifford's birthday party.* New York: Scholastic.

Clifford, M.M. (1991). Risk taking: Theoretical, empirical and educational considerations. *Educational Psychologist, 26*, 263–297.

Collins, A., Brown, J.S., & Newman, S. (1989). Cognitive apprenticeship: Teaching the crafts of reading, writing, and mathematics. In L.B. Resnick (Ed.), *Knowing, learning, and instruction.* Hillsdale, NJ: Erlbaum.

Corno, L. (1992). Encouraging students to take responsibility for learning and performance. *Elementary School Journal, 93*, 69–83.

Csikszentmihalyl, M. (1990). Literacy and intrinsic motivation. *Daedalus, 119*, 115–140.

Decl, E.L., Vallerand, R.J., Pelletier, L.G., & Ryan, R.M. (1991). Motivation and education: The self-determination perspective. *Educational Psychologist, 26*, 325–346.

Hoberman, M.A. (1978). *A house is a house for me.* Bergenfield, NJ: Viking Press.

Lepper, M.R., & Hodell, M. (1989). Intrinsic motivation in the classroom. In C. Ames & R. Ames (Eds.), *Research on motivation in education* (Vol. 3, pp. 73–105). San Diego: Academic Press.

Mullis, I.V.S., Campbell, J.R., & Farstrup, A.E. (1993). *Executive summary of the NAEP 1992 reading report card for the nation and the states.* Washington, DC: U.S. Department of Education.

Newman, R.S., & Schwager, M.T. (1993). Students' perceptions of the teacher and classmates in relation to reported help seeking in math class. *Elementary School Journal, 94*, 3–17.

Paris, S.G., & Byrnes, J.P. (1989). The constructivist approach to self-regulation. In B.J. Zimmerman & D.H. Schunk (Eds.), *Self-regulated learning and academic achievement* (pp. 169–200). New York: Springer-Verlag.

Paris, S.G., & Turner, J.C. (1994). Situated motivation. In P. Pintrich, D. Brown, & C.E. Weinstein (Eds.), *Student motivation, cognition, and learning: Essays in honor of Wilbert J. McKeachie* (pp. 213–237). Hillsdale, NJ: Erlbaum.

Resnick, L.B. (1987). Learning in school and out. *Educational Researcher, 16*, 13–20.

Ryan, R.M., & Grolnick, W.S. (1986). Origins and pawns in the classroom: Self-report and projective assessments of individual differences in children's perceptions. *Journal of Personality and Social Psychology, 50*, 550–558.

Schiefele, U. (1991). Interest, learning, and motivation. *Educational Psychologist, 26*, 299–323.

Schunk, D.H. (1989). Social cognitive theory and self-regulated learning. In B.J. Zimmerman & D.H. Schunk (Eds.), *Self-regulated learning and academic achievement* (pp. 83–110). New York: Springer-Verlag.

Slavin, R.E. (1987). Cooperative learning: Where behavioral and humanistic approaches to classroom motivation meet. *Elementary School Journal, 88*, 29–37.

Turner, J. (1995). The influence of classroom contexts on young children's motivation for literacy. *Reading Research Quarterly.*

Weiner, B. (1979). A theory of motivation for some classroom experiences. *Journal of Educational Psychology, 71*, 3–25.

Wells, R. (1973). *Noisy Nora.* New York: Scholastic.

Developing Motivation to Write

Roger Bruning and Christy Horn
University of Nebraska—Lincoln

Random scribbles on paper or a handy wall signal the beginning of a lifetime of writing for most children. From these humble beginnings, writing's course moves ahead predictably, although certainly not at the same pace for every child. Scribbles soon become more letter-like, giving way to true letters and words. As writing development proceeds in the school years, we see increases in young writers' range of lexical choices, sentence complexity, and topical coherence. They begin to shift away from list-like writing and localized control (e.g., linking to vocabulary used in the previous sentence, repeating familiar syntactic frames) toward a more goal-directed, strategic approach (Berninger, Fuller, & Whitaker, 1996). Their writing has more topical and thematic coherence (e.g., Flower et al., 1990), as purpose, planning, and revising play an increasing role. A growing metacognitive capability gives them the potential to shift from a knowledge-telling to a knowledge-transforming approach (Bereiter & Scardamalia, 1987) and to use information about audience, genre, and rhetorical stance to accomplish a variety of writing purposes (Berninger et al., 1996).

Ideally, these developmental processes result in highly capable and motivated writers, able to deploy a variety of approaches as their purposes and audiences change. They see writing as entering a kind of conversation (Boice, 1994) leading to self-understanding and interaction with others. They hold positive views not only about writing's utility, but about engaging in its processes, and approach writing with anticipation, feelings of control, and minimal anxiety. Their writing production is steady and relatively stress free; they somehow have struck balances between impatience and procrastination, between dull habit and anxious waiting for inspiration.

For many of us, unfortunately, this idealized portrait of writing development may not be a particularly accurate depiction of our own writing development. More important for our purposes here, our collective shortcomings in developing our students' ability and motivation to write are all too apparent. The latest National Center for Education Statistics (1997)

writing assessment, for example, shows that although more than 80% of eleventh graders in the United States can begin to write focused and clear responses to tasks, fewer than one third can write complete responses containing sufficient information to support their claims. Only 2% can write effective responses containing supporting details and discussion.

On the attitudinal side, evidence of our failing to develop positive beliefs and motivation toward writing abounds. There is, of course, the lore of great writing—that if it isn't spontaneously inspired it must be heroically painful. Writing is easy, said Gene Fowler in a famous quip, you ". . . simply sit staring at a blank sheet of paper until the drops of blood form on your forehead." From the vantage point of his clinical practice in helping people who want and need to write, Boice (1994) observed that his clients, typically individuals who have experienced a fair amount of writing success, too often "force writing with a hurried pace, a lagging confidence, and a lingering malaise," remaining ambivalent about writing and "inconsistent about turning intentions into actions" (p. 1). These feelings are no strangers to the masses of our students; although they believe that writing is important and are quite certain of its link to success in school and life (e.g., Shell, Colvin, & Bruning, 1995), the thought of writing, especially extended writing, evokes in them what could best be described as a mixed reaction. For too many, the motivational balance tilts negatively—toward feelings of anxiety and dread, lack of control, and avoidance (Cleary, 1991).

Writers need to develop strong beliefs in the relevance and importance of writing and ... learn to be patient, persistent, and flexible.

Although it seems that we have much to learn about developing motivation to write, we do have a solid understanding about the processes of writing itself, much of it acquired in the past two decades. Research both in the cognitive sciences (e.g., Bereiter & Scardamalia, 1987; Flower & Hayes, 1981; Flower et al., 1990; Flower, Wallace, Norris, & Burnett, 1994; Levy & Ransdell, 1996) and in the literary tradition (e.g., Applebee & Langer, 1984; Elbow, 1994; Langer, 1992; Spaulding, 1992) has provided a converging picture of writing as a process of meaning making and

From Bruning, R. and Horn, C. (2000) Developing motivation to write. *Educational Psychologists*, 35(1), 25–37. Mahwah, NJ; Lawrence Erlbaum Associates. Used with permission.

has shifted emphasis away from writing mechanics to an emphasis on communication. We now recognize skilled writing for what it is—a tremendously complex problem-solving act involving memory, planning, text generation, and revision (Flower et al., 1990, 1994). In solving writing's ill-defined problems, writers must juggle multiple goals (Hayes, 1996) and satisfy many constraints—of topic, audience, purpose, and of physically creating the text itself. They also must switch back and forth among a variety of frames of reference, including critical thinking (e.g., perspective, logic), rhetorical stances (e.g., description, persuasion), and writing conventions (e.g., tone, mechanics, spelling). In a difficult and complex task like this, motivational issues will assume particularly prominent status. Writers need to develop strong beliefs in the relevance and importance of writing and, as they grapple with writing's complexities and frustrations, learn to be patient, persistent, and flexible. Although we believe that these beliefs and attitudes ultimately fall clearly within the realm of intrinsic motivation, their development is in the hands of those who set the writing tasks and react to what has been written.

The Need to Emphasize Motivation to Write

This article focuses on conditions affecting the development of motivation to write. As rich as cognitive research has been in helping us understand writing, it has only scratched the surface of the issue of motivational and social-cognitive variables (e.g., see Bergin & LaFave, 1998; Hayes, 1996; Spaulding, 1992). We argue, therefore, for an expansion of our models to more explicitly recognize the social-cognitive variables implicit in these cognitive analyses. Literacy researchers have long recognized this need—of not only helping students learn how to write, but learn how to want to write (Spaulding, 1992). A vast number of books and articles, many in the whole-language tradition (e.g., Calkins, 1994; Graves, 1991, 1994), have addressed issues of student interest, engagement, and motivation. As Spaulding pointed out, however, most of these have remained largely unconnected to the rapidly growing research in motivation. Although there is a wealth of practical knowledge about writing instruction, there is still relatively little in the way of scientific analysis aimed at the motivational factors critical to writing development.

In this article, we examine issues affecting development of motivation to write and provide a general framework for research aimed at understanding its development. We make several assumptions. The first is that the root source of motivation to write is a set

of beliefs about writing, many of them tacit. As Flower et al. (1990) pointed out, writers' conceptions of the writing task—tacit or not—inevitably affect what they write. Their task representations guide a set of critical decisions, setting up strategies for completing the tasks and creating bridges between writing processes and products. Motivational considerations are an integral part of their vision as writers make trade-offs between costs and benefits of various goals and ways to use resources (Flower et al., 1994; Hayes, 1996). In any writing task—from a child's brief book report to the reading-to-write assignment of college composition—writers must negotiate between what is expected and what can be done. Students need to be motivated to enter, persist, and succeed in this ill-defined problem space we call writing.

... the wellspring of motivation is experiencing writing as purposeful, authentic communication.

A second assumption is that the wellspring of motivation is experiencing writing as purposeful, authentic communication (Crystal, 1997). Like speakers, writers must express themselves in writing, seeing it not so much as a product but as a way of entering and participating in a discourse community (Boice, 1994). In such communities, the central guiding and nurturing force is the teacher whose conceptions of writing will provide a model for and shape students' beliefs. Thus, we argue, programs for developing writing motivation will rest on the beliefs that teachers themselves hold.

A third assumption is that understanding motivation to write requires an appreciation of writing's relation to oral language. A comparison is useful if for no other reason than the phenomenal success children have learning to speak. By the age of four, virtually every child has learned to speak and has done so in the absence of any forml instruction. Many of the conditions supporting this remarkable developmental achievement can be enlisted to support children's writing. However, understanding how writing development differs from speech development is also critical. We believe the comparability argument is overextended by those who argue that simply creating a literacy-rich environment is sufficient. Learning to write is an extraordinarily complex linguistic and cognitive task requiring close attention to the conditions for developing motivation and skill. Because it is typically further removed from experience, writing often lacks the accompanying web of context that supports oral discourse. The challenge for the writer is to recreate the experience—in other words, recontextualize it—without the immediacy of oral discourse (C. A. Cameron, Hunt, & Linton, 1996). Snow (1983) argued that learning to read is facilitated by oral language experiences where parents scaffold understanding by speaking in literate ways. Writing needs the same kind of structure. Because written discourse contains many unfamiliar elements (e.g., new discourse forms, conventions of writing) and exposes writers' thoughts and feelings to much closer scrutiny, careful planning is required to develop positive motivation for the act and process of writing.

Learning to write is an extraordinarily complex linguistic and cognitive task requiring close attention to the conditions for developing motivation and skill.

Table 1 contrasts the oral language capabilities most children bring to school and the challenges that writing presents. Our portrayal, which draws on Calfee's views (e.g., see Calfee & Patrick, 1995), emphasizes the natural language dimensions of children's early oral language experience, contrasting them with the features of language that children encounter through becoming literate. By its very nature, writing typically is a more deliberate, formal act than speech, one that reveals the linguistic and cognitive processes supporting it (Olson, 1994).

Although posing considerable motivational challenges, writing's formal qualities are what give it its potential for developing students' abilities to understand, organize, and express their thoughts and feelings. Developing writers are challenged to do far more than simply set down a sequence of words. They must learn a new communication framework involving an intricate set of formal language conventions. They must spell out what topics are about, organize information, and provide causal explanations. The feedback students receive soon uncovers another feature of written language—its ability to show the quality and authenticity of a writer's thoughts and feelings. When language is written down, anybody can see whether ideas are logical and fit together, or whether emotions ring true. Students doing an investigative report on, for instance, the safety of school playground equipment not only need to state important facts, but express them well and persuasively. Student writing seldom rises to be as vivid and engaging as the stories and word pictures of conversation, but it serves vital developmental purposes by placing new demands on the student. The motivational challenge is to help students see that writing's benefits outweigh its considerable effort and risks.

Developing Motivation to Write

We now turn to the factors we believe are most important for developing and maintaining motivation to write. In describing them, we draw on our analysis of the nature of written discourse, on the relatively small

Table 1 Typical Features of Children's Experience with Oral and Written Discourse

Oral Discourse	Written Discourse
Rapid, transitory, inexact, variable. Provision of additional information is major mechanism for refining meanings and correcting errors.	Slow developing, stable, and reproducible. Revision in light of communication purpose and audience is critical for clarifying ideas and communicating effectively.
Contextual and implicit. Listeners can "fill in" meaning using a variety of contextual clues.	Decontextualized and explicit. Writers must establish common ground for understanding, considering factors such as purpose, audience, and writing conventions.
Early, high, continuing exposure. Most children immersed in rich discourse communities that link oral language to all parts of their lives.	Later, lower, more intermittent exposure. Most children entering school are relative novices at writing, unsure about writing's uses and their own capabilities.
Highly varied pragmatic uses. Most beginning students skilled at using natural language to describe things, tell stories, and express their feelings.	Narrower range of uses. Most entering students will not yet have used writing pragmatically and need to discover writing's utility for description, self-expression, and persuasion.
Narrative structures dominate. Communication success depends on imagery, memorability, implicit meanings.	Descriptive, logical structures dominate. Writing permits careful examination of cognitive and emotional dimensions of communication.
	Successful writing requires mastery of formal language conventions.

Table 2 Factors in Developing Motivation to Write

Cluster	Related Motivation-Enhancing Conditions
Nurturing functional beliefs about writing	• Creating a classroom community supporting writing and other literacy activities • Displaying the ways that teachers use writing personally • Finding writing tasks that assure student success • Providing opportunities for students to build expertise in areas they will write about • Using brief daily writing activities to encourage regular writing • Encouraging writing in a wide variety of genres
Fostering student engagement through authentic writing goals and contexts	• Having students find examples of different kinds of writing (e.g., self-expressive, persuasive, entertaining) • Encouraging students to write about topics of personal interest • Having students write for a variety of audiences • Establishing improved communication as purpose for revision • Integrating writing into instruction in other disciplines (e.g., science, math, social studies)
Providing a supportive context for writing	• Breaking complex writing tasks into parts • Encouraging goal setting and monitoring of progress • Assisting students in setting writing goals that are neither too challenging nor too simple • Teaching writing strategies and helping students learn to monitor their use • Giving feedback on progress toward writing goals • Using peers as writing partners in literacy communities
Creating a positive emotional environment	• Modeling positive attitudes toward writing • Creating a safe environment for writing • Giving students choices about what they will write • Providing feedback allowing students to retain control over their writing • Utilizing natural outcomes (e.g., communication success) as feedback source • Training students to engage in positive self-talk about writing • Helping students reframe anxiety, stress as natural arousal

current research literature directly linking motivational constructs and writing, and, as appropriate, on the much larger literatures relating to motivation in general and to writing instructional practices. Table 2 provides the four clusters of conditions we consider most critical in developing writing motivation, together with exemplars of interventions likely to affect writing motivation's development. These clusters also provide a framework for research leading to a comprehensive understanding of how writing motivation develops.

Heading the list of motivation-enhancing conditions, in our judgment, is *nurturing functional beliefs about the nature of writing and its outcomes*. These beliefs have multiple dimensions, starting with a realistic appraisal of the difficulties and challenges of writing. They also include beliefs in writing's potential, in one's capabilities as a writer, and in having control over writing tasks. A second cluster is designed *to foster student engagement through authentic goals and contexts*—in other words, writing that students will see as meaningful, purposeful, and allowing them to express their own voice (Elbow, 1994; Oldfather, 1993; Oldfather & Dahl, 1994). The goal is to find tasks that generate engagement through their intrinsic qualities and require a minimum of externally managed rewards to keep students involved. A third group of conditions involves *providing a supportive context to develop requisite writing skills*. They include task framing, practice, and feedback conditions likely to build skills and motivation. The final cluster of conditions focuses on *creating a positive emotional environment*, where ideas and feelings can be expressed safely. Because even the most ideal course of writing development involves challenge and frustration, students' anxieties and frustrations with writing also must be addressed. For each of these clusters, we outline possibilities for research on writing motivation.

Cluster 1: Nurturing Functional Beliefs About Writing

Except when carried out mechanically or under duress, writing is a volitional act of problem solving (e.g., Flower et al., 1990; Hayes, 1996). Success in almost any writing task requires extended periods of concentration and engagement in which writers must marshal all of their cognitive, motivational, and linguistic resources. Beliefs about writing must be sufficiently potent to carry the writer through the difficult and often emotion-laden processes of writing.

A reasonable starting point is the perception that writing has value (Codling & Gambrell, 1997). Most students, in fact, seem to believe that it does, at least for achieving academic and vocational goals. Shell et al. (1995) and Pajares and his associates (Pajares & Johnson, 1996; Pajares, Miller, & Johnson, 1999; Pajares & Valiante, 1997), for instance, showed that perceived usefulness of writing is already high by the upper-elementary grades, with writing continuing to be highly valued into high school and college (Shell, Murphy, & Bruning, 1989).

Belief in one's competence as a writer also seems essential to writing motivation. Because of its consistent relation to writing performance (Pajares & Johnson, 1996; Pajares et al., 1999; Pajares & Valiante, 1997; Shell et al., 1989, 1995) and solid theoretical grounding (Bandura, 1997; Schunk, 1991), self-efficacy has emerged as a major focus in studies of writing motivation. Extending self-efficacy theory to writing leads to predictions of a reciprocal relation between writing skill and efficacy, with such assumed benefits for high efficacy writers as lower anxiety, greater persistence, and higher toleration for frustration in writing tasks.

Writing self-efficacy appears to follow a developmental course, most likely linked to growth in writing competence; compared to fourth graders, both seventh and tenth graders have higher self-efficacy for completing writing tasks (Shell et al., 1995). Writing efficacy also increases as a result of interventions that provide students with tools for improving their writing skills. Graham and Harris (1989a, 1989b) and Schunk and Swartz (1993) showed, for example, that the development of self-efficacy for writing is linked to whether students have strategies for writing and to the kinds of feedback they receive. In Graham and Harris's work, students who were learning disabled who were taught strategies for writing stories and essays increased both their writing skills and self-efficacy, changes that were maintained and transferred to other settings. In studies with upper elementary students, Schunk and Swartz highlighted *process goals*, involving strategies that upper-elementary students could use to improve their writing, and *progress feedback*, where experimenters provided students with information on how well they were learning to use a writing strategy. Process goals appear to have some independent effects, and combining process goals with progress feedback not only brings about improvements in self-efficacy, but also increases both strategy use and writing skill. Schunk and Swartz argued that, in general, progress feedback raises efficacy by conveying a belief to learners that they are capable of continuing to improve their skills. It may also heighten learners' sense of volitional control over their writing (Corno, 1993; Deci, Vallerand, Pelletier, & Ryan, 1991; Turner, 1995).

Gender also appears to play a role in the development of writing efficacy. Pajares and Valiente (1997) found, for example, that fifth-grade boys and girls did not differ in their writing performance but that girls perceived writing as more useful than boys, had greater self-efficacy, and worried less about it. In a sample of ninth graders, however, girls reported lower self-efficacy than boys, even though their actual writing performance did not differ. These findings may reflect a general downward trend for girls in perceptions of their academic competence (Phillips & Zimmerman, 1990). It may also be, as Cleary (1996) argued, that secondary schools and colleges emphasize a male-biased form of discourse requiring females to adapt to structures that may be less intuitive, interesting, or intrinsically motivating.

Writers, no doubt, hold a range of important motivation-relevant beliefs that extend well beyond ideas of its value and their own writing competence. Some of these likely parallel the implicit beliefs shown to have important motivational consequences in other areas (e.g., Dweck & Leggett, 1988; Schraw & Bruning, 1996, 1999). Dweck and Leggett, for example, demonstrated that individuals holding so-called incremental views about intelligence (i.e., that intelligence is changeable) tend to have a learning or mastery orientation and, when faced with challenging conditions, respond with more persistent and flexible problem solving. Complex literacy tasks have been found to promote mastery responses because they challenge students (Miller, Adkins, & Hooper, 1993). Environments that provide students the opportunity for input and choice, promote student interaction, and provide challenging tasks particularly impact the goal orientations of lower ability students in positive ways (Meece & Miller, 1999). Similarly, Schraw, Bruning, and their associates (Bruning, Horn, & Sodoro, 1998; Schraw & Bruning, 1996) showed that individuals' implicit beliefs that reading is transactional lead to higher levels of reading engagement and affects reading choices.

Directions for future research.   Although there has been substantial research on writing self-efficacy, plus some work on attributions for writing success (e.g., Shell et al., 1995) and writing apprehension (e.g., Madigan, Linton, & Johnson, 1996), less is known about the patterns of other beliefs that students hold about writing and how they develop. Is there, for example, a parallel to the belief structures identified by Dweck and Leggett (1988), where some students take an entity view of writing, assuming that their writing ability is largely fixed? If so, are there negative motivational consequences, such as those that accompany a performative outlook (e.g., excessive concern with evaluation, risk aversion)? The work of Palmquist and Young (1992) hinted at this possibility; students who believe strongly that writing is a gift (i.e., an entity view) show significantly more writing anxiety and assess their own capabilities more negatively. Similarly, comparable to Schraw and Bruning's (1996, 1999) findings on the structure of reading beliefs, do some see writing as an act of information transmission, whereas others see it as much more transactional? If patterns of writing beliefs vary along this dimension, how do they relate to the likelihood of adopting, for example, a knowledge-telling versus a knowledge-transforming approach in writing (Bereiter & Scardamalia, 1987)? Also, how may such beliefs relate to willingness to revise and to choices about the kinds of revisions to make (Graham, 1997), two critical factors in shaping writers' development?

Several additional dimensions potentially important for developing writing motivation also remain largely unexplored. One of these is beliefs about writing's social role. In many classrooms, writing is structured as a dispassionate and possibly gender-biased activity where only the "academic voice" is valued (Cleary, 1996; McCracken, 1992). Likewise, idea generation, information gathering, writing, and revising can be solitary and potentially isolating acts. Contrasting to these conditions is writing in literacy-oriented classrooms where writing and talk about writing are central features of the classrooms' intellectual and social life and where a variety of expressive forms are honored. Features of such classrooms are well-known (Bruning & Schweiger, 1997; Calfee & Patrick, 1995; Guthrie & Alao, 1997; Guthrie & McCann, 1997; Graves, 1991; Turner, 1995); they include making literacy activities the classroom centerpiece, encouraging cooperative activities, creating project-oriented tasks, giving students responsibility, and scaffolding student responses to insure success. The centrality of literacy and writing in particular seem likely to widen students' understanding of the social functions of written language and to help fulfill a host of social and relational needs. Key questions for the development of motivation to write are whether these experiences affect students' beliefs about writing and, if so, which of the conditions are most critical.

Cluster 2: Fostering Student Engagement Through Authentic Writing Goals and Contexts

Schools provide the best and often the only real opportunities most children have to write. Beyond the simple opportunity to write, of course, is the quality of the writing experience, which is largely determined by how teachers use writing in their classes. Their actions and the enthusiasm they portray toward writing provide the models for student perceptions of writing. Teachers play a vital role by choosing appropriately challenging literacy assignments that foster student engagement and motivation (Ames & Archer, 1988, Guthrie & Alao, 1997; Guthrie & McCann, 1997; Lepper & Hodell, 1989). Another critical role comes in providing guidance and ongoing feedback on writing.

For elementary-level students, in particular, teacher guidance and feedback has a significant impact on the development of strategies, confidence, and actual writing performance (Pajares & Johnson, 1996; Skinner, Wellborn, & Connell, 1990). Teachers can help break writing tasks into manageable parts, which not only reduces the processing demands of a complex task, but also allows students to monitor their progress and experience success during the writing process. Embedded in the tasks teachers assign is the information that shapes students' beliefs about their ability, the amount of effort they are willing to expend, and satisfaction (Ames, 1992). Cycles of goal setting coupled with feedback regarding progress toward the goals often are necessary to activate a full capability for self-monitoring and self-regulation (Cervone, 1993).

Whether teachers enact these important steps depends greatly on what they believe about writing. Their decisions about writing's place in the curriculum—and their reactions to student writing—trace back to their own understanding of writing's nature, its uses, and their own feelings toward it. Thus, the beginning point for building student writing motivation is teacher beliefs about writing. If teachers' experiences with writing are narrow-gauge, socially isolating, evaluation oriented, and anxiety provoking, they are very unlikely to be able to create positive motivational conditions for their students' writing. On the other hand, if teachers see writing as a critical tool for intellectual and social development and as serving a broad range of important student aims—for cognitive stimulation and growth, self-expression, or social affiliation—they will provide settings aimed at fostering similar beliefs.

School writing often takes place under conditions that are artificial, at least from the students' perspective. Writing tasks such as abstracting chapters and books, completing essay exams, and writing term papers seem largely of the teacher's making. Even when selected for sound pedagogical reasons, writing activities often are not set within larger social or communication frames that can create interest and a sense of writing's relevance. Writing becomes an "assignment" in which the desire for closure around specific conclusions will be very strong (Flower et al., 1990). Absent from such arrangements is the opportunity to see writing's utility for "real" purposes such as persuasion, description, and expressing the writer's voice. What is needed, in the view of many, are authentic literacy tasks (e.g., Cleary, 1991; Turner, 1995).

School writing often takes place under conditions that are artificial, at least from the students' perspective.

Hiebert (1994) described authentic literacy tasks as activities that involve children in the immediate use of literacy for enjoyment and communication, distinguishing them from activities where literacy skills are acquired for some unspecified future use. Traditionally, pursuing activities within real-world social and physical contexts has been strongly emphasized (e.g., Brown, Collins, & Duguid, 1989). Many also would add the criterion of meaningfulness, of students acquiring skills within rather than separate from the contexts in which they will be used. Ideally, authentic tasks have much in common with the best of real-world experience—affording opportunities for challenge and self-improvement, student autonomy, interest-based learning, and social interaction (Turner, 1995).

Having genuine reasons for writing almost certainly has motivational consequences. Authentic tasks would seem to afford students the opportunity to express and refine their voice (e.g., Elbow, 1994; Schiwy, 1996). Words set down on a page to a real audience for a real purpose are their own, not borrowed (Elbow, 1994). Authentic tasks are likely to help students develop one or more distinctive styles of writing and to determine if these styles are "theirs." They may also develop more complex dimensions of voice, such as learning to write with authority or ironically. Such writing has potential for expressing "the person behind the words" (Elbow, 1994) and for revealing dimensions of the writer's identity, character, and goals. Writers' discoveries of their own voice and their growing ability to express it would seem to have considerable potential for developing motivation to write (Oldfather, 1993; Oldfather & Dahl, 1994).

Interest is another powerful motivator. It has been shown to have two primary functions; determining how long students persist at tasks and the level of attention they are willing to commit (Hidi, 1990) and influencing the goals students set for themselves, particularly

if they see writing as a mechanism by which they can meet their communication needs (Csikszentmihalyi & Rathunde, 1993). The research on the impact of interest on writing has revealed a complex relation between knowledge, interest, and writing performance (Benton, Corkill, Sharp, Downey, & Khramtsova, 1995; Hidi & Anderson, 1992). Benton et al. (1995), for example, found that students with high topic knowledge and high interest wrote essays that included content-relevant information that was logical and well-organized, whereas writers with relatively less interest and knowledge generated more ideas unrelated to the topic. Although there was a strong relation between knowledge and interest, they were found to be separate constructs. Studies with middle-school children conducted by Pintrich and DeGroot (1990) showed that students who believed that they were engaged in important and interesting tasks were more cognitively strategic.

Directions for future research.   Although a host of theoretical and practical considerations strongly recommend use of authentic tasks and contexts for writing, there is as yet little empirical support for their use or even understanding of their nature. In general, we know that tasks involving variety and diversity are more likely to create interest in learning and a mastery orientation (Ames, 1992). In writing, however, we do not have any kind of taxonomy relating different kinds of writing tasks to either skill or motivational development. What effects do response journals or personal essays, for example, have on the quality of students' creative self-expression and on their desire to write?

More generally, what are the motivational effects exerted by the set of conditions that we refer to as *authentic writing contexts?* It may be useful to approach this question by systematically inquiring into those features of writing contexts, goals, and feedback conditions that most affect motivation to write. For instance, what are the motivational effects if there are pragmatic purposes for writing beyond completion of the assignment itself, or when writing tasks are embedded in larger task contexts? How is writing affected when the audience shifts to one the writer sees as important—to younger students or pen pals in a partner school, for example, or to parents, business people, or public officials?

We also need to inquire of students themselves—about those purposes of writing they consider to be most meaningful and motivating. Are their conceptions consonant with ours? Of all the features of context and purpose, which contribute systematically to student perceptions that writing is interesting and meaningful? How can these features be operationalized for writers of different ages and abilities? Finally, is it always necessary or even desirable to set writing within "real-world" social and physical environments, or are factors such as the opportunity for challenge, student autonomy, interest, and social interaction (Turner, 1995) more reliable keys to student motivation to write?

Cluster 3: Providing a Supportive Context for Writing

Writing successfully is a complex and effortful activity requiring systematic attention to motivational conditions. Each act of writing takes place in a context that defines the initial nature of the writing task, affects the goals that writers set, and influences the decisions they will make as writing progresses (Hayes, 1996). Context also determines the level of skill required to complete a writing task successfully. For students to engage fully and succeed in writing, they need to be able to tap motivational resources embedded in the task itself (e.g., its perceived utility), in their own interest and motivational histories, and in the feedback they receive or give themselves during the writing process.

Gaining and maintaining control of a writing task almost certainly are critical motivationally. No matter what the writer's developmental stage or ability level, each act of writing poses a formidable challenge, having much in common with other ill-defined problems (Flower et al., 1990). In creating the problem space and in its later refinements, writers must balance the potential costs of various courses of action with their hypothesized benefits (Hayes, 1996). Do I need more information? Do I need to change the focus of what I'm writing? Do I have time to revise? Should I read over the paper one more time? Parameters defining this fluctuating problem space include the writer's purposes for writing, the norms of the discourse community (as embodied by the teacher or other audiences), and the writer's own knowledge and writing skill. Framed too broadly, this ill-defined problem has the potential of overwhelming the writer—unless the writer has clear goals and can deploy strategies to reach them. If a writer embarks on a writing journey with a too-complex problem definition, the results can be disastrous, especially if approaches are abandoned midstream (Cervone, 1993).

Given a choice between complexity and simplicity, however, it seems better to err in the direction of complexity in selecting writing tasks. Students find cognitively complex learning activities inherently more interesting and demanding of mental effort (Meece & Miller, 1992); such tasks lead to higher levels of motivation because they create interest, allow for self-improvement, and afford opportunities to control one's own learning (Turner, 1995). They prefer complex literacy assignments for much the same reasons (Miller

et al., 1993). Writers need to believe, however, that if the task is complex it can be accomplished with reasonable effort. This belief can be fostered by helping students define tasks in terms of proximal goals with clear definitions of what constitutes success, learn to observe and judge their own performance against these goals, and react appropriately to these judgments (e.g., by working harder or changing strategies; Schunk & Zimmerman, 1994). In addition, students' engagement levels increase when they consider tasks to be meaningful and connect their accomplishments to their effort (Lepper & Hodell, 1989; Meece, 1991; Nicholls, 1984; Wigfield, Eccles, & Rodriguez, 1998).

Although complex writing tasks can be desirable, students' responses to them need careful monitoring. When they perceive tasks as too difficult or ambiguous, cooperation and interest may decrease and they may try to negotiate requirements downward (Doyle, 1986). Needlessly complex assignments or immature writers' own poor judgments also can place them in situations too complex for them to handle and push them, as Larson (1995) stated, outside their "performance envelopes." When writing tasks take students beyond their ability, the result likely will be anxiety that will lead to poorly controlled writing. If anxiety rises to a high level, the result may be emotional and cognitive thrashing that disrupts writing entirely. Again, at the other end of the spectrum, the result if expectations are too low will be low motivation characterized by apathy, boredom, or disinterest.

Helping students set specific challenging goals. Successful writing depends on students' ability to manage an ongoing relation between themselves and their writing, establishing a level of engagement that maintains their attention and keeps them motivated and involved (Larson, 1995). The challenges are to engage developing writers in writing tasks that match their abilities and current motivational levels and to help them develop the habits and strategies that keep them moving ahead productively (e.g., Graham, 1997). A large amount of motivational literature points to goal setting and progress monitoring as two consistently facilitative variables in this regard. Goals, especially if they are specific and challenging, will lead to higher levels of performance. They will have their greatest effect, however, when students have accurate and useful feedback during task engagement (Locke & Latham, 1990).

Writers necessarily alter their goals as they compose; a key to maintaining motivation to write lies in how these alterations take place. For novice writers and even for quite skilled ones, abandoning one set of goals and starting toward others can create a situation from which it is difficult to recover. Writers instead need to maintain a balance between the challenges presented by the task at any given point and their skills, interest level, and confidence to successfully complete the task (Larson, 1995).

Work by Graham, Harris, and their colleagues (e.g., Graham, 1997; Graham & Harris, 1989a; Graham, MacArthur, & Schwartz, 1995) and by Schunk and his associates (Schunk & Rice, 1991; Schunk & Swartz, 1993) points toward the utility of a combination of goal setting, goal-related strategies, and process feedback. Specific goals for writing, coupled with strategy instruction, facilitate both writing quality and efficacy (e.g., Graham, 1997; Graham et al., 1995). The addition of procedural support for strategies (Graham, 1997) and feedback on how students are progressing toward acquiring writing strategies provides information that the strategies being employed are useful and the students are increasing their skills (Borkowski, Weyhing, & Carr, 1988; Graham & Harris, 1993). These factors are particularly critical in improving self-efficacy and intrinsic motivation because developing writers realize that they are capable of improving their skills (Schunk & Swartz, 1993). The greater their sense that strategies are useful and help give them control over their writing, the more likely they will be to make use of them. Strategy use, in turn, will promote skill acquisition (Bandura, 1997; Graham et al., 1995; Schunk, 1989).

Feedback is crucial for writers because it allows them to see the discrepancies between their current performance and their goals. The feedback helps move them from where they are to where they would like to be and provides direction on what strategies to utilize to achieve their goals (Schutz, 1993). Once they isolate discrepancies and their causes through either internal or external feedback, additional strategies or effort can be applied. On simple activities, the response to feedback will most likely be increased effort, which often results in a removal of the discrepancy (Bandura & Cervone, 1983). On complex tasks, however, the response often is to engage in multiple strategies that may not result in narrowing the discrepancy, but instead creates cognitive overload (Cervone, 1993). In the complex task of writing, this can lead to less, not more, productive activities.

Therefore, the most useful feedback on writing will likely involve specific knowledge about how to move toward one's writing goals. Case study research has indicated that students respond favorably to specific and explicit ways to improve their writing (Straub, 1996, 1997); students are quite clear about their need for specific coaching about their writing. In a number of studies examining student response to teacher comments, students responded very well to comments that dealt with organization, development, and matters of form, but resisted comments that dealt with the value of their ideas or issues they did not consider

germane to the writing task (Cleary, 1996; Larson, 1995; Straub, 1997). Those providing feedback need to contribute in useful ways to the ongoing process of balancing the writing challenge with the writer's skills and motivations. How readers of student writing choose to make that contribution sends strong signals about who controls the writing process. Students appear to be very aware of control issues in writing and recognize when the person giving feedback begins to exert too much control (Straub, 1996).

The most useful feedback on writing will likely involve specific knowledge about how to move toward one's writing goals.

Although we strongly believe that developing motivation to write is best conceived of as a process of building intrinsic motivation, rewards may play a productive role. Rewards can help build achievement-directed motivation when they are made contingent on student effort (Brophy, 1987; Stipek & Kowalski, 1989) and on progress in relation to short-term goals (Schunk, 1989). A further positive factor may come when individuals are rewarded for putting a large amount of cognitive or physical effort into writing. The sensation of high effort can acquire secondary reward properties that ameliorate, to some degree, the aversiveness of writing for some students. Reducing the aversiveness through reward may increase young writers' general readiness to expend effort in goal-directed writing tasks (Eisenberger & Cameron, 1996). Of course, the possible negative effects of rewards need to be considered, especially if rewards are offered for engaging in writing tasks without consideration of performance (J. Cameron & Pierce, 1994). This could occur if students were, say, promised tangible rewards simply for engaging in writing.

Directions for future research.   An important area for future research involves attempting to better understand task conditions that support motivational development. For example, how do students' cognitive, linguistic, and self-regulatory abilities affect the kinds of writing tasks that they find motivating? What students find motivating to write about will be highly contextualized, of course, involving some combinations of personal and situational interest, knowledge about the topic, processes by which the writing topic was selected, and the extent to which writing has purposes students consider authentic. Another area for research is examining ways of parsing goals within complex, real-life writing tasks (e.g., see Zimmerman & Kitsantas, 1999). What is the effect, for example, of teachers' carefully framing and systematically revisiting mid- to long-term classroom goals to which a given piece of writing relates? How in fact do students approach complex, multifaceted writing tasks? What kinds of classroom structures and coaching best facilitate steady, stress-free progress toward writing goals and produce the highest quality writing products? Systematic pursuit of answers to questions such as these should lead to better specification of the conditions that develop and maintain motivation to write.

Close examination also is needed of the motivational fluctuations that occur during the writing process as students make decisions in complex writing tasks. We have learned a great deal about writing's cognitive processes from the work of pioneers like Flower, Hayes, Bereiter, and Scardamalia. We now need to more systematically examine motivation-related factors such as writing efficacy, goal setting, and choices about revision during the processes of writing. How does motivation factor into students' beginning conceptions of writing tasks and their later reconceptualizations? Is it true for writing, as the general motivational research implies, that writing tasks conceived of too simply in fact become boring and mechanical? At the other end of the continuum,

---

Although we strongly believe that developing motivation to write is best conceived of as a process of building intrinsic motivation, rewards may play a productive role.

---

is Larson's (1995) surmise correct that many young writers exceed their performance capabilities? If so, what are the motivational consequences? And is it also true, as Cervone's (1993) work would indicate, that making too many simultaneous changes in a complex and challenging writing task can result in information overload and overpower the writer's processing capacity? Better identification of the conditions that may produce such effects—based on observing student writing and attitudes in naturalistic settings or experimental conditions—would seem to be very important. Finally, how do successful writers maintain a balance of multiple factors such as their knowledge, skills, interest levels, and writing confidence at the outset, during, and as they near the end of writing tasks? When something must be sacrificed, what is? Again, developmental studies of student writers in natural or simulated settings are likely to help us better understand what we need to pay attention to motivationally.

Cluster 4: Creating a Positive Emotional Environment

Anyone who writes has experienced at least some negative feelings about writing. A considerable number of people develop even stronger negative feelings, including writing-related emotional distress and a strong distaste for its processes (Daly, 1985; Madigan

et al., 1996). The reasons seem as varied as writers' experiences. Even in the best of circumstances, the conditions under which children begin to write often are far from ideal motivationally. For the novice writer, especially, writing may seem excruciatingly

---

Even successful writers can get into trouble.

---

slow and the products, filled with erasures and strikeouts, bleak testimonies to the writer's lack of skill. It may be, as Boice (1994) states, that our productive abilities grow more slowly than our critical ones. What is certain is that novice writers are entering an unfamiliar discourse community with new norms and standards. For many, little in their background has prepared them for functioning well in it. They may initially have only a dim conception of writing's usefulness for helping them achieve their intellectual and social goals. Some may find that writing exposes their knowledge and thinking to an uncomfortable level of scrutiny. With this exposure can come feelings of loss of control and its attendant anxieties (Bandura, 1997), which can be amplified when conditions for successful performance and feedback are unclear.

Even successful writers can get into trouble. They may be hypercritical about their own work. Because of anxiety, they may lapse into procrastination or other unproductive habits, such as impulsively starting to write without gathering the necessary information or writing in unhealthy "binges" (Boice, 1994). As affect turns negative, the natural consequence is that students will begin to avoid writing wherever possible. A cycle can thus begin in which lack of writing leads to lack of writing improvement, resulting in even less inclination to continue. Somehow this cycle must be broken for students to have a chance of experiencing the intrinsic motivation writing can bring. At least four conditions seem promising for creating a positive emotional environment for writing.

An obvious starting point is removing conditions that make writing a negative experience. Structurally, this involves eliminating unnecessary stresses related to writing and trying to ensure that students are engaged in enjoyable, successful writing activities. Larson and his colleagues (Larson, Hecker, & Norem, 1985) found enjoyment of the task of writing to make a qualitative difference in student writing. Hayes and Daiker (1984) found that the single most important principle of response in a writing environment was positive reinforcement. Teachers should spend as much energy on praising good writing as they do in pointing out errors and suggesting improvements. In addition, a safe environment needs to express an openness to all kinds of written and oral self-expression, what Oldfather (1993) has called "honored voice." In such an environment, teachers pay careful attention to what students write and say, and students learn to treat each others' ideas with respect.

Engagement is another component essential to fostering a positive emotional environment. Csikszentmihalyi (1975) defined engagement as a balance between a challenging task and the ability to carry out the task. Wigfield et al. (1998) proposed that the critical components for task involvement are allowing adequate time based on student needs and helping students plan and organize their writing process. Clearly (1991) found that students with teachers who assisted them in breaking down their writing into manageable pieces viewed complex assignments as challenging rather than overwhelming. Children's engagement also has been found to be directly influenced by their perceptions of teacher warmth and interest (Skinner & Belmont, 1993). In classrooms where teachers create a climate of trust, caring, and mutual concern, students are motivated to engage (Connell & Wellborn, 1991; Wentzel, 1997).

A second factor in countering negative attitudes toward writing is giving students a significant measure of control. Several factors likely contribute to feelings of control. Perhaps most basic is knowledge—having something to say. Too often, students are assigned writing tasks on topics where they have little content mastery. Creating a writing problem space (Flower et al., 1990) with diffuse and poorly structured knowledge is unlikely to lead to a successful writing experience. Also, simply having knowledge may motivate writing—as information collections grow, so will interest, organization, and the belief that communicating that information is worthwhile (Boice, 1994). Second, there is growing evidence that writing-strategy training (e.g., Graham & Harris, 1989b, 1993) and building efficacy for using strategies (Schunk & Zimmerman, 1997) strengthen both writing skills and efficacy. As Bandura (1997) pointed out, anxiety decreases as efficacy for a task increases. Third, certain kinds of feedback—especially feedback giving information on progress toward writing goals—appear to enhance student feelings of control (Schunk & Swartz, 1993; Straub, 1996, 1997). Finally, and perhaps most simply, is giving students manageable writing tasks. Major writing tasks can be broken into subtasks, retaining the positive motivational effects of challenge but making the task manageable. Breaking writing tasks into sections also affords students multiple opportunities to revise and improve their work.

Many students' negative attitudes about writing seem to stem from their patterns of self-talk. Interestingly, there is at least some evidence that both attitudes and self-talk are independent of how students actually write and task difficulty (Madigan et al., 1996). No matter what their ability or how easy or hard the writing task, students variously may tell themselves that they aren't capable of writing well, blame themselves for waiting too long to write, consider writing to be a special talent that only others have, compare themselves unfavorably to an unrealistic standard of perfection, or assure themselves they can't begin writing because conditions aren't exactly right.

A large body of research on self-management (see, e.g., Kazdin, 1994) has shown, however, that systematic programs countering negative self-talk can change attitudes and promote positive responses for problems ranging from smoking to poor social skills. The keys to most such programs are monitoring negative thought patterns (e.g., "I don't know how to begin") and systematically substituting positive ones (e.g., "I don't have to start with the introduction. Why don't I just start here and come back to the introduction later?"). Closely related to monitoring negative self-talk is an approach Bandura (1997) proposed for increasing efficacy—helping individuals reinterpret their physiological responses to stress-inducing situations in more positive terms. In writing, this would involve helping students understand their feelings of anxiousness before or during writing as a normal physiological response to a challenging and stimulating task—not as a signal that they are about to fail. Of course, this reframing can complement more direct routes to increasing efficacy—enactive task mastery (i.e., writing successfully), seeing successful models for performance (e.g., by the teacher, by peers, or by looking at other examples of writing), and encouragement.

Conclusions

Writing is an immensely valuable intellectual and social tool but presents extraordinary motivational challenges. The act of writing is a complex, protracted, problem-solving task in which motivation is critical but difficult to establish and maintain. Writing also represents mysterious new forms of discourse for many children; we often do not do a good job of showing them writing's potential for enhancing their ability to think and communicate. In school, writing's use for evaluative purposes often dominates, with assigned writing and writing on tests taking precedence over writing to share knowledge, points of view, and feelings. Building lasting motivation to write requires careful attention to the conditions under which students write.

We see a number of keys to developing motivation to write, all related to intrinsic motivation. We first need to build student beliefs about writing's nature and potential. These include not only a sense of writing's power, but also a realistic appraisal of its difficulty. Students need to see writing's value as an intellectual and social tool, as well as develop confidence in their writing ability. Second, authentic writing goals and contexts are likely to provide motivational support. Real purposes and audiences clearly convey writing's pragmatic purposes and help students develop a sense of their own writing voice. Third, developing writers need to experience writing task conditions supportive of motivation. These would include encountering complex writing tasks in manageable parts; being helped to set specific, proximal goals; receiving feedback on progress toward goals; and learning writing strategies and when to use them. Fourth, because of writing's complexity and students' prior experiences in many classrooms, many students will have negative feelings about writing and have unproductive writing habits. Approaches are needed that help students deal with negative affect and establish new, productive writing approaches.

Programs that develop student motivation for writing are most likely to be designed and implemented by those who understand, implicitly, the power and pleasure of writing.

Extensive basic and applied research is needed to explicate the factors affecting the development of writing motivation. At least some of this research needs to focus on teachers because of their roles as models for student writing beliefs and feedback providers. Programs for strengthening student writing motivation likely need to start by building teachers' conceptions of the transactional, constructive, problem-solving nature of writing; its intellectual and social utility; and its unique motivational challenges. Teachers' views of writing are very likely to carry over into the design and conduct of their students' writing experiences. Programs that develop student motivation for writing are most likely to be designed and implemented by those who understand, implicitly, the power and pleasure of writing.

References

Ames, C. (1992). Classrooms: Goals, structures, and student motivation. *Journal of Educational Psychology, 84,* 261–271.

Ames, C., & Archer, J. (1988). Achievement in the classroom: Student learning strategies and motivational processes. *Journal of Educational Psychology, 80,* 260–267.

Applebee, A. N., & Langer, J. (1984). *Contexts for learning to write: Studies of secondary school instruction.* Norwood, NJ: Ablex.

Bandura, A. (1997). *Self-efficacy: The exercise of control.* New York: Freeman.

Bandura, A., & Cervone, D. (1983). Self-evaluative and self-efficacy mechanisms governing the motivational effects of goal systems. *Journal of Personality and Social Psychology, 45,* 1017–1028.

Benton, S. L., Corkill, A. J., Sharp, J. M., Downey, R. G., & Khramtsova, I. (1995). Knowledge, interest, and narrative writing. *Journal of Educational Psychology, 87,* 66–78.

Bereiter, C., & Scardamalia, M. (1987). *The Psychology of written composition.* Hillsdale, NJ: Lawrence Erlbaum Associates, Inc.

Bergin, D., & LaFave, C. (1998). Continuities between motivation research and whole language philosophy of instruction. *Journal of Literacy Research, 30,* 321–356.

Berninger, V.W., Fuller, F., & Whitaker, D. (1996). A process model of writing development across the lifespan. *Educational Psychology Review, 8,* 193–218.

Boice, R. (1994). *How writers journey to comfort and fluency.* Westport, CT: Praeger.

Borkowski, J. G., Weyhing, R. S., & Carr, M. (1988). Effects of attributional retraining on strategy-based reading comprehension of learning-disabled students. *Journal of Educational Psychology, 80,* 46–53.

Brophy, J. (1987). On motivating students. In D. Berliner & B. Rosenshine (Eds.), *Talks to teachers* (pp. 201–245). New York: Random House.

Brown, J., Collins, A., & Duguid, P. (1989). Situated cognition of learning. *Educational Researcher, 18,* 32–42.

Bruning, R, Horn, C., & Sodoro, J. (1998, December). *What readers believe about transactions with texts: A closer look.* Paper presented at the National Reading Conference, Austin, TX.

Bruning, R, & Schweiger, B. (1997). Integrating science and literacy experiences to motivate students' learning. In J. T. Guthrie & A. Wigfield (Eds.), *Reading engagement: Motivating readers through integrated instruction* (pp. 149–182). Newark, DE: International Reading Association.

Calfee, R., & Patrick, C. (1995). *Teach our children well.* Stanford, CA: Stanford Alumni Association.

Calkins, L. M. (1994). *The art of teaching writing.* Portsmouth, NH: Heinemann.

Cameron, C. A., Hunt, A.K., & Linton, M.J. (1996). Written expression as recontextualization: Children write in social time. *Educational Psychology Review, 8,* 125–150.

Cameron, J., & Pierce, W. D. (1994). Reinforcement, reward, and intrinsic motivation: A meta-analysis. *Review of Educational Research, 64,* 363–423.

Cervone, D. (1993). The role of self-referent cognitions in goal setting, motivation, and performance. In M. Rabinowitz (Ed.), *Cognitive science foundations of instruction* (pp. 57–95). Hillsdale, NJ: Lawrence Erlbaum Associates, Inc.

Cleary, L. M. (1991). Affect and cognition in the writing processes of eleventh graders. *Written Communication, 8,* 473–507.

Cleary, L. M. (1996). I think I know what my teachers want now: Gender and writing motivation. *English Journal, 85*(1), 50–57.

Codling, R.M., & Gambrell, L.B. (1997). *The motivation to write profile: An assessment tool for elementary teachers.* College Park: University of Maryland.

Connell, J.P., & Wellborn, J.G. (1991). Competence, autonomy, and relatedness: A motivational analysis of self-system processes. In M. R. Gunnar & L.A. Stroufe

(Eds.), *Self-processes and development: The Minnesota Symposium and Child Development* (Vol. 23, pp. 43–78). Hillsdale, NJ: Lawrence Erlbaum Associates, Inc.

Corno, L. (1993). The best laid plans: Modern conceptions of volition and educational research. *Educational Researcher, 22* (2), 14–22.

Crystal, D. (1997). *The Cambridge encyclopedia of language*. Cambridge, England: Cambridge University Press.

Csikszentmihalyi, M. (1975). *Beyond boredom and anxiety*. San Francisco: Jossey-Bass.

Csikszentmihalyi, M., & Rathunde, K. (1993). The measurement of flow in everyday life: Toward a theory of emergent motivation. In J. Jacobs (Ed.), *Developmental perspectives on motivation: Nebraska symposium of motivation, 1992* (pp. 57–98). Lincoln: University of Nebraska Press.

Daly, J. A. (1985). Writing apprehension. In M. Rose (Ed.), *When a writer can't write* (pp. 42–82). New York: Guilford.

Deci, E.L., Vallerand, R.J., Pelletier, L.G., & Ryan, R.M. (1991). Motivation and education: The self-determination perspective. *Educational Psychologist, 26*, 325–346.

Doyle, W. (1986). Classroom organization and management. In M. Wittrock (Ed.), *Handbook of research on teaching* (pp. 392–431). New York: Macmillan.

Dweck, C., & Leggett, E. (1988). A social-cognitive approach to motivation and personality. *Psychological Review, 95*, 256–273.

Eisenberger, R., & Cameron, J. (1996). Detrimental effects of reward. *American Psychologist, 51*, 1153–1166.

Elbow, P. (1994). *Landmark essays on voice and writing*. Davis, CA: Hermagoras Press.

Flower, L., & Hayes, J. (1981). Plans that guide the composing process. In C. Frederiksen & J. Dominic (Eds.), *The nature, development and teaching of written communication* (pp. 39–58). Hillsdale, NJ: Lawrence Erlbaum Associates, Inc.

Flower, L., Stein, V., Ackerman, J., Kantz, M.J., McCormick, K., & Peck, W.C. (1990). *Reading-to-write: Exploring a cognitive and social process*. New York: Oxford University Press.

Flower, L., Wallace, D.L., Norris, L., & Burnett, R. A. (1994). *Making thinking visible: Writing, collaborative planning, and classroom inquiry*. Urbana, IL: National Council of Teachers of English.

Graham, S. (1997). Executive control in the revising of students with learning and writing difficulties. *Journal of Educational Psychology, 89*, 223–234.

Graham, S., & Harris, K. R. (1989a). Components analysis of cognitive strategy instruction: Effects on learning disabled students' compositions and self-efficacy. *Journal of Educational Psychology, 81*, 353–361.

Graham, S., & Harris, K. R. (1989b). Improving learning disabled students' skills at composing essays: Self-instructional strategy training. *Exceptional Children, 56*, 210–214.

Graham, S., & Harris, K. R. (1993). Self-regulated strategy development: Helping students with learning problems develop as writers. *Elementary School Journal, 94*, 169–181.

Graham, S., MacArthur, C., & Schwartz, S. (1995). The effects of goal setting and procedural facilitation on the revising behavior and writing performance of students with writing and learning problems. *Journal of Educational Psychology, 87*, 230–240.

Graves, D.H. (1991). *Build a literate classroom*. Portsmouth, NH: Heinemann.

Graves, D. H. (1994). *A fresh look at writing*. Portsmouth, NH: Heinemann.

Guthrie, J.T., & Alao, S. (1997). Designing contexts to increase motivations for reading. *Educational Psychologist, 32*, 95–105.

Guthrie, J.T., & McCann, A. D. (1997). Characteristics of classrooms that promote motivations and strategies for learning. In J. T. Guthrie & A. Wigfield (Eds.), *Reading engagement: Motivating readers through integrated instruction* (pp. 128–148). Newark, DE: International Reading Association.

Hayes, J.R. (1996). *The science of writing*. Mahwah, NJ: Lawrence Erlbaum Associates, Inc.

Hayes, M., & Daiker, D. (1984). Using protocol analysis in evaluating responses to student writing. *Freshman English News, 13*, 1–5.

Hidi, S. (1990). Interest and its contribution as a mental resource for learning. *Review of Educational Research, 60*, 549–571.

Hidi, S., & Anderson, V. (1992). Situational interest and its impact on reading and expository writing. In K. Reinninger, S. Hidi, & A. Krapp (Eds.), *The role of interest in learning and development* (pp. 215–238). Hillsdale, NJ: Lawrence Erlbaum Associates, Inc.

Hiebert, E.H. (1994). Becoming literate through authentic tasks: Evidence and adaptations. In R. B. Ruddell, M.R. Ruddell, & H. Singer (Eds.), *Theoretical models and processes of reading* (pp. 391–413). Newark, DE: International Reading Association.

Kazdin, A. E. (1994). *Behavior modification in applied settings*. Belmont, CA: Brooks/Cole.

Langer, J.A. (1992). *Literature instruction: A focus on student response*. Urbana, IL: National Council of Teachers of English.

Larson, R. (1995). Flow and writing. In M. Csikszentmihalyi & I. S. Csikszentmihalyi (Eds.), *Optimal experience: Psychological studies of flow in consciousness* (pp. 150–171). Cambridge, England: Cambridge University Press.

Larson, R., Hecker, B., & Norem, J. (1985, October/November). Students' experience with research projects: Pains, enjoyment, and success. *High School Journal, 61–69*.

Lepper, M.R., & Hodell, M. (1989). Intrinsic motivation in the classroom. In C. Ames & R. Ames (Eds.), *Research on motivation in education* (pp. 73–105). San Diego, CA: Academic.

Levy, C.M., & Ransdell, S. (1996). *The science of writing: Theories, methods, Individual differences, and applications*. Mahwah, NJ: Lawrence Erlbaum Associates, Inc.

Locke, E.A., & Latham, G.P. (1990). *A theory of goal setting and task performance*. Englewood Cliffs, NJ: Prentice Hall.

Madigan, R., Linton, P., & Johnson, S. (1996). The paradox of writing apprehension. In C.M. Levy, & S. Ransdell (Eds.), *The science of writing theories, methods, individual differences, and applications* (pp. 295–307). Mahwah, NJ: Lawrence Erlbaum Associates, Inc.

McCracken, N. M. (1992). *Gender issues and the teaching of writing*. Portsmouth, NH: Heinemann.

Meece, J.L. (1991). The classroom context and students' motivational goals. In M. L. Maehr & P. R. Pintrich (Eds.), *Advances in motivation and achievement* (pp.261–286). Greenwich, CT:JAI.

Meece, J.L., & Miller, S.D. (1992, April). *Promoting independent literacy skills and motivation to learn in low achieving elementary school students*. Paper presented at the annual meeting of the American Educational Research Association, San Francisco.

Meece, J. L., & Miller, S. D. (1999). Changes in elementary school children's achievement goals for reading and writing: Results of a longitudinal and an intervention study. *Scientific Studies of Reading, 3*, 207–229.

Miller, S.D., Adkins, T., & Hooper, M.L. (1993). Why teachers select specific literacy assignments and students' reactions to them. *Journal of Reading Behavior, 25*, 69–95.

National Center for Education Statistics. (1997). *Report in brief: NAEP 1996 trends in academic progress*. Washington, DC: U.S. Department of Education.

Nicholls, J.G. (1984). Achievement motivation: Conception of ability, subjective experience, task choice, and performance. *Psychological Review, 91*, 328–346.

Oldfather, P. (1993). What students say about motivating experience in a whole language classroom. *Reading Teacher, 46*, 672–681.

Oldfather, P., & Dahl, K. (1994). Toward a social constructivist reconceptualization of intrinsic motivation for literacy learning. *Journal of Reading Behavior, 26*, 139–158.

Olson, D.R. (1994). *The world on paper: The conceptual and cognitive implications of writing and reading*. Cambridge, England: Cambridge University Press.

Pajares, F., & Johnson, M.J. (1996). Self-efficacy beliefs and the writing performance of entering high school students. *Psychology in the Schools, 33*, 163–175.

Pajares, F., Miller, M. D., & Johnson, M. J. (1999). Gender differences in writing self-beliefs of elementary school students. *Journal of Educational Psychology, 91*, 50–61.

Pajares, F., & Valiante, G. (1997). The predictive and mediational role of the writing self-efficacy beliefs of upper elementary students. *Journal of Educational Research, 90*, 353–360.

Palmquist, M., & Young, R. (1992). The notion of giftedness and student expectations about writing. *Written Communication, 9*, 137–168.

Phillips, D.A., & Zimmerman, M. (1990). The developmental course of perceived competence and incompetence among competent children. In R.J. Sternberg & J. Kolligian (Eds.), *Competence considered* (pp. 41–67). New Haven, CT: Yale University Press.

Pintrich, P. R., & DeGroot, E. V. (1990). Motivational and self-regulated learning components of classroom academic performance. *Journal of Educational Psychology, 82*, 33–40.

Schiwy, M. (1996). *A voice of her own: Women and the journal-writing journey*, New York: Simon & Schuster.

Schraw, G., & Bruning, R. (1996). Readers' implicit models of reading. *Reading Research Quarterly, 31*, 290–305.

Schraw, G., & Bruning, R. (1999). How implicit models of reading affect motivation to read and reading engagement. *Scientific Studies of Reading, 3*, 281–302.

Schunk, D.H. (1989). Learning goals and children's reading comprehension. *Journal of Reading Behavior, 21*, 279–293.

Schunk, D.H. (1991). Goal setting and self-evaluation: A social cognitive perspective on self-regulation. In M. L. Maehr & P.R. Pintrich (Eds.), *Advances in motivation and achievement* (pp. 85–113). Greenwich, CT: JAI.

Schunk, D.H., & Rice, J.M. (1991). Learning goals and progress feedback during reading comprehension instruction. *Journal of Reading Behavior, 23*, 351–364.

Schunk, D.H., & Swartz, C. W. (1993). Goals and progress feedback: Effects on self-efficacy and writing achievement. *Contemporary Educational Psychology, 18*, 337–354.

Schunk, D.H., & Zimmerman, B. (1994). *Self-regulation of learning and performance: Issues and educational applications*. Hillsdale, NJ: Lawrence Erlbaum Associates, Inc.

Schunk, D.H., & Zimmerman, B.J. (1997). Developing self-efficacious readers and writers: The role of social and self-regulatory processes. In J. T. Guthrie & A. Wigfield (Eds.), *Reading engagement: Motivating readers through integrated instruction* (pp. 34–50). Newark, DE: International Reading Association.

Schutz, P. A. (1993). Additional influences on response certitude and feedback requests. *Contemporary Educational Psychology, 18*, 427–441.

Shell, D., Colvin, C., & Bruning, R. (1995). Self-efficacy, attributions, and outcome expectancy mechanisms in reading and writing achievement: Grade-level and achievement-level differences. *Journal of Educational Psychology, 87*, 386–398.

Shell, D., Murphy, C., & Bruning, R. (1989). Self-efficacy and outcome expectancy mechanisms in reading and writing performance. *Journal of Educational Psychology, 81*, 91–100.

Skinner, E.A., & Belmont, M.J. (1993). Motivation in the classroom: Reciprocal effects of teacher behavior and student engagement across the school year. *Journal of Educational Psychology, 85*, 571–581.

Skinner, E.A., Wellborn, J.G., & Connell, J.P. (1990). What it takes to do well in school and whether I've got it: A process model of perceived control and children's engagement and achievement in school. *Journal of Educational Psychology, 82*, 22–32.

Snow, C. E. (1983) Literacy and language: Relationships during the preschool years. *Harvard Educational Review, 53*, 165–187.

Spaulding, C. (1992). The motivation to read and write. In M. Doyle (Ed.), *Reading/writing connections* (pp. 177–201). Newark, DE: International Reading Association.

Stipek, D., & Kowalski, P. (1989). Learned helplessness in task-orienting versus performance-orienting testing conditions. *Journal of Educational Psychology, 81*, 384–391.

Straub, R. (1996). The concept of control in teacher response: Defining the varieties of "directive" and "facilitative" commentary. *College Composition and Communication, 47*, 223–251.

Straub, R. (1997). Students' reactions to teacher comments: An exploratory study. *Research in the Teaching of English, 31*, 91–119.

Turner, J.C. (1995). The influence of classroom contexts on young children's motivation for literacy. *Reading Research Quarterly, 30*, 410–441.

Wentzel, K.R. (1997). Student motivation in middle school: The role of perceived pedagogical caring. *Journal of Educational Psychology, 89*, 411–419.

Wigfield, A., Eccles, J.S., & Rodriguez, D. (1998). The development of children's motivation in school contexts. *Review of Research in Education, 23*, 73–118.

Zimmerman, B.J., & Kitsantas, A. (1999). Acquiring writing revision skill: Shifting from process to outcome self-regulatory goals. *Journal of Educational Psychology, 91*, 241–250.

The Role of Parents in Motivating Struggling Readers

Linda Baker
University of Maryland—Baltimore County

Parents play a critical role in the literacy development of their children. What parents believe, say, and do does make a difference. Interest is currently high among researchers and practitioners on the role of the family and the value of home-school collaborations. The two key goals of this article are (1) to inform practitioners working with struggling readers of the latest research on home influences on reading motivation, and (2) to provide research-based suggestions to teachers as to how they might enlist the assistance of parents in motivating struggling readers. A survey of elementary school teachers indicated that six of the ten most frequently cited concerns were directly pertinent to the focus of this article: creating interest in reading, intrinsic desire for reading, parent-school partnerships, instructional programs for children placed at risk, increasing the amount and breadth of children's reading, and the role of teachers, peers, and parents in motivation (O'Flahavan, Gambrell, Guthrie, Stahl, & Alvermann, 1992).

The article begins with a brief discussion of the perspectives on motivation and motivation development guiding this synthesis. The next section focuses on home influences on the development of reading motivation. The third section examines home-school collaborations that can enhance motivation for reading, followed by a section that contains suggestions for how families can enhance the motivation of struggling readers.

Perspectives on Reading Motivation and Its Development

The conception of motivation guiding this synthesis is the multi-dimensional framework developed by Wigfield and Guthrie (1997) and further validated by Baker and Wigfield (1999). According to this framework, reading motivation consists of eleven dimensions of reading that fall into three broad categories.

One category includes competence and efficacy beliefs; *self-efficacy*, the belief that one can be successful at reading; *challenge*, the willingness to take on difficult reading material; and *work avoidance*, or the desire to avoid reading activities. The second category concerns the purposes and goals children have for reading, whether intrinsic or extrinsic. The intrinsic (learning) goals are *curiosity*, the desire to read about a particular topic of interest; *involvement*, the enjoyment experienced from reading certain kinds of literary or informational texts; and *importance*, the belief that reading is valuable. The extrinsic (performance) goals are *recognition*, the pleasure in receiving a tangible form of recognition for success in reading; reading for *grades*, the desire to be favorably evaluated by the teacher; and *competition*, the desire to outperform others in reading. The third category addresses social aspects of reading: *social*, the sharing of the meanings gained from reading with others; and *compliance*, reading to meet the expectations of others.

Researchers often use different terminology to refer to some of these same dimensions. For example, Chapman and Tunmer's (1995) reading self-concept questionnaire contains items assessing perceptions of competence at reading, perceptions of reading difficulty, and attitudes or feelings toward reading. These are similar to our efficacy, challenge, and curiosity dimensions. The measure of reading attitudes by McKenna, Kear, and Ellsworth (1995) assesses how much children like to read in school and for recreation. This scale is related conceptually to the curiosity and involvement dimensions. Thus, many of the sources cited in the present article do not actually use the term "motivation" but rather terms such as "self-concept" or "attitudes."

The perspective on motivation development guiding this synthesis is an ecological one that recognizes the overlapping influences of teachers, parents, siblings, peers, and the child himself or herself. Bricklin (1991) articulated an ecological approach to the concept of self as learner, detailing the reciprocal interactions that lead children with reading disabilities to label themselves as unable to learn to read. Most children start off with optimism and interest in learning to read. Those who experience difficulties quickly develop a concept of the self as a poor reader, and their motivation for reading declines (Baker, Sonnenschein, & Switkin, 2001b). They read less, both in school and out, than children who are succeeding. The amount that children read influences further growth in reading (Baker, Dreher, & Guthrie, 2000; Stanovich, West, Cunningham, Cipielewski, & Siddiqui, 1996). How parents respond when their children are struggling to read interacts with teachers' responses and the child's own developing self-system (Bricklin, 1991; Castle, 1994; Chapman & Tunmer, 2003). Castle (1994) emphasized the need for teachers to include parents in improving the self-concept of children with reading difficulties because improvements in self-concept are not likely unless all significant parties are involved.

Home Influences on Motivation for Reading

With the recognition that motivation is a central ingredient of reading success (Baker et al., 2000; Snow, Burns, & Griffin, 1998) has come the acknowledgment that parents play a critical role in its nurturance. Baker, Scher, and Mackler (1997) reviewed the growing body of research on home influences on motivation for reading, beginning in the preschool years. The focus in this article is on work most directly relevant to school-aged children. It is well established that demographic factors such as parental education and income level are correlated with the quantity and quality of children's home literacy experiences. These factors are of little interest from a practical standpoint because they are not readily amenable to intervention; what is of more interest are the experiences themselves and whether they foster motivation, voluntary reading, and achievement. Teachers and other professionals can use the information summarized here in working with parents to design more supportive literacy environments.

The Importance of Home Experiences with Print

Several studies have shown that parental support for reading is associated with greater amounts of voluntary reading by students in the intermediate grades (Braten, Lie, Andreassen, & Olaussen, 1999; Greaney & Hegarty, 1987; Neuman, 1986; Rowe, 1991; Shapiro & Whitney, 1997). Parental support includes such factors as the availability of reading materials in the home, parental reading behavior, and the frequency of reading to the child. Students from supportive environments also have more positive attitudes toward reading, and they more strongly endorse the view that enjoyment is an important, reason for reading (Greaney & Hegarty, 1987). Rowe (1991) further extended this line of research by demonstrating that attitudes toward reading and reading activity at home predicted achievement in a large sample of Australian students aged 5–14 years. In addition, reading activities at home predicted the children's reading attitudes, and these relations grew stronger with increasing age.

Longitudinal studies have provided evidence that early interest in reading influences subsequent achievement. For example, Olofson and Niedersoe (1999) reported that children whose parents said they showed a very low interest in books and story reading before age 5 had weak reading skills in Grade 4. Similarly, Weinberger (1996) found that children who were experiencing reading difficulties at age 7 were less likely to have a favorite book at age 3 and were read to less frequently by their parents at age 5.

… children who have more opportunities to engage in literacy-relevant activities at home have more positive views about reading, engage in more leisure reading, and have higher reading achievement.

The data from the available research converge in suggesting that children who have more opportunities to engage in literacy-relevant activities at home have more positive views about reading, engage in more leisure reading, and have higher reading achievement. Nevertheless, research has documented large numbers of "aliterate" students, that is, capable readers who do not choose to read (Shapiro & Whitney, 1997). In other words, enhancing reading motivation should be a concern not only for struggling readers but all readers.

The Importance of Parents' Perspectives and Beliefs

Snow et al. (1998) suggested that one critical mechanism in the intergenerational transmission of literacy is enjoyment and engagement. Parents need to convey the perspective that reading is pleasurable and worthwhile. In a longitudinal study known as the Early Childhood Project, Baker, Serpell, and Sonnenschein demonstrated that variations in parents' perspectives are associated with differences in children's home reading activities, motivation, and achievement (Baker et al., 1998; Sonnenschein et al., 1997; Sonnenschein, Baker, Serpell, & Schmidt, 2000). Parents first described in diaries the everyday activities of their children either as preschoolers or as first graders. The print-related experiences parents mentioned were categorized in terms of their functions. Parents then were asked their views on the most effective ways of helping their child learn to read. The two sources of information together suggested that parents have three different perspectives on the nature of literacy: (1) literacy is a source of entertainment, book reading itself is fun, and there are many other enjoyable activities in which literacy plays a role; (2) literacy consists of a set of skills that should be deliberately cultivated; children should be given opportunities to practice their emerging competencies; (3) literacy is an intrinsic ingredient of everyday life; by virtue of their participation in daily living routines such as shopping and food preparation, children come to see the functional value of literacy.

The entertainment and skills perspectives were related to several indices of early literacy development. (The daily living perspective was not systematically related to other variables.) Children raised in homes that were predominantly oriented toward the view that literacy is a source of entertainment were more advanced in their development of reading-related competencies than children raised in homes where literacy was more typically viewed as a set of skills to be acquired. The entertainment perspective was a better predictor of phonological awareness and knowledge about print than the skills perspective (Baker et al., 1998; Sonnenschein et al., 1997). An early emphasis on entertainment also predicted scores on the Woodcock Johnson Word Identification test in Grades 1, 2, and 3, as well as the Passage Comprehension test in Grade 3 (Sonnenschein et al., 2000).

Parental beliefs are related not only to home literacy practices and children's reading achievement, but also to children's motivation for reading. Parents who endorse an entertainment perspective on how children learn to read tend to provide more opportunities in the home for children to acquire this perspective themselves than parents who emphasize a skills perspective (Sonnenschein et al., 2000). Parental endorsement of pleasure as a reason for reading was associated with higher scores on a scale assessing motivation for reading in first grade (Baker & Scher, 2002).

Parental perspectives were associated with income level, providing one clue as to why reading achievement is also linked with income level. Middle-income parents gave greater endorsement to the perspective that literacy is a source of entertainment than did low-income parents, whereas low-income parents gave more emphasis to the perspective that literacy is a skill to be deliberately cultivated. Other researchers have also found that parents with low income and less education tend to emphasize drill and practice of reading skills over more informal and playful opportunities for literacy learning (Fitzgerald, Spiegel, & Cunningham, 1991; Goldenberg, Reese, & Gallimore, 1992).

The Importance of the Affective Quality of Home Literacy Interactions

When children in the Early Childhood Project were in kindergarten, their shared reading with a parent or sibling was observed. The affective features of the interaction were analyzed, along with verbal features (Sonnenschein & Munsterman, 2002). The affective quality of the interaction predicted children's self-reported motivation for reading in first grade and in second grade. Thus, children who experienced reading in a comfortable and supportive social context at age 5 were more likely to recognize the value of reading, report enjoyment of reading, and have positive concepts of themselves as readers in subsequent years.

Moreover, the affective quality of shared bookreading is associated with subsequent voluntary reading. Also within the Early Childhood Project, Baker, Mackler, Sonnenschein, and Serpell (2001a) examined how parents interact with their first grade children during shared storybook reading, both in terms of what was said and the affective context in which the interactions occurred. Positive affective interactions were associated with meaning-related talk, and negative interactions were associated with parental attempts to have children use decoding skills or other strategies to identify words they did not know. If the child is a struggling reader and needs considerable help in recognizing words, he or she may find the experience unpleasant rather than rewarding, with potential long-term implications for motivation and achievement. Indeed, affective quality of shared reading in first grade was an important contributor to children's reading of challenging materials in third grade, even after controlling for Grade 1 word recognition skills.

Experiences that focus on accurate word recognition may extinguish struggling readers' already wavering motivation for reading and learning to read.

In the Baker et al. (2001a) study, children who were poorer readers received more error correction feedback when they read aloud than those who were better readers. Tracey and Young (1994) similarly observed more error correction utterances by mothers of third graders who were at-risk readers rather than advanced readers. The parental emphasis on skills and getting the words right that has been observed with poorer readers likely contributes to their well-documented conception of the reading process as mechanistic. For example, Padak, Vacca, and Stuart (1993) interviewed 29 struggling readers at primary and intermediate levels and found a predominant focus on the word level. For all of these children, reading was sounding out words or knowing words rather than getting meaning or enjoyment. Padak et al. suggested that the type of instruction the children received in school contributed to this perception, but the research summarized here also supports a home influence. Experiences that focus on accurate word recognition may extinguish struggling readers' already wavering motivation for reading and learning to read.

Home-School Collaborations to Foster Motivation in Struggling Readers

Struggling readers will benefit from effective collaborations involving home and school. As discussed in this section, teachers should provide advice to parents to help them assist their children at home, and parents should provide advice to teachers to help them motivate children at school. Two approaches to intervention are described, one focusing on increasing home reading activity and the other on enlisting parents as tutors for their children.

How Teachers Can Facilitate Parental Assistance at Home

To what extent do teachers attempt to involve parents in their children's literacy learning? In a comprehensive survey of elementary reading instruction practices in the United States, Baumann, Hoffman, Duffy-Hester, and Ro (2000) found that 93% of 1207 pre-K to 5 teachers indicated that they encourage parents to read to their children at home regularly, and 91% reported encouraging parents to listen to their children read at home regularly. However, only 55% said they regularly send home books for their students to practice reading with their parents, indicating that access to appropriate reading materials could be a problem for some families. Furthermore, only 10% of the teachers said they invite parents to school for special workshops on how they can support literacy at home, indicating that lack of sufficient knowledge as to how to help may be an obstacle for some parents. (All data were provided by J. Baumann, personal communication, August 9, 2000).

Consistent with the results of the Baumann et al. (2000) survey, McNaughton, Parr, Timperly, and Robinson (1992) reported that teachers in New Zealand routinely ask parents to listen to their children read to them. However, a majority of teachers who asked parents to hear their children read to them did not follow up with parents to find out what they were actually doing. Most teachers thought they had provided specific guidance, but most parents thought they had not. McNaughton et al. concluded that parents are not likely to be able to help struggling readers effectively without focused and supported instruction.

Teachers should provide specific advice on what to read, how much to read, how long to read, how to respond to mistakes, what kind of discussions to hold with children, and how to keep the experience enjoyable.

Teachers should not assume parents know how to help their children who are struggling. It is important to provide guidance to parents to help them gain confidence in their ability to help (Castle, 1994). Teachers should provide specific advice on what to read, how much to read, how long to read, how to respond to mistakes, what kind of discussions to hold with children, and how to keep the experience enjoyable (Ollila & Mayfield, 1992).

Working with parents to scaffold their ways of interacting with their children is worthwhile, as Rubert (1994) demonstrated. He conducted case studies of three families of at-risk first-grade readers to learn how parents interact with children when they read aloud at home. Mothers recorded their shared reading on a tape recorder over a three-month period and participated in a series of workshops. Three forms of support reading were modeled for the parents: echo reading, in which the parent reads a sentence and the child repeats; partner reading, in which the parent and child each take turns reading sentences; and independent reading, in which the child reads without the help of a parent. Parents listened to the audiotapes with an instructor and thought aloud about what they had been doing with their children. In the early shared readings, parents tended to focus on phonics and word-level assistance. With the instructor's scaffolding, they came to give more attention to comprehension and they provided more effective support.

What is the appropriate role for parents in helping their children with reading? Parents and teachers do not necessarily agree. McNaughton et al. (1992) questioned New Zealand teachers and parents about the roles parents should take when hearing their young children read to them at home. Fifty-six percent of parents and 92% of teachers believed the parental role is one of support. However, 34% of the parents saw their role as teaching, whereas none of the teachers thought parents should have this role. These data make it clear that teachers need to be explicit about their goals for parental involvement; an overly didactic approach may be counter-productive if it creates an unpleasant affective atmosphere (Baker et al., 2001a).

How should teachers communicate their goals? Rasinski and Fredericks (1988) suggested using school and community media to communicate information that is short and to-the-point, allowing classroom visits for parents to observe models of effective practice and offering courses and workshops to give parents guided hands-on opportunities to engage in effective interactions with their children. As the Baumann et al. (2000) survey indicated, few teachers opt for the latter mode of communication.

Teachers need to recognize that many parents of struggling readers are not skilled readers themselves. The parents may not even be able to read the communications that the teacher sends home from school, let alone be motivated to read on their own or with their children. More complex intervention strategies, some of which are discussed in subsequent sections, may be needed to address problems of intergenerational illiteracy or aliteracy. For example, teachers could turn to interventions that do not rely as heavily on the parents' own reading skills and proclivities, such as those involving older siblings as reading motivators or technological resources such as audiotaped books.

Why Teachers Should Draw on Parental Expertise to Create More Motivating Contexts for Struggling Readers in School

Many children who are struggling readers do not see a connection between what they learn at school and what happens in their lives beyond the classroom. McCarthey (2000) and Gentile and McMillan (1991) cautioned that a cultural disconnect between home and school creates motivational problems. If school seems irrelevant, students will be less likely to put forth the effort needed to read effectively. One way to establish stronger connections between home and school is for teachers to learn about the literacy resources and opportunities available to their students at home. Drawing on students' home culture and interests in classroom activities puts teachers in a better position to reach struggling readers and children who are unmotivated by what they are experiencing in school (Gentile & McMillan, 1990, 1991; McCarthey, 2000; Sonnenschein & Schmidt, 2000). Soliciting information from parents has an added benefit, as Dickinson and DeTemple (1998) noted: "Acknowledgment of parental expertise could go far

toward establishing a teacher-parent relationship based on trust and mutual respect" (p. 256).

Drawing on students' home culture and interests in classroom activities puts teachers in a better position to reach struggling readers.

Teachers may discover that many students they perceive to be unmotivated readers are in fact simply unmotivated for school reading. Ivey (1999) described a struggling sixth grade reader who was not motivated to read at school but in fact read frequently for fun at home, especially information texts. Teachers can learn a great deal about children's reading motivation by enlisting parent participation. For example, Overturf (1997) described a reading portfolio project involving middle school students, their parents, and their teachers. Students kept a portfolio that they discussed with their parents in response to specific prompts provided by the teacher. The portfolios provided teachers with valuable information about their students' interests and motivations and also revealed how parents influence their children's views about reading. Chandler (1999) studied the home reading of adolescents and the interactions they had with their parents surrounding the reading of popular fiction. The positive attitudes toward reading that the parents fostered contrasted sharply with attitudes toward school reading. Chandler recommended that teachers build on the successful reading relationships children have with their parents. If teachers design reading activities with input from parents, this might help ensure that true home-school partnerships can be created.

Interventions Focused on Increasing Home Reading Activity

Many home-school collaborations focus on increasing access to books, a particular concern for children from low income backgrounds (Baker, 1999). Sending books home is a simple and effective strategy for enhancing motivation, but unfortunately, many school and classroom libraries are not well-stocked with books that will entice unmotivated and struggling readers. Schools should make an effort to allocate funds to their classroom libraries, or perhaps they could participate in externally funded incentive programs.

Running Start is one such incentive program where students are challenged to read or have someone read to them 21 books in a 10-week period. The prize for meeting the challenge is a book for the student to own. In an evaluation of the program's effectiveness, Gambrell (1998) compared Running Start participants (inner-city first graders) with a comparable group of students and parents on several measures of motivation and participation in literacy activities. Running Start students spent more time in independent reading, discussed books more with family members, took more books home from school, participated in more family reading activities, and had higher levels of motivation for reading. These advantages were still apparent six months later.

Many home-school collaborations include a school-based instructional component in combination with increased access to literacy materials at home. For example, Morrow and Young (1997) extended a school-based program to the home by engaging parents and children in reading story-books, writing journals, and using the magazine *Highlights for Children*. Monthly meetings were held with teachers, parents, and students, sharing ideas and working together. Students in inner-city first through third grades who participated in the program were compared with a similar group of students who did not participate. Participants demonstrated higher reading achievement and motivation for reading than the nonparticipants.

As another example, Koskinen et al. (2000) demonstrated the value of sending books home from the classroom, either with or without an audio-taped version of the book. In a 7-month intervention involving linguistically diverse first graders, children in one group were asked to read each book at home two or three times, and children in another group were asked to listen to the audiotapes and read along two or three times. Parents were encouraged to listen to the children's reading, but children could also read on their own. Children were given support at school in reading the books so that their home reading attempts would be successful. Evaluation results indicated enhanced motivation, interest, reading activity, and comprehension relative to comparison groups who did not participate in the home reading component. (See Koskinen et al., 1999, for details on how teachers can implement the program in their own classrooms.)

Sharing books with friends and family is an important motivator for reading, as these studies have suggested, and it is an activity in which even struggling readers can take the role of "expert" reader. Fox and Wright (1998) designed a program called Storymates to give 9–11-year-old struggling readers from high-poverty neighborhoods an opportunity to read books to their younger siblings, relatives, or neighbors. The students' reading skills were too low to permit successful reading of grade-level appropriate books, but books appropriate for younger children could be read independently and with confidence because they had the support of illustrations, predictable language patterns, and so on. Pairs of students worked together to practice reading the storybooks they would later read aloud at home. Parents who completed a questionnaire at the end of the 9-week program responded overwhelmingly that their child was reading more at home than at the beginning of the program, that he/she enjoyed reading to the younger children, and, as an added plus, that the younger children also enjoyed the experience.

Interventions Involving Parent Tutoring

Some efforts to help parents help their struggling readers involve explicit teaching of tutoring techniques. These efforts typically do not have enhanced motivation as a primary goal, but it is often considered secondarily. Paired Reading is one such approach that has been widely used in England and increasingly used in the United States (Topping, 1995). This approach is considered particularly valuable for struggling readers who lack the confidence and competence to read independently. Evaluations have revealed that Paired Reading improves attitudes toward reading and that it is more effective than simply having parents listen to their children read (e.g., Cupolillo, Silva, Socorro, & Topping, 1997; Topping, 1995).

The key components of Paired Reading were summarized by Hayden (1998) in an article written for teachers. Briefly, parents are given a short training session with their child in a group setting of 20–30 parents. A follow-up session is conducted after a few weeks to make sure the approach is being followed. Parents commit to using the approach five times a week, ten minutes each, over an eight- to twelve-week period. The child selects a book he/she wants to read with the parent. They start reading aloud in unison. When the child does not read a word correctly, the parent repeats the word correctly and points to it. When the child feels ready to read independently, he/she does so and is praised for the efforts. If the child makes a mistake, the parent waits four seconds for the child to self-correct. If the child does not self-correct, the parent points to the word while saying it and the child repeats it. Parent and child again read together in unison until the child once again signals he/she wants to go ahead independently. Discussion about what is being read takes place at appropriate points in the text.

A major limitation of the Paired Reading approach from a motivational standpoint is that it does not give systematic attention to getting meaning from the story. The affective atmosphere of shared reading is more positive when parents and children discuss story content rather than focus on accurate word reading (Baker et al., 2001a; Leseman & de Jong, 1998). Extending Paired Reading to include discussion is more likely to motivate struggling readers. Support for this suggestion comes from Overett and Donald (1998), who taught parents and their fourth grade children from a working class community how to engage in paired reading and in discussions that extended the literal story content. The emphasis was on promoting brief, regular, positive, and enjoyable interactions around the reading material (they suggested five minutes a day, five days a week). In comparison to a control group, children who participated in the intervention increased in reading accuracy, comprehension, and attitude.

Interventions Focused on Parents' Views and Expectations About Their Children's Performance

Parents play an important role in socializing achievement beliefs in their children, conveying beliefs, values, expectations, and attributions both directly and indirectly. It is therefore important that parents be made aware of the impact of their beliefs (Bricklin, 1991). Parents who hold high expectations for their children's reading achievement in fact have children who are high achievers; the reverse is also true (Halle, Kurtz-Costes, & Mahoney, 1997). In addition, children and parents make similar causal attributions for reading achievement (O'Sullivan & Howe, 1996). Because attributions to effort are more adaptive than those to ability, it is important to provide attributional retraining to children as well as to their parents in programs designed to help struggling readers and to help parents help their children (see Chapman & Tunmer, 2003, for further discussion). Children need support, concern, and interest from parents, but if aspirations, expectations, and pressures are too high, there can be a negative impact. Bricklin (1991) recommended that school personnel work with parents to help them change their perceptions of their struggling readers away from labels such as "lazy" and "not trying" to perceptions that allow them to provide the child with appropriate support.

Counseling is also beneficial for parents of struggling readers in that it can help them better understand their children's difficulties and how to assist their children, as well as how to deal with their own feelings of guilt, anger, frustration, embarrassment, and/or disappointment. Navin and Bates (1987) conducted an intervention in which parents of struggling readers in grades 4–8 attended group counseling sessions over a 5-week period, led jointly by a school counselor and a reading specialist. The children were assessed on attitude and comprehension before and after their parents participated in the counseling sessions, and they were compared with another group of struggling readers whose parents would participate later. All children received individual tutoring for their reading problems at school. Children whose parents had counseling showed improved attitudes and comprehension skills relative to the comparison group.

What Parents Can Do on Their Own to Motivate Struggling Readers

Practices of value for motivating struggling readers in the classroom that are discussed in the other articles in this issue also apply to the home. Just as teachers should provide children with choice, challenge, collaboration, learning goals rather than performance goals, and risk-free environments, so too should parents. Table 1 lists a variety of recommendations culled from the literature (e.g., Baker et al., 1997; Bricklin, 1991; Beers, 1996; Castle, 1994; Gains, 1989; Navin & Bates, 1987; Rasinski & Fredericks, 1988).

It should not be assumed, however, that all students find the same kinds of activities motivating. Beers

Table 1   Recommendations for Home Reading Activities that Promote Motivation

1. Keep shared reading a pleasurable activity without anger, frustration, or excessive emphasis on decoding.
2. Read entertaining books, newspapers, and magazine articles with the child. Encourage diverse reading of a variety of genres.
3. Talk to the child about things read in school and out. Extend discussions about books beyond the literal content.
4. Take advantage of technology to stimulate children's motivation, whether audiotapes, television, or computers.
5. Encourage children to experience a wide range of activities besides reading. These activities do not displace reading, as some might fear, but rather they nurture students' interests.
6. Engage in functional reading tasks where the rewards are built in, such as reading a cookie recipe or directions to build a model.
7. Involve the child in selecting materials that are related to his/her immediate life and interests.
8. Play board games or computer games that involve reading. Draw siblings and friends into the activities . when possible
9. Be patient and tolerant. Provide support and encouragement within a risk-free environment.

(1996) compared motivated and unmotivated 7th graders on their preferences for various reading-related activities and found some dramatic differences. Unlike more motivated readers, the unmotivated students did not like to buy books at a book fair, go to the library, keep a reading journal, take part in book discussions, or share books with friends. Unmotivated readers preferred personal choice from a narrowed selection rather than an entire library, nonfiction, illustrations, seeing movies based on a book and then reading the book, listening to the teacher read an entire book aloud, and completing book-related art activities and magazines.

The preference for listening to stories has been well documented in struggling readers of different ages. For example, Yochum and Miller (1993) reported that first through sixth graders attending a reading clinic had more positive attitudes toward listening to a story rather than reading independently. Similarly, Ivey (1999) learned that a struggling sixth grade reader was much more engaged when listening to stories than when reading them herself. Dreher (2003) argued the value of teacher read-alouds; this argument should be extended to family read-alouds as well. Duchein and Mealey (1993) wrote, "We need to continue educating parents and teachers about the benefits of reading aloud from a variety of materials, both narrative and expository, to children beyond the primary grades and throughout the curriculum, at home and in school" (p. 26).

Teachers can inform parents about the variety of materials likely to capture the interest of struggling and unmotivated readers. Worthy (1998) has compiled a set of recommendations that extend beyond traditional literature to magazines, series books, nonfiction, poetry, and jump rope and street rhymes. Information text is more motivating to many children than stories (Dreher, 2003), and this seems to be particularly true for struggling readers (Ivey, 1999; Worthy, 1998). Parents may be concerned that their child is not benefitting if he or she chooses to read comic books or joke books, but personal choice is key. Materials should be selected to meet children's individual interests.

Parents are not limited in their options to traditional print materials. Researchers have advocated books on tape for struggling readers (Bircham, Shaw, & Robertson, 1997; Graham & Harris, 2000). Listening to audiotaped stories helps maintain students' attention and increases their motivation, as shown by Koskinen et al. (2000). Audiotaped books are particularly beneficial when the parents are unable to provide much support because of limitations in their own literacy levels, their facility with the English language, or their availability.

Even television can be a valuable home resource for enhancing the motivation of struggling readers. Reading Rainbow exposes children directly to good literature as they listen to stories read aloud. As discussed, unmotivated readers often prefer read-alouds. Many television shows that pique a child's interest may stimulate reading or writing. In addition, the closed captioning available on most modern televisions provides a nonthreatening opportunity for struggling readers to connect with print in a meaningful context (Graham & Harris, 2000).

Other forms of technology with motivation-enhancing potential are becoming increasingly common in the home. A majority of American families now have computers, giving them access to educational software, the Internet, and electronic books. Electronic books hold promise for helping struggling readers in the support they provide for word recognition and fluency (Graham & Harris, 2000). However, it is not sufficient to make these books available to the children; teachers or parents should provide guidance in how to take advantage of their features (McNabb, 1998). In addition, it is important that parents move carefully in using these resources, because not all children find them motivating (Lewin, 2000).

With increased public attention to the importance of reading well by age 9 (Snow et al., 1998), more and more parents of struggling readers are being lured by advertisements for expensive products that claim dramatic success in teaching children to read. Many parents lack the expertise or objectivity to meet these claims with the skepticism they deserve. Teachers can provide valuable assistance in this regard. As Castle (1994) put it, "Clearing up parents' misunderstandings about reading terminology and . . . misplaced allegiance to commercially available quick-fix programs will benefit the child" (p. 166).

Finally, what advice should parents be given about providing their children with extrinsic rewards for reading? There is a long-standing controversy as to whether rewards such as money or pizzas undermine children's intrinsic motivation for reading. Flora and Flora (1999) concluded, based on a survey of undergraduates' childhood reading habits, that extrinsic rewards for reading set the conditions where intrinsic motivation for reading may develop. McQuillan (1997) concluded that the available research did not provide clear evidence that incentives were of benefit and that, therefore, money should be devoted to books rather than rewards. A good compromise would be for parents to reward children for reading with a book of their own (Gambrell, 1998). After all, many children are simultaneously motivated by both extrinsic and intrinsic goals for reading (Baker & Wigfield, 1999).

Conclusions

Our knowledge about parental influences on children's motivation for reading has grown considerably in recent years. Children whose early encounters with literacy are enjoyable are more likely to develop a predisposition to read frequently and broadly in subsequent years. This in turn improves their reading achievement. Shared storybook reading plays an important role in promoting reading motivation; when the affective climate is positive, children are more interested in reading and more likely to view it as enjoyable. The beliefs held by children's parents about the purposes of reading and how children learn to read relate to children's motivations for reading. Parents who believe that reading is a source of entertainment have children with more positive views about reading than parents who emphasize the skills aspect of learning to read.

Parents who believe that reading is a source of entertainment have children with more positive views about reading than parents who emphasize the skills aspect of learning to read.

It should be clear from the research reviewed in this article that scholars vary considerably in the kinds of recommendations they provide to parents. On the one hand are advocates of teaching parents how to tutor their children in reading, using tightly prescribed methods. On the other are those who suggest that parents can have the greatest impact by providing enjoyable experiences with print; they endorse a more relaxed and flexible approach. This latter view receives considerable empirical support in longitudinal analyses of home influences on reading activity, motivation, and achievement. An excessive focus on skills development undermines the affective quality of parent-child interactions, which in turn impacts reading engagement. The same conditions that enhance motivation in classrooms will enhance motivation at home: choice, collaboration, and risk-free environments.

References

Baker, L. (1999). Opportunities at home and in the community that foster reading engagement. In J. T. Guthrie & D. Alvermann (Eds.), *Engagement in reading: Processes, practices, and policy implications* (pp. 105–133). New York: Teachers College Press.

Baker, L., & Scher, D. (2002). Beginning readers' motivation for reading in relation to parental beliefs and home reading experiences. *Reading Psychology, 23,* 239–269.

Baker, L., & Wigfield, A. (1999). Dimensions of children's motivation for reading and their relations to reading activity and reading achievement. *Reading Research Quarterly, 34,* 452–477.

Baker, L., Dreher, M. J., & Guthrie, J. T. (2000). Why teachers should promote reading engagement. In L. Baker, M. J. Dreher, & J.T. Guthrie (Eds.), *Engaging young readers: Promoting achievement and motivation* (pp. 1–16). New York: Guilford.

Baker, L., Mackler, K., Sonnenschein, S., & Serpell, R. (2001a). Parents' interactions with their first-grade children during storybook reading and relations with subsequent home reading activity and reading achievement. *Journal of School Psychology, 39,* 415–438.

Baker, L., Scher, D., & Mackler, K. (1997). Home and family influences on motivations for literacy. *Educational Psychologist, 32,* 69–82.

Baker, L., Sonnenschein, S., Serpell, R., Scher, D., Fernandez-Fein, S., Munsterman, K., Hill, S., Goddard-Truitt, V., & Danseco, E. (1998). Early literacy at home: Children's experiences and parents' perspectives. In R. L. Allington (Ed.), *Teaching struggling readers: Articles from The Reading Teacher* (pp. 262–266). Newark, DE: International Reading Association.

Baker, L., Sonnenschein, S., & Switkin, M. (2001b, April). *Relations between motivation and achievement in a summer reading program for rising third graders.* Paper presented at the meeting of the Society for Research in Child Development, Minneapolis.

Baumann, J. F., Hoffman, J. V., Duffy-Hester, A. M., & Ro, J. M. (2000). The First R yesterday and today: U.S. elementary reading instruction practices reported by teachers and administrators. *Reading Research Quarterly, 35,* 338–377.

Beers, G. K. (1996). No time, no interest, no way! The three voices of aliteracy: Part 2. *School Library Journal, 42,* 110–113.

Bircham, A., Shaw, S., & Robertson, A. (1997). Enhancing reading development using audiotaped books. *Educational Psychology in Practice, 13,* 181–188.

Braten, I., Lie, A., Andreassen, R., Olaussen, B. S. (1999). Leisure time reading and orthographic processes in word recognition among Norwegian third-and fourth-grade students. *Reading & Writing, 11,* 65–88.

Bricklin, P. M. (1991). The concept of "self as learner": Its critical role in the diagnosis and treatment of children with reading disabilities. *Journal of Reading, Writing & Learning Disabilities International, 7,* 201–217.

Castle, M. (1994). Promoting the disabled reader's self-esteem. *Reading & Writing Quarterly: Overcoming Learning Difficulties, 10,* 150–170.

Chandler, K. (1999). Reading relationships: Parents, adolescents, and popular fiction by Stephen King. *Journal of Adolescent & Adult Literacy, 43,* 228–239.

Chapman, J. W., & Tunmer, W. E. (1995). Development of young children's reading self-concepts: An examination of emerging subcomponents and their relationship with reading achievement. *Journal of Educational Psychology, 87,* 154–167.

Chapman, J. W., & Tunmer, W. E. (2003). Reading difficulties, reading-related self-perceptions, and strategies for overcoming negative self-beliefs. *Reading & Writing Quarterly, 19* (1), 5–24.

Cupolillo, M., Silva, R., Socorro, S., & Topping, K. (1997). Paired reading and Brazilian first-year school failures. *Educational Psychology in Practice, 13,* 96–100.

Dickinson, D. K., & DeTemple, J. (1998). Putting parents in the picture: Maternal reports of preschoolers' literacy as a predictor of early reading. *Early Childhood Research Quarterly, 13,* 241–261.

Dreher, M. J. (2003). Motivating struggling readers by tapping the potential of information books. *Reading & Writing Quarterly, 19* (1), 25–38.

Duchein, M. A., & Mealey, D. L. (1993). Remembrance of books past . . . long past glimpses into aliteracy. *Reading Research and Instruction, 33,* 13–28.

Fitzgerald, J., Spiegel, D. L., & Cunningham, J. W. (1991). The relationship between parental literacy level and perceptions of emergent literacy. *Journal of Reading Behavior, 23,* 191–192.

Flora, S. R., & Flora, D. B. (1999). Effects of extrinsic reinforcement for reading during childhood on reported reading habits of college students. *Psychological Record, 49,* 3–14.

Fox, B. J., & Wright, M. (1998). Connecting school and home literacy experiences through cross-age reading. In R. L. Allington (Ed.), *Teaching struggling readers: Articles from The Reading Teacher* (pp. 267–275). Newark, DE: International Reading Association.

Gains, K. F. S. (1989). The use of reading diaries as a short-term intervention strategy. *Reading, 23,* 160–167.

Gambrell, L. B. (1998). Creating classroom cultures that foster reading motivation. In R. L. Allington (Ed.), *Teaching struggling readers: Articles from The Reading Teacher* (pp. 108–121). Newark, DE: International Reading Association.

Gentile, L. M., & McMillan, M. M. (1990). Literacy through literature: Motivating at-risk students to read and write. *Journal of Reading. Writing, & Learning Disabilities International, 6,* 383–393.

Gentile, L. M., & McMillan, M. M. (1991). Reading, writing, and relationships: The challenge of teaching at risk students. *Reading Research & Instruction, 30,* 74–81.

Goldenberg, C., Reese, L., & Gallimore, R. (1992). Effects of literacy materials from school on Latino children's home experiences and early reading achievement. *American Journal of Education, 100,* 497–536.

Graham, S., & Harris, K. (2000). Helping children who experience reading difficulties: Prevention and intervention. In L. Baker, M. J. Dreher, & J. T. Guthrie (Eds.), *Engaging young readers: Promoting achievement and motivation* (pp. 43–67). New York: Guilford.

Greaney, V., & Hegarty, M. (1987). Correlates of leisure-time reading. *Journal of Research in Reading, 10,* 3–27.

Halle, T. G., Kurtz-Costes, B., & Mahoney, J. L. (1997). Family influences on school achievement in low-income, African American children. *Journal of Educational Psychology, 89,* 527–537.

Hayden, R. (1998). Training parents as reading facilitators. In R. L. Allington (Ed.), *Teaching struggling readers: Articles from The Reading Teacher* (pp. 296–299). Newark, DE: International Reading Association.

Ivey, G. (1999). A multicase study in the middle school: Complexities among young adolescent readers. *Reading Research Quarterly, 34,* 172–192.

Koskinen, P. S., Blum, I. J., Bisson, S. A., Phillips, S. M., Creamer, T. S., & Baker, T. K. (1999). Shared reading, books, and audiotapes: Supporting diverse students in school and at home. *The Reading Teacher, 52,* 430–444.

Koskinen, P. S., Blum, I. J., Bisson, S. A., Phillips, S. M., Creamer, T. S., & Baker, T. K. (2000). Book access, shared reading, and audio models: The effects of supporting the literacy learning of linguistically diverse students in school and at home. *Journal of Educational Psychology, 92,* 23–36.

Leseman, P. P. M., & de Jong, P. F. (1998). Home literacy: Opportunity, instruction, cooperation, and social emotional quality predicting early reading achievement. *Reading Research Quarterly, 33,* 294–313.

Lewin, C. (2000). Exploring the effects of talking book software in UK primary classrooms. *Journal of Research in Reading, 23,* 149–157.

McCarthey, S. J. (2000). Home-school connections: A review of the literature. *Journal of Educational Research, 93,* 145–153.

McKenna, M. C., Kear, D. J., & Ellsworth, R. A. (1995). Children's attitudes toward reading: A national survey. *Reading Research Quarterly, 30,* 934–955.

McNabb, M. L. (1998). Using electronic books to enhance the reading comprehension of struggling readers. In T. Shanahan & F. V. Rodriguez-Brown (Eds.), *National Reading Conference Yearbook 47* (pp. 405–414). Chicago, IL: National Reading Conference.

McNaughton, S., Parr, J., Timperley, H., & Robinson, V. (1992). Beginning reading and sending books home to read: A case for some fine tuning. *Educational Psychology, 12,* 239–247.

McQuillan, J. (1997). Effects of incentives on reading. *Reading Research and Instruction, 36,* 111–125.

Morrow, L. M., & Young, J. (1997). A family literacy program connecting school and home: Effects on attitude, motivation, and literacy achievement. *Journal of Educational Psychology, 89,* 736–742.

Navin, S. L., & Bates, G. W. (1987). Improving attitudes and achievement of remedial readers: A parent counseling approach. *Elementary School Guidance & Counseling, 21,* 203–209.

Neuman, S. (1986). The home environment and fifth-grade students' leisure reading. *Elementary School Journal, 86,* 333–343.

O'Flahavan, J., Gambrell, L. B., Guthrie, J. T., Stahl, S., & Alvermann, D. (1992, April). Poll results guide activities of research center. *Reading Today,* 12.

Ollila, L. O., & Mayfield, M. I. (1992). Home and school together: Helping beginning readers succeed. In S. J. Samuels & A. E. Forstrup (Eds.), *What research has to say about reading instruction* (pp. 17–45). Newark, DE: International Reading Association.

Olofson, A., & Niedersoe, J. (1999). Early language development and kindergarten phonological awareness as predictors of reading problems: From 3 to 11 years of age. *Journal of Learning Disabilities, 32,* 464–472.

O'Sullivan, J. T., & Howe, M. L. (1996). Causal attributions and reading achievement: Individual differences in low-income families. *Contemporary Educational Psychology, 21,* 363–387.

Overett, J., & Donald, D. (1998). Paired reading: Effects of a parent involvement programme in a disadvantaged community in South Africa. *British Journal of Educational Psychology, 68,* 347–356.

Overturf, B. J. (1997). Reading portfolios reveal new dimensions of students. *Middle School Journal, 28*, 45–50.

Padak, N. D., Vacca, R. T., & Stuart, D. (1993). Rethinking reading for children at risk. *Reading and Writing Quarterly: Overcoming Learning Difficulties, 9*, 361–368.

Rasinski, T. V., & Fredericks, A. D. (1988). Sharing literacy: Guiding principles and practices for parent involvement. *The Reading Teacher, 41*, 508–512.

Rowe, K. J. (1991). The influence of reading activity at home on students' attitudes towards reading, classroom attentiveness and reading achievement: An application of structural equation modeling. *British Journal of Educational Psychology, 61*, 19–35.

Rubert, H. (1994). The impact of a parent involvement program designed to support a first-grade reading intervention program. In C. K. Kinzer & D. J. Leu (Eds.), *Multidimensional aspects of literacy research, theory, and practice: Forty-third year-book of the National Reading Conference* (pp. 230–239). Chicago: National Reading Conference.

Shapiro, J., & Whitney, P. (1997). Factors involved in the leisure reading of upper elementary school students. *Reading Psychology, 18*, 343–370.

Snow, C. E., Burns, M. S., & Griffin, P. (Eds.) (1998). *Preventing reading difficulties in young children.* Washington, DC: National Academy Press.

Sonnenschein, S., & Munsterman, K. (2002). The influence of home-based reading interactions on 5-year-olds' reading motivations and early literacy development. *Early Childhood Research Quarterly.*

Sonnenschein, S., & Schmidt, D. (2000). Fostering home and community connections to support children's reading. In L. Baker, M. J. Dreher, & J. T. Guthrie (Eds.), *Engaging young readers: Promoting achievement and motivation* (pp. 263–284). New York: Guilford.

Sonnenschein, S., Baker, L., Serpell, R, & Schmidt, D. (2000). Reading is a source of entertainment: The importance of the home perspective for children's literacy development.

In K. A. Roskos & J. F. Christie (Eds.), *Play and literacy in early childhood: Research from multiple perspectives* (pp. 125–137). Mahwah, NJ: Erlbaum.

Sonnenschein, S., Baker, L., Serpell, R., Scher, D., Goddard-Truitt, V., & Munsterman, K. (1997). Parental beliefs about ways to help children learn to read: The impact of an entertainment or a skills perspective. *Early Child Development and Care, 127–128*, 111–118.

Stanovich, K. E., West, R. F., Cunningham, A. E., Cipielewski, J., & Siddiqui, S. (1996). The role of inadequate print exposure as a determinant of reading comprehension problems. In C. Cornoldi & J. Oakhill (Eds.), *Reading comprehension difficulties: Processes and interventions* (pp. 15–32). Mahwah, NJ: Erlbaum.

Topping, K. J. (1995). *Paired reading, spelling, and writing.* London: Cassell.

Tracey, D. H., & Young, J. W. (1994). Mothers' responses to children's oral reading at home. In C. K. Kinzer & D. J. Leu (Eds.), *Multidimensional aspects of literacy research, theory, and practice: Forty-third yearbook of the National Reading Conference* (pp. 342–350). Chicago: National Reading Conference.

Weinberger, J. (1996). A longitudinal study of children's early literacy experiences at home and later literacy development at home and school. *Journal of Research in Reading, 19*, 14–24.

Wigfield, A., & Guthrie, J. T. (1997). Relations of children's motivation for reading to the amount and breadth of their reading. *Journal of Educational Psychology, 89*, 420–432.

Worthy, J. (1998). A matter of interest: Literature that hooks reluctant readers and keeps them reading. In R. L. Allington (Ed.), *Teaching struggling readers: Articles from The Reading Teacher* (pp. 122–133). Newark, DE: International Reading Association.

Yochum, N., & Miller, S. D. (1993). Parents', teachers', and children's views of reading problems. *Reading Research & Instruction, 33*, 59–71.

STUDY GUIDE

1. What are the characteristics of open tasks and closed tasks? Which kind has a more powerful effect on student engagement? What potential challenges do open tasks present to teachers and students? Is there any place for closed tasks in literacy instruction? Why or why not? (Turner & Paris)

2. What can teachers do to foster motivation in literacy classrooms? (Turner & Paris)

3. When children are not engaged in school-based tasks, it is not uncommon for teachers to blame children for not being motivated. What do you think contributes to students' lack of engagement in school-based tasks? (Turner & Paris, Bruning & Horn)

4. What is involved in the writing process? What are the unique challenges of writing when compared with, for example, speaking? (Bruning & Horn)

5. How can teachers foster their students' motivation to write? (Bruning & Horn)

6. How are oral and written discourses similar? How are they different? What implications do these similarities and differences have for fostering student motivation for writing? What strategies can be used to motivate students to read/write in expository genres like science in which language is often uncharacteristic of spontaneous speech? (Bruning & Horn)

7. What are the characteristics of engaged readers/writers? (Turner & Paris, Bruning & Horn, Baker)

8. What are the components of reading motivation? (Baker)

9. What does the research say about the impact of print experience at home on children's literacy development? (Baker)

10. How does the nature of parent-child interaction during reading experience affect the child's motivation for literacy? What is the relationship between parental beliefs about reading and children's motivation for literacy? (Baker)

11. How can teachers enlist parents to help create motivating contexts for struggling readers in school and at home? (Baker)

12. Some reading programs in school, such as Accelerated Readers, emphasize extrinsic rewards as a way to motivate children to read. Do you think this is a good idea? Why or why not? What is the relationship between extrinsic motivation and intrinsic motivation? (Bruning & Horn, Baker)

13. Given the current high-stakes testing climate, how feasible is it to implement the ideas for motivating students suggested in these three articles? (Turner & Paris, Bruning & Horn, Baker)

INQUIRY PROJECTS

1. Observe an effective and a less effective upper elementary grade teacher for one day. Compare and contrast the nature and types of literacy tasks assigned by the two teachers and the impact of these tasks on student engagement.

2. Identify one good reader and one poor reader from an elementary grade. Interview the parents of these two students, asking them about their views on the role of parents in children's literacy development as well as about the nature and extent of their involvement in their children's literacy learning.

3. Locate one reading or writing motivation survey instrument from *The Reading Teacher* (e.g., Bottomley, Henk, & Melnick, 1997/1998; Gambrell, Palmer, Codling & Mazzoni, 1996; Henk & Melnick, 1995; McKenna & Kear, 1990) and administer it to a grade level for which the instrument is appropriate. Discuss your findings. In particular, compare and contrast good and struggling learners' reading/writing motivation.

FURTHER READING

Baker, L., Afflerbach, P., & Reinking, D. (1996). *Developing engaged readers in school and home communities*. Mahwah, NJ: Erlbaum.

Baker, L., Dreher, M., & Guthrie, J. (2000). *Engaging young readers: Promoting achievement and motivation*. New York: Guilford Press.

Gambrell, L., & Almasi, J. (1996). *Lively discussion! Fostering engaged reading*. Newark, DE: International Reading Association.

Ginsberg, M., & Wlodkowski, R. (2000). *Creating highly motivating classrooms for all students: A schoolwide approach to powerful teaching with diverse learners*. San Francisco, CA: Jossey-Bass.

Guthrie, J., & Alvermann, D. (1999). *Engaged reading: Processes, practices, and policy implications*. New York: Teachers College Press.

Guthrie, J., & Wigfield, A. (1997). *Reading engagement: Motivating readers through integrated instruction*. Newark, DE: International Reading Association.

McCombs, B., & Pope, J. (1994). *Motivating hard to reach students*. Washington, DC: American Psychological Association.

Pressley, M., Dolezal, S., Raphael, L., Mohan, L., Roehrig, A., & Bogner, K. (2003). *Motivating primary-grade students*. New York: Guilford Press.

Verhoeven, L., & Snow, C. (2001). *Literacy and motivation: Reading engagement in individuals and groups*. Mahwah, NJ: Erlbaum.

Teaching Phonological Awareness, Phonics, and Spelling

INTRODUCTION

One of the distinguishing characteristics of accomplished teachers is their command of pedagogical content. Traditionally, the content of literacy instruction includes key topics such as phonics, spelling, vocabulary, and comprehension. Phonological awareness and fluency have recently received significant attention, due in part to the release of a high-profile document widely known as the National Reading Panel (NRP) report. The report, commissioned by the National Institute of Child Health and Human Development at the request of the United States Congress, reviews the reading research base on the effectiveness of different instructional techniques, and provides a guide for "scientifically-based reading instruction." While the findings of the NRP report continue to be scrutinized and critiqued, often with good reason and benign intent, federal and state mandates for "evidence-based" and "scientifically-based" reading instruction have intensified.

It seems obvious that the best protection against a nationalized reading instructional methodology is for teachers to develop a deep understanding of the key contents of literacy pedagogy so that they can make sound, informed instructional decisions. The articles in this and the next sections provide a starting point for building this content knowledge.

In this section, the topics of phonological awareness, phonics, and spelling are addressed. The first article, by Holly Lane, Paige Pullen, Mary Eisele, and LuAnn Jordan, defines the concept of phonological awareness and clarifies its relationship to phonemic awareness and phonics, two often-confused terms. Phonological awareness development and its relationship to beginning reading are then discussed. Next, the article presents group-based and individualized methods of assessing phonological awareness. It also describes a number of classroom-based instructional strategies and commercially available programs for developing young children's phonological skills. The authors emphasize that phonological awareness instruction is auditory and interactive in nature and prepares children to be able to benefit from phonics instruction.

In the second article, Louisa Moats addresses the question of "what components of decoding instruction are most effective with learners at what stage with what kind of teaching in what context and in relation to what other components." She advocates aligning decoding instruction with stages of reading development, with the structure of the English language, and with the way children learn it most easily. Specifically, she believes that phonics instruction should (a) proceed from speech to print, rather than from print to speech; (b) focus on pattern recognition, not on rule memorization; (c) be sequential, systematic, explicit, deliberate, and meaningful, rather than sporadic, implicit, and decontextualized; and (d) encourage active, constructive exploration. Throughout the article, the author spotlights some of what she considers to be the common flaws in phonics instruction and suggests alternative strategies. She emphasizes the need for literacy teachers to develop conscious knowledge of, among other things, the phonological and orthographic systems of the English language.

The teaching of spelling is closely tied to that of phonological awareness and phonics, for in order to spell a word correctly, one must be able to not only hear the sounds in the word but use graphemes to represent them. Thus, the teaching of spelling can contribute to the development of phonological and decoding skills, and vice versa. The third article, by Lawrence Sipe, discusses the uses and misuses of invented spelling in classroom practices and calls on teachers to assume a more active, constructive role in scaffolding young children's transition from emergent to conventional literacy. Sipe presents a historical overview of the concept of invented spelling and its theoretical underpinnings. He then discusses the perceived tension among children's invention, literacy convention, and teacher intervention. Finally, the author describes, in detail, several intervention strategies (e.g., hearing and recording sounds, Have-a-Go charting, interactive writing, linking the old to the new) that allow teachers to both honor children's approximations and actively assist them in developing conventional literacy.

Preventing Reading Failure: Phonological Awareness Assessment and Instruction

Holly B. Lane
University of Florida

Paige C. Pullen
University of Virginia

Mary R. Eisele
Education Consultant, Naples, FL

LuAnn Jordan
University of North Carolina, Charlotte

Reading is a foundation skill for school learning and life learning—the ability to read is critical for success in modern society. Learning to read is one of the most important events in a child's school career (Anderson, Hiebert, Scott, & Wilkinson, 1985; Lyon, 1999; National Reading Panel, 2000). Unfortunately, many children experience difficulties in the early stages of learning to read that become barriers to later reading and learning. A primary focus of recent research in education, therefore, has been the prevention of early reading problems (Adams, 1990; Snow, Burns, & Griffin, 1998; Torgesen, 1998). One area of beginning reading research that has received enormous attention in the professional literature is phonological awareness. This research has been called "a scientific success story" (Stanovich, 1987) because phonological awareness has been shown to be both a reliable predictor of reading achievement and a key to beginning reading acquisition (Smith, Simmons, & Kame'enui, 1995).

What Is Phonological Awareness?

Phonological awareness can be defined as conscious sensitivity to the sound structure of language. Children with strong phonological awareness can detect, match, blend, segment, and manipulate speech sounds. Such facility with the sounds of spoken language enables children to learn more readily how to apply these skills to decode print. An understanding of phonemes, the smallest detectable unit of sound in spoken language, is essential to the understanding of grapheme-phoneme (letter-sound) relationships. Numerous studies have demonstrated the importance of phonological awareness, particularly at the phoneme level, as the foundation for skilled decoding and,

therefore, for fluent reading (Blachman, Tangel, Ball, Black, & McGraw, 1999; Cornwall, 1992; Lenchner, Gerber, & Routh, 1990; Liberman & Shankweiler, 1985; Pratt & Brady, 1988; Wagner & Torgesen, 1987).

... phonological awareness has been shown to be both a reliable predictor of reading achievement and a key to beginning reading acquisition.

Phonological awareness tasks have been shown to be excellent predictors of reading ability or reading disability. That is, children who perform well on tasks of phonological awareness typically are or will become good readers, but children who perform poorly on them are or will become poor readers (Blachman, 1991; Catts, 1991; Perfetti, 1991; Perfetti, Beck, Bell, & Hughes, 1987; Snow et al., 1998; Stanovich, 1986, 1992; Torgesen, Wagner, & Rashotte, 1997). To benefit from instruction in decoding and spelling, a child must have a fundamental level of phonological awareness (Chard & Dickson 1999; National Reading Panel, 2000).

Many educators confuse the terminology related to this research. In particular, the terms *phonological awareness, phonemic awareness,* and *phonics* are sometimes used interchangeably. As previously stated, phonological awareness is a child's sensitivity to the sound structure of language. *Phonemic awareness* refers to a child's ability to manipulate individual sounds (phonemes) within words. *Phonics* is an instructional approach used to help children make sense of the connection between sounds and letters. Each is important to early reading instruction.

Phonological Awareness Research

Phonological awareness has gained considerable attention in educational research during the last 15 years. The primary attraction to this relatively new area of reading research is the repeated positive results in studies of phonological awareness interventions. Among the numerous reliable predictors of later reading

From *Preventing School Failure,* 46(3), 101–110, Spring 2002. Reprinted with permission of the Helen Dwight Reid Educational Foundation. Published by Heldref Publications, 1319 Eighteenth St., NW, Washington, DC 20036-1802. Copyright © 2002.

performance (e.g., socioeconomic status, mother's education) that educational researchers have identified phonological awareness is one of the few that educators are able to influence significantly.

Numerous studies of phonological awareness have contributed to the knowledge base in this area. These studies can and should inform future educational research and practice. Syntheses of this research (see, for example, Smith et al., 1995; National Reading Panel, 2000) have yielded several important generalizations:

1. Phonological awareness is directly related to reading ability.
2. Although the relationship is reciprocal, phonological awareness precedes skilled decoding.
3. Phonological awareness is a reliable predictor of later reading ability.
4. Deficits in phonological awareness are usually associated with deficits in reading.
5. Early language experiences play an important role in the development of phonological awareness.
6. Early intervention can promote the development of phonological awareness.
7. Improvements in phonological awareness can and usually do result in improvements in reading ability.

Phonological Skills and Developmental Levels

Several skills that are commonly associated with beginning reading instruction help children develop phonological awareness. Typically, the first phonological skill that children master is the ability to rhyme. Very young children may also master skills such as phoneme detection and sound matching with little instruction. More advanced phonological skills such as phoneme deletion, blending, and segmentation pose problems for many emergent readers. Most instruction designed to increase phonological awareness emphasizes these difficult skills (activities designed to enhance these skills will be described in detail in a subsequent section).

Many educators confuse ... the terms phonological awareness, phonemic awareness, and phonics.

The levels of phonological awareness development are associated with the different phonological components of spoken language, including words, syllables, onsets and rimes, and phonemes (Blachman, 1991; Smith, 1995). In Figure 1, we depict phonological awareness as an umbrella term that includes awareness at each level of spoken language. Effective

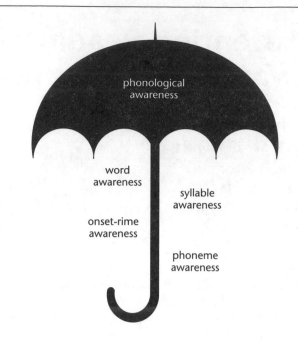

Figure 1   Phonological awareness can be illustrated as an umbrella term that comprises four levels. Phonomic awareness is an understanding of the sound structure of language at the phoneme level.

assessment and instruction should address the various levels of phonological awareness development. In the following sections, we describe each of these four levels of phonological awareness.

Word level.   The awareness that the speech flow is a compilation of individual words is typically achieved at a very young age. The linguistic play of young children, including rhyming and the generation of nonsense words, provides evidence of this early level of phonological awareness (Bradley, 1988). When a child utters a single word that he has only heard in combination with other words, he is demonstrating the word level of phonological awareness.

Syllable level.   Syllables are the most easily distinguishable units within words. Most children acquire the ability to segment words into syllables with minimal instruction (Liberman, Shankweiler, & Liberman, 1989; Lundberg, 1988). Activities such as clapping, tapping, and marching are often used to develop syllable awareness. This level of phonological awareness is useful for initial instruction in detection, segmentation, blending, and manipulation of phonological components of language. The ability to detect, segment, and count syllables is more important to reading acquisition than the ability to manipulate and transpose them (Adams, 1990).

Onset and rime level. The onset-rime or intrasyllabic level of phonological awareness is an intermediate and instructionally useful level of analysis between the syllable and the phoneme (Adams, 1990). The *onset* is the part of the syllable that precedes the vowel (e.g., the /k/ in *cat*, the /br/ in *brown*). The *rime* is the rest of the syllable (e.g., the /og/ in *dog*, the /ack/ in *black*). Because a syllable must contain a vowel, all syllables must have a rime, but not all syllables have an onset (e.g., *and, out, or*).

Treiman (1985) found that children make more errors with consonants at the end of words or with consonant blends than with initial or medial consonants. This finding suggests that children naturally segment words at neither the syllable nor the phoneme level, but at the intrasyllabic level. In addition, most children spell rimes more accurately than individual vowel sounds, which illustrates the level at which they are attending. Onsetrime segmentation skill is an essential component of phonological awareness (Adams, 1990; Goswami & Mead, 1992).

Instruction at the onset-rime level is an important step for many childen (Treiman, 1985, 1991, 1992). Because tasks that require onset and rime analysis require the segmentation of syllables, they are more sophisticated than syllable-level tasks. Yet these same tasks are easier than phoneme-level tasks because they do not require discrimination between individual phonemes. Onset-rime tasks could, therefore, be considered an intermediate step in the development of phonological awareness. The difficulty that many children experience when progressing from syllabic analysis to phonemic analysis may arise because the intermediate step, the intrasyllabic unit, is often omitted from early reading instruction. Providing experience working with onsets and rimes may alleviate this difficulty.

Phoneme level. The most sophisticated level of phonological awareness is the phoneme level, most commonly referred to as phonemic awareness. Children with strong phonemic awareness are able to manipulate individual phonemes, the smallest sound units of spoken language. Phonemic awareness skills include the ability to detect, segment, and blend phonemes and to manipulate their position in words (Adams, 1990; Lenchner et al., 1990).

Because humans coarticulate or overlap sounds in speech, phonemes are impossible to segment in a pure sense. In the speech flow, phonemes are formed and blended in such a way that one phoneme's production is influenced by the surrounding phonemes. For example, the /k/ is formed in slightly different ways in the words *cat* and *cot* due to the influence of the vowel that follows it. Because phonemic analysis requires the reader to detect, segment, and manipulate individual phonemes, it is a much more sophisticated task and, consequently, a much more difficult task than either syllabic or intrasyllabic analysis (Treiman, 1991, 1992).

Assessing Phonological Awareness

Educators face the formidable challenge of determining which children have weaknesses in phonological awareness and, therefore, which children are likely to develop reading problems. Several ways to assess phonological awareness have been developed. Which method to use should be determined based on the number of children to be assessed, the amount of existing information about the children, and the amount of time available. The most reliable and informative method of assessing phonological awareness is through, individual testing. Other methods have been developed, however, that are quick and easy to administer and that have reliability adequate for most classroom purposes. Yopp (1988) investigated some of the most commonly used measures of phonological awareness and determined that the reliability and validity of measurement tasks were greatest when a combination of measures was employed.

Group Assessment

Several methods have been developed for group screening and assessment of phonological skills. Tests of invented spelling can be administered in a group setting, and the analysis of children's attempts to spell words provides the teacher with information about their ability to segment phonemes, their knowledge of the alphabet, and their understanding of letter-sound correspondences (Invernizzi, Meier, Swank, & Juel, 1998; Moats, 2000; Snow et al., 1998). Mann, Tobin, and Wilson (1987) have advocated the use of children's invented spellings as a tool for screening phonological awareness. They developed a system for scoring an invented spelling that can help determine if additional assessment is warranted. In this and other similar scoring methods, points are awarded on the basis of a spelling's phonological accuracy. For example, in an attempt to spell an unfamiliar word, a child may produce a scribble, a random letter string, one or two correctly represented phonemes, or even a phonologically accurate spelling (Figure 2). Each of these attempts represents significant information about that child's phonological knowledge. See Table 1 for a summary of one method for scoring invented spellings.

The Screening Test of Phonological Awareness (STOPA) has been demonstrated to be an effective

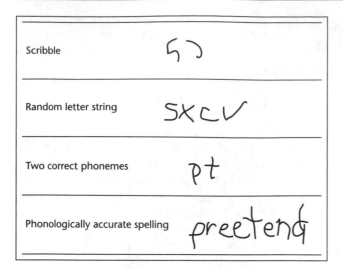

Scribble	ら)
Random letter string	SKCV
Two correct phonemes	pt
Phonologically accurate spelling	preetend

Figure 2 These example spellings for the word *pretend* begin with a series of scribbles and move to a spelling that is phonologically accurate.

group assessment tool (Torgesen, Wagner, Bryant, & Pearson, 1992). The *STOPA,* designed for use with kindergarten students, requires students to identify sounds that are the same and different. The test is simple to administer in a group setting, yet sophisticated enough to detect individual differences in phonological awareness.

Individualized Assessment

To collect the kind of information about a child's phonological knowledge that is necessary to design effective instructional interventions, individual assessments are particularly useful. The assessment method can be informal, criterion-referenced, or norm-referenced.

Clearly, the most direct informal method of measuring a child's phonological awareness is repeated observation by a knowledgeable teacher of the child's ability to perform tasks that require the use of phonological skills. Such observation provides a teacher with an authentic measure of what a child can or cannot do (Valencia, 1997). A variety of skill areas may be examined to measure phonological awareness; these include rhyme detection and production, sound matching, phonemic oddity detection, deletion, segmentation, and blending. Sample questions for informal assessment of a child's phonological awareness appear in Table 2. Several formal measures of phonological awareness have been developed, as well. Descriptions of some of the most widely used appear in Table 3.

Developing Phonological Awareness

Just as assessing phonological awareness is best accomplished by observing students as they perform tasks that demonstrate phonological skills, developing phonological awareness requires practicing phonological skills. Most skill instruction can be easily embedded within the context of meaningful reading or writing (Wadlington, 2000; Yopp, 1992). Some children, however, require more extensive practice with skills. Students who have very low levels of reading ability benefit most from explicit instruction in phonological skills paired with explicit instruction in how to apply those skills in a meaningful context (Cunningham, 1990; Lane, 1994). As these children develop sensitivity to the sound structure of language, instruction in phoneme segmentation and blending should be coupled with instruction using letters (Pullen, 2000).

Instruction in phonological skills can be conducted as formal, structured lessons, as an integrated part of ongoing reading instruction, or as fun activities throughout the school day. Instruction may be individualized, small-group, or whole-class. For students who have significant weaknesses in phonological awareness, 10–20 minutes of individual or small-group instruction each day may be necessary to promote adequate growth. Of course, student needs should dictate the form and amount of instruction provided.

Table 1 Method for Scoring Invented Spelling

Characteristics of spelling	Example spellings	Score
One phoneme accurately represented other than initial phoneme	t	1/2
Initial phoneme accurately represented	f	1
	fesry	
Initial phoneme and one other phoneme accurately represented	ft	2
Initial phoneme and two or more other phonemes accurately represented	fot	3
	flt	
Word is phonologically accurate	flot	4
	flote	

Table 2 Sample Assessment Questions

Assessment	Directions	Sample
Word level		
Tapping words	Teacher reads sentence aloud. Child taps for each word in the sentence	*The little frog is jumping.*
Deleting words	Teacher reads a compound.word, the child deletes one word.	Teacher says, "Say cowboy." Child repeats."Now say *cowboy,* without saying *cow.*"
Syllable level		
Blending syllables	Teacher reads word one syllable at a time. The child listens, then blends the sounds together to make the whole word.	What word do these sounds make? *tea-cher.*
Tapping syllables	Teacher reads word aloud. Child taps for each syllable in the word.	*alligator*
Deleting syllables	Teacher reads child a multisyllable word and the child deletes a specific syllable.	Teacher says, "Say *wonder.*" Child repeats."Now say *wonder* without saying *der.*"
Onset-rime level		
Matching rhymes	Teacher gives child a word pair, the child decides whether or not the pair rhymes.	Do these two words rhyme? *sack/black* Do these two words rhyme? *beat/bean*
Blending onsets and rimes	The teacher segments the word orally between the onset and rime. The child listens, then blends the sounds together to make the whole word.	What word do these sounds make? *n-ote.*
Generating rhymes	The teacher gives child a target word and the child must provide a word that rhymes with the target word.	Tell me a word that rhymes with *sat.*
Phoneme level		
Blending phonemes	Teacher segments a word into phonemes and the child is asked to blend the sounds to make the whole word.	What word do these sounds make? *b-o-th.*
Segmenting phonemes	Teacher reads child a whole word and the child is asked to produce the word sound by sound.	I will say a word, then you say it sound by sound. *mat.*

Commerically Available Instructional Programs

As educators have become aware of the research on phonological awareness, publishers have recognized the demand for classroom materials. Numerous commercial programs are currently available. Several of these programs have undergone field testing and evaluation. We provide a list and brief description of research-based materials for teachers in Table 4. In addition to these classroom materials, several programs for computer-assisted instruction have become available. A listing of these software programs is provided in Table 5.

Informal Methods of Instruction

Most activities in commercial programs such as those described can be incorporated informally within existing reading instruction. The following tasks are useful for practicing and developing phonological skills. The tasks are sequenced in an order that approximates the developmental sequence. However, the sequence and rate of skill development vary from child to child, and skills overlap during development. We also wish to stress that these activities are auditory and interactive in nature; children do not develop phonological skills by doing independent written work.

Tapping words. Children can be taught to tap with a rhythm stick or finger for each word in a sentence or phrase. Most children acquire this skill with minimal instruction. Teacher modeling and guidance are useful for those children who have difficulty with this task. Children who struggle with this activity typically confuse words and syllables. Care should be taken to make this distinction explicit.

Table 3   Assessments of Phonological Awareness

Assessment	Author/publisher	Description
Lindamood Auditory Conceptualization Test (LAC)	Lindamood and Lindamood/ Pro-Ed	The *LAC* is a comprehensive, individually administered assessment for both children and adults. It is effective for a wide range of ages; however, it is difficult for very young children (kindergarten).
Comprehensive Test of Phonological Processing (CTOPP)	Wagner, Toregesen and Rashotte/Pro-Ed	The *CTOPP* is an individually administered assessment that measures (a) phonological awareness (e.g., sound blending, elision); (b) phonological memory (memory of matching, digits, nonword repetition); and (c) rapid serial naming (rapid naming of objects, numbers, and letters).
Test of Phonological Awareness (TOPA)	Toregesen and Bryant/ Pro-Ed	*TOPA* is a measure of young children's ability to isolate individual phonemes in spoken words. It can be administered to groups of children and is available in kindergarten and early elementary versions.
Phonological Awareness Literacy Screening (PALS)	Invernizzi, Meier, Swank and Juel/University of Virginia	*PALS* measures the child's rhyming abilities and sound awareness. In addition to these phonological skills, alphabet knowledge, letter sound knowledge, concept of word, and word recognition are also assessed.
The Developmental Spelling Analysis in Word Journey	Ganske/Guilford Press	This assessment includes a screening inventory for determining a child's stage of spelling development and two parallel feature inventories for highlighting strengths and weaknesses in a child's knowledge of specific spelling features.

Counting and tallying words.   Tallying the number of words in a sentence requires a greater degree of cognitive engagement than tapping words and is considered a more sophisticated task. Another method of word counting involves moving a marker to indicate the number of words in a sentence.

Tapping syllables.   Children may be taught to tap out the number of syllables in a word. This task requires auditory attention. The teacher should provide extensive modeling and guided practice to help children understand the concept of syllable. Starting with long but familiar multisyllable words (e.g., refrigerator, motorcycle) makes the acquisition of this skill easy for most children.

Segmenting syllables.   Teaching students to segment multisyllable words into individual syllables can begin in kindergarten. This process can be made into a game in which children separate their names or the names of familiar objects into syllables. Instruction may begin with segmentation of compound words (e.g., football, outside, sidewalk). Children may also be taught to count the number of syllables in other long but familiar words. These tasks require auditory attention and memory.

Rhyme recognition.   Children can be taught to determine if two one-syllable words rhyme. Some children have an inherent understanding of rhymes based on extensive experiences with language and print. Other children who have not developed this understanding may need explicit instruction about what a rhyme is (i.e., words rhyme when they sound the same in the middle and at the end). This instruction should be accompanied by numerous examples and nonexamples of rhymes. Rhyme recognition simply requires the student to indicate whether or not a pair of spoken words rhymes. Instead of simply providing a pair of words, to promote rhyme recognition, the teacher might say, "*Cat* and *sat* both have an *at*. Does *hat* have an *at*?"

Rhyme generation.   Generating a word or list of words that rhyme with a given word is more difficult than determining if two given words rhyme. The additional cognitive and language requirements of rhyme generation make it quite challenging for some children. The ability to generate rhymes, however, is an excellent indicator of a child's ability to apply phonological knowledge. Many children engage in spontaneous word games that employ rhyming skills. This fun way to practice skills should be encouraged.

Table 4 Commercially Available Instructional Programs

Program	Author/publisher	Description
Lindamood Phoneme Sequencing Program for Reading, Spelling, and Speech (LiPS)	Lindamood/ProEd	*LiPS* is designed to provide intensive remedial instruction for students struggling to develop phonological awareness. Sounds are represented with objects and descriptive names to develop students' concrete understanding of distinct sounds by drawing a child's attention to the motoric features of phoneme articulation through individual or small-group instruction. Students learn how to position their mouths to produce sounds and how to distinguish among various typesof sounds.
Road to the Code: A Program of Early Literacy Activities to Develop Phonological Awareness	Blachman, Ball, Black, and Tangel/Brookes	*Road to the Code* includes activities to move students from phonological awareness to letter knowledge. The program gradually moves into activities that encourage the application of these skills in writing and spelling.
Phonological Awareness Training for Reading	Torgesen and Bryant/ ProEd	This program includes games and activities to help children develop sound segmenting and blending, reading and spelling. An audiotape guide for sound pronunciation is included.
Phonemic Awareness in Young Children	Adams, Foorman, Lundberg, and Beeler/Brookes	This curriculum provides a basis for assessment and instruction in phonological awareness. The book includes a variety of language games, listening games, rhyming activities, and activities for developing students' understanding of sounds in words. Several instruments for assessing phonological awareness are also included.
Ladders to Literacy	O'Connor, Notari-Syverson, and Vadasy/Brookes	These preschool and kindergarten activity books provide early literacy activities in phonological awareness, vocabulary development, and letter names and sounds. The program is designed to emphasize the provision of appropriate levels of instructional support for developing students.
Sounds Abound	Catts and Vartiainen/ LinguiSystems	*Sounds Abound* is for children in grades PreK–3. It targets listening and rhyming skills as students work toward matching sounds with letters. Five sections include fun activities in (1) speech sound awareness, (2) rhyming, (3) beginning and ending sounds, (4) segmenting and blendingsounds, and (5) putting sounds together with words.

Using nonsense words in such games reinforces the child's attention to sounds.

Rhyme oddity detection.   This task requires children to indicate which in a list of three or four words does not rhyme with the other words in the list. The familiar song from the television show *Sesame Street* does this well: "Which of these words is not like the others? Which of these words just doesn't belong?"

Rhyme matching.   Given a list of three or four words, students indicate which one from the list rhymes with a target word. For example, the teacher might say, "Which word rhymes with *stamp: map, lip, or lamp?*"

Sound detection.   Given a target phoneme, students determine which words on a list begin or end with that sound. This activity can be used during story or passage reading, as well. While reading connected text, students find all words in the selection that include the target phoneme. As students become comfortable with beginning and ending sounds, activities that include detection of a target medial sound should be added.

Sound matching.   To match sounds, students must determine which in a selection of words begins or ends with the same sound as a given word. For example, the teacher may ask students, "Which word begins with the same sound as *dog: can, must,* or *dish?*

Table 5 Instructional Software Programs

Program	Author/publisher	Description
Earobics	Wasowicz/Cognitive Concepts	*Earobics* is a software program designed to develop phonemic awareness and letter-sound knowledge through engaging games.
Daisy Quest and Daisy's Castle	Erikson, Foster, Foster, and Torgesen/ProEd	*Daisy Quest and Daisy's Castle* are computer programs for the Macintosh. The games are motivating for children while providing opportunities to develop phonological awareness at each level. Research studies have found these software programs to be an effective way to stimulate phonological awareness in young children.
The Waterford Early Reading Program	The Waterford Institute/ Electronic Education	*The Waterford Early Reading Program* is a comprehensive computer program for Kindergarten. It provides activities in phonological awareness, concepts of print, letter names, and letter sounds.
Read, Write, and Type! Learning System	Herron and Grimm/ Talking Fingers	This computer software program merges the teaching of phonics skills with an introduction to typing. Children move through a progressively challenging sequence of games that begins with single letters, advances to whole words, and concludes with complete sentences, including capitalization and punctuation.
Fast ForWord	Merzenich, Tallal, Jenkins, and Miller/Scientific Learning	*Fast ForWord* is an interactive program that stimulates children's phonological skills using acoustically modified speech sounds. This acoustic training is provided in five 20-minute sessions each day. Requires teacher training.

As students master this skill, the activity should be modified to request ending or middle sound-matching, and more words may be added to the list.

Sound oddity detection. The procedures for this activity are very similar to those for rhyme oddity detection. The difference, however, is that students are asked to determine which in a list of words begins or ends with a sound different from a given word. For example, the teacher may ask, "Which of these words does not have the same ending sound as *cat: mutt, lift, cake,* or *bite?*" Again, work with medial sounds should start when students become skilled with beginning and ending sounds.

Rhyme and sound matching using pictures. For these activities, children are asked to look at pictures and generate the sounds themselves by naming the word the picture represents. Students match pictures illustrating words that share a common rime or a common initial, medial, or final phoneme. This activity is somewhat more advanced than activities that begin with the teacher generating the sounds, because some students find it more difficult to detect individual phonemes when they do not hear someone else say the word.

Oddity detection using pictures. As in the previous activity, the student is expected to generate the name of the word the pictures represents. The student then determines which in a set of pictures illustrating words does not share a common rime or a common initial, medial, or final phoneme.

Counting phonemes. Elkonin (1963) introduced a method of developing phonemic segmentation skills that has become quite popular in recent years. This method involves the use of Elkonin boxes—picture cards with boxes under each picture representing the number of phonemes in the word (see Figure 3). While saying the word slowly, sound by sound, the student moves a marker into each box to represent each sound in the word. This activity may be modified to allow the teacher and student to practice the skill orally. The teacher demonstrates using fingers to count phonemes, raising one finger as each phoneme is pronounced. With teacher guidance, the student should be able to learn how to count phonemes independently.

Phoneme deletion. Phoneme deletion activities require students to detect and manipulate sounds in a word. Students are asked to delete a specified sound from a target word. For example, the teacher may say,

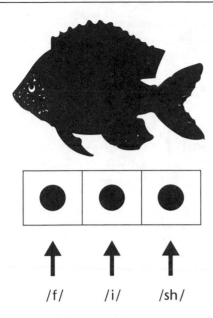

/f/ /i/ /sh/

Figure 3 The teacher models moving one chip into a square for each sound in *fish*. The student then moves the chips into the squares with help from the teacher, until the student is able to move the chips into the squares independently. Eventually, the student learns to write letters in the boxes.

"Say *seat*. Now say *seat* without saying the /t/ sound." Again, practice with this activity should begin with initial sounds and progress to final and, eventually, medial sounds.

Blending and segmenting. Blending and segmenting phonemes are the most sophisticated skills associated with phonological awareness and the most important for application to decoding. Blending and segmenting may be taught in a variety of ways. One of the most useful methods for helping young children to understand the concepts of phonemic blending and segmentation is teaching them to "converse" with a puppet or toy robot in a secret language. Torgesen and Bryant (1994) used this approach in *Phonological Awareness Training for Reading*, but the method is easy to adapt to informal instruction. In this approach, the puppet or robot can only say words and can only understand words when they are said one sound at a time. Young children seem to accept and understand this explanation quite readily and are eager to try communicating in this unusual fashion.

When teaching or assessing blending and segmentation skills, the teacher should be careful to completely segment phonemes before blending them. Many teachers have the tendency simply to say a word slowly, drawing out the phonemes. The teacher should be certain to include a brief but discernible pause between segmented sounds. When children

learn to decode, it is necessary for them to identify the sounds of separate letters and then to blend those letter sounds together. Previous oral blending practice is helpful for students when they are ready to become more fluent with decoding skills.

Another important caution for teachers is that individual phonemes must be pronounced in a manner that will make them blendable. In other words, teachers should be very careful to model correct letter sound pronunciation. Many teachers, in an effort to make short or "stop" consonant sounds more audible, add a vowel sound to the consonant. This additional sound, usually a schwa or short *u* sound, distorts the consonant sound, making it very difficult to blend with other phonemes. For example, a *b* may be incorrectly pronounced "buh," and a *t* may be incorrectly pronounced "tuh." Blending the letters *b*, *a*, and *t* then produces "buh-a-tuh," and many children have serious difficulty identifying the word. It is important to pronounce these stop consonants as quickly as possible, without the confusing "uh." Because it is impossible to pronounce a voiced stop consonant such as *b* or *d* in isolation with no vowel sound attached, the teacher should model saying the sound with an extremely brief short *i* sound following it. The place in the vocal anatomy where the short *i* is produced is closer to the location of more of the other vowel sounds than the short *u*. Teaching children to use this strategy may help them blend stop consonants more readily.

Another way to alleviate this problem is to begin instruction in blending and segmenting using only words with continuous consonant sounds (e.g., /s/, /v/, /z/, /f/, /m/, /n/) at the beginning position. These sounds are much easier to blend than the stop consonants, and their use in early instruction makes the skill of blending more accessible for children. As children are introduced to blending skills, stop consonants may be used at the end of words. In the final position, stop consonants are easier to pronounce quickly and with little distortion. When students become competent with pronunciation, the introduction of stops at the initial position becomes less troublesome.

Including Phonological Awareness Instruction in an Existing Reading Program

Many of the activities we have described can be integrated into any reading activity or used as games during instruction or during noninstructional time. For example, singing and play activities offer many opportunities for kindergarten teachers to incorporate phonological skill development. Stories or poems that include rhyming words may be used as a tool to introduce and develop concepts and skills in rhyming. A teacher of older students could ask them to count the number of syllables or phonemes in the names of story characters or in new vocabulary words. If a teacher encourages the use of carefully invented spellings, students learn to segment words and represent the correct number of phonemes. Modeling how to sound out a word to invent a spelling can help students develop these skills. As students learn about decoding, numerous other opportunities for instruction in blending and segmentation arise.

Instruction in phonological skills can be conducted as formal, structured lessons, as an integrated part of ongoing reading instruction, or as fun activities throughout the school day.

The teacher could make a simple whole-class game out of rhyme or phoneme matching (e.g., "Line up for lunch if your name rhymes with _____," or "if your name has a /t/ at the end"). Teachers can challenge students to think of words that have a particular number of syllables or phonemes. Finding many fun and innovative ways to include such sound play in the school day will address the instructional needs of many students. Additional practice in specific skills will certainly be required for some students who have difficulty acquiring phonological skills, but such informal opportunities to practice throughout the day will help these students, as well.

Combining informal sound play and formal phonological awareness instruction during typical reading and writing activities for all students with explicit skill instruction for students who need additional practice should address the diverse needs in most elementary classrooms. The most important thing for teachers to do is to make the sound structure of language conspicuous to students who do not develop phonological awareness independently.

The activities presented here are designed to develop phonological awareness. Applying these auditory skills to reading requires students to have a working knowledge of sound-symbol relationships, which is typically acquired through phonics instruction. Despite popular misconceptions, phonological awareness instruction is not the same as phonics instruction; instead, phonological awareness instruction prepares students to be able to benefit from instruction in phonics.

Conclusion

Reading research has clearly demonstrated the significance of phonological awareness in the development of early reading skills, and a variety of effective methods for assessment and instruction of phonological skills has been developed. Teachers in remedial and special education programs now have another tool for addressing students' reading problems. Teachers of young children must recognize the importance of incorporating phonological awareness into programs designed to promote emergent literacy, because these teachers now have a tool for preventing reading problems.

References

Adams, M. J. (1990). *Beginning to read: Thinking and learning about print.* Cambridge: MIT.

Adams, M. J., Foorman, B. R., Lundberg, I., & Beeler, T. (1998). *Phonemic awareness in young children: A classroom curriculum.* Baltimore, MD: Brookes.

Anderson, R. C., Hiebert, E. H., Scott, J. A., & Wilkinson, I. A. (1985). *Becoming a nation of readers: The report of the commission on reading.* Washington, DC: National Institute of Education.

Blachman, B. A. (1991). Early interventions for children's reading problems: Clinical applications of the research in phonological awareness. *Topics in Language Disorders, 12*(1), 51–65.

Blachman, B. A., Ball, E. W., Black, R., & Tangel, D. M. (2000). *Road to the code: A phonological awareness program for young children.* Baltimore, MD: Brookes.

Blachman, B. A., Tangel, D. M., Ball, E. W., Black, R., & McGraw, C. K. (1999). Developing phonological awareness and word recognition skills: A two-year intervention with low-income, inner-city children. *Reading and Writing: An Interdisciplinary Journal, 11*, 239–273.

Bradley, L. (1988). Rhyme recognition and reading and spelling in young children. In R. L. Masland & M. W. Masland (Eds.). *Preschool prevention of reading failure* (pp. 143–162). Parkton, MD: York.

Catts, H. W. (1991). Early identification of reading disabilities. *Topics in Language Disorders, 12*(1), 1–16.

Chard, D. J., & Dickson, S. V. (1999). Phonological awareness: Instructional and assessment guidelines. *Intervention in School and Clinic, 34*, 261–270.

Cornwall. A. (1992). The relationship of phonological awareness, rapid naming, and verbal memory to severe reading and spelling disability. *Journal of Learning Disabilities, 25*, 532–538.

Cunningham, A. E. (1990). Explicit versus implicit instruction in phonemic awareness. *Journal of Experimental Child Psychology, 50,* 429–444.

Elkonin, D. B. (1963). The psychology of mastering the elements of reading. In B. Simon & J. Simon (Eds.), *Educational psychology in the U.S.S.R.* (pp. 165–179). Stanford, CA: Stanford University.

Erikson, G. C., Foster, K. C., Foster, D. F. & Torgesen, J. K. (1992). *Daisy Quest.* Austin, TX: Pro-Ed.

Erikson, G. C., Foster, K. C., Foster, D. F. & Torgesen, J. K. (1993). *Daisy's Castle.* Austin, TX: Pro-Ed.

Ganske, K. (2000). *Word journeys: Assessment-guided phonics, spelling, and vocabulary instruction.* New York: Guildford.

Goswami, U., & Mead, F. (1992). Onset and rime awareness and analogies in reading. *Reading Research Quarterly, 27*, 152–162.

Herron, J., & Grimm, L. (2001). *Read, Write, & Type! Learning System*. San Raphael, CA: Talking Fingers.

Invernizzi, M., Meier, J. D., Swank, L., & Juel, C. (1998). *Phonological awareness literacy screening*. Charlottesville, VA: University of Virginia.

Lane, H. B. (1994). *The effects of explicit instruction in contextual application of phonological awareness on the reading skills of first-grade students*. Unpublished doctoral dissertation. University of Florida, Gainesville.

Lenchner, O., Gerber, M. M., & Routh, D. K. (1990). Phonological awareness tasks as predictors of decoding ability: Beyond segmentation. *Journal of Learning Disabilities, 23*, 240–247.

Liberman, I. Y., Shankweiler, D., & Liberman, A. M. (1989). The alphabetic principle and learning to read. In D. Shankweiler & I. Y. Liberman (Eds.), *Phonology and reading disability: Solving the reading puzzle* (pp. 1–33). Ann Arbor: The University of Michigan Press.

Liberman, I., & Shankweiler, D. (1985). Phonology and the problems of learning to read and write. *Remedial and Special Education, 6*, 8–17.

Lindamood, C., & Lindamood, P. (1972). *Lindamood auditory conceptualization test*. Austin, TX: Pro-Ed.

Lindamood, C., & Lindamood, P. (1998). *Lindamood phoneme sequencing program for reading, spelling, and speech*. Austin, TX: Pro-Ed.

Lundberg, I. (1988). *Preschool prevention of reading failure: Does training in phonological awareness work?* In R. L. Masland & M. W. Masland (Eds.), Preschool prevention of reading failure (pp. 163–176). Parkton, MD: York.

Lyon, G. R. (1999). Education research: Is what we don't know hurting our children? *Statement of the Chief of the Child Development and Behavior Branch of the National Institutes of Child Health and Human Development, National Institute of Health, to the House Science Committee*. Washington, DC.

Mann, V. A., Tobin, P., & Wilson, R. (1987). Measuring phonological awareness through the invented spellings of kindergarten children. *Merrill-Palmer Quarterly, 33*, 365–391.

Merzenich, M., Tallal, P., Jenkins, W., & Miller, S. (1996). *Fast ForWord*. Oakland, CA: Scientific Learning.

Moats, L. (2000). *Speech to print: Language essentials for teachers*. Baltimore, MD: Brookes.

National Reading Panel. (2000). *Teaching children to read: An evidence-based assessment of the scientific research literature on reading and its implications for reading instruction*. Washington, DC: National Institute of Child Health and Human Development, National Institutes of Health.

Notari-Syverson, A., O'Connor, R. E., & Vadasy, P. F. (1998). *Ladders to Literacy: A Preschool Activity Book*. Baltimore, MD: Brookes.

O'Connor, R. E., Notari-Syverson, A., & Vadasy, P. F. (1998). *Ladders to Literacy: A Kindergarten Activity Book*. Baltimore, MD: Brookes.

Perfetti, C. A. (1991). Representations and awareness in the acquisition of reading competence. In L. Rieben & C. A. Perfetti (Eds.), *Learning to read: Basic research and its implications* (pp. 33–44). Hillsdale, NJ: Lawrence Erlbaum Associates.

Perfetti, C. A., Beck, I., Bell, L. C., & Hughes, C. (1987). Phonemic knowledge and learning to read are reciprocal: A longitudinal study of first grade children. *Merrill-Palmer Quarterly, 33*, 283–319.

Pratt, A. C., & Brady, S. (1988). Relation of phonological awareness to reading disability in children and adults. *Journal of Educational Psychology, 80*, 319–323.

Pullen, P. C. (2000). *The effects of alphabetic word work with manipulative letters on the reading acquisition of struggling first-grade students*. Unpublished doctoral dissertation. University of Florida, Gainesville.

Smith, C. R. (1995, March). *Assessment and remediation of phonological segmentation difficulties*. Paper presented at the annual meeting of the Learning Disabilities Association of America, Orlando, FL.

Smith, S. B., Simmons, D. C., & Kame'enui, E. J. (1995). *Synthesis of research on phonological awareness: Principles and implications for reading acquisition*. Technical Report No. 21, National Center to Improve the Tools of Educators, University of Oregon.

Snow, C. E., Burns, M. S., & Griffin, P. (Eds.). (1998). *Preventing reading difficulties in young children*. Washington, DC: National Academy.

Stanovich, K. E. (1986). Matthew effects in reading: Some consequences of individual differences in the acquisition of literacy. *Reading Research Quarterly, 21*, 360–406.

Stanovich, K. E. (1987). Introduction to special issue. *Merrill-Palmer Quarterly, 33*.

Stanovich, K. E. (1992). Speculations on the causes and consequences of individual differences in early reading acquisition. In P. B. Gough, L. C. Ehri, & R. Treiman (Eds.), *Reading acquisition* (pp. 307–342). Hillsdale, NJ: Lawrence Erlbaum.

Torgesen, J. K. (1998). Catch them before they fall: Identification and assessment to prevent reading failure in young children. *American Educator, 22*, 32–39.

Torgesen, J. K., & Bryant, B. R. (1994). *Phonological awareness training for reading*. Austin, TX: Pro-Ed.

Torgesen, J. K., & Bryant, B. R. (1997). *Test of phonological awareness*. Austin, TX: Pro-Ed.

Torgesen, J. K., Wagner, R. K., & Rashotte, C. A. (1997). Approaches to the prevention and remediation of phonologically based reading disabilities. In B. Blachman (Ed.), *Foundations of reading acquisition and dyslexia: Implications for early intervention* (pp. 287–304). Mahwah, NJ: Erlbaum.

Torgesen, J. K., Wagner, R. K., Bryant, B. R., & Pearson, N. (1992). Toward development of a kindergarten group test for phonological awareness. *Journal of Research and Development in Education, 25*, 113–120.

Treiman, R. (1985). Onsets and rimes as units of spoken syllables: Evidence from children. *Journal of Experimental Child Psychology, 39*, 161–181.

Treiman, R. (1991). The role of intrasyllabic units in learning to read. In L. Rieben & C. A. Perfetti (Eds.), *Learning to read: Basic research and its implications* (pp. 149–160). Hillsdale, NJ: Lawrence Erlbaum.

Treiman, R. (1992). The role of intrasyllabic units in learning to read and spell. In P. B. Gough, L. C. Ehri, & R. Treiman (Eds.), *Reading Acquisition* (pp. 65–106). Hillsdale, NJ: Lawrence Erlbaum.

Valencia, S. W. (1997). Authentic classroom assessment of early reading: Alternatives to standardized tests. *Preventing School Failure, 41*, 63–70.

Wadlington, E. (2000). Effective language arts instruction for students with dyslexia. *Preventing School Failure, 44*, 61–65.

Wagner, R. K., & Torgesen, J. K. (1987). The nature of phonological processing and its causal role in the acquisition of reading skills. *Psychological Bulletin, 101*, 192–212.

Wagner, R., Torgesen, J., & Rashotte, C. (1999). *Comprehensive test of phonological processing* (CTOPP). Austin, TX: Pro-Ed.

Wasowicz, J. (1997). *Earobics 1*. Evanston, IL: Cognitive Concepts.

Wasowicz, J. (1999). *Earobics 2*. Evanston, IL: Cognitive Concepts.

Waterford Institute. (1993). *Waterford early learning program*. Sunnyvale, CA: Electronic Education.

Yopp, H. K. (1988). The validity and reliability of phonemic awareness tests. *Reading Research Quarterly, 23*, 159–177.

Yopp, H. K. (1992). Developing phonemic awareness in young children. *The Reading Teacher, 45*, 696–703.

Teaching Decoding

Louisa C. Moats, Education Consultant

As it has become increasingly apparent that substantial numbers of children are failing to become skilled readers, a consensus is emerging among reading researchers, practitioners, and policy makers concerning the critical role that decoding plays in the reading process (Snow, Burns, & Griffin, 1998). Cognitive scientists have shown beyond doubt that fluent, accurate decoding is a hallmark of skilled reading (Adams, Treiman, & Pressley, 1997; Fletcher & Lyon, 1998; Rack, Snowling, & Olson, 1992; Share, 1995; Stanovich & Siegel, 1994; Vellutino, Scanlon, & Sipay, 1997). Automatic word recognition, which is dependent on phonic knowledge, allows the reader to attend to meaning; likewise, slow, belabored decoding overloads short-term memory and impedes comprehension.

While this renewed interest in phonics is certainly a welcome development, we will make limited progress unless decoding instruction is grounded in what we know about the stages of reading development, the structure of the English language, and the strategies students employ to learn it. With rare exception, classroom practice is not informed by these principles. As we shall see, problems abound not only with the approaches to decoding typically found in whole-language and "literature-based" programs but also with programs associated with traditional phonics.

Align Decoding Instruction with the Stages of Reading Development

That decoding is learned early by good readers is established in studies of reading development (Chall, 1983; Cunningham & Stanovich, 1997; Ehri, 1994). The ability to sound out new words accounts for about 80 percent of the variance in first-grade reading comprehension, and continues to be a major factor in text comprehension as students progress through the grades (Foorman, Francis, Shaywitz, et al., 1997). Moreover, a series of studies have traced how beginners learn to read and spell words (e.g., Ehri, 1994; Treiman, 1993; Wagner & Barker, 1994). The learner progresses from global to analytic processing, from approximate to specific linking of sound and symbol, and from

context-driven to print-driven reading as proficiency is acquired. The instruction we deliver should be compatible with the emerging competence of the student.

Logographic Reading

Young children, typically before mid-kindergarten, may learn to recognize a limited vocabulary of whole words through incidental cues such as a picture, color, or shape (Ehri, 1994; Gough, Juel, & Griffith, 1992), but in this beginning stage of reading, do not associate sounds with symbols. Children will string letters together when they write and assign changing messages to them, or will look to context to guess at what a word says. A printed word may be remembered for its unique appearance, as in "pizza" or "D'Antoine." If asked about the sound that begins "pizza," however, the student might say "hot" or "m m m m." This visual cue reading typically precedes the insight that alphabet letters correspond to speech sounds. Children at this level have not realized that words are composed of phonemes, that letters represent those speech sounds, and that words can be decoded by matching symbol to sound.

Appropriate activities at the pre-alphabetic level include phonological awareness tasks (carried out orally) such as rhyming; counting, adding, and deleting syllables; matching beginning consonants in words; recognizing odd sounds; substituting sounds and identifying that a sound exists in selected words (Adams, Treiman, & Pressley, 1997; Brady, Fowler, Stone, & Winbury, 1994; Foorman et al., 1997; Torgesen, Wagner, & Rashotte, 1997). In addition, the development of print awareness includes alphabet matching and letter naming, following print with the finger during read-alouds, and much interactive engagement with appealing books. All these activities develop awareness of the alphabetic principle: that letters roughly represent segments of one's own speech.

Novice or Early Alphabetic Reading

To progress in reading, children must develop the insight that alphabet letters represent abstract speech segments (phonemes) and must be able to compare the likeness and difference of similar-sounding words (Liberman, Shankweiler, & Liberman, 1989). Children begin to spell a few salient consonants in words when

Reprinted with permission from the Spring/Summer, 1998, issue of the *American Educator,* the quarterly journal of the American Federation of Teachers.

they write (KR/car; I L T G (I like to go); I LIK LAFFZ (I like elephants). Letter sounds and letter names such as /w/ and "Y", and /y/ and "U" may be confused. At this juncture, teaching affects the development of decoding strategies (Tunmer & Chapman, 1996); children may not develop the habit of sounding a word out unless they are taught how and are given sufficient practice. Instead, they may learn to rely excessively on pictures or context to decipher the pronunciation of unfamiliar words, a habit of doubtful utility (Adams, 1990; Iversen & Tunmer, 1993)[1]

Once an association between sound and letter(s) is taught, children need cumulative practice building words with letters they know. Systematic programs begin with a limited set of sound-symbol correspondences—a few consonants (b, f, h, j, k, m, p, t) and one or two vowels (ā, i)—so that words can be built right away. Other consonants and vowels are added gradually to those already known. Vowels may be represented in a different color. Coupled with practice dividing words into phonemes and blending them back into wholes, children can build words with letter cards and play "chaining" games in which one sound is changed at a time to make a new word (*hat, bat, bit, hit, him, hip, hap, map*). The core activity in systematic, explicit decoding instruction is blending single sounds into words. After the children have learned a few sound-letter correspondences through a rhyme or other mnemonic, blending proceeds sequentially:

T.	(Writing letter <u>h</u> on the board.) What's the sound?
S.	/h/
T.	(Writing letter <u>a</u> on the board.) What's the sound?
S.	/ā/
T.	Blend it. (Sweeping hand under the letters.)
S.	/hā/
T.	(Writing letter <u>t</u> on the board.) What's the sound?
S.	/t/
T.	Blend it. (Sweeping hand under the letters.)
S.	/hāt/

After ten to fifteen words with known sound-symbol connections are blended, they are used immediately in sentences. Even if the written sentences are short, the teacher can ask the children to expand the sentences verbally, as in "Mat has a hat. Tell me what kind of hat he has!"

Mature Alphabetic Stage

At the next stage of early reading, children know associations for the basic sound-spellings and can use them to decipher simple words. Well-taught first graders achieve this by mid-year. When associations to letter patterns are secure, children can decode most predictable syllables. Attention to the internal structure of words, in both speech and spelling, supports whole word identification; it is linguistic awareness, not rote

visual memory, that underlies memory for "sight" words after children enter this stage (Ehri, 1994; Share, 1995). As they become more automatic and efficient, children quickly begin to recognize the redundant "chunks" of orthography. Phonograms (ell, ack, ame, old) and word endings (-ing, -ed, -est) are read as units.

Orthographic Stage: Syllables and Morphemes

Knowledge of sound-symbol associations and lots of practice reading contribute to fluency in word recognition. As whole words, morphemes, and print patterns become increasingly familiar, knowledge of these larger units of print allows students to read efficiently and spend less and less attention on sounding words out letter by letter (Share, 1995). At this stage, students read new words by analogy to known words (*build, guild*) especially if their teachers model and reinforce this strategy (Gaskins, Ehri, Cress et al., 1996). Beyond phonics, the study of word structures comprises syllables and morphemes, the units from which our Latin- and Greek-derived words are created (Henry, 1997).

Fluency in reading is gained by digesting many books at the right level—not too hard, not too easy. Authors invented "series" books for students at this stage, endless sagas of boxcar children, horses, and prairie characters that hook children into independent reading for themselves.

Learning to read unfolds predictably.

Within the sequence of early reading development, many strategies for reading instruction can fit Learning to read unfolds predictably: Phoneme awareness, letter recognition, and concepts of print allow a child to learn the written alphabetic code; knowledge of the alphabetic code, beginning with the elemental units, allows fast, automatic word recognition; fast and accurate word recognition allows fluency in reading connected text for meaning; and comprehension is most likely when children can name the words, interpret the words, and employ various reasoning strategies to understand what they are reading. The question regarding decoding can then be reframed: What components of instruction are most effective with learners at what stage with what kind of teaching in what context and in relation to what other components? This, in fact, is the overarching question for the intervention studies supported by the National Institute of Child Health and Human Development (Lyon & Moats, 1997). Phoneme awareness instruction may no longer be helpful for students who can spell words phonetically; word families may "work" when students have the underpinnings of sound-symbol correspondence; repeated readings for fluency may be less effective if students do not know basic phonics, and so forth. Scientific investigation, with deliberate testing of competing hypotheses, will eventually map best practice at each stage. Given what we already know about language and how students learn it, however, what are the principles by which we should teach children to read the print?

Align Decoding Instruction with the Structure of the English Language

Put the Spelling System in Historical Perspective

Our writing system is an amalgam of Anglo-Saxon, Latin, and Greek, and to a lesser extent, includes spellings from French, German, Italian, and Spanish. Each of these languages contributed spelling conventions that within the language of origin were predictable but that violate the patterns of another. For example, *ch* is used to spell /ch/ in Anglo-Saxon words such as *chair;* is used to spell /k/ in Greek-derived words such as *chorus;* and spells /sh/ in French-derived words such as *charade* and *Charlotte.*

The Phoenicians and Greeks, over several centuries, invented the alphabet first to spell consonant phonemes and then, later, to include vowels. The system they invented, when appropriated by the Romans and spread throughout Europe, was used creatively by scribes to accommodate evolutions in language pronunciation and the interweaving of several languages that became Modern English. Our brand of English has at least forty speech sounds or phonemes: twenty-five consonants and fifteen vowels. (The official count of phonemes is different in every linguistics textbook, evidence itself of the abstractness and difficulty of phoneme classification.)

Scribes who appropriated the Greco-Roman alphabet for Germanic Anglo-Saxon words were equipped with an insufficient number of letters for the phonemes, a problem they solved by combining letters to use as spelling units (graphemes), such as *wh, th, sh, ch, oi, ou,* and *aw,* and using letters for several jobs. The letter *y,* for example, has four spelling jobs: it spells a consonant /y/ at the beginnings of words such as *yes,* and spells three vowels—/i/ in Greek-derived words such as *gym;* ¯eat the ends of two-syllable words such as *baby;* and /ī/ at the ends of one-syllable words such as *cry, why,* and *by.* Further, the scribes gradually developed conventions for letter sequences. Certain spellings would be used for sounds in specified locations only. For example, when single-syllable words ended in /f/, /s/, /l/, or /z/, the consonant letters would be doubled, as in *stiff, mess, full,* and *jazz.* The sound /s/ could be spelled with *s* or *c* followed by *e, i,* or *y.* Although the possibilities for vowel spellings were more varied, those also were used within constraints. For example, *oi* was used only when the vowel occurred before a consonant (*toil, coin*); *oy* was used at the ends of words (*soy, cloy*).

The relational units of English orthography—the written symbols for sounds—are not simply single letters. English does not use a phonetic alphabet, wherein one letter represents a speech sound. It does use a deep alphabetic system that shows speech sounds and meaningful units, often in a somewhat complex and variant manner, directly related to the history of the English language.

Teach Speech to Print, Not Print to Speech

One of the most fundamental flaws found in almost all phonics programs, including traditional ones, is that they teach the code backwards. That is, they go from letter to sound instead of from sound to letter. Such programs disregard the fact that speech evolved at least 30,000 years before writing. Alphabetic writing was invented to represent speech; speech was not learned from reading. Following the logic of history, we should teach awareness of the sound system (phonology) and anchor letters to it.

The print-to-sound (conventional phonics) approach leaves gaps, invites confusion, and creates inefficiences.

The print-to-sound (conventional phonics) approach leaves gaps, invites confusion, and creates inefficiences.[2] The first problem with such a system is its incompleteness; it typically teaches only part of the code. This is because instruction follows from the alphabet sequence and the sounds of its 26 letters. However, if beginning instruction in decoding is organized around the alphabet letter-sounds, the identities of consonants /wh/, /th/ (voiceless), /th/ (voiced), /sh/, /ch/, /ng/, /zh/, and vowels /oi/, /ou/, /aw/, /oo/, and /ǝ/ (schwa) are obscured because no single letters of the alphabet represent these phonemes. Twelve phonemes out of 40 remain "hidden" when the alphabet is the organizing basis of instruction. A few letters also have no defined job. The letter *c* is redundant for /k/ and /s/. The letter *q* is redundant for the sound of /k/, and the letter *x* redundant for the combination /ks/ or the phoneme /z/.

The alphabet-to-sound approach in phonics instruction also overlooks the fact that some letter names bear little relationship to the sounds the letters represent and interfere with learning the sounds. If the child learns letter names without a clear conceptual and associative emphasis on the sounds the letters symbolize, confusions in reading and/or spelling will occur. Consider these pairs:

Letter	Name	Sound	Typical Reading Errors	/	Typical Spelling Errors
Y	/wi/	/y/	will = yell	/	YL (will) BOU (boy)
U	/yu/	/u/	use = us	/	UESTRDA/yesterday
W	/double yu/	/w/	when =	/	UEN
X	/eks/	/ks/ or /z/	exam =	/	ECKSAM
H	/aitch/	/h/	watch =	/	WOH

In the first example, the first grader who recently read me the word "yell" as "will" needed much more practice differentiating letter sounds from letter names. Likewise, the children who confused the name "Y" with the sounds of /w/ and /yû/ was unaware of the difference. The child who did not know how to spell /ch/ turned to the letter name that has that sound in it: "aitch" (H). In the phonics lesson, children would not have pronounced the first sound of "laugh" as "el" and the first sound of "fish" as "ef" if they had been clear about these associations. However, such responses are common unless children are routinely and explicitly expected to distinguish letter names from sounds, especially during the early alphabetic stage of reading.

The alphabet orientation to phonics underlies the "word wall" idea that has proliferated in primary classrooms. Alphabet letters are posted along a colorful bulletin board; under each are high-frequency words for which children are to develop automatic recognition. The resulting array typically includes lists of words under the vowel letters such as:

Aa	Ee	Ii	Oo	Uu
apple	egg	it	orange	under
and	eight	is	of	use
away	eat	in	on	us
all	end	I'm	out	united
are			once	
			open	
			off	

What can a child conclude who is shown that words starting with the letter "o" begin with as many as six different sounds, including the /w/ in *one* and *once*? Any observant child would surmise that letters are irrelevant to sound and must be learned by some magical memory process. The display directs children away from a sound-symbol connection and toward a rote, visual-cue orientation, like that taken by my student whose decoding approach was to "look harder at the word." Sight words do need to be learned, gradually and cumulatively, but bulletin board space can be used to better advantage for predictable patterns and correspondences.

How much easier and more logical to teach children each sound, then anchor the sound to a grapheme (letter, letter group, or letter sequence) with a keyword mnemonic (see chart below). This mimics the way alphabetic writing was invented. The sound /s/, then, would be associated first with "snake" and the letter s, and later with the *ci* and *ce* combinations (*city, race*). With an instructional goal of teaching eighty to 120 spellings for forty phonemes, and then moving to syllables and morphemes, teachers can teach the whole system in a comprehensive, clear, logical sequence over several years. Instruction can begin with high-utility, low-complexity consonant and vowel units, and move gradually to less common, conditional, and more complex graphemes. Spelling units of several letters (-tch, -igh, -mb, ce-, -ough) will be treated as the blocks from which words are built, rather than as mysterious combinations of "sounded" and "unsounded" letters.

With the sound to spelling approach, spelling units (graphemes) are used to represent the forty sounds and often are more than one letter. For example, "eight" has two phonemes and two graphemes—the vowel /â/ spelled *eigh* (also in *weigh, weight, sleigh*) and the consonant /t/. Teachers are less likely to try to "blend" /t/ + /h/ to make /th/ or /s/ + /h/ to make /sh/ if the letter combinations are understood to operate as symbolic units known as digraphs. I taught for years before a linguist showed me that *ng* stood for one nasal speech sound that shared features with /m/ and /n/ but was different from each. Surprise: it was not a blend of /n/ + /g/! The word *thank* included this phoneme, spelled with the letter *n*.

Consonant spellings, sound-to-symbol organization:

/p/	/b/	/t/	/d/	/k/	/g/
pot	bat	tent	dime	cup	go
		walked	stayed	kettle	ghost
				deck	fatique
				school	
				oblique	

/f/	/v/	/th/	/s/	/z/	/sh/
fish	very	thin	see	zoo	shop
phone		then	fuss	jazz	sure
stiff			city	Xerox	Chicago
tough			science	rose	-tion
					-sion

/ch/	/j/	/m/	/n/	/ng/	/h/
cheer	judge	man	net	king	hair
batch	wage	tomb	knight	lanky	who
	gent, gym	autumn	sign		
	gist				

/l/	/r/	/y/	/w/	/wh/	
lake	run	yes	want	whistle	
tell	wrist	use	one		

A few orthographic rules or patterns are somewhat arbitrary and do not relate to sound. For example, no words in English can end in *v* or *j*. Thus, all words ending in /v/, regardless of the vowel sound preceding the /v/, must have an *e* on the end (*love, dove, shove, live, give, grieve, leave*). Unfortunately, many words such as *give* are taught to children as "sight" or "outlaw" words, in spite of the fact that they are completely regular by orthographic rule. Similarly, all words ending in /j/ must spell it *ge* or *dge; dge* occurs only after accented short vowels (*dodge, wedge, badge, ridge, fudge*). A word such as *Raj* is clearly non-English for this reason.

Teach Word study Beyond Second Grade

Understanding word structure for reading, vocabulary and spelling necessitates knowledge of syllable patterns and morphology, grist for the fourth-grade mill and beyond. Good readers will learn to parse longer words into segments, if necessary, supply accent, and relate familiar word parts to meaning when possible. Each level of orthography—sounds, syllables, and morphemes—has its own organization, and each of those levels will differ according to the language from which a word was derived. Thus, the comprehensive domain of word structure (Henry, 1989, 1997; Bear, Templeton, Invernizzi, & Johnson, 1996) will be part of language teaching through at least sixth grade.

Learning the structure of words at the syllable and morpheme levels supports word recognition, spelling, and vocabulary development (Nagy & Anderson, 1984). About 60 percent of the words in English running text are of Latin or Greek origin (Henry, 1997). The meaningful parts (morphemes) of these words are often recombined with others in compounds and affixed forms and are thus extremely productive; many words can be deciphered from a few familiar parts. Roots such as *scribe, rupt, struct,* and *port* are each found in scores of related words. For example, students who know that *rupt* means *to break* will find it much easier to add words such as *erupt, corrupt, disrupt, interrupt, rupture,* and *bankrupt* to their vocabulary.

Children learn all of these patterns in a more or less predictable sequence (Templeton & Bear, 1994). Syllables without consonant blends are easier than syllable structures that include consonant blends (e.g., *am, Sam, slam, lamp, clamp, scram, cramps* represent progressive levels of complexity). Patterns within words are learned before the patterns of syllable combination. Inflectional morphemes (word endings) are learned before derivational morphemes (Latin roots, prefixes, suffixes). If word study lessons include a hodge-podge of thematically related but structurally unrelated words (*weather, cloudy, precipitation, solar, atmosphere*), children will not be exposed to enough examples of structural relationships in the orthography (as in *solar; insolation*) to internalize them.

Layer of language	Sound	Syllable	Morpheme
Anglo-Saxon	*Consonants* single blends	closed open	compounds (*highlight; scatterbrain*)
	digraphs *Vowels* short	v-c-e r-control c-le	inflections (*-ed, -s, -ing, -er, -est*)
	long (v-c-e) teams diphthong r-control	vowel team (schwa)	
Romance (Latin)			prefixes (*mis-; in-*) suffixes (*-ment; -ary*) roots (*-fer, -tract*) plurals (*curricula; alumnae*)
Greek	/i/ = y (*gym*) /k/ = ch (*chorus*) /f/ = ph (*photo*)		combining forms: (*biography, micrometer*) plurals (*crises, metamorphoses*)

Teach the Code the Way Children Learn It Most Easily

Teach Explicitly and Systematically

Systematic, explicit instruction leaves little to chance and thus ensures the success of most children. The phonic elements are taught in a logical order, simple to complex, informed by the structure of language itself. Predictable, common correspondences are taught before the variant, less common correspondences. One linguistic concept at a time, a sound or a spelling, is spotlighted in a lesson and constitutes the organizing principle of the lesson. That component of language is then contrasted with others that are potentially confusable (*yell/well; yak/whack*) based on catalogues of typical children's errors (Treiman, 1993). The sound-symbol unit is then read and spelled in words; those words, in turn, are couched in sentences; and the sentences, in turn, are placed in simple stories. Automatic association of symbol with sound is the outcome, the foundation of fluent reading for meaning.

Systematic, explicit instruction contrasts with incidental, implicit instruction. In incidental teaching, sound-symbol elements are taught without intention to follow a sequence from easier to more difficult. A phonic element or pattern may be pointed out by a teacher in the context of words in a book (e.g., find the ⌐ e / in *James and the Giant Peach*). The student would not learn that *ea* is a less predictable spelling than *ee* and would be exposed to many vowel spelling patterns simultaneously, instead of learning one or two at a time in order of predictable to variant. In implicit teaching, the sound stays embedded in whole words, not sounded in isolation or contrasted with other vowels. For example, a student might be asked to infer that the middle sound of *peach* is /ē/ and that it is spelled with *ea,* but for implicit instruction to result in learning, the child must already be able to do what the task presumably teaches: to match a phoneme with a grapheme and differentiate it from others.

The "mini-lesson" approach, whereby a phonic element is illustrated after reading has been practiced, is often incidental and implicit (Cooper, 1997). Without very strong preparation, teachers who teach phonics as a supplement may provide disconnected drills that provide too little information about the system being learned and too little practice with each component. If a teacher runs her first graders through the list *bug, tug, hug, mug, hum, drum, such, tuck, duck, stuck,* and *much,* without ever identifying the vowel in contrast to others, spelling the words, blending the sounds together, or reading the words in books, the activity may be a write-off. If students learn this way, it may be in spite of the way we teach them.

In systematic code instruction, decodable books are used that are aligned with the sound-symbol association taught in the lesson. These books, created to make independent reading possible for a beginner, are a device to provide practice reading words that have specific spelling patterns or letter-sound correspondences and to encourage sounding words out. Many children can retain new sound-spelling patterns only with cumulative, distributed practice. Several recent studies have shown an advantage for early reading programs that include decodable texts (Felton, 1993; Foorman et al., 1998; Iversen & Tunmer, 1993; Juel & Roper-Schneider, 1985), and at least one shows a disadvantage for "predictable" books that are not organized to provide practice with phonic patterns (Johnston, 1998).

Decodable text includes a high percentage of words with the phonic associations already taught and a few high-frequency sight words that make the sentences less stilted. Contrary to the negative stereotype "Dan Can Fan the Man," decodable text can be appealing. Adult distaste for decodable books fails to respect the child's need to exercise a skill: Children want to be self-reliant readers and are delighted when they can apply what they know. Creative solutions to contrived language patterns include interspersing text for an adult to read with text for the child to read, using attractive illustrations, and developing a good story line.

Of course, the use of decodable text should never replace oral reading of quality literature in a comprehensive reading program. Indeed, this is a good juncture at which to point out that, while this article discusses the decoding aspect of reading, a comprehensive reading program attends to meaning and comprehension from the start. Oral language development, vocabulary development, the steady building of background knowledge, extensive exposure to quality children's literature, discussion and retelling and dramatization of stories should begin with the earliest years of preschool. At each succeeding level, students can learn and practice simple comprehension strategies that will help secure their understanding of text. And at every stage of their schooling, children should be surrounded by books and take part in a wide and engaging array of print experiences.

Teach Pattern Recognition, Not Rule Memorization

Most individuals learn to decode words in print because they accumulate explicit and tacit knowledge of linguistic patterns—phonological, orthographic, and morphological. Any audience of literate adults can be cajoled into displaying their unconscious knowledge of orthographic constraints. Ask a group to spell "throige." The majority will use *oi,* not *oy,* although many will have trouble explaining that *oi* is used in the middle of words for /oi/, and *oy* is used at the end of words. Most will also use *ge* instead of *dge,* because a diphthong (vowel with a glide) is never followed by "dge." If a group is asked to read a nonword such as "pertollic," the middle syllable will be stressed and the vowel /o/ will be short. Readers of English know intrinsically that in the Latin layer of the language, the root is usually stressed, not the prefix or suffix, and a doubled consonant following a vowel causes it to be short.

Awareness and use of such organizational patterns, not memorization of rules, facilitates learning; the goal of insight is to read more fluently, not to recite orthographic trivia. Sometimes critics of phonics instruction lament that there are too many rules to teach, the rules don't always apply, or the rules are too complicated to be taught. This criticism is apt if the correspondence system is conceived as a series of letter sequence rules, instead of a layered system for representing both sound and meaning. Examples abound.[3]

> If a vowel letter is at the end of the word, the letter usually stands for the long sound.
>
> W is sometimes a vowel and follows the vowel digraph rule.
>
> The letter *a* has the same sound when followed by *1, w,* and *u.*

These observations, among many others, obscure what is at work in speech-to-print correspondence and are not what children should be asked to learn. With reference to the first of these "rules," children can simply sort, read, and spell groups of words that share a single-letter, long-vowel spelling: *me, he, she, we, be; go, so, no,* and *yo-yo.* With reference to the second, the letter W is never a vowel; it is used in vowel digraphs *aw, ow, ew.* As for the third, it makes more sense to explain that *aw* and *au* are two spellings for /aw/ and give students practice sorting, reading, and writing many examples to discover the system. *Au* is used internally in a syllable (*applaud, laundry, taut*), and *aw* is used in word-final position and before word-final /n/ and /l/ (*saw, thaw; brawn, brawl; drawn, drawl*). Part of teaching decoding well is to select what is useful, understandable, and applicable and represent it as directly and logically as possible.

What does worthwhile practice entail, beyond phoneme awareness, sound-symbol linkage, and sound blending? Many teaching strategies apply. Words can be analyzed in a student-teacher dialogue so that their structures are discovered and then generalized to new words; patterns may be sorted so that groups of words are compared and classified (see Templeton, Bear, Invernizzi, and Johnson, 1996); phonic concepts may be applied to reading "foreign" words, names, low frequency words, or nonwords; and sentence completion exercises can require students to make fine discriminations of words that look or sound alike in text reading. Writing words after reading them reinforces pattern knowledge. Some children with significant reading impairments need to be taught every code element explicitly, but others will begin to generalize independently if they have a solid basis from which to proceed (Share, 1995). Thus, we teach the major spellings for /k/ as a beginning decoding skill (*c, k, ck*), but wait to highlight the Greek *ch* and the French *-que* until entries from those languages are considered as an etymological group (*chorus, orchestra, school, chlorox, pachyderm; antique, pique, mystique*).

Encourage Active, Constructive Exploration

Workbooks are great for independent practice when concepts have been well taught. They are not categorically despicable, just often misused as a substitute for teaching. Concepts, however, should be developed in the context of student-teacher interaction and activities designed to encourage reflection about language form. The brain responds to novelty and sensory involvement; that's why we learn better by doing than by listening. Some powerful approaches to phonological awareness, for example, emphasize mouth position and the ability to compare how words feel when they are spoken. Some decoding programs ask children to stand at the chalkboard and write words as they are analyzed, sounded out, and explained. Others use manipulative letters and trays. Still others give children small lap slates to write words as they are created, dictated, or illustrated on an overhead. Letter cards can be manipulated in personal pocket charts that are made with manila folders. Hand gestures are employed for sweeping through sounds and blending them into words. All of these active techniques require the learner to select, classify, and consciously manipulate sounds and letters so that more thorough word learning occurs.

Anticipate, Prevent, and Correct Confusions

Sound representation. Organizing and sequencing the content is only the beginning of good decoding instruction. Ensuring that code associations become useful for children is yet another challenge, one for which few teachers are well prepared because our training did not emphasize the specifics (Moats, 1995). Just speaking the phonemes can be tricky. Phonemes combined in words are not what they become in isolation. Coarticulation—the folding of speech sounds into one another in natural speech—makes the identity of single phonemes an abstract exercise for the learner. But the closer the teacher gets to producing a "pure" form of the phoneme, a prototype that can be used for classification, the easier it is for the learner to establish a point of reference. When teachers ask the class to blend "kuh, a, ruh" only the lucky students will recover "car." On the other hand, if they say /k/ - /ar/, blending can result in "car." If the teacher says "fuh, a, tuh" only the children who can already spell are likely to blend "fat." /f/ /ā/ /t/, however, is closer to the real thing.

Knowing the basics of language structure can boost any teacher's effectiveness. For example, let's look at consonant features. What phonics books seldom tell us is that nine consonant pairs in English differ only in a feature called voicing. The consonants are spoken in the same manner but one of the pair is quiet (voiceless) and the other is vocalized (voiced). The pairs, and words that contrast because of those consonants, are:

/p/, /b/	pest, best
/t/, /d/	tide, died
/k/, /g/	cut, gut
/f/, /v/	ferry, very
/ th/, /th/	bath, bathe
/s/, /z/	fussy, fuzzy
/sh/, /zh/	fission, vision
/ch/, /j/	batch, badge
/wh/, /w/	whether, weather

Children learning to decode and spell often confuse these consonant pairs. An excerpt from Samantha's composition in third grade included the words HOSPIDAL/hospital, UNGL/uncle, EFRY/every, and LONJ/lunch. Clearly, no one had been clear with her about the voicing feature of consonants. A knowledgeable instructor could ask Sam to articulate the phonemes, look in a mirror, feel her own throat for resonance, and ask Sam to identify which sound was spoken in target words. Sam should read and spell contrasting pairs of words designed to highlight the distinctions before she practices them in context to be sure the speech basis for spelling is established.

Ryan, in first grade, sat through a well-taught lesson on the speech sound /ch/ and then returned to his desk to write: *Chuck lix to ent some jele and some joclet.* (Chuck likes to eat some chili and some chocolate). Rather than confusing /ch/ with the fricative /sh/, as the teacher anticipated, he confused it with its voiced equivalent, /j/. Ryan needed to be shown again that /ch/ is quiet and /j/ is noisy or sounded, and needed practice reading and spelling words with each of these sounds.

It is because children do confuse similar speech sounds that their features may need to be spotlighted. Accurate word learning requires identification of the sounds and letters in the word. Without such clarity, meanings are harder to learn; *build, built,* and *bill* differ only by one phoneme, as do *bruise* and *breeze,* and *goal* and *gold.* One of my fifth graders, years ago, was sure for weeks that the Gold Rush had something to do with soccer ("goal rush"), a semantic confusion directly tied to phonological unawareness.

To be able to analyze children's confusions and errors, teachers need to know sounds, spellings, and syllables. Otherwise selection of appropriate examples is impossible. Creative but pointless strategies abound, especially in vowel instruction. "Egg" is not a great keyword for /e/. *Edward, echo, etch,* and *bed* are all better bets. Chanting "long vowels, short vowels, rah rah rah" with wild hand gestures, as I have seen, might build enthusiasm but not reading skill. The word "arm" does not have a "long a" in it. The abbreviation *Mrs.* is not a consonant-vowel-consonant configuration, as a national reading expert was

recently seen to claim. And *kiss* is not a two-syllable word. Poor examples arise from forcing vowels into two arbitrary categories rather than teaching the whole system of vowel production and representation. Programs that define vowels as 6 letters are missing the essence: Vowels are 15 open sounds around which syllables are organized. Every syllable has one vowel sound, even though print does not correspond as directly as we would like.

Corrective feedback.   Children's misperceptions can often be resolved quickly and effectively if feedback leads to insight about how language works. Targeted feedback, however, requires understanding of language and confidence that, armed with good strategies, children can figure out new words. If a child reads "net" and the word is "neat," the first comment from the teacher might be "ea says /e/ in this word; now try to blend it." Such feedback supports the learner and reinforces the idea that sounding out is generally possible if context is used as a backup. Asking children to say the letters they see, refer to a keyword mnemonic for a sound, or recognize a familiar part of a word (*eat* in *neat*) all reinforce the habit of looking carefully at words before guessing or skipping.

The Current Trend

One of the most ironic consequences of the current trend in publishing is the reappearance of workbooks and readers intended to "supplement" whole-language classroom reading programs. The original design of many programs omitted or obscured instruction in phoneme awareness, letter recognition, sound-symbol association, blending and word attack, spelling, and the application of phonics in reading decodable text. Millions of dollars were invested by schools in the literature-based basals of the early 1990s and they will not be discarded lightly. Districts will be tempted to spend money on gap-filling phonics, phoneme awareness, and spelling kits that will have to be taught as separate components of a language arts block rather than as integrated parts of a coherent lesson. Fragmentation of instruction is a likely consequence—the very problem that whole-language programs were designed to combat.

One of the consequences of fragmentation in lesson design and curriculum is inefficiency. It will take longer to teach children what they need to learn; it will be less likely that all children who are capable will learn to read well. Although needed skills may be addressed if combinations of core programs and their supplements are used, the whole process may take longer than necessary and result in superficial learning. Better results are obtained if the necessity of code instruction is confronted early, directly, and wisely.

Summary

Decoding instruction might be termed the "technical" part of teaching reading. It requires knowledge of language, including phonology and the structure of orthography; knowledge of how children learn language; and strategies for teaching a writing system incrementally even as the purpose of reading is kept in focus.

"Decoding instruction ... requires knowledge of language ...; knowledge of how children learn language; and strategies for teaching a writing system incrementally ...."

In a well-designed and executed program, decoding is taught in relation to the student's stage of reading development. The inherent structure of language provides the scaffold for program organization. Teaching itself is explicit, systematic, and connected to meaning. It respects the ways that children learn language, through active extraction of patterns and successive approximations. Selected linguistic elements are highlighted in a lesson. The lesson teaches a sound-symbol pattern within the context of many examples applied to reading and writing single words, sentences, and texts. Blending sounds in words is emphasized.

Students learn to rely on what they know about speech-print connections. They develop fluency and independence in word recognition with sufficient practice. Instruction in component skills, practice applying those skills in controlled texts, and reinforcement in games and workshops is balanced with listening to and reading literature of all kinds.

If they are taught with care, children can gain sufficient reading skill by the end of first grade to read many books independently. Competence is reinforcing; those who can read are more likely to read. Those who do read are more likely to be educated. And therein lies our responsibility: to teach with knowledge, skill, and artistry the alphabetic invention that makes all this possible.

Notes

1. Once words are pronounced, meaning must be attached. The process of word identification is supported by sound-symbol decoding; the process of learning a word's meaning is supported by contextual analysis.
2. A point developed in great detail by Dianne McGuinness (1997).
3. These are from Lapp & Flood, but many others can be found.

References

Adams, M. (1990) *Beginning to read: Thinking and learning about print.* Cambridge, MA: MIT Press.

Adams, M., Treiman, R. & Pressley, M. (1997). Reading, writing, and literacy. In I. E. Sigel and K. A. Renninger, eds., *Handbook of Child Psychology, 5th edition, Vol 4: Child Psychology in Practice.* (pp. 275–355). New York: Wiley.

Bear, D. R., Templeton, S., Invernizzi, M., & Johnston, F. (1996). *Words their way: Word study for phonics, vocabulary, and spelling instruction.* Englewood Cliffs, NJ: Merrill.

Brady, S., Fowler, A., Stone, B., & Winbury, N. (1994). Training phonological awareness: A study with inner-city kindergarten children. *Annals of Dyslexia, 44,* 26–102.

Chall, J. (1983). *Stages of reading development.* New York: McGraw-Hill.

Cooper, J. D. (1997). *Literacy: Helping children construct meaning.* Boston: Houghton Mifflin.

Cunningham, A. E. & Stanovich, K. E. (1997) Early reading acquisition and its relation to reading experience and ability ten years later. *Developmental Psychology,* 33 (6), 934–945.

Ehri, L. (1994). Development of the ability to read words: Update. In R. Ruddell, M. Ruddell, & H. Singer (eds.), *Theoretical models and processes of reading* (4th ed., pp. 323–358). Newark, DE: International Reading Association.

Felton, R. H. (1993). Effects of instruction on the decoding skills of children with phonological processing problems. *Journal of Learning Disabilities, 26,* 583–589.

Fletcher, J. & Lyon, R. (1998). Reading: A research-based approach. In W. Evers (Ed.), *What's Gone Wrong in America's Classrooms* (pp. 49–90). Stanford, CA: Hoover Institution Press.

Foorman, B. R., Francis, D. J., Fletcher, J. M., Schatschneider, C., & Mehta, P. (1998). The role of instruction in learning to read: Preventing reading failure in at-risk children. *Journal of Educational Psychology,* 90, 1–15.

Foorman, B.R., Francis, D. J., Shaywitz, S. E., Shaywitz, B. A., & Fletcher, J. M. (1997). The case for early reading intervention. In B. Blachman (ed.) *Foundations of reading acquisition and dyslexia* (pp. 243–264). Mahwah, NJ: Lawrence Erlbaum.

Gaskins, I., Ehri, L., Cress, C., O'Hara, C. & Donnelly, K. (1996). Procedures for word learning: Making discoveries about words. *The Reading Teacher, 50,* 312–327.

Gough, P. Juel, C. & Griffith, P. (1992). Reading, spelling, and the orthographic cipher. In P. Gough, L. Ehri, & R. Treiman (eds.), *Reading Acquisition* (pp. 35–48). Hillsdale, NJ: Lawrence Erlbaum.

Henry, M. (1989). Children's word structure knowledge: Implications for decoding and spelling instruction. *Reading and Writing: An Interdisciplinary Journal, 2,* 135–152.

Henry, M. (1997). The decoding/ spelling continuum: Integrated decoding and spelling instruction from preschool to early secondary school. *Dyslexia, 3,* 178–189.

Iversen, S. & Tunmer, W. (1993). Phonological processing skills and the Reading Recovery program. *Journal of Educational Psychology, 85*, 112–126.

Johnston, F. R. (1998) The reader, the text, and the task: Learning words in first grade. *The Reading Teacher, 51*, 666–675.

Juel, C. (1988). Learning to read and write: A longitudinal study of 54 children from first through fourth grades. *Journal of Educational Psychology, 80*, 437–447.

Juel, C. & Roper-Schneider, D. (1985). The influence of basal readers on first grade reading. *Reading Research Quarterly, 20*, 134–152.

Lapp, D. & Flood, J. 1992. *Teaching reading to every child,* 3rd ed. New York: Macmillan.

Liberman, I. Y., Shankweiler, D., & Liberman, A. M. (1989). The alphabetic principle and learning to read. In D. Shankweiler & I. Y. Liberman (eds.), *Phonology and reading disability: Solving the reading puzzle* (IARLD Research Monograph Series). Ann Arbor: University of Michigan Press.

Lyon, G. R. (1998). Why learning to read is not a natural process. *Educational Leadership,* March, 14–18.

Lyon, G. R. & Moats, L. C. (1997). Critical conceptual and methodological considerations in reading intervention research. *Journal of Learning Disabilities,* 30, 578–588.

McGuinness, D. (1997). *Why our children can't read and what we can do about it.* New York: The Free Press.

Moats, L. C. (1995) The missing foundation in teacher preparation. *American Educator,* 19, 9, 43–51.

Nagy, W. E. & Anderson, R. C. (1984). How many words are there in printed school English? *Reading Research Quarterly, 19*, 304–330.

Rack, J., Snowling, M., & Olson, R. (1992). The nonword reading deficit in developmental dyslexia: A review. *Reading Research Quarterly, 27*, 28–53.

Share, D. (1995). Phonological recoding and self-teaching: Sine qua non of reading acquisition. *Cognition,* 55, 151–218.

Snow, C.E., Burns, S. M., & Griffin, P. (eds.) 1998. *Preventing Reading Difficulties in Young Children.* Washington, D.C.: National Academy Press.

Stanovich, K. & Siegel, L. S. (1994). The phenotypic performance profile of reading-disabled children: A regression-based test of the phonological-core variable-difference model. Journal of Educational Psychology, 86, 24–53.

Templeton, S. & Bear, D. (1992). Teaching the lexicon to read and spell. In S. Templeton and D. Bear (eds.), *Development of orthographic knowledge and the foundations of literacy: A memorial Festschrift for Edmund H. Henderson* (pp. 333–352). Hillsdale, NJ: Lawrence Erlbaum.

Torgesen, J. K., Wagner, R., & Rashotte, C. (1997) Approaches to the prevention and remediation of phonologically based reading disabilities. In B. Blachman (ed.), *Foundations of Reading Acquisition and Dyslexia: Implications for Early Intervention.* (pp. 287–304) Mahwah, NJ: Lawrence Erlbaum.

Treiman, R. (1993). *Beginning to spell.* New York: Oxford University Press.

Tunmer, W. & Chapman, J. (1996) Language prediction skill, phonological reading ability, and beginning reading. In C. Hulme & R. M. Joshi (eds.), *Reading and Spelling: Development and Disorder.* Mahwah, NJ: Lawrence Erlbaum Associates.

Wagner, R. & Barker, T. (1994). The development of orthographic processing ability. In V. Berninger (ed.), *The varieties of orthographic knowledge I: Theoretical and developmental issues* (pp. 243–276). Dordrecht, The Netherlands: Kluwer.

Vellutino, F. R., Scanlon, D. M., & Sipay, E. R. (1997). Toward distinguishing between cognitive and experiential deficits as primary sources of difficulty in learning to read: The importance of early intervention in diagnosing specific reading disability. In B. Blachman (ed.), *Foundations of reading acquisition and dyslexia* (pp. 347–379). Mahwah, NJ: Lawrence Erlbaum.

Invention, Convention, and Intervention: Invented Spelling and the Teacher's Role

Lawrence R. Sipe
University of Pennsylvania

The following two vignettes of first-grade children and their writing are used to indicate subtle confusions and tensions that seem to be present in both teachers' and children's ideas about early attempts to spell. All names are pseudonyms.

Kelly is in first grade and is receiving individual help in reading. She's doing very well, and her reading teacher thinks that she is probably functioning in the average range of her fellow classmates, but Kelly's classroom teacher disagrees. She shows the reading teacher Kelly's classroom journal, and the two teachers confer. It seems Kelly is able to spell many words on her own when she writes with her reading teacher, but the same words are not spelled conventionally in her journal. The reading teacher decides to talk to Kelly about this. The next time Kelly comes to her lesson, she places her classroom journal and her writing folder side by side. "Kelly," she says, "you spelled all these words correctly when you were with me, but look at your journal—you spelled them any which way in here. Why?" Kelly shrugs her shoulders. "My teacher gives me a break— she just wants me to come close."

Fred chews thoughtfully on his pencil as he tries to encode the word *down*. For the past 30 minutes, he has been deeply engaged in writing the sentence "Bats hang upside down" following a group lesson about bats. The process has been full of signs of metacognition, as he thinks aloud, rereads his message, evaluates it, and changes it when it doesn't match what he has in mind. He's justifiably proud of his effort, and beckons to his teacher, reading the sentence to her. She praises his efforts, and asks him if he could write one more thing about bats. He immediately thinks of writing, "Bats sleep in the daytime," while the teacher moves on to another child. He copies *bats* from his previous sentence. Then, while saying "bats sleep" to himself, he writes a *B* and a *T*, followed by a series of scribbles and letter-like shapes,

ending with a backwards *N,* a lowercase *n,* and a *Y.* This is done very quickly, with no sounding out or apparent subvocalization. He calls his teacher again, and the following exchange occurs:

Fred	Mrs. Myron, I'm done. "Bats hang upside down."
Teacher	What else did you write? You have two things. What does the other thing say?
F.	This one? Bats hang up—I mean Bats...sleep...in...the day...time (pointing to the words and the scribbles in the second sentence).
T.	Good. You wrote two things down.

Then something very interesting happens:

Fred	I didn't get this right, did I? (pointing to the second sentence)
Teacher	What didn't you get right?
F.	Words.
T.	Did you get some of it right?
F.	Yeah.
F.	Well, You just need to get as many right as you can. You don't need to spell all of these words yet. When you do, then you'll get 'em all right, but right now I just want you to get as many right as you can. Good for you. You did a good job.

What is happening in these two situations?

Kelly had mistakenly concluded that her classroom teacher's expectations were not the same as those of her reading teacher; "coming close" was good enough, even when she knew how to spell the word. Fred was demonstrating a form of mature metacognitive self-evaluation. He knew that what he had written was nonsense; he wasn't satisfied with it, and in his own way he let the teacher know. Fred was self-aware to the point of being able to realistically evaluate his writing, isolating the sentence in which he had merely pretended to write.

In this article, I argue that we need to look closely at children's emerging capacities as writers, focusing especially on the issue of invented (or temporary) spelling, and its use and misuse in classroom practice. In order to understand the current situation, we need to examine the history of the concept of invented spelling and its theoretical underpinnings in the general context of the paradigm of emergent literacy. We need to deal with perceived tensions between the honoring of children's approximations and our desire to assist them in making the transition to conventional literacy. In the second part of the article, I describe in detail several teacher interventions that both honor children's attempts and actively assist them in their journey to becoming more mature readers and writers.

The Concept of Invented Spelling

The idea that children achieve mastery of the conventional forms of literacy through gradual and successive approximations is one of the most important concepts in the emergent literacy model. Invented spelling is an elegant example of this approximation (DeFord, 1980). Discussions of invented spelling often begin with the seminal work of Charles Read (1971), who examined preschool children who constructed their own spellings of words before they received formal instruction. Longitudinal case studies of children's writing (Bissex, 1980) found that spelling progressed from scribbles to letter-like shapes to sequences of letters. When the alphabetic principle was grasped, children often encoded words by their initial consonants, followed by ending sounds. Medical sounds were the last to be heard and encoded. The whole process seemed to be like a camera lens coming very slowly into focus, as the spellings gradually came closer to conventional forms. Such research showed that, contrary to the behaviorist view that incorrect spellings contributed to confusion and the formation of bad habits, children's attempts at writing were evidence of the active process of meaning making that had sustained them when they had learned spoken language (Temple, Nathan, & Burris, 1982). Parents had responded to their meaning when they had asked for "wa-wa," ignoring the incorrect pronunciation; in a similar way, researchers argue that children's incorrect spellings should be seen in a developmental light as well. Just as children had eventually learned correct syntax and articulation of oral language, they would gradually self-construct the generative rules which would lead them into more mature and conventional uses of written language.

Spelling errors ... provided a window on the process children were engaged in ....

From this perspective, spelling errors made during the process of writing were not viewed as impediments to learning, but as opportunities for the observant teacher to notice how children were making sense of sound-letter relationships. They provided a window on the process children were engaged in, and they could be analyzed: A child's spelling of *monster* as "MSTR" tells us about the sophistication of that child's understanding of the way words work (Henderson, 1980). In a parallel way, children's miscues in reading were valued as indications of their attempts at using visual, semantic, and syntactic information and integrating this information to make meaning. The miscues could be analyzed to gain insight on children's internal theories of reading (Goodman, 1969).

Accentuating the positive qualities of children's attempts at meaning making and communication, whether in reading or writing, is another of the major legacies of the paradigm shift from a readiness model to an emergent model of literacy. Researchers and teachers let children show what they could do and what they did know rather than what they had not yet mastered. Clark's (1988) research indicated that children's writing and the ability to spell regularly are developed by invented spelling. Closely connected to this positive emphasis was the idea that children are empowered by our acceptance of their invented spelling. They are able to write purposefully and with communicative intent from the very beginning of school, and even before. They can say, "I can do this myself. I am a writer" (Hansen, 1987).

In reading, the message is not known, but in writing the writer already knows the message.

Finally, by engaging in the process of invented spelling, children discover for themselves more about the relationships between sounds and letters. They practice applying the alphabetic principle and gain in phonemic awareness (Gentry, 1981, 1987). One first-grade teacher called the invented spelling her children did during writing her "applied phonics program." Invented spelling thus assists in the development of reading, and is one powerful component of reciprocal gains afforded by the connections between reading and writing. Writing slows down the whole process of dealing with text, so that children can see relationships between sounds and words more clearly (Clay, 1991a). It is possible that, at least for some children, writing may be an easier "way into" literacy than reading. In reading, the message is not known, but in writing the writer already knows the message. In reading, the task involves going from letters and letter sequences to sounds, whereas in writing the process is reversed: going from sounds (which are already known and automatic) to letters. In this way, writing can be viewed as an easier task than reading, because it proceeds from the known to the unknown, rather than from what is unknown to what is known (Chomsky, 1971, 1979).

Where is the Teacher?

The theoretical and descriptive research, therefore, has been quite rich in describing what is happening cognitively as children learn to spell. What is still lacking is an equally rich articulation of *what adults do* that assists children's development. As Cazden (1992) wrote, "We now know much about the active child, but we still have much to learn about the active teacher" (p. 15). The stage was set for the careful *descriptive* research about children's invented spellings to be interpreted in a *prescriptive* way. The way it was falsely interpreted was "hands off." The message received (though not necessarily the message given) was this: Children will learn to spell in their own good time, and teacher interventions of any kind are suspect. Perhaps the most critical voice in questioning an "anything goes" approach to invented spelling was that of Marie Clay: "[C]hildren use what they know to solve their new problems, and that, young though they are, they form hypotheses about what might work in print. I have a sense that many teachers are directing children to produce writing nonsense and children are obliging them, as they typically do" (1991b, p. 268).

In the last two decades, educators have rediscovered a theoretical voice that provides a way of conceptualizing the teacher as an active participant in the classroom without ignoring the child as the constructor of his or her own meaning. Vygotsky's (1978, 1986) theories came as a welcome antidote to the hands-off approach. Although Vygotsky felt that peers could also assist, he did not argue that interaction with peers was the *primary* way in which learning occurred. Whereas a Piagetian model places perhaps greater emphasis on social interaction of peers (Kamii & Randazzo, 1985), for Vygotsky interactions between the learner and an "expert other" are crucial, and his concept of "mediation" provides a way of conceptualizing a strong role for the teacher in assisting the child in that "zone of proximal development" between what was already grasped firmly and what was unknown. He argued that what children can do with assistance today, they can do independently tomorrow; he described learning in such a way as to emphasize its dynamic process rather than its products.

Yet, for many teachers, the hands-off message remains. We seem to have created inaccurate metaphors, which limit our understanding of the learning process. Newkirk (1991) wrote,

> We are trapped by organic metaphors that suggest that the child's "unfolding" will be hindered if the teacher has objectives for that unfolding. We use misleading metaphors of property—"ownership"—that invariably imply that the teacher is an outsider in the learning process. (p. 69)

When we use organic metaphors, we are trapped into thinking that children's rate of growth is predetermined, as if any attempt to assist were an intrusion and a dangerous action, like forcibly opening the petals of a flower bud, and thereby ruining the flower. Power, empowerment, and "ownership" are falsely conceived as a zero-sum game, where if the teacher exerts more influence, the children will necessarily exert less (e.g., Garan, 1994). Even the use of the common metaphor of "construction" implies the same thing: The teacher stands on the sidelines and observes while the real activity, the real construction of meaning, is accomplished by children alone. Perhaps we need to think more of the "co-construction" of meaning, so that the partnership among children, their peers, *and* adults is emphasized.

The dichotomies we have set up are subtly false, as well: process versus product; children's invention versus teachers' imposition of convention; student ownership versus teacher intervention; risk-taking versus passive reception; transaction versus transmission. The realities of the classroom are much more subtle, fluid, and dynamic than this, and should not be dichotomized in this way. The sensitive teacher will sometimes find it appropriate to emphasize products and conventions. According to Newkirk (1991),

> If we stress child-centeredness and the lack of teacher direction, the almost divine right of the child to choose from a wide array of options the teacher helps place before him or her, then we may appear more permissive than we are. We are often trapped into a rhetoric of freedom that makes it difficult to acknowledge our own influence in the process classroom. By stressing process over product (as if they can be separated), we fail to demonstrate that we expect a high quality of writing from students—and usually get it. (p. 70)

An active role for the teacher is suggested by Calkins (1986), Cazden (1992), Routman (1993), Schickedanz (1990), and Weaver (1990) who feared that the constructivist theory of literacy learning has been translated into laissez-faire classrooms, and who argued for both active students and active teachers. It may be that some children (particularly children whose culture does not match the school's "culture of power") will fare best when teachers are explicit in their directions and in their teaching, without harming children's independence and sense of self-worth (Delpit, 1988; Ladson-Billings, 1994).

Some Examples of Helpful Teacher Intervention

It is important to recognize that teachers' activities during the drafting stage of writing, when children are first getting down ideas, must not inhibit children's willingness and desire to write. How can we help children make the transition to more conventional forms of spelling? This is of particular concern for children who don't seem to be taking on the tasks of reading and writing. If the answer is not simply more time and more immersion in purposeful and meaningful literacy activities, then how can the teacher help? What does instruction look like when both the child and the teacher are active participants? What does scaffolding look like?

Hearing Sounds in Words

One of the techniques used in the writing portion of the Reading Recovery lesson (Clay, 1993) provides an elegant example of scaffolding in a one-to-one situation. It can also be adapted for classroom use during conferences. During the lesson, the child generates her or his own sentence or story, which is composed on the bottom portion of a double page. The top portion is the "practice page," for trying out words of which the child is unsure. After having read the book *Mrs. Wishy-Washy* (Cowley, 1999), for example, Kenny decides to write his own story about it. He generates the sentence, "She got them all clean." He confidently writes *She* and then rehearses the sentence again. "*Got* has a *g*," he says, "but I know it has some more letters." The teacher says, "Let's make a box for it." She quickly draws a rectangle on the practice page, and draws partitions within it so that it has three compartments, corresponding to the three sounds in *got*.

This is a technique adapted from the Russian psychologist Elkonin (Clay, 1979), who developed it in order to assist children in hearing the sounds in words. The teacher places three round markers or pennies under each of the compartments. As Kenny says *got* slowly, he pushes the markers up into the boxes.

The teacher has taught him to synchronize the pushing with his articulation of the sounds. He knows that he has to "stretch out" the word so that he is saying the last sound just as he comes to the final box. As Kenny says the /t/, his finger pushes the third marker into the box above it. "I heard the *g* here," he says, pointing to the first box, and he writes it there.

He then moves the markers down below the boxes, and pushes them up again, saying the word slowly. This time, he says, "I hear a *t* here," pointing to the third box, and writes it as well. The third time, he hears the medial vowel, and writes *o* in the middle box. He's then ready to add the word to his story. For the word *them,* he pauses, and the teacher says, "It starts like a word you know." Kenny thinks for a minute and says "*the*—it starts like *the*." He writes *th,* and the teacher says, "It has an *e* like *the,* too." After

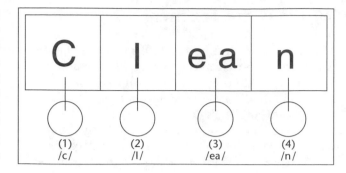

Figure 1   Sound box.

saying the word slowly, Kenny hears the final sound and writes the *m*. He's able to write *all* independently, but needs another sound box for *clean*. The same procedure is employed as for *got*: The teacher draws a rectangle with four boxes (corresponding to the four phonemes in *clean*).

Kenny pushes up the markers, saying the word slowly. He says "k" for the first sound, and the teacher praises him, saying, "Yes, it could be a *k*; is there anything else it could be?" He writes *c*, then *l*, saying, "I heard an *l*, too." Pushing up again, he hears the long *e*, and the teacher tells him that it is spelled the same way as *eat*, a word she knows he can write. He is able to hear the *n* by himself. Kenny has made some links to words he already knows, and the similarity between *k* and *c* has been made clearer to him. He has learned that the way words sound is not necessarily the way they look—it sounds like there is only an *e* in *clean*, but it turns out that there are two letters; this has been linked with another word he knows, *eat*. Kenny has contributed a great deal to the task, and the teacher has assisted him with the parts that are difficult; she has "scaffolded" the task. At the end of the process (see Figure 1), the words are spelled conventionally, but *that was not the purpose of the task*: The purpose was to help him hear sounds in words. In a sense, we might say that it has helped to prepare him for invented spelling.

Most children may not need this kind of help; but without it, independent writing time would be a frustrating and defeating activity for Kenny. He now has a tool that can help him to write. For the teacher to say, "Write it like it sounds, and I'll be able to read it" is not useful for Kenny, because that is precisely what he is unable to do. Children who know this procedure have been observed pushing up with their fingers as they say words slowly, and then being able to write a tricky word. When children have been introduced to the technique, the teacher can employ it quickly while circulating during independent writing time. For children who are already good at invented spelling, the technique can stretch their capacities and help them make links to what they already know. A further refinement of the technique (used with more advanced children) is to make boxes corresponding to the number of letters (rather than sounds) in the word. Children who are ready for this can consider what *looks right* as well as what *sounds right.*

If Kenny were writing a multisyllable word, he would be taught to clap the syllables. The purpose is not to tell how many parts the word has, but rather to assist him in segmenting the parts of the word so that it can be more easily written. If a child is trying to write the word *yesterday*, for example, it is easier to hear the sounds (and represent them in writing) in three smaller segments. Classroom teachers have found this simple technique to be greatly effective in helping children to hear sounds in words and record them.

Have-a-Go

A variety of activities can be used to support students in identifying and correcting mispelled words with guidance from the teacher or peers. An additional activity that also involves attention to syllabication, teacher scaffolding, and sounding out syllables is the use of a Have-a-Go chart (Bolton & Snowball, 1993). When the student is interested in working on words within his text, he gets the Have-a-Go chart (see Figure 2). The chart is divided into four columns. The student begins with the left column, writing the word or words that he or she has identified as incorrect and would like assistance in spelling. In the second column, "Have-a-Go," he or she attempts to spell the word correctly with assistance from the teacher or a peer. As demonstrated in the previous examples, the teacher can scaffold understanding with a variety of instructional techniques, including the use of clapping syllables or "stretching" the word. The student then writes a revision of the word. If this is incorrect, the teacher either refers the student to a dictionary or writes the word for the student. In the final column, the student rewrites the word after finding out the correct spelling. Students should be encouraged to recall the correct spelling when writing in the last column in order to commit the spelling to memory.

Word from text	Have-a-Go	Correct spelling	Copied spelling
Brids	Birds		Birds
Luch	Lnch	Lunch	Lunch

Figure 2 Have-a-Go chart.

Interactive Writing

Interactive writing (Pinnell & McCarrier, 1993) is a technique of group composition intended for use with emergent writers. It is both similar to and different from the traditional language experience approach. Like the language experience approach, it is done with a group of children and their teacher, the children deciding as a group on the message they wish to write. Like language experience, interactive writing places a high value on using children's own words to ensure that the message relates to their own experience and use of oral language. Another similarity is that the message is written on a large piece of paper with lettering of a size that can easily be seen by the children. In interactive writing, however, the children are more involved in the actual writing of the message. The children contribute what they know about spelling and letter formation, and the teacher scaffolds their attempts by supplying spellings and other items of knowledge they lack. Thus the pen is shared between the teacher and the children, and the children do most of the recording of the text. Interactive writing is done for a wide range of purposes. Like traditional language experience, it demonstrates that what we say can be written down and then read, making clear the vital links between reading, writing, listening, and speaking. Unlike language experience, it not only models conventional reading and writing behavior, but also scaffolds children's participation in the process. By actively involving the children, interactive writing helps them feel that they are "members of the literacy club," through structuring an environment for taking risks. Children draw upon their fund of literacy knowledge and have the experience of integrating and using that knowledge for a real and functional purpose.

Interactive writing does not occur in isolation. It is set in the context of a holistic early literacy framework (Glasbrenner, 1989), which includes several other literacy activities: reading aloud, both collaborative and independent familiar rereading, shared reading, various activities done as text extensions, and independent writing. In order to explain interactive writing more fully, I will present a summary of an interactive writing session conducted by a Kindergarten teacher.

The children have been working for several days on activities related to *The Three Billy Goats Gruff* (Galdone, 1981). They have heard the story read several times by the teacher and have also written a list of characters and words to describe the setting. These words have been written on chart paper and posted on the wall.

To begin the interactive writing lesson, the teacher reads the book aloud again. The children frequently chime in with words and phrases they remember. Then the teacher is ready to begin the interactive writing itself, which is done on a horizontally ruled piece of chart paper on an easel that is low enough for the children to use. The teacher sits on a low chair beside it. She connects what the children are going to do with what they have already done by saying that the class has written about the characters and the setting, but they now need to "tell our story." The children decide to write the sentence, "The three billy goats gruff were hungry." What follows is not a transcript, but is a fairly detailed record of the interactions.

1. The teacher asks what word should be written first. The task is writing *the*, and a child comes up to the chart to write it.

2. A child writes *the*, but the *e* is backwards. The teacher points this out, saying it's all right to make a mistake—we just fix it with correction tape. The child writes *e*.

3. The children remember the entire sentence again, in order to locate the next word that needs to be written—*three*.

4. Children call out various letters. One spells *three* correctly. The teacher acknowledges this.

5. A child [not the one who spelled *three* correctly] comes to the easel and writes the numeral 3. Another child helps to make a "three-finger space" at the teacher's request.

6. The children reread what has been written so far: *The 3*.

7. When they get to the next word, *billy,* several children call out *b*.

8. The teacher asks a child to come write "her" *b* (because this letter begins her name). Another child helps by making a space after 3.

9. The teacher encourages children to say the word *billy* slowly. Several children say *i*.

10. The teacher says there are two *l*'s "and an *i* in here that you can't hear so well." (She's already put in the *i* herself because she knows that most children in the group are not at the stage where they use medial vowels in their writing.)

11. For the long-*e* sound at the end of *billy,* the teacher asks, "Who remembers when we talked about this sound?" Some children say *e,* but the teacher reminds them that it sounds like the sound at the end of *Suzy,* one of the children's names. Children say *y*.

12. Suzy writes the *y*.

13. This child also rereads what is written so far: *The 3 billy*.

14. The children proceed similarly for the word *goats*. The teacher assists with a prompt for the final *s* by saying. "What do I need to make it more than one?"

15. The teacher says, "Now we want to write *gruff.*" Several children call out letters.

16. A child comes to write. The teacher says, "We have a problem—there's not enough room [at the right side of the page]. So where do we go?" The child shows where to start a new line and writes the *g*.

17. Children are prompted to say the word slowly. Several call out different letters. The same child who wrote *g* also writes *r*.

18. The teacher says, "Then there's a *u* (writing it). And then finish it."

19. Children call out *f*.

20. The teacher says, "It's Frank's *f*, and mine," (the teacher's first name begins with *F*). A child writes two *f's*, as the teacher says that there are two *f's*.

21. The children proceed similarly for the words *were* and *hungry*.

22. The teacher prompts for a period, and a child writes it.

23. The child who wrote the period reads the whole sentence, pointing to the words.

24. The teacher calls on a few more children to come up and read the sentence. One child makes a matching mistake, realizes it, and goes back to the beginning of the sentence to reread.

25. When she is finished, the teacher says, "I like the way you went back [to make it match]. When you say *hungry,* where do you get to?" Children say, "the end," and one child points to *hungry* in the sentence.

This interactive writing lesson lasted 13 minutes and 30 seconds. All of the children were involved in writing and reading the sentence. The children had done interactive writing many times before; they frequently anticipated what question the teacher would ask next. A number of children had a clearly developed sense of the initial and final letters in words: They could hear the sounds in these positions, and represent them with letters. Medial vowels and internal nasals (*bi̱lly; hu̱ngry*) were much more difficult, as research suggests (Read, 1971). The teacher dealt with some variants (for example the final *y* having the long-*e* sound) as the opportunity arose. One word (*the*) was written fluently without any analysis. The teacher accepted a child's decision to write the numeral 3 instead of the word. One structural feature was dealt with (*s* to indicate plurals in *goats*). Conventions of writing (left to right; top to bottom; spacing; punctuation) were modeled by both the teacher and the children. After rehearsing the sentence, the children were able to remember the text they had decided upon, and rereading the sentence kept this fresh in their minds. Some children were clearly more able than others, but the teacher was able to find ways for everyone to be actively involved and to feel successful. The completed sentence was the first part of the retelling of a story that the children had heard and discussed several times before, and thus was heavily contextualized. The teacher later added a few more sentences to complete the short summary of the story in several more interactive writing lessons.

Linking the Known to the New

A third teacher intervention for spelling is one that can be done with the whole class, small groups, or individuals. This technique draws from a variety of sources, including the word sort method (Zutell, 1996), schema theory (Anderson, 1984), Goswami's research on onset and rime (1986), other research on phonemic awareness, and the work of Clay (1979, 1991a, 1991b). The phrase "known to new" is Clay's. The basic idea is that learning anything new is a matter of linking this new knowledge in some way with what is already known. This theoretical principle of all learning is naturally applied by many children without help from the teacher. Mike, for example, was trying to write the word *like,* and had already written an *l*. He knew how to spell his own name; and he looked up at the top of his paper at his name as he vocalized "like—Mike." Then he was able to complete the spelling of *like* because he had made a link between a known word and the new word he was working on.

It may be that many (or most) children grasp this powerful principle of linking the known to the new. Whenever children "overgeneralize" a spelling pattern, they are making use of this principle. However, some children need to be explicitly taught the ways and means of linking new spellings with words they already know how to spell. The level of teacher scaffolding varies with what the child needs. Here is one possible sequence of increasing support, based on Brad's desire to write *bright*:

1. "Do you know a word that starts like (rhymes with, is like) *bright*?" Brad may need no more than this to make a link and proceed.
2. If Brad cannot think of a word that is like the word he wants to write, the teacher may suggest a word, asking, "Do you know how to write *light*?" If this is a known word, this may be enough of a scaffold to get the child started.
3. Often, children can read a word which they cannot write conventionally. The teacher may write a word, for example, *light,* and say, "I'm writing a word you know that will help you with *bright*." If Brad can read *light,* he may be able to use that knowledge to spell *bright*.

All of these examples show joint problem-solving situations where the child becomes a co-constructor of meaning along with an "expert other." The creativity and independence of children who participate in such activities is not hampered, but rather is enhanced by the teacher's active involvement and scaffolding.

Active Teaching and Active Learning

In the last two decades, educators have made enormous strides in theory and classroom practice related to writing. No one would want to return to the days of delaying writing until children could spell conventionally. Writing without being overly concerned with conventions that may impede the flow of thoughts is one of the most powerful literacy activities for children (Adams, 1990). It has made it possible for children to engage in writing meaningful, communicative text far earlier than we ever dreamed. It honors children as active participants in their own construction of literacy in a way that enables the development of phonemic awareness and fosters independence and control.

Active intervention by the teacher and judicious use of direct, explicit instruction can help children along the literacy road.

But an active child does not imply an inactive teacher. Teachers should be more than just close observers of children, as important as that is. Active intervention by the teacher and judicious use of direct, explicit instruction can help children along the literacy road (Spiegel, 1992). For some children, this is critical; simply waiting for them to bloom will not help (Clay, 1991a). Though our intentions were good, the dichotomies we have created—invention versus convention; process versus product; meaning versus surface features; even independence versus dependence—have probably made the transition to conventional literacy harder, not easier, for children. The metaphors we use—"ownership"; "growing"; "unfolding"—have become traps rather than heuristic guides. In an essay entitled "The Enemy Is Orthodoxy," Graves (1984) pointed out that age and extensive use produce rigid ways of interpreting and implementing even the most robust theories. He argued that the writing process approach was being applied in inflexible ways, and that teachers needed to be aware of this natural tendency. In the same way, perhaps, we need to reexamine the orthodoxies that have grown up around the concept of invented spelling and the way it is applied in the classroom. In another book on writing, Graves (1994) stated that "when first-grade children learn to spell, they need much more teaching than I've demonstrated in the past" (p. xvi). We need to grapple long and hard with the concept of "development," and consider how learning (and teaching) may enhance and encourage development. We need to recognize that active teaching and active learning go hand in hand. Kelly and Fred, the two children whose stories began this article, deserve that clearer vision.

References

Adams, M. (1990). *Beginning to read: Thinking and learning about print.* Cambridge, MA: MIT Press.

Anderson, R. (1984). Role of the reader's schema in comprehension, learning and memory. In R. Anderson, J. Osborn, & R. Tierney (Eds.), *Learning to read in American schools: Basal readers and content texts* (pp. 243–257). Hillsdale, NJ: Erlbaum.

Bissex, G. (1980). *Gnys at wrk: A child learns to write and read.* Cambridge, MA: Harvard University Press.

Bolton, F., & Snowball, D. (1993). *Ideas for spelling.* Portsmouth, NH: Heinemann.

Calkins, L. (1986). *The art of teaching writing.* Portsmouth, NH: Heinemann.

Cazden, C. (1992). *Whole language plus: Essays on literacy in the United States and New Zealand.* New York: Teachers College Press.

Chomsky, C. (1971). Write first, read later. *Childhood Education, 47,* 296–299.

Chomsky, C. (1979). Approaching reading through invented spelling. In L. Resnick & P. Weaver (Eds.), *Theory and practice of early reading* (Vol. 2, pp. 43–65). Hillsdale, NJ: Erlbaum.

Clark, L.K. (1988). Invented versus traditional spelling in first graders' writings: Effects on learning to spell and read. *Research in the Teaching of English, 22,* 281–309.

Clay, M.M. (1979). *The early detection of reading difficulties: A diagnostic survey with recovery procedures.* Auckland, New Zealand: Heinemann.

Clay, M. (1991a). *Becoming literate: The construction of inner control.* Portsmouth, NH: Heinemann.

Clay, M. (1991b). Developmental learning puzzles me. *Australian Journal of Reading, 14,* 263–275.

Clay, M. (1993). *Reading Recovery: A guidebook for teachers in training.* Portsmouth, NH: Heinemann.

DeFord, D. (1980). Young children and their writing. *Theory Into Practice, 19,* 157–162.

Delpit, L. (1988). The silenced dialogue: Power and pedagogy in educating other people's children. *Harvard Educational Review, 58,* 280–298.

Garan, E. (1994). Who's in control? Is there enough "empowerment" to go around? *Language Arts, 73,* 192–199.

Gentry, J.R. (1981). Learning to spell developmentally. *The Reading Teacher, 34,* 378–381.

Gentry, J.R. (1987). *Spel ... is a four-letter word.* New York: Scholastic.

Glasbrenner, C.C. (1989). Elements of a literacy lesson. In G. S. Pinnell & A. McCarrier (Eds.), *Literacy matters, 13* (p. 306). Columbus, OH: The Martha L. King Language and Literacy Center, The Ohio State University.

Goodman, K.S. (1969). Analysis of oral miscues: Applied psycholinguistics. In F. Smith (Ed.), *Psycholinguistics and reading* (pp. 158–176). New York: Holt, Rinehart & Winston.

Goswami, U. (1986). Children's use of analogy in learning to read: A developmental study. *Journal of Experimental Psychology, 42,* 413–424.

Graves, D. (1984). The enemy is orthodoxy. In *A researcher learns to write: selected articles and monographs* (pp. 184–193). Exeter, NH: Heinemann.

Graves, D. (1994). *A fresh look at writing.* Portsmouth, NH: Heinemann.

Hansen, J. (1987). *When writers read.* Portsmouth, NH: Heinemann.

Henderson, E.H. (1980). *Developmental and cognitive aspects of learning to spell: A reflection of work knowledge.* Newark, DE: International Reading Association.

Kamii, C., & Randazzo, M. (1985). Social interaction and invented spelling. *Language Arts, 62,* 124–133.

Ladson-Billings, G. (1994). *The dreamkeepers: Successful teachers of African American children.* San Francisco: Jossey-Bass.

Newkirk, T. (1991). The middle class and the problem of pleasure. In N. Atwell (Ed.), *Workshop 3 by and for teachers: The politics of process* (pp. 63–72). Portsmouth, NH: Heinemann.

Pinnell, G.S., & McCarrier, A. (1993). Interactive writing: A transition tool for assisting children in learning to read and write. In E. Hiebert & B. Taylor (Eds.), *Getting reading right from the start: Effective early literacy interventions* (pp. 149–170). Needham Heights, MA: Allyn & Bacon.

Read, C. (1971). Pre-school children's knowledge of English phonology. *Harvard Educational Review, 41,* 1–34.

Routman, R. (1993). The uses and abuses of invented spelling. *Instructor, 102,* 36–39.

Schickedanz, J.A. (1990). Developmental spelling: What's the teacher's role? *Orbit, 21,* 10–12.

Spiegel, D.L. (1992). Blending whole language and systematic direct instruction. *The Reading Teacher, 46,* 38–44.

Temple, C., Nathan, R., & Burris, N. (1982). *The beginnings of early writing.* Boston: Allyn & Bacon.

Vygotsky, L. (1978). *Mind in society.* Cambridge, MA: Harvard University Press.

Vygotsky, L. (1986). *Thought and language.* Cambridge, MA: MIT Press.

Weaver, C. (1990). *Understanding whole language: From principles to practice.* Portsmouth, NH: Heinemann.

Zutell, J. (1996). The directed spelling thinking activity (DSTA): Providing an effective balance in word study instruction. *The Reading Teacher, 50,* 98–109.

Children's Books Cited

Galdone, Paul. (1981). *The three billy goats gruff.* New York: Houghton Mifflin.

Knowley, Joy. (1999). *Mrs. Wishy-Washy.* New York: Philomel.

STUDY GUIDE

1. Define and give one example for each of the following: phonological awareness, phonemic awareness, and phonics. What are the relationships among them? (Lane et al.)

2. Identify and familiarize yourself with at least five group-based and individualized instruments for assessing phonological awareness. Evaluate these tools for their reliability, validity, and usability. (Lane et al.)

3. How can teachers promote the development of phonological skills in a meaningful and engaging way? Brainstorm at least 10 activities. (Lane et al.)

4. Locate and familiarize yourself with three to five commercial instructional programs for developing phonological awareness. Evaluate the quality of these programs in terms of their potential effectiveness with young children. (Lane et al.)

5. Some people oppose the teaching of phonemic awareness on the grounds that even many proficient adult readers are unable to segment words into discrete sounds. Others oppose it based on their interpretations of "scientific" research. What do you think is the role of phonemic awareness in learning to read? Could you cite relevant research studies to support your position? (Lane et al.)

6. Identify the stages of reading development. Why is it important to align decoding instruction with these stages? How can it be done? (Moats)

7. Give specific examples to illustrate how English orthography has been influenced by other Indo-European languages such as Greek, Latin, French, German, and Spanish. (Moats)

8. Why should phonics instruction proceed from speech to print, rather than from print to speech? (Moats)

9. Some people oppose the use of decodable texts on the grounds that they are boring and senseless. What do you think is the role, if any, of decodable texts in phonics instruction specifically and in a comprehensive reading program generally? (Moats)

10. Opponents of systematic phonics instruction often argue that because English is too complex and irregular, it is practically impossible to teach the rules of the language systematically. Do you agree? Why or why not? Should phonics instruction be done sequentially and systematically or incidentally based on student needs? Cite evidence to support your argument. (Moats)

11. Why is it important to encourage active, constructive exploration in decoding instruction? What is the role of the worksheet in a phonics program? (Moats)

12. Compare/contrast a readiness model with an emergent model of literacy. What are the implications of each model for literacy teaching and learning? (Sipe)

13. What is the teacher's role in an emergent model of literacy? (Sipe)

14. What is the significance of children's spelling errors for the learning and teaching of literacy? (Sipe)

15. Identify and describe at least three activities in which teachers actively scaffold children's transition from invented spelling to conventional spelling. (Sipe)

16. Drawing on your own teaching, as well as learning, experiences, discuss your prior understanding of the teacher's role in an emergent, constructivist, or process-oriented model of literacy development. (Sipe)

INQUIRY PROJECTS

1. Read a summary of the National Reading Panel report online at *www.nichd.nih.gov/publications/ nrp/smallbook.html* and then read one of the following books listed in Further Reading: Allington, 2002; Coles, 2002; Garan, 2002. Discuss your thoughts and reactions to the nature of this debate on scientifically based reading research/instruction and its impact on classroom teachers.

2. Locate two or three popular commercial phonics programs and examine whether the decoding instruction prescribed in them is consistent with the basic principles articulated in Louisa Moats' article. Be sure to provide examples from the programs.

3. Select a random sample of primary grade teachers at different grade levels and then observe them teaching phonics for at least two sessions

each. Compare their decoding instruction with that suggested by Louisa Moats. What can you say about the current status of phonics instruction in the elementary school?

4. Read Louisa Moats' *Speech to Print* (2002). Construct and then conduct a survey of what elementary school teachers know about the phonological and orthographic structures of the English language, as well as about effective strategies for teaching phonological awareness, phonics, and spelling. Discuss your findings and their implications for teacher education.

5. The issue of which kind of text is best for beginning reading instruction has been debated with intense heat and considerable rancor in recent years. Suppose that as a beginning first grade teacher, you are allocated a small budget to start up your own classroom library. You seek advice from experienced teachers. Some of them suggest buying decodable texts, leveled books, and easy readers, whereas others urge you to purchase only authentic literature. What would you do? Justify your spending by citing relevant research.

FURTHER READING

Allington, R. (2002). *Big brother and the national reading curriculum: How ideology trumped evidence.* Portsmouth, NH: Heinemann.

Bear, D., Invernizzi, M., Templeton, & Johnston, F. (2000). *Words their way: Word study for phonics, vocabulary, and spelling instruction* (2nd ed.). Upper Saddle River, NJ: Merill/Prentice Hall.

Brown, K. (1999). What kind of text—for whom and when? Textual scaffolding for beginning readers. *The Reading Teacher, 53* (4), pp. 292–307.

Chall, J. (1996). *Stages of reading development.* Fort Worth, TX: Harcourt Brace.

Cunningham, P. (2004). *Phonics they use: Words for reading and writing* (4th ed.). Boston: Allyn & Bacon.

Fromkin, V., Rodman, R., & Hyams, N. (2003). *An introduction to language* (7th ed.). Boston: Heinle and Heinle.

Garan, E. (2002). *Resisting reading mandates: how to triumph with the truth.* Portsmouth, NH: Heinemann.

Kress, G. (2000). *Early spelling: Between convention and creativity.* New York: Routledge.

Moats, L. (2001). *Speech to print: Language essentials for teachers.* Baltimore: Brookes.

Scarborough, H., & Brady, S. (2002). Toward a common terminology for talking about speech and reading: A glossary of the "phon" words and some related terms. *Journal of Literacy Research, 34* (3), pp. 299–336.

Stahl, S., Duffy-Hester, A., & Stahl, K. (1998). Everything you wanted to know about phonics (but were afraid to ask). *Reading Research Quarterly, 33* (3), pp. 338–355.

Taylor, D. (1998). *Beginning to read and the spin doctors of science: The political campaign to change America's mind about how children learn to read.* Urbana, IL: National Council of Teachers of English.

Venezky, R. (1999). *The American way of spelling: The structure and origins of American English orthography.* New York: Guilford Press.

Teaching Fluency, Vocabulary, and Comprehension

INTRODUCTION

This section continues the discussion of the major content of literacy education, focusing on fluency, vocabulary, and comprehension. While each of the five major components of reading—phonological awareness, phonics, fluency, vocabulary, and comprehension—is important, one must remember that the ultimate goal of reading is comprehension. Furthermore, the five components are interactive and closely related. They are not learned, and should thus not be taught, in a sequential, stepwise manner. Development in one area leads to advancement in others.

Although fluency has recently become one of the top items on the instructional agenda, it is a construct that continues to cause confusion among many educators. The article by Susan Strecker, Nancy Roser, and Miriam Martinez helps clarify the concept. It reviews research on oral reading fluency, identifying factors affecting fluency development as well as issues associated with the measurement and interpretation of the construct. It also discusses the reciprocal relationship between fluency and comprehension. Further, the article describes several research-based instructional strategies for promoting fluency development (e.g., rereading, modeling, explicit instruction, wide reading of manageable/appropriate texts). Various approaches to assessing fluency are then presented. Finally, directions for future research in fluency are identified.

Unlike fluency and phonological awareness, vocabulary has been somewhat overlooked in recent years. Yet, like other components of reading, vocabulary is a critical aspect of successful reading. The article by

Patricia Herman and Janice Dole explores the relationship between vocabulary knowledge and reading comprehension and discusses the role of direct instruction in vocabulary development. The authors describe the strengths and limitations of three commonly used approaches to vocabulary instruction—definitional, contextual, and conceptual. They suggest that no single approach suffices in a comprehensive program for vocabulary development. They assert that appropriate instruction depends to a large extent on target words and surrounding context, as well as on the goal of the lesson. The article concludes with recommendations for future research on vocabulary instruction.

The last article, by E. D. Hirsch, Jr., examines factors that contribute to reading comprehension and suggests ways for teachers to support students' comprehension development. The author argues that fluency at the word and sentence levels, breadth of vocabulary, and domain knowledge are the fundamental building blocks of reading comprehension. Thus, the key to improving reading comprehension is, Hirsch asserts, to build strong oral language foundations, develop automaticity in word recognition, expand vocabulary, and increase domain knowledge. The author spotlights some of the common problems in classroom comprehension instruction and offers a framework, as well as strategies, for building an effective literacy curriculum that can systematically improve students' reading comprehension. This article offers an alternative perspective to the prevailing paradigm of comprehension instruction that seems to over-emphasize the application of cognitive strategies such as predicting, questioning, inferencing, visualizing, and synthesizing.

Toward Understanding Oral Reading Fluency

Susan K. Strecker and Nancy L. Roser
University of Texas at Austin

Miriam G. Martinez
University of Texas at San Antonio

Reading fluency has long been considered a critical factor in reading development and achievement. A preponderance of empirical and clinical evidence supports the relationship of fluent oral reading and overall reading ability (Carver & Hoffman, 1981; LaBerge & Samuels, 1974; Reutzel & Hollingsworth, 1993). As young children move beyond the emergent stages of reading, development of fluency is purported to be "a step in developing effective and efficient readers" (Allington, 1983, p. 561).

Investigations of classrooms and inspections of teachers' editions of reading textbooks, however, reveal that little attention is directed toward helping children become fluent (Allington, 1983; Hoffman, 1987; Zutell & Rasinski, 1991). Calling for renewed awareness of fluency's role in reading proficiency, some reading educators have decried this inattention. For example, Allington (1983) declared fluency "the neglected goal"; Dowhower (1991) called prosody "the forgotten bedfellow," and Anderson (1981) labeled fluency "the missing ingredient" in reading instruction. Our review of the literature on oral reading fluency offers a comprehensive picture of factors associated with fluency development by clarifying and refining the variant ways researchers have interpreted the fluency construct. Additionally, we recommend research-based instructional principles that foster fluency development, examine approaches used to measure fluency, and identify areas of fluency research for further investigation.

One reason fluency instruction has been ignored may be that conflicting views exist over the role of fluency in skilled reading. Another explanation may be the difficulty of examining a construct, such as fluency, when there is no unified view of that construct. Whereas some reading researchers consider oral reading fluency to be an *outcome* of decoding and

comprehension (Gough, 1972; Rumelhart, 1977), others assert that fluent oral reading is a *contributor* to both decoding and comprehension (Breznitz, 1987). Fluency is sometimes defined as the ability to recognize words rapidly and accurately (LaBerge & Samuels, 1974). Others (e.g., Schreiber, 1991), however, define fluency in terms of the reader's making connections between the prosodic features of speech and the prosodic features of reading. Notions of fluency have also expanded to include the suprasegmental features of prosodic reading. In this definition, fluency involves reading in expressive rhythmic and melodic patterns (Dowhower, 1987). Thus, fluency, as a feature of reading performance, continues to be variantly viewed. Table 1 shows which aspects of fluency have been emphasized in various studies.

Reading fluency has long been considered a critical factor in reading development and achievement.

Investigators also differ in their assumptions about the underlying causes of disfluency. Some researchers (e.g., LaBerge & Samuels, 1985) assert that fluent reading is dependent upon the rapid and accurate use of graphophonic information to quickly identify words. Others (e.g., Clay, 1979; Goodman, 1967) argue that readers perform fluently when they focus on construction of meaning using multiple sources of information. Still others (e.g., Rhodes & Dudley-Marling, 1988) contend that the lack of fluency may be the result of factors such as inadequate sight word knowledge or anxiety about reading orally. Stanovich (1986) argues that disfluency is the result of lack of opportunity to interact with print and to practice reading. Responding to the differing opinions about the causes of disfluent reading, Rasinski (1986) and Lipson and Lang (1991) assert that researchers have viewed fluency too narrowly. The problem, Rasinski argues, is lack of awareness of fluency's complexity. He asserts that researchers have "made the tacit assumption that each factor [e.g., rate, accuracy,

Table 1 Aspects of Fluency Included in Each Study

Researchers	Rate	Accuracy	Phrasing	Punctuation	Stress	Expression	Pitch	Juncture	Intonation	Duration
Allington & Brown (1970)			x	x	x	x				
Aulls (1978)	x		x	x		x				
Clay & Imlach (1975)					x		x	x		
Cutler & Isard (1986)			x		x				x	
Dowhower (1987)					x		x		x	x
Kleiman et al. (1979)			x							
Nathan & Stanovich (1991)	x	x								
Pinnell et al. (1995)	x	x	x			x				
Samuels (1979)	x	x								
Schreiber (1980)			x		x				x	x
Zutell & Rasinski (1991)	x	x	x		x		x		x	

phrasing, prosody] alone was responsible for fluent reading" (Rasinski, 1986, p. 3). Rasinski (1980) offers evidence to support the notion that reading fluency is a multidimensional reading construct.

In spite of differing notions regarding the features of fluency, there is general agreement regarding oral reading behaviors of nonfluent readers. Reviewing the research in fluency, Reutzel (1996) summarized the "at-risk indicators" for oral reading fluency: (a) slow, labored pace; (b) poor flow or continuity indicated by pauses, false starts, regressions; and (c) poor phrasing evidenced by choppy reading, improper stress, and intonation.

There may also be general agreement about the period of reading development in which a young reader begins to develop fluency. Researchers who have described the oral reading behavior patterns for children at different stages of reading development point to a critical juncture at which readers' focus shifts from features of print and decoding toward greater attention to meaning and improved fluency (Chall, 1979; Ehri & Wilce, 1983; LaBerge & Samuels, 1985). Chall (1979) reported that speed and fluency are gained during "Stage Two," a period she identified in her investigations of early readers and early reading instruction as a time in which the reader internalizes decoding skills and begins to rely on personal knowledge and use of context. During this stage the reader is no longer "glued to print" (Chall, 1979, p. 41) but rather rereads familiar texts, delighting in the "redundancies of

language and the redundancies of stories read" (Chall, 1983, p. 19). LaBerge and Samuels (1985) describe a similar scheme as the reader moves from "nonautomatic processing" to "automatic processing" when word recognition is immediate and effortless and the reader begins to focus on the meaning of the words. Ehri and Wilce (1983) use the term "unitization," to refer to speed of word recognition. They contend that unitization occurs when the phonological, orthographic, and semantic aspects of the words presented in print have been fully amalgamated.

Although there is some disagreement about the durations and onsets of the "stages," all models suggest that children read in qualitatively different ways over time. There is a convergence of evidence that transitional readers "need to shift their focus from the individual word to connected discourse and to integrate their fragmented knowledge. It is the larger picture that they need help with, in learning to attend to the semantics and syntax of a written passage ..." (Chomsky, 1976, p.289).

Aspects of Fluency

Rate and Accuracy

Traditionally, accuracy and speed have been considered the primary indicators of oral reading fluency. This conception of fluency, focusing on the student's ability to identify words quickly and correctly, is supported by

LaBerge and Samuels' theory of automaticity in reading (LaBerge & Samuels, 1974; Samuels, 1979). LaBerge and Samuels propose that fluency develops as readers move toward automatic decoding, enabling them to read more accurately and more rapidly. They, and others (Perfetti & Hogaboam, 1975; Stanovich, 1980), further argue that, as the reader devotes fewer cognitive resources to word recognition, more attention is available for comprehending text.

Accordingly, as automaticity in word recognition develops, students read faster and have greater opportunity to gain meaning from the text. Difficulty in recognizing individual words hampers the ability to gain meaning from a passage (Samuels, 1979). As a reader pauses to decode unfamiliar words, thoughts about that portion of text may be disrupted. Berliner and Casanova (1988) point out that readers also need to make connections between ideas within a text. If reading proceeds too slowly, such connections are difficult to make. Thus, accuracy alone is not enough; accurate word recognition must be completed rapidly for fluency to occur (Nathan & Stanovich, 1991).

Phrasing

Alternative explanations stress the importance of processes beyond word identification to fluent oral reading. Some investigators of oral reading fluency look to linguistics for insight regarding fluency (Schreiber, 1980; O'Shea & Sindelar, 1983). Modern linguistic study emphasizes phrase structure as the crucial organizing principle of syntax. Researchers of speech contend that the duration of spoken segments is heavily influenced by syntactic structures (Cooper & Paccia-Cooper, 1980). That is, oral language relies heavily on prosodic cues to indicate the appropriate syntactic phrasing of spoken sentences. Drawing on this linguistic-based research, some reading educators assert that fluency is an indicator of a reader's ability to apply his knowledge of spoken language to the reading of written text. Support for this argument comes from research in which single word automaticity training failed to demonstrate gains in reading comprehension (Grant & Standing, 1989; Spring, Blunden, & Gatheral, 1981). Additionally, studies show that providing young readers with text that has been segmented into phrases results in improved comprehension (Amble & Kelly, 1970; O'Shea & Sindelar, 1983).

Schreiber (1980, 1987) proposed an explanation for such results. Schreiber's (1987) work documented that children are especially sensitive to prosodic signals of syntactic structure in oral speech. In written language, such phrase boundaries are not as clearly marked. Accordingly, Schreiber asserted that the "Stage Two" reader (Chall, 1983) must "learn to rely more heavily on morphological and abstract syntactic cues … to assign syntactically appropriate phrasing to the written sentence" (1987, p. 264). Thus, Schreiber explained the development of fluency in terms of the reader's making connection between the phrase boundaries of speech and the corresponding phrase boundaries of reading. Because written text contains only minimal parsing cues such as punctuation, young readers must learn to segment text by attending to other markers of phrase boundaries such as syntactic segments. Fluency, then, provides evidence that the reader understands the basic syntactic structure of the material being read because fluent reading requires recognition of the phrasal structures of sentences. Conversely, word-by-word reading provides evidence that the reader cannot yet organize written code into syntactically appropriate phrases. Other investigations suggest that word-by-word reading is caused by the inability of the reader to chunk the words into meaningful clauses (Clay & Imlach, 1971; Coots, 1982; Golinkoff, 1976; Schreiber, 1991).

It is interesting to note that some reading educators argue that fluency takes into account both automaticity of word recognition *and* phrasing. For example, Bear (1991) views fluency as occurring on two levels, the word and the phrase. At the word level, the reader must be able to recognize words and orthographic patterns quickly. At the phrase level, the reader must have the ability to group words together in a meaningful way.

Prosody

Investigators have examined the prosodic features of oral reading (Clay & Imlach, 1971; Dowhower, 1987). These prosodic features include pitch (rise and fall of voice), juncture (placement and duration of pauses), stress (loudness or emphasis), intonation (voice inflections), smoothness (lack of hesitations and repetitions), and expressiveness (dramatic interpretation). Researchers have documented the differences in these prosodic behaviors in disfluent and fluent readers.

The pattern-of-pitch change that creates the melody of the read-aloud sentence is called the intonation contour. Research indicates that intonation contours yield important clues to the reader's ability to chunk units of text (Cooper & Sorensen, 1981; Dowhower, 1987). Examining young children's oral reading and intonation contours. Clay and Imlach (1971) found that the most proficient readers used a falling pitch at terminal markers, whereas poorer readers used a sustained or rising pitch.

Stress is the intensity with which a phoneme or syllable is uttered, as well as the word emphasis within multiword phrases. Readers use stress to convey appropriate meaning or to emphasize significance.

Clay and Imlach (1971) examined the stress, pitch, and juncture of 7-year-olds. They discovered that the good readers stressed one word in every 4.7 words. The poorest readers paused between almost every word and often stressed each word as if reading a list.

In a review of literature related to the prosodic features of fluency, Dowhower (1987) examined her own findings and those of other studies and summarized the prosodic indicators of fluent oral reading: (a) lack of "pausal intrusions" (inappropriate hesitations), (b) appropriate phrase duration, (c) grouping of words into units that are grammatically and semantically acceptable, (d) lengthening of final phrase vowels, and (e) use of intonation contours. Snow and Coots (1981) also claimed that final phrase lengthening is an indication that the reader is attuned to the prosodic features of spoken language. They found that fluent readers elongate the stressed vowel in final word of a sentence.

Cutler and Isard (1980) likened prosody to a good sauce; that is, there is a "blend of different ingredients, none of which can be separately identified in the final product" (p. 245). Analyzing the "sauce," however, Cutler and Isard identified four categories of prosodic effects: (a) lexical stress within individual words, (b) placement of sentence accent, (c) syntactic structure, and (d) intonation contour. They note, however, that all aspects of prosody interact when the oral reader gives utterance to the words in print.

Fluency and Comprehension

Some educators view fluency as "prerequisite" skill, an instrument for achieving comprehension. Others argue that comprehension fosters fluency. The issue of whether fluency is an outgrowth of or a contributor to comprehension is unresolved. There is empirical evidence to support both positions. What *is* undisputed is the interrelatedness of fluency and comprehension. As Pinnell et al. (1995) reported in their analysis of the most recent data from the National Assessment of Education Progress (NAEP), which monitors and assesses the academic achievement of American students, "A major finding from the fourth grade oral reading fluency study demonstrated a significant relationship with reading comprehension. Increasingly higher levels of fluency were associated with increasingly higher overall reading proficiency" (p. 2).

Cognitive psychologists who study reading, such as Samuels, Perfetti, and Stanovich, traditionally conceive of reading fluency as the by-product of the ability to recognize words rapidly and accurately (LaBerge & Samuels, 1974; Perfetti & Hogaboam, 1975; Stanovich, 1980, 1986). They assert that quick

and accurate word identification is the key to good reading comprehension.

The work of various reading researchers (Allington, 1983; Anderson, Wilkenson, & Mason, 1991; Hoffman & Isaacs, 1991; Rhodes & Dudley-Marling, 1988), however, reflects that fluency results from good comprehension and from attention focused on meaning rather than accuracy. Research evidence to support this position is provided by studies that show that word recognition alone does not directly facilitate fluency. Dahl and Samuels (1974) showed that repeated readings of continuous text produced better rate and accuracy than did training in word recognition. Clay (1985) found that oral reading fluency was more directly linked to text comprehension processes than to word recognition.

The issue of whether fluency is an outgrowth of or a contributor to comprehension is unresolved.

In their study of students' segmentation of written text into phrases, Kleiman, Winograd, and Humphrey (1979) offered research evidence indicating that the ability to read in meaningful phrases is important to understanding text. They claimed that segmenting sentences into meaningful phrases is an "essential step in comprehension." Clay and Imlach (1971) and Golinkoff (1976) also offered empirical evidence that children who cannot chunk words together into meaningful units during oral reading suffer comprehension failure. Explanation for these findings (also offered by Schreiber and discussed earlier) asserts that when readers learn to apply the phrasal and prosodic cues of oral language to written text comprehension is enhanced.

Investigating the role of the prosodic features of fluency in comprehension, Bear (1991) reported that students who could read at a good rate but lacked expressiveness in their oral reading showed a lack of understanding. Cutler and Swinney (1987) conducted experiments with both children and adults that clearly indicated a semantic role for stress in the listener's understanding of oral reading. They hypothesized that stress, or emphasis, is interpreted by both listener and reader as indicative of idea importance; that is, words stressed in a sentence are likely to be the most important elements of that sentence's meaning.

Several studies, however, found little relationship between prosodic oral reading and comprehension. Karlin (1985) examined the relationship between the prosodic features in the oral reading of adults in the Virgin Islands and their reading comprehension. Karlin found no significant connection between the two in this special population. Similarly, Snow, Coots, and

Smith (1982) found no clear effect of prosody on comprehension among fifth graders.

Rasinski (1986) tested various models of the relationship between reading and comprehension and concluded that the reader's automatic word identification, contextual word identification, and ability to phrase the text appropriately all act together to contribute to comprehension. Stayter (1990) provided evidence to support the position that comprehension influences both decoding and oral reading fluency. Zutell and Rasinski (1991) describe the "reciprocal relationship" between fluency and comprehension. Stayter and Allington (1991) also articulated the "reciprocal benefits" for children's reading growth when attention is paid to both oral reading fluency and the constructive nature of the comprehension process. Perhaps many reading educators would agree with Snow and colleagues (1982) in concluding that fluency and comprehension "are linked, but 'how' is still unclear" (p. 170).

Fluency Instruction

In their effort to help young readers move from slow, word-by-word reading to more fluent reading, many researchers have identified various instructional factors to promote oral reading fluency. Different goals for reading fluency and different conceptions of reading fluency led to experimentation with different instructional routines to promote fluency. As a result, these researchers suggest various ways to foster more fluent reading, including rereading, modeling, explicit instruction, and reading manageable and appropriate texts.

Rereading

There is considerable evidence that repeatedly reading the same passage (also called *rereading*) significantly increases reading rate and accuracy (Carver and Hoffman, 1981; Chomsky, 1976; Dahl & Samuels, 1974; Dowhower, 1987; Herman, 1985; Rashotte & Torgesen, 1985; Samuels, 1979). As described by Samuels (1979), repeated reading instruction requires students to repeatedly read a short passage on their own until they can read the text at a predetermined speed. Then the students repeat the process with a new text. Chomsky (1978), Samuels (1979), and others provide evidence that (a) with each successive rereading of a passage, rate increases and errors decrease; and (b) with each new passage fewer rereadings are needed to attain mastery speed levels. Repeated reading led to increases in college level students' fluency, and they were able to transfer these fluency gains to new material (Carver & Hoffman, 1981).

Some instructional models have combined repeated reading with other instructional elements, such as modeling and discussion, to produce growth in students' fluency (Rasinski, Padak, Linek, & Sturtevant, 1994). Carbo (1978) and Chomsky (1976) experimented with assisted rereadings by adding a read-along component using a teacher model or taped text. Both reported gains in oral reading fluency. Hoffman's (1987) Oral Recitation Lesson (ORL) incorporated discussion of text and teacher modeling of fluent reading with individual rereading practice for a "performance." Reutzel and Hollingsworth (1993) compared the use of Samuel's unassisted repeated reading model with Hoffman's ORL for a group of second graders. They found that ORL was more effective in promoting oral reading fluency.

Research has also documented that rereading promotes both the meaningful segmentation of text and prosody in oral reading. Dowhower (1987) reported that word-by-word readers, after repeated practice, read in longer phrases and segmented text more appropriately. Schreiber (1980) proposed that rereading allows the transfer of aural prosodic knowledge to the visual form, so that the reader can then effectively segment the sentence into appropriate phrases. Dowhower (1987) agreed, concluding that rereading "allows a series of approximations that help students learn to operate at a phrasal level, practicing word groups until the phrasing and rhythm sound right to the ear" (p. 404). Herman (1985) studied the effects of repeated reading on the prosodic features of oral reading. His findings suggest that rereading eases the beginning reader's transition from word-by-word reading to more prosodic reading.

Modeling

Research has also documented the value of good models of fluent reading on students' oral reading. Chomsky (1978) found that remedial third graders made significant gains in reading rate and prosody by repeatedly listening to a text read aloud while following along in the book when compared with students who read the same books without tape assistance. Eldredge (1990) also studied the effects of repeated listening on oral read fluency. In his investigation, students who tracked each word with their finger as the teacher read the selection and then repeatedly read the text for themselves made significant gains over comparison students who read without teacher assistance. Holdaway's (1979) "Shared Reading" offers a teacher model of fluent oral reading with voluntary student participation in choral reading. Holdaway attests to the effectiveness of Shared Reading with young readers.

Bear and Cathey (1989) found that third-grade students' oral reading fluency improved when they first listened to a story read by an adult model and then practiced reading selected passages themselves. Coots (1982) conducted a study with fifth-grade students and found that the more modeling the children were given the more they were able to parse text into meaningful units.

Schreiber (1987) argued that fluent models of oral reading provide direct prosodic indications of phrasal organization. Similarly, Snow, Coots, and Smith (1982) hypothesized that having an adult demonstrate fluent oral reading is effective because it "provides a rich model of the phrasal organization of written text that otherwise contains few reliable cues guiding its segmentation into meaningful units" (p. 20). Supporting this hypothesis, Dowhower (1987) found that second-grade students who received assistance with a read-along procedure segmented text more appropriately than did students who practiced independently. Neville's (1968) earlier work also indicated that first graders who participated in echoic reading of a text with a teacher before independent practice demonstrated significant improvement in reading phrasing over those students who had no teacher model.

Investigations also have supported the effects of modeling on students' ability to "read with expression" (Chomsky, 1976; Hoffman, 1987). Students who are exposed to an effective oral reading model of a text subsequently read that text with greater prosody than other students (Dowhower, 1987; Snow, Coots, & Smith, 1982). Attesting to the value of modeling, Dowhower (1991) asserts that a fluent model is "powerful" in encouraging prosodic reading because it offers students understanding of what it means to "read with expression."

Not all evidence, however, supports the notion of modeling as a facilitator of fluency gain. Both Dowhower (1987) and Rasinski (1990) compared the oral reading fluency of students using assisted reading (a read-along procedure) followed by repeated readings with the fluency of students who used only repeated readings. Both researchers found that the treatments resulted in significant gains in reading rate and accuracy with no significant differences between the two instructional methods. In spite of this contrary evidence, modeling appears to offer promise for effective instruction in fluency.

Explicit Instruction

Although few scholars have addressed the issue, there may be support for explicit instruction, including explanation of aspects of fluency and feedback, as a component of fluency instruction. Schreiber (1987) asserted that when readers recognize that the task is to assign appropriate phrasing in the absence of graphic cues, their reading fluency shows "steady improvement." He encouraged teachers to provide instruction specifically designed to focus attention on phrasing. He urged educators to find ways to teach children to look for cues to segment text into phrases, using punctuation, inflectional endings, word order, and meaning. Aulls (1978) also argued for instruction to help children "in becoming very aware of how they segment information auditorily and then to teach them to transfer this knowledge to visual segmentation of continuous text" (p. 283). Reflecting on the results of her study of transitional readers' prosody, Dowhower (1987) additionally recommended that teachers provide frequent feedback to students regarding their oral reading.

Although there have been no experimental studies to date that explicitly examine the effect of direct instruction, fluency researchers have alluded to the benefits of explanation and discussion of factors associated with improved fluency. The implication is that instructional attention to the aspects of fluency enhances students' metacognitive awareness of fluency production. As Aulls (1982) states, "In order to break out of word-by-word reading and to begin to group words, beginners must be *aware* that it is possible to read in some other way than word by word" (p. 348).

Manageable and Appropriate Texts

Reading educators and researchers have also addressed the role that reading material itself plays in fluency development. They have documented the importance of practice in manageable texts, texts that "fit" the reading level of the student, for the development of reading fluency (Gambrell, Wilson, & Gantt, 1981; Guszak, 1992). Only when readers can read the material with ease do they have opportunity to develop fluency. Lipson and Lang (1991) asserted that poor readers especially benefit from careful selection of text to match their abilities, so that they can identify the words in the text without difficulty. Reporting on instructional factors that facilitated prosodic reading among second graders, Dowhower (1987) recommended the use of passages that students can read with at least 85% accuracy on the first reading. Guszak (1992) recommended fluency practice in passages that students can read with at least 95% accuracy.

Reading researchers have identified other textual factors that positively influence young readers' oral reading and reading comprehension. Peterson (1991) and Rhodes (1981) underscored the importance of familiar concepts and familiar story lines in assisting young readers in gaining meaning from text. Zutell and Rasinski (1991) emphasized the importance of a well-written text with natural dialogue for oral reading fluency development. They asserted that young readers need to practice word recognition in the context of appropriate segments of natural language in order to develop fluency. Sloyer (1982), a leader in oral interpretation, outlined similar characteristics of stories recommended for oral reading; suspense or humor and a well-designed plot with compelling characters. Although there is evidence that fit, familiarity, natural language, and predictable characters support, engage, and motivate young readers, there is no evidence that these factors have been of prime interest in fluency studies.

Wide Reading

Although research evidence documents that students who do the most reading on their own are the most proficient readers (Anderson, Wilson & Fielding, 1988; Applebee, Langer, & Mullis, 1988; Pinnell et al., 1995), researchers studying oral reading fluency development have not incorporated documentation of wide, extensive reading into their research designs. Pinnell and colleagues found that higher oral reading fluency was associated with fourth-grade students' use of libraries and daily recreational reading. Although better readers may read more because reading is easier for them, Anderson et al.'s (1988) analysis of data suggests a cause-effect relationship. They assert that students read better because they read more.

Thus, research clearly points to the value of extensive practice (repeated reading) and to the importance of effective modeling in fostering oral reading fluency. There is also some evidence that textual factors, specifically, matching the difficulty of the text with the ability of the student and selecting engaging and appropriate texts, can promote the development of fluency. Furthermore, evidence shows that wide reading contributes to proficient reading, and that direct teaching about aspects of fluency may assist young readers in attending to fluency.

Measures of Fluency

The traditional approach to measuring fluency has been to mark student errors in reading or to calculate oral reading rate in words per minute with graded passages. Because no large-scale norms currently exist for oral reading fluency (Hasbrouck & Tindell, 1992), investigators such as Samuels (1974), Hoffman (1987), and Guszak (1992) established their own words per minute criteria (between 70 and 85 wpm reading second-grade materials).

Dowhower (1987) argues that quantifying rate and accuracy to indicate fluency leaves prosody "unattended." She and others (e.g., Zutell & Rasinski, 1991) assert that prosodic features, including expressiveness, need to be included in measurements of oral reading fluency.

To measure students' ability to phrase text appropriately, another group of investigators asked students to mark phrase boundaries in a text, or they compared a students' phrasing performance in oral reading with the phrasing agreed upon by a group expert readers (Kleiman et al., 1979). Cutler and Swinney (1987) concur that examination of oral reading prosody involves assessing the "correctness" of the prosody with respect to a fluent adult model.

Studies point to three key instructional opportunities that foster fluency development: reading manageable text, repeated reading of the same text, and observing effective models of fluent reading.

Allington (1983) addressed the difficulty of measuring oral reading fluency, noting that no perfect scale exists with demonstrated reliability. Allington and Brown (1979) offered a six-category holistic scale for judging fluency that included phrasing, expression, and intonation as indicators of fluent reading. To assess the quality of fourth graders' fluency, the National Assessment of Education Progress (Pinnell et al., 1995) implemented a four-level scale that emphasized phrasing and adherence to author's syntax. The NAEP assessment also measured students' reading rate and accuracy. Close examination of these holistic measures of fluency, however, reveals that the same components and criteria are not identified at each level of proficiency. For example, the NAEP Oral Reading Fluency Scale for Level 1 only describes phrasing. The same scale for Level 4 describes phrasing, text deviations, preservation of author's syntax, and expressive interpretation.

Rasinski (1990) examined measures of fluency to determine which measures were reliable predictors of reading comprehension and overall reading proficiency. By conducting factor analysis of fluency measures (reading rate, miscue scores, measures of text phrasing, retelling and comprehension scores) at Grades 3 and 5, Rasinski identified three distinct factors of reading fluency. He determined that rate, accuracy, and phrasing measure different aspects of reading fluency. Rasinski's work seems to underscore the need for a multidimensional scoring measure of reading fluency. Zutell and Rasinski (1991) offered a "multidimensional fluency scale" that includes four proficiency levels on the three dimensions of phrasing, smoothness, and pace. They challenged fluency investigators to work to refine fluency measures.

Summary

Oral reading fluency has been viewed variantly, often with researchers assuming that a single factor is responsible for fluent reading. A closer examination of evidence suggests, however, that fluency depends upon a confluence of variables. For example, accuracy needs to be accompanied by appropriate rate. Moreover, processes beyond word recognition contribute to fluency, including phrasing by syntactically meaningful units and appropriate use of prosodic features such as intonation, stress, and pauses. Fluency has been shown to have a "reciprocal relationship" with comprehension, with each fostering the other. Studies point to three key instructional opportunities that foster fluency development: reading manageable text, repeated reading of the same text, and observing effective models of fluent reading. There is some evidence that explicit instruction in the components of fluency and wide reading of many texts may also foster fluency development, but further studies are needed to document the extent and nature of its contribution.

Greater understanding of the construct of fluency will depend upon more informative fluency assessment. Measures that incorporate phrasal and prosodic features, such as appropriate pauses and stress, and that offer the rater consistent scoring criteria, should provide a clearer picture of fluency. Such measures, used with assessments of rate and accuracy, could provide educators with valuable insights concerning which component(s) of fluency require instructional support for each reader.

Further Research

It is apparent that further studies are needed both to define the construct of fluency and to inform instructional delivery. Studies are needed to examine the effect of direct instruction in the different aspects of fluency on students' fluency growth and to identify at what stage in a child's reading development instructional intervention to promote fluency has greatest effect. Before concerns regarding instructional delivery can be addressed, however, the first step may be to develop a measure that examines different aspects of reading fluency. Such a measure must articulate oral reading behaviors consistently across each scoring level. A refined, consistent fluency measure may allow researchers to identify the variables that impact fluency independently, and thus, to clearly define the construct of fluency. Such investigation may also provide educators with valuable information regarding how best to foster the growth of oral reading fluency.

References

Allington, R. L. (1983). Fluency: The neglected goal. *Reading Teacher, 36*, 556–561.

Allington R. L., & Brown, S. (1979). *FACT: A multimedia reading program,* Milwaukee, WI: Raintree.

Amble, B. R., & Kelly, F. J. (1970). Phrase reading development training with fourth grade students: An experiment and comparative study. *Journal of Reading Behavior, 2*, 85–96.

Anderson, B. (1981). The missing ingredient: Fluent oral reading. *Elementary School Journal, 81*, 173–178.

Anderson, R. C. Wilkinson, I. A. G., & Mason, J. A. (1991). A microanalysis of small-group, guided reading lesson: Effects of an emphasis on global story meaning. *Reading Research Quarterly, 26*, 417–441.

Anderson, R. C., Wilson, P. T., & Fielding, L. G. (1988). Growth in reading and how children spend their time outside of school. *Reading Research Quarterly, 23*, 285–303.

Applebee, A. N., Langer, J. A., & Mullis, I. V. S. (1988). *Who reads best? Factors related to reading achievement in grades 3, 7, and 11.* Princeton, NJ: Educational Testing Service.

Aulls, M. W. (1978). *Developmental and remedial reading in the middle grades.* Boston: Allyn & Bacon.

Aulls, M. W. (1982). *Developing readers in today's elementary school.* Boston: Allyn & Bacon.

Bear, D. R. (1991). "Learning to fasten the seat of my union suit without looking around": The synchrony of literacy development. *Theory into Practice, 30*, 145–157.

Bear, D., & Cathey, S. (1989, November). *Writing and reading fluency and orthographic awareness.* Paper presented at the meeting of the National Reading Conference, Tucson, AZ.

Berliner, D., & Casanova, U. (1988). Should we raise the reading speed limit? *Instructor, 97*, 14–15.

Breznitz, A. (1987). Increasing first graders' reading accuracy and comprehension by accelerating their reading rates. *Journal of Educational Psychology, 79*, 236–242.

Carbo, M. (1978). Teaching reading with talking books. *Reading Teacher, 32*, 267–273.

Carver, R. P., & Hoffman, J. V. (1981). The effect of practice through repeated reading on gain in reading ability using a computer-based instructional system. *Reading Research Quarterly, 16*, 374–390.

Chall, J. S. (1979). The great debate: Ten years later, with a modest proposal for reading stages. In L. B. Resnick, & P.A. Weaver (Eds.), *Theory and Practice of Early Reading* (Vol. I. pp. 29–55). Hillsdale, NJ: Erlbaum.

Chall, J. S. (1983). *Stages of reading development.* New York: McGraw-Hill.

Chomsky, C. (1976). After decoding: What? *Language Arts, 53*, 288–296.

Chomsky, C. (1978). When you still can't read in third grade: After decoding, what? In S.J. Samuels (Ed.), *What research has to say about reading instruction* (pp. 13–30). Newark, DE: International Reading Association.

Clay, M. (1979). *Reading: The patterning of complex behavior* (2nd ed.), Exeter, NH: Heinemann.

Clay, M. (1985). *The early detection of reading difficulties* (3rd ed.). Portsmouth, NH: Heinemann.

Clay, M. M., & Imlach, R. H. (1971). Juncture, pitch, and stress as reading behavior variables, *Journal of Verbal Learning and Verbal Behavior, 10,* 133–139.

Cooper, W. E., & Paccia-Cooper, J. (1980). *Syntax and speech.* Cambridge, MA: Harvard University Press.

Cooper, W. E., & Sorensen, J. M. (1981). *Fundamental frequency in sentence production.* New York: Springer-Verlag.

Cools, J. H. (1982). *Reading comprehension: Instructional Implications of SWRL research* (Tech. Reps. 052 and 120). Los Alamitos, CA: Southwest Regional Laboratory. (ERIC Document Reproduction Service No. ED 241 902)

Cutler, A., & Isard, S. D. (1980). The production of prosody. In B. Butterworth (Ed.), *Language production: Speech and Talk* (pp. 245–270). New York: Academic.

Cutler, A., & Swinney, D. A. (1987). Prosody and the development of comprehension. *Journal of Child Language, 14,* 145–167.

Dahl, P. R., & Samuels, S. J. (1974). *A mastery based experimental program for teaching poor readers high speed word recognition skills.* Unpublished manuscript, University of Minneapolis, MN.

Dowhower, S. L. (1987). Effects of repeated readings on selected second grade transitional readers' fluency and comprehension. *Reading Research Quarterly, 22,* 389–406.

Dowhower, S. L. (1991). Speaking of prosody: Fluency's unattended bedfellow. *Theory into Practice, 30,* 165–175.

Ehri, L. C., & Wilce, L. S. (1983). Development of word identification speed in skilled and less skilled beginning readers. *Journal of Educational Psychology, 75,* 3–18.

Eldredge, J. L. (1990). *An experiment using a group assisted repeated reading strategy with poor readers.* Unpublished manuscript. Brigham Young University, Provo, UT. (ERIC Document Reproduction Service No. ED 314 721).

Gambrell, L. B., Wilson, R. M., & Gantt, W. M. (1981). Classroom observations of task-attending behaviors of good and poor readers. *Journal of Educational Research, 74,* 400–404.

Golinkoff, R. M. (1976). A comparison of reading comprehension processes in good and poor readers. *Reading Research Quarterly, 4,* 623–656.

Goodman, K. S. (1967). Reading: a psycholinguistic guessing game. *Journal of the Reading Specialist, 6,* 126–135.

Gough, P.B. (1972). One second of reading. In F. Kavanagh & G. Mattingly (Eds.), *Language by ear and by eye* (pp. 331–358). Cambridge, MA: MIT Press.

Grant, E., & Standing, L. (1989). Effects of rapid decoding training on reading speed and comprehension. *Perceptual and Motor Skills, 69,* 515–521.

Guszak F. J. (1992). *Reading for students with special needs,* Dubuque, IA: Kendall-Hunt.

Hasbrouck, J. E., & Tindal, G. (1992). Curriculum-based oral reading fluency norms for students in grades 2 through 5. *Teaching Exceptional Children 24,* 41–44.

Herman, P. A. (1985). The effect of repeated readings on reading rate, speech pauses, and word recognition accuracy. *Reading Research Quarterly, 20,* 553–564.

Hoffman, J. V. (1987). Rethinking the role of oral reading in basal instruction. *Elementary School Journal, 87,* 367–374.

Hoffman, J. V., & Isaaes, M. E. (1991). Developing fluency through restructuring the task of guided oral reading. *Theory into Practice, 30,* 185–194.

Holdaway, D. (1979). *Foundations of literacy.* Sydney, Australia: Ashton Scholastic.

Karlin, A. (1985). Intonation in oral reading and reading comprehension. *Reading Horizons, 25,* 169–175.

Kleiman, G. M., Winograd, P. N., & Humphrey, M. H. (1979). *Prosody and children's parsing of sentences* (Tech. Rep. No. 123), Urbana: University of Illinois. Center for the Study of Reading.

LaBerge, D., & Samuels, S. J. (1974). Toward a theory of automatic processing in reading. *Cognitive Psychology, 6,* 193–323.

LaBerge, D., & Samuels, S. J. (1985). Toward a theory of automatic information processing in reading. In H. Singer & R. Ruddell (Eds.), *Theoretical models and processes of reading* (3rd ed., pp. 689–718). Newark, DE: International Reading Association.

Lipson, M. Y., & Lang, L. B. (1991). Not as easy as it seems: Some unresolved questions about fluency. *Theory into Practice, 30,* 218–227.

Nathan, R. G., & Stanovich, K. E. (1991). The causes and consequences of differences in reading fluency. *Theory into Practice, 30,* 176–184.

Neville, M. H. (1968). Effects of oral and echoic responses in beginning reading. *Journal of Educational Psychology, 59,* 362–369.

O'Shea, L. J., & Sindelar, P. T. (1983). The effects of segmenting written discourse on the reading comprehension of low- and high-performance readers. *Reading Research Quarterly, 18,* 458–465.

Perfetti, C. A., & Hogaboam, T. (1975). Relationships between single word decoding and reading comprehension skill, *Journal of Educational Psychology, 67,* 461–469.

Peterson, B. (1991). Selecting books for beginning readers. In D. E. DeFord, C. A. Lyons, & G. S. Pinnell (Eds.), *Bridges to literacy: Learning from Reading Recovery* (pp. 119–147). Portsmouth, NH: Heinemann.

Pinnell, G. S., Pikulski, J. J., Wixson, K. K., Campbell, J. R., Gough, P. B., & Beatty, A. S. (1995). *Listening to children read aloud: Oral fluency.* Washington, DC: U.S. Department of Education, National Center for Education Statistics.

Rasinski, T. V. (1986). *Developing models of reading fluency,* Newark, DE: International Reading Association. (ERIC Document Reproduction Service No. D 269 721)

Rasinski, T. V. (1990). Investigating measures of reading fluency. *Educational Research Quarterly, 14*(3), 37–44.

Rasinski, T. V., Padak, N., Linck, W., & Sturtevant, E. (1994). Effects of fluency development on urban second-grade readers. *Journal of Educational Research, 87,* 158–165.

Reutzel, D. R. (1996). Developing at-risk readers' oral reading fluency. In L. Putnam, (Ed.), *How to become a better reader: Strategies for assessment and intervention* (pp. 241–254). Englewood Cliffs, NJ: Merrill.

Reutzel, D. R., & Hollingsworth, P. M. (1993). Effects of fluency training on second graders' reading comprehension. *Journal of Educational Research, 86*, 325–331.

Rhodes, L. (1981). I can read! Predictable books as resources for reading and writing instruction. *Reading Teacher, 34*, 511–518.

Rhodes, L. K., & Dudley-Marling, C. (1988). *Readers and writers with a difference.* Portsmouth, NH: Heinemann.

Rumelhart, D. (1977). Toward an interactive model of reading. In S. Dormic (Ed.), *Attention and performance* (Vol. 6. pp. 573–603). Hillsdale, NJ: Erlbaum.

Samuels, S. J. (1979). The method of repeated reading. *Reading Teacher, 32*, 403–408.

Schreiber, P. A. (1980). On the acquisition of reading fluency. *Journal of Reading Behavior, 12*, 177–186.

Schreiber, P. A. (1987). Prosody and structure in children's syntactic processing. In R. Horowitz & S. J. Samuels (Eds.), *Comprehending oral and written language* (pp. 243–270). New York: Academic.

Schreiber, P. A. (1991). Understanding prosody's role in reading acquisition. *Theory into Practice, 30*, 158–164.

Sloyer, S. (1982). *Readers' theater: Story dramatization in the classroom.* Urbana, IL: National Council of Teachers of English.

Snow, D. P., & Coots, J. H. (1981), *Sentence perception in listening and reading* (Tech. Note 2-81/15). Los Alamitos, CA: Southwest Regional Laboratory.

Snow, D. P., Coots, J. H., & Smith, K. (1982). *Speech prosody and children's perception of sentence organization* (Tech. Note 2-82/34). Los Alamitos. CA: Southwest Regional Laboratory. (ERIC Document Reproduction service No. ED 222 890)

Spring, C., Blunden, D., & Gatheral, M. (1981). Effect on reading comprehension of training to automaticity in word reading. *Perceptual and Motor Skills, 53*, 779–786.

Stanovich, K. E. (1980). Toward an interactive-compensatory model of individual differences in the development of reading fluency. *Reading Research Quarterly, 16*, 32–71.

Stanovich, K. E. (1986). Matthew effects in reading: Some consequences of individual differences in the acquisition of literacy. *Reading Research Quarterly, 21*, 360–407.

Stayter, F. Z. (1990). Talking with texts: Conversations with six readers. Unpublished raw data. Cited in D. R. Reutzel, & P. M. Hollingsworth. Effects of fluency training on second graders' reading comprehension. *Journal of Educational Research, 86*, 3–30.

Stayter, F. Z., & Allington, R. L. (1991). Fluency and the understanding of texts. *Theory into Practice, 30*, 143–148.

Zutell, J., & Rasinski, T. (1991). Training teachers to attend to their students' oral reading fluency. *Theory into Practice, 30*, 212–217.

Theory and Practice in Vocabulary Learning and Instruction

Patricia A. Herman
Kamehameha Schools, Hawaii

Janice Dole
University of Utah

This article describes principled, research-based ways to consider vocabulary instruction. We first review research about vocabulary and reading comprehension and demonstrate that the relation between the two is not as simple and straightforward as it might seem. We then examine three major approaches to teaching word knowledge, highlighting the strengths and weaknesses of each. Finally, we discuss future research needed in vocabulary learning and instruction.

Research Review

Vocabulary Knowledge and Reading Comprehension

Teachers often assume that vocabulary is an important part of a comprehensive reading program because they believe that students who understand words in a selection will comprehend what they read. In fact, researchers have demonstrated a strong link between vocabulary knowledge and reading comprehension; that is, most students who do well on vocabulary tests also do well on reading comprehension tests (Davis, 1944, 1968; Thorndyke, 1973). Therefore, it is not surprising that vocabulary development exercises and activities appear in workbooks and teacher's manuals of most basal reading programs. Nor is it surprising that many teachers direct their students to use these exercises and activities in hopes of improving vocabulary knowledge and comprehension.

Although a number of factors contribute to the relation between vocabulary knowledge and reading comprehension, the most obvious explanation for the relation is that a reader must know the meanings of words—at least most of them—in order to comprehend a text (Freebody & Anderson, 1983). This implies that if teachers want to improve students' comprehension, they must teach them the meanings of words in the text. However, the inadequacy of this view is demonstrated by the fact that several approaches to vocabulary instruction—learning definitions, learning antonyms/synonyms, doing workbook pages—have failed to produce improvement in comprehension of passages containing the words covered in instruction (e.g., Jackson & Dizney, 1963; Tuinman & Brady, 1974). Stahl and Fairbanks (1986, p. 101) concluded from their meta-analysis of vocabulary instruction that "... methods that provided *only* [italics added] definitional information about each to-be-learned word did not produce a reliable effect on comprehension. ... Also, drill-and-practice methods, which involve multiple repetitions of the same type of information about a target word using *only* [italics added] associative processing did not appear to have reliable effects on comprehension."

... only fairly thorough word knowledge produces measurable gains in comprehending a to-be-read text.

Stahl and Fairbanks found that vocabulary instruction needed to include considerably more than just definitions or short sentences containing the word to improve comprehension. A combination of methods may be needed to provide the necessary depth of knowledge about each to-be-learned word (see also Mezynski, 1983). Thus, in order to increase comprehension, instruction must often go beyond the passive, somewhat superficial act of memorizing definitions or doing vocabulary worksheets. Instead, instruction needs to help students develop fairly thorough understandings of words important to the to-be-read text. Several studies support this position (e.g., Bos, Anders, Filip, & Jaffe, 1985, Mckeown, Beck, Omanson, & Perfetti, 1983, Vaughn, Castle, Gilbert, & Love, 1982).

Apparently only fairly thorough word knowledge produces measurable gains in comprehending a to-be-read text. For example, adults have a thorough breadth of knowledge about the word *wedding*. They know events leading up to a wedding and the significance of each part of the ceremony. They know trivia

From Herman, P. and J. Dole, "Theory and practice in vocabulary learning and instruction," *The Elementary School Journal,* 89(1), 42–54. ©1988 by the University of Chicago. All rights reserved. Reprinted with permission.

and folk wisdom connected to weddings. This means that they thoroughly understand the concept of wedding, its relations with similar concepts, and the words that label those concepts. That is, adults have a well-developed wedding schema. Such knowledge extends beyond a simple definition of a wedding.

Vocabulary Learning and Instruction

Researchers do not know exactly how children learn words in the massive numbers and at the amazingly fast rates that they do (Carey, 1978; Dickinson, 1984; Nagy, Herman, & Anderson, 1985a). Nagy and Herman (1987) estimate that between grades 3 and 12, average students gain knowledge of around 3,000 words each year.

Researchers suspect that vocabulary learning cannot be accounted for by instruction alone (Jenkins & Dixon, 1983; Nagy & Herman, 1987). First, there is at least some observational evidence that teachers do not spend much time teaching vocabulary (Durkin, 1979; Jenkins & Dixon, 1983; Roser & Juel, 1982; for common basal practices see Beck, McCaslin, & McKeown, 1980; Durkin, 1981). Second, even if teachers directly taught every new word encountered in a typical basal reading program, those words would account for fewer than 500 words per year (Nagy & Herman, 1987). And, although teachers probably teach vocabulary words in language arts and other subjects (but see Roser & Juel, 1982), it is still highly unlikely that the explicit teaching of vocabulary could account for the high numbers of words children learn during their school years.

Nagy et al. (1985a, 1985b) and Herman, Anderson, Pearson, and Nagy (in press) have documented that much vocabulary learning occurs *incidentally* through reading. Students ranging from third to eighth grade and from low to high ability gained vocabulary knowledge while reading school texts without any instructional intervention. These researchers estimate that an average reader learns the meaning of 800–1,200 words per year through free reading alone.

... much vocabulary learning occurs incidentally through reading.

Teachers have an instructional dilemma. Students' vocabulary knowledge must be extensive and thorough in order to improve their comprehension. However, instruction to develop thorough word knowledge is time consuming and can cover only a few words (Graves & Prenn, 1986). On the other hand, students learn the meaning of hundreds of words each year simply through reading, without any apparent instruction. In light of this paradox, what kind of instruction makes sense for teachers to use as part of a comprehensive reading program? The next section addresses this question.

Approaches to Vocabulary Instruction

The purpose of this section is to describe methods of vocabulary instruction, particularly those exemplified in basal reading programs, and to examine the utility of the different approaches in relation to the theory and research already discussed. Although there are many ways to approach vocabulary instruction, in this article we classify the approaches into one of three major categories:

1. *Definitional* Student learns a phrase or synonym that defines a word. Example: *hamal*—a porter or bearer.
2. *Contextual*
   a. Student reads one or more sentences provided by the teacher that specifically illustrate the meaning of a word. Example: *A hamal, or strong man hired to carry goods, trudged down the path with many heavy boxes on his back.*
   b. While reading, a student learns part or all of the meaning of a word incidentally through using clues in context.
3. *Conceptual* Student learns how the meaning of the word fits with related words or concepts. Example: Student compares and contrasts a hamal, a busboy, and a backpacker.

Definitional Approach

The traditional approach to vocabulary instruction is to require students to learn definitions of words, either by drill or by looking words up in a glossary or a dictionary (Manzo & Sherk, 1972; Petty, Herold, & Stoll, 1968). There are two clear advantages to this approach: A large number of words can be covered, and learning, or at least being exposed to, a definition is not very time consuming. Although this approach is practical for teaching a large number of words, it also has several limitations.

For example, there is no guarantee that having students learn definitions of words or look them up in a glossary or dictionary will improve their comprehension of a selection. Teaching students only definitions of difficult words before they read a selection has improved the comprehension of that selection in some studies (e.g., Kameenui, Carnine, & Freschi, 1982) but not in others (e.g., Ahlfors, 1979; Tuinman & Brady, 1974).

Teachers must consider the relation between the to-be-learned word and the concept it represents in order to use the definitional approach more effectively (see Graves, 1984; Jenkins & Dixon, 1983). How effective the definitional approach is depends on how much knowledge readers have about a topic. Definitions can be very effective in teaching vocabulary when students already understand the underlying concept or closely related concepts. For example, if students already know the meaning of "porter" or "bearer" and they know how these words fit into a network of concepts, or schema, such as "ways of moving things" or "occupations," then a definitional phrase that links that knowledge to a word label may be sufficient for establishing an understanding of hamal.

On the other hand, if a word represents a more complex and little understood concept like *heterodyne,* then providing readers with a definitional phrase such as the following one falls far short of the kind of information needed to understand the meaning of the word.

> *heterodyne:* adj., of or relating to the production of an electrical beat between two radio frequencies of which one usually is that of a received signal-carrying current and the other that of an uninterrupted current introduced in the apparatus. [*Webster's Third New International Dictionary,* 1981, p. 1062]

Using only this definition, could students write the word in a sentence that clearly demonstrates its meaning, write specific examples of contexts where the word can be used (Shefelbine, 1984), or explain how heterodyne is similar to but different from descriptions of other frequencies? When the definitional approach alone is used to teach such a word, most students fail to understand the word because they do not understand the underlying concept, nor do they know how it is like and unlike other closely related words or concepts (see Graves, 1984).

The usefulness of the definitional approach also depends on how much knowledge readers need to have about a word in relation to a particular reading task (Mezynski, 1983). When comprehension of a passage depends on having a thorough understanding of a word, and students lack knowledge of the underlying concept, then more than the definitional approach is needed to learn that word. However, if a word plays a relatively minor role in a passage, students may need to know only some partial meaning of the word, and reading a definition may provide that information. For example, to comprehend a mystery story, students may only need to know that heterodyne has something to do with frequencies.

The definitional approach is most effective, then, when students already know the underlying concept or closely related words or concepts. Then a synonym or short phrase alone may encourage students to make meaningful connections. When knowledge of underlying concepts is missing, learning definitions is unlikely to result in anything more than partial knowledge. Some researchers believe that even partial knowledge may be useful it if provides a base for learning more about a word in future encounters (Beck & McKeown,

1985; Nagy & Herman, 1985, 1987). Most of the time, however, learning definitions does not foster integration of new knowledge with existing knowledge. Without achieving this integration, students fail to understand the word, and comprehension suffers. This approach therefore should not be used as the only method of instruction.

Contextual Approach

The contextual approach to vocabulary instruction is designed to teach students the meanings of new words by having them study the context of surrounding words. Two kinds of context often get confused in discussions about this approach (Beck, McKeown, & McCaslin, 1983). The first type of context can be labeled pedagogical or instructional. This context refers to sentences specifically written to introduce the meanings of words. A second type, natural contexts, refers to text sentences written to communicate ideas and not to teach word meanings specifically.

An underlying assumption of the contextual approach is that students already possess some knowledge relevant to the topic of the text in which an unknown word is embedded. Students are then expected to reason from this knowledge to figure out a meaning for the word. Needless to say, if students do not possess appropriate background knowledge, they will profit little from this method. For example, it would be difficult for lay readers to develop a definition of "heterodyne" from reading a physics text.

Instructing students about how they can use context to reveal some or all of the meaning of a word is important in view of the fact that children learn most words incidentally rather than through any formal instruction (Jenkins & Dixon, 1983; Nagy et al., 1985a, 1985b; Sternberg, 1987). If students could be taught to reason effectively about the meaning of a word from its context, their vocabulary knowledge might increase, especially the vocabularies of students who frequently read for recreation (Nagy & Herman, 1985). However, no research outlines exactly how this might be accomplished. Therefore, as we discuss the contextual approach, we draw on conventional wisdom and instructional research whose aim was not to study vocabulary instruction, but comprehension instruction.

Instructional Context Approach

Many basal reading programs and experienced teachers use pedagogical context to teach vocabulary words, especially to preteach words before students read a selection. For this method, sentences are specifically constructed so that students can learn something about the meaning of words by thoughtfully examining context clues. For example, consider the following sentences: "Mastodons became *extinct* years ago when the last one died," and "The old farmer *trudged* down the dusty road to the village." Both sentences have been created for instructional purposes to provide enough information so that students can reason about the meaning of the italicized word.

Teachers and basal authors need to be careful as they use this approach to vocabulary instruction. Not all sentences provide sufficient context clues to derive the meaning of a given word. For example, a careful consideration of the two sentences above shows important differences between them. In the first sentence, the meaning of *extinct* can be gained directly from the context of the sentence. In the second sentence, the correct meaning of *trudged* could possibly be inferred, but so could incorrect meanings (e.g., *trudged* could mean *whistled, drove, limped*). So, a sentence that provides sufficient context clues for adults who already know the concept underlying a word can be baffling to students who do not.

The instructional context approach alone, like the definitional approach alone, is unlikely to provide readers with enough information about a word to affect comprehension of a given passage, especially if the word also represents a new concept. To improve comprehension, students may need more active, intense instruction in word meanings (e.g., a combination of definitional and contextual information; Stahl & Fairbanks, 1986), more knowledge about the topic of the passage, or explicit instruction in comprehension skills. Furthermore, instructional sentences rich in meaning may not prepare students for becoming independent word learners because most texts do not provide rich contexts. Students need practice in learning how to use context while reading trade books and articles to gain meaning of unknown words. This is especially important considering the potential for learning words while reading.

Natural Context Approach

To become independent word learners, students are encouraged, and even expected, to figure out the meanings of words on their own. Most texts, however, whether they are in basal reading programs or in trade books, are not written to provide rich context for every potentially difficult word but to communicate ideas. Learning the meanings of words simply by reading a sentence or even a group of sentences is far from guaranteed. Even when sufficient information is available, some children do not know how to go about using text information to reason about the meanings of words. Research has shown that lower-ability readers often have this difficulty (McKeown, 1985;

van Daalen-Kapteijns & Elshout-Mohr, 1981; but see Nagy & Herman, 1987).

Part of vocabulary instruction in every classroom should include teaching students the process of deriving information about the meanings of words that appear in natural context. Mentioning that one can obtain information about word meanings from surrounding context is probably not sufficient. Instead, teachers need to demonstrate the process of using context to gain meaning from text (Graves, 1987). One way to do this is for teachers to verbalize their thought processes as they use in-text clues to figure out word meanings, as in the following example:

Text: *One day a wise hamal passed the castle. On his back he carried the furniture of a whole house.*

Teacher models the use of text clues to obtain word meaning:

"Let's see, what do I know about the word *hamal* based on these two sentences? Well, it's probably a man because it says 'he,' although it could be an animal, I suppose. I know he is wise, but I don't know whether all hamals are wise or just this one. I know this hamal is strong, because he carried furniture on his back. But I don't know whether *all* hamals are this strong. Oh, I also know that this hamal probably lived a long time ago, because the sentence says he passed a castle, and so that makes me think that the story took place some time ago near a castle. I guess that's all the information I can use in these sentences. I don't see any prefixes or suffixes that might help me get some of the word meaning. I'll have to do more reading to see if I can find other clues to help me figure out what a *hamal* is."

In this example, the teacher considered semantic or meaning clues directly in the text and from the teacher's background knowledge, considered word part clues, suggested a strategy for finding out more, and modeled an active, problem-solving approach to understanding text.

After the teacher demonstrates how to think through a variety of clues in different contexts, students need opportunities to encounter words in other texts and to reason about word meanings under the guidance of the teacher. Such opportunities require that teachers not preteach every difficult word before students read a basal selection. After reading a selection, students can think aloud about how they constructed some or all of the meaning for a difficult word as they were reading. Ultimately, responsibility for deriving information about word meanings is released entirely to students.

One important advantage of having teachers model how to use context clues to gain word meanings is that it does not fragment instruction by using isolated examples. Instead, students are shown explicitly how a rather complex process works in the continuous task of constructing meaning while reading.

Research on instruction aimed specifically at helping students become independent word learners is relatively new (Carr, 1985; Schwartz & Raphael, 1985). Support for this instruction comes from the work of Duffy et al. (1986), Duffy, Roehler, and Rackliffe (1986), and Paris, Lipson, and Wixson (1983). In the Teacher Explanation Project, Duffy and his colleagues demonstrated the effectiveness of explicit teacher explanations of reading comprehension strategies to lower-ability students. In their project, teacher explanations consisted of modeling several strategies to help students gain meaning from texts. One strategy was the use of context to gain word meaning. Duffy et al. did not test directly the effectiveness of using a modeling approach to derive word meanings, but their findings suggest the usefulness of explicit teacher explanations in helping students to become independent word learners.

The limitations of this approach need to be recognized as well. Not all contexts lead readers to full meanings of words. In fact, students need to realize that surrounding context clues often do not give enough information to infer complete meanings of words (Schatz & Baldwin, 1986). Furthermore, some contexts are "misdirective" (Beck et al., 1983). Consider the following example taken from a fifth-grade social studies book: "In Brazil, the national religion is Roman Catholicism. The religion most workers follow is a combination of Christianity and African and Indian beliefs." These sentences might lead readers to infer wrongly that Catholicism is a combination of African, Indian, and Christian beliefs rather than a major branch of Christianity. However, readers could still infer correctly that Catholicism is some type of religion, even though the exact type is unclear.

When students infer meanings from a text, they are more likely to gain partial word knowledge that is specific to that text and thus are unlikely to develop full understanding of words after a few exposures to them (Mezynski, 1983; Stahl & Fairbanks, 1986). However, even with one exposure, students can gain some knowledge, which, when coupled with considerable reading, can result in substantial gains in overall vocabulary knowledge over time (Nagy & Herman, 1987).

A contextual approach that includes teacher modeling appears to be most valuable in developing students' understanding and awareness of how context can reveal some or all of the meaning of words. Students are expected to construct meaning actively by drawing on their background knowledge, knowledge of affixes, and their unfolding understanding of the text. This approach can play an important part in a comprehensive reading program because it has the potential of helping students become better independent word learners—a valuable strategy considering the large number of words involved.

Conceptual Approach

When students do not know underlying concepts related to words, as is the case in many content areas, a definitional or contextual approach to vocabulary instruction may be inadequate, especially when understanding those concepts is important for establishing or maintaining comprehension. The following example illustrates the inadequacy of the definitional and contextual approaches in providing readers with enough information about the word *grafting* to comprehend the passage.

The Granny Smith Apple

When John Smith moved to Seattle, Washington, in 1895, he found that he had inherited an orchard of apple trees. One tree was different from the rest and bore the most delicious apples he had ever tasted.

John tried to figure out how he could create a whole orchard of these delicious apples. He knew that the seeds from an apple generally produce trees with smaller and poorer fruit than the original. So, he could not simply plant seeds from his delicious apple and expect to grow more apples of the same quality.

One day, John's grandmother gave him some help. She showed John how to put branches from the first tree onto other apple trees so that these trees also could bear the delicious apples that John loved. Branches from those trees were later cut and grafted onto still other trees. Thus, many orchards today have trees that produce Granny Smith apples.

If students look *grafting* up in the dictionary, they may encounter the following definition: "uniting a shoot or bud with a growing plant by insertion or placing in close contact." However, this definition does not explain why the act of grafting branches from one tree onto another produces the Granny Smith apple. Readers need more knowledge about the grafting process itself, as well as other related knowledge. That is, students need to understand a network of concepts, or schema (e.g., to know that when a cut branch from one plant is grafted onto another plant, the branch will grow on the host plant and be just like the plant from which it was cut). So, in the case of the Granny Smith apple, the cut branch of the Granny Smith is grafted onto another tree, which grows a new branch with Granny Smith apples. This important piece of information explains how the farmers managed to grow Granny Smith apples in other places.

Using context clues alone in the grafting text will not help students either. They can probably figure out on their own that grafting is something done with branches and trees, but that information is inadequate for comprehension of this text.

The goal of the conceptual approach to vocabulary instruction is to develop extensive knowledge of a word, which leads to a thorough understanding of the word—how the word is similar to and different from related concepts and how the word is used in a variety of situations.

How might a teacher implement a conceptual approach to vocabulary instruction? The key is having students understand a concept at a personal level and then understand its relations to similar concepts (Blachowicz, 1986; Carr & Wixson, 1986; Thelen, 1986). Following are a series of activities that demonstrate a conceptual approach to teaching the word *grafting*.

1. *Teacher begins with what students already know:* "Do your parents have plants? Have you ever seen your parents put a leaf or stem of a plant in water? What happens to the leaf when you do? What does the new plant look like?" (Note: If students are not familiar with this concept, the teacher can provide direct experience by having students root leaves in water. This activity then provides a basis for further learning.)
2. *Teacher connects new information to what students already know:* "*Grafting* is like putting a plant in water to grow a new plant—only you place a shoot of one plant onto the stem of another plant and you'll end up with a new plant that looks like the first plant." (Note: An actual demonstration of the grafting technique by using a few small branches would help students grasp the concept more readily.)
3. *Teacher leads a discussion that centers on how the new concept is like and unlike related, known concepts:*
   a. *regeneration*—starfish—cut one arm off and the starfish regrows a whole new arm in that place; new part looks just like old.
   b. *reproduction*—need male and female—new plant or animal will look different from either of its parents.
   c. *grafting*—connect piece of a new plant to a host plant—a new plant grows on host plant and looks just like the parent plant.
4. *Teacher draws together experiences and discussions into a visual display* so that concepts and relations among them are clearer. One such display is

a semantic features grid (Johnson & Pearson, 1978) (see bottom of p. 50).

To construct the grid, the teacher lists the words/concepts to be compared and contrasted on the left and elicits from the students facts associated with each word. Together, the students and teacher fill in the grid by discussing how each match fits or does not fit. For example, the "yes" in the upper left-hand box indicates that grafting and "new, looks just like old" fit. Such discussions help students hone their word knowledge by fitting new knowledge with knowledge already acquired.

Instruction that leads to a thorough understanding of words has been demonstrated to affect reading comprehension (Anders, Bos, & Filip, 1984; Bos et al., 1985; McKeown et al., 1983; Stahl & Fairbanks, 1986). Such instruction is beneficial in that students are more likely to retain the new information over time (Bos et al., 1985; McKeown et al., 1983) and to make important associations between new information and related knowledge acquired previously (Graves & Prenn, 1986).

At first glance, the benefits of the conceptual approach seem considerable. However, there are disadvantages to this type of instruction, which requires lengthy teacher planning time (Graves & Prenn, 1986). The realities of classroom life suggest that teachers do not have time to prepare the kind of varied and extensively rich lessons necessary for the conceptual approach. In addition, teachers will not get much assistance from basal programs—even the newer programs are only beginning to incorporate aspects of the conceptual approach (Dole, Osborn, & Rogers, 1987).

Another problem with the conceptual approach is that it is instructionally time consuming. Teachers may need to spend 30 minutes a day teaching vocabulary in order to provide students opportunities to develop deep understanding of words (Graves & Prenn, 1986). Therefore, teachers need to choose carefully which words to teach. Words central to the main point of a story and words representing key concepts in an exposition would be good candidates for the conceptual approach.

	new, looks just like old	new, looks different	new, grows one part from old
grafting	yes		
reproduction			
regeneration			

Conclusion

No simplistic solutions exist to the instructional dilemmas teachers face as they approach the teaching of vocabulary. On the one hand, they know that students learn most of their knowledge about words informally through encounters with oral and written language. On the other hand, they know that students can also be taught new words effectively.

Appropriate instruction most often depends on the to-be-learned words and the given text for which a word is important. Sometimes students can simply be given definitions of words and such knowledge is sufficient for understanding words and for enhancing comprehension of a given text. Other times students will need a strategy for using context to figure out word meanings in order to maintain comprehension. At still other times, students will need more extensive instruction to learn new words because definitions alone and context alone are not sufficient for a thorough enough understanding of words crucial to comprehending a given text.

Appropriate instruction most often depends on the to-be-learned words and the given text for which a word is important.

Little research exists on how students learn to use context in conjunction with their unfolding understanding of a passage to figure out the meaning of new words. Merely mentioning that students should use context or briefly instructing students about various types of context clues probably does not go far enough (Graves, 1987) to ensure that students have enough understanding of the process to employ it on their own (see Duffy, Roehler, & Rackliffe, 1986). Basal programs are just now beginning to include information about how teachers can help students understand the thought processes in deriving word meaning from context (e.g., *Houghton-Mifflin Reading,* 1986).

Research on specific kinds of context instruction is needed, for example, to determine how effective the instructional context approach is. Basal programs have used this approach for years, perhaps assuming that providing sentences that are rich in context clues will somehow lead students to become independent users of the process of deriving information from a variety of texts. However, what students learn from such instruction is unclear. In addition, how students might transfer that knowledge to more natural contexts is unclear. The modeling approach appears to be one good candidate. If this strategy is effective, could it be used effectively with high- and low-ability students? Perhaps high-ability students already know how to use context and would not benefit from such instruction (Pearson & Dole, in press).

The conceptual approach to vocabulary instruction also needs more research; for example, what is the role of concept development in such an approach to vocabulary instruction? Research using more elaborate teaching of vocabulary words (e.g., Carr, 1985; McKeown et al., 1983) has incorporated some, but not all, concept development principles (e.g., Tennyson & Cocchiarella, 1986). Yet it makes sense to include such principles in vocabulary programs.

Research is needed on the role of recreational reading in vocabulary learning. We need to learn more about how students learn new words through reading and what can be done to encourage their learning more words while reading. Such knowledge will help teachers understand the relative importance of learning words directly through vocabulary instruction and indirectly through reading. Teachers can then use this information to allocate appropriate instructional time to each activity.

Note

We gratefully acknowledge the help and support of Isabel Beck, University of Pittsburgh, and William Nagy, University of Illinois. Their ideas have been instrumental to us in the formulation of this article. We also appreciate the helpful comments of Kathryn Au.

References

Ahlfors, G. (1979). *Learning word meanings: A comparison of three instructional procedures.* Unpublished doctoral dissertation, University of Minnesota.

Anders, P., Bos, C., & Filip, D. (1984). The effect of semantic feature analysis on the reading comprehension of learning-disabled students. In J. Niles & L. Harris (Eds.), *Changing perspectives on research in reading/language processing and instruction* (pp. 162–166). Rochester, NY: National Reading Conference.

Beck, I., McCaslin, E., & McKeown, M. (1980). *The rationale and design of a program to teach vocabulary to fourth-grade students* (LRDC Publication 1980/25). Pittsburgh: University of Pittsburgh, Learning Research and Development Center.

Beck, I., & McKeown, M. (1985). Teaching vocabulary: Making the instruction fit the goal. *Educational Perspectives, 23,* 11–15.

Beck, I., McKeown, M., & McCaslin, E. (1983). Vocabulary development: All contexts are not created equal. *Elementary School Journal, 83,* 177–181.

Blachowicz, C. (1986). Making connections: Alternatives to the vocabulary notebook. *Journal of Reading, 29,* 643–649.

Bos, C., Anders, P., Filip, D., & Jaffe, L. (1985). Semantic feature analysis and long-term learning. In J. Niles & R. Lalik (Eds.), *Issues in literacy: A research perspective* (pp. 42–47). Rochester, NY: National Reading Conference.

Carey, S. (1978). The child as word learner. In M. Halle, J. Bresnan, & G. Miller (Eds.), *Linguistic theory and psychological reality* (pp. 359–373). Cambridge, MA: MIT Press.

Carr, E. (1985). The vocabulary overview guide: A metacognitive strategy to improve vocabulary comprehension and retention. *Journal of Reading, 28*, 684–689.

Carr, E., & Wixson, K. (1986). Guidelines for evaluating vocabulary instruction. *Journal of Reading, 29*, 588–595.

Davis, F. (1944). Fundamental factors of comprehension in reading. *Psychometrika, 9*, 185–197.

Davis, F. (1968). Research in comprehension in reading. *Reading Research Quarterly, 3*, 499–545.

Dickinson, D. (1984). First impressions: Children's knowledge of words gained from a single exposure. *Applied Psycholinguistics, 5*, 359–373.

Dole, J., Osborn, J., & Rogers, T. (1987). *A guide to selecting basal reading programs.* Champaign-Urbana: University of Illinois, Center for the Study of Reading.

Duffy, G., Roehler, L., Meloth, M., Vavrus, L., Book, C., Putnam, J., & Wesselman, R. (1986). The relationship between explicit verbal explanations during reading skill instruction and student awareness and achievement: A study of reading teacher effects. *Reading Research Quarterly, 21*, 237–254.

Duffy, G., Roehler, L., & Rackliffe, G. (1986). How teachers' instructional talk influences students' understanding of lesson content. *Elementary School Journal, 87*, 3–16.

Durkin, D. (1979). What classroom observations reveal about reading comprehension instruction. *Reading Research Quarterly, 14*, 481–533.

Durkin, D. (1981). Reading comprehension instruction in five basal reader series. *Reading Research Quarterly, 26*, 515–544.

Freebody, P., & Anderson, R. (1983). Effects on text comprehension of differing proportions and locations of difficult vocabulary. *Journal of Reading Behavior, 15*, 19–39.

Graves, M. (1984). Selecting vocabulary to teach in the intermediate and secondary grades. In J. Flood (Ed.), *Promoting reading comprehension* (pp. 245–260). Newark, DE: International Reading Association.

Graves, M. (1987). The roles of instruction in fostering vocabulary development. In M. McKeown & M. Curtis (Eds.), *The nature of vocabulary acquisition* (pp. 165–184). Hillsdale, NJ: Erlbaum.

Graves, M., & Prenn, M. (1986). Costs and benefits of various methods of teaching vocabulary. *Journal of Reading, 29*, 596–602.

Herman, P., Anderson, R., Pearson, P., & Nagy, W. Incidental acquisition of word meaning from expositions that vary text features. *Reading Research Quarterly.*

Houghton-Miffin reading. (1986). Boston, MA: Houghton-Mifflin.

Jackson, J., & Dizney, H. (1963). Intensive vocabulary training. *Journal of Reading, 6*, 221–229.

Jenkins, J., & Dixon, R. (1983). Vocabulary learning. *Contemporary Educational Psychology, 8*, 237–260.

Johnson, D., & Pearson, P. D. (1978). *Teaching reading vocabulary.* New York: Holt, Rinehart & Winston.

Kameenui, E., Carnine, D., & Freschi, R. (1982). Effects of text construction and instructional procedures for teaching word meanings on comprehension and recall. *Reading Research Quarterly, 17*, 367–388.

Manzo, A., & Sherk, J. (1972). Some generalizations and strategies for guiding vocabulary. *Journal of Reading Behavior, 4*, 81–88.

McKeown, M. (1985). The acquisition of word meaning from context by children of high and low ability. *Reading Research Quarterly, 20*, 482–496.

McKeown, M., Beck, I., Omanson, R., & Perfetti, C. (1983). The effects of long-term vocabulary instruction on reading comprehension: A replication. *Journal of Reading Behavior, 15*, 3–19.

Mezynski, K. (1983). Issues concerning the acquisition of knowledge: Effects of vocabulary training on reading comprehension. *Review of Educational Research, 53*, 253–279.

Nagy, W., & Herman, P. (1985). Incidental vs. instructional approaches to increasing reading vocabulary. *Educational Perspectives, 23*, 16–21.

Nagy, W., & Herman, P. (1987). Breadth and depth of vocabulary knowledge: Implications for acquisition and instruction. In M. McKeown & M. Curtis (Eds.), *The nature of vocabulary acquisition* (pp. 19–35). Hillsdale, NJ: Erlbaum.

Nagy, W., Herman, P., & Anderson, R. (1985a). *Learning word meanings from context: How broadly generalizable?* (Tech. Rep. No. 347). Champaign-Urbana: University of Illinois, Center for the Study of Reading.

Nagy, W., Herman, P., & Anderson, R. (1985b). Learning words from context. *Reading Research Quarterly, 20*, 233–253.

Paris, S., Lipson, M., & Wixson, K. (1983). Becoming a strategic reader. *Contemporary Educational Psychology, 8*, 293–316.

Pearson, P. D., & Dole, J. Explicit comprehension instruction: A review of the research and a new conceptualization of instruction. *Elementary School Journal.*

Petty, W., Herold, C., & Stoll, E. (1968). *The state of the knowledge about the teaching of vocabulary* (Cooperative Research Project No. 3123). Champaign, IL: National Council of Teachers of English.

Roser, N., & Juel, C. (1982). Effects of vocabulary instruction on reading comprehension. In J. Niles & L. Harris (Eds.), *New inquiries in reading research and instruction* (pp. 110–118). Rochester, NY: National Reading Conference.

Schatz, E., & Baldwin, S. (1986). Context clues are unreliable predictors of word meanings. *Reading Research Quarterly, 21*, 439–453.

Schwartz, R., & Raphael, T. (1985). Concept of definition: A key to improving students' vocabulary. *Reading Teacher, 39*, 198–205.

Shefelbine, J. (1984). *Teachers' decisions about the utility of dictionary tasks and the role of prior knowledge.* Unpublished manuscript, University of Texas at Austin.

Stahl, S., & Fairbanks, M. (1986). The effects of vocabulary instruction: A model-based meta-analysis. *Review of Educational Research, 56*, 72–110.

Sternberg, R. (1987). Most vocabulary is learned from context. In M. McKeown & M. Curtis (Eds.), *The nature of vocabulary acquisition* (pp. 89–106). Hillsdale, NJ: Erlbaum.

Tennyson, R. & Cocchiarella, M. A. (1986). An empirically based instructional design theory for teaching concepts. *Review of Educational Research, 56*, 40–71.

Thelen, J. (1986). Vocabulary instruction and meaningful learning. *Journal of Reading, 29*, 603–609.

Thorndyke, R. (1973). *Reading comprehension education in fifteen countries.* New York: Wiley.

Tuinman, J., & Brady, M. (1974). How does vocabulary account for variance on reading comprehension tests? A preliminary instructional analysis. In P. Nacke (Ed.), *Interaction: Research and practice for college-adult reading* (pp. 176–184). Clemson, SC: National Reading Conference.

van Daalen-Kapteijns, M., & Elshout-Mohr, M. (1981). The acquisition of word meanings as a cognitive learning process. *Journal of Verbal Learning and Verbal Behavior, 20*, 386–399.

Vaughn, J., Castle, G., Gilbert, K., & Love, M. (1982). Varied approaches to preteaching vocabulary. In J. Niles & L. Harris (Eds.)., *New inquiries in reading research and instruction* (pp. 94–97). Rochester, NY: National Reading Conference.

Webster's third new international dictionary. (1981). Springfield, MA: Merriam-Webster.

Reading Comprehension Requires Knowledge—of Words and the World

Scientific Insights into the Fourth-Grade Slump and the Nation's Stagnant Comprehension Scores

E. D. Hirsch, Jr.
University of Virginia

While educators have made good progress in teaching children to decode (that is, turn print into speech sounds), it's disheartening that we still have not overcome the "fourth-grade slump" in reading comprehension. We're finding that even though the vast majority of our youngest readers can manage simple texts, many students—particularly those from low-income families—struggle when it comes time in grade four to tackle more advanced academic texts.

To help these students, we must fully understand just where this "fourth-grade slump" comes from. The "slump" was the name that the great reading researcher Jeanne Chall used to describe the *apparently* sudden drop-off between third and fourth grade in the reading scores of low-income students. In her research, Chall found that low-income students in the second and third grades tended to score at (and even above) national averages in reading tests and related measures such as spelling and word meaning. But at the fourth grade, low-income students' scores began a steady drop that grew steeper as the students moved into the higher grades.[1] I describe this drop-off as *apparently* sudden because there is now good evidence that it is there, unmeasured, in earlier grades. A large language gap—not just a reading gap—between advantaged and disadvantaged students exists also in third grade, not to mention second, first, and even earlier.

Researchers have known about the fourth-grade slump in poor children's reading comprehension for several decades, but it was only recently, especially in the work of Betty Hart and Todd Risley, that solid data on children's early language development have been available.[2] We now believe that reading tests make the comprehension gap *seem* much greater in

fourth grade because the tests used in earlier grades are heavily focused on testing early reading skills (like decoding) and do not try to measure the full extent of the vocabulary differences between the groups.

Yet it would be a mistake to assume that problems with comprehension are limited to disadvantaged students. According to the most recent evidence from the National Assessment of Educational Progress, most students' reading comprehension scores remain low despite many years of concentrated efforts to improve reading instruction.[3] Effective teaching of reading comprehension to all children has turned out to be a recalcitrant problem. Now that we have good programs that teach children to decode text accurately and fluently, the task of creating programs and methods that teach students to *comprehend* text accurately and fluently is the new frontier in reading research.

It's a challenging problem. The U.S. Department of Education is currently soliciting research proposals to help solve it. That's a very good sign. With renewed scientific attention to this fundamental problem, we can expect real progress in equity and in student achievement—some day. Meanwhile, we already know things about reading comprehension that have immediate implications for teachers. I will try to summarize some of the most important findings and their implications for classroom practice.

I. A Growing Scientific Consensus

For most of my scholarly life (going back to my first technical publication on the subject in 1960) my research has been concerned with the nature of text comprehension: How do we know we have correctly understood a text? Is reading a displaced version of ordinary oral communication? My active interest in relating that subject to student achievement and educational equity dates to the '70s when I began to study some of the advances being made in cognitive

Reprinted with permission from the Spring 2003 issue of the *American Educator*, the quarterly journal of the American Federation of Teachers.

science and psycholinguistics (the study of how our minds produce and comprehend language spoken and written). Now, after several decades of researching this difficult subject of reading comprehension from varied angles in the humanities and sciences, I can report that although what we don't know still far exceeds what we do, there is current scientific agreement on at least three principles that have useful implications for improving students' reading comprehension. The three principles (which subsume a number of others) are these:

1. Fluency allows the mind to concentrate on comprehension;
2. Breadth of vocabulary increases comprehension and facilitates further learning; and
3. Domain knowledge, the most recently understood principle, increases fluency, broadens vocabulary, and enables deeper comprehension.

Fluency Is Important

"Fluency" means "flowing," and in this context it also means "fast." There is a general, though not perfect, correlation between how fast you can comprehend a text and how well you can comprehend it. To most psychologists, including those who don't specialize in reading, it would be surprising if that weren't the case. A person who reads fast has "automated" many of the underlying processes involved in reading, and can, therefore, devote conscious attention to textual meaning rather than to the processes themselves. What's more, fluency is greatly enhanced by word and domain knowledge: While word knowledge speeds up word recognition and thus the process of reading, world knowledge speeds up comprehension of textual meaning by offering a foundation for making inferences.[4] A few of the principles underlying the relationship between fluency and comprehension are explained below.

If decoding does not happen quickly, the decoded material will be forgotten before it is understood. Have you ever tried to understand what is being said in a movie in a foreign language (say in French) that you have studied in school? Even if you know the words, isn't it frustrating that they speak so fast? While you are trying to work out what the actors just said, they are already saying something else, and your mind gets overloaded. The basic difficulty regarding speed and reading comprehension is even more serious than that. If you were able to slow down the movie so that you could concentrate on identifying the words and translating them, you would find in that situation, too, that your understanding would *still* be less than adequate. By

having to focus on the sounds, turn them into French words and subsequently into English ones, you tend to lose track of the connections between one sentence and another, and between groups of sentences. You are in the same position as a child who has to translate consciously and slowly from print to sound. Things disappear from your mind before you have a chance to ponder the significance of what is being said. In slowly translating from French to English, you have been handicapped by the severe limits of what cognitive scientists call your "short-term memory" or "working memory."

I vividly remember when I first learned about the severe limits of human working memory and their importance in communication. It was in a wonderful book called *The Psychology of Communication* by the distinguished cognitive scientist George A. Miller.[5] The second chapter was one of the most famous articles ever written in the field of psychology, "The Magical Number Seven, Plus or Minus Two: Some Limits on Our Capacity for Processing Information." The "magical number seven" turned out to be the approximate number of items (whether simple facts, or numbers, or words representing complex concepts) that you can hold in your conscious mind at one time before they start evaporating into oblivion. This "magical number seven" is a limitation that (with some variation) afflicts everyone—including geniuses. One way we overcome this limitation of working memory while reading is by learning how to make a rapid, automatic deployment of underlying reading processes so that they become fast and unconscious, leaving the conscious mind (i.e., the working memory) free to think about what a text means.

This is why fast and accurate decoding is important. Experiments show that a child who can sound out nonsense words quickly and accurately has mastered the decoding process and is on the road to freeing up her working memory to concentrate on comprehension of meaning. Decoding fluency is achieved through accurate initial instruction followed by lots of practice. Typically, it takes several years of decoding practice before children can process a printed text as rapidly as they can process that same text when listening to it.

Students also overcome the limitations of working memory by rapidly grasping what kind of text this is, rapidly identifying words, and by understanding the grammatical connections between them at the basic level of the sentence.[6] This kind of fluency at the sentence level increases with practice and with knowledge of different kinds of writing. Such general language fluency is also intimately connected with well-practiced vocabulary knowledge, meaning how familiar the words and their various connotations are to the student. Take, for example, the following sentence: "Besides having had a lot of useful time in the trenches, Claire will also make a good assistant principal because she is able to keep her eyes on the ball." Educators, with their knowledge of the conventions of language and vocabulary use, will have no problem surmising that Claire has worked with students (probably as a classroom teacher) and is good at staying focused. But notice that to process this simple sentence, you had to interpret two metaphors (trenches and ball); and if you were to make a judgment regarding Claire's qualifications to be an assistant principal, you would draw on your domain knowledge as to the demands of that particular job.

Finally, fluency is also increased by domain knowledge, which allows the reader to make rapid connections between new and previously learned content; this both eases and deepens comprehension. An expert in a subject can read a text about that subject much more fluently than she can read a text on an unfamiliar topic.[7] Prior knowledge about the topic speeds up basic comprehension and leaves working memory free to make connections between the new material and previously learned information, to draw inferences, and to ponder implications. A big difference between an expert and a novice reader— indeed between an expert and a novice in any field— is the ability to take in basic features very fast, thereby leaving the mind free to concentrate on important features.

A big difference between an expert and a novice reader is the ability to take in basic features very fast, thereby leaving the mind free to concentrate on important features.

This insight was dramatized in a famous experiment. Dutch psychologist Adrian de Groot[8] noticed that chess grand masters have a remarkable skill that we amateurs cannot emulate. They can glance for five seconds at a complex mid-game chess position of 25 pieces, perform an intervening task of some sort, and then reconstruct on a blank chess board the entire chess position without making any mistakes. Performance on this task correlates almost perfectly with one's chess ranking. Grand masters make no mistakes, masters very few, and amateurs can get just five or six pieces right. (Remember the magical number seven, plus or minus two!) On a brilliant hunch, de Groot then performed the same experiment with 25 chess pieces in positions that, instead of being taken from an actual chess game, were just placed at random on the board. Under these new conditions, the performances of the three different groups—

grand masters, masters, and novices—were all exactly the same, each group remembering just five or six pieces correctly.

The experiment suggests the skill difference between a master reader who can easily reproduce the 16 letters of "the cat is on the mat" and a beginning reader who has trouble reproducing the same letters: t-h-e-c-a-t-i-s-o-n-t-h-e-m-a-t. If, instead of providing expert and child with that written sentence, we change the task and ask them to reproduce a sequence of 16 random letters, the performance of the first-grader and master reader would be much closer. On average, neither would get more than a short sequence of the random letters right. Practiced readers, chess grand masters, and other experts do not possess any special brain centers that novices lack, and they do not perform any better than novices on structurally similar yet unfamiliar tasks. Nonetheless, experts are able to perform remarkable feats of comprehension and memory with real-world situations such as remembering mid-game chess positions or the meanings and even spellings of actual sentences and paragraphs. How do they manage?

They do so partly by chunking—a word used by George A. Miller to denote the way knowledgeable people concentrate multiple components into a single item that takes up just one slot in working memory. "The cat is on the mat" is an easily remembered sentence, and expert readers can easily reproduce the 16 letters not because the letters are individually remembered, but because the sentence is remembered as a chunk out of which the sub-elements can be reconstructed from prior knowledge of written English. Remember, working memory can hold roughly seven items—but those items can be anything from simple numbers to complex previously-learned concepts that can be concentrated in a single word or image. What de Groot found, and what subsequent research has continually confirmed, is that the difference in fluency and higher-order skill between a novice and an expert does not lie in mental muscles, but in what de Groot called "erudition," a vast store of quickly available, previously acquired, knowledge that enables the mind to take in a great deal in a brief time. So, when shown a mid-game board, the chess grand masters were not *separately* remembering the placement of 25 pieces—they were able to draw quickly on previous knowledge of similar past games and the one or two ways in which the pieces were aligned differently from those games.

Experiments have shown that when someone comprehends a text, background knowledge is typically integrated with the literal word meanings of the text to construct a coherent model of the whole situation implied by the text. An expert can quickly make multiple connections from the words to construct a situation model. But a novice will have less relevant knowledge and less well-structured knowledge, and will therefore take more time to construct a situation model. Suppose the text contained the term "World War II." Someone who has the requisite knowledge of that war will be able to take in the term very fast, and, like the chess grand masters, be able to unpack its many layers of meaning when needed. The novice's limited background knowledge will not be as readily accessible as the expert's, and so the novice will only slowly make the few connections that his limited knowledge enables. Inevitably, he will comprehend the text poorly.

Breadth of Vocabulary Is Important

Vocabulary knowledge correlates strongly with reading (and oral) comprehension. This seems so obvious that it might seem pointless to discuss vocabulary in a brief review of research on reading comprehension. True enough. But we know a few significant things about vocabulary acquisition that might be useful in enhancing students' ability to comprehend texts. These are not obvious things, and some aspects of vocabulary acquisition are deeply surprising. A few important insights are discussed next.

In vocabulary acquisition, a small early advantage grows into a much bigger one unless we intervene very intelligently to help the disadvantaged student learn words at an accelerated rate. Hart and Risley[9] have shown that low-income homes on average expose young children to far fewer words and far simpler sentence structures than middle-class homes. A high-performing first-grader knows about twice as many words as a low-performing one and, as these students go through the grades, the differential gets magnified.[10] By 12th grade, the high performer knows about four times as many words as the low performer.[11]

The reason for this growing gap is clear: Vocabulary experts agree that adequate reading comprehension depends on a person already knowing between 90 and 95 percent of the words in a text.[12] Knowing that percentage of words allows the reader to get the main thrust of what is being said and therefore to guess correctly what the unfamiliar words probably mean. (This inferential process is of course how we pick up oral language in early childhood and it sustains our vocabulary growth throughout our lives.)

This means that the communications students read or hear hold very different knowledge and word-acquisition possibilities for advantaged and disadvantaged students. Those who know 90 percent of the words in a text will understand its meaning and, because they understand, they will also begin to learn the other 10 percent of the words. Those who do not know 90 percent of the words, and therefore do not comprehend the passage, will now be even further behind on both fronts: They missed the opportunity to learn the content of the text and to learn more words. The prominent reading researcher Keith Stanovich termed this growing gap the "Matthew Effect" from the passage in the Gospel of Matthew: "Unto every one that hath shall be given, and he shall have abundance: but from him that hath not shall be taken away even that which he hath."

Overcoming this initial disadvantage is a huge challenge. To do so, we need to engage in the best, most enabling kinds of vocabulary building. As we will see, that means explicit vocabulary instruction done in the best possible way and providing an environment that accelerates the incidental acquisition of vocabulary, which is how most vocabulary growth takes place.

A well educated 12th-grader knows an enormous number of words, mostly learned incidentally. But, there is also an important place for explicit vocabulary development, especially in the early years, and especially for children who are behind. Isabel Beck and her colleagues[13] in their excellent guide to explicit vocabulary instruction estimate that students can be taught explicitly some 400 words per year in school. These 400 words can be of immense importance to those children who are behind and need to be brought to the point of understanding key words as fast as possible. But that is just the beginning. If we want all of our children to comprehend well, they must learn many, many more words each year through incidental means. A 12th-grade student who scores well enough on the verbal portion of the SAT to get into a selective college knows between 60,000 and 100,000 words. There is some dispute among experts regarding the actual number so we might split the difference and assume that the number is about 80,000 words. If we assume that a child starts acquiring vocabulary at age two, and that the 12th-grader is 17 years old, he has acquired 80,000 words in 15 years. Multiplying 365 days times 15 we get 5,475 days. We divide that number into 80,000, and we find that the high-achieving 12th-grader has learned some 15 words a day—over 5,000 words a year. But of course, the 15-words-a-day estimate is just a mathematical average that describes a haphazard and complex process occurring along a very broad front.

Most vocabulary growth results incidentally, from massive immersion in the world of language and knowledge. Recent work in cognitive science holds promise for making progress on this incidental learning front. It has long been known that the growth of word knowledge is slow and incremental, requiring multiple exposures to words. One doesn't just learn a word's meaning and then have the word. One gradually learns the word's denotations and connotations and its modes of use little by little over many, many language experiences.[14] The high-performing 12th-grader who knows 80,000 words knows them with very different degrees of complexity and precision, and has learned them not by learning 15 words a day, but by accruing tiny bits of word knowledge for each of the thousands of words that he encounters every day. As I shall discuss below, this and other considerations mean that we should immerse students for extended periods in the sorts of coherent language experiences that are most conducive to efficient vocabulary learning.

Domain Knowledge Is Important

More than vocabulary knowledge is needed to understand most texts. To make constructive use of vocabulary, the reader also needs a threshold level of knowledge about the topic being discussed—what we call "domain knowledge." Consider the following examples.

Domain knowledge enables readers to make sense of word combinations and choose among multiple possible word meanings. A typical newspaper article shows why it's important to know in advance something about the subject matter of a text in order to understand it. If we are reading a story about a baseball game in the newspaper sports section, we must typically know quite a lot about baseball in order to comprehend what is being said. Think of the quantity of baseball knowledge that has to be already in mind to understand the simple sentence "Jones sacrificed and knocked in a run." Strung together in this fashion, the literal words are almost meaningless. A baseball-ignorant Englishman reading that sentence would be puzzled even if there were nothing amiss with his fluency or general knowledge of words like "sacrificed." Words have multiple purposes and meanings, and their meaning in a particular instance is cued by the reader's domain knowledge. The word "sacrifice" has different connotations in a baseball story and in the Bible.

Domain knowledge is necessary to give meaning to otherwise confusing sentences. I once read an anecdote about an elderly person who went to hear the great Albert Einstein lecture on relativity at Princeton University. She is reported to have said after the lecture: "I understood all the words. It was just how they were put together that baffled me."

What she meant was that the everyday words that Einstein used in his lecture referred to a particular knowledge domain. If we don't know that domain, we can't construct a meaningful mental model of what's being said. Here's a sentence by Einstein such as might have been heard in his Princeton lecture: "It will be seen from these reflections that in pursuing the general theory of relativity we shall be led to a theory of gravitation, since we are able to produce a gravitational field merely by changing the system of coordinates." I know all those words, but since I can't imagine how changing coordinates will "produce" gravity, I can't comprehend what that sentence means.

If we don't know the domain, we can't construct a meaningful mental model of what's being said.

For a more everyday example, take this sentence from the February 2003 issue of *National Geographic:* "Gigantic and luminous, the earliest star formed like a pearl inside shells of swirling gas." Most adults, drawing on their knowledge of the Big Bang theory, pearl formation (and the use of metaphor, which I return to below), and gasses, can comprehend this sentence. But we would expect different degrees of comprehension among, say, physicists, amateur astronomers, and you and me. Likewise, we should expect little comprehension among average sixth-graders—not just because of the words used, but because of the extensive domain knowledge those words represent in this context.

Reading (and listening) require the reader to make inferences that depend on prior knowledge—not on decontextualized "inferencing" skills. Many basal reading series direct teachers to use valuable teaching time to instruct students in "inferencing skills." But a simple example illustrates that inferencing itself is a fairly basic skill that most children already have: If somebody says to a child, "Hey, shut up. I'm trying to read," most children, advantaged or disadvantaged, can infer the connection between the first statement and the second. They have prior knowledge of the fact that hearing somebody talk can be distracting and make reading difficult. So they are able to construct a mental model that meaningfully connects the sentence "Hey shut up" with the sentence "I'm trying to read." In contrast, many children may not understand the simple sentence, "I wanted to take a vacation in Mexico this year, but my wife can only be away from her job in July." The children who don't understand the connection between the clauses don't lack an inferencing skill; they lack the geographical knowledge that Mexico is extremely hot in July—and not most people's idea of a pleasant vacation spot.

Speaking and writing always convey meanings that are not explicitly given by the words themselves. If speakers or writers tried to make everything explicit, they would take far too much time to say anything, and the message would become impossibly long and digressive. We learn from infancy that oral language comprehension requires readers to actively construct meaning by supplying missing knowledge and making inferences. Of course, the need for prior knowledge is not unique to oral communication but is also necessary to comprehend written texts.

In comprehension, the need for making inferences by activating already existing domain knowledge has been shown by a number of researchers since the 1960s. But the basic insight goes back further than that. In Greek antiquity it was understood that communication involves the drawing of inferences based on knowledge that is taken for granted. The Greek term for such an implicit argument was "enthymeme," from *en* (in) and *thumos* (mind)—that is, something kept in mind and taken for granted but not expressed.[15] One example of this characteristic of speech is a truncated syllogism: "All men are mortal, so Socrates is mortal." To make strict logical sense of this statement, we have to infer the missing premise that Socrates is a man.

Likewise, reading comprehension depends on the reader filling in blanks and silently supplying enough of the unstated premises to make coherent sense of what is being read. Once print has been decoded into words, reading comprehension, like listening comprehension, requires the active construction of inferences from utterances that are chock full of unstated premises and unexplained allusions.

Irony, metaphor, and other literary devices require background knowledge for their comprehension. Besides filling out logical connections, there are other ways in which relevant background knowledge is activated in reconstructing meaning from a text. One of the most immediately obvious examples is irony, which, by definition, refrains from explicitly stating its meaning. If it did so, it would cease to be irony and become explicit statement. "He's a bright boy." Is the statement straight, in which case he is thought to be intelligent, or is it ironical, in which case he is thought to be stupid? Irony is subject to two contrary interpretations, the straight and the ironical. To decide between these two possibilities the reader has to activate relevant world knowledge not stated in the sentence.

Another important illustration of the way in which background knowledge is activated in the process of comprehending language is metaphor—an almost omnipresent element of speech. "Victory is sweet" is easily and quickly understood by students. So is "War

is hell" or "Don't be a wet blanket." We know these can't be meant literally because we know what is being referred to. Researchers have shown that metaphors are often processed just as rapidly as literal meaning—indicating that we are constantly activating background knowledge in comprehension. In part two of this article, I'll show that this idea of taken-for-granted knowledge is an important clue to the sort of instruction that can help students improve their ability to comprehend written texts.

In recent years, efforts to improve reading have focused on how best to teach decoding. And, of course, fluent decoding is an absolute prerequisite to comprehension. But we can easily see from this quick summary of research that comprehension—the goal of decoding—won't improve unless we also pay serious attention to building our students' word and world knowledge.

II. Rethinking the Language Arts Curriculum

To improve reading, schools across the country have been steadily increasing the amount of time allocated to language arts. For example, in Baltimore, Chicago, and the entire state of California, early-grade teachers are already expected to devote 2½ hours a day to language arts. In an AFT poll, 80 percent of elementary teachers said their schools recommended a language arts block of two hours or more each day. (If the poll were limited to teachers in the lower elementary grades, the percentage might have been even higher.) Even given the large challenge we face, this is a lot of time—especially since it's usually during the precious morning hours. We need to use the time optimally. As we shall see, we're not. What's happening in that time? Given what we've just reviewed about reading comprehension, how should it be used?

Start Early to Build Word and World Knowledge

As I mentioned above, the typical disadvantaged child enters kindergarten knowing only half as many words as the typical advantaged child. Because of the Matthew Effect, it may never be possible *entirely* to overcome this initial disadvantage on a large scale: As we have seen, word-rich children learn more vocabulary and content than word-poor children from the very same language experiences. On the other hand, intelligent remediation is possible, especially if we start early by encouraging optimal vocabulary growth in preschool and kindergarten. Acquiring word knowledge and domain knowledge is a gradual and cumulative process. Since early learning of words and things is the only way to overcome early disadvantage, the argument for including optimal content in language arts as early as possible seems compelling.

There are strong theoretical and practical advantages to teaching early decoding through simple "decodable texts" that enable the child to progress rapidly in decoding skill. But the top research in this area suggests that 40 minutes of daily decoding instruction is plenty in first grade; and for most second-graders, 20 minutes is ample.[16] That leaves between one and two hours daily (depending on the time allocated to language arts) for activities that foster vocabulary, domain knowledge, and fluency. Such knowledge could be conveyed through read-alouds, well-conceived vocabulary instruction, and a variety of cumulative activities that immerse children in word and world knowledge. But no published basal program I have seen systematically pursues this goal. Wasted opportunity abounds.

Build Oral Comprehension and Background Knowledge

Thomas Sticht has shown that oral comprehension typically places an upper limit on reading comprehension; if you don't recognize and understand the word when you hear it, you also won't be able to comprehend it when reading.[17] This tells us something very important: Oral comprehension generally needs to be developed in our youngest students if we want them to be good readers.

From the earliest ages, reading is much more than decoding. From the start, reading is also accessing and further acquiring language knowledge and domain knowledge. This means that instruction and practice in fluency of decoding need to be accompanied by instruction and practice in vocabulary and domain knowledge. If we want to raise later achievement and avoid the fourth-grade slump, we need to combine early instruction in the procedures of literacy with early instruction in the content of literacy, specifically: vocabulary, conventions of language, and knowledge of the world.

In the earliest grades, before students can read substantive texts on their own, this content will be best conveyed orally. An important vehicle is teacher read-alouds, in which texts selected for their interest, substance, and vocabulary are read aloud to children and followed by discussion and lessons that build children's understanding of the ideas, topics, and words in the story. Most of the popular basal reading series include read-alouds in their curriculum, but the content is almost always banal, and read-alouds are generally phased out in second grade despite the fact that research has found that students benefit from read-alouds until eighth grade.[18] Further, the basal series' teacher guides instruct teachers to build background knowledge, but usually on topics that are thoroughly ordinary, like pets, sharing, and even what spreads taste best on toast!

Another problem is that the early grades language-arts curriculum, both in terms of read-alouds and decoding texts, is overwhelmingly devoted to fiction. Literature is a very important domain of knowledge in its own right, but I have seen no convincing challenge to the argument made by Jeanne Chall, who wrote that we need to place a far greater emphasis on nonfiction in early language-arts classes. This emphasis is essential for children to learn the words and concepts they need to understand newspapers, magazines, and books addressed to the general public.[19] But the problem is not just the disproportionate attention to fiction; in addition, the fiction that is offered is typically trivial in content and simple in its language conventions. Fiction can build knowledge and understanding of peoples, lands, times, and ideas that are very important but totally unknown to children. A fine example of such fiction is *The Hole in the Dike,* included in one basal series. The famous legend acquaints students with Holland, its geography, and the power of water and the ingenious dike system that restrains it. But such fiction is the exception. Far more typical, especially before grades three and four, are stories based in the here and now that address in pedestrian ways the "ideas" children already know about school, friendship, families, and the like.

Don't Spend Excessive Time Teaching Formal Comprehension Skills

A great deal of time in language arts is currently being spent on teaching children formal comprehension strategies like predicting, classifying, and looking for the main idea. In most language-arts textbooks, these exercises persist throughout the year and over many years. Every researcher believes that there is *initial* value in practicing these comprehension strategies. They teach children to construe a text in the same meaning-seeking way that they already construe the oral speech of adults and their peers. It helps children understand that the text, like a person, is trying to communicate something. But after an initial benefit, further conscious practice of these formal skills is a waste of time, according to Barak Rosenshine, who reviewed the research on the effects of using such methods. Rosenshine found that spending six classes on teaching these skills had the same effect on students' reading comprehension as spending 25 classes on them. After a quick initial bump, there's a plateau or ceiling in the positive effects, and little further benefit is derived.[20]

Rosenshine's finding might have been predicted from the rest of what we know about comprehension. Children have been strategically inferring meaning from speech most of their lives. (Remember: Every child can construe the inference implicit in "Shut up! I'm trying to read.") Students don't lack inferring techniques so much as they lack relevant domain knowledge. So while it's good to devote only a small amount of time to explicitly teaching comprehension skills, this does not mean that the skills will then be abandoned. They will be activated in the course of becoming increasingly familiar with the vocabulary and domain of what is being read. The point of a comprehension strategy is to activate the student's relevant knowledge in order to construct a situation model. That's great, but if the relevant prior knowledge is lacking, conscious comprehension strategies cannot activate it.

Systematically Build Word and World Knowledge

Let's consider why the current basals have failed to advance reading comprehension scores. First of all, they have failed significantly to advance students' vocabulary. Vocabulary researchers agree that to get a good start in learning the connotations of a word, a person needs multiple exposures to the word in different contexts. Such exposure is not supplied by a fragmented selection of reading in which topics leap from a day at the beach to a trip to the vegetable section of the supermarket.

The point of a comprehension strategy is to activate the student's relevant knowledge. That's great, but if the relevant prior knowledge is lacking, conscious comprehension strategies cannot activate it.

That is the more superficial defect of current programs; another goes deeper. With their very heavy orientation to trivial literature, these programs do not take it upon themselves to enhance students' general knowledge in any coherent way. Wide vocabulary and broad knowledge go together. Language is not an isolated sphere of activity but our fundamental human instrument for dealing with the world. The best way to expand students' language is to expand their understanding of what language refers to. If we want students to know the connotations of the word "apple," the best instruction will include references to real apples—not just to verbal associations like "sweet," round," and "crisp," but to the actual objects that unify those traits. An ideal language program is a knowledge program. It is a program that anchors and consolidates word meaning in the students' minds by virtue of their knowing what the words actually refer to.

The late Jeanne Chall was distressed at the nullity of the world knowledge being conveyed to students by the helter-skelter fictional sketches that did so little to enhance their breadth of knowledge and their vocabulary. She pointed out that world knowledge is an essential component of reading comprehension, because every text takes for granted the readers' familiarity with a whole range of unspoken and unwritten facts about the cultural and natural worlds.

World knowledge is an essential component of reading comprehension, because every text takes for granted the readers' familiarity with a whole range of unspoken and unwritten facts about the cultural and natural worlds.

It is now well accepted that the chief cause of the achievement gap between socioeconomic groups is a language gap. Much work on the subject of language and vocabulary neglects a fundamental element of word acquisition that is so basic as to be almost invisible: The relationship between language and the world knowledge to which language refers is extremely strong. In human beings, knowledge of a subject is automatically accompanied by language use that represents that knowledge. It is this language/knowledge nexus that establishes the key principle of a language arts curriculum: A coherent and extended curriculum is the most effective vocabulary builder and the greatest contributor to increased reading comprehension.

In the classroom, reading comprehension and vocabulary are best served by spending extended time on reading and listening to texts on the same topic and discussing the facts and ideas in them. The number of classes spent on a topic should be determined by the time needed to understand and become familiar with the topic—and by grade level. In kindergarten and first grade, students might listen to and discuss single topics for just three classes. In fourth grade, the immersion might last two weeks, and in later grades longer. Needless to say, this principle applies to good fictional stories as well as good nonfiction. These texts and topics must be compelling enough that both the teacher and the children want to talk about what they read, and deep enough that there is enough reason to revisit the topic.

Such immersion in a topic not only improves reading and develops vocabulary, it also develops writing skill. One of the remarkable discoveries that I made over the many years that I taught composition was how much my students' writing improved when our class stuck to an interesting subject over an extended period. The organization of their papers got better. Their spelling improved. Their style improved. Their ideas improved. Now I understand why: When the mind becomes familiar with a subject, its limited resources can begin to turn to other aspects of the writing task, just as in reading. All aspects of a skill grow and develop as subject-matter familiarity grows. So we kill several birds with one stone when we teach skills by teaching stuff.

Moreover, there is evidence that by teaching solid content in reading classes we increase students' reading comprehension more effectively than by any other method. Some very suggestive research conducted by John Guthrie and his colleagues shows that reading instruction that focuses on a coherent knowledge domain over an extended time not only enhances students' general vocabularies compared to a control group but also improves their general fluency and motivation to read.[21] This is exactly what we would predict from what has been determined about the processes of reading comprehension and vocabulary growth. For instance, take the rule of thumb that you need to know 90 percent of the words to comprehend a text. As exposure to the domain is extended over time, the percentage of text words familiar to the child will increase. This means that incidental word learning of all the words of the text, both general words and domain-specific words, will be continually enhanced with extended immersion in a subject matter. At the same time, general fluency will also be enhanced as the child becomes more familiar with the domain. In short, the principle of content immersion can make language-arts classes become not just more interesting experiences for students but also much more effective vehicles for enhancing their reading and writing skills.

The great sociologist James S. Coleman, after spending a career examining the characteristics of effective schools and programs, concluded that the most important feature of a good school program is that it makes good academic use of school time. The consistent theme of Coleman's work had been "equality of educational opportunity"— the title of his monumental "Coleman Report" of 1966.[22] Making good use of school time, he concluded, was the single most egalitarian function the schools could perform, because for disadvantaged children, school time was the only academic-learning time, whereas advantaged students learned a lot outside of school. The main conclusion that people gleaned from Coleman's work was that social advantage counted for more in academic results than schooling did—as schools were then constituted. But there was a second, much more hopeful finding in the Coleman Report that Coleman himself pursued in his later career—the inherently egalitarian and compensatory character of a really good school program. A poor program adversely affects low-income students more than middle-income students who are less dependent on the school in gaining knowledge. By contrast, a good program is inherently compensatory because it has a bigger effect on low-income than middle-income students. This is because low-income students have more to learn—and in an effective program they begin to catch up.

Making good use of school time is the single most egalitarian function the schools perform, because for disadvantaged children, school time is the only academic learning time, whereas advantaged students can learn a lot outside of school.

A good, effective language-arts program that is focused on general knowledge and makes effective use of school time will not only raise reading achievement for all students, it will, by virtue of the Coleman principle, narrow the reading gap—and the achievement gap—between groups.

Notes

1. Chall, J.S., Jacobs, V.A., & Baldwin, L.E. (1990). *The Reading Crisis: Why poor children fall behind.* Cambridge, Mass.: Harvard University Press.
2. Hart, B., & Risley, T.R. (1995). *Meaningful Differences in the Everyday Experience of Young American Children.* Baltimore, Md.: Paul H. Brookes Publishing Co.
3. Campbell, J.R., Hombo, C.M., & Mazzeo, J. (2000). *NAEP 1999 Trends in Academic Progress: Three Decades of Student Performance.* NCES 2000469.
4. Recht, D.R., & Leslie, L. (1988). Effect of prior knowledge on good and poor readers' memory of text. *Journal of Educational Psychology,* vol. 80(1), pp. 16–20. American Psychological Association.
5. Miller, G.A. (1969). *The Psychology of Communication: seven essays.* Baltimore, Md.: Penguin Books.
6. Kintsch, W. (1998). *Comprehension: A Paradigm for Cognition.* N.Y.: Cambridge University Press.
7. Ericsson, K.A., & Charness, N. (1994). Expert performance: Its structure and acquisition. *American Psychologist,* vol. 49(8), pp. 725–747.
8. de Groot, A. (1965). *Thought and Choice in Chess.* The Hague, Mouton, in translation.
9. See endnote 2.
10. Graves, M.F., Brunetti, G.J., & Slater, W.H. (1982). The reading vocabularies of primary-grade children of varying geographic and social backgrounds. In J.A. Harris & L.A. Harris (eds), *New inquiries in reading research and instruction,* pp. 99–104. Rochester, N.Y.: National Reading Conference. Also see Graves, M.F., & Slater, W.H. (1987). The development of reading vocabularies in rural disadvantaged students, inner-city disadvantaged and middle-class suburban students. Paper presented at the meeting of the American Educational Research Association, Washington, D.C.
11. Smith, M.K. (1941). Measurement of the size of general English vocabulary through the elementary grades

and high school. *Genetic Psychological Monographs, 24,* pp. 311–345.

12. Nagy, W.E., and Scott, J. (2000). Vocabulary processes. In Kamil, M. et al., *Handbook of Reading Research,* vol. III. Mahwah, N.J.: Erlbaum.

13. Beck, I.L., McKeown, M.G., & Kucan, L. (2002) *Bringing Words to Life.* New York: Guilford Press.

14. See endnote 12.

15. Singer, M., Revlin, R., & Halldorson, M. (1990). Bridging-inferences and enthymemes. In A.C. Graesser & G.H. Bower (eds), *Inferences and Text Comprehension,* pp. 35–52. San Diego, Calif.: Academic Press.

16. Personal communication with Louisa Moats.

17. Sticht, T.G. (1975). Auding and reading: A developmental model. *Catalog of Selected Documents in Psychology,* vol. 5, Winter.

18. Chall, J.S., & Jacobs, V.A. (1996). The Reading, Writing, and Language Connection. In J. Shimron (ed.), *Literacy and Education: Essays in Memory of Dina Feiselson,* pp. 33–48. Cresskill, N.J.: Hampton Press, Inc.

19. See endnote 1.

20. Rosenshine, B., & Meister, C. (1994). Reciprocal Teaching: A Review of the Research. *Review of Educational Research,* vol. 64, pp. 479–530, Winter.

21. Guthrie, J.T., Anderson, E., Alao, S., & Rinehart, J. (1999). Influences of concept-oriented reading instruction on strategy use and conceptual learning from text. *Elementary School Journal,* vol. 99(4), March, pp. 343–366. See also Guthrie, John T., Wigfield, Allan, & Von-Secker, Clare. Effects of integrated instruction on motivation and strategy use in reading. *Journal of Educational Psychology*, vol. 92(2), June 2000, pp. 331–341. American Psychological Association.

22. Coleman, J.S. (1966). *Equality of Educational Opportunity.* U.S. Department of Health, Education and Welfare, Office of Education, Print Office, Washington, D.C.

STUDY GUIDE

1. What is fluency? Identify and describe its components and ways of measuring those components. (Strecker, Roser, & Martinez; Hirsch)

2. What causes dysfluent reading? What are the symptoms, as well as consequences, of dysfluent reading? (Strecker, Roser, & Martinez)

3. At what stage of reading development does emphasis on developing fluency need to be placed? How can reading fluency be improved? (Strecker, Roser, & Martinez; Hirsch)

4. What are the relationships among fluency, vocabulary, and comprehension? (Strecker, Roser, & Martinez; Herman & Dole; Hirsch)

5. Where and how do successful students learn the words they know? What implications does your answer have for vocabulary instruction? (Herman & Dole; Hirsch)

6. What is the role of direct instruction in vocabulary development? How has vocabulary traditionally been taught? What are the strengths and weaknesses of each approach? What would a sensible vocabulary-building program look like in the classroom? (Herman & Dole; Hirsch)

7. Describe the "fourth-grade slump" phenomenon. What is its likely cause? (Hirsch)

8. What do we now know about the factors that contribute to reading comprehension? Give examples from your own experience as a reader to illustrate each of those factors. (Hirsch)

9. Some reading educators have emphasized the need for instruction in comprehension strategies such as inferencing, predicting, visualizing, and summarizing. However, Hirsch argues that more emphasis should be placed on building up children's domain/subject-specific knowledge, rather than on isolated strategies instruction. With whom do you agree? Why? What do you think is the role of formal strategy instruction in developing comprehension? (Hirsch)

10. How can you build a coherent, effective reading/language arts curriculum that supports the development of reading comprehension across grade levels? Identify 3 to 5 characteristics of such a program. (Hirsch)

11. It has been suggested that listening comprehension places an upper limit on reading comprehension. Do you think it is possible for one to comprehend a text when it is read, but not when it is heard? What does this mean for reading comprehension instruction? For example, have someone read the sentence that follows aloud to you, and then read it silently to yourself. "What de Groot found, and what subsequent research has continually confirmed, is that the difference in fluency and higher-order skill between a novice and an expert does not lie in mental muscles, but in what de Groot called *erudition,* a vast store of quickly available, previously acquired, knowledge that enables the mind to take in a great deal in a brief time." (Hirsch)

12. Research has documented a large language gap between low-income and middle-income children. This gap is believed to be partially responsible for the disparity of reading achievement between the two groups. What are the roles of school and of home in narrowing this gap? Brainstorm some practical strategies that both teachers and parents could use to address this disparity. (Hirsch)

INQUIRY PROJECTS

1. Find one or two basal reading programs and examine the ways in which vocabulary and comprehension are taught in the programs. Use the principles and guidelines suggested in this section's articles to evaluate the quality of these programs.

2. Observe comprehension instruction in one primary and one upper grade classroom. Compare and contrast comprehension instruction in these classrooms. Discuss the relative strengths and weaknesses of each classroom.

3. Have a struggling reader read 2–3 grade-appropriate texts and record his/her reading. Play the recordings back and go over his/her reading, paying particular attention to dimensions of fluency such as accuracy, rate, phrasing, and prosody. Come up with a system of measuring each of these fluency components. Make plans to help the child improve his/her oral reading fluency.

FURTHER READING

Vocabulary

Anderson, R., & Nagy, W. (1992). The vocabulary conundrum. *American Educator*, *16*(4), 14–18, 44–47.

Baumann, J., & Kame'enui, E. (2003). *Vocabulary instruction: Research into practice.* New York: Guilford Press.

Beck, I., McKeown, M., & Kucan, L. (2002). *Bringing words to life: Robust vocabulary instruction.* New York: Guilford Press.

Blachowicz, C., & Fisher, P. (1996). *Teaching vocabulary in all classrooms.* Columbus, OH: Merrill.

Nagy, W. (1988). *Teaching vocabulary to improve comprehension.* Newark, DE: International Reading Association.

Fluency

Johns, J., & Berglund, R. (2002). *Fluency: Questions, answers, and evidence-based strategies.* Dubuque, IA: Kendall/Hunt.

Kuhn, M., & Stahl, S. (2000). *Fluency: A review of developmental and remedial practices* (Report No. 2–0008). Ann Arbor, MI: Center for the Improvement of Early Reading Achievement.

Rasinski, T., & Padak, N. (2001). *From phonics to fluency: Effective teaching of decoding and reading fluency in the elementary school.* Boston : Allyn & Bacon.

Comprehension

Block, C., Gambrell, L., & Pressley, M. (2002). *Improving comprehension instruction: Rethinking research, theory, and classroom practice.* Newark, DE: International Reading Association.

Block, C., & Pressley, M. (2002). *Comprehension instruction: Research-based best practices.* New York: Guilford Press.

Fountas, I., & Pinnell, G. S. (2000). *Guiding readers and writers (grades 3–6): Teaching comprehension, genre, and content literacy.* Portsmouth, NH: Heinemann.

Harvey, S., & Goudvis, A. (2000). *Strategies that work: Teaching comprehension to enhance understanding.* Portland, ME: Stenhouse.

Sweet, A., & Snow, C. (2003). *Rethinking reading comprehension.* New York: Guildford Press.

Tovani, C. (2000). *I read it, but I don't get it: Comprehension strategies for adolescent readers.* Portland, ME: Stenhouse.

Van Dijk, T. A., & Kintsch, W. (1983). *Strategies of discourse comprehension.* San Diego, CA: Academic Press.

Exploring the Language of School–Based Texts

INTRODUCTION

The books that children read have the potential to make an impact on, among other things, their conception of reading, their acquisition of reading skills, their motivation to read, and their writing. Because text matters, it is vitally important that children be exposed to books that are of high quality and rich variety. What are the linguistic and discursive features of different school-based texts? What are the defining characteristics of high quality books? How can teachers help students develop communicative competence in school-based discourses? The readings in this section provide some of the answers to these questions. They offer a glimpse into the practicalities of a language-based theory of education that foregrounds the role of language in literacy teaching and learning.

In the first article, Katharine Perera, a British educational linguist, argues that books for young children should support their initiation into literacy, be enjoyable and rewarding, and provide good models for their own writing. Applying these criteria, she identifies the three linguistic features of good storybooks for beginning readers as (a) having a recognizable, satisfying story structure, (b) using rhythmical, familiar, and natural-sounding language, and (c) containing motivated vocabulary repetition. Based on an examination of 45 sample books from several early reading series, the author concludes that the selection of beginning reading books for children will often involve some compromise because it is indeed very difficult to write entertaining stories in natural, rhythmic language using a controlled vocabulary.

The article by Australian applied linguist Len Unsworth, on the other hand, describes some of the linguistic features of expository texts in science and social studies. He demonstrates that the grammar of written language in curriculum content areas is distinctively different from that of everyday interactional spoken language in that the former makes an unusually heavy use of extended noun phrases and has a greater density of information. He suggests that learning to read and write in curriculum content areas is synonymous with learning the unique lexical and syntactic features that construe the curricular knowledge. He further argues that it is critical for both teachers and students to develop a conscious understanding of the ways in which the grammatical resources of language are deployed to construct different kinds of meanings that are appropriate for different contexts and purposes.

Finally, as trade books that juxtapose narrative and expository language features have become more common in recent years, the educational potential of these "hybrid" texts in comparison to prototypical storybooks and informational books needs to be examined. In the third article, American literacy scholars Carol Donovan and Laura Smolkin present analyses of the genre, content, and visual features of four types of trade books commonly used in science instruction: storybooks, narrative informational books, non-narrative informational books, and dual purpose books. The authors suggest that each of the four text types contains different textual features that allow it to offer something unique to the complex enterprise of science teaching and learning. They conclude that different types of trade books can be used to serve different instructional purposes.

Taken together, these three articles offer a functional description of, as well as practical strategies for exploring, the language of school-based texts. They provide potent models of discourse analysis that can yield useful insights into the language of schooling. A conscious understanding of the nature, characteristics, and functions of such school-based language will enable teachers not only to make informed decisions in selecting appropriate books for particular learners, purposes, and tasks at hand, but also to provide productively explicit guidance in apprenticing children to the practices of school-based discourses.

The 'Good Book': Linguistic Aspects

Katharine Perera
University of Manchester, UK

What Is Required of Early Reading Books?

Ideally, the reading books that are available for children in their first year or so at school need to be able to do three things. First, they need to provide the kind of text which will support children as they begin to learn to read. Secondly, they need to show children that reading is enjoyable and rewarding. And thirdly, they need to offer good models for children's own writing.

[Early] reading books ... need to ... support children as they begin to learn to read ... show children that reading is enjoyable and rewarding ... [and] offer good models for children's own writing.

The first requirement is necessary unless children have already acquired the foundations of literacy at home, or unless the teacher teaches reading using other means, such as the published 'Language Experience' approach *Break-through to Literacy*. In practice, in many schools the reading books that children are given provide the main basis of their reading instruction. The second requirement—that books should be enjoyable—is important for all children but particularly for those who have had no experience of books and story-telling at home. If the first books they meet are dull, pointless and unappealing, it is hard to see how they can discern any reason for making the effort to learn to read. The third requirement—that books should be well written—is justified by the evidence (e.g., Eckhoff, 1983) that children tend to write in the style of the books they are currently reading.

Taking these three requirements as a starting point, and focusing in this chapter solely on stories and only on their linguistic aspects, it is possible to outline in broad terms some features that characterise good books for beginning readers.

From Perera, K. (1993), The 'good book': Linguistic aspects. In R. Beard (Ed.), Teaching literacy: Balancing perspectives (pp. 95–113). Reprinted by permission of Hodder Arnold.

Some Linguistic Features of Good Story Books for Beginning Readers

1. Stories should have a recognisable story structure. Typically, stories are written in the past tense and include characters, a setting, an action or event or situation that motivates what follows, and a satisfying conclusion. Such a structure encourages the reader to keep going because it holds out the promise that the effort of reading will be rewarded. This plays a very important part in making reading enjoyable. It also provides a necessary and valuable model for the young writer.

2. Stories should be written in flowing, rhythmical language as this is pleasant to read aloud and, again, provides a good model for the young writer. There is also a case to be made for the use of the kind of sentence patterns that children are likely to hear, and to use in their own speech. This case rests on the evidence from research by people like Rose-Marie Weber (1970) that beginning readers who are reading aloud say what they expect to find rather than necessarily what is printed. This suggests that familiar language patterns will lead to more successful prediction and, therefore, to a greater sense of achievement.

The structure of written language has characteristic differences from spoken language.

However, the structure of written language has characteristic differences from spoken language (there is an account of these differences in Perera, 1984). One aspect of children's development as writers is their growing ability to use appropriately those structures that are more common in writing than in speech. This grammatical ability is acquired chiefly through experience of a literary style in books—first by hearing stories read aloud and then by reading them for themselves. Therefore, at some point in children's literacy development, there is a place for stories written in language which does not depend exclusively on an oral style. Teachers who are sensitive to their pupils' level of language development and knowledgeable about their experience of listening to stories will be in a position to decide when that point has been reached. For some children at least, a judicious blend of familiar and more literary grammatical structures will be just the right combination.

Whether the language of early reading books is familiar or more literary, what is important is that it should be language that people really use, rather than a kind of language, sometimes known as 'readerese', that occurs exclusively in books written to teach children to read.

3. Stories that are to be used by children who are beginning to learn to read should have a higher level of vocabulary repetition than is usual in books written for proficient readers. It is partly by seeing the same word many times in different contexts that children gradually develop the essential skill of rapid and effortless word recognition (Juel and Roper/Schneider, 1985). But word recognition is also aided by familiarity with frequent spelling patterns and their pronunciation. Marilyn Adams, who has carried out a thorough review of the research literature, says this:

> *Proficient reading depends on an automatic capacity to recognise frequent spelling patterns visually and to translate them phonologically. Differences in this capacity are principal separators of good from poor readers.* (Adams, 1990, p. 293)

Therefore, children are likely to be helped if their reading books contain at least some words that demonstrate a consistent relationship between spelling and pronunciation. We can note at this point that this does *not* mean language of the 'Can Nan fan Dan?' variety; indeed, Marilyn Adams herself comments that such language is 'inordinately difficult to process' (1990, p. 322). Rather, it means that if a book contains, say, the word *reading,* it will be more helpful if it also has words like *leader* and *teacher* than if it includes other *-ea-* words with a different pronunciation, such as *head* or *great.*

It is hard to write entertaining stories in natural, rhythmical language using a limited and constrained vocabulary.

To fulfill all these criteria is very difficult. It is hard to write entertaining stories in natural, rhythmical language using a limited and constrained vocabulary. Therefore, the selection of reading books will often involve some compromise.

Reading Books Examined

In order to discover how far different kinds of reading books do meet the criteria, I have analysed the language of a number of books that are used with children in the early stages of learning to read. These books come from the following five reading schemes: 'New Way', 'Reading 360', 'Oxford Reading Tree', 'Story Chest' and 'Book Bus'. In each case, I have examined between 1000 and 1200 words. I have also looked at roughly 1200 words from books that do not form part of any scheme and have not been written with the aim of teaching children to read; they are the kind of books that are used by many teachers to supplement or, in some cases, to replace a reading scheme. (They are often called 'real books', but I believe that this is an unfortunate label as it implies, misleadingly, that any book that is written with the purpose of helping children to read is not real. I prefer to call them 'individual books', as what they have in common is that they stand alone and do not form part of any set of graded or sequenced books.) The selection of these books was made by a children's book specialist, who has considerable experience both as a teacher of reading and as an adviser to teachers who want to replace a reading scheme with individual books.

Between them, the forty-five stories I have examined represent a range of different views about the kind of reading material that should be presented to beginning readers. We can reveal the extent of that range by seeing how many of the characteristics that are typically associated with a reading scheme are displayed by each of the six sets of books. Archetypal reading schemes are sets of books with most or all of the following objective characteristics: (1) they are produced with the aim of teaching children to read; (2) they are explicitly and finely graded into ascending levels of difficulty; (3) they have strict vocabulary control within and across books; (4) they focus on consistent spelling patterns; (5) they feature the same set of characters in all the stories; (6) they have a common authorship; (7) they have a uniform format; and (8) they are supplemented by other activities, materials and a teachers' manual.

The early stages of 'New Way', 'Reading 360' and 'Oxford Reading Tree' display most of these characteristics, with slight differences of emphasis. 'New Way', for example, gives more prominence than the other two to consistent spelling patterns but does not use the same set of characters in all the stories. The early stories in 'Story Chest' have some reading scheme features (notably (1), (3), (6) and (8)) but the books are not finely graded for difficulty; they come in different formats; they are written in different styles about completely different characters; and they do not aim to teach consistent spelling patterns. (Sound-spelling relationships are taught separately in this scheme by means of rhymes.) The stories in the 'emergent' and 'early' phases of 'Book Bus' have been broadly graded and put together by the publisher to provide teachers with a collection of individual books that can be used to teach reading. Other than that they have none of the characteristics of a reading scheme: they are written by different authors; they have different formats; there are no shared characters; there is no vocabulary control between books; and there is no focus on spelling patterns. As the five schemes differ in the extent to which they can be considered archetypal reading schemes, I shall from now on refer to them collectively as 'publishers' schemes' rather than 'reading schemes'. The individual books are not written with the aim of teaching children to read, and they are published by different publishers so, not surprisingly, they have none of the objective characteristics of reading schemes.

In order to make the comparisons between these six rather different sets of books as fair as possible, I have used the measure of the number of different words within any one story and have restricted the selection of stories to those which contain fewer than 120 different words. (Many individual books that are in use with beginning readers use over 200 different words.) More detailed information about all of the stories is given in Table 2.

In the rest of this chapter I shall use the analysis of the language of these forty-five stories to illustrate in more detail the linguistic features I have already outlined.

Story Structure

We can consider some stories which, despite being very simple, nevertheless demonstrate in an embryonic way the characteristics of well-formed story structure.

In *Lots of Caps* ('New Way'), a cap-seller puts all his caps on top of his head and then sits down under a tropical tree and falls asleep. While he is sleeping, monkeys in the tree steal all the caps except one. When he wakes up he stamps his feet in anger but the monkeys merely imitate him. He is so cross that he throws down his remaining cap—and the monkeys imitate that too and the cap-seller retrieves all his caps. So the story presents a character in a clearly defined setting who has a problem that is solved in a satisfyingly humorous way. There is also a humorous ending to *New Trainers* ('Oxford Reading Tree'): in this story a boy gets a new pair of trainers and then plays in them so that they get wet and muddy. His father is so preoccupied with telling him off that he doesn't notice that he is walking into wet concrete in *his* new pair of shoes. Here the conclusion depends on a pleasing role reversal.

Sometimes the conclusion is signalled by a change of language after a number of repetitions. For example, in *Sleeping Out* ('Story Chest') some children are sleeping out in the open with their mother. Every time they hear a strange noise they ask her what it is and she tells them, e.g.

What's that going sniffle, sniffle?
A hedgehog. Go to sleep.

What's that going yowl, yowl?
A cat. Go to sleep.

The last strange noise is 'zzzz-zzzz':

What's that going zzzz-zzzz?
It's Mum. She's gone to sleep.

Caspar's week (Individual) uses the same technique. Caspar is an accident-prone cat who creates a different kind of havoc on every day of the week:

On Monday ...
Caspar fell in the toilet.
There was water everywhere!
On Tuesday ...
Caspar knocked a plant off the windowsill.
There was dirt everywhere!

The story ends with a departure from the pattern that has been established:

Tomorrow is Sunday ...
Maybe Caspar will rest!

Not all early reading books handle story structure well, though. It may be that the characters are not properly introduced at the beginning. For example, the story *At the Zoo* ('Reading 360') begins like this:

'This is the zoo, Ben,' said Tom.
'You will like it here.'

Mum appears on the next page but it is not until another four pages further on that it becomes apparent that Dad is there too, when Ben says, 'Come here, Dad.' This is rather disconcerting at this late stage in the story and is similar to what children sometimes do in their own story writing.

Another weakness is when there are sudden, unsignalled shifts of time or setting. There is an example in *The Storm* ('Oxford Reading Tree'):

It was bedtime.
Biff was in her room.
Biff looked outside.
There was a storm.
It was time for school.
Wilf and Wilma came.

The last two sentences would read more smoothly, and would provide a better model for children's own writing, if they were written like this: The next day, when it was time for school, Wilf and Wilma came.

Sometimes there is inconsistency in the use of tenses. For example, *Bear hunt* (Individual) begins like a typical story with a formulaic opening and past tense verbs:

One day Bear went for a walk.
Two hunters were hunting.

When Bear is in danger, the narrator addresses him directly, e.g. 'Look out! Look out, Bear!' Such interventions are sometimes followed, appropriately, by the past tense, e.g. 'Quickly bear *began* [my italics] to draw'. But sometimes they are followed, rather oddly, by a present tense verb, before the narrative reverts to the past again, e.g.

> *Look up, Bear!*
> *Bear is caught.*
> *But Bear still had his pencil ...*

Given children's tendency to muddle tenses in their writing anyway, it is unfortunate if what they read reinforces that tendency.

Probably the most serious failure of story structure is the absence of a satisfying and clearly final conclusion. In *At the Zoo* ('Reading 360') the children go to see the goats:

> *'Hello, little goat,' said Ted.*
> *'What do you want?'*
> *'Can't you see,' said Kay.*
> *'It wants to play.'*
> *'No,' said Ted.*
> *'It wants something to eat.'*
> *'But we can't feed the animals,' said Tom.*
> *'The zoo man will feed the goats.'*

And that is the end of the story. It simply stops, without there being any sense that it is complete and rounded off. The same is true of one of the individual books, *If I had a sheep*. Here, a young girl fantasises about the things she would do if she had a sheep: she would teach it to count, play games with it where they would pretend to be grown-ups or pirates or princesses, and so on. The story ends like this:

> *If she fell over ...*
> *... I would make her better.*
> *I would read her a story ...*
> *... and take her to bed.*

As the fantasies have not been confined to a single day, there is no reason why going to bed should signal the end of the story—it would be perfectly possible for it to continue the next day. Having a satisfying conclusion matters so much because it gives a point to the story. Without one, all that has gone before is undermined: if there is no point to the tale, then why tell it? And, even more, why read it? In a study of children's oral story-telling, Arthur Applebee (1978) found that fewer than half of his five-year-old subjects gave their story a formal conclusion, although nearly all of them handled the other aspects of story structure successfully. This finding emphasises how important it is for children's reading books to provide good examples of well-concluded stories.

Rhythmical Language

The rhythm of English derives from the alternation of stressed and unstressed syllables. Typically, nouns, verbs, adjectives and adverbs are stressed while the articles, prepositions, auxiliaries and pronouns are unstressed. In the following sentence the words that would normally be stressed are printed in capital letters, the unstressed words are in lower case:

> THIS is the BEAR who FELL in the BIN.

When children first begin to read, it is very common for them to give all words equal stress, so the sentence sounds like this:

> THIS—IS—THE—BEAR—WHO—FELL—IN—THE—BIN.

Although beginning readers tend to stress every word, they do not generally stress every syllable, so 'parrot' and 'elephant' are pronounced PARrot and ELephant, not PAR-ROT and EL-E-PHANT. Therefore, an excellent way to introduce the alternation of stressed and unstressed syllables into children's oral reading is to give them books that contain polysyllabic as well as monosyllabic words. I counted the monosyllables and polysyllables in each of the forty-five stories to see what the proportion of polysyllabic words was. Some of the early books in 'New Way' and 'Reading 360' contain only monosyllabic words. This is likely to lead to jerky reading with too many strong stresses, e.g.

> BEN—THE—DOG
> WENT—DOWN—THE—HILL.
> LOOK—AT—ME.
> LOOK—AT—ME—SAID—BEN.

(*Down the hill*, 'New Way')

None of the stories analysed in these two schemes has more than 20 per cent polysyllabic words. In contrast, the other four sets of books each has at least one story with more than 25 per cent polysyllabic words. This should lead to more rhythmical reading, even if the child is still stressing the grammatical words that are unstressed in adult speech, e.g.

> 'GET TEDdy,' SAID KIPper.
> BIFF COULDn't GET TEDdy.

(*By the stream*, 'Oxford Reading Tree')

Language That Children Use or Hear

Variety of Sentence Length

We can expect that children will read more readily language that they themselves either use or hear,

Table 1 Variety of Sentence Length in 'Individual' Books

Title	Range of sentence length in words	Mean	s.d. (standard deviation)
Have you seen the crocodile?	2–24	10.8	8.0
*Rosie's walk**	32	32.0	—
Caspar's week	3–11	6.1	2.6
Bear hunt	1–11	4.1	2.2
You'll soon grow into them, Titch	4–22	11.2	5.5
If I had a sheep	8–14	9.5	1.9
Charles Tiger	5–16	10.6	3.4
Mr Gumpy's outing	4–52	9.8	10.8
Mr McGee	6–15	11.2	2.8

*This story consists of one 32-word sentence.

than language that no one is likely either to say or to read aloud for pleasure. A number of grammatical features contribute to natural-sounding language. The first to consider is variety of sentence length. Taking the individual books as a yardstick (since their authors have not been constrained by ideas about what makes sentences readable), we can see in Table 1 the kind of variation in the length of written sentences that occurs naturally.

It is clear that there is considerable variation of sentence length within most of the books. *Mr Gumpy's outing* is highly unusual in having a difference of 48 words between the longest and the shortest sentence, but it is not abnormal for there to be a difference of 10 or 11 words (e.g. *Charles Tiger*). The comparable figures for the publishers' schemes are given in Table 3. The 'Book Bus' selection is very similar to the set of individual books, even containing one very unusual book, *The pet show,* which has a difference of 48 words between the longest and the shortest sentence. The other publishers' schemes generally have rather less variation of sentence length within each book, with a difference of 6 or 7 words between the longest and the shortest sentence being normal.

The figures in Table 2 and Table 3 also reveal the fact that sentences are, on average, longer in the individual books than in the publishers' schemes. Mean sentence length in *Charles Tiger,* for example is 10.6 words, whereas in *Fat Pig's car* ('New Way') it is 5.7; in *Help me* ('Story Chest') it is 5.2; and in *The storm* ('Oxford Reading Tree') it is only 4.7. As sentences are units of meaning, it may be that a heavy concentration of long sentences impedes understanding and is rather daunting for those children who are reading slowly and with some difficulty. Where short sentences are interspersed with occasional longer ones, the variation makes the language sound natural, while the general pattern of fairly short sentences probably makes the young reader's task easier. The closing sentences of *The sports day* ('New Way') illustrate this:

> *Tom got up.*
> *He went very fast.*
> *'Hello Tom,' said his Dad.*
> *You have jumped fast but*
> *you have jumped back*
> *to the start.*

In contrast, an unrelieved sequence of short sentences—particularly when they have a similar sentence structure—can sound rather stilted, e.g.

> *The witch opened the door.*
> *Gran pushed the witch.*
> *Chip took the witch's keys.*
> *They ran out of the room.*
> *Chip locked the door.*

(*Castle adventure*, 'Oxford Reading Tree')

Appropriate Use of Pronouns

Another grammatical characteristic of natural-sounding language is the appropriate use of pronouns. Once we have mentioned someone or something in a conversation, we generally refer to them after that with a pronoun, so long as the reference is clear, e.g., 'I saw my sister yesterday. She was looking well. She's just come back from a cycling holiday.' It would be very odd to say, 'I saw my sister yesterday. My sister was looking well. My sister has just come back from a cycling holiday.' Yet this is what happens in some early reading books, e.g.

> *Jill said,*
> *'We want to help the tortoise.*
> *What can we do?'*
> *Miss Hill said,*
> *'What do you think the tortoise wants?'*
> *'The tortoise wants a home,' said Kay.*

(*The tortoise*, 'Reading 360')

Table 2 Reading Books Examined

Scheme	Publisher	Date	Author(s)	Title	Level	Total no. of words	No. of sentences
'NEW WAY'	Macmillan Education	1987	Anonymous	*Down the hill*	2	60	12
			"	*Sam wants to play*	2	68	12
			"	*Help me*	2	56	10
			"	*The sports day*	3	114	21
			"	*Fat Pig's birthday*	3	125	16
			"	*Lots of caps*	3	194	31
			"	*Fat Pig's car*	4	212	37
			"	*Looking for a letter*	4	221	30
			"	*Bad cow*	4	168	28
						1218	197
'READING 360'	Ginn	1978	H. Keenan-Church	*Ben and Lad*	2	68	23
			T. Clymer	*The tortoise*	3	469	84
			"	*At the zoo*	4	402	75
			"	*The hare and the tortoise*	5	166	27
						1105	209
'OXFORD READING TREE'	OUP	1986	R. Hunt	*A new dog*	2	52	12
			"	*New trainers*	2	34	9
			"	*By the stream*	3	71	16
			"	*Nobody wanted to play*	3	80	16
			"	*House for sale*	4	109	23
			"	*The storm*	4	188	40
			"	*Gran*	5	309	58
			"	*Castle adventure*	5	306	57
						1149	231
'STORY CHEST'	Arnold-Wheaton	1982	J. Cowley & J. Melser	*Feet*	Get ready	18	4
			"	*Who's going to lick the bowl?*	Ready, set go	16	6
			"	*Plop!*	Ready, set go	30	6
			"	*Sleeping out*	Ready, set go	49	15
			"	*Mrs Wishy Washy*	Read together	102	14
			"	*Help me*	2	170	33
			"	*Two little mice*	2	302	48
			"	*Let me in*	3	354	43
						1041	169
'BOOK BUS'	Collins	1990	K. Hayles	*I don't like fish*	Emergent	76	15
			S. Wilde	*Yum, Yum!*	Emergent	85	17
			M. Shepherd	*The enormous turnip*	Early	302	35
			S. Andrews	*Greedy Stanley*	Early	192	26
			R. Green & B. Scarffe	*The pet show*	Early	274	9
			D. Blackburn	*There's a monster in my house*	Early	91	12
			E. Reeves	*Flower shop Fred*	Early	196	24
						1216	138

(Continued)

Table 2   *Continued*

Scheme	Publisher	Date	Author(s)	Title	Level	Total no. of words	No. of sentences
'INDIVIDUAL'	Walker	1986	C. West	*Have you seen the crocodile?*	—	151	14
	Puffin	1970	P. Hutchins	*Rosie's walk*	—	32	1
	Macdonald	1988	C. Ward	*Caspar's week*	—	85	14
	Scholastic	1979; 1982	A. Browne	*Bear hunt*	—	81	20
	Puffin	1983; 1985	P. Hutchins	*You'll soon grow into them, Titch*	—	191	17
	Macmillan	1988	M. Inkpen	*If I had a sheep*	—	104	11
	Collins	1987; 1989	S. Dodds	*Charles Tiger*	—	138	13
	Puffin	1970; 1978	J. Burningham	*Mr Gumpy's outing*	—	283	29
	Puffin	1987; 1989	P. Allen	*Mr McGee*	—	202	18
						1267	137

Table 3   Variety of Sentence Length in Publishers' Schemes

Scheme and title	Range of sentence length in words	Mean	s.d. (standard deviation)
'NEW WAY'			
Down the hill	3–7	5.0	1.5
Sam wants to play	5–7	5.7	1.0
Help me	4–7	5.6	1.0
The sports day	3–12	5.4	2.0
Fat Pig's birthday	5–12	7.8	1.9
Lots of caps	2–15	6.3	3.3
Fat Pig's car	3–10	5.7	1.7
Looking for a letter	4–14	7.4	2.5
Bad cow	1–13	6.0	2.6
'READING 360'			
Ben and Lad	1–7	3.0	1.3
The tortoise	1–14	5.6	2.5
At the zoo	1–10	5.4	2.0
The hare and the tortoise	3–11	6.2	2.3
'OXFORD READING TREE'			
A new dog	4–6	4.3	0.7
New trainers	2–5	3.8	0.8
By the stream	1–7	4.4	1.6
Nobody wanted to play	1–6	5.0	1.4
House for sale	3–7	4.7	0.9
The storm	3–8	4.7	1.2
Gran	3–10	5.3	1.6
Castle adventure	2–9	5.4	1.3
'STORY CHEST'			
Feet	4–6	4.5	1.0
Who's going to lick the bowl?	1–6	2.7	1.8
Plop!	3–6	5.0	1.1

(Continued)

Table 3 *Continued*

Scheme and title	Range of sentence length in words	Mean	s.d. (standard deviation)
Sleeping out	2–5	3.3	1.2
Mrs Wishy Washy	4–12	7.3	3.0
Help me	2–10	5.2	1.5
Two little mice	1–13	6.3	2.5
Let me in	4–20	8.2	3.8
'BOOK BUS'			
I don't like fish	2–8	5.1	1.8
Yum! Yum!	4–9	5.0	1.3
The enormous turnip	5–21	8.6	4.0
Greedy Stanley	3–15	7.4	3.0
The pet show	8–58	30.4	16.5
There's a monster in my house	5–12	7.6	3.1
Flower shop Fred	3–17	8.2	4.2

Here it would be more natural if one or more of the tortoise phrases were replaced by 'it'. The under use of pronouns is not confined to reading schemes, however. The individual book *Mr Gumpy's outing* begins like this:

> *This is Mr Gumpy.*
> *Mr Gumpy owned a boat and his house*
> *was by a river.*
> *One day Mr Gumpy went out in his boat.*
> *'May we come with you?' said the children.*
> *'Yes,' said Mr Gumpy,*
> *'if you don't squabble.'*

Although it might be argued that this is a special kind of repetition of the proper noun Mr Gumpy, characteristic of a particularly literary style, it seems likely that the following literary example, with its combination of the proper noun 'Mr Wolf' and the pronoun 'he', provides a more helpful model for young children's own writing:

> *Along came old Mr Wolf.*
> *He went up to the house made of straw.*
> *And old Mr Wolf said,*
> *'Little pig,*
> *little pig,*
> *let me come in.'*

(*Let me in.* 'Story Chest')

The appropriate use of pronouns also entails avoiding them when their reference would not be clear. In their writing, young children sometimes use a pronoun without the necessary noun having been explicitly mentioned. There is an example of this in *I don't like fish* ('Book Bus'):

> *'Hello, Seal. What's your favourite food?'*
> *'Fish of course,' said Seal.*
> *'What do you think about fish, Walrus?'*

> *'Fish are FANTASTIC,' said Walrus.*
> *'Do you eat fish too?' said Polar Bear.*
> *'Sometimes, but beans on toast is best!'*

The last 'you' in this extract refers to an Eskimo boy, but this is only apparent from the picture. It is obviously unfortunate when a reading book provides a misleading model for children's own writing.

Reduced Forms

In speech, we generally use the reduced forms of words like 'is', 'are', 'have', 'will' and 'not' unless we want to emphasise them. So we are more likely to say, 'I don't know if she'll like the present I've bought her' than, 'I do not know if she will like the present I have bought her'. In the individual books these speech-like reductions are used extensively, e.g.

> *'We'll walk home across the fields,'*
> *said Mr Gumpy. 'It's time for tea.'*

(*Mr Gumpy's outing,* 'Individual')

'Oxford Reading Tree', 'Story Chest' and 'Book Bus' also generally use reduced forms, e.g.

> *'I don't like witches,' said Gran.*
> *She put a net over the witch.*
> *The witch couldn't get out.*

(*Castle adventure,* 'Oxford Reading Tree')

In the other two publishers' schemes there is some inconsistency. For example, in *Fat Pig's birthday* ('New Way') 'don't' is given in the reduced form but 'it is', 'I will', 'will not' and 'did not' are all given in full:

> *It is Fat Pig's birthday.*
> *I will have a party,*

said Fat Pig.
Don't forget to come
to my party, said Fat Pig.
We will not forget,
said Meg and Ben.
...
Look, I did not forget
to come to the party, said Deb.

If that passage is read aloud with reduced forms throughout, it sounds rather less stilted. It would be easy for publishers to replace unreduced forms with reduced ones when books are reprinted; in some cases, the resulting increase in naturalness would be quite marked.

Vocabulary Control

The real challenge that faces authors of early reading books is to produce interesting well-structured stories written in rhythmical, natural-sounding language while using only a strictly controlled vocabulary and endeavouring to repeat the most important words frequently enough for children to be able to become familiar with them. Some stories are unappealing to read at least partly because they contain unmotivated repetition. By that I mean repetition that does not contribute to the story but is there purely to provide reading practice, e.g.

Ben can run.
Look.
We can run.
We can run like this.
...
We can run.
We can run fast.

(*Ben and Lad*, 'Reading 360')

In the forty-five stories I have examined there is very little of that kind of repetition. Authors seem to take considerable pains to use *motivated* repetition—that is, repetition which plays a key role in the telling of the story. For example, when Charles Tiger searches for his lost roar, his quest leads him to different places and different creatures:

He looked in the long grass
and found a snake
—but no roar.
He looked in a deep river
and found a crocodile
—but no roar.

Here there is repetition both of vocabulary and of grammatical structure, with the pattern 'He looked in a *adjective noun* and found a *noun*' occurring again

and again. Not only does this nicely reflect the insistent nature of his search; it also makes possible the breaking of the pattern at the end off the story when the lost roar is found:

Under a stone he found a spider
—and his
> *great*
>> *big*
>>> *roar.*

(*Charles Tiger*, 'Individual')

Some of the publishers' scheme stories have a similar kind of motivated repetition. For example, in *Bad cow* ('New Way') when a cow gets into the garden, Ben tries to chase her out without success:

Moo, said the cow
but she did not go.

He then enlists the help first of a dog and then of a horse, each time with the same result. The pattern changes, though, when a bee intervenes:

The bee buzzed round the cow.
Buzz, buzz, buzz, said the bee.
The cow ran out of the garden.

The motivated repetition in *Charles Tiger* means that each different word is repeated, on average, 2.1 times, but some of the individual books have much lower word repetition rates than this, e.g. *Bear hunt* – 1.5, and *Rosie's walk* – 1.3. In contrast, the publishers' scheme books have higher word repetition rates, e.g. *Bad cow* ('New Way') – 3.2, *Gran* ('Oxford Reading Tree') – 3.5, *Two little mice* ('Story Chest') – 4.0, and *At the zoo* ('Reading 360') – 6.2. But at least as important as these figures are the repetition rates *between* books. Not surprisingly, the individual books share very little vocabulary with each other. So if a child were to read *Charles Tiger* (which has 66 different words) and then to read *You'll soon grow into them* (with 62), he or she would find only seven words (11 per cent) in common between the two books. In this respect, the books in 'Book Bus' are more like individual books than reading scheme books. Between two of the 'Book Bus' books—*There's a monster in my house* and *The enormous turnip*—there is an overlap of 16 per cent. In contrast, the overlap between the pairs of books I examined in the remaining schemes ranged between 24 per cent (*Fat Pig's car* and *Looking for a letter*, 'New Way') and 45 per cent (*Two little mice* and *Let me in*, 'Story Chest'). When children move from one book to another within a scheme, they are to some extent building on what they already know. When they move from one individual book to another they may well be virtually starting afresh each time. Clearly this is possible only if there is a great deal of adult support available, either in the classroom or at home.

Conclusions

As Roger Beard (1990, p. 91), and many others, have demonstrated, it is very easy to catalogue the weaknesses in the earlier generation of reading schemes, with their dull, pointless 'stories' and their unnatural language. If we imagine a situation where an infant teacher is stocking her bookshelves from scratch but is forced to choose between such a scheme and individual books, then we may predict that she would reject the old-fashioned reading scheme. But, fortunately, the choice is not so stark. Recently published schemes have benefited greatly from some of the ideas that have gained currency during the last twenty years or so. These ideas include the centrality of meaning in the reading process; the importance of story structure; the need for natural-sounding language that can be read, and re-read, with pleasure; the interplay between words and pictures; the contribution that print in the environment can make to learning to read, and so on. In spite of the marked improvements in the newer schemes, much current discussion about books for teaching reading still draws a sharp dividing line between reading schemes on the one hand and 'real' books on the other.

I have tried in this chapter to show that, by examining a range of books and relating their linguistic features to the needs of children who are beginning to learn to read, it is possible to identify the strong and weak points of both kinds of book and to recognise the contribution that both kinds can make to the learning process. If the teacher knows there is enough adult support available to make it feasible for her pupils to learn to read solely from individual books, then she may choose this approach, and the children will encounter some appealing books. Even so, those of average and below average ability may find the sentences in some books dauntingly long and the rate of introduction of new vocabulary unmanageably rapid. If, on the other hand, the teacher chooses to use a good reading scheme which has well-constructed interesting stories written in reasonably natural language, then she can still try to keep a sizeable number of the best individual books in the classroom, so that the whole class can enjoy them together at storytime, or so that children can read them by themselves when they are ready to. It is worth making the point that the greatest need for the simplification, structure and support offered by a reading scheme is in the early stages, when there is so much to be learnt at once. After that, once children can read simple stories fluently and independently, many of them will be ready to enjoy for themselves the rich delights offered by individual books.

Bibilography

Adams, M.J. (1990) *Beginning to Read: Thinking and Learning about Print.* Cambridge. Mass.: MIT Press.

Applebee, A.N. (1978) *The Child's Concept of Story: Ages Two to Seventeen.* Chicago: University of Chicago Press.

Beard, R. (1990) *Developing Reading 3–13,* 2nd edn. London: Hodder and Stoughton.

Eckoff, B. (1983) How reading affects children's writing, *Language Arts,* 60, 607–16.

Juel, C. and Roper/Schneider, D. (1985) The influence of basal readers on first grade reading, *Reading Research Quarterly,* 20, 134–52.

Weber, R.M. (1970) A linguistic analysis of first-grade reading errors, *Reading Research Quarterly,* V, 3, 427–51.

Some Practicalities of a Language-Based Theory of Learning

Len Unsworth
University of Sydney, Australia

If we compare the examples of factual writing in Figure 1, we will quickly see that the piece in the left-hand column is very much like speech written down, while the piece on the right shows much more use of the distinctive grammatical features of written language (for additional related comparisons see Christie, 1984: p. 96, and Gilbert, 1990: p. 75).

We can only speculate as to why this is the case, but we can be reasonably confident that the writer of the piece on the right is better prepared for reading and writing the kinds of curriculum area texts that s/he will increasingly need to negotiate as s/he progresses through the education system. There is now a good deal of evidence to show that, in curriculum areas like

Do you know what this is? A pond is the answer (coloured picture). Fish (coloured picture). Water spider (coloured picture). These are just two of the things that live in the pond. Of course there are more things. A fish breathes through its mouth and can only live in water like we would die if we were put in water for a long while and could not come out, a water spider lives in a bubble of air underneath the water. It can also run across the water without getting its feet wet...	A pond is full of life. A whole city in miniature may exist in a pond. The animals are either carnivorous or vegetarian. Of all the things that live in the pond the caddis fly lava is the one with the best camouflage. It makes a kind of shed out of the substance around it. The water spider has an ingenious method of breathing underwater. He makes his den and then he brings down air bubbles in his hind legs. The fish breathe by breathing in water and then extracting its properties of oxygen by means of a type of grid (drawing).

(From N. Martin, 1983: p. 110–12)

Figure 1 Comparison of two samples of factual writing.

science and technology and human society and its environment, developing knowledge and understanding and learning to control the specialised language of such curriculum areas is one and the same thing (Wells, 1994; Halliday & Martin, 1993; Martin, 1993a; 1993b; Lemke, 1989, 1990; Kress, 1984). The practical question for teachers is: 'How do we intervene to support children in developing the kinds of grammatical resources used by the writer of the right-hand column in Figure 1?'

There are, of course, some obvious moves such as ensuring access to appropriate factual texts and working with children on these as a part of close classroom study and also as a part of 'wider reading' programs. But we shall propose here that a fairly modest level of teacher expertise in functional grammar can greatly enhance such practical interventions. Theoretical knowledge of

just what are the grammatical features that characterise the specialised language of curriculum areas makes it practically possible for teachers to effectively integrate the teaching and learning of these grammatical features and curriculum area concepts.

We will look at just two aspects of the grammar of written language in curriculum areas, emphasising how they are different from the language of everyday talk. The first of these is the greater density of information in the written texts of information books. This density is achieved partly through the use of longer and more complex noun groups in the written medium. The second aspect is the greater abstraction of written language. This is partly due to the greater use of nouns to express actions and events, whereas in everyday talk they are typically expressed by verbs.

We will illustrate these aspects of written language in primary school texts, indicating how they are essential to the construction of curriculum area knowledge and understanding. We will argue that children need to control these linguistic resources to read factual texts efficiently and to improve the relative effectiveness of their writing of factual genres in curriculum areas. In the final section we will note current approaches to teaching based on the ideas discussed and offer some additional practical activities for building and consolidating children's knowledge of selected grammatical resources central to the language of curriculum area learning.

Characteristics of Curriculum Area Language

Lexical Density

In English, written medium tends to pack information more densely than spoken medium. This is achieved through greater use of lexical items (content words) in comparison with grammatical items (structure words). The lexical items are underlined in the following text taken from Hammond (1990: p. 36) where a student is talking about the novel *Z for Zachariah* (O'Brien, 1975).

> Like I <u>reckon</u> he would have been really <u>nice</u> but now that he's been to all the <u>towns</u> and <u>seen</u> like there's no <u>life</u> or anything and he <u>comes</u> into the <u>valley</u> and <u>sees</u> <u>Ann</u> and <u>sees</u> <u>life</u> and he just <u>wanted</u> <u>power</u> over her because he's never had <u>power</u> or anything before.

Lexical items form part of open sets: for 'know' we might have 'consider', 'thought', 'believe', 'appreciate' and so on. Grammatical items, on the other hand, are part of closed sets: 'I' can be substituted for only by a few items such as 'we', 'they', 'you' ... in fact, the list of English personal pronouns. So grammatical items are words like pronouns, prepositions (in, on, under, to, from, etc) and words like 'each', 'every', 'either', 'neither', etc.

In the text commenting on *Z for Zachariah* there are fourteen lexical items distributed over ten clauses, thus the text has a lexical density of 1.4. This is fairly typical of spoken medium.

The written medium of many information books is more lexically dense. Consider the following excerpt from a book for primary school children called *Spiders* (Bender, 1988: p.6).

> <u>Spiders</u> are not <u>insects</u>. ‖ They always <u>have eight joint-ed legs</u>, not <u>six</u> ‖ as <u>insects have</u> ‖ and they never <u>have</u> <u>wings</u>. ‖ The <u>feeling organs</u> on their <u>head</u> are not <u>ant-ennae</u> but <u>leg-like structures called palps</u>. ‖ <u>Spiders</u> all <u>have</u> a <u>pair</u> of <u>poison fangs</u> and several <u>pairs</u> of <u>spin-nerets</u> ‖ which <u>produce silk</u>.

Here there are 28 lexical items and seven clauses—a lexical density of 4. So there is much more content or information packed into this text. How is this achieved? In contrast to the 'Zachariah' excerpt, many of the lexical items in the *Spiders* text occur within 'groups' of words that act as single participants—'feeling organs', 'leg-like structures called palps', 'poison fangs'. These groups of words realising single participants are known as *nominal groups*. By expanding the nominal groups to include more lexical items (content words), a greater amount of information is able to be included within each clause. If we can draw children's attention to the way information is packaged in these nominal groups and show them how to build more complex nominal groups in their own writing, we will facilitate their growing control of the distinctive grammar of written language and hence their capacity to negotiate the language forms of the powerful institutions within the culture.

As an initial step toward the basis for this kind of teaching, we will firstly look at where the nominal group fits into what makes up a clause in English. We will then look at the functional parts of the nominal group in order to understand how it can be expanded.

The nominal group as part of the clause. The basic unit of grammatical analysis is the clause. The clause is made up of groups or phrases and these groups or phrases are made up of words. This is illustrated in Figure 2 (for a more detailed discussion, see Halliday, 1994: p. 179–214).

In this clause the nominal groups are 'Next year' and 'our best men'. The verbal group is 'are going to swim'. The final clause constituent 'in the competition' is a prepositional phrase. We will investigate only the nominal group.

Functional parts of the nominal group. Once we know the grammatical structure of the nominal group, we can appreciate the often expanded forms that occur in information books and we can also show children how to expand the nominal groups in their own writing (in doing this we also need to point out when expanded nominal groups are appropriate and when it is better to use simpler smaller nominal groups). What follows is a brief account of the grammatical structure of the nominal group and how it can be expanded. To begin with we will consider the large nominal group in the following clause:

> These two small, sleepy dingo pups have eaten six warm milk meals during the night.

CLAUSE	CONSTITUENTS
These two small, sleepy dingo pups	NOMINAL GROUP
have eaten	VERBAL GROUP
six warm milk meals	NOMINAL GROUP
during the night	PREPOSITIONAL PHRASE

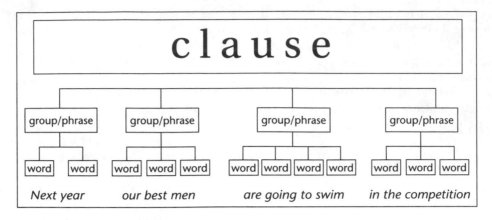

Figure 2

What are the functional parts of the nominal group?

	these two small, sleepy dingo pups
Which one(s)?	these
	Deictic (or Pointer)
How many?	two
	Numerative
What like?	small
	sleepy
	Epithet (or Describer)
What kind?	dingo
	Classifier
What?	pups
	Thing
More details?	e.g. without a mother
	Qualifier

Traditional school grammar would refer to 'small', 'sleepy' and 'dingo' all as adjectives qualifying the noun 'pups'. Note, however, that you can *intensify* the first two, i.e. 'very small', 'really small' and they could be 'really cuddly', but you can't intensify 'dingo', i.e. you can't say 'very dingo' or 'really dingo' or 'extremely dingo'. So these elements of the nominal group have different *functions*. The first two describe, and are called Epithets (or Describers) in functional grammar. The role of 'dingo' is to put the pups into a category or to classify—they are not 'kelpie' or 'seal' pups, for example—so in functional grammar this role is called Classifier.

Not all nominal groups include all possible constituents, but when they do occur they always occur in the same order: Deictic^Numerative^Epithet^Classifier^Thing^Qualifier.

There are two groups of items which function as Pointers:

1. The, this, that, these, those, which, what, whose, my, your, our, his, her, its, their, one's, John's, my father's, etc.

2. Each, every, either, neither, some, any, both, all.

The nominal group can be expanded by increasing the number of Describers and Classifiers.

These two small, <u>cuddly</u>, sleepy <u>Queensland</u> dingo pups ...

But much greater expansion can be achieved through the Qualifier.

The dingo pups <u>with the injuries</u>.

Note that the Qualifier in the nominal group for which 'pups' is the Thing consists of a preposition and a nominal group. Now it is possible to expand the nominal group in the Qualifier by adding more Describers and Classifiers.

The dingo pups ... with the <u>serious leg</u> injuries.

But it is also possible to add a Qualifier to the nominal group within the original Qualifier.

The dingo pups ... with serious leg injuries <u>to both front limbs</u>.

In this way the nominal groups can be very long with a lot of information packed into them, but they are still only functioning in a single grammatical role. In the following clause, for example, the very long (underlined) nominal group is all included in the role Subject (in functional grammar this nominal group is also simultaneously Actor and Theme).

<u>These two small, sleepy dingo pups with serious leg injuries to both front limbs</u> have survived.

Practical uses of expanded nominal groups. Being able to put a lot of information into one nominal group and then locating that nominal group at the beginning of a clause can be very useful in giving the reader a very comprehensive and clear orientation or background for the new information that comes at the end of the clause. News reports may use expanded nominal group structure in their opening sentences in this way to provide a substantial background to the story which follows. In the following examples the long nominal groups pack a lot of information into the overview in the first sentence of the report.

1. <u>Arsonists believed responsible for five school fires around Parramatta in a week</u> have struck again overnight.

Arsonists believed responsible for five school fires around Parramatta in a week.	
Thing	Qualifier (embedded clause)

1. <u>A light plane in which five people were killed yesterday is now the target of an investigation by investigators from the Bureau of Air Safety</u>.

A	light	plane	in which five people were killed yesterday
Deictic	Classifier	Thing	Qualifier (embedded clause)

the	target	of an investigation by investigators from the Bureau of Air Safety.
Deictic	Thing	Qualifier (embedded clause)

Examples from Primary School Books of Lexically Dense Text with Extended Nominal Groups

As in the news reports above, long nominal groups in the first sentence of a factual text allow a lot of information to be packed in so that the readers get a clear overview of what the text will be about. In the following example this technique is used to foreshadow how the content of the text will develop.

One	animal	caught in the clash between wildlife conservation and the cosmetics industry is the male musk deer.
Numerative	Thing	Qualifier (embedded clause)

Bright, M. (1988). *Killing for Luxury*. London: Franklin Watts.

Definitions in factual books also frequently require long nominal groups. These summarise the meanings that are to be equated with a technical term. In the following example the single technical term 'tundra' and the long nominal group 'the largest continuous tract of wilderness and wildlife habitat remaining in the northern hemisphere' are one and the same thing!

The tundra is the	largest	continuous	tract	of wilderness and wildlife habitat remaining in the northern hemisphere.
Deictic	Epithet	Classifier	Thing	Qualifier

Simon, N. (1987), *Vanishing Habitats*. London: Franklin Watts.

When we use the term 'tundra' subsequently, it carries with it all of those meanings compacted into the long nominal group and we don't have to repeat them

in the text. So long nominal groups are an important part of how meanings are condensed into technical terms—an important part of how definitions work.

Nominalisation—Realising Events as Things

The usual view of 'things' at a commonsense level is that they are nouns, entities like chairs, tables, money, animals, etc. But in English, Things (in the technical sense) in a nominal group can realise events or happenings (Halliday, 1994: p. 340-63). Consider the first two clauses in the introduction to *Killing for Luxury* (Bright, 1988: p. 4):

Man has always killed animals. The killing was traditionally for food and clothing ...

In the first clause the nominal groups (Man; animals) are indeed things. But in the second clause, the first nominal group is 'The killing'. It is a simple nominal group structure:

The	killing
Deictic	Thing

But the Thing is actually realising an event. This is a very common resource in English. Consider the following excerpt from *Vanishing Habitats* (Simon, 1987: p. 21):

All over <u>the world</u> <u>wetlands</u> are threatened by <u>drainage</u> and <u>conversion to arable land</u>.

The nominal groups are underlined. The first two (the world; wetlands) are clearly 'Things' in the everyday sense. But 'drainage' and 'conversion' are 'Things' only in language—they are abstract or pseudo things. In a more 'spoken' explanation of this phenomenon the events would be realised as material processes (verbs):

All over the world people <u>are draining</u> more and more of the wetlands and <u>converting</u> them to arable lands so there is a danger that the wetlands will disappear.

One advantage of realising events as Things in nominal groups, rather than as Processes (verbs) is that in English there are many more resources for modifying the nominal group than there are for the verbal group. In the 'wetlands' excerpt, for example, the nominal groups 'drainage' and 'conversion to arable land' could be extensively expanded:

All over the world wetlands are being threatened by <u>immediate</u>, <u>large-scale</u> drainage and <u>dangerous</u>, <u>ill-conceived</u>, <u>rapid</u> conversion to arable land.

The Role of Nominalisation in Explanation

Nominalisation is an essential resource in explanations. By expressing in language a series of events as a Thing, those summarised events can then assume a participant role in the next part of the explanation. So nominalisation is one of the means by which the explanation is able to progress through the cause and effect sequence. You can see this is in the following explanation of 'bending light' from *Science Starters: Bouncing and Bending Light* (Taylor, 1989).

> Light travels more slowly through glass or water than it does through air. If light hits glass or water at an angle, this slowing-down makes it change direction. The bending of light is called refraction.
>
> Have you ever looked down at your legs when you are standing in a swimming pool? Refraction makes your legs look shorter than they really are.

The use of nominalisation in the explanation can be seen in Figure 3, which shows how events are initially expressed as verbs and subsequently summarised and expressed as Things in the nominal group.

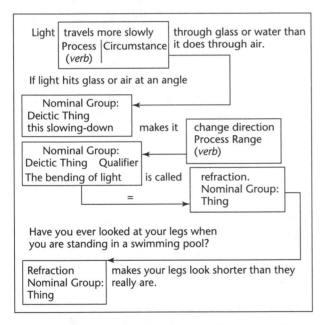

Figure 3 Nominalisation in an explanation of 'refraction'.

So 'travels more slowly' becomes 'this slowing down' and then the 'Thing' ('this slowing down') is what makes the air change direction. Similarly, the verbal structure 'change direction' becomes a Thing in the nominal group, 'The bending of light'. This is equated with another Thing, 'refraction' and this 'makes your legs look shorter than they really are'.

A further example of this can be seen in Figure 4, which shows an explanatory excerpt from *Science Workshop: Water, Paddles and Boats* (Robson, 1992).

This use of nominalisation is not typical of everyday spoken language and children need to be made familiar with it if they are to read and write effectively the language of curriculum areas like science.

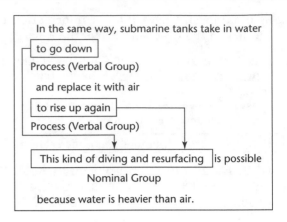

Figure 4 Nominalisation in an explanation of 'submarines'.

Lexical Density and Nominalisation in Children's Writing

We can now look again, in Figure 5, at the pieces of writing we compared in the opening section of this article. These were done by English children of about 9-10 years of age after a science excursion. The nominal groups in each piece are underlined in Figure 5.

In the left-hand example there is really only one long nominal group ('two of the things that live in the pond'). But notice in the right-hand example there are many more long nominal groups ('A whole city in miniature'; 'all the things that live in the pond'; 'the one with the best camouflage'; 'an ingenious method of breathing underwater'; 'its properties of oxygen').

Notice also the use of nominalisation in the right-hand example ('an ingenious method of breathing underwater'). This is a nominal group.

an	ingenious	method	of breathing underwater
Deictic	Epithet	Thing	Qualifier

The nominal group is realising an event or action, which would usually be realised by a Process (verbal) structure in spoken language:

> The water spider <u>breathes</u> underwater in a very clever (ingenious) way.

Children who write effective explanations are clearly able to make appropriate use of nominalisation. One further example (supplied by R. Cusworth) is from the child's explanation of why rainwater isn't salty.

> ...The vapour condenses into droplets of liquid water, forming clouds. If the vapour is chilled enough, it condenses into ice crystals and falls as snow. <u>This great unending circulation of the earth's waters</u> is called the water cycle.

This	great	unending	circulation	of the earth's waters
Deictic	Epithet	Classifier	Thing	Qualifier

Do you know what <u>this</u> is? <u>A pond is the answer</u> (coloured picture). <u>Fish</u> (coloured picture). <u>Water spider</u> (coloured picture). <u>These</u> are just <u>two of the things that live in the pond</u>. Of course there are <u>more things</u>. <u>A fish</u> breathes through <u>its mouth</u> and can only live in <u>water</u> like <u>we</u> would die if <u>we</u> were put in <u>water</u> for *a* long while and could not come out, <u>a water spider</u> lives in <u>a bubble of air</u> underneath <u>the water</u>. It can also run across <u>the water</u> without getting <u>its feet</u> wet...	<u>A pond</u> is <u>full of life</u>. <u>A whole city in miniature</u> may exist in <u>a pond</u>. <u>The animals</u> are either <u>carnivorous</u> or <u>vegetarian</u>. Of <u>all the things that live in the pond the caddis fly lava</u> is <u>the one with the best camouflage</u>. <u>It</u> makes <u>a kind of shed</u> out of <u>the substance around it</u>. <u>The water spider</u> has <u>an ingenious method of breathing underwater</u>. <u>He</u> makes <u>his den</u> and then <u>he</u> brings down <u>air bubbles</u> in <u>his hind legs</u>. <u>The fish</u> breathe by breathing in <u>water</u> and then extracting <u>its properties of oxygen</u> by means of <u>a type of grid</u> (drawing).

Figure 5   Comparison of two samples of factual writing for lexical density and nominalisation.

This expanded nominalisation is used to compact previous meanings and equate them with the technical term, 'the water cycle'.

Incorporating Knowledge of Nominal Group Structure into Teaching

The Importance of Meaningful Context

Shared reading and deconstruction of informational texts is important in teaching all aspects of knowledge about language (Macken et al., 1989; Christie et al., 1990a, 1990b, 1992). This should include 'talking out the text'—in discussing the text, shunting between the more familiar grammar of spoken language and the less familiar grammar of the written texts. For more practical information see Lemke (1989) and Unsworth (1993: p. 326–45).

Joint construction of texts with the children when teaching writing should also model the use of complex nominal groups and nominalisation, showing the children how these forms are derived from the more 'concrete' spoken grammar.

The following are some additional ideas for further consideration and development.

- Have children work in groups of three to produce a radio science show series based on the work you are currently doing in class. Each group produces a single episode of about five minutes, which is recorded on cassette tape. They are given one (or more) passages from an information book on the topic and their task is to turn this into a spoken script. (You will have to provide a demonstration of the task first.) The children write out their script and then practice speaking it onto the tape. You can then put the scripts and the original texts on an overhead projector slide; over the next few lessons, listen to the tapes and have the children explain what they did to the language to make it more 'spoken'.

- Have the children in groups of three again interview a knowledgeable adult to obtain an explanation of some phenomenon relevant to the curriculum area topic you are studying. For example, in a unit on sound, interview the principal to find out how the portable megaphone works, or a music teacher on why the keys at one end of a piano produce different sounds from those at the other end. The children then need to transcribe the explanation and turn it into a written form to accompany a table display of their work on that topic. Again the children might be asked to discuss how they had changed the spoken version, or they might be supplied with a written explanation from an information book and be asked to describe how that explanation differed from their own. (In all work of this kind it is essential that the teacher provide a demonstration of the completed task before the children are asked to undertake it.)

- A variation is to provide each group with an explanatory diagram of a topic they have been working on with you (e.g. the water cycle; how a torch works) and ask some groups to produce a spoken explanation for a radio science spot and other groups to produce written versions to a accompany a display of class work. You can then 'regroup' the children so that the new groups contain some children who produced the spoken versions and some who produced the written versions. They can then collaboratively work out an explanation of the differences between the language of the two versions.

Teaching Children the Actual Structure of the Nominal Group—Playing Language Games!

Exaggerations.   This can be focussed on any topic and can be played orally or in writing. Begin with a simple Deictic^Thing structure, for example, 'This hamburger'. Each child in the game must then add a component of nominal group structure.

These two hamburgers	Numerative
These two delicious hamburgers	Epithet
These two delicious MacDonald's hamburgers	Classifier
These two delicious MacDonald's hamburgers with extra cheese.	Qualifier

The exercise becomes more interesting as children expand the number of Epithets or Classifiers or expand the Qualifier, each time nominating which part of the nominal group they are going to modify. For instance, the next child may nominate Epithet:

These two delicious, <u>cheap</u> MacDonald's hamburgers with extra cheese,

and the next one might nominate Qualifier:

These two delicious, cheap MacDonald's hamburgers with extra cheese [[<u>sitting on the tray</u>]].

A variation is to have one child nominate the part of the nominal group to be expanded and the next child has to do it. If successful, that child nominates the next part of the nominal group to be expanded (if not successful s/he is out). Obviously it is essential to demonstrate and practice in order for the game to be successful.

Nominal group category search. The children work in small groups to search for nominal groups in various categories, e.g. 'political'; 'funny'; 'gruesome', 'scientific'; 'insult'; 'compliment', etc. They can search in newspapers, magazines, poetry books, etc., then within each group—e.g. the 'funny' group—some members look for nominal groups with lots of Epithets and Classifiers and some members look for nominal groups with extended Qualifiers. Each group either cuts and pastes its findings on butchers' paper or pins them on a sections of the pinboard. Groups report on and describe their findings. The results can then be 'regrouped' according to the type of nominal group structure, e.g. embedded clauses as Qualifier, and a new display assembled.

Political (Sydney Morning Herald, 30 November 1995):

<u>The superficially good news in yesterday's figures</u> is likely to be an important consideration ...

<u>The capacity of this royal commission to conduct covert operations and the extent of its intelligence bank</u> should now be obvious.

...<u>the benefits of securing severance of the corrupt from the Police Service and the collection of intelligence and evidence against other police</u> heavily outweigh <u>the punishment or deterrent effect of recovery of proceeds.</u>

Nominal groups from book titles:

Conrad: <u>The hilarious adventures of a factory-made child</u> (Nostlinger)

<u>The turbulent term of Tyke Tiler</u> (Kemp)
Alexander and <u>the terrible horrible no good very bad day</u> (Viorst)
<u>The boy who was followed home</u> (Mahy)

Funny:

<u>The dong with the luminous nose.</u> (Edward Lear)
Beware the Jabberwock, my son!
<u>The jaws that bite</u>, <u>the claws that catch!</u>
Beware the Jubjub bird, and shun the frumious Bandersnatch! (Lewis Carroll)

Definitions. The teacher prepares a number of acceptable definitions of key terms from a current unit of work and writes these in large letters on cardboard. These definitions are cut up in single word cards. Also make a number of sets of nominal group cards (Deictic, Numerative, Epithet, Classifier, Thing, Qualifier). Children can play the game in groups of three or four. The nominal group cards are shuffled and face down. The cards containing the terms to be defined (like monotreme, platypus, marsupial, etc., which could be a different colour) are placed in the middle of the table. Each player must take a nominal group card from the pile and then select a corresponding item from the definition cards to put beside the relevant term to be defined. For example, if the nominal group card selected turns out to be Classifier, the student could pick up amphibian, and put it beside platypus. Each correct placement scores a point. Students can be strategic in working toward a longer definition they have worked out, which may not be obvious to their peers, hence they have more correct placements and win. (Note, for example, the definition of platypus in Figure 6.) As each child has his/her turn the definitions are built and the knowledge of the elements of the nominal group is consolidated (the teacher may need to be a roving referee!). The children are learning grammar and learning content at the same time.

Of course you could generate may other such games, but it is important to remember that these are simply a heuristic to introduce and consolidate the technical description of the language. The starting point would be pointing out the functionality of the nominal group structure in the context of shared reading of information texts on the topic being investigated. This might mean simply underlining or boxing in coloured text the long nominal groups realising a substantial Theme to orient the reader, as illustrated earlier in this article. You could then take one or two examples of these and show and explain the elements of the nominal group to indicate how it is expanded. Subsequent lessons might include some game ideas similar to those above to build familiarity with the possible structures of the nominal group. These should then be applied in the next lesson where

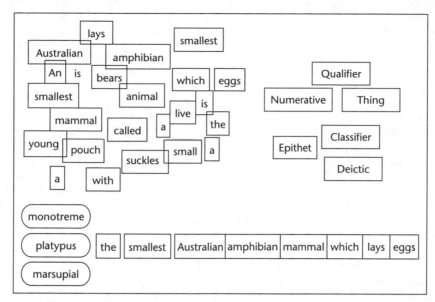

Figure 6 'Definitions' game to teach nominal group structure.

a text on the topic of study is read together so that the children understand the role of these grammatical structures. The most productive work is then using these understandings in critical consideration of texts children are reading and writing.

Conclusion

The material presented in this article simply elaborates and applies the very substantial work of Australian educators and systemic functional linguists on literacy development and learning (e.g. Christie, 1989a, 1989b, 1990; Derewianka, 1990; Halliday & Martin, 1993; Martin, 1989; Martin & Rothery, 1988; Collerson, 1988; Rothery, 1986; Kress, 1984). The international significance of this work has been widely acknowledged and is clearly indicated in a recent article by Gordon Wells (1994) from the Ontario Institute for Studies in Education. In discussing the complementary contributions of Vygotsky and Halliday to a language-based theory of learning', Wells notes that:

> in learning to reconstrue experience in terms of the semantic structures of written language, children construct what Vygotsky refers to as 'smallest scientific concepts.' That is to say, it is written texts—and the talk about them—that provide the means for the development of the 'higher mental functions' ...

(Wells, 1994: p. 82).

He goes on to discuss the prevalence of nominalisation in 'the written texts in which discipline-based, school knowledge is presented' and further notes that:

> The reorganisation of the grammar and the concomitant reconstrual of experience that is required in order to use

written text as a tool for thinking and communicating does not occur spontaneously for most children

(Wells, 1994: p. 82).

This article has attempted to demonstrate that a very modest excursion into functional grammar provides immediate practical payoff in enhancing teachers' efforts to facilitate children's 'reorganisation of the grammar and the concomitant reconstrual of experience', which is essential to effective curriculum area learning.

References

Christie, F. (ed.). (1984). *Children Writing: Study guide.* Geelong: Deakin University Press.

Christie, F. (ed.). (1989a). *Writing in Schools: Reader.* Geelong: Deakin University Press.

Christie, F. (ed.). (1989b). *Writing in Schools: Study guide.* Geelong: Deakin University Press.

Christie, F. (ed.). (1990). *Literacy for a Changing World.* Hawthorn: Australian Council for Educational Research.

Christie, F., Gray, P., Gray, B., Macken, M., Martin, J. & Rothery, J. (1990a). *Language: A Resource for Meaning— Exploring Reports (Teachers' Book).* Sydney: Harcourt Brace Jovanovich.

Christie, F., Gray, P., Gray, B., Macken, M., Martin, J. & Rothery, J. (1990b). *Language: A Resource for Meaning— Exploring Procedures (Teachers' Book).* Sydney: Harcourt Brace Jovanovich.

Christie, F., Gray, P., Gray, B., Macken, M., Martin, J. & Rothery, J. (1992). *Language: A Resource for Meaning— Exploring Explanations (Teachers' Book).* Sydney: Harcourt Brace Jovanovich.

Collerson, J. (ed.) (1988). *Writing for Life.* Sydney: Primary English Teaching Association.

Derewianka, B. (1990). *Exploring How Texts Work.* Sydney: Primary English Teaching Association.

Gilbert, P. (1990). Authorising disadvantage: Authorship and creativity in the language classroom. In F. Christie (ed.), *Literacy for a Changing World.* Hawthorn: Australian Council for Educational Research.

Halliday, M. (1993). Towards a language-based theory of learning. *Linguistics and Education,* 5, 1. pp. 93–116.

Halliday, M. (1994). *An Introduction to Functional Grammar* (2nd ed.). London: Edward Arnold.

Halliday, M. & Martin, J. (eds). (1993). *Writing Science: Literacy and discursive power.* London: Falmer Press.

Hammond, J. (1990). Is learning to read and write the same as learning to speak? In F. Christie (ed.), *Literacy for a Changing World.* Hawthorn: Australian Council for Educational Research.

Kress, G. (1984). Things children read, and things children write. In L. Unsworth (ed.), *Fifth Macarthur Reading/Language Symposium.* pp. 2-23. Sydney: Macarthur Institute of Higher Education.

Lemke, J. (1989). Making text talk. *Theory into Practice,* 28. pp. 136–41.

Lemke, J. (1990). *Talking Science: Language, learning and values.* Norwood, New Jersey: Ablex.

Macken, M., Kalantzis, M., Kress, G., Martin, J. & Cope, B. (1989). *A Genre-based Approach to Teaching Writing, Years 3–6, Book 1: Introduction.* Sydney: Directorate of Studies, NSW Department of Education and Literacy and Education Research Network.

Martin, J. (1989). *Factual Writing: Exploring and challenging social reality.* Oxford: Oxford University Press.

Martin, J. & Rothery, J. (1988). Classification and framing: Double dealing in pedagogic discourse. Paper presented to the Post World Reading Congress Symposium, Brisbane.

Martin, N. (1983). Writing: What for? In R. Parker and F. Davis (eds), *Developing Literacy.* Newark: International Reading Association.

Morgan, S. (1987). *My Place.* Fremantle, WA: Fremantle Arts Centre Press.

O'Brien, R. (1975). *Z for Zachariah,* New York: Atheneum.

Rothery, J. (1986). Teaching writing in the primary school: A genre-based approach to the development of writing abilities. In *Working Papers in Linguistics,* 4. pp. 3–62. Sydney: Department of Linguistics, University of Sydney.

Unsworth, L. (ed.). (1993). *Literacy Learning and Teaching: Language as social practice in the primary school.* Melbourne: Macmillan.

Wells, G. (1994). The complementary contributions of Halliday and Vygotsky to a 'Language-based Theory of Learning'. *Linguistics and Education,* 6, 1. pp. 41–90.

Primary school information book references

Bender, L. (1988). *Spiders,* London: Franklin Watts.

Bright, M. (1988). *Killing for Luxury.* London: Franklin Watts.

Robson, P. (1992). *Science Workshop: Water, paddles and boats.* London: Franklin Watts.

Simon, N. (1987). *Vanishing Habitals.* London: Franklin Watts

Taylor, B. (1989). *Science Starters: Bouncing and bending light.* London: Franklin Watts.

Considering Genre, Content, and Visual Features in the Selection of Trade Books for Science Instruction

Carol A. Donovan
University of Alabama

Laura B. Smolkin
University of Virginia

Teachers have been encouraged for some time to use trade books as part of the science curriculum (Barlow, 1991; Butzow & Butzow, 1988; Mayer, 1995; Smardo, 1982). Their use has been advocated to enhance textbooks (e.g., Moss, 1991), to replace textbooks (e.g., Barlow, 1991; Butzow & Butzow, 1988; Mayer, 1995; Smardo, 1982), and to supplement activity-based science curriculum (e.g., Anderson, 1998; Morrow, Pressley, Smith, & Smith, 1997; Palincsar & Magnusson, 2000; Roth, 1991).

Fictional storybooks (e.g., McClure & Zitlow, 1991), informational storybooks (e.g., Leal, 1992; 1993), and information books (e.g., Duke, 2000; Moss, 1991; Pappas, 1991) have all been encouraged for use in science instruction for various reasons. However, teachers have received little guidance on the many factors that should be considered when selecting books to enhance science instruction. This article presents analyses of different aspects of various types of texts so teachers may make informed decisions when selecting books to enhance their science program.

We first provide an overview of three major categories—genre, content, and visual features—that the literature supports as important in the selection of books for science. We then "walk through" the analyses of four books, one representing each of the different text types or genres frequently recommended for teachers to use in their science instruction: (a) story, (b) nonnarrative information, (c) narrative information, and (d) dual purpose. Finally, we pull together factors from the analyses with findings from current research to argue the importance of considering genre, content, and visual features when selecting books to enhance the science curriculum.

An Overview of Categories to Consider

When selecting trade books for science there are three key categories, each represented in Figure 1, that deserve attention and consideration: genre, content, and visual features. *Genre* refers to the type of text (e.g., an information book, a storybook), but in linguistics genre may also refer to the structure of the text—the

> *When selecting trade books for science there are three key categories ... that deserve attention and consideration: genre, content, and visual features.*

distinguishing features of the text and how they are put together to make the text suitable for a particular purpose. *Content,* or ideas, may be presented either through text or through particular visual features. Textual content describes the informational ideas communicated by the written, or linguistic, portion of the text; these ideas, as we will discuss, may be explicitly stated or they may be implied. The *visual features* of science-related trade books have been created to present, support, and enhance textual content. While both content and visual features are commonly addressed in discussions of information books (e.g., Horning, 1997; Huck, Helper, Hickman, & Kiefer, 2001) and are likely better known to teachers, the role of genre has been much less frequently discussed. For that reason, as we examine each of these three major categories and the features they encompass in the sections that follow, we will devote much of our attention to genre.

Considering the Genre of the Book

Genre, as we will be using the term in this article, is the way in which texts are structured to serve different purposes in specific social contexts (Kress, 1994).

Genre

Four typical genres found in schools
  Story, nonnarrative information, narrative information, dual purpose

Features that determine genre
  1. Linguistic features—how meaning is related within and across sentences, including vocabulary and syntax
  2. Global elements—the overall structuring of "chunks" of the text, such as setting, initiating event, and so forth
  3. Global structure—relationships among ideas as represented visually by a tree, or skeletal, diagram

---

Content

Features that determine content
  1. Accuracy—the degree to which information is precise, straightforward, and reliable or wrong, misleading, and unreliable
  2. Complexity—includes the following:
     • depth and breadth (the complexity of topic coverage—how much, in how much detail)
     • informational ideas (the number of ideas in text relevant to the topic)
     • lexical density (measure of content's compactness: clauses divided by ideas)
     • reading level (the difficulty of the text; readability)

Visual features

  • Illustrations/photographs—attributes of the pictures created or photographed to accompany the text; particular attention must be given to captions and their purpose
  • Diagrams—charts, tables, graphs, and other structures used to plot information
  • Text—features of the actual print, in terms of placement, size, amount per page, and fonts

---

Figure 1 An overview of the elements to consider when selecting books for science.

Science, for example, is one such social context in which the language used is "a powerful and specialized way of talking about the world" (Lemke, 1990, p. xi). Specialized ways of using language are detectable in content, organization, and syntax. In linguistic terminology, there are three aspects that may be seen as differentiating genre: linguistic features operating at the sentence level (specific word choice or syntax), global elements (specific information or content), and global structure (hierarchical relationships between elements). We first briefly describe the general elements that we are considering in our analysis of genre for each book and then provide specific examples of each of these elements for different genres typically recommended for and found in elementary science.

Linguistic Features

Linguistic features include cohesion, tense, vocabulary, and syntax. The meaning that is created within and between sentences holds a text together and creates its unity, or cohesion. Certain types of meaning relations are created in genres through the different uses of tense (e.g., past, present) and cohesive devices (e.g., focus on a character's action throughout the story—"Babar walked along the road," as opposed to considering the nature of elephants in general—"Elephants travel in herds"). Genres are also distinguished by their vocabulary (e.g., commonsense words like *rain* or discipline-specific words like *precipitation*) and syntax (grammatical constructions specific to different genres—"She peered down the long dark tunnel"). These features, specific to different genres, are described in detail in our analysis of specific books.

Global Elements

Within each genre, there are some elements of information that tend to recur (e.g., the setting of a fairy tale or the comparison of two specific cases of a more general topic, such as Labrador and poodle as two types of dog in an informational text). These global elements help organize a text at its overall, or macrolevel, indicating "chunks" or "grammars" (Pappas, Kiefer, & Levstik, 1999) of different genres. Grammars of different genres have been defined and described by researchers such as Hasan (1984) and Pappas (1986) who were particularly interested in determining which elements are essential—that is, must be present for a text to fall within a particular genre—and which are optional. For stories, a common grammar includes the elements of setting, initiating event, and conflict and its resolution (Stein & Glenn, 1979). The grammar of a topical information book, one that provides information about one topic such as dogs, generally includes an orientation to the topic followed by descriptions of characteristic attributes and events (Pappas, 1986).

Global Structure

Linguistic features at the sentence or intersentential level and global elements at the macrolevel combine to create the global structure of the genre, as defined by Donovan (2001). This definition varies from those offered by others in its expansion of the term *global structure* to include not only the more commonly recognized grammar, or text structure, but also hierarchical links in text content. Tree diagrams of the clauses of each text can create a visual representation of how the content is connected hierarchically (see Figure 2 for an example). Simple texts have very little breadth (introduce few ideas), and provide very little depth (elaboration is minimal). Complex texts provide many ideas about the topic, or subtopics (greater breadth), and provide much more elaboration (greater depth) of these ideas (Langer, 1986; Meyer, 1975). Tree diagrams, as will be apparent in the next section, reveal differences in the structural, or macrolevel, organization of different genres, as well as displaying the overall structure of a particular text.

Generic Distinctions in Science-related Texts

As we noted in our introduction, various genres have been suggested for use in science instruction. Informational texts, in our framework, may be classified as nonnarrative, those in which the temporal sequencing of events is not a particularly significant feature (Newkirk, 1987), or narrative, describing the sequence of factual events over time. Generally, both of these text types are written in present tense on a single topic, frequently identified by the title. In the sections that follow, we present our four generic categories—storybooks, nonnarrative informational texts, narrative informational texts, and dual-purpose texts—and consider how the genre features we have defined work in these texts.

Storybooks.   If genre is determined by purpose, stories serve to entertain, and "do not pretend to be factual" (Kress, 1994, p. 11). Figure 2 provides the genre-specific features of stories.

The linguistic features of story texts are quite familiar; cohesion is created by the actions of characters and the various words that refer to them as they move across time in the evolution of the plot. Stein and Glenn's (1979) well-known story grammar considers the global elements of a well-formed story to center on the goal-directed action of the main character and include a setting, initiating event, internal reaction, internal plan, attempts, consequence, and reaction. Hasan's (1984) framework is very similar and includes an optional placement (orients reader to the setting and characters), an initiating event (introduces the problem or conflict), sequent events (attempts to solve the problem), final events (resolves

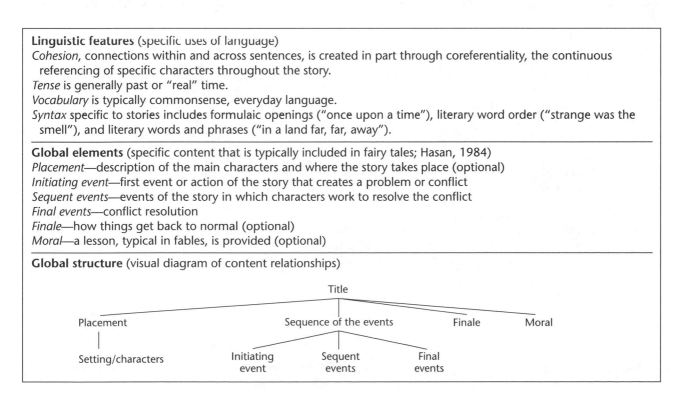

Figure 2   Specific features of story genre.

conflict), and an optional finals and moral. The global structure of the story genre is typically dominated by the temporal sequencing of events.

Multiple sources suggest that stories be included in science instruction. Lake (1993), for example, indicated that effective science programs will begin with picture storybooks to create a love of science and then move to informational texts. McClure and Zitlow (1991) believed that an aesthetic stance, achieved through science ideas presented in poetry and fiction, serves to dispel a meaningless presentation of facts. Camp (2000) and Crook and Lehman (1991) suggested that content material may best be presented through a pairing of fiction and nonfiction. Also recommending stories for science instruction are sources such as GEMS, Great Explorations in Math and Science (Barber et al., 1993). Stories that have been suggested by various sources for use in science include Eric Carle's *The Very Hungry Caterpillar* (1969), *The Tiny Seed* (1987), and *The Very Quiet Cricket* (1997); Barbara Cooney's *Miss Rumphius* (1982), and Simon James's *Dear Mr. Blueberry* (1996).

Information books: Nonnarrative. Nonnarrative, topic-oriented information books are sometimes classified by linguists as "reports." According to Kress (1994), these "are factual texts that describe the way things are" (p. 9). Figure 3 presents the genre-specific aspects of nonnarrative informational texts.

In terms of notable linguistic features, cohesion in these texts is created in part through coclassification,

the focus on a general class of the topic (elephants) and not on specific characters (Dumbo). Tense is generally present or timeless, and vocabulary is typically technical. Syntax specific to nonnarrative informational texts includes formulaic openings (topic introductions such as "Elephants are mammals"). The global elements first identified by Pappas (1986) include both obligatory elements—topic presentation, description of attributes, and characteristic events— and optional elements—category comparison, final summary, and afterword. Many of Gail Gibbons's books fall into the nonnarrative category, such as *Beacons of Light: Lighthouses* (1990), *Catch the Wind! All about Kites* (1995), *Sharks* (1992), and *Check It Out! The Book About Libraries* (1995). Seymour Simon's *Sharks* (1995), *Volcanoes* (1995), and *Whales* (1989), and Aliki's *My Five Senses* (1990) are additional examples.

Information books: Narrative. As we noted previously, narrative informational texts relate factual events over time. Figure 4 provides the genre-specific aspects of narrative informational texts. Comparing Figures 3 and 4, we can note differences between narrative and nonnarrative information books in the linguistic feature of tense and, more noticeably, in global structures. Regarding differences in tense, narrative informational texts sometimes recount the events of a specific case in order to generalize to all cases. When this approach is used, authors will occasionally employ the past tense. When

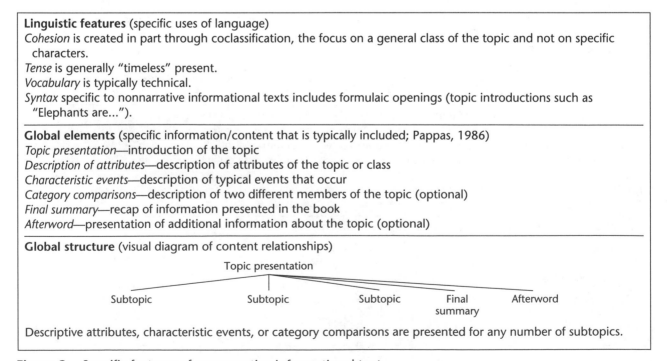

Figure 3 Specific features of nonnarrative Informational text.

Linguistic features (specific uses of language)
Cohesion is created in part through coclassification, the focus on a general class of the topic and not on specific characters.
Tense may be present if the information provided is "how it always is" (e.g., how to conduct Experiment X) or past if the information provided is a recounting of "how it was for a particular case" (e.g., how we conducted Experiment X yesterday).
Vocabulary is typically technical (e.g., caudal fin, dorsal fin, pectoral fins, gills, ampullae).
Syntax specific to narrative Informational texts includes formulaic openings (topic introductions such as "The female trapdoor spider chooses a place for her nest...").

Global elements (specific information/content that is typically included; Pappas, 1986)
Topic presentation—introduction of the topic
Description of attributes—description of attributes of the topic or class
Characteristic events—description of typical events that occur
Category comparisons—description of two different members of the topic (optional)
Final summary—recap of information presented in the book
Afterword—presentation of additional Information about the topic (optional)

Global structure (visual diagram of content relationships—characteristic events dominate)

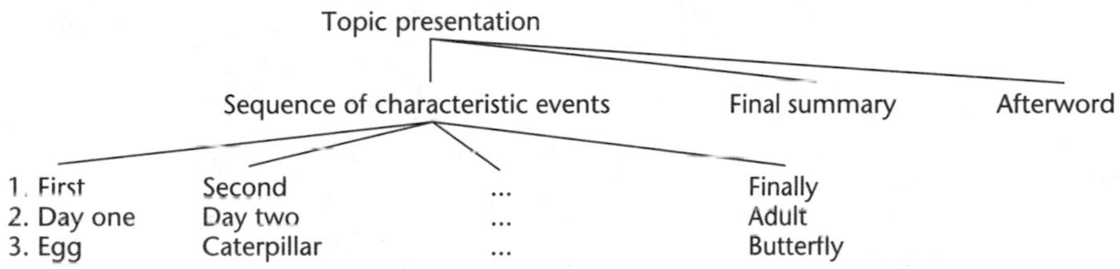

```
                        Topic presentation
                       /        |         \
        Sequence of characteristic events   Final summary   Afterword
         /        |         \
  1. First    Second    ...        Finally
  2. Day one  Day two   ...        Adult
  3. Egg      Caterpillar ...      Butterfly
```

Descriptive attributes or category comparisons may be presented for any of the events or subtopics covered with the events. Numbers 1–3 represent different sequences.

Figure 4　Specific feature of narrative informational text.

authors are describing the general case, as in Millicent Selsam's (1970) *Egg to Chick* in which no specific chick's life is recounted, they most commonly use the present tense. Comparing the two distinct tree diagrams of Figures 3 and 4 shows that rather than depicting a hierarchy of the topic and related subtopics, the global structure of narrative informational texts includes a sequence of factual events or occurrences over time.

Narrative informational texts include those that describe sequences, such as the life cycle of plants or animals (e.g., Denise Burt's 1988 *Birth of a Koala*, Ron Goor and Nancy Goor's 1990 *Insect Metamorphosis: From Egg to Adult*), or processes, which provide the procedure for how something is done (e.g., Aliki's 1991 *Milk: From Cow to Carton*) or how to do something (e.g., Janet VanCleave's 1989 *Chemistry for Every Kid: 101 Easy Experiments That Really Work*). Additional examples of narrative information books include Alice Provensen and Martin Provensen's *Year at Maple Hill Farm* (1978), Donald Hall's *Ox-Cart Man* (1983), and Gail Gibbons's books including *New Road!* (1987), *Sunken Treasure* (1990), and *From Seed to Plant* (1991). Joanna Cole's *A Chick Hatches* (1976) and the new series of Magic School Bus books based on episodes of the television series (e.g., Cole and Degen's 1996 *The Magic School Bus Gets Ants in Its Pants: A Book About Ants*) are also examples of narrative information books.

Dual-purpose books. Since the early 1990s, researchers have been discussing the fact that authors sometimes combine text types (Leal, 1993; Pappas et al., 1999; Skurzynski, 1992). While each of these writers has suggested a term for this phenomenon, we have chosen the term *dual purpose*. To us, this best captures the idea that these texts (a) are intended by their authors to present facts and provide a story, and (b) use a dual format that allows them to be accessed by readers like a nonnarrative information book or like a storybook. In many cases, the running text in these books carries the story and must be read from beginning to end. Although information is sometimes found in the running text, more frequently the content appears in insets and diagrams. So, to access the informational content, a child may "enter" on virtually any page to read

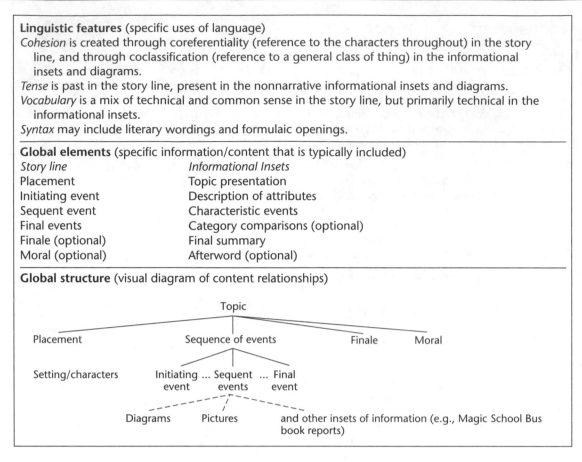

Figure 5 Specific features of dual-purpose texts.

specific facts. As Figure 5 indicates, for these texts, linguistic features and global elements follow the patterns of stories when appearing in the story line, and the patterns of informational texts when in the diagrams and insets. The global structure is determined by the story line; the insets and diagrams, often only loosely connected to the story, create depth, a phenomenon we will discuss in our section on complexity.

Tomie de Paola's *The Quicksand Book* (1977) and *The Popcorn Book* (1978) fall within this category. Well-known examples in this category are Joanna Cole's entire original series of Magic School Bus books (e.g., *The Magic School Bus Inside the Earth,* 1987, and *The Magic School Bus at the Waterworks,* 1986).

Considering the Textual Content of the Book

As children's literature experts (e.g., Horning, 1997; Huck et al., 2001) have said for years, when considering books for science we must examine the content. Our first concern, of course, is accuracy of information. Books that provide misinformation or inadvertently reinforce children's misconceptions serve our students badly. Also important in considering the textual content is the complexity of the text. How much informational depth does a text supply? How difficult is it for children to access that information?

Accuracy

Unfortunately, many books suggested for science instruction deliver incorrect information (Mayer, 1995; Rice & Rainsford, 1996; Trundle, 2000). Horning (1997) supplied excellent guidance for teachers on this topic. She suggested checking whether an author has the subject matter knowledge to write on the topic and whether the acknowledgments indicate that content specialists checked the text for accuracy. She also directed attention to documentation of sources, which may include bibliographies, endnotes, information on nonprint resources, and even a brief description of the author's research process. Teachers who are concerned with the accuracy of the information in particular children's books can turn to the journal *Appraisal: Science Books for Young People* currently published by Northeastern University in Boston, Massachusetts, USA (*http://www.appraisal.neu.edu*). Though published somewhat irregularly, this journal offers teachers two differing but important perspectives of each book reviewed. Half of the review is written by a librarian who points out features and uses of the book; the second half is written by a scientist who examines the text for the correctness of its content and also makes suggestions for its use.

Complexity

Textual content complexity can be measured in many ways. Each measure provides different information and perspectives about the book's potential for supporting science instruction. We will consider the more linguistically oriented concepts of depth and breadth of ideas, ideas presented explicitly or implicitly, and lexical density of a text. We will then address the more standard consideration of readability.

Depth and breadth.   Tree diagrams, as seen in the Global Structure sections of Figures 2 through 5, supply a skeleton upon which the global elements of a text may be hung. Each of these elements may contain informational ideas that contribute to the content. They may have breadth of information (consider the possibility of adding more and more subtopics under Topic Presentation in Figure 3). They may also have depth of information as more and more information is supplied, or elaborated, for a particular subtopic, a point to which we will return in our contrast of two books in the next section.

Tree diagrams are useful in understanding the relationship between and among sections of content; they also let us see how information may be connected hierarchically (Meyer, 1975). However, their creation can be somewhat time consuming. The models we present here are designed to supply teachers with an idea of how texts are shaped rather than to serve as examples of what should be done every time we examine a new text for science use.

Informational ideas: Explicit and implicit.   Closely tied to the depth of the information presented is the number of informational ideas in a text, which may be determined by examining clauses within the text. For example, the simple sentence "Plants grow roots" in Colin Walker's *Seeds Grow* (1992) has one informational idea, whereas "Mount Everest in the Himalayas is the highest mountain above sea level" in Seymour Simon's *Mountains* (1994) has three. The first idea identifies Mount Everest as located in the Himalayas, the second identifies Mount Everest as the highest mountain above sea level, and the third implies that there may be taller mountains below sea level. Determining an average number of informational ideas

per page allows us to think about the text's potential for conveying concepts.

Implicit informational ideas are those that are suggested, but not explicitly stated, in the text, as seen in the Mt. Everest example. For us, these ideas seem effort-laden in that teachers must go beyond what is written to make these ideas explicit for the children if the book is being read aloud, or children reading to themselves must construct more inferences to understand the text. For example, in Eric Carle's *The Tiny Seed* (1987), the sentences "After a few months the snow has melted. It is really spring" hold the implicit information that snow melts in spring. Unless the reader makes this connection for children, the implied information may go unnoticed. Thus, for books with much implicit information, teachers who use the text for science instruction (e.g., to teach about the life cycle of plants) must make the effort to explicate these informational ideas for most children. Still, greater numbers of implicit ideas may be seen as positive in certain ways. They do offer opportunities for elaboration upon a text as well as affording opportunities to talk with children about what texts do not tell readers.

Lexical density.   Another measure of text complexity, lexical density, is easily determined for any passage (Halliday, 1993; Unsworth, 1999). Halliday (1993) defined lexical density as "a measure of the density of information in any passage of text, according to how tightly the lexical items (content) words have been packed into the grammatical structure" (p. 76). To determine lexical density in a passage of text, we can count the number of lexical items (nouns, content-related modifiers, content-carrying verbs) and then divide that number by the number of clauses (clauses are groups of words that contain a subject and predicate, which can constitute part of or an entire sentence). For example, in the previously mentioned book *Seeds Grow,* the text reads "*Plants grow roots.*" As indicated by the italics, each word is considered a lexical item in this single-clause sentence. Therefore, 3 lexical items divided by 1 clause equals a lexical density of 3.0. In the other example, "*Mount Everest in the Himalayas is the highest mountain above sea level,*" 6 lexical items divided by 1 clause equals a lexical density of 6.0.

Written and spoken language differ in terms of how many lexical items appear in a clause. According to Halliday (1993), spoken language generally has a much lower lexical density (about 2 content words per clause), whereas written texts have a higher lexical density (about 4 to 6 lexical items per clause). For scientific texts, however, the lexical density can be even greater (about 10–13 items per clause). Halliday explained that as lexical density increases, so too do difficulties in reading the text. So, the "Mount Everest" example is not only difficult for its implicit ideas but also because of its greater lexical density.

Readability.   Finally, the readability of a text provides yet another measure of its complexity. While a rough measure of readability can be derived through an examination of the relationships between numbers of sentences and syllables in a given passage (Fry, 1977), we have known for quite some time (Klare, 1976) that such formulas are unable to indicate whether a particular text is easy or difficult for a particular reader. Other factors, more difficult to measure than syllables and sentences, are also a part of the difficulty equation. These factors include, but are not limited to, readers' motivation, their background knowledge, and their sophistication in language use. Children who have read many books about volcanoes would likely have less difficulty with a text on volcanoes that contained many implicit ideas and technical terms than peers on the same reading level whose reading interests have chiefly focused upon sharks.

Considering the Visual Features

As books are planned for children, decisions are made on physical aspects—the size, the shape, and the cover. Design decisions extend to the appearance of individual pages, including what Caldecott-winning artist Uri Shulevitz (1985) described as an artist's readability, "all the visual elements on the page—and breathing space, the white space around both the type and the pictures that provides rest for the eyes" (p. 46). Design in nonfiction, particularly in terms of type styles, sizes, and colors, serves a special comprehension function in that these elements help readers link information-containing portions of the texts. Most visually notable in today's information books are the incredible illustrations. These information-bearing units—of various media, colors, and styles—merit special consideration, especially given that current research during interactive read-alouds (Oyler, 1996; Pappas, Varelas, Barry, & O'Neill, 2000) indicates that the illustrations contain much of the information to which children will attend.

Within the reading field, there has been considerable research on the relationship between illustrations and textual content. From that research, we have come to know that pictures that illustrate textual content lead to enhanced comprehension (Levie & Lentz, 1982), while those that serve an embellishing function (unrelated to textual content) do not. We have also come to understand that captions for pictures or diagrams have an especially important purpose. According to Peeck (1993), captions serve to "enable learners to understand and interpret illustrations correctly, to direct their attention to relevant elements, and prevent information from being overlooked" (p. 230). Peeck also informed us that the ability to actually integrate pictures with text is developmental; children need assistance in directing their attention to the most important, meaning-bearing sections of an illustration. If children relate to pictures in superficial ways, the pictures will not support any additional concept construction or comprehension activity (Weldenmann, 1989). We also know that poorly designed, low information-bearing pictures can actually affect children negatively, making them less interested in learning more about a topic than if no pictures were present at all (Peeck, 1987).

In examining the illustrations of informational texts (and here we are speaking of both representational efforts such as photography and painting as well as other types of visual displays of information such as graphs, diagrams, maps, tables, and charts), we need to ask ourselves several key questions. What is the relationship of the illustration to the textual content? Does it reinforce or elaborate upon the information in the text or does it simply serve as an embellishment, unrelated to the information (Hunter, Crismore, & Pearson, 1987)? Are there easy-to-read captions for the pictures and labels for diagrams." Do these captions help direct readers' "attention to relevant elements, and prevent information from being overlooked" (Peeck, 1993, p. 230)?

We will also need to ask ourselves about the motivational qualities of the included illustrations. As Huck et al. (2001) pointed out, today's amazing photographs, now the medium of choice in informational texts, can invite readers to pose numerous questions. From our own experiences (Smolkin & Donovan, 2001) we know that aesthetically engaged children will respond to text through their comments. Will children respond to the pictures they see with comments such as "Wow!" or "Gross! What's that?" or "Ooh, that's neat!"? Do the illustrations have the power to elicit immediate wonder and awe and open the door to complex meaning making about the topic?

Analyzing Books for Genre, Content, and Visual Features

Having introduced and explored variables we think important in considerations of science trade books, we now analyze four distinct text types—a storybook, a nonnarrative information book, a narrative information book, and finally a dual-purpose text—to illustrate how the factors we have described work.

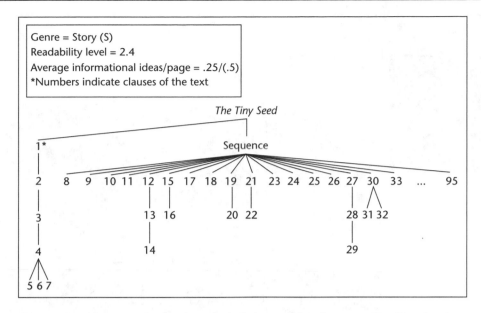

Figure 6 Diagram of a book typical of the storybook genre: *The Tiny Seed.*

Storybook: The Tiny Seed

Eric Carle's (1987) story *The Tiny Seed* is organized around goal-directed action, as the implied goal is for the "Tiny Seed" to grow into a plant. The story begins by presenting the setting (Autumn) and introducing the protagonist, "Tiny Seed": "One of the seeds is tiny, smaller than any of the others" (p. 1). You can see this description of the setting in numbers 1–7 of our tree diagram (Figure 6).

The initiating event (labelled 8 in the diagram, Figure 4) emerges in the sentence "One of the seeds flies higher than the others" (p. 2). The remainder of the book relates the various events, or episodes, as the Tiny Seed confronts and escapes obstacles until it realizes the end goal (final event) of becoming a plant. Many of these obstacles are fanciful in nature (e.g., "It flies too high and the sun's hot rays burn it up").

These fanciful aspects, certainly appropriate in story genre, may create or reinforce misconceptions about seed travel or the relationship of the earth to the sun. Some of these events are elaborated upon, as shown in the diagram, but the overall structure is the sequence of events.

Informational ideas in *The Tiny Seed* average .25 explicit and .5 implicit items per page. Few informational ideas in general, most of which are implicit, mean that a teacher will have to work hard to ensure that this book strengthens children's understanding of the life cycle of plants. Additional discussion may be necessary to counter the misconceptions we've previously noted.

In the illustrations, Carle's tissue paper collage artwork depicts the text on each page. His efforts produce good illustrations for a picture storybook in that the story's message is conveyed equally well through two media—print and picture—with the illustrations helping to "bear the burden of narration" (Huck et al., 2001, p. 168). However, if we view the illustrations in terms of supporting scientific concepts, they are far less successful. For example, if a key scientific understanding is that seeds expand and then send down roots and send up stems and leaves, the birds, the sun, and the overbearing weed found on one double-page spread may all be seen as details that distract from a clear presentation of a concept.

Nonnarrative Information Book:
Seeds Grow

Although the Wright Group's books are not technically trade books, they are commonly found in early elementary classrooms. So we are using Colin Walker's (1992) *Seeds Grow* for our example of a nonnarrative informational text (see Figure 7).

This text provides information about the general nature of plants, demonstrated through the use of plurals and the timeless present as in "Seeds need air and water" and "Plants grow." The text is nonnarrative, meaning there is no sequence of events, which would be the case if the objective were to describe the growth from seed to mature plant. Instead, this text provides information about seeds and what they need to grow. The text in Figure 5 presents the topic orientation, "Seeds are baby plants waiting to grow," on page 1. The remaining information in this book is grouped into subtopics supporting the initial orientation along with characteristic attributes about the topic. The subtopics "baby plants" and "plants grow seeds" have little elaboration, whereas more

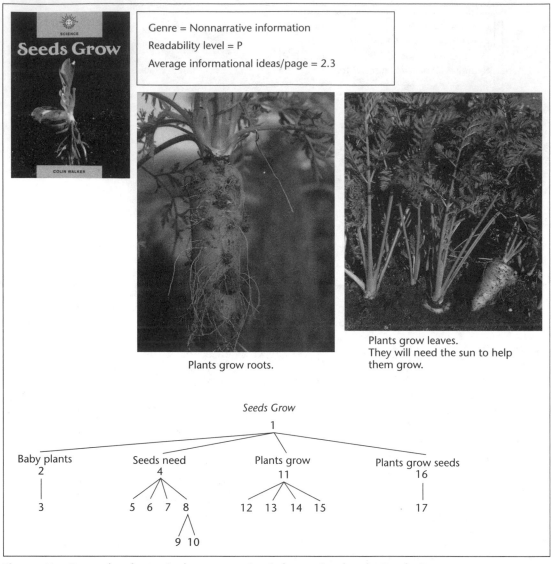

Genre = Nonnarrative information
Readability level = P
Average informational ideas/page = 2.3

Plants grow roots.

Plants grow leaves.
They will need the sun to help
them grow.

Figure 7 Example of a typical nonnarrative information book: *Seeds Grow.*

From *Seeds Grow* by Colin Walker, 1992. Bothell, WA: The Wright Group. Copyright 1992 by Wright Group Publishing, 1920 1 120th Avenue NE, Bothell, WA 98011 (1-800-523-2371). Reprinted with permission. Photos used with permission of G.R. Roberts, Nelson, New Zealand.

information is provided about the other two subtopics, with "seeds' needs" being the most elaborated upon.

This text has an average of 2.3 explicit informational ideas per page. The vivid color photographs contain information as well. For example, the double-page spread that goes with the text "Seeds are baby plants waiting to grow" (p. 2) contains photographs of 11 different types of seeds and their corresponding seed packets, with the name and picture of the fruit or vegetable clearly visible. Of course, such labels might be considered implicit information in that the teacher would have to attend to the photographs and make the information explicit. Still, even without considering implicit information, *Seeds Grow* contains three times the amount of information about seeds that Carle's story *The Tiny Seed* does.

In terms of the illustrations for the folio, or two-page spread, shown in Figure 7, the simple sentences serve as captions for the photographs. On page 10, the roots mentioned in the text are clearly visible in the photograph, just as the leaves in the text on page 11 are dominant in the photograph on page 12. Both of these photographs directly support the content of the text, and their crisp detail should lead to discussions that expand children's understanding of the functions of roots and leaves in a way that Carle's beautiful artwork does not.

Narrative Information Book: Hornets' Nest

Kate Scarborough's (1997) *Watch It Grow: Hornets' Nest* is an example of a narrative informational text

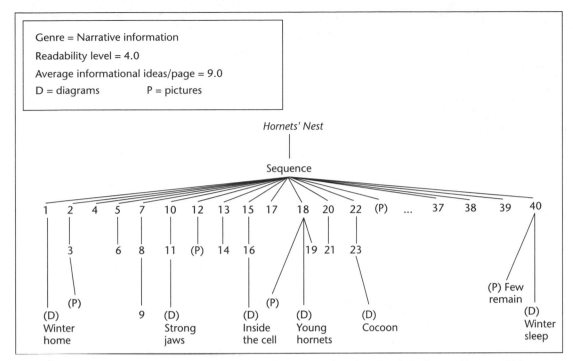

Figure 8 Diagram of a typical narrative information book: *Watch It Grow: Hornets' Nest.*

that details how hornets build their nests. As the building of nests sustains the hornet population, the book also covers the life cycle of hornets. Because *Hornets' Nest* focuses on the sequence hornets follow in building their nest as well as their life cycle, the book's diagram (Figure 8) looks very much like that for the fictional story *The Tiny Seed.*

The overall structure, then, is the sequence with some events receiving additional elaboration: The pictures (P) that go with each page of text, as well as the diagrams (D), seen as insets on each page, provide additional information on concepts presented in the running text. Unlike the sequence of a story, however, the major purpose of this narrative text is to provide information. Written in present tense, as informational texts usually are, this book refers to a general class, all hornets, not to specific events that happened to specific characters. The lexical density measures an average of 9.3 informational ideas per page, including information provided in the text of the diagram inserts and the subtext of the illustrations describing the stages of the nest construction.

In a typical two-page spread, the depiction of a forest fills both pages completely. Set within the center of that scene is a close-up of a particular tree. On the left-hand page, the tree's bark has worn away, leaving a surface on which the running text paragraph, describing what happens on "Day Fifty Two," is presented. Immediately below that paragraph, an inset diagram and its accompanying paragraphed text serve to elaborate upon the running text ("They have taken 20 days to turn into adults") by showing five

phases of development. On the facing page, a cutaway reveals the hatching female workers, reinforcing the idea presented in the running text.

Dual-purpose Text: The Magic School Bus Inside a Beehive

Figure 9 provides the diagram of a dual-purpose text, Joanna Cole's (1996) *The Magic School Bus Inside a Beehive,* designed both to relate an entertaining fantasy as well as to supply information about bees and related topics.

The numbers in Figure 9 represent the clauses of the running text, which contain the story line of Ms. Frizzle and her students' fanciful journey into a beehive. Each page of the book includes short reports (R) of information and diagrams (D) of the topic under investigation; these are also represented on the tree diagram. Not surprisingly, this structural diagram is very similar to that of the fictional story. A setting and characters are introduced immediately, as represented by the initial portion of the tree diagram (1–9) that describe these elements. The sequence of events begins as the class leaves to "meet [the beekeeper] there" and they all board the bus. The story line is presented through the running text, supported by the dialogue in the characters' speech bubbles (SB). Diagrams and reports appearing on each page need not be read to follow the developing story line.

On average, each page contains 9.0 informational ideas. However, the bulk of the information is concentrated in the diagrams and reports in the following

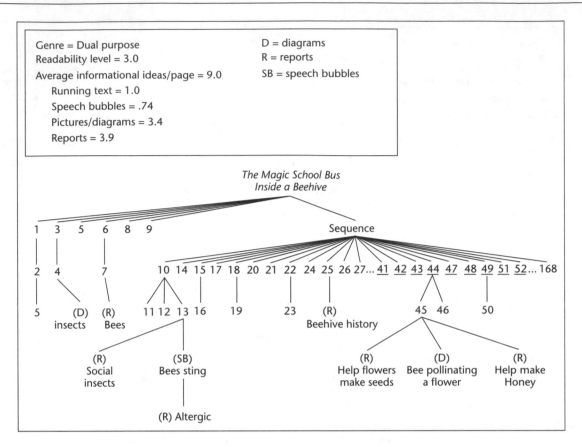

Figure 9   Diagram of a typical dual-purpose book: *The Magic School Bus Inside a Beehive.*

manner: running text (1.0), speech bubbles (.74), diagrams (3.4), and reports (3.9). What these numbers indicate is that children who are simply listening to the fanciful adventure of the running text will not gain as much information as those who also have the diagrams and reports called to their attention.

The two-page spread of pages 16 and 17 is typical of the original Magic School Bus books. On this folio, the story line of the bee transformed Miss Frizzle and her students and the accompanying illustrations (complete with characters and their speech balloons) are presented in the center of the visual environment. Framing this story environment are reports and diagrams, ostensibly produced by Miss Frizzle's students upon their return to her classroom. Reports by John and Alex serve to define key words, but John's definition of crop plants seems to have little to do with Miss Frizzle and the students' pictured activity. The untitled diagram set in the middle of Alex's report accurately uses labels to point out the key features in the fertilization of a flower; this information, though interesting and important, also has very tenuous links to the action in the story. The untitled picture below John's report on food requires readers to infer that the pictured plants are crop producers. An

While we are not saying that a single text type should dominate and be used for all science-related instruction, we will say that all genres have specific purposes and uses to which they are best suited.

additional graphic element is found at the bottom of the left-hand page; two humor-inducing figures represent an informational conversation between smiling flowers and a flower-carrying bee with a pun on bee/be. A final graphic element found at the lower outside corner of the right-hand page, children holding crops and advocating for bees, is linked to John's report.

What These Analyses Tell Us About Books for Science

Drawing from our analyses of the storybook, the information books, and the dual-purpose book, it becomes easier to see what each genre offers science instruction in terms of concept development, specific language features, and possible uses in instruction.

Children's books of different genres

Stories

Carle, Eric, (1969). *The very hungry caterpillar.* New York: Philomel.

Carle, Eric, (1987). *The tiny seed.* New York: Scholastic.

Carle, Eric. (1997). *The very quiet cricket.* New York: Philomel.

Cherry, Lynn. (1990). *The great kapok tree: A tale of the Amazon Rain Forest.* New York: Harcourt Brace.

Cherry, Lynn, & Plotkin, Mark J. (1998). *The shaman's apprentice. A tale of the Amazon Rain Forest.* New York: Harcourt Brace.

Cooney, Barbara. (1982). *Miss Rumphius.* New York: Puffin.

Hall, Donald. (1983). *Ox-cart man,* New York: Puffin.

James, Simon. (1996). *Dear Mr. Blueberry.* New York: Aladdin.

Nonnarrative information books

Aliki. (1990). *My five senses.* New York: Harper Trophy.

Gibbons, Gail. (1990). *Beacons of light: Lighthouses.* New York: William Morrow.

Gibbons, Gail. (1992). *Sharks.* New York: Holiday House.

Gibbons, Gail. (1995). *Catch the wind! All about kites.* New York: Little, Brown.

Gibbons, Gail. (1995). *Check it out! The book about libraries.* New York: Harcourt Brace.

Simon, Seymour. (1989). *Whales.* New York: Harper-Collins.

Simon, Seymour. (1994). *Mountains.* New York: Mulberry.

Simon, Seymour. (1995). *Sharks.* New York: HarperCollins.

Simon, Seymour. (1995). *Volcanoes.* New York: Mulberry.

Walker, Colin. (1992). *Seeds grow.* Bothell, WA: Wright Group.

Narrative information books

Aliki. (1992). *Milk: From cow to carton.* New York: HarperCollins.

Burt, D. (1988). *Birth of a koala.* Melbourne, Australia: The Australian Book Source.

Cole, Joanna. (1976). *A chick hatches.* New York: William Morrow.

Cole, Joanna, & Degen, Bruce. (1996). *The magic school bus gets ants in its pants: A book about ants.* New York: Scholastic.

(Continued)

Stories

Given the long-held assumption that stories are primary and dominate all early reading and writing experiences (Pappas, 1993), it is no surprise that storybooks have been emphasized by many to help enhance students' interest and achievement in science (Lake, 1993; McClure & Zitlow, 1991). However, looking back at Figure 1, it becomes clear that the analysis of stories reveals several issues that must be considered before teachers opt to select them to support science instruction.

First and foremost, in terms of the accuracy of content, stories suggested for science use often contain errors (e.g., Mayer, 1995; Rice & Rainsford, 1996). With so many teachers reporting that they have little confidence in their knowledge of science concepts and their ability to teach science (e.g., Czerniak & Lumpe, 1996; Harlen, 1997; Tilgner, 1990), using texts in which there is a high probability of incorrect information (that may go unnoticed) is problematic.

Second, also in terms of content, the low number of informational ideas presented in many stories means that these will not support concept development in the same ways as texts that present higher numbers of ideas to connect with, discuss, and think about. Also important in terms of informational ideas is the number of implicit ideas a text has, for teachers may need to spend considerable time working to make them explicit. As to children's reactions to the content of stories during interactive read-alouds, our own research has indicated that stories do not provide the same context for engaging with the content or organization of the book as informational texts do (Smolkin & Donovan, 2001). Other researchers who have looked at long-term retention of science information, have found that children did not retain as many ideas about a science concept when the information was embedded in a story (Jetton, 1994; Maria & Junge, 1994).

Continued heavy reliance upon stories in science instruction neither supports acquisition of the language of science nor familiarizes children with science texts and their structures, a point made by Hunter et al. (1987).

> When publishers do not take advantage of opportunities to use maps to show locations, diagrams to show geological information ..., or charts to summarize the importance of findings, they also deprive students of opportunities to read and understand visual displays like those they will meet in their content area textbooks—again reduced opportunity to learn important conventions. (p. 133)

We consider this to be an absolutely critical point for the "fourth-grade slump" in achievement has been linked to students' lack of familiarity with expository

---

Children's books of different genres

(continued)

Gibbons, Gail. (1987). *New road!* New York: HarperCollins.

Gibbons, Gail. (1990). *Sunken treasure.* New York: Harper Trophy.

Gibbons, Gail. (1991). *From seed to plant.* New York: Holiday House.

Goor, Ron, & Goor, Nancy. (1990). *Insect metamorphosis: From egg to adult.* New York: Aladdin.

Provensen, Alice, & Provensen, Martin. (1978). *Year at Maple Hill farm.* New York: Aladdin.

Scarborough, Kate. (1997). *Watch it grow: Hornets' nest.* London: Marshal Editions.

Selsam, Millicent. (1970). *Egg to chick.* New York: HarperCollins.

VanCleave, Janet P. (1989). *Chemistry for every kid: 101 easy experiments that really work.* New York: John Wiley & Sons.

Dual-purpose books

Cole, Joanna. (1986). *The magic school bus at the waterworks.* New York: Scholastic.

Cole, Joanna. (1987). *The magic school bus inside the earth.* New York: Scholastic.

Cole, Joanna. (1996). *The magic school bus inside a beehive.* New York: Scholastic.

de Paola, Tomie. (1977). *The quicksand book.* New York: Holiday House.

de Paola, Tomie. (1978). *The popcorn book.* New York: Holiday House.

---

texts (Chall, Jacobs, & Baldwin, 1990). Our analyses presented here have shown the differences in generic features (linguistic features, global elements, and global structures), content, and visual features between stories and informational texts. Stories simply do not offer environments that help children know about or use the features of informational texts, the very texts on which later school success in science is dependent.

However, we would never wish to deny the potential motivational power of particularly well-considered stories for science instruction. Outstanding examples of powerful science stories are Lynn Cherry's *The Great Kapok Tree* (1990) and *The Shaman's Apprentice* (1998). Both of these stories are set in rain forests that Cherry has personally visited and studied; her intensive research and consultation with experts are documented and support both stories. Both books depict events that could occur in these settings so neither introduces potential misconceptions through texts or illustrations. *The Shaman's Apprentice,* in particular, encourages further science

studies through its story in which a shaman is able to effect cures through his plant knowledge; its exceptionally informative end pages display the many medicinally important plants found in the South American rain forest. This book directly leads children to wonder about other plants and their medicinal value, and it is exactly the kind of book that supports science as inquiry (Austin & Buxton, 2000).

Dual-purpose Books

Because they include both stories and informational content, dual-purpose books have been a source of researchers' interest. Leal (1992), for example, found that, following a read-aloud of an informational storybook, the elementary school children she studied retained more information and had better discussions than they did following the story or informational book she supplied. Other researchers, however, have had very different results, finding instead, as we mentioned above, that story ideas impeded students' learning of the embedded informational content (Jetton, 1994; Maria & Junge, 1994).

The mixed results of these studies, and the in-depth analyses of genre, content, and physical features, lead us to suggest some caution in the use of dual-purpose books. If teaching science concepts is the purpose for reading these texts, teachers must keep in mind that our analyses found very little science content located in the actual running texts of the story. In fact, over 80% of the informational ideas were found in the diagrams and reports; these visual displays could actually be read independently of the story. If the informational insets and diagrams are read, explained, discussed, and connected to one another, then we see these dual-purpose texts as offering great potential for concept development and the acquisition of the language of science.

Information Books

Our analyses reveal how fundamentally different information books are from storybooks, in terms of their generic features, their content, and even their visual features. Particularly important in these texts are their linguistic features and global structures, for these elements combine to make the language of science quite different from the language of stories. Whether informational science texts are more difficult for children to listen to, engage with, read, and write or whether they are, as Lemke (1990) stated, "no more intellectually complex or difficult than those of any other subject ... only less familiar, less like what we are already used to" (p. 139), we are not prepared to say definitively at this time.

However, given our reviews of the literature, our own research with teachers on the selection of books for science (Donovan & Smolkin, 2001) and Duke's (2000) study, we are quite sure that primary-grade children have not had nearly the number of experiences with information books that they have had with stories. Counter to assumptions that informational texts are "unfun" or that "children need stories first" (e.g., Pappas, 1991, 1993), mounting evidence demonstrates that children do enjoy information books (Caswell & Duke, 1998; Donovan, Smolkin, & Lomax, 2000; Horowitz & Freeman, 1995; Oyler, 1996; Pappas, 1991; Smolkin & Donovan, 2001). And, quite importantly, they supply children opportunities to make meaning from less familiar texts as well as acquainting children with the discourse of science.

Scott (1992) suggested that language plays a role in science learning, that science can play a role in language development, and that increased knowledge of language goes "hand in hand with the development of scientific ideas" (p. ix). While Scott may have been referring to oral language development, we see these statements as particularly applicable to science-related informational texts: Listening to and talking about science information books changes children's ways of making meaning. Encountering the many terms critical to the presentation of scientific concepts offers opportunities for teachers and students to connect new ideas to known ideas through the use of metaphors and similes, thus strengthening existing language while solidly inserting new vocabulary and concepts. In turn, new vocabulary and concepts ease students' ways into the unique structures of textbooks from which much of their upper level learning in science will develop.

Concluding Thoughts

Our work in the study of science texts continues to evolve. If this article has a bias toward informational texts, it is only because we have encountered so many teachers who worry that these books will be "unfun" for their students. As we work with more teachers, more children, and more texts, we become increasingly aware of the different ways teachers make use of different texts in different classrooms. So, until we complete controlled quasi-experimental studies, we will not be able to say for sure that experience with information books leads to greater achievement in science or greater facility with the language of science and written genres crucial to science achievement. We will also need further study to determine how the different structures of information books (nonnarrative versus narrative) affect science learning and the ability to learn from unfamiliar informational texts, and whether experience with informational texts alleviates in any way the "fourth-grade slump."

Lemke (1990) offered some important ideas for those of us who work with science and children.

> If we are to effectively teach against the mystique of science we are going to have to stop making it seem that science is intrinsically a harder subject than any other. We are going to have to present science not as an arcane mystery that only the super intelligent can understand, but as one specialized way of talking about the world. (p. 159)

We have offered this intensive look at the texts of elementary school science with the hope that our guidelines and discussion serve to slice away some of the mysterious and foreboding aura attached to informational texts in particular. Though stories are lovely, and enjoyed by children of all ages, it is our stance that we need not make one genre serve for all purposes. Instead, we can recognize that information books also excite interest in the world of science, foster discoveries in science and language use, and invite connections to life within classroom walls and outside as well.

References

Anderson, E. (1998). Motivational and cognitive influences, conceptual knowledge: The combination of science observation and interesting texts. *Dissertation Abstract, International, A. (Humanities and Social Sciences). 59* (6–1913).

Austin, P., & Buxton, C. (2000). Science as inquiry. *Book Links, 10*(2), 10–15.

Barber, J., Bergman, L., Hosoume, K., Kopp, J., Sneider, C., & Willard, C. (1993). *Once upon a GEMS guide: Connecting young people's literature to great explorations in math and science.* Berkeley, CA: Lawrence Hall of Science, University of California at Berkeley.

Barlow, D. (1991). Children, books, and biology. *BioScience, 41*(3), 166–169.

Butzow, C., & Butzow, J. (1988). Facts from fiction. *Science & Children, 25*(6), 27–29.

Camp, D. (2000). It takes two: Teaching with twin texts of fact and fiction. *The Reading Teacher, 53,* 400–408.

Caswell, L. J., & Duke, N. K. (1998). Non-narrative as a catalyst for literacy development. *Language Arts, 75,* 108–117.

Chall, J. S., Jacobs, V., & Baldwin, L. (1990). *The reading crisis: Why poor children fall behind.* Cambridge, MA: Harvard University Press.

Crook, P. R., & Lehman, B. A. (1991). Themes for two voices: Children's fiction and nonfiction as "whole literature." *Language Arts, 68,* 34–41.

Czemiak, C.M., & Lampe, A.T. (1996). Relationship between teacher beliefs and science education reform. *Journal of Science Teacher Education, 7,* 247–266.

Donovan, C. A. (2001). Children's development and control of written story and informational genres: Insights from one elementary school. *Research in the Teaching of English, 35*, 394–447.

Donovan, C. A., & Smolkin, L.B. (2001). Genre and other factors influencing teachers book selections for science. *Reading Research Quarterly, 36*, 412–440.

Donovan, C. A., Smolkin, L. B., & Lomax, R.G. (2000). Beyond the independent-level text: Readability of first graders' self-selections. *Reading Psychology, 21*, 309–333.

Duke, N. K. (2000). 3.6 minutes per day: The scarcity of informational texts in first grade. *Reading Research Quarterly, 35*, 202–224.

Fry, E. (1977). Fry's readability graph: Clarification, validity, and extension to level 17. *Journal of Reading, 21*, 242–252.

Halliday, M. A. K. (1993). Some grammatical problems in scientific English. In M. A. K. Halliday & J. R. Martin (Eds.), *Writing science: Literacy and discursive power* (pp. 69–85). London: Falmer.

Harlen, W. (1997). Primary teachers' understanding in science and its impact in the classroom. *Research in Science Education, 27*, 323–337.

Hasan, R. (1984). The nursery tale as a genre. *Nottingham Linguistic Circular, 13*, 71–102.

Horning, K. T. (1997). *From cover to cover: Evaluating and reviewing children's books.* New York: HarperCollins.

Horowitz, R., & Freeman, S. H. (1995). Robots versus spaceships: The role of discussion in kindergartners' and second graders' preferences for science text. *The Reading Teacher, 49*, 30–40.

Huck, C. S., Hepler, S., Hickman, J., & Kiefer, B. (2001). *Children's literature in the elementary school* (7th ed.). Boston: McGraw Hill.

Hunter, B., Crismore, A., & Pearson, P.D. (1987). Visual displays in basal readers and social studies texts. In D. M. Willows & H.A. Houghton (Eds.), *The psychology of illustration: Vol. 1. Basic research* (pp. 116–135). New York: Springer-Verlag.

Jetton, T. L. (1994). Information-driven versus story-driven: What children remember when they are read informational stories. *Reading Psychology, 15,* 109–130.

Klare, G. R. (1976). A second look at the validity of readability formulas. *Journal of Reading Behavior, 8*, 129–152.

Kress, G. (1994). *Learning to write* (2nd ed.). New York: Routledge.

Lake, J. (1993). *Imagine: A literature-based approach to science.* Bothell, WA: Wright Group.

Langer, J. A. (1986). *Children reading and writing: Structures and strategies.* Norwood, NJ: Ablex.

Leal, D. J. (1992). The nature of talk about three types of text during peer group discussions. *Journal of Reading Behavior, 24*, 313–338.

Leal, D. J. (1993). Storybooks, information books, and informational storybooks: An explication of the ambiguous grey genre. *The New Advocate, 6*, 61–70.

Lemke, J. L. (1990). *Talking science: Talking, learning, and values.* Norwood, NJ: Ablex.

Levie, W. H., & Lentz, R. (1982). Effects of text illustrations: A review of research. *Educational Communication & Technology Journal, 30*, 195–232.

Marin, K., & Junge, K. (1994). A comparison of fifth graders' comprehension and retention of scientific information using a science textbook and an informational storybook. In C. K. Kinzer & D. J. Len (Eds.), *Multidimensional aspects of literacy research, theory, and practice. 43rd yearbook of the National Reading Conference* (pp. 146–152). Chicago: National Reading Conference.

Mayer, D. (1995). How can we best use literature in teaching. *Science and Children, 32*, 16–19.

McClure, A. A., & Zitlow, C. S. (1991). Not just the facts: Aesthetic response in elementary content area studies. *Language Arts, 68*, 27–33.

Meyer, B. J. F. (1975). *The organization of prose and its effects on memory.* Amsterdam: North-Holland.

Morrow, L. M., Pressley, M., Smith, J. K., & Smith, M. (1997). The effect of a literature-based program integrated into literacy and science instruction with children from diverse backgrounds. *Reading Research Quarterly, 32*, 54–76.

Moss, B. (1991). Children's nonfiction trade books: A complement to content area texts. *The Reading Teacher, 45*, 26–32.

Newkirk, T. (1987). The non-narrative writing of young children. *Research in the Teaching of English, 21*, 121–144.

Oyler, C. (1996). Sharing authority: Student initiations during teacher-led read-alouds of information books. *Teaching & Teacher Education, 12*, 149–160.

Palincsar, A. S., & Magnusson, S. J. (2000). *The interplay of first-hand and text-based investigations in science education* (Rep. No. 2-007). Ann Arbor, MI: University of Michigan, Center for the Improvement of Early Reading Achievement.

Pappas, C. C. (1986). *Exploring the global structure of "Information books"* (Rep. No. CS-008-683). Paper presented at the annual meeting of the National Reading Conference, Austin, TX. (ERIC Document Reproduction Service No. ED 278 952)

Pappas, C. C. (1991). Fostering full access to literacy by including information books. *Language Arts, 68*, 449–462.

Pappas, C. C. (1993). Is narrative "primary"? Some insights from kindergarteners' pretend readings of stories and information books. *Journal of Reading Behavior, 25*, 97–129.

Pappas, C. C., Kiefer, B. Z., & Levstik, L. S. (1999). *An integrated language perspective in the elementary school: An action approach* (3rd ed.). White Plains, NY: Longman.

Pappas, C. C., Varelas, M., Barry, A., & O'Neill, A. (2000, April). *Exploring young children's science discourse registers in integrated primary-grade science-literacy inquiries.* Paper presented at the annual meeting of the American Educational Research Association, New Orleans, L. A.

Peeck, J. (1987). The role of illustrations in processing and remembering illustrated text. In D. M. Willows & H. A.

Houghton (Eds.), *The psychology of illustration: Vol. 1. Basic research* (pp. 115–151). New York: Springer-Verlag.

Peeck, J. (1993). Increasing picture effects in learning from illustrated text. *Learning and Instruction, 3*, 227–238.

Rice, D., & Rainsford, A. (1996). *Using children's trade books to teach science: Boon or boondoggle?* Paper presented at the annual meeting of the National Association for Research in Science Teaching, St. Louis, MO. (ERIC Document Reproduction Service No. ED 393 700)

Roth, K.J. (1991). Learning to be comfortable in the neighborhood of science: An analysis of three approaches to elementary science teaching. In W. Saul & S.A. Jagusch (Eds.), *Vital connections: Children, science, and books: Papers from a symposium sponsored by the Children's Literature Center* (pp. 143–161). Washington, DC: Library of Congress.

Scott, J. (1992). *Science & language links.* Portsmouth, NH: Heinemann.

Shulevitz, U. (1985). *Writing with pictures: How to write and illustrate children's books.* New York: Watson-Guptill.

Skurzynski, G. (1992). Up for discussion: Blended books. *School Library Journal, 38*(10), 46–47.

Smardo, A. (1982). Using children's literature to clarify science concepts in early childhood programs. *The Reading Teacher, 36*, 267–273.

Smolkin, L.B., & Donovan, C.A. (2001). The contexts of comprehension: The information book read aloud, comprehension acquisition, and comprehension instruction in a first grade classroom. *Elementary School Journal, 102*, 97–122.

Stein, N.L., & Glenn, C.G. (1979). An analysis of story comprehension in elementary school children. In R.O. Freedle (Ed.), *New directions in discourse processing* (Vol. 2, pp. 53–120). San Francisco: Jossey-Bass.

Tilgner, P.J. (1990). Avoiding science in the elementary school. *Science & Education, 74*, 421–431.

Trundle, K.C. (2000). *Misrepresentation of the moon.* Paper presented at the Association for the Education of Teachers in Science, Akron, OH.

Unsworth, L. (1999). Developing critical understanding of the specialised language of school science and history texts: A functional grammatical perspective. *Journal of Adolescent & Adult Literacy, 42*, 508–521.

Weidenmann, B. (1989). When good pictures fail: An information-processing approach to the effect of illustrations. In H. Mandl & J.R. Levin (Eds.), *Knowledge acquisition from text and pictures* (pp. 157–171). Amsterdam: Elsevier.

STUDY GUIDE

1. What contributions should early reading books make to children's literacy development? (Perera)

2. Why is it important for children to read "good" books? Identify three linguistic features of good storybooks for beginning readers. (Perera)

3. What constitutes "motivated repetition"? Why is it important for beginning reading books to contain motivated, rather than unmotivated, lexical and syntactic repetition? (Perera)

4. What does the author mean when he states that "... in curriculum areas like science and technology and human society and its environment, developing knowledge and understanding and learning to control the specialized language of such curriculum areas is one and the same thing"? (Unsworth)

5. How and why is the grammar of curriculum area language different from that of the everyday interactional spoken language? What implications do such differences have for literacy instruction in content areas? (Unsworth)

6. What is a nominal group? What does it consist of? Some people argue that native speakers of English already know the order of the constituents of a nominal group and that bringing this information to children's conscious attention may lead to confusion. What do you think? (Unsworth)

7. What is lexical density? How can it be calculated? How can the lexical density of a text be increased or reduced? What impact does such change have on a text's readability? Also think about this in conjunction with the next question. (Unsworth)

8. What does nominalization involve? Compare the following three sentences from Michael Halliday's (1985, p. 79) *Spoken and Written Language* and discuss the impacts nominalization

and lexical density have on a text's comprehensibility. (Unsworth)

a. You can control the trains this way and if you do that you can be quite sure that they'll be able to run more safely and more quickly no matter how bad the weather gets.

b. If this method of control is used, trains will unquestionably (be able to) run more safely and faster (even) when the weather conditions are most adverse.

c. The use of this method of control unquestionably leads to safer and faster train running in the most adverse weather condition.

9. How is the functional grammar presented in the article different from traditional grammar? Identify 3–5 activities that can be used to enhance children's understanding of the grammar of curriculum content area language. (Unsworth)

10. What kinds of trade books are commonly used in elementary school science instruction? What are the genre, content, and visual features of each text type? What are the potentials of each text type for science instruction? (Donovan & Smolkin)

11. What are the benefits and potential problems associated with using educational novels, in which the contents of technical topics are fictionalized, in the teaching and learning of science and social studies? (Donovan & Smolkin)

12. All three articles in this section stress that it is important for teachers and students to develop a conscious understanding of the language of school-based texts. Explain how such explicit knowledge of functional discourse grammar can be useful in guiding the teaching and learning of school-based literacies. Give clear examples. (Perera; Unsworth; Donovan & Smolkin)

INQUIRY PROJECTS

1. In recent years there has been a proliferation of leveled books in beginning reading instruction. The criteria for leveling these texts are many and varied. These books have often been criticized for their lack of literary quality. Identify 1–2 reading series of leveled books and collect a random sample of 10–12 storybooks from each series. Analyze these books according to Perera's

criteria and determine whether they are "good books." Discuss the challenges of writing/selecting good books for beginning readers.

2. Select an excerpt on a familiar topic from an elementary science textbook and 5–10 writing samples on the same topic from an upper elementary or middle grade class. Compare the number, complexity, and functions of nominal

groups in, as well as the lexical density of, these sample expository texts. Discuss the implications of your findings for reading and writing instruction in curricular content areas.

3. Decide on one science topic and then collect one trade book that addresses the topic in each of the following text types: story, narrative informational, non-narrative informational, and dual-purpose. Compare and contrast the genre, content, and visual features of these texts. Discuss the pros and cons of using each text for teaching the selected science topic.

FURTHER READING

Chall, J., Bissex, G., Conard, S., & Harris-Sharples, S. (1996). *Qualitative assessment of text difficulty: A practical guide for teachers and writers.* Cambridge, MA: Brookline Publishers.

Derewianka, B. (1990). *Exploring how texts work.* Victoria, Australia: Primary Education Teacher Association.

Fountas, I. C., & Pinnell, G. S. (1999). *Matching books to readers: Using level books in guided reading, K–3.* Portsmouth, NH: Heinemann.

Halliday, M. A. K. (1985). *Spoken and written language.* Geelong, Victoria, Australia: Deaking University Press.

Halliday, M. A. K., & Hasan, R. (1989). *Language, context and text: Aspects of language in a social-semiotic perspective.* Oxford, UK: Oxford University Press.

Halliday, M. A. K., & Martin, J. R. (1993). *Writing science: Literacy and discursive power.* London: Falmer.

Hiebert, E. H. (1999). Text matters in learning to read. *The Reading Teacher, 52,* 552–566.

Hiebert, E. H. (2002). Standards, assessments, and text difficulty. In A. Farstrup & S. Jay Samuels (Eds.). *What research has to say about reading instruction* (pp. 337–369). Newark, DE: International Reading Association.

Hoffman, J. (2002). Words (on words in leveled texts for beginning readers). In D. Schallert, C. Fairbanks, J. Worthy, B. Maloch, & J. Hoffman (Eds.). *51st Yearbook of the National Reading Conference* (pp. 59–81). Oak Creek, WI: National Reading Conference.

Martin, J., & Veel, R. (1998). *Reading science: Critical and functional perspectives on discourses of science.* London: Routledge.

Perera, K. (1984). *Children's writing and reading: Analysing classroom language.* London: Basil and Blackwell.

Peterson, B. (2001). *Literary pathways: Selecting books to support new readers.* Portsmouth, NH: Heinemann.

Schleppegrell, M. (2004). The Language of schooling: A functional linguistics approach. Mahwah, NJ: Lawrence Erlbaum.

Wellington, J., & Osborne, J. (2001). *Language and literacy in science education.* Philadelphia: Open University Press.

Teaching Struggling Readers

INTRODUCTION

In almost every school in America, there are students who are at risk of reading failure. These students have been variably referred to as struggling readers, poor readers, low-achieving readers, slow readers, reluctant readers, at-risk readers, delayed readers, backward readers, and disabled readers. The population of these readers is heavily and nonproportionately represented in urban and poor neighborhood schools. While there is a general consensus on the importance and urgency of helping these children succeed in school, approaches to accomplishing this goal have been controversial.

In the first article, Anne McGill-Franzen and Richard Allington suggest that common policy and pedagogical responses to struggling readers are often predicated on outdated assumptions about learners and learning. Based on a review of low-achieving readers' experiences in classroom instruction and in remedial and special education programs, the authors suggest that the problem of underachievement is not one of poverty or linguistic/cultural differences, but of restricted access to high-quality school instruction. They propose that in order to break the gridlock of low reading achievement, policy makers and educators must radically rethink their responses by promoting a more sociocognitively and socioculturally oriented approach that emphasizes ownership, meaning, coherence, and acceleration in instruction. This article, although written a decade ago, is still very relevant today because schools are facing mounting pressure to comply with rapidly multiplying federal and state mandates. Although criticized for their narrow and simple views of reading, these government mandates are nevertheless being promoted as the solution to meeting the needs of struggling readers.

Darrell Morris' article describes some of the persistent issues and concerns surrounding the teaching of struggling readers in grades K–3 and outlines a grade-by-grade action plan for supporting those children's reading growth. The author reviews the classroom context in beginning reading instruction over the past 50 years, suggesting that the methods, materials, and management techniques of the present and past can both be used to address the unique needs of struggling readers. He further argues, based on a comparison of two notorious early intervention programs (Reading Recovery and Success for All), that, although different instructional schemes can be effective with struggling readers, providing carefully graded texts and instruction in alphabetic code both seem to be particularly critical. He urges educators to utilize the existing professional knowledge base and to continue searching for new and more effective ways to meet the needs of struggling readers.

There is, however, more to teaching struggling readers than merely providing high-quality instruction. As Irene Gaskins argues in her article, successful school-based initiatives for struggling readers require, in addition, ongoing staff development, persistent support services, congruence between remedial and regular instructional programs, and ample instructional time. Her description of the design, implementation, and revision of the reading programs at Benchmark, a school for struggling readers in grades 1–8, is a vivid testimony to the complexities, challenges, and possibilities of meeting the needs, as well as ensuring the continued success, of children who experience reading difficulties.

The Gridlock of Low Reading Achievement: Perspectives on Practice and Policy

Anne McGill-Franzen
University of Florida

Richard L. Allington
University of Florida

Low achieving children do not read very well, but then, why should they? We have institutionalized stratified achievement and the expectation that some children will do less well than others through our standardized testing policies (Johnston, 1989; Martin, 1988). We have built a separate educational system for the lowest achieving children in the form of compensatory and special education programs, and we maintain children in these programs and support these practices through a complex interaction of professional beliefs, pedagogy, and local, state, and federal regulations (Gartner & Lipsky, 1987; McGill-Franzen, 1987).

We have institutionalized stratified achievement and the expectation that some children will do less well than others through our standardized testing policies

Neither policy nor regulation nor instruction typically reflects the goal of developing independent, self-monitoring, actively comprehending readers among children whose literacy development lags behind that of their peers. Over the past 20 years, theories of literacy development have advanced from behaviorist to constructivist and connectionist models of comprehension (Adams, 1990), but federal and state regulations and pedagogy for children who find learning to read difficult have remained relatively static, locked in a reductionist model of learning (Allington, 1990). All around us, notions of the nature of literacy development and the form of appropriate instruction are shifting dramatically (Willinsky, 1990). For the at-risk reader, however, both policy and pedagogy remain firmly entrenched in the assumptions about learners and learning that were prominent a quarter century ago. Three assumptions, each incorrect, undergird the most common policy and pedagogical responses to children who experience difficulty learning to read.

The first incorrect assumption is that children and their families are the problem. We do not deny that children of poverty and minorities are most often at risk in our schools, but we believe that schools, not children and their families, are the problem. Learning to read, like all other learning, is embedded in the context of the whole, and children come to know the form of written language because they understand the uses of text in their lives. Schools are typically organized in ways that limit the access of low achieving or at-risk children to experiences that promote literacy development and that build on the culture of the family and community.

The second incorrect assumption is that specialists and separate programs are the solution. An alternative understanding is that special programs, albeit well intentioned, ultimately reduce professional accountability for the progress of low achieving children by dispersing responsibility for teaching these children to read. At best, such programs create fragmented instructional experiences for participating children and, at worst, trivialize learning and waste the time and motivation of children who are already at risk of failure.

The third incorrect assumption is that children who find learning to read difficult are best served by a "slow it down and make it more concrete" version of instruction. An alternative to this assumption is that learning can and indeed must be accelerated, and that coherent literacy lessons that engage students in reading and writing of extended text are needed to facilitate such acceleration.

Each of these wrong assumptions is at least implicit in the educational policies and regulatory statues that govern school programs for low achieving, poor, and minority children. These incorrect assumptions are the underpinnings of conventional wisdom about how best to teach these children to read and write. No issue should be more critical in the elementary school than ensuring literacy for all children. But, although we have literacy programs, funds, categories, specialists, and such, we have relatively little evidence that our current efforts substantially alter the educational futures of at-risk children (Carter, 1984; Juel, 1988; Singer & Butler, 1987;

Slavin, 1989). In this paper, we discuss why we think the assumptions raised above are wrong and how else we might frame the problem of low achieving children who do not read and write well.

Access to School Knowledge

Despite good intentions on the part of teachers, optimism on the part of parents, and more than two decades of investment in compensatory and special education services at-risk children rarely perform at the same level as their more advantaged and majority peers. Rather than blame the child and the family (see, e.g., "Mothers Who Don't Know How," by columnist George Will, in *Newsweek*, April 23, 1990), contemporary educators, psychologists, linguists, and sociologists have proposed varying reasons why children from poor and minority communities read less well than children from mainstream communities (Cazden, 1988; Delpit, 1988; Fraatz, 1987; Heath, 1983; Hyde & Moore, 1988; Mehan, 1978; Moll, 1990).

The limited resources available to poor families and aspects of the cultural and linguistic differences ... may contribute somewhat to low reading achievement, but schools themselves contribute the most.

The limited resources available to poor families and aspects of the cultural and linguistic differences in language interactions within minority communities may contribute somewhat to low reading achievement, but schools themselves contribute the most. We believe that schools provide instructional experiences to low achievers that are often qualitatively different from those of their high achieving peers. Because simple texts and trivial tasks are emphasized, such experiences rarely accelerate the literacy development of low achievers and often restrict the kinds of knowledge available to these learners.

Family Resources and Access to School Knowledge

Limited family or school resources may contribute to a differential access to school knowledge, but neither because of class bias on the part of teachers and schools nor because of a lack of caring on the part of poor parents. Contrary to the findings of earlier research, the ethnographer Lareau (1989) found that teachers did not appear to expect less of first graders who were poor than of those from middle class families. Teachers' expectations for children's work and parental participation were uniform across socioeconomic classes. What differed by social class was the family's expectations of the school in general and the family's ability to muster resources to compensate for a weak curriculum or incompetent teacher, particularly for low achieving children.

Poorer families regarded teachers as their social superiors and they typically respected without question the professional judgment of the teacher concerning their children. Poorer families also believed that the curriculum was the purview of the school, that it was the teacher's job to teach, not the parents'. The parents' job, according to those interviewed by Lareau, was to "ready" the child for school, to make sure that the child was well fed, clothed, and on time for school. These parents did not think that they were qualified to teach the curriculum to their children, even when the school requested that they do so to bolster the achievement of a child who was falling behind. By contrast, middle class parents believed themselves to be the teacher's professional equal: parents were knowledgeable about grade-level curriculum and about the strengths and weaknesses of their child's teacher. In the case of low achieving children, middle class parents were able to supplement an inadequate instructional program and compensate for a weak or incompetent teacher by obtaining tutoring (or teaching the children themselves) outside the school.

Unlike low achieving children from poor families, low achieving middle class children were often able to "keep up" with their peers because their parents had the resources to recognize when the school was not doing its job, to speak on the child's behalf, and to help create an intervention tailored specifically for their child. Low achieving poor children had no personalized parental intervention. Nonetheless, schools cannot adhere to organizational patterns that penalize children for the resources of their parents. In our view, the continued low achievement demonstrated by many poor children is largely a function of the quality of their instructional experiences.

Cultural Difference

Besides poverty, linguistic and cultural difference has also been proposed as a potential barrier to school success. An improvement over the assumption of the 1960s—that children from poor, minority, and bilingual communities were linguistically and culturally deprived—this alternative assumption acknowledges that children, no matter how poor, participate fully in the language and culture of their communities. This alternative assumption holds that educators need to be cognizant of the ways children create and express meaning outside the school in order to build appropriate discourse structures within the classroom. The difficulty in applying this assumption to classroom practice lies in the inability of most of us to decide which cultural and linguistic variations are important for instructional purposes and, having determined the important variations, to recast our instructional strategies for a better match with the children's "ways of knowing" (Cazden, 1988). Fortunately, some models in the research literature suggest how we might make the most of the cultural and linguistic knowledge children bring to school.

Schools provide instructional experiences to low achievers that are often qualitatively different from those of their high achieving peers.

Well-known examples are the Kamehameha Early Education Project (KEEP) in Hawaii (Au & Jordan, 1980), studies of the Warm Springs Indian children in central Oregon (Philips, 1983), and the linguistic descriptions of working class and black family interactions in the Piedmont Carolinas (Heath, 1983). Children in each of these communities were notably unsuccessful and frequently perceived as uncooperative in school, but were quite competent participants in activities outside the classroom. By identifying variations in the ways children were socialized to participate in verbal interactions in the family and community versus the dominant interactional structures of the classroom, researchers were able to suggest classroom adaptations that helped to bridge the gap between the culture of the home and community and that of the school.

Among the Hawaiian children, for example, educators were able to improve the children's reading comprehension by allowing the "talk story" to evolve as the preferred method of responding to text. Rather than answering individually, children jointly contribute to the recitation, and responses may overlap, simulating the structure of interactions within the Hawaiian family. Likewise, Warm Springs Indian children, perceived as extremely shy and soft spoken, were more involved and more successful when they were encouraged to engage in group learning activities with their peers than when they were called upon to individually and publicly display their knowledge as in typical teacher-dominated reading group interactions. In the Carolinas, teachers and their students were encouraged to observe and document ways of using written language within their communities so that awareness of different "ways with words" might serve as a first step in bridging discontinuities between home and school. Although such home and cultural continuities and discontinuities are important in addressing the education of at-risk children, so too are the school programs that we create for these children.

Access to Knowledge: Tasks and Texts of the Bottom Group

Although differential access to school knowledge, particularly the high-status knowledge embedded in the instruction of the highest achieving groups, is an issue that has received much attention in studies of high school tracking (Goodlad & Oakes, 1988; Oakes, 1985), it has not been well researched at the elementary level. Nonetheless, we believe this issue has profound implications for at-risk and low achieving children. In our classroom observations of reading instruction for low achieving children, and in similar studies reported by others, it appears that such children do not have access to large amounts of high-quality instruction (Allington, 1980, 1983; Allington & McGill-Franzen, 1989a, 1989b; Haynes & Jenkins, 1986; McGill-Franzen & Allington, 1990).

Children in the bottom reading group spend fewer minutes than other students actually reading text and more time on isolated skill work, but it is the experience of reading text that is related to improved reading achievement in both decoding and comprehension. A close examination of the types of tasks that low achieving children are required to do in general classroom literacy activities suggests an emphasis on tasks at the letter or word level with scant opportunity to read connected text silently. Teachers appear to interrupt poor readers more often as these children try to read connected text orally, a tendency that aborts the flow of meaning, increases the error rate, focuses children's attention on letter-sound correspondences instead of the continuity of the text itself, and develops habits of helplessness and dependency in reading (Johnston & Winograd, 1985).

Although there have been no large-scale studies of the types of curriculum texts provided to low achieving children or those in the bottom reading group, our observations suggest that the texts selected for poor readers have fewer words per page, vocabulary that is more controlled for phonetic regularity or frequency of use, sentences that are syntactically simple and very unlike children's natural language, and narrative and expository text structures that are not well formed. Different types of text do appear to influence children's comprehension of the material (Armbruster & Anderson, 1984). Complex concepts are more clearly understood by all children when the relationships between ideas are explicitly laid out in text that is cohesive and interesting. A steady diet of text that is poorly written and uses only monosyllabic words, letter-sound patterns, or simple syntax could not adequately address complex issues of content, and probably would diminish the richness and complexity of the language children use to express their ideas in writing or speaking.

Over a decade ago, when we first began to examine the differential instructional experiences of children classified as poor readers, we were struck by how well these children "learned what they were taught" and how much of the knowledge children displayed actually reflected the instructional emphases of their teachers and their texts. The writing of children in the bottom reading group, in particular, was compelling testimony to the kinds of texts these children read and the focus of the instruction they received (McGill-Franzen, 1979).

To illustrate the powerful effects of instruction on children's cognitive functioning, we share two writing samples (see Figure 1) collected on the same day—one from a child in the average reading group and the other from a child in the bottom reading group. Both children had the same first-grade teacher and the same writing assignment ("write a story") but used different texts in their reading groups. As these writing samples suggest, the child in the bottom group used a phonemically regular text for reading group; the focus of instruction was accurate decoding. This child wrote a "story" that conformed to mostly short *u* and short *a* trigrams (i.e., three-letter words) in a format and style (one sentence per line) that reflected the structure of the phonetically regular text he read in his reading

Average group member

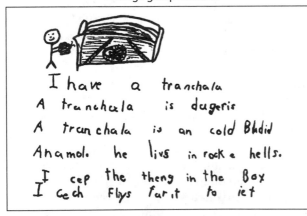

Bottom group member

Figure 1 These writing samples are from children in the average and bottom reading groups.

group. The child in the average group used language that was much more complex and natural sounding, also reflecting the text he read in his reading group.

It is interesting to note that the child in the low reading group spelled the majority of his words accurately but wrote a fairly nonsensical story similar to the story patterns in phonemically regular reading texts. The child in the average group took many more "risks" with his spelling, using words that he did not know how to spell but that he needed to say what he wanted about the topic. If it is true that children's academic work shapes much of their thinking, as Marx and Walsh (1988) and Doyle (1990) suggested, then low achieving children are relegated to school tasks that require little comprehension and discourage risk taking, self-monitoring, and independence, and, in fact, these tasks may restrict the range of thinking children do.

We have expended enormous energy and resources examining children and their families for differences and deficiencies that would account for failure to learn to read. Unfortunately, we have only rarely and recently begun to seriously examine the appropriateness of the instruction offered to those children who have found learning to read difficult.

Remedial and Special Education for Low Achieving Readers

The second incorrect assumption holds that when learning problems appear, the best solution is to export the child to a specialist for "special" instruction. When the achievement of children in the bottom reading group is substantially below their peers on standardized tests, these children usually are referred to either compensatory education or special education programs for additional reading services.

Based on our studies of children's experiences in remedial and special services, and the research reported by others, students placed in these programs do not usually have access to instruction that will accelerate their development and enable them to catch up to their peers (Allington & McGill-Franzen, 1989a, 1989b; Haynes & Jenkins, 1986; Johnston, Allington, & Afflerbach, 1985; McGill-Franzen & Allington, 1990; Rowan & Guthrie, 1989; Ysseldyke, O'Sullivan, Thurlow, & Christenson, 1989). Instead, low achieving children who participate in these programs rarely receive more instructional time, and frequently are scheduled for less instruction than children whose achievement is average. Not only do children who "go down the hall" for reading often receive less classroom time for reading instruction, but these children also miss the presentation of curriculum in other content areas as well. Although the effect of less scheduled classroom instruction in math, for example, has not been studied, it is not farfetched to predict difficulty in math among students who regularly miss substantial time in a math group because they participate in remedial or special services while their classmates have math. These same arguments apply to all content areas.

Elementary-age students are being asked to demonstrate competency not only in reading, writing, and math, but also in science and social studies. In some states, children who do not meet competency standards in these subjects are required to participate in more remedial courses and are precluded from participating in other more content-rich courses. Thus, it seems to us that participation in remedial and special services can further limit access to other kinds of curriculum knowledge for participating children. One special education teacher recognized the dilemma for students placed in resource rooms. She said that a problem with such tests is that "some of our children are tested on things that they weren't taught. In the general classroom they might not be taught it specifically, [but] if they were there, there was some exposure to it."

The organization of instruction in remedial and special education programs is itself problematic and works against the idea of sustained, personalized intervention to accelerate literacy development.

Certainly, recent studies of reading vocabulary development (White, Graves, & Slater, 1990) suggest a substantial knowledge gap between mainstream, average achieving suburban children and their lower achieving peers who attend school in disadvantaged areas. By the end of third grade, the mainstream, suburban children have vocabularies that are 50% larger, a gap of about 5,000 words. For the low achieving child, roughly 2,000 of these unknown words may be attributed to less skilled decoding, since these children could not actually read as many words as the suburban children (the reading achievement scores of the suburban children were higher than those of the disadvantaged children). However, the meanings of 3,000 more words were inaccessible to these children, even when the words were decoded for them. In our view, it should not be surprising that low achieving readers know the meanings of fewer words. Given the restrictions noted for their reading instruction, the lack of time they spend reading connected texts on topics of any consequence, and the predilection on the part of classroom teachers to send low achieving readers to remedial or special education for part of the school day, we would expect these children to know less than their peers because they have experienced less relevant instruction.

In addition, "the organization of instruction in remedial and special education programs is itself problematic and works against the idea of sustained, personalized intervention to accelerate literacy development." Because specialist teachers are considered a "resource" to children across a wide span of ages, grades, and achievement, they often must schedule children together who collectively demonstrate a range of achievement much greater than would be found in the average classroom. Specialist teachers deal with such diversity in much the same way that classroom teachers deal with diversity in achievement: They group children together, they teach the same things to everyone in a particular group, and they assign seatwork to the others.

Separate Curricula

The reason classroom teachers give for referring children to a specialist is to provide them with "individualized" or "one-to-one" help to improve their reading and enable them to participate more successfully in their regular classroom. We found scant evidence, however, that the academic work assigned to children in remedial reading or special education was related to either improving the performance of individuals or the curriculum of the classroom. Rather, specialist teachers seemed to have created yet another literacy curriculum for children who were already experiencing difficulty with the curriculum of the general classroom (McGill-Franzen & Allington, 1990).

The specialists' curriculum varied from specialist teacher to specialist teacher. If the specialist teacher believed that drawing pictures and dictating "stories" were good ideas, then all children did them, albeit at different times during the day. If doing symbol/sound drills was viewed as beneficial, all children did them, perhaps different pace. It did not seem to matter whether the activities were "whole language," such as journal writing or generating "prediction" questions, or whether they were "discrete skills," such as working their way through progressive levels of "find the main idea" workbooks, specialist teachers seemed to have created a separate "curriculum"—different from that of the regular classroom, but a curriculum nonetheless. Children's academic work in these specialist programs was every bit as routinized as their work in the general classroom, with no evidence that instruction was personalized to address the needs or performance of individuals.

The specialist instruction also was not designed to promote the success of individual children back in the classroom. Rarely were tasks related across settings. Most often the specialist instruction simply added more fragmented tasks to the already confusing array of worksheets that confronted the low achieving child. These tasks were generally not related to each other, or to the academic work of the general classroom. One second grader, for example, unsuccessfully read a grade-level basal reader in his classroom, making three errors in the single sentence he read orally, and then proceeded to remedial reading. In remedial reading, he was given a spelling test on words with *ew, ue,* and *oo* patterns, was asked to copy a list of vocabulary into a "word bank," was asked to correctly pronounce another list of vocabulary words from a basal reader (different from his classroom reader), listened to an audiotaped activity on five more vocabulary words (different from all the others), completed a phonics worksheet on words with the *ope* and *oat* patterns, and read two short text selections, one on a primer level and one at a second-grade level. Such disjointed bits and pieces of commercial supplementary reading materials were not idiosyncratic to this particular child and his remedial program, but were the most common form of special services curricula that we observed.

Collective Instruction

Even the difficulty of the tasks varied greatly from classroom to special program. Instruction was not coordinated to focus on particular types of texts, themes, strategies, or even vocabulary or concepts, and children were asked to participate in activities that were widely divergent in difficulty. Students assigned to remedial or special education spent considerably more of their instructional time doing seatwork. This is particularly true of special education resource rooms, where children were less often engaged in text reading or writing and special education teachers less often taught children directly, but rather assigned workbook pages or skillsheets to complete "independently" (Allington & McGill-Franzen, 1989b).

One fourth grader, for example, was observed performing without difficulty on grade-level materials in his fourth-grade classroom, but in the resource room routinely worked only with prereading-level materials, reportedly because he did not like "challenging work." On the other hand, some students were clearly struggling with the academic tasks assigned by the specialists. A Chapter 1 student, for example, who obviously could not orally read a worksheet he was given, was admonished by his teacher to perform this task, telling him that he "was not looking at [the] little words in [the] big words." Usually, but not always, instruction was easier in the specialist program, but among the children working on particular tasks, there would be some who could not do the work at all and others who were not challenged at all.

This situation is common in elementary classrooms where teachers feel that all children must be "exposed" to the curriculum of a particular grade level, but such a lack of "fit" between the performance levels of individual children and the instructional tasks was unexpected in the remedial and special education classrooms. Fraatz (1987) described the dilemma of the classroom teacher as "the paradox of collective instruction," the idea that reading instruction must be provided on equal terms to all children even though individual children may have very different personal understandings or "needs." Classroom teachers in our studies and those described by Fraatz believed that specialist teachers were able to overcome this paradox and actually "individualize" instruction for children having difficulty.

Unfortunately, our observations only demonstrated that the specialist teachers had constructed a separate curriculum with separate tasks and texts. These separate curricula were neither coordinated with the work of the general classroom nor consistently an improvement over the classroom curriculum. This is the case even though the academic work of the classroom was not typically differentiated beyond reading group work. Language arts work, including writing, was rarely differentiated for any child, yet the classroom language arts and reading group work frequently was a more appropriate "match" for the children than the specialist's "different" curriculum. For the most part, the coordination between the classroom and the specialist teachers was "catch as catch can," a situation that is not surprising given the exigencies of school life (McGill-Franzen & Allington, 1990).

Fragmented Responsibility

Finally, Pugach and Sapon-Shevin (1987) argued that the use of the specialist instructional model dilutes responsibility for the academic achievement of at-risk children. Support for their hypothesis is found in our work (Allington & McGill-Franzen, 1989a; McGill-Franzen & Allington, 1990) and Winfield's (1987), where classroom teachers assigned primary responsibility for reading instruction to specialist teachers, even though the children spent the vast majority of the day in their classrooms and the specialist teachers rarely acknowledged accepting primary responsibility for these childrens' reading instruction. We found similar difficulties in the responses of school administrators, with principals disavowing responsibility for remedial and special education students and the categorical programs administrator assigning responsibility to the principal. As Hyde and Moore (1988) suggested, when children participate in reading instruction in several different settings, no one teacher believes himself or herself to be responsible for teaching the children to read. When responsibility is diffused, so also is accountability for the child's progress. Classroom teachers claimed they had "no idea" what low achieving children actually did during their remedial or resource room instruction, and no clear ideas on who was supposedly in charge of the child's program. In short, it seems to us that the larger the number of professionals and programs a child is assigned, the less likely it is that anyone accepts responsibility for the academic outcomes achieved or not achieved.

How Policy and Regulation Influence Instruction

Although we do not want to minimize the influence of particular teachers or teaching that individual children may encounter, the experiences of the low achieving child are also influenced by federal, state, and local policy and regulations. At the broadest level, the federal government makes resources available to the states for programs for low achieving children that conform to certain regulatory models. Regulatory language determines in large part which categories of children are eligible, which types of services may be put into place, and what the instruction should look like. The relative availability of funds and the regulations governing the use of these funds also influence school procedures for identifying targeted populations and providing services. (Allington & McGill-Franzen, 1989a; McGill-Franzen, 1987).

The relative availability of funds and the regulations governing the use of these funds also influence school procedures for identifying targeted populations and providing services.

Although the federal legislation that created remedial and special education programs was drafted in response to what policy makers perceived as discrete educational problems—that is, providing an educational program for children who have handicaps and compensating for the effects of poverty—in practice, these problems and the children who are targeted for intervention often overlap (Birman, 1981; Jenkins, 1987). What these children have in common and what alerts teachers to the need for special attention is a problem learning to read. During the late 1970s and 1980s, when money for compensatory education decreased and, concomitantly, the money available for handicapped services increased,

children who were low achieving readers were often classified as handicapped rather than eligible for remediation because handicapped services were readily available and remedial services were not (McGill-Franzen, 1987). Such designations influence the instruction that low achieving children experience. According to our observations, which we discussed earlier, special education students are less likely to participate in classroom reading instruction, they receive less instructional time in reading, and they spend more of this time doing seatwork. Although obviously unintended, the shifts in federal fiscal policy shaped the nature of instruction experienced by many low achieving students.

Even at the building or "street" level, local policy and regulation influence instruction for low achievers. District policy determines the resources allocated to each school, and each building administrator allocates school resources to the classroom teacher (Barr & Dreeben, 1983; Hyde & Moore, 1988). Class size and class heterogeneity are two forms of resources not typically considered in analyses of this sort, but both conditions have enormous impact on the pace of instruction and the curriculum selected, particularly when low achieving children are grouped together in a single homogeneous class. Conventional wisdom, or what we described as our third incorrect assumption, holds that low achieving children should proceed at a slower pace in material that is broken down into discrete steps, an approach that is based in reductionistic learning theory prominent several decades ago. When this "slow it down" approach is applied to whole classrooms of low achieving children, there is little possibility that the educational status of any of these learners will improve. Research on the relation between the pacing and appropriateness of instruction and achievement seems to support this gloomy prediction. As Barr and Dreeben (1983) and Gamoran (1986) demonstrated, the content covered over the course of the school year determines in large part what the achievement of individual children will be at the close of the school year. Children who are equally able students at the onset of instruction will have greatly different achievement profiles by the end of the term. These differences in achievement are linked not to within-child variations, but rather to differences in the pace and appropriateness of instruction. Thus, children who are behind their peers in reading do not need slower and different instruction, but more sustained instruction of the kind that facilitates active, self-improving literacy development in all students. The lack of explicit strategy instruction in the classroom (Duffy, Roehler, & Rackliffe, 1986) and in remedial and special education rooms leaves those children who most need to be taught instead having to puzzle through on their own.

In other words, we do not have to look beyond the school for the reasons why low achieving children do not read and write well. The way instruction is organized in schools and the kinds of tasks and texts given to the children limit their access to knowledge and ensure their continued low achievement.

Learning Theory in a Time Warp

Shortly after the turn of the century, and concurrent with the development of standardized tests of reading and intelligence, nationally known educators called for differential outcomes for different children, differences as measured on the newly developed tests (Johnston & Allington, 1991). As the concept of the "slow learner" emerged, programs and curricula for these students were developed. Because reductionism was the primary learning theory of the era (Shannon, 1989), most of the instructional recommendations fell into the "slow it down and make it more concrete" category. Thus, reduced academic outcomes for these "slow learning" students were widely accepted, and educational programs were created that virtually ensured slow academic progress and academic outcomes that were different from "normally" achieving students.

By the 1960s, the historical slow learner was represented by several categories of learners: the educational mentally handicapped (not necessarily intellectually retarded), the educationally disadvantaged, and the emerging "brain damaged/learning disabled" category. Each of these categories had grown from the earlier slow learner concept and each, by and large, brought the dominant thinking of the slow learner tradition along with them. As the accountability pressure on schools grew, so too did procedures for demarcating what students were to be taught, with behavioral objectives foremost among the recommendations.

This history is needed to put the Pupil Educational Plans (PEP) of the Chapter 1 remedial program and the Individualized Educational Plans (IEP) of special education in proper perspective and, likewise, the focus on identifying specific subskill deficiencies as part of the instructional planning process. Contrary to more contemporary views of the learning process, reductionism emphasized a task analytic approach that attempted to reduce complex learning to a series of hierarchically arranged sequences of component tasks. We argue that the IEP required for handicapped students trivializes reading instruction into small easily measured steps and, similarly, that the mandated PEP and achievement testing for Chapter 1 accountability fosters a subskills focus in the instructional program. By contrast, current connectionist (Adams, 1990) and sociocognitive theories (Willinsky, 1990) emphasize the importance of children's involvement in the whole of complex tasks, the inter-relatedness of learning activities, and the social nature of learning, particularly language learning opportunities such as reading and writing.

Convention is reinforced by other state and federal regulations. Another example is the regulation that compensatory education must supplement, not supplant, the classroom reading instruction. Districts on the whole have misinterpreted this regulation to mean that the same curriculum or curriculum materials could not be used in the compensatory program, thus leading to widespread use of "supplementary" remedial reading materials (Allington, 1986). This use of supplementary curriculum materials produces, at best, a fragmented curriculum experience for participating children. Although this practice seems to derive from an inappropriate interpretation of a federal regulation, we found that a similar situation existed in special education resource rooms, even though those programs operate under no similar regulatory mandate.

It may be that the "differential teaching hypothesis" that has long dominated both remedial and special education (Johnston et al., 1985) is still the most influential pedagogical theory among practitioners. The perceptual deficit, modality preference, and learning styles approaches all arose from this hypothesis. Although each has been fully discredited in the research, the associated pedagogical approaches are alive and well (Allington, 1982; Walmsley & Walp, 1989). It was common in our studies to find teachers and administrators who believed that instruction in remedial and special education should be different from that in the classroom—different in content, pedagogy, and, often, philosophy. The end result was a confusing and often incoherent array of learning activities for participating children.

Funding requirements, particularly requirements for districts to maintain clear fiscal "trails" for auditing purposes, also influenced the establishment of separate curricula in remedial and special education programs. To establish the uniqueness of the students and the instructional programs, many remedial and special education personnel used the categorical funds to purchase materials different from the classroom. These different materials also reinforced the uniqueness of the teachers in these special programs. With separate curriculum in place, specialist teachers no longer had the responsibility of coordinating instruction with regular educators, a difficult task in many cases given the organization of the school day.

As we discussed earlier, the importance of the texts and tasks assigned to low achieving children has long been overlooked in the design of both remedial and special education. Within the separate curricula used in remedial and special education, the most commonly used materials are basically content-free workbooks, skillsheets, and other isolated skill and drill type activities on such topics as the Loch Ness monster, Bigfoot, killer bees, and other topics with little relevance to the core curriculum of the school. The importance of background knowledge in school learning cannot be overestimated, yet most of what is read in remedial and special education classes offers little content that could prove useful in other classes. Thus, children who would seem most likely to benefit from a rich, integrated, and coherent curriculum were those least likely to experience it. When coupled with absence from the general education classroom for part of the day, usually during one or more content-area classes, the potential and actual loss of useful school knowledge places participating students in an even more risky situation.

This brief history may also help explain why so few have been concerned until recently about the lack of demonstrated achievement effects either program has had on participating children. We would suggest that conventional wisdom has long held that there has to be a bottom group and, thus, few saw the primary mission of remedial and special education as resolving learning problems of participating students and fewer still saw accelerated learning and normalized achievement as the goals of these programs.

Even federal and state funding agencies have historically evidenced little concern for the achievement effects of remedial and special education programs (Gartner & Lipsky, 1987; Singer & Butler, 1987). Federal agencies in particular have been more concerned about whether the funds were distributed to the appropriate group of children than in whether the programs supported by the funding achieved some positive academic effect. For instance, Gartner and Lipsky (1987) noted that the federal office that distributes special education funds had no plans to even address that issue. Currently, more energy at all levels goes into identifying the appropriate recipients of these categorical funds than into determining the nature, quality, or effectiveness of the program that the funds support. As long as the appropriate children are selected and scheduled for the minimum time required, reimbursements have followed.

Summary

Contemporary policies and pedagogical practices for low achieving readers have been driven by the conventional wisdom or learning theories of the 1960s. These regulations thus encourage teaching that conforms to a reductionist model of learning and discourages teaching that does not.

We know that children who find learning to read difficult do not make adequate progress when exposed only to the standard curriculum. However, in our attempts to address these childrens' needs, we have created a patchwork of overlapping categories and programs for these categories and special teachers and special programs for each category. The end result is that few schools have any coherent instructional support program, and fewer still have programs with a demonstrated record of successfully and substantially changing the status of low achieving readers. Nevertheless, virtually all such programs are in compliance with the various policies and regulations that define them!

It is a question of will. We know how to accelerate the literacy development of low achieving children (Clay, 1987; Clay & Cazden, 1990; Pinnell, 1989). We can organize our schools so that all children are entitled to literacy (Madden, Slavin, Karweit, Liverman, & Dolan, 1989). It will require changing not only the way we teach, but also our beliefs about the capabilities of low achieving children. It will require both more and better instruction than is available in the regular education program today. State and federal policies and program regulations are changing, but the changes we see as necessary will require far more radical rethinking than seems popular (Timar & Kirp, 1987). We have evidence that better programs can be implemented and for long-term costs not substantially different than what we now spend. Will we wait for policy to lead us in the right direction? Or will we shape policy?

References

Adams, M. J. (1990). *Beginning to read: Thinking and learning about print.* Cambridge, MA: MIT Press.

Allington, R. L. (1980). Poor readers don't get to read much in reading groups. *Language Arts, 57,* 872–877.

Allington, R. L. (1982). The persistence of teacher beliefs in facets of the perceptual deficit hypothesis. *Elementary School Journal, 82,* 351–359.

Allington, R. L. (1983). The reading instruction provided readers of differing abilities. *Elementary School Journal, 83,* 548–559.

Allington, R. L. (1986). Policy constraints and effective compensatory reading instruction: A review. In J. Hoffman (Ed.), *Effective teaching of reading: Research and practice* (pp. 261–289). Newark, DE: International Reading Association.

Allington, R. L. (1990). How policy and regulation influence instruction for at-risk learners or why poor readers rarely comprehend well and probably never will. In L. Idol & B. F. Jones (Eds.), *Educational values and cognitive instruction: Implications for reform.* (pp. 529–542). Hillsdale, NJ: Erlbaum.

Allington, R. L., & McGill-Franzen, A. (1989a). Different programs, indifferent instruction. In A. Gartner & D. Lipsky (Eds.), *Beyond separate education: Quality education for all* (pp. 75–98). Baltimore: Brookes.

Allington, R., & McGill-Franzen, A. (1989b). School response to reading failure: Chapter 1 and special education students in grades 2, 4, & 8. *Elementary School Journal, 89,* 529–542.

Armbruster, B. B., & Anderson, T. H. (1984). Content area textbooks. In R. C. Anderson, J. Osborn, & R. Tierney (Eds.), *Learning to read in American schools: Basal readers and content texts* (pp. 193–226). Hillsdale, NJ: Erlbaum.

Au, K., & Jordan, C. (1980). Teaching reading to Hawalian children: Finding a culturally appropriate solution. In H. T. Trueba, G. P. Guthrie, & K. Au (Eds.), *Culture and the bilingual classroom* (pp. 139–152). Rowley, MA: Newbury House.

Barr, R., & Dreeben, R. (1983). *How schools work.* Chicago: University of Chicago Press.

Birman, B. F. (1981). Problems of overlap between Title I and P.L. 94–142: Implications for the federal role in education. *Educational Evaluation and Policy Analysis, 3,* 5–19.

Carter, L. (1984). The sustaining effects study of compensatory and elementary education. *Education Researcher, 12,* 4–13.

Cazden, C. B. (1988). *Classroom discourse: The language of teaching and learning.* Portsmouth, NH: Heinemann.

Clay, M. M., (1987). Learning to be learning disabled. *New Zealand Journal of Educational Studies, 22,* 155–171.

Clay, M. M., & Cazden, C.C. (1990). A Vygotskian interpretation of 'Reading Recovery.' In L. C. Moll (Ed.), *Vygotsky and education: Instructional implications and applications of socio-historical psychology.* New York: Cambridge University Press.

Delpit, L. (1988). The silenced dialogue: Power and pedagogy in educating other people's children. *Harvard Educational Review, 58,* 281–298.

Doyle, W. (1990). Classroom tasks: The core of learning from teaching. In M.S. Knapp & P. M. Shields (Eds.), *Better schooling for the children of poverty: Alternatives to conventional wisdom* (commissioned Paper X, pp. 1–19). Menlo Park, CA: SRI International.

Duffy, G. G., Roehler, L. R., & Rackliffe, G. (1986). How teachers' instructional talk influences students' understanding of lesson content. *Elementary School Journal, 87,* 4–16.

Fraatz, J. M. B. (1987). *The politics of reading: Power, opportunity, and prospects for change in America's public schools.* New York: Teacher's College Press.

Gamoran, A. (1986). Instructional and institutional effect of ability grouping. *Sociology of Education, 59,* 185–198.

Gartner, A., & Lipsky, D. (1987). Beyond separate education: Toward a quality system for all students. *Harvard Educational Review, 57,* 367–395.

Goodlad, J. I., & Oakes, J. (1988). We must offer equal access to knowledge. *Educational Leadership, 45,* 16–22.

Haynes, M. C., & Jenkins, J. R. (1986). Reading instruction in special education resource rooms. *American Educational Research Journal, 23,* 161–190.

Heath, S. B. (1983). *Ways with words: Language, life and work in communities and classrooms.* New York: Cambridge University Press.

Hyde, A. A., & Moore, D. R. (1988). Reading services and the classification of students in two school districts. *Journal of Reading Behavior, 20,* 301–338.

Jenkins, J. R. (1987). Similarities in the achievement levels of learning disabled and remedial students. *Counterpoint, 7,* 16.

Johnston, P. (1989). Constructive evaluation and improvement of teaching and learning. *Teachers College Record, 90,* 509–528.

Johnston, P., & Allington, R. L. (1991). Remediation. In R. Barr, M. Kamil, P. Mosenthal, & P. D. Pearson (Eds.), *Handbook of reading research* (Vol. 2, pp. 984–1012). New York: Longman.

Johnston, P., Allington, R. L., & Afflerbach, P. (1985). The congruence of classroom and remedial reading instruction. *Elementary School Journal, 85,* 465–478.

Johnston, P., & Winograd, P. (1985). Passive failure in reading. *Journal of Reading Behavior, 17,* 279–301.

Juel, C. (1988). Learning to read and write: A longitudinal study of 54 children from first through fourth grade. *Journal of Educational Psychology, 80,* 437–447.

Lareau, A. (1989). *Home advantage: Social class and parental intervention in elementary education.* Philadelphia: Falmer.

Madden, N. A., Slavin, R.E., Karweit, N. L., Liverman, B. J., & Dolan, L. (1989). *Success for all: Effective student achievement, retentions, and special éducation referrals* (Report No. 30). Baltimore: Johns Hopkins University, Centers for Research on Elementary and Middle Schools.

Martin, A. (1988). Screening, early intervention, and remediation: Observing children's potential. *Harvard Educational Review, 58,* 488–501.

Marx, R. W., & Walsh, J. (1988). Learning from academic tasks. *Elementary School Journal, 88,* 207–219.

McGill-Franzen, A. (1979, August). *Teachers' conceptions of reading project.* Unpublished case studies, Michigan State University, Institute for Research on Teaching, East Lansing.

McGill-Franzen, A. (1987). Failure to learn to read: Formulating a policy problem. *Reading Research Quarterly, 22,* 475–490.

McGill-Franzen, A., & Allington, R. L. (1990). Comprehension and coherence: Neglected elements of literacy instruction in remedial and resource room services. *Journal of Reading, Writing, and Learning Disabilities, 6,* 149–180.

Mehan, H. (1978). Structuring school structure. *Harvard Educational Review, 48,* 32–64.

Moll, L. (1990). Social and instructional issues in educating disadvantaged students. In M. S. Knapp & P. M. Shields (Eds.), *Better schooling for the children of poverty: Alternatives to conventional wisdom* (Commissioned Paper III, pp. 1–22). Menlo Park, CA: SRI International.

Oakes, J. (1985). *Keeping track: How schools structure inequality.* New Haven, CT: Yale University Press.

Philips, S. (1983). *The invisible culture: Communication in classroom and community on the Warm Springs Indian reservation.* New York: Longman.

Pinnell, G. S. (1989). Reading recovery: Helping at-risk children learn to read. *Elementary School Journal, 90,* 161–183.

Pugach, M., & Sapon-Shevin, M. (1987). New agendas for special education policy: What the national reports haven't said. *Exceptional Children, 53,* 295–299.

Rowan, B., & Guthrie, L. F. (1989). The quality of Chapter I instruction: Results from a study of twenty-four schools. In R. E. Slavin, N. Karweit, & N. Madden (Eds.), *Effective programs for students at risk* (pp. 195–219). Boston: Allyn & Bacon.

Shannon, P. (1989). *Broken promises: Reading instruction in twentieth-century America.* Granby, MA: Bergin & Garvey.

Singer, J.D., & Butler, J.A. (1987). The Education for All Handicapped Children Act: Schools as agents of social reform. *Harvard Educational Review, 57,* 125–152.

Slavin, R. E. (1989). Students at risk of school failure: The problem and its dimensions. In R.E. Slavin, N. Karweit, & N. Madden (Eds.), *Effective programs for students at risk* (pp. 3–22). Boston: Allyn & Bacon.

Timar, T. B., & Kirp, D. L. (1987). Educational reform and institutional competence. *Harvard Educational Review, 57,* 308–330.

Walmsley, S.A., & Walp, T.P. (1989). *Teaching literature in the elementary school* (Report series 1.3). Albany, NY: State University of New York, Center for the Learning and Teaching of Literature.

White, T. G., Graves, M. F., & Slater, W. H. (1990). Growth of reading vocabulary in diverse elementary schools: Decoding and word meaning. *Journal of Educational Psychology, 82,* 281–290.

Will, G. (1990, April 23). Mothers who don't know how. *Newsweek,* p. 80.

Willinsky, J. (1990). *The new literacy: Redefining reading and writing in the schools.* New York: Routledge.

Winfield, L. F. (1987). Teachers' estimate of test content covered in class on first grade students' reading achievement. *Elementary School Journal, 87,* 437–454.

Ysseldyke, J.E., O'Sullivan, P. J., Thurlow, M. L., & Christenson, S. L. (1989). Qualitative differences in reading and math instruction received by handicapped students. *Remedial and Special Education, 10,* 14–20.

Preventing Reading Failure in the Primary Grades

Darrell Morris
Appalachian State University

Addressing the problem of reading failure in the primary grades is a complex and humbling task, one that has occupied the best minds in our field for over a half-century. In just the past 15 years, there have been three major, book-length reviews of the research on beginning reading: *Becoming a Nation of Readers* (Anderson, Hiebert, Scott, & Wilkinson, 1983), *Beginning to Read* (Adams, 1990); and the recent, *Preventing Reading Difficulties in Young Children* (Snow, Burns, & Griffin, 1998). Although these reports have contributed significantly to our understanding of beginning reading, they have been less successful in realizing a professional consensus regarding the *teaching* of reading. One can make a strong case that beginning reading instruction is as controversial today as it was in the 1960s, the era of the First Grade Studies (Bond & Dykstra, 1967).

Here I will take a different tack. Those who are familiar with my work realize that I am part practitioner and part applied researcher. I direct a university-based reading clinic and, for the past decade, I have helped public schools in several states set up early intervention programs for at-risk readers. It is from the vantage point of my own practice that I wish to review the research on preventing reading failure. If this conceptual review is less comprehensive than some would prefer, perhaps it compensates by raising practical pedagogical issues that are in need of more study.

I will begin with a true story that defines the problem. This past year, I helped a mid-sized urban school district in the Southeast set up a first-grade reading intervention program in six of its neediest Title 1 schools. In the intervention, reading teachers and first-grade teachers participated in a year-long practicum in which they tutored at-risk beginning readers and reflected on the process with a visiting consultant. The intervention went well, and, in February, one of the young first-grade teachers was telling how much she had learned. Then, she abruptly changed course:

> You know. Dr. Morris, the problem is bigger than first grade. I feel really sorry for third graders in my school. On days their teacher is absent, eight third graders visit my class (our school has a hard time getting substitutes). Anyway, at the beginning of the school year the third graders were happy to visit my classroom. They helped me with my first graders, and seemed to enjoy doing the work in my class. Now [in February] the third graders are becoming a big problem; they are angry, uncooperative, and hard to manage when they come into my classroom. I think I know what's going on. With the help of your intervention and my trying new things, most of my students are learning to read this year. *The third graders sense that they cannot read as well as my first graders*, and they are mad . . . frustrated. I don't blame them. They are way behind in reading and have a long road ahead of them.

After 20 years in the profession, I was still taken aback by the young teacher's story. I knew that in February her first graders were reading at no better than a preprimer 3 to primer level. How could a large number of third graders in the school be reading still lower? How could children spend 4 years in school and be reading at a preprimer level? What would be their academic chances when they entered fourth grade in a few short months?

Death at an Early Age is the title of a book written by Johnathon Kozol (1967). It is an apt description of what happens academically to far too many children in this country who do not learn to read in their first 3 years of school. I am certain that we can do a better job with these children. I am equally certain that we should not wait for a breakthrough study or "state-of-the-art" reading program to lead the way. We have been waiting for 100 years. In truth, much good research, both theoretical and applied, has been done. What confronts us, in my view, is an engineering problem. How do we apply what we know; how do we structure schooling so that all children have a real chance of learning to read?

In this paper, I begin by citing a goal that we should aim for in our work with at-risk primary-grade readers. Next, I discuss two critical contexts

From "Preventing reading failure in the primary grades," by D. Morris in T. Shanahan and F. Rodriquez-Brown (Eds.) 1999, *National Reading Conference Yearbook*, 48, pp. 17–38. Copyright 1999 by the National Reading Conference. Reprinted with permission.

for reading instruction: the classroom, including materials, methods, and management concerns; and the one-to-one tutorial. Finally, I outline a grade-by-grade "action plan" for increasing the number of children who can read proficiently by the end of third grade.

The Educational Goal

Most American children learn to read in the first 3 years of school and are ready for the grade-level narrative and subject-matter texts that await them in fourth grade. If this were not the case, we would have seen a citizen rebellion against the field of reading education. On the other hand, our schools have historically had difficulty teaching a sizeable minority of children to read—15% to 40%, depending on socioeconomic circumstance (Allington, 1994; National Assessment of Educational Progress, 1995). Finishing third grade a year or more behind in reading leaves children at a serious disadvantage in an educational system that, from fourth grade on, demands grade-level reading ability.

Finishing third grade a year or more behind in reading leaves children at a serious disadvantage in an educational system that, from fourth grade on, demands grade-level reading ability.

In a sense, low-reading primary-grade students are in a race against time. No matter how slow their start, by the end of third grade they need to be reading at or near grade level. In effect, they need to reach the *fluency stage* (Level 2) in Chall's (1983) developmental scheme, automatizing their print-processing skill to the point where they can give full attention to the task of comprehension.

Although the goal of grade-level reading ability by the end of third grade is easier stated than accomplished, assessing progress towards it is straightforward enough. On a yearly basis, teachers can administer a set of graded reading passages to individual students, taking measures on their word reading accuracy, rate, and comprehension. Such informal assessment—at the end of grades one, two, and three—provides sufficient evidence of student progress. Moreover, the worth of a given instructional program for low readers should be judged pragmatically—that is, by its results. Those reading programs that move low readers farthest toward the goal of fluent, third-grade-level reading should be judged most effective.

There is, of course, an affective side to this issue. That is, we want children not just to be able to read but to enjoy reading. I would argue, however, that for a student who has struggled with the reading process, nothing is more satisfying than "catching up" and being able to participate in grade-level reading activities with one's peers. I also hasten to point out that the goal of fluent, third-grade-level reading in no way diminishes the importance of teaching comprehension in the primary grades. Teachers bear responsibility for continually encouraging students to think about what they are reading and to share their thoughts with others via discussion and writing. As students advance through the primary grades, however, their text comprehension will depend, to a large degree, on their reading fluency—on their ability to process efficiently the words on the page.

Contexts for Instruction

The Classroom

The classroom context for teaching beginning reading has remained much the same over the course of this century. That is, in first- or second-grade classrooms, there is usually one teacher, 24 or more children, a set of published reading materials, and approximately 90 minutes of instructional time. These constants notwithstanding, the basal reader programs used to teach children have changed over the past 50 years, and these changes raise important questions about the teaching of at-risk or low-readiness readers. A brief historical sketch is warranted.

From the 1920s to the 1960s, *whole-word* or look-say basal readers dominated the market. These programs, such as Scott Foresman's *New Basic Readers* (Gray, Monroe, Artley, & Arbuthnot, 1951), featured (a) carefully controlled repetition of high frequency vocabulary, (b) slow but systematic introduction of phonics principles (consonants in first grade, vowels in second grade), (c) an emphasis on reading for meaning, and (d) the use of ability grouping to address individual differences in reading skill.

The 1960s was a period of controversy and ferment in the field of beginning reading. Sentence-based, language-experience approaches (Lee & Allen, 1963; Stauffer, 1970), as well as new phonics approaches (Engelmann & Bruner, 1968; Fries, 1963), rose up to challenge the word-control basal readers. Some scholars argued for more natural language in early reading materials and a reduction in isolated skills work. Others, including Jeanne Chall (1967), argued for a greater emphasis on phonics or code instruction in grades one and two.

Interestingly, the traditional basal reader did not disappear or even change in form after the 1960s' assault. Like "Old Man River," it simply widened its banks a little—incorporating suggestions for more intensive phonics—and kept on rolling. The basal readers of the 1970s and 1980s continued to feature controlled vocabulary in the first- and second-grade books and guided reading in small ability groups. Commenting on the resilience of the programs, Henderson (1986) stated:

> To be sure these materials are easy to criticize on a variety of counts. They are too gaudy. They often lack taste. They are too prescriptive and claim an infallibility that they do not merit. They are too littered with skills and gimmicks, and overstuffed with right answers. . . . *Still, they do reflect with considerable accuracy many of the empirical needs of teachers and children.* (p. 76, emphasis added)

But beneath the seeming stasis of beginning reading instruction in the 1980s, important forces were at work. An objective history of this period has yet to be written, but it is clear that several factors conjoined to produce radical changes in the field of beginning reading. Among these factors were the objections to basal reader instruction leveled by a group of well-known university-based critics (e.g., Goodman, 1985; Harste, 1989; Smith, 1981); the existence of an alternative model of instruction (including published materials) in another English-speaking country (New Zealand); and teacher dissatisfaction with the 1980s' basals, particularly with the cumbersome, mechanized, skills-accountability systems (Jerrolds & Thompson, 1995). The traditional basal reader had weathered criticism before, but this time its critics, coalescing under the banner of "whole language," succeeded in producing a groundswell of teacher support across the nation—enough support that the realities of the publishing marketplace changed (Pearson, 1989). By 1990, U.S. teachers and schools were asking for a new kind of basal reader, a new kind of beginning reading instruction.

The new, literature-based basal readers of the 1990s are not a variation on the same theme; they are different. They use shared, Big-Book experiences instead of readiness workbooks to establish early reading skills. They feature considerably less vocabulary control in the first- and second-grade reading selections. The new basals advocate whole-class, teacher-guided reading with follow-up rereading of the selection to be done in student dyads. Finally, the new basals deemphasize the systematic teaching of phonics (a hallmark of the old basals), opting instead for a more contextualized approach to helping students learn letter-sound relationships (Hoffman et al., 1994).

Teachers need materials to teach reading, and the basal programs provided to them certainly influence their classroom instruction (Barr, 1982). It is surprising, therefore, that there has been so little study of the unprecedented change from the pre-1990 traditional basals to the post-1990 literature basals.

Hoffman and his colleagues did examine the nature of the new materials (Hoffman et al., 1994) and, in a follow-up study, the use of the new basals by a small group of teachers (Hoffman et al., 1998). However, no one, to my knowledge, has investigated how these new basal programs have affected the learning of low-reading primary-grade children. I would like to consider this question from three perspectives: (a) controlled-vocabulary versus natural-language reading materials, (b) systematic versus contextually-based phonics instruction, and (c) small-group versus whole-class guided reading instruction.

Vocabulary Control

The "old," pre-1990's basals attempted to stamp into children's minds an initial sight vocabulary via rote practice in readiness workbooks and through the reading of stilted preprimer books. This initial vocabulary was then repeated and gradually expanded as the students progressed through successive levels of carefully controlled text (primer through 2-2). The new literature basals are designed differently. They use the natural language and rhythmic predictability of Big Books to help beginners establish basic concepts about print, including an initial sight vocabulary. Then, eschewing formulaic word control at the primer to 2-2 levels, the new basals use rereadings of stories to help students advance their reading ability.

Although the new basals may be preferable aesthetically, their basic design raises questions. For example, what is the effect on low-reading students when first-grade basals increase the number of words to be learned while decreasing the repetition of these words within and across stories? Does having students reread selections (as advocated in the new manuals) actually counterbalance the need for systematic repetition of a core vocabulary? These critical questions have not been addressed by the research community.

A more complicated but equally important issue has to do with the timing of word control in early reading materials. That is, a forced choice between systematic word-control text and natural-language text may not be desirable. In the early stages of learning to read, wholistic approaches such as shared-book experience (Holdaway, 1979; Routman, 1988) and language experience (Stauffer, 1970) can help children acquire early concepts about print. Nonetheless, once beginners understand how print works (i.e., that we read from left to right, that words are separated by spaces, that letters correspond to sounds), they may well benefit from word-control text that allows them to develop basic sight vocabulary and spelling pattern knowledge. By mid-to-late second grade, word-control text may have served its purpose, making it possible for even low readers to tackle more natural or less formulaic text. To my knowledge, such a developmental text progression—natural text, word-control text, natural text—has not been considered by researchers or basal publishers.

Advocacy of more word control in beginning reading materials begs the question of what type of word control; that is, repetition of high-frequency words (e.g., *boy, mother, look*) or patterned words (e.g., *man, bat, sad*)? Writers of basal stories, understandably, do not look fondly on either option. One possibility is to include both types of words in first-grade-level stories. This would give authors more words to work with and expose children to a diverse but manageable set of word features. The elusive goal is to produce a set of interesting stories that feature a reasonable degree of vocabulary control.

Phonics Instruction

The 1990s' basals decreased the amount of systematic phonics instruction while increasing the vocabulary load at the first- and second-grade levels (Hoffman et al., 1994). The underlying assumption was that predictable language, rereadings, and contextual attention to letter/sound relationships would adequately support children's word learning, thereby lessening the need for intensive phonics instruction. Again, we may ask, what is the effect of this change on low-reading students?

At this point, allow me to digress briefly to what we know about word recognition in the learning-to-read process. First, we know that phoneme awareness plays a central role in learning to read words in an alphabetic language (Bradley & Bryant, 1983; Gough & Hillinger, 1980; Liberman & Liberman, 1992; Wagner, Torgesen, & Rashotte, 1994). Beginning readers must become aware that words are composed of phonemes that match to letters if they are to commit printed words to memory (Ehri & Wilce, 1985). Second, we know that children follow a discernible path in developing phonological awareness and spelling pattern knowledge. Developmental spelling research clearly shows that children first become aware of the beginning consonants in words, then the beginning and ending consonants, and finally the medial vowels. Later, they come to understand that long vowels are often marked with an extra or silent letter (e.g., *late, mail*) (Henderson & Templeton, 1986; Morris & Perney, 1984). Third, we know that skillful reading ultimately depends on accurate, automatic processing of words. Such automaticity frees mental resources for comprehending text (Adams, 1990; Perfetti, 1985, 1992). The achieving reader's change in reading rate from first grade (60–70 wpm) to third grade (90–100

wpm) is indicative of this movement toward automatic word processing (Carver, 1990).

Struggling beginning readers, by definition, have difficulty establishing automatic word recognition processes. They are often slow in developing phonological awareness, slow in establishing an initial sight vocabulary, slow in mastering frequently-occurring spelling patterns (e.g., CVC, CVCe, CVVC), and slow in reading text. What role then can phonics instruction play in their development?

Direct phonics or letter-sound instruction can actually enhance beginning reader's phoneme awareness. As noted above, full phoneme awareness or segmentation ability does not emerge spontaneously, but rather in stages. If initial phonics instruction is carefully paced to the readiness of the learner, with beginning consonants taught first and vowel instruction awaiting a stable understanding of consonant boundaries, then almost all children will develop requisite phoneme awareness.

A second task facing low readers is to ferret out and over-learn the regular patterns in our spelling system. Although children who successfully are learning to read often accomplish this pattern-detecting task with seeming ease, low readers need help. Phonics instruction, when paced appropriately by the teacher, helps low readers master the high-frequency, short- and long-vowel patterns. Given this foundation, they can begin to make sense of other spelling patterns they come upon in contextual reading. In a sense, good phonics instruction should highlight or "bring into focus" critical spelling patterns that are within the learner's developmental grasp (Henderson, 1990; Invernizzi, Abouzeid, & Gill, 1994). Then, purposeful reading and writing can drive the patterns into memory, leading to the important goal of fluent reading.

Despite a consensus in the psychological research community about the importance of letter/sound and spelling pattern knowledge in reading acquisition (Adams, 1990; Stanovich, 1998), pragmatic questions about phonics instruction continue to divide reading educators. For example: What kind of phonics instruction is best (synthetic or analytic, systematic or incidental, isolated or contextual)? How much phonics instruction is needed? Do all students require the same amount? Should systematic phonics be taught directly to the whole class or should instruction be timed to the developmental readiness of individuals or small groups? How closely should phonics concepts be coordinated with the material students read (e.g., are decodable texts preferable)? Can phonics be taught effectively through the writing process?

Although definitive answers to such instructional questions are lacking (and thus, the controversy will continue), I believe that it is illogical to withhold systematic phonics instruction from beginning readers who are struggling with word recognition. It is true that teachers must learn to provide such instruction in a timely and interesting manner; it is equally true that phonics should be only one part of an instructional program that features large amounts of meaningful reading and writing. Still, we cannot teach the hard-to-teach by ignoring their learning difficulties; we cannot facilitate word recognition by avoiding the study of words.

Ability Grouping

Up until the late 1980s, ability grouping for reading (low, middle, and high groups) was a standard procedure in most first- and second-grade classrooms (Barr, 1995; Slavin, 1987). The underlying assumption was that grouping provided a practical way for teachers to address reading ability differences among their students. By matching text difficulty to ability-group level, the teacher could provide appropriate challenge to low, middle, and high readers alike.

It is illogical to withhold systematic phonics instruction from beginning readers who are struggling with word recognition.

Unfortunately, there are problems associated with reading ability groups. For example, children's self-esteem may be harmed by placement in the low-reading group (Barr, 1995). Children who are "locked into" a low-group placement across several grades can fall significantly behind their peers in reading (Hiebert, 1983; Juel, 1988). The instruction offered to the low group is different than and, some critics argue, inferior to that offered to higher achieving groups (Allington, 1983). And finally, the very practice of ability grouping presents classroom teachers with significant organizational and management problems, such as, "What do I do with the children who are not with me in the reading circle?"

Perhaps it is understandable that little opposition was raised when the new 1990s' basals proposed an alternative to within-class ability grouping. The new basals recommended whole-class, teacher-guided story reading, followed up by rereadings of the story in student pairs. This was a seemingly democratic change and one that made classroom management easier for many teachers. Nonetheless, whole-class reading instruction raises a basic question: Can one story or selection—no matter how many times it is modeled and reread—meet the needs of children who are reading at different levels? Can we make one size fit all in beginning reading instruction?

Those who would look to research to resolve the issue of ability grouping versus whole-class instruction

will be disappointed. Research is lacking for the simple reason that historically no one was asking the question. That is, up until 1990, nearly all primary-grade teachers did ability group for reading; influenced by the traditional basal reader, they did not see whole-class instruction as a viable alternative (Barr, 1995; Slavin, 1987). In a sense then, the new basals' change from ability grouping to whole-class instruction, like their change from word-control to natural-language text, was guided not by research, but rather by philosophy or belief. The impact of these changes, particularly on low-reading students, has yet to be systematically studied.

The changes in the 1990s' basal readers were not cosmetic, but instead represented a clear break with the past. Moreover, these basals have had far-reaching effects on classroom reading instruction in this country, with both experienced and novice teachers opting to use the new texts. These materials may have led to an improvement in beginning reading instruction for many children. However, by deemphasizing vocabulary control, systematic phonics instruction, and ability grouping, I suggest that the new basals have adversely affected the learning of low readers, the very children who are most in need of help.

In taking this position, I am not advocating a blind retreat to the old basal routine—a return to small-group, round-robin reading of stilted preprimer text, with a heavy dose of workbook phonics thrown in. This did not serve low readers well in the past, nor will it do so today. Instead, as a profession, we need to think anew how classroom instruction can be designed to better meet the needs of low readers. We might begin by considering the characteristics of early-intervention tutorial models that have proven successful in helping at-risk first-grade readers.

Tutorial Models

Marie Clay (1979, 1993), a New Zealand developmental psychologist, deserves considerable credit for drawing our attention to the effectiveness of early, tutorial-based interventions in reading. In the late 1970s, when American schools were concentrating on small-group remedial reading instruction beginning no earlier than second grade, Clay argued forcefully that effective "catch-up" instruction would have to *begin earlier*—in first grade when the child had not yet fallen too far behind, and be *more intensive*—one-to-one as opposed to small-group. This logic led Clay to develop Reading Recovery, a groundbreaking early intervention program that is being used today throughout the English-speaking world (Clay, 1993; Pinnell, 1989).

Reading Recovery and Success for All, early intervention programs developed in Baltimore during the late 1980s (Slavin, Madden, Karweit, Dolan, & Wasik, 1994), have garnered much attention. Both programs have been extensively field tested, and both have proven to be replicable with regard to raising reading achievement (Pinnell, Lyons, Deford, Bryk, & Seltzer, 1994; Shanahan & Barr, 1995; Slavin et al., 1996). Daily one-to-one tutoring is the core of Reading Recovery and also a major component of the more comprehensive Success for All program. Wasik and Slavin (1990) have argued, and Clay would agree, that a one-to-one setting ensures that the child is taught consistently at the appropriate level, and is provided with timely reinforcement and corrective feedback during reading. Such individually paced instruction is not possible in "even one-to-two or one-to-three instruction, where adaptation to individual needs becomes progressively more difficult" (Wasik & Slavin, 1990, p. 6).

A shared commitment to one-to-one tutoring notwithstanding, the differences between Reading Recovery and Success for All are large and striking. First, the programs use markedly different instructional schemes. For example, Reading Recovery uses natural-language text, whereas Success for All uses highly-controlled phonetic text. Reading Recovery embeds phonics instruction within the context of reading a story or writing a sentence, whereas Success for All teaches phonics skills in an isolated, systematic manner, using the phonetic text to reinforce the specific skills. In effect, the two intervention programs tend to represent opposite sides in the long-standing debate between meaning- and code-emphasis advocates (Adams, 1990; Chall, 1967).

A second difference between the two intervention models pertains to coordination with the regular classroom program. The tutoring component of Success for All is closely connected with the reading instruction children receive in their classroom. In fact, the same materials and methods are used in both contexts. Reading Recovery, on the other hand, is essentially a free-standing, pull-out program. Although Reading Recovery teachers undoubtedly prefer some degree of curricular coordination with the classroom reading program, they do not modify their unique intervention model to attain such coordination.

A third difference pertains to the duration of the tutoring experience. Reading Recovery provides intensive tutoring in first grade only, with the intent of producing a qualitative change in the first grader's reading behavior (a "self-improving system") that will hold up over time. Success for All students, depending on their rate of progress, may receive tutoring for up to 3 full years. As one of its architects, Bob Slavin, has argued, Success for All is an "unrelent-

ing" program that provides tutorial assistance as long as a low-reading child needs it.

A final difference between the two intervention programs relates to the mode of teacher training. Reading Recovery teachers-in-training tutor for a full year under the close guidance of an experienced trainer. The trainees learn not only teaching techniques but also how to think about the developing reading process within a credible theoretical framework. This expensive and unprecedented investment in training speaks to the importance Reading Recovery places on the active decision-making or problem-solving role of the reading tutor. In contrast, Success for All is more program driven than teacher driven. Certainly, a competent teacher is needed to deliver the systematic, skills-based program. Nonetheless, the Success for All reading materials and accompanying teacher's manual propel day-to-day instruction, and teacher training is limited to helping teachers understand and make efficient use of the carefully sequenced curriculum.

The documented effectiveness of both Reading Recovery and Success for All presents a quandary for the reading field. That is, what lessons can be drawn from two reading programs that employ such different methods, materials, and modes of teacher training? Perhaps the first lesson is simply to acknowledge that, in a tutorial context, different instructional approaches can be effective with low-reading first graders. A second lesson might be to look beyond differences and focus on underlying similarities between the two programs. Two immediately come to mind.

First, both programs employ a large set of carefully graded reading materials. Although the nature of the text differs across these programs, both include 15 or more difficulty levels within the first grade (many more levels than are found in a classroom basal reader). In Reading Recovery, there are 10 or more books at each level, allowing for needed repetition of high-frequency vocabulary (e.g., *of, have, but, to, for*). In Success for All, phonetically regular words are gradually introduced and systematically repeated at each level. This careful leveling of books in both programs facilitates "instructional level" placement, and allows for gradual and efficient movement through the graded reading curriculum.

A second similarity between Reading Recovery and Success for All is that both programs provide at-risk readers with ongoing help in mastering the alphabetic code. Success for All features direct instruction in phonological awareness and letter/sound relationships. Reading Recovery has been criticized for teaching phonics more indirectly through sentence writing and context-based attention to letter/sounds (Center, Wheldall, Freeman, Outhred, & McNaught, 1995; Iversen & Tunmer, 1993). Nonetheless, both tutoring programs, on a daily basis, encourage and monitor the student's use of letter-sound cues in the act of reading.

These basic principles—carefully graded text and instruction in the alphabetic code—are relevant not just to the tutorial context, but also to the classroom.

I maintain that these basic principles—carefully graded text and instruction in the alphabetic code—are relevant not just to the tutorial context, but also to the classroom. It is difficult, of course, to meet the needs of at-risk readers in a first-grade class of 24 students. The difficulty is exacerbated when the number of at-risk readers in a classroom is large, the teacher's training or experience is deficient, or appropriate reading materials are lacking (Barr, 1982; Barr & Dreeben, 1983). Still, the ultimate responsibility facing the classroom teacher and the tutor is the same; to pace low readers efficiently through a set of graded reading materials, ensuring that they acquire sufficient word or orthographic knowledge along the way.

A Plan for Preventing Reading Failure

Kindergarten

If low readers are in a race against time (the goal being fluent reading by the end of third grade), then the race begins in kindergarten. In truth, it begins even earlier. Entering kindergartners who have been read to extensively in the home often demonstrate a keen interest in books, a feel for the rhythm of written language, a good concept of story, alphabet knowledge, and even rudimentary phonological awareness (alliteration and rhyme). Other children, lacking a rich literacy environment in the home, do not enter school with this crucial print-related knowledge. Thus, one can argue that a "haves versus have-nots" situation is in place even prior to kindergarten year.

How should a kindergarten teacher respond to the needs of children who show deficits in literacy-related knowledge? Obviously, reading aloud to the class from a wide variety of books should be a basic staple of the kindergarten curriculum. Only by listening to books read aloud can young children begin to sense the special cadence of written language and learn to construct and sustain meaning across pages of text (Wells, 1986). Kindergarten children who have not been read to on a regular basis at home may not at first be avid classroom listeners, but they are the ones who have the most to gain from read-aloud activities

(Dickinson & Smith, 1994; Elley, 1989; Feitelson, Goldstein, Iraqi, & Share, 1993).

The kindergarten teacher must also attend to more concrete aspects of children's print-related knowledge: for example, directionality, concept of word in text, and alphabet knowledge. Meaning-centered activities such as language experience approach (Nessel & Jones, 1981; Stauffer, 1970) and shared-book experience (Holdaway, 1979; Routman, 1988) are excellent vehicles for teaching kindergartners that we read from left to right, that spoken words match to printed words in text, and that we can use beginning consonant cues along with sentence context to facilitate word recognition. Alphabet knowledge is not taught as easily in such a natural language context. That is, a child who knows only 4 alphabet letters will not learn the other 22 by simply reading and rereading a favorite Big Book. Kindergarten teachers have developed a myriad of ways for teaching the alphabet, and the value of a given method should be determined by its results. Two things are certain: the alphabet is important (Ehri, 1983) and, for some kindergartners, the 52 upper- and lower-case letters are learned only through systematic teaching over an extended period of time.

Phoneme awareness is yet another reading-related understanding that must be addressed in kindergarten. Twenty-five years of research has clearly established an important causal relationship between phoneme awareness and reading acquisition. It is not until young children become aware that spoken words are composed of a sequence of sounds (phonemes), that they can begin to exploit the alphabetic code and to match letters to sounds in reading and writing (Ehri & Wilce, 1985; Stuart & Coltheart, 1988).

Phoneme awareness is often wrongly equated with full segmentation ability; that is, the ability to attend to each sound in a syllable (/bit/ = /b/ /i/ /t/). Instead, phoneme awareness is a complex, multilayered understanding that for most children develops slowly over time. In kindergarten, beginning consonant discrimination, the most basic form of phoneme awareness, should be prioritized and taught right along with the alphabet. This can be accomplished by simply having children sort picture cards (e.g., *ball, bike, sun, sock, ring, rose*) into columns by beginning sound (Bear, Invernizzi, Templeton, & Johnston, 1996; Morris, 1999). It is true that some kindergartners will grasp the concept of beginning consonant sound more quickly than others, just as some will learn the alphabet letters more easily. Nonetheless, given daily instruction and adequate review across the school year, nearly all children can learn their letters and sounds before leaving kindergarten.

Beyond beginning consonant discrimination, phoneme awareness can be addressed in different ways in kindergarten and first grade. For example, a direct approach, favored by most cognitive psychologists and some educators, is to provide children with explicit training in segmenting spoken words into phonemes (Elkonin, 1973; Lundberg, Frost, & Peterson, 1988; Torgesen, 1997). Over several months' time, the teacher guides students in segmenting, first, two-phoneme words (e.g., /at/ = /a/ /t/) and, later, three- and four-phoneme words (e.g., /sat/ = /s/ /a/ /t/:/flat/ = /f/ /l/ /a/ /t/). Several studies (e.g., Ball & Blachman, 1991; Bradley & Bryant, 1983) have reported positive gains in young children's reading and spelling ability when such explicit phoneme segmentation training is paired with letter/sound instruction.

A less direct approach to developing phoneme segmentation ability is to engage young children in supported reading and writing activities and allow the writing system, itself, to teach them about the phonemic properties of words. For example, as kindergartners finger-point read and reread simple texts (Big Books, dictations), they come to learn, with a teacher's guidance, how spoken words match to printed words (Clay, 1991; Morris, 1993) and how printed words are composed of letters that match to sounds (Holdaway, 1979). As the children begin to write their own texts, they learn to focus on individual words within a sentence and individual sounds within a word. In fact, at this early stage, "invented" spelling is an ongoing exercise in attending to phonemes within spoken words (Chomsky, 1979; Ehri, 1989).

Although there is little experimental evidence supporting the effectiveness of a "reading/writing" approach to developing phoneme segmentation ability (but see Morris, 1993; Perfetti, Beck, Bell, & Hughes, 1987), the approach rightly appeals to many kindergarten and first-grade teachers. After all, the teacher of beginning readers faces a dual responsibility: to facilitate phonemic awareness *and* to heighten young children's interest in becoming literate (Meek, 1985). Perhaps, direct versus indirect phonemic segmentation instruction should not be an either/or choice; instead, both methods of instruction should be in the skillful teacher's repertoire, to be used as needed.

First Grade

First grade is a critical year in literacy development, particularly for the at-risk child. Children who fall behind significantly in first-grade reading tend to struggle with the process throughout the primary grades (Clay, 1993; Juel, 1988). To ensure that all first graders get off to a good start in reading, comprehensive planning is needed; planning that addresses both classroom instructional issues and intervention-based tutorial issues.

Classroom issues. At the beginning of the year, at-risk first-grade readers require the same type of foundational instruction that was or should have been provided in kindergarten. Concepts of print and an initial sight vocabulary can be developed through guided reading of Big Books and dictations; alphabet and beginning consonant knowledge through direct teaching; and familiarity with written language through the teacher reading aloud to the class. At this early stage, a knowledgeable first-grade teacher must instill a "literacy set" (Holdaway, 1979) in low readers, preparing them for the more formal reading instruction that will follow.

Eventually, low-reading first graders should be placed in a set of graded reading materials and advanced through the materials with all deliberate speed. Unfortunately, securing appropriate materials for low readers continues to be a major problem. Arthur Gates (1969) argued 30 years ago that a single basal reader program would not meet the needs of every child in a classroom. He argued for multiple sets of graded reading materials, with the teacher deciding which materials to use with different groups of children. I agree with Dr. Gates, but I do not believe that today our choices should be limited by the warring philosophical camps. Many low readers may benefit most from materials that "split the difference"; that is, carefully graded texts that feature decent stories and a moderate amount of vocabulary control (e.g., the Laidlaw basal reader [Eller & Hester, 1980], the Wright Group's *Starpol* series [Tully, 1988]). In any case, effective classroom instruction for low readers is impossible without a set of carefully graded reading materials geared to the children's interests and needs.

Children who struggle learning to read usually experience difficulty with decoding or word recognition. Thus, phonics needs to be taught to these students, and it needs to be taught well. To do so, a teacher must first understand the content or developmental continuum of phonics instruction (e.g., beginning consonants, word families or rhyming words, short-vowel patterns, long-vowel patterns, syllabication). Second, he or she must determine individual student's levels of word knowledge or where they should be instructed along the developmental continuum (Invernizzi, Abouzeid, & Gill, 1994). Third, the teacher must possess a systematic method for teaching phonics—a method that engages children in practicing (overlearning) important letter-sound relationships and spelling patterns.

One historically divisive issue that has yet to be satisfactorily resolved is whether phonics instruction for low readers needs to be reinforced with the reading of decodable or phonetically regular text. Foorman, Francis, Fletcher, Schatschneider, and Metha

(1998) found that a group of low-reading first graders, who received explicit phonics instruction and reading practice with decodable text, outperformed two control groups who received less intensive phonics instruction that was embedded in the reading of natural-language text. Success for All also features decodable text, as does the Orton-Gillingham approach (Gillingham & Stillman, 1997), which is used successfully with severely disabled readers. But note that Reading Recovery and other successful first-grade intervention programs, such as Book Buddies (Invernizzi, Rosemary, Juel, & Richards, 1997) and Early Steps (Santa & Holen, 1999), use natural-language text. This suggests that the majority of at-risk readers, if provided with systematic code instruction, can progress by reading carefully graded natural-language text. A small subset of children, however, may require the extra support provided by decodable text (Vellutino et al., 1996).

Commenting recently on the need for phonics instruction in the schools, Chall stated (1997):

> We need to find quick and effective ways to train and retrain teachers in phonics and other beginning reading skills. Teachers need to know why phonics should be taught, what needs teaching, when, and how. They need to know the research literature on phonics and beginning reading and how to read the research. And they need to know the history of reading instruction, for in reading as in other aspects of life, those who ignore history are doomed to repeat its errors. (p. 262)

I agree with Dr. Chall's appraisal, except that I do not believe we can produce effective teachers of phonics quickly or easily. Research may support phonics instruction and publishers may hasten to provide the requisite materials. (This occurred in the 1960s and 1970s and is occurring again today.) Nonetheless, simply dispensing phonics materials and mandating their use will not get the job done. The abstractness and complexity of phonics instruction—for children and teachers, alike—has been underestimated. Until teachers come to understand the structure of the spelling system, the developmental nature of printed word learning, and a viable instructional method, they will experience difficulty teaching phonics to the children who most need it. This is truly a problem of teacher training, a problem that has yet to be adequately addressed.

Although controversial today, within-class ability grouping, historically, has been a common-sense attempt to meet the needs of first-grade children reading at different levels. Earlier I noted several problems connected with ability grouping. Nonetheless, it is less than clear how the alternative—that is, whole-class instruction—can meet the needs of low-reading first graders. It stands to reason that when the pace of whole-class instruction exceeds the abilities of low readers, these children will make minimal progress.

Ability grouping offers advantages. Foremost among these is that low readers, on a daily basis, can read stories and study phonics concepts that are at the appropriate difficulty level. The small-group environment also affords increased opportunity for low readers to participate in story discussions (Stauffer, 1970; Tharp & Gallimore, 1988). The criticism that ability grouping isolates low readers from their higher achieving peers can be addressed by beginning each school day with a whole-class literature circle for 45–60 minutes. Here, all children in the class can join in choral-reading dictations, Big Books, and poems, and listening to stories read aloud by the teacher (Holdaway, 1979; Routman, 1988). A second criticism of ability groups is not as easily dismissed. This is the contention that low readers are often "locked into" slowly paced, low-group instruction over several years' time; that is, once placed in the low reading group, a child remains there (Hiebert, 1983; Juel, 1988). However, even in this area of instructional pacing, there is room for hope, as we will see.

Intervention issues.   The effectiveness of one-to-one tutoring in preventing reading failure in first grade has been well documented. But keep in mind that tutoring is most effective when it works in concert with the classroom instructional program. When a beginning reader starts to "catch on" and makes quick progress in tutoring, this presents an opportunity to move him or her to a higher reading group in the classroom. Such a move can produce a spiraling effect on achievement, for now the child is being taught at the cutting edge of his or her ability in both contexts. In this way, tutoring can actually prevent students from being locked into a low-reading-group placement; it can make flexible grouping in the classroom a reality.

Some first-grade reading intervention programs contain a powerful teacher-training component. In Reading Recovery, for example, a teacher-in-training tutors a low reader for a full year under the watchful eye of a skilled clinician. Such a sustained apprenticeship, although costly in time and money, can deepen a teacher's understanding of the beginning reading process, instill a problem-solving mind set (Schon, 1987), and, most important, give the teacher confidence that he or she can teach an at-risk child to read.

While acknowledging the power of such training, we must also consider its "spread effect" within a school. For example, if, after training, there is only one Reading Recovery teacher in a school with four first-grade classes and 30-plus at-risk readers, then that teacher will be able to serve less than one-quarter of the children who need help. Moreover, if the intervention teacher is trained and works in isolation from classroom teachers, as is often the case, then he or she will have little effect on the classroom instruction of low readers.

One way around this problem is to provide intervention training (supervised one-to-one tutoring experience) simultaneously to the reading teacher and first-grade teachers within a school (Morris, 1995; Santa & Holen, 1999). Training of this kind provides participating teachers with a shared knowledge base, language, and experiences that should lead to meaningful dialogue and, ultimately, to coordination of instruction for low readers. More research is needed, but we may eventually find that a supervised tutoring experience is the most effective way to train classroom teachers to work with low readers; if this is true, reading education will have rediscovered its clinical tradition (Broaddus & Bloodgood, in press; Morris, 1999; Schon, 1987).

Second Grade

In the enthusiastic response to first-grade intervention programs (particularly Reading Recovery), the role of second grade in preventing reading failure has been all but overlooked. This is unfortunate because most at-risk readers will require more than one year of quality instruction if they are to attain grade-level reading status by the end of third grade. Even those low readers who make good progress in a first-grade intervention program often need an extra boost in second grade if they are to keep up with their peers.

Good classroom instruction for low readers in second grade involves the same elements that were important in first grade: graded reading materials that contain some degree of word control; appropriate phonics instruction that develops students' orthographic knowledge; and grouping arrangements that allow students to read at their instructional level. In addition, the second-grade teacher must pace the instruction of low readers efficiently, paying sufficient attention to decoding, fluency, and comprehension.

Rarely do low-reading second graders receive one-to-one tutorial instruction. The cost of using certified teachers to tutor is high, and when money for tutoring is available, it is usually targeted for first grade (Success for All is an exception, providing tutoring help, as needed). This brings us to a recent and interesting development in our field, the proposed use of volunteer tutors to assist low-reading primary-grade students.

Volunteer tutors (college students, parents, retirees, etc.) can potentially provide the one-to-one instruction that is needed by, but generally unavailable to, low-reading second graders. In fact, a handful of studies (Invernizzi, Rosemary, Juel, & Richards, 1997; Juel, 1991; Morris, Shaw, & Perney, 1990) have shown that volunteer tutoring programs can raise the achievement of at-risk readers. Nonetheless, few things in this world are completely free of cost, and an effective volunteer tutoring program is no exception. In a recent review, Wasik (1998) noted that successful volunteer programs seem to require close, on-site supervision by a reading specialist. It is through the reading specialist's lesson-planning and vigilant supervision, Wasik argues, that volunteer tutors are able to make a difference with low-reading children.

Reading educators should be the first to understand that simply sending hordes of unsupervised volunteers into the schools will not the get the job done. The real challenge is not recruiting volunteers, but rather readying schools to make effective use of those who do volunteer. Two things are needed: preparatory training for reading teachers who will supervise the volunteers, including information on teaching method, materials selection, lesson planning, modeling, provision of feedback, and so on; and time, during or after school, for the teacher to supervise the tutoring lessons (Johnston, Invernizzi, & Juel, 1998; Morris, 1999).

There is something inherently right about involving the larger community in helping at-risk children learn to read. The Book Buddies program in Charlottesville, Virginia (Invernizzi et al., 1997) is a wonderful example of what can be accomplished. However, volunteer tutoring programs, to be successful, will require resources, careful planning, and ongoing, diligent supervision. Further research is needed to document the effectiveness of such programs and to identify the specific characteristics that make them effective.

Third Grade

The instructional issues in third grade are similar to those in second. In the classroom, low-reading third graders need to read at their instructional level in both narrative and expository text. Literature circles (Daniels, 1994) are promising, particularly if they are used to put low readers in novels and information books that they can actually read. Low-reading third graders also need to study spelling patterns at the appropriate difficulty level (Henderson, 1990; Morris, Blanton, Blanton, Nowacck, & Perney, 1995). Finally, they need to develop reading fluency. Here again, volunteer tutors, if adequately supervised, can provide third graders with badly needed contextual reading practice. With thoughtful, intensive instruction, third grade can be an important "catch up" year for children who get off to a slow start in reading.

Conclusion

To many reading educators and researchers, the issues I have raised may appear old, mundane, and less than cutting-edge. However, for low readers and their teachers, these "old" issues have never been adequately resolved. And that is why they are important. At-risk beginning readers need interesting reading materials that support word learning, they need help in mastering critical spelling patterns, and they need to read consistently at their instructional level. As reading professionals, we cannot in good conscience ignore or sidestep these issues. Instead, we must continue to confront them with commitment, creativity, and practicality.

Our challenge is to hold on to what we know to be sound theory and practice . . . while at the same time searching for new and more efficient ways to meet the needs of low readers.

Along with the old, I have touched on some newer issues—specifically, early reading intervention and volunteer tutoring. In a field that is dominated by changing trends. I am heartened by the fact that first-grade intervention programs like Reading Recovery and Success for All have been around for over a decade now, and do not appear to be waning in influence. I attribute this to the indisputable logic that supports early intervention and also to the positive achievement results that these programs have produced.

I am less optimistic about the shelf life of volunteer tutoring. I believe in the idea; I believe volunteers, if appropriately used, could make a huge difference in the achievement of low-reading children. However, the concept of volunteer tutoring was, in a sense, sprung on the reading field a few years ago in the midst of a national political campaign. We were not adequately prepared for it. We do have a few promising models, but volunteer tutoring needs to be thought through and researched more carefully if it is to have a significant and lasting impact on our field.

Volunteer tutoring needs to be thought through and researched more carefully if it is to have a significant and lasting impact on our field.

Allington (1994) recently pointed out that we are relatively new at this job of preventing reading failure. He noted that it was only about 30 years ago that the federal government began to focus on this huge societal problem by passing the Elementary and Secondary Education Act, including the authorization of Title 1. As a field, we have made important steps forward over the past three decades, both in our understanding of the reading acquisition process and in program development. Our challenge is to hold on to what we know to be sound theory and practice (and this includes elements of both whole-language and direct instruction), while at the same time searching for new and more efficient ways to meet the needs of low readers. There is no excuse for further pendulum swings. Given what we presently know about effective classroom and intervention instruction, I firmly believe that we can teach almost all children in this country to read by the end of third grade. The knowledge base is there. What we need are adequate resources and a relentless professional commitment to low-reading children. It is past time to roll up our sleeves and get the job done.

References

Adams, M. J. (1990). *Beginning to read: Thinking and learning about print*. Cambridge. MA: MIT Press.

Allington, R. (1983). The reading instruction provided readers of differing reading ability, *Elementary School Journal, 83*, 548–559.

Allington, R. (1994). Critical issues: What's special about special programs for children who find learning to read difficult? *Journal of Reading Behavior, 26*, 95–115.

Anderson, R. C., Hiebert, E., Scott, J., & Wilkinson, I. (1983). *Becoming a nation of readers: The report of the Commission on Reading*. Washington, DC: National Academy of Education.

Ball, E., & Blachman, B. (1991). Does phoneme segmentation training in kindergarten make a difference in early word recognition and developmental spelling? *Reading Research Quarterly, 26*, 49–66.

Barr, R. (1982). Classroom reading instruction from a sociological perspective. *Journal of Reading Behavior, 14*, 375–389.

Barr, R. (1995). What research says about grouping in the past and present and what it suggests about the future. In M. Radencich & L. McKay (Eds.), *Flexible grouping for literacy in the elementary school* (pp. 1–24). Boston: Allyn & Bacon.

Barr, R., & Dreeben, R. (1983). *How schools work*. Chicago: University of Chicago Press.

Bear, D., Invernizzi, M., Templeton, S., & Johnston, F. (1996). *Words their way*. Columbus, OH: Prentice Hall.

Bond, G. L., & Dykstra, R. (1967). The cooperative research program in first-grade reading instruction. *Reading Research Quarterly, 2*, 1–142.

Bradley, L., & Bryant, P. (1983). Categorizing sounds and learning to read: A causal connection. *Nature, 30*, 419–421.

Broaddus, K., & Bloodgood, J. (1999). "We're supposed to already know how to teach reading": Teacher change to support struggling readers. *Reading Research Quarterly*.

Carver, R. (1990). *Reading rate: A review of the research and theory*. San Diego, CA: Academic Press.

Center, Y., Wheldall, K., Freeman, L., Outhred, L., & McNaught, M. (1995). An evaluation of Reading Recovery. *Reading Research Quarterly, 30*, 240–263.

Chall, J. (1967). *Learning to read: The great debate*. New York: McGraw-Hill.

Chall, J. (1983). *Stages of reading development*. New York: McGraw-Hill.

Chall, J. (1997). Are reading methods changing again? *Annals of Dyslexia, 47*, 257–263.

Chomsky, C. (1979). Approaching reading through invented spelling. In L. Resnick & P. Weaver (Eds.), *Theory and practice of early reading* (Vol. 2, pp. 43–65). Hillsdale, NJ: Erlbaum.

Clay, M. (1979). *The early detection of reading difficulties*. Auckland: Heinemann.

Clay, M. (1991). *Becoming literate: The construction of inner control*. Auckland: Heinemann.

Clay, M. (1993). *Reading Recovery: A guidebook for teachers in training*. Auckland: Heinemann.

Daniels, H. (1994). *Literature circles: Voice and choice in the student-centered classroom*, York, ME: Stenhouse.

Dickinson, D., & Smith, M. (1994). Long-term effects of pre-school teachers' book readings on low-income children's vocabulary and story comprehension. *Reading Research Quarterly, 29*, 104–122.

Ehri, L. (1983). A critique of five studies related to letter-name knowledge and learning to read. In L. Gentile, M. Kamil, & J. Blanchard (Eds.). *Reading research revisited* (pp. 143–153). Columbus, OH: Merrill.

Ehri, L. (1989). The development of spelling knowledge and its role in reading acquisition and reading disability. *Journal of Learning Disabilities, 22*, 356–365.

Ehri, L., & Wilee, L. (1985). Movement into reading: Is the first stage of printed word learning visual or phonetic? *Reading Research Quarterly, 20*, 163–179.

Elkonin, D. (1973). U.S.S.R. In J. Downing (Ed.). *Comparative reading: Cross-national studies of behavior and processes in reading and writing* (pp. 551–578). New York: MacMillan.

Eller, W., & Hester, K. (1980). *The Laidlaw reading program* (Levels 4–8). River Forest, IL: Laidlaw Brothers.

Elley, W. (1989). Vocabulary acquisition from listening to stories. *Reading Research Quarterly, 24*, 174–187.

Engelmann, S., & Bruner, E. (1968). *DISTAR*. Chicago: Science Research Associates.

Feitelson, D., Goldstein, Z., Iraqi, J., & Share, D. (1993). Effects of listening to story reading on aspects of literacy acquisition in a diglossic situation. *Reading Research Quarterly, 28*, 70–79.

Foorman, B., Francis, D., Fletcher, J., Schatschneider, C., & Metha, P. (1998). The role of instruction in learning to read: Preventing reading failure in at-risk children. *Journal of Educational Psychology, 90*, 37–55.

Fries, C. (1963). *Linguistics and reading*. New York: Holt, Rinehart & Winston.

Gates, A. (1969). The tides of time. In J. Figurel (Ed.). *Reading and realism* (pp. 12–20). Newark, DE: International Reading Association.

Gillingham, A., & Stillman, B. (1997). *The Gillingham manual: Remedial training for students with specific disability in reading, spelling, and penmanship* (8th ed.). Cambridge, MA: Educators Publishing Service.

Goodman, K. (1985). *What's whole in whole language*. Toronto: Scholastic Canada.

Gough, P., & Hillinger, M. (1980). Learning to read: An unnatural act. *Bulletin of the Orton Society, 30*, 180–196.

Gray, W. S. Monroe, M., Artley, A. S., & Arbuthnot, M. H. (1951). *The new basic readers*. Chicago: Scott, Foresman.

Harste, J. (1989). The basalization of American reading instruction: One researcher responds. *Theory into Practice, 28*, 265–273.

Henderson, E. H. (1986). Understanding children's knowledge of written language. In D. Yaden & S. Templeton (Eds.), *Metalinguistic awareness and beginning literacy* (pp. 65–77). Portsmouth, NH: Heinemann.

Henderson, E. H. (1990). *Teaching spelling*. Boston: Houghton Mifflin.

Henderson, E. H., & Templeton, S. (1986). A developmental perspective of formal spelling instruction through alphabet, pattern, and meaning. *Elementary School Journal, 86*, 305–316.

Hichert, E. (1983). An examination of ability grouping for reading instruction. *Reading Research Quarterly, 18*, 255–331.

Hoffman, J., McCarthey, S., Abbott, J., Christian, C., Corman, L., Curry, K., Dressman, M., Elliot, B., Matherne, D., & Stahle, D. (1994). So what's new in the new basals? A focus on first grade. *Journal of Reading Behavior, 26*, 47–74.

Hoffman, J., McCarthey, S., Elliot, B., Bayles, D., Price, D., Ferree, A., & Abbot, J. (1998). The literature-based basals in first-grade classrooms: Savior, Satan, or same-old, same-old? *Reading Research Quarterly, 33*, 168–197

Holdaway, D. (1979). *The foundations of literacy*. Auckland: Heinemann.

Invernizzi, M., Abouzeid, M., & Gill, J. T. (1994). Using students' invented spellings as a guide for spelling instruction that emphasizes word study. *Elementary School Journal, 95*, 155–167.

Invernizzi, M., Rosemary, C., Juel, C., & Richards, H. (1997). At-risk readers and community volunteers: A three-year perspective. *Journal of Scientific Studies of Reading, 3*, 277–300.

Iversen, S., & Tunmer, W. (1993). Phonological processing skills and the Reading Recovery program. *Journal of Educational Psychology, 85*, 112–126.

Jerrolds, B., & Thompson, R. (1995). History of the whole language concept. *Georgia Journal of Reading, 20*, 10–15.

Johnston, F., Invernizzi, M., & Juel, C. (1998). *Book Buddies: Guidelines for volunteer tutors of emergent and early readers*. New York: Guilford.

Juel, C. (1988). Learning to read and write: A longitudinal study of fifty-four children from first through fourth grade. *Journal of Educational Psychology, 80*, 437–447.

Juel, C. (1991). Cross-age tutoring between student athletes and at-risk children. *Reading Teacher, 45*, 178–186.

Kozol, J. (1967). *Death at an early age: The destruction of the hearts and minds of Negro children in the Boston Public Schools*. Boston: Houghton Mifflin.

Lee. D., & Allen, R. V. (1963). *Learning to read through experience*. New York: Appleton Century Crofts.

Liberman, I. Y., & Liberman, A. M. (1992). Whole language versus code-emphasis: Underlying assumptions and their implications for reading instruction. In P. Gough,

L. Ehri, & R. Treiman (Eds.). *Reading acquisition* (pp. 343–366). Hillsdale, NJ: Erlbaum.

Lundberg, I., Frost, J., & Peterson, O. (1988). Effects of an extensive program for stimulating phonological awareness in preschool children. *Reading Research Quarterly, 23,* 263–284.

Meek, M. (1985). *Learning to read.* Portsmouth, NH: Heinemann.

Morris, D. (1993). The relationship between children's concept of word in text and phoneme awareness in learning to read: A longitudinal study. *Research in the Teaching of English, 27,* 133–154.

Morris, D. (1995). *First Steps: An early reading intervention program.* (ERIC Documentation Reproduction Service No. ED 388 956)

Morris, D. (1999). *The Howard Street tutoring manual: Teaching at-risk readers in the primary grades.* New York: Guilford.

Morris, D. (1999). The role of clinical training in the teaching of reading. In D. Evensen & P. Mosenthal (Eds.), *Advances in reading/language research (vol. 6).* Greenwich, CT: JAI.

Morris, D., & Perney, J. (1984). Developmental spelling as a predictor of first-grade reading achievement. *Elementary School Journal, 84,* 441–457.

Morris, D., Shaw, B., & Perney, J. (1990). Helping low readers in grades two and three: An after-school volunteer tutoring program. *Elementary School Journal, 91,* 133–150.

Morris, D., Blanton, L., Blanton, W., Nowacck, J., & Perney, J. (1995). Teaching low-achieving spellers at their instructional level. *Elementary School Journal, 96,* 163–177.

National Assessment of Educational Progress (1995). *NAEP 1994 Reading: A First Look—Findings from the National Assessment of Educational Progress* (Revised Edition). Washington, DC: Government Printing Office.

Nessel, D., & Jones, M. (1981). *The language-experience approach to reading: A handbook for teachers.* New York: Teachers College Press.

Pearson, P. D. (1989). Commentary: Reading the Whole Language movement. *Elementary School Journal, 90,* 231–241.

Perfetti, C. (1985). *Reading ability.* New York: Oxford University Press.

Perfetti, C. (1992). The representation problem in reading acquisition. In P. Gough, L., Ehri, & R. Treiman (Eds.), *Reading acquisition* (pp. 145–174). Hillsdale, NJ: Erlbaum.

Perfetti, C., Beck, I., Bell, L., & Hughes, C. (1987). Phonemic knowledge and learning to read are reciprocal: A longitudinal study of first-grade children. *Merrill-Palmer Quarterly, 33,* 283–319.

Pinnell, G. S. (1989). Reading Recovery: Helping at-risk children learn to read. *Elementary School Journal, 90,* 161–183.

Pinnell, G. S., Lyons, C., Deford, D., Bryk, A., & Seltzer, M. (1994). Comparing instructional models for the literacy education of high-risk first graders. *Reading Research Quarterly, 29,* 8–39.

Routman, R. (1988). *Transitions from literature to literacy.* Portsmouth, NH: Heinemann.

Santa, C., & Holen, T. (1999). An assessment of Early Steps: A program for early intervention of reading problems. *Reading Research Quarterly, 34,* 54–79.

Schon, D. (1987). *Educating the reflective practitioner.* San Francisco: Jossey-Bass.

Shanahan, T., & Barr, R. (1995). Reading Recovery: An independent evaluation of the effects of an early instructional intervention for at-risk learners. *Reading Research Quarterly, 30,* 958–996.

Slavin, R. (1987). Ability grouping: A best-evidence synthesis. *Review of Educational Research, 57,* 293–336.

Slavin, R., Madden, N., Karweit, N., Dolan, L., & Wasik, B. (1994). Success for All: Getting reading right the first time. In E. Hiebert & B. Taylor (Eds.), *Getting reading right from the start* (pp. 125–147). Boston: Allyn & Bacon.

Slavin, R., Madden, N., Dolan, L., Wasik, B., Ross, S., Smith, L., & Dianda, M. (1996). Success for All: A summary of the research. *Journal of Education for Students Placed At Risk, 1,* 41–76.

Smith, F. (1981). Demonstrations, engagements, and sensitivity: The choice between people and programs. *Language Arts, 58,* 634–642.

Snow, C., Burns, S., & Griffin, P. (1998). *Preventing reading difficulties in young children.* Washington, DC: National Academy Press.

Stanovich, K. (1998). Twenty-five years of research on the reading process: The Grand Synthesis and what it means for our field. In T. Shanahan & F. V. Rodriguez-Brown (Eds.), *47th Yearbook of the National Reading Conference* (pp. 44–58). Chicago: National Reading Conference.

Stauffer, R. (1970). *The language-experience approach to the teaching of reading.* New York: Harper & Row.

Stuart, M., & Coltheart, M. (1988). Does reading develop in a sequence of stages? *Cognition, 30,* 139–181.

Tharp, R., & Gallimore, R. (1988). *Rousing minds to life: Teaching, learning, and schooling in social context.* New York: Cambridge University Press.

Torgesen, J. (1997). The prevention and remediation of reading disabilities: Evaluating what we know from the research. *Journal of Academic Language Therapy, 1,* 11–47.

Tully, J. (1988). *Starpol series.* San Diego, CA: The Wright Group.

Vellutino, F., Scanlon, D., Sipay, E., Small, S., Pratt, A., Chen, R., & Denekla, M. (1996). Cognitive profiles of difficult-to-remediate and readily remediated poor readers: Early intervention as a vehicle for distinguishing between cognitive and experiential deficits as basic causes of specific reading disability. *Journal of Educational Psychology, 88,* 601–638.

Wagner, R., Torgesen, J., & Rashotte, C. (1994). Development of reading-related phonological processing abilities: New evidence of bidirectional causality from a latent variable longitudinal study. *Developmental Psychology, 30,* 73–87.

Wasik, B. (1998). Volunteer tutoring programs in reading: A review. *Reading Research Quarterly, 33,* 266–291.

Wasik, B., & Slavin, R. (1990). *Preventing early reading failure with one-to-one tutoring: A best evidence synthesis.* Paper presented at the meeting of the American Educational Research Association, Boston.

Wells, G. (1986). *The meaning makers.* Portsmouth, NH: Heinemann.

There's More to Teaching At-risk and Delayed Readers than Good Reading Instruction

Irene W. Gaskins
Benchmark School, Media, PA

Here's the story of the Benchmark School, a most interesting place where children with severe reading difficulties learn to read.

Historically, longitudinal and follow-up studies of children delayed in reading have suggested that gains made during reading remediation are rarely maintained and that delayed readers who have concluded a course of remediation usually function in regular classes at a level below what their potential would predict (Bronfenbrenner, 1974; Muehl & Forell, 1973–74; Page & Grandon, 1981; Spache, 1981; Strang, 1968). Recently there has been agreement among experts that if we could intercept these at-risk children in kindergarten or first grade and provide them with an exemplary program, the prognosis for their success in regular classes would improve (Pikulski, 1994; Spiegel, 1995). Reading Recovery (Pinnell, Lyons, DeFord, Bryk, & Seltzer, 1994) and Success for All (Slavin, Madden, Karweit, Dolan, & Wasik, 1994) are well-known examples of such attempts to guarantee at-risk children a brighter future by intervening early. Unfortunately, as laudable as these attempts have been, there is evidence that even when at-risk children are intercepted early, exemplary reading instruction may not be sufficient to prevent school difficulties for these vulnerable children (Center, Wheldall, Freeman, Outhred, & McNaught, 1995; Hiebert, 1994; Shanahan & Barr, 1995). What is missing? What do schools need to provide to increase the probability that delayed readers eventually will meet with success in regular classrooms?

Questions like these prompted the founding of Benchmark School almost 3 decades ago. Benchmark is a school for children who read below grade level, have average or better potential, and whose reading delay cannot be attributed to primary emotional or neurological problems. Most enter the school as non-

readers. During the early years of the school some children attended the school for a half-day reading program, returning in the afternoon to their regular schools, and others attended full day for a total elementary program. Both options included a daily, $2\frac{1}{2}$-hour reading block that featured a great deal of reading and responding to what was read (Gaskins, 1980). The half-day program was phased out during the early years of the school because it separated the teaching of reading from the rest of the curriculum. Now all children who attend the school receive a full elementary or middle school curriculum. At present the student body consists of 125 lower school students and 50 middle school students.

During Benchmark's first 25 years, the staff taught over 3,000 delayed readers who were enrolled in either the regular school year or summer school programs. The responses of these students to instruction at Benchmark, and at the schools they attended after Benchmark, as well as study of the professional literature, have led us to make some tentative hypotheses about what works in teaching delayed readers. We hope that our hypotheses about programming for at-risk and delayed readers will lead to fruitful discussions with other professionals as we continue to refine our understanding of how best to meet students' needs.

The article begins with a brief overview of four elements that provide a foundation for the success of school-based initiatives to teach at-risk and delayed readers. These include staff development, quality instruction and support services, congruence between "remedial" and regular programs, and ample instructional time for learning to occur. Following this description is the story of program development at Benchmark, which is based on an extensive menu of staff development opportunities and has as its goal quality instruction and support services that are congruent with the skills and strategies students need to succeed in regular Grades 1–8 classrooms. This second section on program development at Benchmark describes the evolution of programs to address students' difficulties in reading narrative text, expressing ideas in writing, reading in the content areas, learning sight words and decoding, understanding what it means to be actively involved in learning, applying strategies across the curriculum, being aware of personal road-blocks, and taking charge of personal style and motivation.

Foundation Upon Which Successful Programs Are Built

Research suggests that the foundation of a school initiative to provide at-risk and delayed readers with the skills and strategies they need to meet with and maintain success in regular classrooms is composed of at least four critical elements.

Staff Development

The cornerstone of instructional programs that produce significant results in student progress is staff development (Darling-Hammond, 1996). Staff development needs to be ongoing, collaborative, and in-depth as it engages teachers and support staff in exploring and understanding research-based principles and theories about instruction, curriculum, and cognition. The goal is that staff development will lead to the staff creating, and taking ownership of, quality programs that meet the needs of at-risk and delayed readers. Understanding instructional principles and theories allows teachers to make informed decisions about long-term program planning and on-the-spot instruction. Another important aspect of staff development is principals and supervisors spending time in classrooms to support, coach, and collaborate with teachers as they meet the daily challenges of providing at-risk and delayed readers with quality instruction.

The cornerstone of instructional programs that produce significant results in student progress is staff development.

When Benchmark was founded, a small group of teachers who enjoyed reading and applying the research literature was selected as the initial staff. Their aim was to study the literature and plan research-based instruction for remediating reading problems. A weekly $1^1/_2$-hour seminar was instituted to study and reflect on the professional literature related to the school's instructional goals. This weekly seminar continues today as the heart of staff development. Based on what is learned, the staff collaborates to develop or fine-tune instructional practices. Teachers meet individually each week with their supervisors to plan instruction, and the supervisors and I spend a portion of each day in classrooms teaching and observing. New staff members are provided with

regular professional development meetings both prior to the start of and throughout the school year. Staff development also includes monthly inservice meetings for the entire staff conducted by well-known experts in literacy and cognition; weekly team meetings; and the circulation, reading, and discussion of professional journals. Staff members are also encouraged to write for publication and to share their drafts with the staff. Writing about what we are doing, and receiving input about these drafts, help us clarify our thinking.

Quality Instruction and Support Services to Address Roadblocks

A second critical ingredient is quality instruction and support services tailored to address the academic and nonacademic roadblocks that stand in the way of success in regular classrooms (Dryfoos, 1996). For example, delayed readers, unlike their more successful classmates, often do not figure out on their own how to learn a word or make an inference. For them, learning these skills may be contingent upon instruction from the very best teachers—instruction that includes explicit explanations, modeling, and scaffolded practice that is engaging and meaningful.

Our experience at Benchmark suggests that teaching delayed readers how to read is only a first step in dealing with their roadblocks to academic success.

And, more than likely, they will need this kind of high-quality instruction not merely during reading instruction, but across the curriculum. Our experience at Benchmark suggests that teaching delayed readers how to read is only a first step in dealing with their roadblocks to academic success. In addition to high-quality instruction across the curriculum, students often need additional support services to address social and emotional needs and maladaptive cognitive styles.

Quality instruction at Benchmark means meeting students where they are with respect to affect, motivation, and cognition; explicitly teaching them strategies for taking charge of tasks, situations, and personal styles; and scaffolding the successful completion of academic tasks. The staff believes that all we can change is ourselves and that children change as a result of the changes we make in our approach to them. We look at what works and does not work and build on what works. Our focus is on solutions to academic and nonacademic roadblocks rather than on explanations for why students experienced school difficulties prior to attendance at Benchmark. The staff identifies goals and plots the most efficient route to achieving them. This route often includes orchestrating additional services from mentors, psychologists, social workers, and counselors.

Congruence

The third critical ingredient is congruence between the remedial program and regular classroom programs. Although there is movement in the United States toward an inclusion model that brings specialists into regular classrooms to collaborate with the classroom teacher in teaching at-risk and delayed readers, many programs continue to pull students out of their regular classrooms for remedial instruction that is poorly coordinated with the curriculum and instruction of the regular classroom (Johnston, Allington, & Afflerbach, 1985). No matter how good, pull-out instruction is not usually sufficient to create successful students. At-risk and delayed readers have the best chance for success if classroom instruction and remedial instruction are not only of high quality but also congruent. Research has consistently shown that even when academic progress of at-risk and delayed readers is accelerated as a result of remedial programs, these learning gains are difficult to maintain unless there is congruence between remedial and regular classroom instruction (Shanahan & Barr, 1995). Remedial teachers must prepare delayed readers with the skills and strategies they need for success in regular classrooms.

Time

Missing in most initiatives to teach at-risk and delayed readers is sufficient time to accomplish the goal of preparing students to be successful in the mainstream. Most initiatives envision support in terms of a year or two. The Benchmark staff's experience suggests that (a) preparation for success in the mainstream requires that delayed readers spend more time receiving quality instruction than their peers in regular classes, and (b) delayed readers continue to need support over many years. Thus, ideally, programs for every at-risk and delayed reader should begin as early as possible and continue across the curriculum throughout the elementary and middle school years.

What follows is the story of a program development journey to provide quality instruction and support services that address at-risk and delayed readers' roadblocks to success in regular classrooms. Staff development, congruence with regular school programs, and ample time to learn and practice the skills and strategies needed for success in regular classrooms were major considerations in the development of the programs described.

The Development of Programs for Delayed Readers

Benchmark School was founded as a laboratory school to design and evaluate programs for teaching delayed readers between the ages of 6 and 14. The goal in 1970, as it is now, was to create a research-based curriculum for teaching delayed readers the skills and strategies they need to perform in regular classrooms at levels commensurate with their abilities and no lower than the median of their classes. To accomplish this, a small staff of reading specialists was brought together to form a school.

Throughout the first 5 years of the school's existence, the staff's total focus was on teaching reading and on the volume of reading completed by students. This focus continues today, but the scope is much broader than just reading. Our study of the research suggested that the key to progress in reading might be the number of words that children read.

Reading Lots of Books

During the 1970s, Benchmark students were taught reading in small groups of 2 to 4 students who had similar needs; groups progressed through basal reader levels at rates $1^1/_2$ to 2 times that of students in regular schools, for example, moving from the 1–2 level to the 3–1 level in one year. While regular school students typically read one basal per level and spent hours completing workbook pages and skillsheets, our students read 5 to 10 basal readers at each level, as well as many trade books. Workbooks and publishers' skillsheets were seldom used. In the early years of the school, we used out-of-date basals discarded by other schools and trade books donated by schools, staff, and parents. Parents supported their children's reading by making sure that their children read each evening for 30 minutes at their independent level, and by reading to their children for an additional 20 minutes from children's literature supplied by the school. In class each day teachers held individual book conferences with students about their home reading. These home and school reading activities continue today.

As a result of a great deal of reading and discussion about what was read, most students not only learned to read but also became avid readers. Their success in reading was a testament to the fact that the number of words read correlates with progress in reading. On average in our early years, students entered the program at 10 and 11 years of age, reading 2 to 5 years below level. They usually left the program 2 years later, having advanced 2 or more years in basal reader level and achieving at or above the mean for their grade level on standardized achievement tests in reading.

We were excited about our students' ability to read! However, when we followed the progress of our students once they returned to regular schools, we often found that, although we had created readers, our students did not do as well in other areas of the curriculum as intelligence tests suggested they should.

During the mid-1970s we decided that the age of entry to the Benchmark program might be a factor in the difficulties some of our former students experienced when they returned to the mainstream. As a result, we began giving first preference in admissions to the youngest students. These younger children exhibited less emotional overlay and fewer behavior problems than the older students, confirming our suspicions that entering Benchmark after years of failure made remediation more difficult. As with the older students, we were successful in teaching these younger children to read.

We were excited about our students' ability to read! However,. . .we often found that, although we had created readers, our students did not do as well in other areas of the curriculum.

In following the progress of these students as they returned to regular schools, we learned that they were often found happily engaged in reading trade books (even when they should have been attending to other aspects of the curriculum) and that they made insightful contributions to discussions about what they had read. Our follow-up also revealed that these former students had difficulty demonstrating in writing their understanding of trade books, basal reader stories, and content area subject matter. Difficulty expressing themselves in writing, difficulty handling content area assignments, and difficulty exhibiting style and dispositional characteristics of successful students (e.g., attentiveness, organization, conscientiousness) were the problems most often cited when discussing the poor academic performance of former Benchmark students. As a result, we became convinced that merely accelerating the reading ability of delayed readers was not sufficient for school success. Many, if not most, of our students seemed to need reading instruction, plus something more. Consequently, our search for an appropriate program for delayed readers widened beyond teaching students how to read trade books and basals. We identified problem areas among our students who had graduated to regular schools and researched instructional techniques that we could add to our program to address these problems.

Expressing Ideas in Writing

One problem that concerned us was our students' poor written expression. We searched professional journals for insights into how to teach our delayed readers to express themselves adequately in writing. We discovered, and our experience confirmed, that children with reading problems usually demonstrate an even greater and more enduring lag in writing skills than they do in reading (Critchley & Critchley, 1978; Frauenheim, 1978; Kass, 1977). In our literature search we came across the early work of Donald Graves (1977). His ideas about process writing made sense, especially for our population of reluctant writers. We invited Graves to present several inservice programs at Benchmark. With these inservice meetings as a catalyst, the staff collaborated to develop a process approach to writing that not only succeeded in teaching our reluctant writers to write, but also seemed to enhance their reading ability (Gaskins, 1982). In the years since we implemented a process approach, we have continued to refine our writing program and, through explicit explanations, teach students how to write both expository and narrative text.

Once the process writing program was in place, we added hand-me-down computers to our classrooms, so that students could learn word processing skills. Students found revising and editing much more palatable when revised copies of their pieces could be produced by computer rather than by recopying drafts. Word processing also improved the legibility, spelling, and organization of students' writing.

Reading in the Content Areas

Another newly discovered problem we addressed about the same time as we initiated a process approach to writing was the difficulty our students experienced reading and learning from content area textbooks. Once again, a review of the research was conducted. At our weekly research seminars the staff studied and discussed the work of Cunningham and Shablak (1975), Herber (1978), Manzo (1969, 1975), Preston and Botel (1981), Reder (1980), Robinson (1961), Strange (1980), and Tuinman (1980). Based on our study and the needs of our students, the staff developed methods to address intent to learn; schema development; active involvement in searching for meaning; and the synthesis, reorganization, and application of what was learned (Gaskins, 1981). A key feature of these lessons was providing students with advance organizers, discussions about what was to be accomplished, what they presently knew, and an overview of the new content. Lessons also featured the scaffolding necessary for success, including daily reviews, homework checks, guided practice, and corrective feedback. We later learned that explicit strategy instruction that would put students in charge of their own learning was missing from these lessons. We had developed excellent lessons in how to read a text, but these lessons were too teacher driven to create students who understood how to be self-regulated learners, thinkers, and problem solvers.

Learning Words and Decoding

In the early 1980s we became convinced that instruction in neither synthetic phonics nor context clues was meeting all of our students' needs in decoding. For example, many of our students were able to recall and match the individual sounds represented by letters or letter combinations but had difficulty blending the sounds into words they recognized. Other students who used their background knowledge and the sense of a sentence to decode ran into difficulty decoding words if the information was new and they could not guess from context. Thus we undertook a literature search to learn more about teaching decoding. As a result of this search, we became aware of an analogy approach to decoding (Cunningham, 1975–76; Glushko, 1979; Santa, 1976–77). This approach made sense from both a linguistic and pedagogical perspective.

With Patricia Cunningham and Richard Anderson as consultants, we developed a Grades 1–8 program for teaching students to identify unknown words using analogous known words (Gaskins et al., 1988). In this program students are taught key words for the 120 most common phonograms (spelling patterns) in our language, as well as how to use these key words to decode unknown words (Gaskins, Downer, & Gaskins, 1986). For example, knowing the key word *king* helps a student decode *sing*, and knowing the key words *can* and *her* helps a student decode *banter*. As a result of being taught to use known words to decode unknown words, our students improved significantly in their decoding ability (Gaskins, Gaskins, Anderson, & Schommer, 1995). The program has proved successful in other schools and clinics as well (Dewitz, 1993; Gaskins, Gaskins, & Gaskins, 1991, 1992; Lovett et al., 1994).

Between 1970 and 1994 the staff continued to evaluate our reading program, study the professional literature, and make changes to address our delayed readers' needs; yet as we began our 25th year, two literacy issues still puzzled us. These were how to help all students achieve automaticity in reading words and how to improve students' spelling ability. Although by the early 1990s the vast majority of our students read with automaticity and good comprehension upon graduation from Benchmark, about 15% were exceedingly slow readers, and these same students tended to be poor spellers. We suspected that we had designed a word identification program that eventually worked for most of our students, but not all.

Once again we studied the professional literature in search of what might be missing from our present word identification program. In our reading, as well as in conversations with basic literacy researcher Linnea Ehri, we became aware that our analogy program made assumptions about word learning that were not necessarily true for all, or even most, of our students when they began the program. According to Ehri (1991) and Perfetti (1991), in order to apply an analogy approach to decoding, students need to have progressed through several phases of word learning, from the early phases of using selected visual and phonological clues to the alphabetic phase where entire words are stored in memory. According to Ehri's theory (1994), only when words have been fully analyzed with each sound matched to its corresponding letter or letters can sight words be used to decode unknown words by analogy.

Although the analogy approach to word identification that we designed in the early 1980s produced better results than our previous attempts to teach delayed readers to decode, we had a hunch we could make it even better. We had observed that nearly all of our students arrived at Benchmark stranded in the early phases of word learning. Even after a year of instruction, many still had not learned the key words with high-frequency phonograms in a fully analyzed way. Thus they were unable to call them to mind to use in decoding unknown words. In 1994 we added a sight-word-learning strategy to our word identification program. We now teach students how to learn sight words by analyzing the sounds they hear in each word and matching those sounds to the letters they see. Our initial data suggest that current students who have been taught to fully analyze words in this way are making significantly better progress in word learning than a comparison group who received only the analogy program but were not instructed in word learning (Gaskins, Ehri, Cress, O'Hara, & Donnelly, 1996).

Understanding How to Learn

Despite the changes we made in our curriculum during the late 1970s and early 1980s, we still did not produce students who could enter regular schools and be successful across the curriculum. Some students who were reading on a level commensurate with their regular school peers when they graduated from Benchmark were not as successful as we would have expected. Teachers in the regular schools often described our former students as employing unproductive strategies for learning, remembering, and completing assignments. Thus, during the 1980s, teaching students how to learn became the focus for inservice meetings, research seminars, and teacher-supervisor classroom collaboration.

We discovered that students who are delayed in reading also usually do not figure out on their own the strategies that are characteristic of successful students (Chan & Cole, 1986; Wong, 1985). They have few intuitions about how the mind works nor have they discovered, as most successful students have, how to take control of the learning process. We began to explore the literature about the cognitive and metacognitive strategies that are characteristic of successful students and, as a result of this study, set about developing a comprehensive strategies instructional program (Gaskins, 1988; Gaskins & Elliot, 1991). In developing this program we were influenced by the work of Anderson and Pearson (1984), Duffy and Roehler (1987a, 1987b), Palincsar and Brown (1984), Paris, Lipson, and Wixson (1983), and Pressley et al. (1990) and were fortunate to work with each of these experts in the development of our own program. In fact, Anderson and Pressley were frequent collaborators in Benchmark's research and development projects (e.g., Gaskins, Anderson, Pressley, Cunicelli, & Satlow, 1993; Pressley et al., 1992; Pressley, Gaskins, Wile, Cunicelli, & Sheridan, 1991).

In 1986–87 a social studies teacher, Jim Benedict, and I piloted a program to infuse cognitive and metacognitive strategies into the teaching of content-area subject matter. Jim taught middle school students American history, and I joined two of his classes each day to share information about how the brain works and what learners can do to enhance learning. Students loved learning information usually reserved for college psychology students, and the rationale this knowledge provided for strategy use seemed to convince most that it made sense to learn and employ strategies. Jim began incorporating knowledge about how the brain works, as well as strategies for enhancing learning, into his daily teaching. By spring I was out of the classroom, and Jim was teaching social studies classes infused with strategies instruction. (See Gaskins & Elliot, 1991, for the story of 8 months of collaborative teaching.)

Applying Strategies Across the Curriculum

The success of Jim's social studies classes generated interest and curiosity among the staff. Thus, the following year I began teaching a course called Psych 101 to middle school students and LAT (Learning and Thinking) to lower school students. We organized these courses around a formula for intelligent behavior (IB): IB = knowledge + control + motivation (Gaskins & Elliot, 1991). With respect to the first element of intelligent behavior, we guided students to the awareness that acquiring knowledge includes knowledge about more than the content of school subject matter. They also need knowledge about skills

and strategies, as well as about the traits and dispositions that undergird successful school performance. Each of these was discussed with students as it related to how they learn. For example, students learned that it was easier to remember new information if it is organized into 5 to 7 ideas, because most of us can only remember 5 to 7 pieces of information at one time. Experiments were conducted to prove the points that were made about how the mind works. Acquisition of different kinds of knowledge, however, is only one part of what it takes to be intelligent. *How* and *if* knowledge is used were issues central to our students' success or failure.

The "how" and "if" involve control, the second element of intelligent behavior. We taught students that being in charge of how their brains work—the control element of intelligent behavior—requires active involvement and the ability to reflect on and manage one's thinking. Students were taught that they needed to take charge of tasks, situations, and their own personal learner characteristics and were shown how to do it. The *how* was to be accomplished by learning strategies for acquiring, understanding, remembering, and completing tasks, as well as by learning how to select, apply, and monitor these strategies.

The third element of intelligent behavior is motivation—the affective component of intelligent behavior. We shared with students that motivation is the result of one's beliefs, attitudes, values, and interests. Examples were given of how approaching learning opportunities believing that you are not intelligent, or that you have an enduring ability deficit, can be self-fulfilling. The examples illustrated that such beliefs are not conducive to taking charge of learning. In fact, these beliefs tend to result in such learning characteristics as lowered expectations for success, nonpersistence, and passivity (Johnston, 1985; Torgesen, 1977).

We also taught that motivation to use strategies was specific to students' beliefs about the relationship of effort to success for a particular task. Because of this, teachers guided students to connect their successes with what they did to achieve success. Teachers emphasized that the critical factor in a successful performance is not how much time a student spent working *hard*, but rather what the student did to work *smart*.

Teachers attended Psych 101 and LAT with their students and, as a result, began to incorporate what they had heard into their own teaching. Two of the most valuable outcomes of Psych 101 and LAT lessons are that they provide students and staff with both a rationale and a common language for strategies instruction.

Some of the first comprehension strategies we taught in small reading groups were surveying, predicting, and setting purposes; identifying key elements in fiction—the characters, setting, central story problem, and resolution; and summarizing using the key elements. Other strategies followed: accessing background knowledge, making inferences, monitoring for understanding and taking remedial action when necessary, noticing patterns in text, identifying main ideas in nonfiction, organizing information, summarizing nonfiction in one's own words, and analyzing and taking charge of tasks. Our research suggested that, as compared to a comparison group, the students who received several years of strategies instruction made significant progress in understanding what they read both on reading achievement tests and on performance-based tests in social studies (Gaskins, 1994). Others have reported similar results (e.g., Dole, Brown, & Trathen, 1996). As we continued this program it was fascinating to watch how each additional year of strategy instruction at Benchmark built on the strategies learned the previous year. Those who had 4 or 5 years of this instruction tended to flourish in the regular schools they attended after Benchmark.

Teacher reports and follow-up data, however, from the early years of Benchmark's strategies instruction made us aware that our students did not automatically transfer the strategies they were learning in reading and social studies classes to the areas of the curriculum in which the strategies had not been taught. This was not unlike what other researchers have found with respect to transfer (e.g., Olsen, Wong, & Marx, 1983). Therefore, the next 3 years were devoted to applying to the teaching of mathematics and science what we had learned about teaching comprehension strategies in reading and social studies.

For example, in the year prior to applying the strategies program to science, Eleanor Gensemer and I cotaught social studies and developed a program centered on major concepts. Students were guided to discover concepts that were true of one historic episode that might also serve as an organizing schema for learning about other aspects of history. An example of this occurred in studying about the settlement of the Americas by the Native Americans. Students concluded that the geography of the land determined the culture that developed in a specific location. Once the concept was established that geography influenced the culture that developed in an area, students had a powerful schema for learning about not only the history of Native Americans of the United States, Canada, and Central America, but also the history of people in other areas of the world. For example, when they studied Mesopotamia, Egypt, Greece, and Italy, students were delighted to find that geography also influenced these cultures. Our next challenge was not only to apply what we learned

about specific strategies, such as surveying, purpose setting, and summarizing, to teaching mathematics and science, but also to apply the general strategy of using major concepts as a means of organizing and remembering ideas.

Our project focused on developing a science program that was conceptually oriented, problem-based, collaborative, and constructivist. For example, one concept that organizes science information is that all systems are interrelated; a change in one affects the rest. This concept applies to the human body or the ecology of a coral reef. In our middle school unit about the human body, students were given a problem about a family's health issues that they were to solve in collaborative groups. All the health issues were related to the circulatory system. Over a period of 6 weeks students studied these health issues, constructing understandings of heart attacks, strokes, high cholesterol, varicose veins, and other health problems related to the circulatory system. The conclusion of each collaborative group was that body systems do not operate in isolation; rather what affects one system has an impact on all the other body systems.

The research-based axioms that drive instruction for delayed readers in all areas of the curriculum, including science and mathematics, were present in the unit about body systems; employ every-pupil-response activities, encourage collaboration, focus on real-life problems, emphasize a few important concepts, teach students how to learn, and guide the construction of understanding (Gaskins, Satlow, Hyson, Ostertag, & Six, 1994). During our 3-year project to develop a strategy-based science program, we were able to integrate the teaching of science, reading, and writing in a conceptually based, constructivist curriculum and to document that students actually learned the processes that were taught (Gaskins, Guthrie et al., 1994). Mathematics teachers followed the lead of language arts, social studies, and science teachers in implementing a conceptually based, constructivist curriculum that incorporates both domain specific and general learning strategies.

The results of our strategies programs were and continue to be exciting, but we have not found a way to develop strategic students quickly. Becoming strategic across the curriculum takes many years of instruction and scaffolded practice in all subject areas, as well as instruction tailored to students' developmental levels.

Identifying Roadblocks to School Success

The schoolwide focus during the past several years has been to revisit an earlier concern about students' maladaptive styles that interfere with academic success. Our awareness of the need to address styles began 20 years ago. During the late 1970s we became increasingly aware that something about the way our students approached academic tasks was different from the way successful students approached school tasks. Beginning in 1978, we gathered data regarding 32 possible academic and nonacademic roadblocks to school success that our teachers had observed in our students. Academic roadblocks, for example, include poor comprehension, poor written expression, and poor handwriting; nonacademic roadblocks include poor attention, inflexibility, impulsivity, lack of persistence, poor home support, frequent absences, and disorganization. Data gathering was a first step in developing a plan to help individual students overcome roadblocks to academic success. Each spring teachers complete a 32-item Roadblock Questionnaire for each of their students.

In analyzing the results of our first 5 years of roadblocks data (1978–1983), we concluded that it was unlikely that just addressing academics would meet our students' needs. In the spring of 1979, for example, just 9% of 149 students were viewed as having only one roadblock; the remainder had up to 10 academic or nonacademic roadblocks. In addition, each year our students' nonreading problems varied greatly from student to student. For example, in the spring of 1980 the most common roadblock was poor written expression, yet teachers viewed this as a major roadblock to school success for only 17% of our students because many nonacademic roadblocks were of greater concern. Our review of the literature confirmed, just as Monroe (1932) had found over 50 years earlier, that in teaching delayed readers we are dealing with students who usually have more than one roadblock to school success and who have more differences than similarities (Gaskins, 1984). In light of these findings, it appeared that our program for at-risk and delayed readers had to be more comprehensive than we had initially envisioned.

We concluded that poor reading might result from, or even cause, a number of the roadblocks, and that these might persist even if the reading problem itself were solved. In view of the variety of characteristics exhibited by our delayed readers, we began to suspect that at least some of our students might need an educational program that included remedial reading, writing, and strategy instruction plus something extra to address cognitive styles, dispositions, and feelings.

Taking Charge of Personal Style and Motivation

Based on a review of the research, we developed a training program in the early 1980s to teach students how to cope with maladaptive cognitive styles

(Gaskins & Baron, 1985). For our initial research project we chose to address three of our students' problematic thinking styles: impulsivity, inflexibility, and nonpersistance. Students in the experimental group were instructed in small groups for several months about how to take charge of their maladaptive styles. Following that training and for the remainder of the school year, they met once a week with their trainer to review the goal cards that their teachers completed daily and to receive coaching about taking charge of their styles. After 8 months of small-group and individual training, students in the experimental group demonstrated significantly more awareness of and control over their maladaptive styles than did the control group.

In teaching students how to take charge of unproductive thinking styles, we also created the prototype for a staff-student mentor program. During the decade that followed the initial cognitive style training study, mentors at Benchmark were staff members who volunteered to be special adult coaches and friends to students who were experiencing difficulties in their Benchmark classes. Mentors met individually with their students at least once a week, and students could contact their mentors at other times as well. In more than a few cases mentors made the critical difference in the success of Benchmark students (Gaskins, 1992).

Our program for at-risk and delayed readers had to be more comprehensive than we had initially envisioned.

In the early 1990s the middle school staff attempted to build on these programs and find better ways to coach students to take charge of their personal styles and their learning and to apply the strategies they had been taught. The goals of the middle school staff were for students to learn to be self-regulated learners and advocates for themselves. For example, the staff wanted students to monitor more effectively their progress as they completed school tasks and to seek out the support they needed to understand and complete assignments. Psych 101 and strategies instruction had provided students with a rationale for employing strategies and knowledge of how to implement them, yet some of our middle school students were not acting on what they knew. We wondered if it was a motivation problem or whether maladaptive cognitive styles were getting in the way.

This question became the topic of research seminar study and discussion. As a result of our study, we theorized, as does Deci (1995), that choice, collaboration, and competence provide the foundation for motivation. Choice was built into most middle school activities and assignments, but some of our students did not make good choices, sometimes because they had not been attentive to the guidance given about how to make a reasoned choice and sometimes because they were not reflective in considering their options. In theory, collaboration was also part of middle school courses, but in actuality many of our students did not know how to collaborate fruitfully. They tended to be inflexible, for example, when their way of doing or thinking was challenged. Some students were not as actively involved or persistent as other group members would have liked. With respect to competence, we discovered that the staff viewed some students as more competent than the students viewed themselves.

We believe that programs that work are the result of dedicated teachers and support staff who, based on a foundation of sound theory and research, evaluate their programs and are open to new possibilities for meeting students' needs.

During the 1995–96 school year Joanne Murphy (1996) completed a follow-up study of 118 graduates of Benchmark who were in the age range 18 to 25. She found that reading level at the time of graduation from Benchmark was not as good a predictor of success in future academics as was the number of roadblocks indicated by students' teachers at the time of graduation from Benchmark. The fewer roadblocks, the more likely the student would be to do well in his or her schools after Benchmark, regardless of reading level. Based on this study and our earlier work, we were convinced that, in addition to teaching students strategies across the curriculum for reading, writing, understanding, and remembering, we also needed to do a better job of making students aware of their unproductive styles and of providing them with the rationale and strategies that would enable control of them. Styles that we targeted for emphasis were attentiveness, active involvement, persistence, reflectivity, and adaptability. Knowledge of and control over sounds, letters, words, and text were necessary, but learning how to control one's cognitive style would assure that students could put to good use what they knew about words and text. We were convinced that if we did not address maladaptive styles we would invite continued school difficulties.

In the fall of 1994 the middle school staff responded to these motivational and style issues by beginning to revamp the mentor program to better meet our 50 middle school students' needs for choice, collaboration, competence, and productive cognitive styles. The middle school staff felt that, while the present mentor program was working for our lower

school students, the middle school mentor program could be improved. In their weekly team meetings, the middle school staff decided that each staff member would be asked to mentor 4 or 5 students and that a portion of each team meeting would be devoted to staff training in mentorship by psychologist Meredith Sargent.

The middle school staff agreed to meet with their small groups during a half-hour mentor period 4 days a week to supervise and coach these students as they completed school assignments, as well as to meet with them individually to set goals and resolve issues, especially cognitive style issues, that seemed to be getting in the way of their success. During that same half-hour period one day a week middle school students met with members of the support services staff (psychologists, social workers, and counselors) for a class meeting. Class meetings were held once a week throughout the school.

Middle school mentors have become students' contact people with staff and parents. They keep track of students' progress in all courses and are in regular contact with parents. Most important, the 4 or 5 students have become each mentor's mission in life. Mentors tend to leave no stone unturned in coaching these students to adapt their styles, make smart choices, and develop interdependent collaborative relationships with staff and students. In individual and small-group mentor meetings, students are guided to understand how to take charge of both their style and their learning and how to become self-advocates. As the bonds with mentors grow, so does each student's trust. As this happens, students begin to risk implementing suggestions made by their mentors. In addition, because students have become accustomed to seeking out the help they need from their mentors, this attitude of self-advocacy carries over to other situations. Now students are more likely to approach content area and homeroom teachers for help and advice.

Staff Development and Change

As we have become aware of the special needs of our delayed readers during the past 28 years, we have searched the professional literature for insights into how to improve our program and have provided a variety of training opportunities to engage our staff in learning research-based methods for teaching and supporting delayed readers. (See Gaskins, 1994, for details of professional development opportunities at Benchmark.) As a result, the Benchmark program for delayed readers has been and is dynamic in responding to students' needs. We believe that programs that work are the result of dedicated teachers and support staff who, based on a foundation of sound theory and research, evaluate their programs and are open to new possibilities for meeting students' needs. The staff is never satisfied that they have it right. They continually adjust the way they teach and coach students. They also watch students' responses to determine what works. Because the staff engages in studies of the research literature to meet specific needs of their students, there is a sense of ownership of the programs they develop. Change is not made for the sake of change. Rather, ideas for change are carefully researched, discussed, adapted, piloted, and evaluated before being widely employed in the school.

Conclusions Based on Benchmark Experiences

At Benchmark we have discovered that, although necessary, providing an exemplary reading program adapted to the needs of individual students is not sufficient to assure the academic success of delayed readers. Other researchers have reached similar conclusions. Remedial reading programs do not usually produce successful students (e.g., Allington, 1994). Our students, originally identified for remediation because of a delay in reading, tend to exhibit additional school difficulties, even after they become readers.

It appears that children who are delayed in learning to read require more than reading instruction. They need quality programs across the curriculum characterized by staff development, congruence with regular programs, and ample time in which to learn and apply what has been taught. Such programs are grounded in teachers' understanding of instructional theory and research. These programs need to be matched to where students are, proceed according to the competencies they develop, and teach explicitly what they do not figure out on their own (Gaskins, 1997). Such instruction would be ideal for all students, but it appears to be essential for delayed readers.

Our work at Benchmark School suggests that, contrary to what we had hoped, providing delayed readers with 2 or 3 years of remedial instruction is usually not sufficient to prepare them for success in regular classes. Most delayed readers need much more. Throughout elementary and middle school they need an integrated, full-day program taught by well-trained and caring teachers who collaborate with parents; orchestrate conditions that are motivating; and teach students the strategies they will need in regular classrooms for reading, writing, understanding, remembering, completing tasks, and taking control of maladaptive styles. The program must be undergirded by ongoing and reflective professional development, including follow-up of former students. Further, it must be distinguished by its quality.

Teaching at-risk and delayed readers the skills and strategies that are congruent with success in the mainstream must begin early and continue for many years. There are no shortcuts. But, given instruction by the best teachers that is congruent with instruction in regular classrooms and that is provided over ample time, at-risk and delayed readers can be successful in the mainstream. A few will even perform better than we ever dreamed possible . . . because taking charge of one's style and being strategic about reading, writing, and learning works miracles in and out of the classroom!

References

Allington, R.L. (1994). The schools we have. The schools we need. *The Reading Teacher, 48*, 14–29.

Anderson, R.C., & Pearson, P.D. (1984). A schema-theoretic view of basic processes in reading comprehension. In P.D. Pearson (Ed.), *Handbook of reading research* (pp. 255–291). New York: Longman.

Bronfenbrenner, U. (1974). Is early intervention effective? In M. Guttentag & E. Streuning (Eds.), *Handbook of evaluation research* (Vol. 2, pp. 519–603). Beverly Hills, CA: Sage.

Center, Y., Wheldall, K., Freeman, L., Outhred, L., & McNaught, M. (1995). An evaluation of Reading Recovery. *Reading Research Quarterly, 30,* 240–263.

Chan, L.K.S., & Cole, P.G. (1986). The effects of comprehension monitoring training on the reading competence of learning disabled and regular class students. *Remedial and Special Education, 7*, 33–40.

Critchley, M., & Critchley, E.A. (1978). *Dyslexia defined*. London: William Heinemann Medical Books.

Cunningham, D., & Shablak, S.L. (1975). Selective reading guide-o-rama: The content teacher's best friend. *Journal of Reading, 18*, 380–382.

Cunningham, P.M. (1975–76). Investigating a synthesized theory of mediated word identification. *Reading Research Quarterly, 11*, 127–143.

Darling-Hammond, L. (1996). The quiet revolution: Rethinking teacher development. *Educational Leadership, 53*, 4–10.

Deci, E.L. with Flaste, R. (1995). *Why we do what we do: The dynamic of personal autonomy*. New York: G.P. Putnam's Sons.

Dewitz, P. (1993, May). *Comparing an analogy and phonics approach to word recognition*. Paper presented at the Edmund Hardcastle Henderson Roundtable in Reading, Charlottesville, VA.

Dole, J.A., Brown, K.J., & Trathen, W. (1996). The effects of strategy instruction on the comprehension performance of at-risk students. *Reading Research Quarterly, 31*, 62–88.

Dryloos, J.G. (1996). Full-service schools. *Educational Leadership, 53*, 18–23.

Duffy, G.G., & Roehier, L.R. (1987a). Improving reading instruction through the use of responsive elaboration. *The Reading Teacher, 40*, 514–520.

Duffy, G.G., & Roehier, L.R. (1987b). Teaching reading skills as strategies. *The Reading Teacher, 40*, 414–418.

Ehrl, L.C. (1991). Development of the ability to read words. In R. Barr, M. Kamil, P. Mosenthal, & P.D. Pearson (Eds.), *Handbook of reading research* (Vol. II, pp. 383–417). New York: Longman.

Ehrl, L.C. (1994). Development of the ability to read words: Update. In R. Ruddell, M. Ruddell, & H. Singer (Eds.), *Theoretical models and processes of reading* (4th ed., pp. 323–358). Newark, DE: International Reading Association.

Frauenhaim, J.G. (1978). Academic achievement characteristics of adult males who were diagnosed as dyslexlo in childhood. *Journal of Learning Disabilities, 11*, 476–483.

Gaskins, I.W. (1980). *The Benchmark story.* Media, PA: Benchmark Press.

Gaskins, I.W. (1981). Reading for learning—Going beyond basals in the elementary grades. *The Reading Teacher, 35*, 323–328.

Gaskins, I.W. (1982). A writing program for poor readers and the rest of the class, too. *Language Arts, 59*, 854–861.

Gaskins, I.W. (1984). There's more to a reading problem than poor reading. *Journal of Learning Disabilities, 17*, 467–471.

Gaskins, I.W. (1988). Teachers as thinking coaches: Creating strategic learners and problem solvers. *Journal of Reading, Writing, and Learning Disabilities, 4*, 35–48.

Gaskins, I.W. (1994). Classroom applications of cognitive science: Teaching poor readers how to learn, think, and problem solve. In K. McGilly (Ed.), *Classroom lessons* (pp. 129–154). Cambridge, MA: MIT Press.

Gaskins, I.W. (1997). Teaching the delayed reader: The Benchmark School model. In J. Flood, S. Health, & D. Lapp (Eds.), *Handbook of research on teaching literacy through the communicative and visual arts* (pp. 677–687). New York: Macmillan.

Gaskins, I.W., Anderson, R.C., Pressley, M., Cunicelli, E.A., & Satlow, E. (1993). Six teachers' dialogue during cognitive process instruction. *The Elementary School Journal, 93*, 277–304.

Gaskins, I.W., & Baron, J. (1985). Teaching poor readers to cope with maladaptive cognitive styles: A training program. *Journal of Learning Disabilities, 18*, 390–394.

Gaskins, I.W., Downer, M.A., Anderson, R.C., Cunningham, P.M., Gaskins, R.W., Schommer, M., & the teachers of Benchmark School. (1988). A metacognitive approach to phonics: Using what you know to decode what you don't know. *Remedial and Special Education, 9*, 36–41, 66.

Gaskins, I.W., Downer, M.A., & Gaskins, R.W. (1986). *Introduction to the Benchmark School word identification/vocabulary development program.* Media, PA: Benchmark Press.

Gaskins, I.W., Ehri, L.C., Cress, C., O'Hara, C., & Donnelly, K. (1996). Procedures for word learning: Making discoveries about words. *The Reading Teacher, 50*, 2–18.

Gaskins, I.W., & Elliot, T.T. (1991). *Implementing cognitive strategy instruction across the school: The Benchmark manual for teachers.* Cambridge, MA: Brookline.

Gaskins, I.W., Guthrie, J.T., Sallow, E., Ostertag, J., Six, L., Byrne, J., & Conner, B. (1994). Integrating instruction of science, reading, and writing: Goals, teacher development, and assessment. *Journal of Research in Science Teaching, 31*, 1039–1058.

Gaskins, I.W., Sallow, E., Hyson, D., Ostertag, J., & Six, L. (1994). Classroom talk about text: Learning in science class. *Journal of Reading, 37*, 558–565.

Gaskins, R.W. (1992). When good instruction is not enough: A mentor program. *The Reading Teacher, 45*, 568–572.

Gaskins, R.W., Gaskins, I.W., Anderson, R.C., & Schommer, M. (1995). The reciprocal relationship between research and development: An example involving a decoding strand for poor readers. *Journal of Reading Behavior, 27*, 337–377.

Gaskins, R.W., Gaskins, J.C., & Gaskins, I.W. (1991). A decoding program for poor readers—and the rest of the class, too. *Language Arts, 68*, 213–225.

Gaskins, R.W., Gaskins, J.C., & Gaskins, I.W. (1992). Using what you know to figure out what you don't know: An analogy approach to decoding. *Reading and Writing Quarterly, 8*, 197–221.

Glushko, R.J. (1979). The organization and activation of orthographic knowledge in reading aloud. *Journal of Experimental Psychology: Human Perception and Performance, 5*, 674–691.

Graves, D.H. (1977). Research update—Language arts textbooks: A writing process evaluation. *Language Arts, 54*, 817–823.

Herber, H.L. (1978). *Teaching reading in content areas* (2nd ed.). Englewood Cliffs, NJ: Prentice-Hall.

Hieberl, E.H. (1994). Reading Recovery in the United States: What differences does it make to an age cohort? *Educational Researcher, 23*(9), 15–25.

Johnston, P. (1985). Understanding reading disability: A case study approach. *Harvard Educational Review, 55*, 153–177.

Johnston, P.H., Allington, R.L., & Afflerbach, P. (1985). Congruence of classroom and remedial reading instruction. *The Elementary School Journal, 85*, 485–478.

Kass, C.E. (1977). Identification of learning disability (dyssymbolia). *Journal of Learning Disabilities, 10*, 425–432.

Lovelt, M.W., Borden, S.L, DeLuca, T., Lacerenza, L., Benson, N., & Brackstone, D. (1994). Treating the core deficits of developmental dyslexia: Evidence of transfer of learning after phonologically- and strategy-based reading training programs. *Developmental Psychology, 30*, 805–822.

Manzo, A.V. (1969). ReQuest: A method for improving reading comprehension through reciprocal questioning. *Journal of Reading, 12*, 123–126, 163.

Manzo, A.V. (1975). Guided reading procedure. *Journal of Reading, 18*, 287–291.

Monroe, M. (1932). *Children who cannot read.* Chicago: University of Chicago Press.

Muehl, S., & Forell, E. (1973–74). A follow-up study of disabled readers: Variables related to high school reading performance. *Reading Research Quarterly, 9*, 110–123.

Murphy, J. (1996). *A follow-up study of delayed readers and an investigation of factors related to their success in young adulthood.* Unpublished doctoral dissertation, University of Pennsylvania, Philadelphia.

Olsen, J.L., Wong, B.Y.L., & Marx, R.W. (1983). Linguistic and metacognitive aspects of normally achieving and learning-disabled children's communication process. *Learning Disabilities Quarterly, 6,* 289–304.

Page, E.B., & Grandon, G.M. (1981). Massive intervention and child intelligence. The Milwaukee project in critical perspective. *Journal of Special Education, 15,* 239–256.

Palinscar, A.S., & Brown, A.L. (1984). Reciprocal teaching of comprehension-fostering and comprehension-monitoring activities. *Cognition and Instruction, 1,* 117–175.

Paris, S.G., Lipson, M.Y., & Wixson, K.K. (1983). Becoming a strategic reader, *Contemporary Educational Psychology, 8,* 293–316.

Perfetti, C.A. (1991). Representations and awareness in the acquisition of reading competence. In L. Rieben & C.A. Perfetti (Eds.). *Learning to read: Basic research and its implication* (pp. 33–44). Hillsdale, NJ: Erlbaum.

Pikulski, J.J. (1994). Preventing reading failure: A review of live effective programs. *The Reading Teacher, 48,* 30–39.

Pinnell, G.S., Lyons, C., DeFord, D., Bryk, A., & Selizer, M. (1994). Comparing instructional models for the literacy education of high-risk first graders. *Reading Research Quarterly, 29,* 9–39.

Pressley, M., El-Dinary, P.B., Gaskins, I., Schuder, T., Bergman, J.L., Almasi, J., & Brown, R. (1992). Beyond direct explanation: Transactional instruction of reading comprehension strategies. *The Elementary School Journal, 92,* 513–555.

Pressley, M., Gaskins, I.W., Wile, D., Cunicelli, B., & Sheridan, J. (1991). Teaching literacy strategies across the curriculum: A case study at Benchmark School. In S. McCormick & J. Zutell (Eds.), *Learner factors/teacher factors: Issues in literacy research and instruction, 40th yearbook of the National Reading Conference* (pp. 219–228). Chicago: National Reading Conference.

Pressley, M., Woloshyn, V., Lysynchuk, L.M., Martin, V., Wood, E., & Willoughby, T. (1990). A primer of research on cognitive strategy instruction: The important issues and how to address them. *Educational Psychology Review, 2,* 1–58.

Preston, R.C., & Botel, M. (1981). *How to study.* Chicago: Science Research Associates.

Reder, L.M. (1980). The role of elaboration in comprehension and retention of prose: A critical review. *Review of Educational Research, 50,* 5–53.

Robinson, F.P. (1961). *Effective study* (rev. ed.). New York: Harper & Row.

Santa, C.M. (1976–77). Spelling patterns and the development of flexible word recognition strategies. *Reading Research Quarterly, 12,* 125–144.

Shanahan, T., & Barr, R. (1995). Reading Recovery: An independent evaluation of the effects of an early instructional intervention for at-risk learners. *Reading Research Quarterly, 30,* 958–996.

Slavin, R.E., Madden, N.A., Karwelt, N.L, Dolan, L.J., & Wasik, B.A. (1994). Success for All: A comprehensive approach to prevention and early intervention. In R. Slavin, N. Karweit, & B. Wasik (Eds.), *Preventing early school failure: Research, policy, and practice* (pp. 175–205). Needham Heights, MA: Allyn & Bacon.

Spache, G. (1981). *Diagnosing and correcting reading disabilities* (2nd ed.). Boston: Allyn & Bacon.

Spiegel, D.L. (1995). A comparison of traditional remedial programs and Reading Recovery: Guidelines for success for all programs. *The Reading Teacher, 49,* 86–96.

Strang, R. (1966). *Reading diagnosis and remediation.* Newark, DE: International Reading Association.

Strange, M. (1980). Instructional implications of a conceptual theory of reading comprehension. *The Reading Teacher, 33,* 391–397.

Torgesen, J.K. (1977). The role of nonspecific factors in the task performance of learning-disabled children: A theoratical assessment. *Journal of Learning Disabilities, 10,* 27–34.

Tuinman, J.J. (1980). The scheme schemers. *Journal of Reading, 23,* 404–419.

Wong, B.Y.L. (1985). Self-questioning instructional research: A review. *Review of Educational Research, 55,* 227–268.

STUDY GUIDE

1. What are the popular assumptions that under-gird government policy and pedagogical responses to struggling readers? Why are these assumptions problematic? (McGill-Franzen & Allington)

2. How can the needs of struggling readers be best supported: through the context of regular classroom reading programs, special/compensatory education programs, or a combination of both? (McGill-Franzen & Allington; Morris; Gaskin)

3. Identify 2–3 classroom reading programs (e.g., Success for All) and 2–3 tutorial models (e.g., Reading Recovery) that have documented success with struggling readers. Compare and contrast the components and key features of these programs. (McGill-Franzen & Allington; Morris)

4. Why is it critical that we make sure children learn to read by the end of third grade? (Morris)

5. How is today's pedagogical context for struggling readers similar to and different from that of the past few decades? What do we learn about teaching struggling readers by tracing pedagogical shifts over time? (Morris)

6. What can primary grade teachers do to ensure that their struggling readers are reading at grade level by the end of the school year? (Morris)

7. In her second edition of *An Observation Survey of Early Literacy Achievement* (2002), Marie Clay wrote, "For a good programme [for children of low achievement in classroom settings] you need a very experienced teacher who has been trained to think incisively about the reading process and who is sensitive to individual differences; a teacher who has continued to seek professional development, and under-

stands the literacy issues of the day, and the particular programme the school is delivering" (p. 25). This is not what happens in many American schools, however. For example, many tutoring programs for struggling readers use volunteers or other paraprofessionals. Given limited personnel and financial resources facing these schools, how can the effectiveness of these tutoring programs be maximized? (Morris)

8. Compared to typical public schools in your area, what is unique about the Benchmark School? (Gaskins)

9. Identify and describe 3–5 elements that are critical for the success of school-based initiatives in teaching struggling readers. (Gaskins)

10. What does Irene Gaskins mean when she states that there is more to teaching struggling readers than just good reading instruction? (Gaskins)

11. Identify at least five roadblocks to success that are experienced by struggling readers. Describe how the Benchmark School addresses these roadblocks. (Gaskins)

12. What does the experience of the Benchmark School tell us about the complexities, challenges, and promises of teaching struggling readers? (Gaskins)

13. The three articles in this section suggest that teaching struggling readers is an incredibly complex and challenging task. Do you think regular classroom teachers have the will, expertise, and resources to provide such demanding instruction in the current high-stakes testing and standards-based educational climate? Support your argument with research evidence and practical examples. (McGill-Franzen & Allington; Morris; Gaskins)

INQUIRY PROJECTS

1. In the current accountability-driven and high-stakes testing educational climate, schools are under immense pressure to improve instruction for struggling readers. Many turn to scripted commercial reading programs for a "quick fix," hoping that the programs will do the trick. While such pre-packaged programs claim to feature "best current practices" and be based on "scientifically-based reading

research," their quality has been a source of constant concern among literacy educators. Suppose that you serve on a school district textbook adoption committee. What criteria or principles do you think should be considered for adopting a remedial reading program? Identify one or two classroom remedial reading programs and evaluate their quality based on your criteria.

2. Identify a low-performing elementary school in your local area and interview a representative sample of struggling readers on what they perceive to be the roadblocks to their success in the classroom. Then interview the school principal, curriculum resource teacher, classroom teachers, special education teachers, and parents on what they consider to be the barriers to, as well as solutions for, supporting the literacy growth of struggling readers. Compare and contrast the views of these different stakeholders.

3. In an elementary classroom, observe one good reader and one struggling reader (as identified by their classroom teachers) for one typical day. Document the nature and type of reading/literacy instruction provided to these two students. Compare and contrast their experiences in the classroom. Discuss the educational implications of your findings.

FURTHER READING

Allington, R. L. (1998). *Teaching struggling readers: Articles from* The Reading Teacher. Newark, DE: International Reading Association.

Allington, R. L. (2001). *What really matters for struggling readers.* New York: Longman.

Allington, R. L., & Walmsley, S. A. (1995). *No quick fix: Rethinking literacy programs in American elementary schools.* New York: Teachers College Press and Newark, DE: International Reading Association.

Barone, D. (1999). *Resilient children: Stories of poverty, drug exposure, and literacy development.* Newark, DE: International Reading Association and Chicago, IL: National Reading Conference.

Block, C. (2003). *Literacy difficulties: Diagnosis and instruction for reading specialists and classroom teachers* (2nd ed.). Boston: Allyn & Bacon.

Bryant, P., & Bradley, L. (1994). *Children's reading problems.* Oxford: Blackwell.

Duffy-Hester, A. (1999). Teaching struggling readers in elementary school classrooms: A review of classroom reading programs and principles for instruction. *The Reading Teacher, 52*(5), 480–495.

Knapp, M. S. (1995). *Teaching for meaning in high-poverty classrooms.* New York: Teachers College Press.

Lyons, C. (2003). *Teaching struggling readers: How to use brain-based research to maximize learning.* Portsmouth, NH: Heinemann.

McCormack, R., & Paratore, J. (2003). *After early intervention, then what? Teaching struggling readers in grades 3 and beyond.* Newark, DE: International Reading Association.

Moore, D. W., Alvermann, D. E., & Hinchman, K. A. (2000). *Struggling adolescent readers: Articles from* The Reading Teacher. Newark, DE: International Reading Association.

Rhodes, L. K., & Dudley-Marling, C. (1996). *Readers and writers with a difference: A holistic approach to teaching struggling readers and writers* (2nd ed.). Portsmouth, NH: Heinemann.

Snow, C., Bruns, M. S., & Griffin, P. (1998). *Preventing reading difficulties in young children.* Washington, DC: National Academy Press.

Spear-Swerling, L., & Sternberg, R. (1997). *Off-track: When poor readers become "learning disabled."* Boulder, CO: Westview.

Stanovich, K. E. (2000). *Progress in understanding reading: scientific foundations and new frontiers.* New York: Guilford Press.

Strickland, D., Ganske, K., & Monroe, J. (2001). *Supporting struggling readers and writers: Strategies for classroom intervention 3–6.* Portland, ME: Stenhouse and Newark, DE: International Reading Association.

Teaching Diverse Learners

INTRODUCTION

In a multicultural and multilingual society like ours, tremendous diversity exists in the student population of our public schools. This diversity is manifested in many ways. In addition to differences in ethnic, economic, and cultural backgrounds, we have students who are bilingual, second-language learners, and speakers of nonstandard dialects of English. How can educators capitalize on the opportunities, as well as meet the challenges, that such diversity presents, especially in today's educational climate where legislative attempts to standardize curriculum and pedagogy have intensified? The three articles in this section address this and other important questions surrounding literacy instruction for these diverse learners.

In the first article, Kathryn Au focuses her discussion on the intersection of three prominent topics in the current debate on early literacy instruction: constructivist approaches, phonics, and literacy learning of nonmainstream learners (whom she calls "students of diverse backgrounds"). She expresses her concerns about the impact that the current push for "back to basics" education may have on students, teachers, and the teaching profession. Based on her own work with the Hawaiian children and that of other scholars, the author describes what she has learned about best literacy practices for students of diverse backgrounds. She argues that approaches that use a constructivist framework, such as literature-based instruction and process writing, are more empowering and ultimately more effective for working with students of diverse backgrounds. She encourages teachers to make tough choices in light of the mounting legislative mandates by creating and championing policy alternatives that are consistent with constructivist approaches.

In the second article, Ofelia Miramontes focuses her discussion on literacy instruction for the English-language learners whom she labels "linguistically diverse students." The author challenges the traditional assumptions about bilingualism and about the linguistically diverse students and their families/communities. She presents the typical educational lives and experiences of linguistically diverse learners through the example of an 11-year-old Latino student named Alfredo. She argues that in order to put existing knowledge about effective literacy instruction to use with linguistically diverse learners, we need to break out of our tradition of compensatory thinking about diversity and away from the traditional ways of thinking about and doing school. She suggests that a more equitable and just education for linguistically diverse students will need to attend to both their social and academic development. Finally, she presents 10 basic principles for guiding the development, implementation, and evaluation of sound literacy programs for linguistically diverse students.

In the third article, John Baugh sheds light on some persistent issues of language and literacy among African Americans, the largest population of nonstandard-dialect speakers in the United States. He reminds us that, unlike other immigrants who came to the United States in search of freedom and wealth, people from Africa first came to America involuntarily as slaves. He suggests that this immigration history, coupled with subsequent racial discrimination and segregation, has had a profound impact on the literacy development of African American students. Drawing upon sociolinguistic studies, the author notes that African American Vernacular English (AAVE), as a product of particular historical and social circumstances, is just as logical and coherent as other varieties of English, including Standard English. He proposes that educators adopt a pedagogy that is mindful of the linguistic skills students bring to school and that fosters the development of competence in academic registers/styles as an additional linguistic resource.

Constructivist Approaches, Phonics, and the Literacy Learning of Students of Diverse Backgrounds

Kathryn H. Au
University of Hawaii

Once again we find ourselves faced with a push "back to basics." I am deeply concerned about this push because of the significant strides we have made as a field toward understanding constructivist approaches to literacy instruction and their benefits, especially to the literacy learning of students of diverse backgrounds. In this paper I want to look at the intersection of three topics that figure prominently in the current debate: constructivist approaches to literacy instruction, phonics, and the literacy learning of students of diverse backgrounds.

My perspective on these topics has been shaped by the 24 years I spent working at the Kamehameha Elementary Education Program (KEEP) in Hawaii. The purpose of KEEP was to improve the literacy achievement of students of Hawaiian ancestry enrolled in public schools. These students typically come from low-income families, grow up speaking Hawaii Creole English (a nonmainstream variety of English) and, as a group, score in the lowest quartile on standardized tests of reading achievement. As a beginning teacher, I quickly learned that students could attend school yet still be outsiders to the processes of schooling. In September 1972, we enrolled the first class of kindergarten students at KEEP. I clearly remember the first time I read a story to the class. I called the children to sit in front of me, on the carpet. One of the boys, whom I will-call Keoki, eagerly joined the group but sat with his back to me. I began to read, expecting him to turn around, but he did not. Instead, he sat quietly, studying the expressions on the faces of the other children. Keoki's behavior surprised me, but I realized that he was not being disobedient. Evidently, he had not previously participated in this kind of reading event, and his classmates were of more interest to him than the story. This incident involving Keoki is symbolic of many I have witnessed as a teacher and researcher, incidents in which Hawaiian children literally and figuratively turned their backs on literacy in the classroom.

I do not support the narrow focus of "back to basics" instruction because my research with Hawaiian students, and my experience as a classroom teacher, have shown me that phonics is just one part of children's literacy learning during the first years of elementary school. It is an essential part but as I will explain neither the starting point nor the most important element. In this paper, I draw upon three sources of information. The first is our research at KEEP on a constructivist literacy curriculum, centered on writers' and readers' workshops. The second source of information is the larger body of research conducted by others, and the third is the experience of the teachers with whom I have worked.

Phonics is just one part of children's literacy learning during the first years of elementary school. It is an essential part but . . . neither the starting point nor the most important element.

Let me proceed by outlining some key terms I use in this paper. By *constructivist approaches to literacy instruction* I refer to approaches based on the idea that students create their own understandings of literacy in the context of the various aspects of their lives. A constructivist orientation may be contrasted with a behaviorist orientation, which emphasizes the transmission of knowledge from teacher to students, rather than students' construction of their own understandings (Au & Carroll, 1996). In constructivist approaches, the teacher initiates instruction by getting students interested and involved in the full processes of reading and writing, and skills are taught as part of students' engagement with meaningful literacy activities. Constructivist approaches to literacy instruction include the process approach to writing (Calkins, 1994; Graves, 1983, 1994), literature-based instruction (Raphael & Au, 1998; Roser & Martinez, 1995), whole language (Goodman, 1986;

From Au, K. (1998). Constructivist approaches, phonics, and the literacy of learning of students of diverse backgrounds.[1] In Shanahan, T. & Rodriquez-Brown, F. *National Reading Conference Yearbook, 47, pp. 1–21.* Used with permission.

Weaver, 1990), and balanced literacy instruction (Au, Carroll, & Scheu, 1997; Strickland, 1994–95). These approaches and philosophies are consistent with a constructivist or interpretivist paradigm (Guba & Lincoln, 1994; Spivey, 1997) and the sociocultural or sociohistorial perspective, as exemplified in the work of Vygotsky (1987) and extended to literacy research and education by scholars such as Moll (1990).

I understand *phonics* to be the teaching of letter-sound correspondences. The term phonics is commonly used to refer to the letter-sound correspondences themselves, as in the phrase "phonics instruction" or in the statement, "Children need to know phonics." Certainly, knowledge of letter-sound correspondences is the basis for decoding words. However, phonics is not the only type of word-identification instruction that students need. Students also must learn to recognize nondecodable words (a category that includes many of the most frequently occurring words), to analyze multisyllabic words, and to make use of base words and affixes.

I use the term *students of diverse backgrounds,* within the United States, to refer to students who are African American, Asian American, Latino, or Native American in ethnicity; who speak a first language other than standard American English; and who come from low-income families. (Although I will be making some generalizations about students of diverse backgrounds as a group, I want to begin by recognizing the immense variability in their cultural and linguistic circumstances, as well as important differences among individuals.) I will argue that constructivist approaches to literacy instruction can be highly beneficial for these students. This conclusion is supported not only by our research at KEEP but by studies by Dahl and Freppon (1995). Morrow and her colleagues (Morrow, 1992; Morrow, Pressley, Smith, & Smith, 1997), and others.

As events have transpired, phonics and skills have become the key issues that must be addressed, if constructivist approaches to literacy instruction are to win wider acceptance in schools. These issues must be addressed for both instructional and political reasons. First, as literacy researchers and teacher educators, we do need to have a clear understanding of the role of phonics and skill instruction within constructivist approaches, especially for students of diverse backgrounds. Second, we must be able to communicate clearly with policy makers, parents, and the general public. Many NRC members have already been involved in the acrimonious debates centering on issues of phonics and skill instruction—debates with significant implications in the larger political context (Pearson, 1997). If we fail to establish our standing and credibility in these debates, we will increasingly see literacy instruction in classrooms being deter-

mined by legislative mandate rather than by sound professional judgment built on knowledge of research, theory, and practice.

I have written recently about my reasons for recommending a constructivist, process approach to writing, in the form of the writers' workshop, as the starting point for literacy instruction in classrooms with students of diverse backgrounds (Au, 1997a). In this paper, I focus primarily on a constructivist approach to the teaching of reading and literature-based instruction because at present the major debates in our field and in the political arena revolve around these topics. I turn now to six understandings I have gained, from my own research and the research of others, about the teaching of reading within a constructivist framework.

Understandings from Research

Ownership Is the Overarching Goal Within a Broad View of the Curriculum

My first understanding has to do with the breadth of the elementary language arts curriculum and the shift from reading, narrowly defined, to literacy, broadly defined. In research at KEEP, we worked with a curriculum with six aspects of literacy, as shown in Figure 1. The aspects of literacy were ownership, the writing process, reading comprehension, vocabulary development, word reading and spelling strategies, and voluntary reading (Au, Scheu, Kawakami, & Herman, 1990). This curriculum recognized the connections between reading and writing and the importance of affective dimensions of literacy, as well as cognitive ones.

Perhaps our most important discovery was that ownership of literacy needed to be the overarching goal of the curriculum. Ownership may be defined as students' valuing of literacy (Au, 1997b). Ownership is seen when students not only have positive attitudes about literacy but make it a part of their everyday lives, at home as well as in school. Students

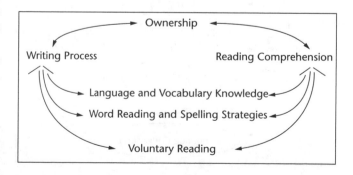

Figure 1 KEEP literacy curriculum.

demonstrate ownership by reading books of their own choosing, keeping journals, and sharing books with one another, even when these activities are not assigned by the teacher. The importance of ownership is supported in recent research on the engagement perspective by Guthrie, Alvermann, and their colleagues at the National Reading Research Center (Guthrie & Alvermann, 1998). The engagement perspective looks beyond the question of *how* people read to the question of *why* someone would want to read in the first place.

The view of the literacy curriculum reflected in the six aspects of literacy is largely process oriented, which I believe is typical of constructivist language arts curricula developed in the late 1980s and early 1990s. Views of the literacy curriculum have now shifted somewhat, as shown in Figure 2, which comes from a recent chapter that Raphael and I wrote (Au & Raphael, 1998).

There are two differences between these curricula that I want to explore. First, the heading *literary aspects* represents a recognition that the literacy curriculum must address content and not just process. Literary aspects include the themes developed through literature, or the ideas that hold the story together and that will be remembered long after details of the plot and setting have faded from memory (Lukens, 1990). Literary elements also include point of view, plot, and characters. Of course, the purpose of addressing literary aspects is to enhance the reader's response to the literature, whether that response is personal, creative, or critical.

Second, the heading *language conventions* reflects the idea that literacy is a social process requiring interactional skills and not just text-based skills and strategies. This element encompasses the aspects of literacy represented in the KEEP framework by the headings *language and vocabulary knowledge* and *word reading and spelling strategies*. Besides addressing the traditional skill areas of vocabulary, word identification, grammar, punctuation, and other

mechanics, this area deals with the conventions of interaction students must know to participate appropriately in literacy events. Many of these language conventions may be more familiar to mainstream students than to students of diverse backgrounds.

In short, current research shows the breadth of the literacy curriculum. Many studies document the importance of all of these curriculum elements in students' development as readers and writers (Guthrie & Alvermann, 1998; Raphael & Au, 1998).

What about the place of phonics in this picture? Phonics is part of one of the five elements in the contemporary literacy curriculum. Phonics cannot be neglected, but there is wide consensus in the literacy research community that it should not be seen as the whole of reading, even at the kindergarten and first-grade levels. As I will explain, research conducted at KEEP indicates that students of diverse backgrounds, who originally turned their backs on literacy in the classroom, may develop greater proficiency in word identification when instruction begins by promoting ownership and not just skills (Au, 1994).

Constructivist Approaches Improve Both Word Identification and Higher Level Thinking About Text

My second understanding concerns the importance of providing students at all grades with instruction in comprehension and composition, complex literacy processes requiring higher level thinking. Teaching all students to think with text must be our highest priority.

In our initial work with a constructivist curriculum at KEEP, we made an interesting discovery. The results shown in Figure 3 illustrate the pattern we observed for 2 consecutive years with nearly 2,000 students in six schools in Grades 1 through 3, as measured by a portfolio assessment system anchored in grade-level benchmarks (Au, 1994). We saw better achievement results in some aspects of literacy than in others. The results for these aspects of literacy are shown above the heavy line in the figure, and they are ownership of literacy, voluntary reading, and word reading strategies. What happened, I believe, was that KEEP teachers focused on promoting students' ownership of literacy, and they encouraged students to read books, at home as well as at school. They set aside time daily for sustained silent reading, and the vast majority of students developed the habit of daily reading. Because of this increase in independent reading, students' fluency and accuracy in word identification improved, as indicated in individually administered running records (Clay, 1985). We were particularly surprised to find 39% of the

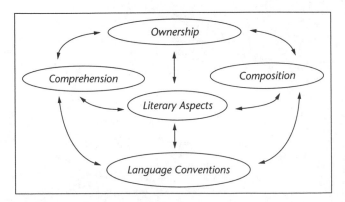

Figure 2 Current literacy curriculum.

second graders performing above grade level, which in this case meant that they could accurately decode texts at the 3.2 level. Achievement lagged in the other three aspects of literacy: the writing process, reading comprehension, and language and vocabulary knowledge.

These initial results show that gains in word identification were somewhat easier to obtain with constructivist curricula than gains in the more complex literacy processes—composition, comprehension, and the learning of concepts and vocabulary. With the KEEP students, and very likely with other students of diverse backgrounds, word identification was neither as difficult for teachers to teach, nor for students to learn, as these more complex processes. In other words, our findings at KEEP contradict the impression that constructivist approaches are somehow detrimental to students' development of word-identification ability.

In our last 2 years of work with the constructivist curriculum at KEEP, we focused on improving students' higher level thinking about text, particularly in the writing process. We found that a constructivist curriculum was effective in improving students' achievement in these areas, but that teachers needed to implement this curriculum fully (Au & Carroll, 1997). Unlike constructivist approaches, basic skill approaches, such as commercial programs that emphasize phonics drills, ignore the more complex literacy processes and cannot lead to improvement in these processes. There is a mistaken tendency to believe that basic skills approaches are particularly beneficial for students of diverse backgrounds, who may appear from a mainstream perspective to be lacking in certain ways of thinking. This unfortunate tendency may prevent these students from receiving instruction that will be the most valuable to them in the long run, and that is instruction in higher level thinking about text.

Our findings at KEEP do not fit with the views of those who put phonics first and foremost, but they will come as no surprise to those familiar with the extensive research base on comprehension instruction developed during the 1980s. We learned early on, most notably from a study by Anderson, Mason, and Shirey (1984), that comprehension does not result naturally as a consequence of students being able to decode every word in a text. Researchers demonstrated that strategy instruction could improve students' comprehension, in terms of their ability to make inferences (Hansen & Pearson, 1983), identify the main idea (Baumann, 1984), summarize a text (Taylor, 1982), and monitor their own understanding (Palincsar & Brown, 1984). Recent work by Beck and McKeown (Beck, McKeown, Sandora, Kucan, & Worthy, 1996), in which students are taught to "question

Aspect of Literacy	% Above	% At	% Below	Missing Data
Ownership	30	19	46	5
Voluntary Reading	71	24	5	0
Word Reading Strategies	39	20	38	2
Writing Process	0	33	55	11
Reading Comprehension	5	31	59	5
Language & Vocabulary	3	37	54	6

Figure 3 Initial results: grade 2.

the author," builds on this foundation and points to the centrality of active engagement with text, including literature.

Concepts of comprehension have been enriched with the growing interest in literature-based instruction, which has its theoretical basis in reader response theory. Rosenblatt's (1978) work established the distinction between the aesthetic and efferent stances and argued persuasively for the predominance of the aesthetic stance in the reading of literature. Our views of what it means to comprehend have been broadened to encompass personal response, which includes the emotions called forth by the literature and the ability to see connections between literature and one's own life.

Phonics Instruction Should Be Properly Timed

In terms of the third understanding, it is clear to me that phonics cannot be the first or only focus for beginning readers, particularly for young children such as Keoki, who are likely to turn their backs on literacy learning in the classroom. The timing of phonics instruction for these children is critical. In fact, in kindergarten and first grade, an overemphasis on phonics instruction, to the exclusion of other literacy activities, may prevent these children from developing the concepts and background necessary for the later development of word-identification ability. Let me explain this point by referring to a discussion in a recent chapter by Stahl (1997). Citing common findings in the work of a number of researchers (Biemiller, 1970; Chall, 1983; Frith, 1985; Lomax & McGee, 1987; McCormick & Mason, 1986), Stahl notes that children go through three broad stages in learning to identify words: awareness, accuracy, and automaticity.

In the first stage, *awareness,* children are developing a conceptual understanding of the nature of written language and its relationship to spoken language. This understanding covers four areas. The first, functions of print, involves understanding, for example, that print can be used to tell stories. The second, conventions of print, includes knowing that one reads from left to right and from the top of the page to the bottom. The third, forms of print, encompasses the letters of the alphabet. The fourth, awareness of phonemes, entails the notion that spoken words can be broken into separate sounds or phonemes, an understanding central to the later learning of letter-sound correspondences. Stahl asserts that these four aspects of the relationship between written and spoken language serve as the foundation for children's later development as readers, and that children will experience difficulty in learning to read if they lack any of these aspects.

To complete the picture: in the second stage, *accuracy*, children learn to decode words accurately. They focus on print and work to identify words correctly. Children read text aloud in a laborious, choppy, word-by-word fashion, a phenomenon usually termed "word calling." Stahl notes that this stage is generally short lived, leading quickly into the third stage, *automaticity*, when children come to recognize words automatically. The transition from accuracy to automaticity usually occupies the time from the end of first grade to the end of third grade, although it may be prolonged for struggling readers. The rapid, automatic recognition of words is, of course, necessary to free up information processing capacity for comprehension of the text.

This overview of the development of word-identification ability suggests to me that phonics instruction should be emphasized when children are in the accuracy stage, not when they are in the awareness stage, or when they are in the automaticity stage. Phonics plays a crucial but temporary role, and phonics instruction must be properly timed to achieve its optimal effect. Literacy researchers agree that phonics cannot be seen as a blanket approach to beginning reading instruction because knowledge of letter-sound correspondences is not the first, or the only thing, that children need to learn as they develop the ability to identify words.

In a conversation about research on emergent literacy in *Reading Research Quarterly*, McGee and Purcell-Gates (1997) draw a conclusion that is not new but is often forgotten in current debates: "Children learn to read and write successfully if their teachers accommodate their instruction *to* the children, and they struggle if they do not" (p. 312). This statement certainly applies to young Hawaiian children, who are in the awareness stage when they first arrive in kindergarten. At KEEP we administered emergent literacy tasks (based on the work of Mason

& Stewart, 1989) to children entering kindergarten. The typical child could name perhaps one to three letters of the alphabet, often letters that appeared in his or her name, but could not use magnetic letters to represent the first or last sounds of any words. When shown the page of a simple book and asked where there was something to read, the typical child pointed to the illustration, not to the print. Clearly, the typical child was not yet attending to print. Many KEEP kindergarteners, like Keoki, had little or no experience with family storybook reading, and most had not attended preschool.

Unless there is good evidence that kindergarten children are already in or near the accuracy stage, it appears harmful to their overall literacy development to begin with an emphasis on the teaching of phonics in isolation. Note that I am not opposed to an early introduction to phonics, but to the teaching of phonics for its own sake, apart from literacy activities that children will find meaningful. Some kindergarten teachers emphasize drill on letter names and sounds in isolation, a form of teaching that is too abstract for many children. In my observations in classrooms with Hawaiian children, I have seen repeatedly that most fail to benefit at all from these isolated activities. Some children are completely mystified, whereas others gain the impression that reading is nothing more than a process of rote learning and sounding out. Neither of these outcomes is desirable.

This type of teaching cannot replace instructional activities, such as shared reading or the writing of their own stories, that provide children with meaningful contexts for the learning of letter-sound correspondences. These activities allow children to develop understandings of the four aspects of written-spoken language relationships that form the foundation for later acquisition of letter-sound correspondences. Phonics instruction can certainly be introduced as part of shared reading and children's writing of their own stories, as I will describe next, but phonics should not be taught apart from these meaningful literacy activities.

Writing Makes a Significant Contribution to Children's Learning of Phonics

My fourth understanding concerns the contributions of writing, specifically invented spelling, to children's learning of phonics. In KEEP primary-grade classrooms, teachers conducted a writers' workshop four or five times a week. For kindergarten teachers, introducing the writers' workshop took courage. In September, most kindergarten students are drawing, and just a few are scribbling or using letter-like forms. In classrooms in rural schools, there is often a child who has not had the experience of holding a pencil or crayon and drawing with it.

During the writers' workshop, kindergarten teachers promoted children's understandings of print in many ways. They modeled writing during the morning message and had children make observations about the print in the message (Crowell, Kawakami, & Wong, 1986). They introduced sounds and letters through lessons in which children associated letters with the names of their classmates or familiar objects. They created word walls and posted charts to which the children could refer, including lists of people (*mommy, brother, cousin*) and actions (*planting, surfing, roller blading*). Gradually, teachers identified children who could use invented spelling to label objects in their drawings. During individual or small-group writing conferences, they assisted these children with labeling and then taught them how to use initial consonants to draft short sentences.

In my experience, the writers' workshop provides the best context in which to teach children letter-sound correspondences—phonics—in a manner that makes that knowledge useful and ensures its application. The following summary of my observations in a kindergarten classroom provides a sense of how phonics fits within the larger context of meaningful literate activity in the writers' workshop. In this classroom the teacher had the children keep four questions in mind when they wrote their stories: Who is in my story? What is happening in my story? Where is my story taking place? What else happened? She did not use the terms "characters," "events," and "setting," but the children clearly understood these concepts. I observed a girl drafting the sentence, "I am popping firecrackers with my friends at home." The teacher had taught the children to isolate the first sound in the word and write that letter. Then they were to say the word slowly, listen for other sounds, and add those letters. The girl who wanted to write *firecrackers* isolated the initial *f* sound, said, "f-f-f," and wrote the letter *f*. As this example shows, children in primary classrooms with writers' workshops create their own phonics exercises because of the stories they want to write. The teacher in this classroom, as well as many others, have told me words to this effect: "I have taught letter sounds in isolation, and this way, through invented spelling, is much faster and more effective."

My observations in classrooms with Hawaiian children are consistent with a growing body of studies pointing to the benefits of invented spelling in children's long-term development as readers and writers (Ehri, 1987; Wilde, 1989). These studies suggest that children who have the opportunity to use invented spelling eventually become better spellers than children who are taught spelling by rote memorization and never have the opportunity to infer for themselves how the English spelling system works. In the case of both spelling and phonics, it is not just a matter of learning skills but of applying these skills in the context of real reading and writing. Teachers commonly observe that students misspell words they wrote correctly on recent spelling tests. Similarly, studies suggest that many children who learn phonics in isolation do not use these skills when they read (Shannon, 1989), and that by fourth grade, students' reading problems are related to a lack of automaticity rather than to the absence of basic reading skills (Campbell & Ashworth, 1995).

Phonics Should Be Embedded in Meaningful Contexts

As far as the fifth understanding, I have become convinced that there is not one best way to teach phonics and that students of diverse backgrounds benefit from a multipronged approach that shows them the usefulness of letter-sound correspondences during both reading and writing. Our research at KEEP supports this contention. Decoding by analogy is an approach to word identification, demonstrated to be effective, that has undergone continual refinement, as shown in the work of Gaskins and her colleagues (Gaskins, Ehri, Cress, O'Hara, & Donnelly, 1996–97; Gaskins, Gaskins, & Gaskins, 1991). At KEEP we asked Cunningham (1991) to provide workshops to our teachers on decoding by analogy, and KEEP teachers taught lessons incorporating word walls. The relative importance of onset-rime segmentation and phonemic segmentation in children's development of word reading and spelling ability continues to be explored in the experimental literature (Nation & Hulme, 1997). However, the KEEP students seemed to benefit both from learning decoding by analogy, which requires onset-rime segmentation, and from learning invented spelling, which led them to employ phonemic segmentation.

Although I know of no research to suggest that there is a single best way to teach phonics (Allington, 1997), I find that there are two principles that underlie effective phonics instruction for Hawaiian students and others of diverse backgrounds. The first principle is that phonics instruction should be explicit. In two controversial and widely cited articles in the *Harvard Educational Review*, Delpit (1986, 1988) presents a convincing case for the explicit instruction of skills within constructivist approaches, for students of diverse backgrounds. Delpit states that, unlike their mainstream, middle-class peers, students of diverse backgrounds generally do not have the opportunity outside of the classroom to acquire the codes of the culture of power. These codes include such skills as phonics and standard English grammar. According to Delpit, teachers handicap students of diverse backgrounds when they fail to provide explicit instruction in these skills. As indicated earlier, teachers in KEEP classrooms provided students with explicit instruction in phonics through a wide variety of activities. Delpit (1988) adds this caveat, with which I agree:

> I am not an advocate of a simplistic "basic skills" approach for children outside the culture of power. It would be (and has been) tragic to operate as if these children were incapable of critical and higher-order thinking and reasoning. (p. 286)

I hesitate to use the word *systematic* along with *explicit* because of the many misunderstandings of what *systematic* might mean when it comes to phonics instruction. There is no evidence for the effectiveness of phonics that is thought to be systematic because the teacher follows a set sequence of skill lessons. As Allington (1997) puts it, "there simply is no 'scientifically' validated sequence of phonics instruction" (p. 15). This rigid concept should be replaced by one in which phonics is understood to be systematic because the teacher provides instruction based on ongoing assessment of the children's needs as readers and writers. Phonics should also be systematic in the sense that teachers devote considerable time and attention to it on a daily basis, when ongoing assessment indicates that such instruction will be beneficial.

The second principle is that this explicit phonics instruction should take place in meaningful contexts in which the reasons for learning letter-sound correspondences can readily be understood by children. In the writers' workshop, described earlier, children understand that they need knowledge of letter-sound correspondences to put their stories down on paper for communication to others. In shared reading and guided reading, children understand that knowledge of letter-sound correspondences enables them to read the words in books for themselves. Children are pursuing certain purposes through literacy and can see the value of knowledge of letter-sound correspondences in achieving these purposes.

McGee (McGee & Purcell-Gate, 1997) presents a thoughtful discussion of these issues in the conversation with Purcell-Gates cited earlier. She notes that "any understandings constructed about phonemic awareness, or any other of the processes and understandings associated with reading and writing, are always embedded with and connected with all the other processes operating in concert" (pp. 313–314). She emphasizes that it is the richness of these embedded and interconnected understandings that supports children's literacy learning. Children who have had many opportunities to learn about reading and writing through interactions in a variety of literacy events develop a deeper and qualitatively different kind of understanding from children whose understandings have developed largely through training—especially if that training has focused on the teaching of letter-sound correspondences or other skills in the absence of a purpose drawn from a larger, meaningful activity. McGee does not object to the game-like activities in these training programs because children on their own do play with language. (And, as described earlier, children create "phonics exercises" for themselves when engaged in invented spelling.) What is at issue is the connections made for children between these activities and their purposeful engagement in the full processes of reading and writing.

Literacy Learning Is Supported by a Continuum of Instructional Approaches

My sixth understanding centers on a continuum of instructional approaches, consistent with a constructivist framework, for promoting students' learning to read during the elementary school grades. These instructional approaches are shown in Figure 4 have observed the use of these approaches in the classrooms of teachers whose success in promoting the literacy of Hawaiian students has been well documented (Au & Carroll, 1997). Two instructional approaches are shown to be useful at all grades: teacher read alouds and sustained silent reading. The other four instructional approaches are arranged in the order in which they would often occur, given students' progress in learning to read. They are shared reading, guided reading, guided discussion, and literature discussion groups. These approaches are often associated with certain grade levels. For example, shared reading is commonly used in kindergarten and first grade, whereas literature discussion groups generally occur after first grade. However, the use of these approaches is not linear. Teachers may use some combination of these approaches with a particular group

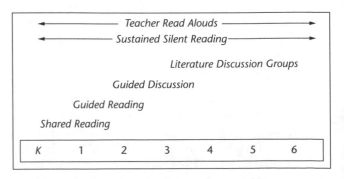

Figure 4   Continuum of instructional approaches.

of students, for example, adding opportunities for extended discussion to shared reading and guided reading. The nature of the text may also influence the teacher's choice of approach. For example, if a novel proves particularly challenging for students, the teacher may decide to use guided discussion in order to provide greater scaffolding, rather than using literature discussion groups.

Literature discussion groups.   I want first to say a few words about literature discussion groups because this is the newest instructional approach in my repertoire as a teacher educator, and the one that caused me seriously to rethink my views of reading instruction. Literature discussion groups may also be called Book Clubs (Raphael & McMahon, 1994) or literature circles (Short & Pierce, 1990). Literature discussion groups promote students' ownership of literacy by giving them the opportunity to shape their own conversations about literature. Talk does not follow the typical pattern of classroom recitation driven by the teacher's quizzing. Rather, as Atwell (1987) puts it, these are conversations around the dining room table, the kinds of conversations that adults might have in the real world when discussing books with family, friends, and colleagues.

In workshops on literature-based instruction, I try to give teachers the opportunity to engage in such conversations. I begin these workshops by having teachers read and write in response to a poem, then share their responses in a literature discussion group. I always choose a poem that appears to offer room for a number of different yet plausible interpretations. O'Hehir's (1988) "Riding the San Francisco Train" is a good example of such a poem. Readers usually agree that it conveys feelings of guilt, but they differ widely in their views of the probable source of the guilt. Participants think that the individual is gay, has just been released from prison, or has left an abusive relationship, and they are always able to support their views by referring to particular lines in the poem. Most teachers are surprised by the extent to which literature discussion groups capture their interest and attention, and they contrast this experience with that of typical school discussions of literature, in which the student's goal is to arrive at the canonical interpretation or that favored by the teacher. This brief experience with literature discussion groups often helps teachers gain insights about the differences between literature-based instruction, rooted in reader response theory (Rosenblatt, 1991), and other ways of teaching reading.

Many teachers are quick to see the value of having their students participate in literature discussion groups. For teachers in the primary grades, the question arises: If students are to gain the background needed for them to participate in and benefit from literature discussion groups, how do we prepare them for this experience? To address this question, I will briefly discuss my views of the other instructional approaches in the continuum, beginning with shared reading.

Shared reading.   As mentioned earlier, many Hawaiian children in low-income communities enter kindergarten without having participated in family storybook reading. Shared reading, in conjunction with the reading aloud of picture storybooks, provides the teacher with a prime opportunity to introduce these children to the joys of reading and of books. When they enter kindergarten, many young Hawaiian children are in the awareness stage in their development of word-identification ability. Shared reading is beneficial because it provides teachers with opportunities to promote all four of the understandings about the relationships between spoken and written language that develop during this stage. Teachers can help children gain knowledge of an important *function of print*, that print can be used to communicate stories. Teachers can model how readers observe *conventions of print*, such as directionality. Teachers can call children's attention to the *forms of print*, including letters of the alphabet and punctuation. Teachers can develop children's *phonemic awareness*, by pointing out or having children identify words that rhyme, or words that begin or end with the same sounds.

In terms of the development of word-identification ability, shared reading serves the crucial function of moving children from paying attention only to pictures to paying attention to print. As Sulzby's (1985) work on young children's storybook reading demonstrates, this shift is a major landmark in literacy development. Teachers worry that children memorize the texts of big books, and they question whether children are actually referring to print. In my observations of young Hawaiian children, I have seen that memorization of the text plays an important role in their development as readers. The ability to associate certain exact words with each page signals their understanding that text is stable and unchanging. This understanding leads to another, that the memorized words they recite can be matched with the print on the page. Teachers can guide children to slow down their recitation of the text and to point to each word as they say it. In this way, memorization of the big book text contributes to development of the children's ability to track print.

Holdaway (1979) notes that, even during the introductory stage with a big book, teachers should "induce sound strategies of word solving by encouraging and discussing suggestions, at an appropriate skill level and without unduly interrupting the story" (p. 72). In one activity, the teacher copies the text of the big book on an overhead transparency. The words are covered with strips of paper and progressively unmasked, letter by letter. When teachers unmask words, they model for children how good readers look at each letter of a word in order, moving from left to right. A critical feature of this and related activities is the requirement that children attend closely to print and break away from a reliance on pictures. Shared reading lays the foundation for independence in word identification encouraged through guided reading.

Guided reading.   A major focus of guided reading is to teach children to use reading strategies—particularly strategies of word identification—independently. A comprehensive treatment of guided reading, based on Clay's (1991) research, is provided in a recent book by Fountas and Pinnell (1996). Guided reading may be introduced when children are moving from the awareness stage to the accuracy stage. Whereas shared reading is usually conducted with the whole class, guided reading takes place with a small group of children whose reading processes are at a similar level. The teacher introduces a previously unseen little book to this small group, and the children read the book on their own, with a minimum of help from the adult. For many Hawaiian children, the move from shared reading to guided reading is quite a leap. For one thing, they must track the print on their own, as they are now looking at their individual copies of the book, not at a big book in which the teacher is tracking the print for them. Also, they are expected to read through a text that has not previously been read aloud to them. I see teachers providing scaffolding as children make the transition from shared reading to guided reading. For example, the teacher may have the children look at her copy of the book. She remains silent but tracks the print as the children read along for a page or two. Then she has the children continue independently in their own books.

During guided reading, the central activity is the children's own independent reading of the text. As the children read the text on their own, the teacher monitors their performance. Fountas and Pinnell use the phrase "small detours" to describe the problem-solving assistance given by the teacher when children need help. They caution teachers to be very quick about individual interventions, so that children can immediately return to their efforts at meaning construction. This view echoes Holdaway's concern that the teacher not "unduly interrupt" the flow of the story during shared reading. By conducting a mini-lesson after the children have finished reading,

the teacher can address the points of difficulty identified earlier.

Guided discussion   As children gain proficiency in word identification, they are able to read more complex texts. These texts include picture storybooks, such as Choi's (1993) *Halmoni and the Picnic*, that contain such elements as a theme, memorable characters, and a plot with a problem and solution. These books offer the possibility for in-depth, guided discussion. In guided discussion, the teacher uses questioning to sharpen students' understanding of the theme and other story elements and to help them make personal connections to the text (Au, 1992).

Teachers at KEEP used the form of guided discussion known as the experience-text-relationship or ETR approach (Au, Carroll, & Scheu, 1997). Lessons of about 20 minutes are taught to small groups of children, and the lessons on a particular story usually take from 3 to 5 days. As in guided reading, these are children whose reading processes are at a similar level. The teacher selects a text the students will be able to read largely on their own, on a topic likely to be of interest, and she identifies a possible theme for the text. In the experience or E phase, the teacher introduces the story and has the students discuss experiences they have had, which relate to the possible theme. As the lesson enters the text or T phase, the teacher has the students read the first segment of the story silently. As in guided reading, she assists students who encounter a problem while reading. After reading, the students discuss this part of the text, with the teacher guiding discussion to focus on key points, such as the characters and events, as well as the emerging theme. The lesson alternates between silent reading and discussion, until students have finished reading the text. In the relationship or R phase, the teacher helps the students to draw relationships between their own experiences and the ideas in the story. It is not uncommon for students to construct their own theme for the story, rather than assenting to the theme planned by the teacher (Au, 1992).

The teacher may focus on one or two teaching points near the end of the 20-minute lesson. As in shared and guided reading, the idea is that skill instruction should intrude as little as possible upon students' ongoing efforts at constructing meaning from text. The teacher has the students return to the text and reread the passage containing the target word, and she and the students discuss how the word might be identified and what it might mean. Often, especially as students reach the third grade, they are beginning to encounter multisyllabic words, such as *ricochet* or *coincidence*, that may not be part of their speaking vocabularies. The need at this point is not usually for phonics but for other strategies useful in identifying and deriving the meaning of un-familiar words. One of these strategies is "look in, look around," which involves looking in the word to find a base word and affixes, and around the passage to gain a sense of what the word might mean (Herman & Weaver, 1988).

For many Hawaiian students, guided discussion provides the background necessary for their later participation in literature discussion groups. Teachers encourage students to read carefully and thoughtfully, in preparation for sharing their ideas with others. In the process, teachers familiarize students with traditional comprehension skills such as identifying the sequence of events and with literary elements such as character development, flashbacks, point of view, and theme. Students engage in in-depth discussions of literature, under the teacher's guidance, and present justifications for their interpretations. Perhaps most importantly, guided discussion can contribute to students' ownership of literacy, as they learn to make personal connections to books and to see that books can have themes of relevance to their lives.

Read alouds and sustained silent reading. In classrooms with Hawaiian students from low-income communities, read alouds serve the important function of allowing teachers to act as literate role models and to convey their own love of books and reading. This function is particularly important in these classrooms, because few such role models may be available to students.

The reading aloud of picture storybooks in kindergarten and first grade, when shared reading and guided reading are the principal instructional approaches, appears to play a critical role in the literacy development of Hawaiian children. The reason is that the majority of texts children can read on their own in these grades are not likely to be high quality works of children's literature or to have many ideas worth discussing at length. Children delight in books with simple but clever texts, such as *Mrs. Wishy-washy* (Cowley, 1990), and these texts help them to acquire a sense of what it is like to be a reader, to develop strategies for identifying words, and to gain confidence. At the same time, the children's development as readers is greatly enhanced if the teacher reads aloud picture storybooks, such as *Mufaro's Beautiful Daughters* (Steptoe, 1987), which are too difficult for the children to read on their own. Many Hawaiian children will not be able to read such mealy texts independently until they are in the second or third grades. Picture storybooks give the teacher the opportunity to engage children in thoughtful discussions of literature. As I have argued, attention to comprehension and other complex literacy processes is required even at the earliest grades.

Teachers effective in teaching reading to young Hawaiian children often put limits on the books that children may read during the time set aside for sustained silent reading (which in kindergarten and first grade is usually not particularly sustained or silent). One first-grade teacher marks books according to difficulty, giving each book a blue, yellow, or red dot, and the children in her class know which books they should be reading. The teacher justified her system to me in these words: "The reason I do that is because I don't want them to start working with books and just read the pictures. I know they can read the pictures already." She wanted to be sure her students were focused on print. If the children were interested in books they could not yet read on their own, they could take these books home and have their parents read them aloud. A similar insistence on students' independent reading of books at an appropriate level of difficulty is observed at Benchmark School, which has a record of success in assisting struggling readers (Center for the Study of Reading, 1991). In both cases, students have a choice of numerous books, but these books must be those that they can read on their own, so that independent reading contributes to students' application of effective reading strategies.

Hawaiian students and others of diverse backgrounds are not expected to develop reading ability through some magical process. Instead, teachers foster reading development through the systematic application of specific instructional approaches.

The general point I wish to make about the continuum of six instructional approaches, consistent with a constructivist framework, is that Hawaiian students and others of diverse backgrounds are not expected to develop reading ability through some magical process. Instead, teachers foster reading development through the systematic application of specific instructional approaches. These approaches enable students to understand the functions of literacy, to identify words and to read them in a fluent and accurate manner, to comprehend text (nonfiction as well as fiction), to construct themes, and to develop personal responses to literature.

Closing Thoughts

Proficiency is an essential goal for the literacy achievement of students of diverse backgrounds, and knowledge of letter-sound correspondences or phonics is, of course, necessary for proficiency in reading. However, the teaching of phonics is not the first task a teacher faces with students such as Keoki. The first task is to make sure that students do not turn their backs on literacy but come to realize that literacy can be meaningful to their lives.

Because of my interest in the literacy learning of Hawaiian students and others of diverse backgrounds, I have had to consider the question of how to motivate students to become excellent readers and writers. The answer, I believe, lies in developing students' understandings of the reasons why people read and write in real life. One of the most compelling reasons is the joy of reading and becoming "lost in a book." Another is the understanding of one's own life that can grow from writing personal narratives. Both these reasons are readily grasped by students of diverse backgrounds when they experience literature-based instruction and the readers' workshop, and the process approach to writing and the writers' workshop.

Swings of the pendulum "back to basics" take place periodically, and other presidents of the National Reading Conference, beginning with Jim Hoffman, have issued calls to action. However, I judge the present situation to be different from those we have seen before, in terms of the power of the political forces at work, and the magnitude of the consequences for students and teachers and for our profession. The choices are clear.[2] Our first choice is that we can actively resist the proposed legislative mandates for a narrowly defined return to basic skill instruction. Our second choice is that we can comply with these mandates and simply do what the new laws require. Our third choice is that we can appear to agree with the new initiatives, but continue to go about our work in the way that we see fit. Our fourth choice is that we can create and champion policy alternatives consistent with constructivist approaches.

Swings of the pendulum "back to basics" take place periodically. . . . However, I judge the present situation to be different from those we have seen before, in terms of the power of the political forces at work, and the magnitude of the consequences for students and teachers and for our profession.

My decision is to make this fourth choice. My greatest fear in the move "back to basics" is for the future of Hawaiian students and others of diverse backgrounds. On one hand, studies demonstrate that these students are the most vulnerable to the negative effects of a narrowing of the curriculum (Allington, 1991). On the other hand, a growing body of research shows that these students can and do benefit from constructivist approaches to literacy instruction (Au & Carroll, 1997; Dahl & Freppon, 1995; Morrow, 1992; Morrow, Pressley, Smith, & Smith, 1997). We have an obligation to educate policy-makers and the general

public about this research and a constructivist vision of the teaching of reading and writing. I have indicated that the present situation is different because of the strength of the political forces at play, but it is also different in terms of our knowledge as researchers. We have come too far as a field in our understanding of literacy learning, constructivist approaches, and their benefits to students, to remain silent or to be silenced. If we are ever to make our voices heard, now is the time.

Notes

1. Presidential Address. The National Reading Conference. Scottsdale, AZ, December 4, 1997. Thanks are due to Taffy Raphael. David Pearson, Barbara Taylor, Diane Stephens, Freddy Hiebert, Jean Osborn, Marcy Stein, Timothy Shanahan, and Dorothy Strickland for their comments on earlier drafts of this paper.
2. I am indebted to David Pearson for his ideas on this topic.

References

Allington, R. L. (1991). Children who find learning to read difficult: School responses to diversity. In E. H. Hiebert (Ed.). *Literacy for a diverse society: Perspectives, practices, and policies* (pp. 237–252). New York: Teachers College Press.

Allington, R. L. (1997, August/September). Overselling phonics. *Reading Today.* pp. 15–16.

Anderson, R. C., Mason, J., & Shirey, L. (1984). The reading group: An experimental investigation of a labyrinth. *Reading Research Quarterly, 20.* 6–38.

Atwell, N. (1987). *In the middle: Writing, reading, and learning with adolescents.* Portsmouth, NH: Boynton/Cook.

Au, K. H. (1992). Constructing the theme of a story. *Language Arts, 69,* 106–111.

Au, K. H. (1994). Portfolio assessment: Experiences at the Kamehameha Elementary Education Program. In S. W. Valencia E. H. Hiebert, & P. P. Afflerbach (Eds.), *Authentic reading assessment: Practices and possibilities* (pp. 103–126). Newark, DE: International Reading Association.

Au, K. H. (1997a). Literacy for all students: Ten steps toward making a difference. Distinguished Educator Series. *Reading Teacher, 51,* 186–194.

Au, K. H. (1997b). Ownership, literacy achievement, and students of diverse cultural backgrounds. In J. T. Guthrie & A. Wigfield (Eds.), *Reading engagement: Motivating readers through integrated instruction* (pp. 168–182). Newark, DE: International Reading Association.

Au, K. H., & Carroll, J. H. (1996). Current research on classroom instruction: Goals, teachers' actions, and assessment. In D. Speece & B. Keogh (Eds.), *Research on classroom ecologies: Implications for inclusion of children with learning disabilities* (pp. 17–37). Hillsdale, NJ: Erlbaum.

Au, K. H., & Carroll, J. H. (1997). Improving literacy achievement through a constructivist approach: The KEEP Demonstration Classroom Project. *Elementary School Journal, 97*, 203–221.

Au, K. H., Carroll, J. H., & Scheu, J. A. (1997). *Balanced literacy instruction: A teacher's resource book.* Norwood, MA: Christopher-Gordon.

Au, K. H., & Raphael, T. E. (1998). Curriculum and teaching in literature-based programs. In T. E. Raphael & K. H. Au (Eds.), *Literature-based instruction: Reshaping the curriculum* (pp. 123–148). Norwood, MA: Christopher-Gordon.

Au, K. H., Scheu, J. A., Kawakami, A. J., & Herman, P. A. (1990). Assessment and accountability in a whole literacy curriculum. *Reading Teacher, 43*, 574–578.

Baumann, J. F. (1984). The effectiveness of a direct instruction paradigm for teaching main idea comprehension. *Reading Research Quarterly, 20*, 93–115.

Beck, I. L., McKeown, M. G., Sandora, C., Kucan, L., & Worthy, J. (1996). Questioning the author: A yearlong classroom implementation to engage students with text. *Elementary School Journal, 96*, 385–414.

Biemiller, A. (1970). The development of the use of graphic and contextual information as children learn to read. *Reading Research Quarterly, 6.* 75–96.

Calkins, L. M. (1994). *The art of teaching writing.* Portsmouth, NH: Heinemann.

Campbell, J. R., & Ashworth, K. P. (Eds.). (1995). *A synthesis of data from NAEP's 1992 integrated reading performance record at grade 4.* Washington, DC: Office of Educational Research and Improvement, U.S. Department of Education.

Center for the Study of Reading. (1991). *Teaching word identification.* In Teaching reading: Strategies from successful classrooms (six-part videotape series). Urbana-Champaign: University of Illinois, available through the international Reading Association.

Chall, J. (1983). *Stages of reading development.* New York: McGraw-Hill.

Choi, S. N. (1993). *Halmoni and the picnic.* Boston: Houghton Mifflin.

Clay, M. M. (1985). *The early detection of reading difficulties* (3rd ed.). Auckland: Heinemann.

Clay, M. M. (1991). *Becoming literate: The construction of inner control.* Portsmouth, NH: Heinemann.

Cowley, J. (1990). *Mrs. Wishy-washy.* Bothell, WA: Wright Group.

Crowell, D. C., Kawakami A. J., & Wong, J. L. (1986). Emerging literacy: Reading-writing experiences in a kindergarten classroom. *Reading Teacher, 40*, 144–149.

Cunningham, P. M. (1991). *Phonics we use: Words for reading and writing.* Glenview, IL: Scott, Foresman.

Dahl. K., & Freppon. P. (1995). A comparison of innercity children's interpretations of reading and writing instruction in the early grades in skills-based and whole language classrooms. *Reading Research Quarterly, 30.* 50–74.

Delpit, L. D. (1986). Skills and other dilemmas of a progressive Black educator. *Harvard Educational Review, 56.* 379–385.

Delpit, L. D. (1988). The silenced dialogue: Power and pedagogy in educating other people's children. *Harvard Educational Review, 58*, 280–298.

Ehri, L. C. (1987). Learning to read and spell words. *Journal of Reading Behavior. 19*, 5–31.

Fountas, I. C., & Pinnell. G. S. (1996). *Guided reading: Good first teaching for all children.* Portsmouth, NH: Heinemann.

Frith, U. (1985). Beneath the surface of developmental dyslexia. In K. E. Patterson, J. C. Marshall, & M. Colheart (Eds.), *Surface dyslexia: Neurophysiological and cognitive studies of phonological reading* (pp. 301–331). Hillsdale, NJ: Erlbaum.

Gaskins, I. W., Ehri, L. C., Cress, C., O'Hara, C., & Donnelly, K. (1996–97). Procedures for word learning: Making discoveries about words. *Reading Teacher, 50*, 312–327.

Gaskins, R. W., Gaskins, J. C., & Gaskins, I. W. (1991). A decoding program for poor readers—and the rest of the class, too! *Language Arts, 68.* 213–225.

Goodman, K. (1986). *What's whole in whole language?* Portsmouth, NH: Heinemann.

Graves, D. (1983). *Writing: Teachers and children at work.* Exeter, NH: Heinemann.

Graves, D. (1994). *A fresh look at writing.* Portsmouth, NH: Heinemann.

Guba. E. G., & Lincoln, Y. S. (1994). Competing paradigms in qualitative research. In N. K. Denzin & Y. S. Lincoln (Eds.), *Handbook of qualitative research* (pp. 105–117). Thousand Oaks, CA: Sage.

Guthrie, J. T., & Alvermann, D. E. (Eds.), (1998). *Engagement in reading: Processes, practices, and policy implications.* New York: Teachers College Press.

Hansen, J., & Pearson, P. D. (1983). An instructional study: Improving the inferential comprehension of fourth-grade good and poor readers. *Journal of Educational Psychology, 75*, 821–829.

Herman, P. A., & Weaver, C. R. (December 1988). Contextual strategies for learning word meanings: Middle grade students look in and look around. Paper presented at the meeting of the National Reading Conference, Tucson, AZ.

Holdaway, D. (1979). *The foundations of literacy.* Sydney: Ashton Scholastic.

Lomax, R. G., & McGee, L. M. (1987). Young children's concepts about print and reading: Toward a model of word reading acquisition. *Reading Research Quarterly, 22.* 237–256.

Lukens, R. J. (1990). *A critical handbook of children's literature* (4th ed.). Glenview. IL: Scott, Foresman.

Mason, J. M., & Stewart, J. P. (1989). *CAP early childhood screening/diagnostic tests.* Pilot version. Iowa City: American Testronics.

McCormick, C. E., & Mason, J. M. (1986). Intervention procedures for increasing preschool children's interest in and knowledge about reading. In W. H. Teale & E. Sulzby (Eds.), *Emergent literacy: Writing and reading* (pp. 90–115). Norwood, NJ: Ablex.

McGee, L. M., & Purcell-Gates, V. (1997). "So what's going on in research on emergent literacy?" *Reading Research Quarterly. 32*, 310–318.

Moll, L. C. (1990). Introduction. In L. C. Moll (Ed.), *Vygotsky and education: Instructional implications and applications of sociohistorical psychology* (pp. 1–27). Cambridge, England: Cambridge University Press.

Morrow, L. M. (1992). The impact of a literature-based program on literacy achievement, use of literature, and attitudes of children from minority backgrounds. *Reading Research Quarterly, 27,* 251–275.

Morrow, L. M., Pressley, M., Smith, J. K., & Smith, M. (1997). The effect of a literature-based program integrated into literacy and science instruction with children from diverse backgrounds. *Reading Research Quarterly, 32,* 54–76.

Nation, K., & Hulme, C. (1997). Phonemic segmentation, not onset-rime segmentation, predicts early reading and spelling skills. *Reading Research Quarterly, 32.* 154–167.

O'Hehir, D. (1988). *Home free.* New York: Atheneum.

Palinesar, A. S., & Brown. A. L. (1984). Reciprocal teaching of comprehension-fostering and comprehension-monitoring activities. *Cognition and Instruction. 2,* 117–175.

Pearson. P. D. (1997). The politics of reading research and practice. *Council Chronicle, 7*(1). 24, 28.

Raphael, T. E., & Au, K. H. (Eds.). (1998). *Literature-based instruction: Reshaping the curriculum.* Norwood. MA: Christopher-Gordon.

Raphael, T. E., & McMahon, S. I. (1994). Book Club: An alternative framework for reading instruction. *Reading Teacher. 48,* 102–116.

Rosenblatt, L. M. (1978). *The reader, the text, the poem: The transactional theory of the literary work.* Carbondale: Southern Illinois University Press.

Rosenblatt, L. M. (1991). Literary theories. In J. Flood, J. M. Jensen, D. Lapp. & J. R. Squire (Eds.), *Handbook of research on teaching the English language arts* (pp. 57–62). New York: Macmillan.

Roser, N. L., & Martinez, M. G. (Eds.). (1995). *Book talk and beyond: Children and teachers respond to literature.* Newark, DE: International Reading Association.

Shannon. P. (1989). *Broken promises: Reading instruction in twentieth century America.* New York: Bergin & Garvey.

Short, K. G., & Pierce, K. M. (Eds.). (1990). *Talking about books: Creating literate communities.* Portsmouth, NH: Heinemann.

Spivey, N. N. (1997). *The constructivist metaphor: Reading, writing, and the making of meaning.* San Diego, CA: Academic Press.

Stahl, S. A. (1997). Instructional models in reading: An introduction. In S. A. Stahl & D. A. Hayes (Eds.). *Instructional models in reading* (pp. 1–29). Mahwah, NJ: Erlbaum.

Steptoe, J. (1987). *Mufaro's beautiful daughters.* New York: Lothrop, Lee & Shepard.

Strickland, D. S. (1994–95). Reinventing our literacy programs: Books, basics, and balance. *Reading Teacher, 48,* 294–306.

Sulzby, E. (1985). Children's emergent reading of favorite storybooks: A developmental study. *Reading Research Quarterly, 20,* 458–481.

Taylor, B. (1982). A summarizing strategy to improve middle grade students' reading and writing skills. *Reading Teacher, 36,* 202–205.

Vygotsky, L. S. (1987). Thinking and speech. In R. W. Rieber & A. S. Carton (Eds.). *The collected works of L. S. Vygotsky, Volume I, Problems of general psychology* (pp. 37–285). New York: Plenum.

Weaver, C. (1990). *Understanding whole language: Principles and practices.* Portsmouth, NH: Heinemann.

Wilde, S. (1989). Looking at invented spelling: A kidwatcher's guide to spelling, part I. In K. Goodman, Y. Goodman, & W. Hood (Eds.). *The whole language evaluation book* (pp. 213–226). Portsmouth, NH: Heinemann.

Language and Learning: Exploring Schooling Issues That Impact Linguistically Diverse Students

Ofelia B. Miramontes
University of Colorado, Boulder

This paper presents a brief sketch of issues and dilemmas faced by linguistically diverse students in schools today and focuses on language acquisition, proficiency, use across contexts, instruction, and policies. The students whose school lives this paper highlights are identified by a wide range of terms: ESL students, second-language learners, limited English-proficient students, language-minority students, bilinguals, non-English speakers, monolingual speakers of another language, native X speakers, and so on. The school attendance of these students is not, and has not been, restricted to the southwest or to urban settings, as many people seem to believe, rather they attend schools throughout this country and their presence in schools is projected to grow even more dramatically over the next decade (Ramirez, 1985).

I will begin by discussing the nature of linguistically diverse communities and the demands that belonging to a bilingual world places on linguistically diverse students. I will then give an example of the schooling trajectory that befalls many of these students. This example will be contrasted with some of the beliefs we hold about the nature of effective instruction, and how education for linguistically diverse students measures up to these beliefs. In the last part of this paper I will explore what it means to become proficient in a second language and finally present some basic premises which provide a framework for developing and assessing programs for these students—a necessity for understanding school failure and for improving instruction.

Language is a major carrier of culture and a principle tool in the development of thought and mind (Mead, 1977; Vygotsky, 1978). For students who live

in bilingual environments, therefore, how each language is used, that is, their opportunities to develop competency in each language across a spectrum of content, plays a significant role in their overall cognitive and affective development, both in and out of school (Commins & Miramontes, 1989). Deficit attitudes and perceptions about minority students' language, culture, and homes have a long history in education and have played a principal role in defining the way schools have chosen to approach linguistically diverse students (Edelsky et al., 1983; Crawford, 1989).

Deficit attitudes and perceptions about minority students' language, culture, and homes have a long history in education and have played a principal role in defining the way schools have chosen to approach linguistically diverse students.

Although there are certainly other sociopolitical factors besides language that contribute to the academic difficulties of these students (McDermott, 1981; McGoarty, 1992), in schools, oral expression is the most visible and immediate vehicle for making judgments regarding student competencies. Research has demonstrated that teachers' beliefs and perceptions about language use create expectations and reinforce deficit perceptions about students' cognitive and academic abilities.

Contrary to many stereotypes, linguistically diverse communities are rich and complex in their language use (Delgado-Gaitan, 1986; Heath, 1983, 1986; Zentalla, 1988). This complexity is reflected in how children speak when they come to school and the skills and proficiencies they exhibit there. Relatively few children come to school totally non-English speaking. More likely their lives reflect the lively and dynamic language use illustrated in the following example of Maysee, a 9-year-old Hmong child:

> Maysee dashes into her house and bumps into her grandmother. She greets her grandmother and tells her

From Miramontes, O. (1993) Language and learning: Exploring school issues that impact linguistically diverse students. In Leu, D. & Kinzer, (Eds.), *Examining central issues in literacy research, theory, and practice* (Forty-second Year book of the National Reading Conference) pp. 25–40. Chicago, IL: National Reading Conference. Used with permission.

briefly about her day—in Hmong. She drops her things on the bed in the room she shares with her sister and asks her to come out and play—in English. As she runs into the kitchen to get a quick snack before going outside, her mother asks about what happened in school today. Although she asks Maysee in Hmong, Maysee answers her mother using both Hmong and English to get her ideas across. Outside her friends are enthusiastically engaged in a boisterous game of soccer and Hmong and English ring through the neighborhood.

Maysee is required throughout the day to negotiate meaning in one or the other of her two languages, depending on the situation and context. Given the almost infinite variety of ways in which the home language and English interact, both within linguistically diverse communities and within families, gaps in particular areas of vocabulary and content may occur, depending on the setting and language in which particular information was encountered.

To be a linguistically diverse student means having to function in two languages. This is true because being able to participate fully in the life of home and community requires facility and fluency in the home language. And, participating in school life requires the ability to handle English fluently and academically. The cognitive challenges for these students are therefore far greater than those faced by majority language and culture students.

For all of the supposed attention given to changing demographics and the needs of linguistically diverse students, as little as 6 years ago Olson (1986) reported in *Education Week* that an estimated 84% of eligible language-minority students received no special services whatsoever. In addition, although research evidence indicates that it takes 5 to 7 years or more for students with limited English proficiency to achieve academic proficiency in English (Cummins, 1989; Wong-Fillmore, 1986), services for those students who receive them are typically only funded for 2 to 3 years (Nadeau & Miramontes, 1988).

Instead of expanded services, it seems that more and more children who come to school needing basic instruction in English and in other areas of the curriculum, are hearing teachers saying to them: "If you don't know your letters and your colors, if you don't know how to read and write, if you don't know English, don't come here because that's not what we do here. We don't teach that here. You'll have to go somewhere else to learn that." One wonders where we expect these children to go? And, how we define our jobs as teachers?

Exclusionary attitudes and the policies they generate have very important negative consequences, as most of us are well aware. I think it is useful, therefore, to explore how some of these policies play out in the educational lives and experiences of linguistically diverse

students. In order to do this I will use the example of Alfredo, an 11-year-old Latino student. Alfredo's story demonstrates a trajectory of educational experiences which is played out all too often in the educational lives of linguistically diverse students, and, that many of you will undoubtedly recognize.

Alfredo's story demonstrates a trajectory of educational experiences which is played out all too often in the educational lives of linguistically diverse students.

Alfredo enters school speaking only his home language at kindergarten. There may or may not be possibilities for instruction in Alfredo's first language, but these are not pursued in his education. Alfredo does receive English as a second language instruction—ESL. (ESL instruction might range from 15 minutes three times per week with a tutor to a more fully developed program, such as an hour or so per day with a certificated, trained ESL teacher). Alfredo receives the latter in a pull-out program. There is no guarantee, however, that Alfredo has received literacy instruction since most beginning ESL programs focus primarily or exclusively on oral language.

Because many states limit the funding for providing "special" services for linguistically diverse students, typically to about 2 years, in 2 years, at the beginning of second grade, Alfredo is "exited" out of the ESL program. What is most important at this juncture in Alfredo's schooling is the question of what his regular classroom teacher understands this exit to mean. Given the lack of preparation in first- and second-language acquisition received by most regular classroom teachers, it is not unlikely that his teacher will assume that Alfredo has been deemed to be a proficient English speaker, since he is no longer classified as eligible to receive English as a second language support.

Because he has missed a good deal of classroom instruction by being pulled out for ESL instruction during the reading and languages arts period, in his regular classroom Alfredo is placed in a lower reading group so that he can catch up to the other students. Although 2 years of English as a second language development cannot transform a native speaker of Spanish into a native speaker of English able to function proficiently and exclusively in English across all areas of the curriculum, children like Alfredo are expected to have developed near-native proficiency in English.

After several months, Alfredo's teacher notices that he is not keeping up with his peers in reading. He has a great deal of trouble figuring out new words, is often unable to express himself clearly about the passages read, and does not seem to be making basic connections to the content. By this time Alfredo is speaking only English at school, and in fact most people in the school have forgotten that he originally spoke anything else. As the year progresses the teacher begins to have real concerns. She decides to refer Alfredo to Chapter I. In her referral statement she says that his reading comprehension is very literal and that he seems to have a very narrow vocabulary (Diaz, Moll, & Mehan, 1986; Ruiz, 1990). He is falling behind in other areas of the curriculum, and she says that he does not seem to understand the readings in other textbooks. He often tunes out during class discussions and is very unmotivated. In addition, he does not contribute to discussions.

Now, let us look at some of the assumptions the Chapter I teacher might make about Alfredo. First, it would be a logical, though not necessarily accurate, assumption for her to believe that Alfredo has received a regular initial reading program and therefore has had the necessary opportunity to learn to read in English. Since he speaks only English at school, she would likely assume that he is proficient in English. These assumptions lead the Chapter I teacher to treat Alfredo as though he were a remedial native English speaker (rather than the initial reader he may be, or the second-language speaker of English he certainly is). Since he is not a native English speaker, many of the approaches that might typically be used for native speakers are likely to be inappropriate for him, and many of the experiences Alfredo needs such as opportunities to develop oral as well as reading and writing fluency, and planned instructional experiences with a wide variety of vocabulary and language forms are probably missing (Allington, 1991; Trueba, 1989).

After a couple of years of remedial reading, Alfredo still seems to be making little progress. During this time, the demands of reading have also been going up, the context has expanded and there has been a shift from narrative to expository text. Alfredo seems to have made little progress in his ability either to decode text or to comprehend what he reads. In addition, he continues to have trouble asking and answering questions about the content he has read, stating his position, providing reasons for his thinking, and generally articulating the important ideas to which he has been exposed.

Seemingly, the next logical step is a referral to special education. And, Alfredo is referred. His Chapter I teacher says that Alfredo seems to have auditory and visual memory problems and she is also concerned about his inability to think clearly about what he has read. His classroom teacher reports that when he is not daydreaming he seems very restless and occasionally acts out, clowning around, and disrupting the class.

The special education teacher, being a well-meaning individual, decides that Alfredo needs to be tested in reading and writing in both English and his home language. Although primary-language testing can be very useful for a number of different purposes, the special education teacher fails to reflect on the fact that Alfredo has received little if any literacy instruction in Spanish along with his restricted experiences with literacy in English. Alfredo tests low in both the English and Spanish achievement tests (Figueroa, 1990). From an assessment on academic subjects in a language in which these subjects have never been taught, and from assessments in a second language that has not had a full chance to develop, it is concluded that something is interrupting Alfredo's ability to learn.

Although it is certainly true that something has interrupted Alfredo's ability to learn, it should be clear at this point in his educational career that it has been the pattern of schooling he has received, rather than a disability that is inherent in Alfredo himself. Unfortunately Alfredo is not an isolated case. Daily this type of instruction for linguistically diverse students can be seen in schools throughout this country, where patterns of assumptions held by teachers and specialists lead to inappropriate, unarticulated programs (Trueba, 1989; Shannon, 1990). And, every day, judgments are made about linguistically diverse students' capabilities without consideration for how their educational experiences have helped or hindered their academic development.

Although it is certainly true that something has interrupted Alfredo's ability to learn, . . . it has been the pattern of schooling he has received, rather than a disability that is inherent in Alfredo himself.

Why do we tend to spend so little time in examining schooling experiences as basic factors of school failure for children like Alfredo? Why are we so quick to label such children needy and at risk, implying, not that we are putting them at risk, but rather that they already come with major deficits that will make it difficult for us to teach them, and difficult for them to learn? How do we begin to shift the onus of deficit away from Alfredo, his language, his ethnicity, and his family? Why is that our first line of explanation?

Broad societal perceptions play an important role in the way all students are viewed, and in how programs for them are developed. Although differences need not be equated with deficits, the compensatory orientation to thinking about ethnic and linguistic diversity that has been pervasive in schools, continues to influence educational decisions for minority students (Hiebert & Fisher, 1990; Miramontes & Commins, 1990; Oakes, 1985).

Such theories have a long tradition. At least as early as 1932, George I. Sanchez was speaking against the narrow ethnocentric formulations of school policies that limited opportunities for culturally and linguistically diverse students. Lower middle-class and minority homes have long been perceived to be limited and inadequate language learning environments. They are often viewed as not being able to provide academically oriented experiences for children, and therefore, as promoting faulty patterns of socialization. Finally, these families are perceived to place little or no value on education. Although each of these perceptions have been clearly refuted by the research literature they continue to influence school instruction and policies (Delgado-Gaitan, 1986; Hakuta, 1986; Labov, 1972).

For linguistically diverse students, these deficit perspectives are compounded by deficit views of bilingualism. For many years bilingualism was believed to cause language-minority students' supposed inability to learn. Many bilingual students are still perceived as lacking development and proficiency in two languages, both English and the home language. As Grosjean (1982) has noted, the notions of children having "no language at all" and of "not possessing the means for logical thought" are familiar characterizations of many language-minority pupils in schools today. Again, the research literature is clear on the faulty assumptions reflected in such views (Hakuta & Diaz, 1984; Lambert, 1977; Wong-Fillmore, 1986). Yet, these negative stereotypes and limited vision have led to the development of educational programs focused on compensating for what students are perceived to be lacking. They are based not on the idea that certain homes and patterns of socialization are merely different, but rather that they are fundamentally deficit environments, lacking the ingredients necessary for the development of the skills demanded by a literate society.

Let us look for a moment now at how Alfredo's educational experience squares with what we consider good instruction for "all" children. Most of us believe that: the knowledge and experience children bring to school should be used to expand their educational experiences and schemata; students should be aided by teachers to work in the zone of proximal development; information should be presented in a way that is comprehensible to students; reading should be meaning centered; students should be asked to demonstrate their understanding of what they have been taught; students need to be able to extrapolate and apply that knowledge to new situations; and learning is developmental, that learners learn by doing, and that they are active participants in constructing their own meaning. These beliefs provide the basic principles we feel should guide students' educational development and

lead us to expect that certain experiences need to occur if schooling is to be successful.

To put this in concrete terms let us think about the education of a native English speaker. Imagine we were living abroad in China. It would not be acceptable—or even advisable—to most of us to have our monolingual English-speaking children begin initial schooling, including literacy instruction, in Chinese instead of in English. Why is this so?

One could argue that our children would not be able to understand the content of instruction, and that therefore learning would move very slowly and their ability to develop academic skills fully would be inhibited. The language and skills the children had learned at home would not easily transfer to school. For example 6-year-olds would not have access to the knowledge they had acquired in the approximately 17,520 hours of listening in their primary language to rely on in school (as they would if they were receiving instruction in their primary language), or the more than 2,190 hours of practice in speaking in their primary language which Asher (1982) has conservatively calculated for children that age. In fact, their primary-language skills might even be ignored by their teachers.

We would also certainly consider it eminently unfair if, in addition to asking our children to begin all their learning in Chinese, the Chinese teachers taught them as if they were native speakers of Chinese (i.e., assuming the same level of background and experience in the language as they do for native speakers). We would also consider it unjust if the teachers asked our children to compete at the same level as native Chinese speakers, and judged their competence as learners only from a native Chinese-language perspective.

Now, if we were confident that we could fully meet our children's English language and academic instructional needs we might feel that the extra effort on their part would be worth the effort to learn Chinese. But, if we felt that there was a danger that our children would lose their English proficiency, we probably would not risk it. If we had a choice between an all-Chinese language school and an English language school, then, it is likely that we would choose the latter, eliminating many of the problems of basic understanding and allowing our children to make direct use of the language and thinking tools they have been developing at home. If we, ourselves, spoke little or no Chinese, an all-English environment would also allow us to participate fully in our children's school experiences and learning.

Suppose, however, we do not have the option of an English language school for our children, and, we will never be able to return to live in an English-speaking country. What would we want with regard to the education of our children? What would make sense to us? Most likely we would hope that the methods used for native Chinese speakers would be adjusted for our English-speaking children to insure that understanding was occurring. We would hope that attention was paid to teaching our children to develop the ability to converse and express their ideas in Chinese. We would want our children to be allowed time to work in small groups where they could practice and develop Chinese skills without continually having to compete for the "floor" with Chinese speakers. In addition, we would hope that if our children's competence and abilities were being assessed, and judgments were being made about their cognitive and academic potential, the fact that they were in the process of developing language skills in Chinese would be taken into account. And, finally we would be very appreciative if the Chinese teachers supported our home and family life with our children and found ways in which we could participate in school with our children.

Now, would we think that our children needed these "special" considerations and approaches because they had deficits? For how long might we expect "special" approaches to their instruction? Would we consider our children ready to compete on an equal footing with native Chinese speakers in school in 2 years? In 4? In 6? How would we feel if teachers and school officials tried to discourage us from speaking to our children in English, the language in which we were fluent? And, how would we feel if the school offered us the possibility of some instruction in English? How might we hope this instruction would be handled?

One major point here is that children do not need primary-language instruction because there is something wrong with them. They need it because it provides them the same basic, normal development provided to English-speaking youngsters in English-speaking schools (Snow, 1989). And yet, bilingual programs that allow full access to cognitive and linguistic development in the first language are considered radical. A second critical lesson is that well-organized and implemented second-language instruction plays a very particular and significant role in the education of second-language students, a point to be discussed later below.

Why does it seem so difficult to extrapolate our theories, ideas, and principles about thinking, learning, and teaching to linguistically diverse learners in this country? A major reason, already discussed, is our tradition of compensatory thinking about diversity. Another reason is the way in which schools function and traditional ways of thinking and doing which simply perpetuate poor programs. In Alfredo's case we clearly saw the trajectory created when unexamined labels and assumptions were blindly followed.

In thinking about what equitable, just education for linguistically diverse students should be, it is important to go back to the question of what it will take for these students to be fully functioning members of their home and school communities. The level of bilingualism demanded of these students across settings requires much more than a broad interpretation of the term bilingual. It is insufficient, for example, for these students to be able to handle social situations in both languages, that is, to be able to get around school and hold social conversations with others (Cummins, 1989). And, although social discourse certainly requires many specific competencies (competencies that we usually take for granted in native speakers), it is insufficient to succeed in school. In schools what we really demand is academic proficiency (Heath, 1983, 1986). Because of this it is very important to recognize how the two aspects of second-language development, social and academic, differ. It is also very important to seriously consider the types of language and learning experiences required for full proficiency, and to recognize how the second-language use we expect of linguistically diverse students in our schools differs from the exposure most of us have had to second-language learning.

For most people, an understanding of the requirements of a second language comes from a foreign language perspective. For many it means high school and/or college-level courses in Spanish, French, or German, with the stakes not much higher than getting a good grade. In order to clarify the difference between these experiences and those of second-language learners in this country, that is, to clarify this question of what it means to function successfully in an academic setting in a second language, and what it takes to achieve native-like fluency, consider the following.

Suppose that you will soon be expected to teach a literacy course in Spanish. In order to prepare, you are attending a Spanish talk on literacy.

> ¿Qué es la lectura? Cuando muchos de nosotros aprendimos a leer, se consideraba muy importante poder decirfrar las palabras en la página, usualmente usando un método fonético. La orientación era hacía a prender las partes de la palabras, de las oraciones y de las ideas, y por la práctica de estos elementos llegaríamos al entendimiento de la totalidad. Ahora hemos adoptado otra manera de pensar en cuanto a la lectura. En vez de enfocarnos en las partes, nos hemos comenzado a enfocar primero en las ideas enteras. De este enfoque, esperamos que el deseo de communicarnos por los símbolos escritos ayudará en el desarrollo de las destrezas de la lectura. Es importante considerar las implicaciones de este cambio de perspectiva para nuestra metodología de instrucción.

Hearing [or reading] some of this information in a language that may be unfamiliar to you undoubtedly restricts, if not totally inhibits, your ability to think about the information and to incorporate it into your existing knowledge base. It may also have seemed stressful and irritating, and might have made you tune out. And yet, you are going to be required to utilize this information to develop a broader understanding for your students of some basic literacy principles.

Let's take this example one step further. You have been working on your language abilities for 9 months. You are now asked to give a lecture on an extension of this topic in Spanish, developing your ideas and rationale. This will take more than the ability to listen [read] and understand a lecture. It will require you to develop the ability to fully articulate ideas about literacy instruction in Spanish. As you do this, you will pass through several stages.

First you will most likely learn to handle the topic at a conversational, nontechnical level, then at a level that allows you to state your positions and explain and defend them simply and clearly. The most difficult level of proficiency will be that of learning to articulate and develop the subtleties and complexity of your ideas aloud for your students, and to answer questions and engage in a spontaneous interchange about the topic. Of course, in addition to being able to present this information orally, you will also be expected to read and write your thoughts on the subject clearly, coherently, and correctly. And, finally to be truly considered fluent, you must strive for native-like syntax and prosody.

The situation above presents some stiff challenges. However, to bolster you, you have a fully developed educational and language repertoire and a good to excellent grasp of the topic to provide the foundation for acquiring this level of proficiency in your second language and that you can transfer to this new task. You have had the opportunity to develop your thinking and articulation skills within the context of a language, culture, and set of experiences familiar to you.

As you just experienced, dealing with a fully familiar topic in a second language is very difficult. Even more difficult is dealing with that topic at a fully academic level, even as an individual with a strong schooling background. It is important to reflect on how much more difficult it is for students who: (a) may have little familiarity with the topics they are asked to learn, (b) are also in the process of developing basic underlying academic competencies, and (c) are trying to gain access to the content at the same time that they are being asked to gain mastery of it. This is the task we have set for limited English-proficient students as they enter many schools, often with little or no support for its accomplishment. Linguistically diverse students do arrive at school with the essential fund of language that English speakers come with, but it is *not encoded* in English.

As the former example suggests, given the level of proficiency students need in schools, schools have at least two major roles to play in relationship to the education of linguistically diverse students: first, to educate these children, that is, to facilitate their learning of processes for acquiring, analyzing, and utilizing information; and second, to develop their English proficiency. As demonstrated in Alfredo's example, many programs developed for linguistically diverse students often ignore the principles of thinking, learning, and development that should guide the education of all students including those where these principles need to be refined and adapted to the development of two languages within the school setting.

Linguistically diverse students do arrive at school with the essential fund of language that English speakers come with, but it is not encoded in English.

There are, of course, two major approaches to meeting the needs of linguistically diverse students—those that use the primary language as an integral part of instruction either fully or partially, and those that use only English. In order to accommodate the needs of students and the resources of schools, there are many different ways in which programs can be configured to provide appropriate and sound support and educational development. Although I am a firm believer in and advocate of bilingual education, I know that full primary-language instruction is not always possible for all language groups in all situations. Where there is a critical mass of students, however, opportunities for supporting students by providing primary-language development can usually be accomplished by rethinking and reconfiguring programs and resources (Berman et al., 1991). If primary-language development is not possible, schools can still always find ways to utilize home language resources to connect and give meaning to students' academic learning within real life experiences. It should not be necessary for children to have to choose between their families and communities, and school. In the long run, everyone loses (Garcia, 1982; Zentalla, 1988).

Whether programs utilize the primary language or only English, basic principles of learning, development, and language acquisition should be used to guide decision making about language use, time in program, strategies for instruction, and so on. But, because these principles are unfamiliar to most educators, and because in schools they are often replaced by pragmatic considerations, where decisions are made to accommodate adults rather than students (McGill-Frazen & Allington, 1993; Sizer, 1985; Trueba, 1989), the result is educational practice that contradicts what we know and believe about good teaching and learning. The faulty practices they engender have tragic academic and life consequences. Among these faulty practices are: students being exited from ESL services after 2 years, regardless of proficiency; ESL students expected to function fully as native English speakers across the curriculum after 2 years; students always separated from English speakers for instruction; or, at the other extreme never being grouped homogeneously by language proficiency and always asked to perform in a setting in which they have to compete with native English speakers for the floor; critical masses of students of a particular language group consistently split up and distributed throughout a school to provide a multi-cultural experience for other children—although their own educational needs may not be met. They include: students taught primarily by paraprofessionals with little or no involvement or direction from certificated staff; students taught in their first language by teachers with very limited proficiency in that language; programs that use translation as a substitute for a true development of thinking in the first language or where the first language is indiscriminately used primarily for directives; reading and writing interventions that ignore the need for the development of oral language and background knowledge; students asked to do their writing in their first language but prepared for it in English, or vice versa; students expected to become native English speakers on a minimum of 15–30 minutes of ESL pull-out a day with no second-language reinforcement in the regular classroom; students' potential for learning being tested, assessed, and judged, and their being labeled, through assessments in areas in which they have had little or no academic experience—in essence, having to bear the blame for their own lack of instruction; students considered to have minimal or no language or cognitive abilities because they are not able to demonstrate them in English. As we interpret and draw conclusions about students' potential, reasons for school failure, and better methods and strategies for instruction from the research, evaluation and assessment data we collect, we need to be acutely aware of the impact of the particular schooling opportunities that have, or have not, existed for students over time.

We have all seen approaches that we advocate and know can enhance instruction for students implemented in ways that are unrecognizable in theory, philosophy, and purpose. It should therefore be no surprise to any of us that programs called bilingual and ESL also represent a great range in quality and effectiveness. We do not abandon or condemn methodologies or strategies on the basis of poor implementation, but rather we work to foster their more accurate and effective use. We should not be fooled, then, by the labels applied to programs, but rather we should

be able to discern, evaluate, and assess the degree and quality of the elements of first- and second-language acquisition included in such programs, and in how they are implemented. Knowledge and understanding of the specifics of student cognitive development and the social context and language in which it occurs is critical to all researchers and educators involved in finding better methods and approaches to: developing literacy; affecting educational policy; making recommendations regarding what constitute reading disabilities; defining levels of potential; and perhaps most importantly preparing the teachers who will teach linguistically diverse children.

How do we identify good programs? What basic principles should we be able to see reflected in their implementation? Listed below are 10 basic principles that research and experience indicate are essential to developing sound programs. In many ways they parallel what we would expect for all children, but they always include the added dimension of first- and second-language acquisition. These principles provide part of the basic framework more fully discussed in Miramontes, Nadeau, and Commins (manuscript in preparation). These basic principles include:

1. *Educational experiences should engage linguistically diverse students actively in meaningful activities, appropriate to students' levels of experience.* This principle acknowledges that learning is not merely acquiring and practicing bits of language or bits of knowledge, but that learning develops through a process of experience, interaction and mediation. It also recognizes that a developmental continuum exists for both first- and second-language development, continua that must be taken into account when organizing instruction (Au, 1984; Ruiz, 1990; Cummins, 1989).

2. *Second-language development cannot be accomplished by simply placing students in a language context designed for native speakers.* As presented earlier, both curriculum and strategies for second-language instruction differ from those for primary-language instruction. And, English as a second language instruction is an essential part of a total curriculum for linguistically diverse students.

3. *Second-language instruction must be organized to provide students the time, experiences, and opportunities they need to fully develop language proficiency across a range of social and academic contexts.* Planning for second-language learning must take into account how long it takes for full proficiency in a second language to develop across contexts. It also must insure that transfer and transition criteria are not determined

arbitrarily (Nadeau & Miramontes, 1989; Krashen, 1981). Oral language, meaning-based strategies, experience with a broader range of vocabulary and linguistic structure, and extensive mediation need to be incorporated into a second-language reading program (Barnitz, 1985). A strong oral-language development component is essential at the beginning levels of second-language development and continues to be important throughout the various levels of acquiring second-language proficiency (Diaz et al., 1986; Ruiz, 1990), as was demonstrated earlier in the Spanish lecture example.

4. *Developing respect and proficiency for a student's home language nurtures cognition, academic achievement, family cohesiveness and student self-concept.* This fourth principle recognizes that the relationship of language, thought, and social context speak to the essential role of the primary language for the development of thinking and learning for all students, regardless of their language backgrounds (Cummins, 1989; Hakuta & Diaz, 1984; snow, 1989; Vygotsky, 1978).

5. *There is a distinction between using the primary language as a crutch for learning English, and developing the primary language as a foundation for thinking and learning.* The level, intensity, and quality of primary-language use plays a major role in the efficacy of bilingual instruction. It requires planning for the purposeful use of the primary language for thinking and learning. This planning is important whether full bilingual programs are implemented or whether programs are focused on a complete transition to English only (Legarreta-Marcaida, 1986).

6. *In order to develop bilingual academic proficiency, clear, separate, and meaning-enriched contexts for each language must be created during instructional time.* Principle 6 speaks to the broader societal context in which linguistically diverse students will be asked to function competently, and deals directly with the use of languages within instruction. Because of the sociopolitical context in which English and the student's first language exist (Carter, 1979; Crawford, 1989), each language must have its own discrete time and domains within the curriculum. This implies the separation of languages in instruction. As discussed, bilingual students will be required to use their languages effectively in three primary domains: (a) with monolingual primary-language speakers, (b) with monolingual English speakers, and (c) with other bilinguals. English is not the only language they require to be successful in the bilingual communities in which they live. Using languages in separate contexts provides students

the opportunity and encouragement to create and expand the domains in each language necessary for academic success in both (Commins & Miramontes, 1989; Wong-Fillmore, 1982).

7. *Assessment and evaluation of students must take into consideration first- and second-language developmental levels. Evaluation of student progress must necessarily include multiple strategies, contexts, instruments, and approaches in order to determine underlying knowledge and competencies.* This does not mean watered-down criteria, but rather appropriate criteria. Such criteria might be suggested by the earlier example of Chinese instruction for English speakers. In terms of assessment, although the performance of all students may vary in different contexts and on different tasks, research indicates that this is certainly true for linguistically diverse students (Diaz et al., 1986; Commins & Miramontes, 1989; Miramontes, 1990; Ruiz, 1990). Too often assessment is focused on the minimum a student can accomplish. A more productive and useful view of assessment would use students' identified competencies as the starting point for new learning, thus shifting from a deficit to an advocacy orientation.

8. *Parents and communities must play a major role in the learning and schooling of their children, and their inclusion is critical.* A principle role that families and community members can play is to provide support for primary-language development and the elaboration of underlying concepts needed for academic achievement (Delgado-Gaitan, 1986, 1992; Commins, 1989).

9. *Schoolwide organization and decision-making processes are important in developing strong, coherent, well-articulated, and successful programs for linguistically diverse students.* Therefore, the education of these students cannot be the sole responsibility of what are considered special programs, such as bilingual or ESL. In addition, both monolingual and bilingual teachers have very important roles to play in the education of these students, and it is unconscionable that we find so many paraprofessionals in this country ultimately responsible for the instructional program of linguistically diverse students. Information and training for teachers is sorely needed if they are to become effective instructors of linguistically diverse students (Berman et al., 1991).

10. *Schools need to deliberately plan and provide many opportunities for all students to interact, learn about, and respect one another.* Mere proximity is not enough. For all students, a knowledge of one's own culture and the cultures of others in the broader society are integral to the development of self-concept and self-knowledge.

Although briefly sketched, these basic premises should provide some food for thought with regard to criteria for examining programs you have observed or studied. As researchers in the field of literacy, a knowledge of the basic processes involved in moving from oral speech to symbolic representations are fundamental to what we do. Knowledge of how this is accomplished across two languages is not extraordinary to what we should know about language and learning, but rather is an essential part of our fundamental understanding of this process for all students. Research in first- and second-language acquisition provides many insights into the learning of other students who may also differ from so-called mainstream norms. In short, research on bilingualism, on first- and second-language acquisition, and on the education of bilingual students is not on the fringes, but rather right in the center of learning in schools.

In our research, we should become more aware of what constitutes a linguistically diverse student. As Alfredo's example points out, by the time he was being assessed for Chapter 1 and special education services, he was no longer speaking his primary language at school. It is also likely that he was not speaking it at home, either. Nevertheless, many of his interactions with family and community still engaged him actively in receiving information in his first language. How would Alfredo be labeled? How would his teachers refer to him: bilingual, a-lingual, mixed dominant, dominant English speaker, English-only speaker? And how are any, or all, of these labels relevant to his school learning?

In summary, what I hope has been established in this paper is that understanding first- and second-language acquisition in schools calls for sophisticated research and instructional strategies, and for teachers who are actively teaching. Interactions between first and second language and school learning are complex and simply ignoring the issues (as seems to be the case for 84% of linguistically diverse students) or attaching labels to kids, sprinkling in a little instruction in either language and hoping for the best, has not worked.

> *Interactions between first and second language and school learning are complex and simply ignoring the issues . . . or attaching labels to kids, sprinkling in a little instruction in either language and hoping for the best, has not worked.*

Linguistically diverse communities are rich and complex in their language environments. This complexity is reflected in how children speak when they come to school and the skills and proficiencies they exhibit there. Making good program-planning deci-

sions will depend on our being able to ask the right questions about a students' home language and school background, and on our understanding of the interrelationship of a variety of factors such as age, previous schooling experiences, language exposure, oral proficiency, and literacy development—in two languages.

Author note   I wish to thank Dr. Kathryn Au and Dr. John Barnitz for their careful reading and helpful suggestions for strengthening the manuscript.

References

Allington, R. L. (1991). Children who find learning to read difficult: School responses to diversity. In E. H. Hiebert (Ed.), *Literacy for a diverse society: Perspectives, practices and policies* (pp. 237–252). New York: Teachers College Press.

Asher, J. J. (1982). *Learning another language through actions: The complete teacher's guide.* Los Gatos, CA: Sky Oaks Products.

Au, K. H. (1984). Participation structures in reading lessons with Hawaiian children: Finding a culturally appropriate solution. In H. Trueba, G. Guthries, & K. Au (Eds.), *Culture and the bilingual classroom: Studies in classroom ethnography* (pp. 139–152). Rowley, MA: Newbury House.

Barnitz, J. (1985). *Reading development of nonnative speakers of English: research and instruction.* Language in Education series, ERIC Clearinghouse on Language and Linguistics. Washington, DC: Center for Applied Linguistics/Harcourt, Brace, Jovanovich.

Berman, P., Chambers, J., Gandara, P., McLaughlin, B. (1991). *Meeting the challenge of language diversity: An evaluation of programs for pupils with limited proficiency in English: Vol. 1. Executive summary.* Berkeley, CA: B.W. Associates.

Carter, T. (1979), *Mexican Americans in school: A decade of change.* New York: The College Board.

Crawford, J. (1989). *Bilingual education: History, politics, theory and practice.* Trenton, NY: Crane.

Commins, N. L. (1989). Language and affect: Bilingual students at home and at school. *Language Arts, 66,* 29–43.

Commins, N. L., & Miramontes, O. B. (1989). A descriptive study of the linguistic abilities of a selected group of low achieving Hispanic bilingual students. *American Educational Research Journal, 26,* 443–472.

Cummins, J. (1989). *Empowering minority students.* Sacramento: California Association for Bilingual Education.

Delgado-Gaitan, C. (1986). Teacher attitudes in diversity affecting student socio-academic responses: An ethnographic view. *Journal of Adolescent Research, I,* 104–114.

Diaz, E., Moll, L. C., & Mehan, H. (1986). Sociocultural resources in instruction: A context specific approach. In *Beyond language: Social and cultural factors in schooling language minority students* (pp. 187–230). Sacramento: Bilingual Education Office, California State Department of Education.

Edelsky, C., Hudelson, S., Flores, B. Altweger, B., & J. Jilbert. (1983). Semilingualism and language deficit. *Applied Linguistics, 4*, 1–22.

Figueroa. R. A. (1989). Psychological testing of linguistic-minority students: Knowledge gaps and regulations. *Exceptional Children, 56*, 145–153.

Garcia, J. (1981). *Teaching in a pluralist society: Concepts, models and strategies*. New York: Harper & Row.

Hakuta, K. (1986). *Mirror of language: The debate on bilingualism*. New York: Basic Books.

Heath, S. B. (1983). *Ways with words*. Cambridge, MA: Cambridge University Press.

Heath, S. B. (1986). Sociocultural contexts of language development. In *Beyond language: Social and cultural factors in schooling language minority students* (pp. 143–186). Sacramento: Bilingual Education Office, California State Department of Education.

Hiebert, E. H., & Fisher, C. W. (1991). Task and talk structures that foster literacy. In E. H. Hiebert (Ed.), *Literacy for a diverse society: Perspectives, practices and policies* (pp. 141–156). New York: Teachers College Press.

Krashen, S. (1981). *Second language acquisition and second language learning*. Rowley, MA: Newbury House.

Lambert, W. (1977). The effects of bilingualism on the individual: Cognitive and sociocultural consequences. In P. Hornby (Ed.), *Bilingualism: Psychological, social and educational implications*. New York: Academic Press.

Labov, W. (1972). *Language in the inner city: Studies in the black English vernacular*. Philadelphia: University of Pennsylvania Press.

Legarretta-Marcaida, D. (1981). Effective use of the primary language in the classroom. In *Schooling and language minority students: A theoretical framework* (pp. 83–117). Sacramento: Bilingual Education Office, California State Department of Education.

McDermott, R., & K. Gospodinoff. (1981). Social contexts for ethnic borders and school failures. In H. T. Trueba, G. Guthrie, & K. Aus (Eds.), *Culture and the bilingual classroom* (pp. 212–230). Rowley, MA: Newbury House.

McGill-Frazen, A. & Allington, R. L. Flunk'em or get them classified: The contamination of primary grade accountability data. *Educational researcher, 22*, 19–22.

McGoarty, M. (1992). The societal context of bilingual education. *Educational Research, 21*, 7–9.

Mead, G. H. (1977). *George Herbert Mead: On social psychology*. Chicago: University of Chicago Press.

Miramontes, O. B. (in press). School restructuring: An opportunity for language minority students, or more of the same? *Journal of Educational Issues of Language Minority Students*.

Miramontes, O. B. (1990). A comparative study of English oral reading skills in differently schooled groups of Hispanic students. *Journal of Reading Behavior, 22*, 373–394.

Miramontes, O. B., & Commins, N. L. (1990). Redefining literacy and literacy contexts. In E. F. Hiebert (Ed.), *Literacy for a diverse society: Perspectives, practices and policies* (pp. 75–89). New York: Teacher's College Press.

Nadeau, A., & Miramontes, O. B. (1988). The reclassification of limited English proficient students: Assessing the inter-relationship of selected variables. *NABE Journal, 12*, 219–242.

Oakes, J. (1985). *Keeping track*. New Haven: CT: Yale University Press.

Olson, L. (1986). Many bilingual pupils unaided, study finds, *Education Week, 5*, 1.

Peal, E. & Lambert, W. E. (1962). The relations of bilingualism to intelligence. *Psychological Monographs, 76*. 1–23.

Ruiz, N. (1990). An optimal learning environment for Rosemary. *Exceptional Children, 56*, 130–144.

Sanchez, G. I. (1932). *The age-grade status of the rural child in New Mexico, 1931–1932*. Santa Fe, NM: State Department of Education.

Shannon, S. (1990). Transition from bilingual programs to all-English programs: Issues about and beyond language. *Linguistics and Education, 2*(4), 323–343.

Sizer, T. (1985). *Horace's compromise*. Boston: Houghton Mifflin.

Snow, C. E. (1989). Rationales for native language instruction: Evidence from research. In A. M. Padilla, H. H. Fairchild, & C. M. Valadez (Eds.). *Bilingual education: Issues and strategies* (pp. 60–74). London: Sage.

Trueba, H. T. (1989). *Raising silent voices*. New York: Newbury House.

Vygotsky, L. S. (1978). *Mind in society: The development of higher psychological processes*. Cambridge, MA: Harvard University Press.

Wong-Fillmore, L. (1986). Teaching bilingual learners. In M. C. Wittrock (Ed.), *Handbook of Research on Teaching* (3rd ed., pp. 648–685). New York: Macmillan.

Wong-Fillmore, L. (1982). Instructional language as linguistic input: Second language learning in classrooms. In L. C. Wilkinson (Ed.), *Communicating in the Classroom*. New York: Academic Press.

Zentalla, A. C. (1988). The language situation of Puerto Ricans. In S. L. McKay & A. C. Wong, *Language diversity, problem or resource* (pp. 140–165). New York: Newbury House.

African American Language and Literacy

John Baugh
Stanford University

Tremendous misunderstanding still surrounds issues of language and literacy among African Americans. This chapter describes the ways that the situation of African Americans differs from that of other immigrants to the United States and highlights the consequences of those differences for the literacy skills development of African American students. It then describes the ways that African American vernacular English differs from standard English and the implications of these differences for literacy development. Finally, it suggests ways that we can adopt a pedagogy that is mindful of the linguistic skills students bring to school at the same time that it helps them move toward achievement of advanced literacy.

The Unique Linguistic Heritage of African Slave Descendants in the United States

As is the case with every racial and ethnic group in the United States, African Americans are highly diverse, and defy monolithic classification in racial or linguistic terms.[1] However, the first people of African descent to arrive in the Americas did so as slaves, and not as immigrants in search of freedom, wealth, and enhanced opportunities. Slaves, as property, were not *free* to exercise the common liberties of other citizens in the postcolonial birth of the United States. At that time it was illegal to teach a slave how to read or write. Even after President Lincoln's *Emancipation Proclamation*, ex-slaves did not gain access to good schools or the high levels of literacy that such schools typically instill. The lingering shadow of racial segregation forces us to seek new ways to overcome the problem of low levels of literacy among African American students.

African American slave descendants have a unique linguistic heritage. Although they were in contact with different European languages, including French, Spanish, and Portuguese, people of African descent in North and South America share common linguistic

attributes that gave rise to the Black English trial in 1979 (see Smitherman, 1981), and the Ebonics[2] controversy of 1997 (see Baugh, 1999, 2000; Rickford & Rickford, 2000). Whereas the typical European immigrants may have arrived in the United States with very little money and no knowledge of English, they did so with other speakers of their indigenous mother tongues, and typically formed communities where they continued to speak those languages. For slave descendents, on the other hand, the situation was quite different.

Whenever possible, slave traders would isolate slaves by language in an attempt to restrict uprisings. This prevented African Americans from using their native tongues, forcing them to adopt the language of the slave owners. Because slaves were overtly denied access to literacy and formal education, their English acquisition was impeded by capricious racial and legal obstacles that reinforced the subordination of enslaved Africans and their posterity. Negative stereotypes about slaves were then reinforced by negative stereotypes about their speech. This speech was further misrepresented in vaudeville, movies, television, advertising, and cartoons that indoctrinated those who saw them with the message that blacks, speaking nonstandard English, were simply less intelligent than whites.

The combination of impoverished education and a devalued linguistic heritage . . . set the wheels in motion that resulted in the Ebonics controversy . . .

These negative images persist today, and it is on this uneven linguistic landscape that teachers seek to nurture literacy. The combination of impoverished education and a devalued linguistic heritage that was reinforced through slavery and racial segregation set the wheels in motion that resulted in the Ebonics controversy and other attempts to increase standard English proficiency and literacy among students of African descent.[3] Many people would like to ignore the unique linguistic legacy of the African slave trade throughout North and South America in the name of asserting that today all are equal. People of African descent are expected to follow the path of other immigrants in adopting the dominant language (and dialect) of the nation where they live.

Baugh, John (2002). African American language and literacy. In Mary Schleppegrell & M. Cecilia Colombi (Eds.). *Developing advanced literacy in first and second language: Meaning with power* (pp. 177–185). Mahwah, NJ: Lawrence Erlbaum Associates. Used with permission.

In an effort to support Oakland educators, and to enlist linguistic expertise, linguists of considerable stature began to embrace the term "Ebonics," but they did so based on Oakland's definition, not that originally proposed by Williams in 1975 (see O'Neil, 1998). As a result, the available literature is divided with respect to the definition of Ebonics.

Ogbu's (1978) distinction between voluntary and involuntary immigration is very relevant to this matter, because those whose ancestors came to the United States voluntarily did so with access to schooling and a desire to master English. But involuntary immigrants, in this instance African slaves, were denied access to their mother tongues and to schools. They learned English through pidginization and creolization rather than through a gradual bilingual transition to English, as did other immigrants.

Pidginization, which results in the birth of a new language born of contact between two or more mutually unintelligible parent languages, took place throughout the world, accompanying the African slave trade. The British, Dutch, Portuguese, and Spanish, and many Africans themselves were merchants of human cargo, and the linguistic consequences of slavery uprooted Africans from their native speech communities into a foreign linguistic context where their native language was not understood.

When the children of these slaves first heard languages, they were often the pidgin languages spoken by their parents and others who interacted with slaves. As a result, the pidgin was transformed into a Creole. Creolization is the evolutionary process whereby a pidgin (which has no native speakers) becomes a creole language as it becomes the first language of the children of the pidgin speakers. There remains considerable controversy over a host of historical, political, and linguistic details surrounding the linguistic legacy of slavery. These controversies, in turn, resonate among scholars who seek ways to improve educational prospects for African American students.

African American Language: a Dialect or Separate Language?

Even linguists have not always valued African American vernacular as a cohesive linguistic system with its own integrity and structure. Because the language of slaves was devalued, so too was the study of their speech. Why would language scholars be concerned with *bad speech* or other *corrupt* forms of the language? In addition, European languages had established writing traditions whereas the African languages—with an oral tradition—did not; thereby also causing some to devalue these languages. But studies of Black speech by language scholars in the 1960s and 1970s

exposed the lack of a linguistic basis for the negative stereotypes associated with this dialect and demonstrated the logical coherence of vernacular African American English (AAE; e.g., Bailey, 1965, 1966; Dillard, 1972; Fasold, 1972; Labov, 1969, 1972; Smitherman, 1978; Wolfram, 1969). Since 1972, linguists have referred to Black speech as "Black English" or "African American English." The misconceptions of nonlinguists about African American language behavior (i.e., in speech and writing) have been identified and dismantled by linguists, but much misunderstanding still exists within the educational community and the community at large.

Whereas dominant dialects, typically spoken by affluent and well educated members of a speech community, are often equated with *correct* or *proper* speech in provincial folk mythology, linguists recognize that nonstandard dialects are also fully formed linguistic systems that serve their speakers well in their lives and communities. Linguists contrast *standard* dialects and *nonstandard* dialects, and reject the notion that some dialects are *bad English*. The antonyms in Table 1 illustrate the contrast between the linguistic and folk notions.

Linguists consistently use *nonstandard English* rather than the derogatory folk terminology, because African American English is a coherent dialect; it is not flawed either logically or grammatically.

The unique linguistic history of the manner in which slaves and their descendants learned English has raised important questions about the classification of dialects and languages, as well as about the social, racial, and geographic parameters that determine where a dialect ends and a language begins. The vast majority of African Americans speak English, albeit through a broad range of socially stratified dialects spread across urban and rural communities. The extent to which their speech conforms to standard American English, or is dissimilar from standard dialects of American English will vary based on a host of personal, circumstantial, and historical variables that are both obvious and inherently complex.

The vast majority of African Americans have learned English natively, but they span a broad range

Table 1 Contrasting Terminology for English Dialects

Preferred Linguistic Terminology		
Standard English	⟷	*Nonstandard English*
Folk terms for standard and nonstandard English		
Correct English	⟷	Incorrect English
Proper English	⟷	Improper English
Good English	⟷	Bad English

of regional, social, and educational dialects. Despite this considerable diversity, many similarities exist among speakers of vernacular African American English across the United States. For example, the use of habitual *be* as in *They be happy*, has been attested in urban and rural African American speakers across the nation.

Those who would like to know more about AAE phonological features, such as the use of /f/ for /th/ in word-final position (as in "boof" for "booth"), or zero usage of final consonants in consonant clusters (as in "lif" for "lift" or "las" for "last") should consult Wolfram (1994) and Bailey and Thomas (1998). Such features have been shown to be dialect differences in pronunciation that are equivalent to other phonological differences in dialects that are typically referred to as different "accents."

Grammatical differences, beyond the "*be*" example previously cited, are described more fully by Rickford (1999), including evidence pertaining to *done, been*, and Preterite Had + Verb-ed structures such as *Bob had kicked the ball* instead of *Bob kicked the ball* or *He had went home* instead of *He went home*. These linguistic details are significant for many reasons. They not only reveal the precise differences between dominant linguistic norms, they confirm potential (and authentic) sources of linguistic confusion and interference for many African American students who encounter academic difficulty in school.

Speaking a nonstandard dialect is not the primary reason for . . . students' difficulties in school.

But these differences are not significant enough to account for the failure of many African American students to develop advanced literacy skills. Speaking a nonstandard dialect is not the primary reason for these students' difficulties in school. In many countries, children who speak nonstandard dialects are very successful in attaining high levels of advanced literacy in the standard dialect. In the United States, however, because of the unique history of African Americans, there is little understanding of the linguistic and educational issues that face these students, and they are often stigmatized for speaking nonstandard English, which is all too often made the primary reason for their failure at school.

Overcoming Linguistic Barriers in Bidialectal African American Communities

The vast majority of U.S. citizens and residents do not understand the plight of African American students who are unsuccessful in school. Based on survey after survey across the country, the vast majority of people lay the blame for educational failure at the feet of the student, and perhaps their parents (or guardians). The linguistic issues are rarely addressed.

Extensive evidence confirms that many African Americans, urban and rural, speak nonstandard vernacular dialects of English that are stigmatized by the larger society, and often by the educational system. Teachers today seldom have linguistic training or adequate resources to understand the language issues that would prepare them to fully cultivate their students' language and literacy skills. Educational policies need to address the educational inequalities that were originally born of slavery, and further incubated through racial segregation and poverty. Linguistic barriers have been recognized as one of the largest hurdles confronting the typical African American student and leading to academic failure. Indeed, this was the primary justification for the Oakland School Board's African American Task Force to pursue Ebonics (see Baugh, 2000; Rickford & Rickford, 2000; Smitherman, 2000).

Teachers today seldom have linguistic training or adequate resources to understand the language issues that would prepare them to fully cultivate their students' language and literacy skills.

Any educational policy that builds on the notion that a dominant dialect is synonymous with the *proper* or *correct* dialect is misguided at its outset. But the general public, and many educators, do not understand what a nonstandard dialect is. Furthermore, the educational implications of students speaking nonstandard dialects are still very controversial. Some strive to eradicate the nonstandard dialect; others urge that we value the dialects students bring to school and build on them as we help students gain literacy skills.

In testimony before the U.S. Senate in 1997, Labov described the situation as follows:

> There are two major points of view taken by educators. One view is that any recognition of a nonstandard language as a legitimate means of expression will only confuse children, and reinforce their tendency to use it instead of standard English. The other is that children learn most rapidly in their home language, and that they can benefit in both motivation and achievement by getting a head start in learning to read and write in this way. Both of these are honestly held and deserve a fair hearing. (Labov, 1997)

Unfortunately, neither of these views adequately addresses the issue of how advanced levels of literacy can be achieved by speakers of AAE. Most of the work in this area has focused on emergent literacy learning in the early years; for example, through the use of dialect readers (Labov, 1994; Rickford & Rickford, 1995).

One way to address this is to focus on students' abilities to shift their style of speech. All speakers modify their speech according to the situations they are participating in (Ervin-Tripp, 1972; Giles & Powesland, 1975). My earliest work on African American language (Baugh, 1983) studied the ways in which these speakers modified their speech to suit their immediate situation. Inspired greatly by the work of Ferguson (1959) and Brown and Gilman (1960), I was seeking to identify those linguistic elements that appeared to be within the conscious control of various African American adults; that is, depending on the relative formality of any given speech event. For example, most African Americans that I interviewed were more likely to use African American English in the presence of familiar acquaintances regardless of race, and their speech was much more formal when they were meeting someone for the first time. This was most evident in terms of phonological and morphological variation; the more intimate the relationship, the more vernacular features of AAE appeared. Less familiar relationships were often marked by striking phonological, morphological, and grammatical movement toward standard English norms.

This kind of adjustment according to situation is not the same as the code-mixing and code-switching that occurs in bilingual communities. Switching between two (often mutually unintelligible) languages is not the same as shifting between two (often highly intelligible) dialects. Under many circumstances, African American students will become bidialectal; that is, they will acquire the skill to shift between their home vernacular and standard English with relative ease and considerable proficiency. But motivating students to make these style shifts is not easy. Many minority students seek to avoid behavior that they consider to be *White*, and language is included among these perceptions (see Fordham & Ogbu, 1986).

Students can be encouraged to adopt new styles or registers in their speaking and writing, however, if they see the value of such linguistic skill. Delpit (1995) suggests some ideas for working with students who speak nonstandard English, including comparing features of the dialects, encouraging students to translate or style shift between dialects, and conducting activities in which standard English is called for, where students need to play roles using standard English. To those who argue that we should not interfere with students' dialects at all, Delpit (1998) argues that teaching academic discourse to African American students is both possible and necessary.

Kutz (1986) also addresses the controversy about using students' language versus initiating them into academic discourse by arguing that although students have the right to their own language, teachers need to focus on helping them develop proficiency with academic discourse. She calls for a middle ground based on what we know about style-shifting, comparing learning a new dialect to learning a new language. She suggests, for example, that writing courses focus on helping students learn to ask questions as experts in a discipline would. She criticizes a focus on error instead of on the growth of the writer, and suggests that teachers need to understand that features will occur in students' writing that reflect neither the source nor the target language. With a conceptual framework that sees student writing as a stage in a developmental process, we can understand their errors as developmental, systematic, rule-governed, predictable, and transitional, and can focus beyond the errors on the whole language production.

We need to focus on the writing development of African American students who are working to achieve advanced literacy. Studies of writing such as Whiteman (1981) demonstrate that all speakers of nonstandard dialects show dialect features in their writing, but that developmental factors also play a role. Students need opportunities to develop advanced writing skills through engagement in motivating tasks that are relevant to their purposes in learning.

Rather than continue the practice of chastising African American students for speaking differently than members of the majority culture, educators . . . are more likely to meet with success if they adopt a pedagogy that is motivational and mindful of the language and culture that students bring with them to school.

Linguistic differences are but the tip of a substantially larger iceberg where differences in the allocation of educational resources, glaring differences in class sizes, and the variable quality of school teachers all contribute substantially to a student's overall academic performance. Rather than continue the practice of chastising African American students for speaking differently than members of the majority culture, educators (and their African American students) are more likely to meet with success if they adopt a pedagogy that is motivational and mindful of the language and culture that students bring with them to school. Rather than attempt to eliminate all traces of African American vernacular, they should help students learn and acquire knowledge of the grammatical differences between standard English and nonstandard vernacular African American English. In much the same manner that we do not demand that representatives of Congress abandon their regional accents in pursuit of their professional careers, so too would it be wrong to demand that African American students cleanse all ethnic traces of their speech in their quest to gain standard English proficiency. The ultimate goal is to enhance the communication and educational prospects for all students, regardless of their background or the languages that they bring to school.

Notes

1. For example, advances in DNA technology remind us that women of African descent often bore the children of their owners, thereby mixing the races since the inception of slavery. It is futile to attempt to provide a biological definition of African American identity; for the purpose of this discussion, we focus on those people of African descent who self-identify as "African American." In some cases such self-identified African Americans are naturalized citizens who emigrated to this country more recently; whereas others—who are the major object of this discussion—can trace all or part of their ancestry to enslaved Africans in America.

2. Psychologist Robert Williams coined the term "Ebonics," defining it as "the linguistic and paralinguistic cues that on a concentric continuum represent the communicative competence of the West African, Caribbean, and United States slave descendant of African origin. It includes the various idioms, patois, argots, idiolects and social dialects of black people, especially those that have been forced to adapt to colonial circumstances" (Williams 1975, p.5). This original definition of Ebonics concentrates not on English, or the United States; rather, it is a term that refers to the linguistic consequences of the African slave trade. The original definition of Ebonics also applies to the Caribbean and West Africa, although Ebonics speakers in Haiti or Brazil do not share the same language as African slave descendants who reside in the United States. However, because events in Oakland catapulted Ebonics onto the world stage, the vast majority of people around the world, including many linguists, have come to equate Ebonics with the speech of Black Americans.

3. The Oakland, California, Unified School District's Board of Education endorsed a resolution in 1997 declaring that "African-American people, and their children, are from home environments in which a language other than the English language is dominant . . ." (see Baugh, 2000, p.39). Oakland's board stated that their primary motivation was to improve the education of the vast majority of African American students who were having considerable difficulty with school. Some journalists speculated that Oakland's board was planing to seek bilingual education funding; funding that is provided to students who are not native speakers of English. Although some African Americans, for example, Haitian Americans, in many instances have learned English as a second language, this is not the case for the majority of African Americans.

References

Bailey, B. (1965). "Toward a new perspective in Negro English dialectology." *American Speech 40*, 171–177.

Bailey, B. (1966). *Jamaican Creole syntax*. London: Cambridge University Press.

Bailey, G., & Thomas, E. (1998). Some aspects of African American English phonology. In S. Mufwene, J. Rickford, G. Bailey, & J. Baugh (Eds.), *African American English, structure, history, and use* (pp. 227–244). London: Routledge.

Baugh, J. (1983). *Black street speech: Its history, structure and survival*. Austin: University of Texas Press.

Baugh, J. (1999). *Out of the mouths of slaves: African American English and educational malpractice*. Austin: University of Texas Press.

Baugh, J. (2000). *Beyond Ebonics: Linguistic pride and racial prejudice*. New York: Oxford University Press.

Brown, R., & Gilman, A. (1960). The pronouns of power and solidarity. In T. A. Sebeok (Ed.), *Style in language* (pp. 253–276). Cambridge, MA: MIT Press.

Delpit, L. (1995). *Other people's children: Cultural conflict in the classroom*. New York: The New Press.

Delpit, L. (1998). The politics of teaching literate discourse. In V. Zamel & R. Spack (Eds.), *Negotiating academic literacies: Teaching and learning across languages and cultures*, (pp. 207–218). Mahwah, NJ: Lawrence Erlbaum Associates.

Dillard, J. L. (1972). *Black English*. New York: Random House.

Ervin-Tripp, S. (1972). On sociolinguistic rules: Alternation and co-occurrence. In J. J. Gumperz & D. Hymes (Eds.), *Directions in sociolinguistics: The ethnography of communication*, (pp. 213–250). New York: Holt, Rinehart and Winston.

Fasold, R. (1972). *Tense and the form 'be' in Black English*. Washington, DC: Center for Applied Linguistics.

Ferguson, C. (1959). Diglossia. *Word*, 15, 325–340.

Fordham, S., & Ogbu, J. (1986). Black students' school success: Coping with the burden of 'Acting White.' *The Urban Review, 8(3)*, 176–206.

Giles, H., & Powesland, P. (1975). *Speech styles and social evaluation*. New York: Academic Press.

Kutz, E. (1986). Between students' language and academic discourse: Interlanguage as middle ground. *College English, 48(4)*, 385–396.

Labov, W. (1969). The logic of nonstandard English. In J. Alatis (Ed.), *Georgetown Monographs on Language and Linguistics* (Vol. 22, pp. 1–31). Washington, DC: Georgetown University Press.

Labov, W. (1972). *Language in the inner-city: Studies in the Black English vernacular*, Philadelphia: University of Pennsylvania Press.

Labov, W. (1994). Can reading failure be reversed: A linguistic approach to the question. In V. Gadsen & D. Wagner (Eds.), *Literacy among African American youths* (pp. 39–68). Cresskill, NJ: Hampton Press.

Labov, W. (1997). U.S. Senate testimony: *Ebonics Hearings*. January 23. Honorable Arlen Specter presiding.

Ogbu, J. (1978). *Minority education and caste*. New York: Academic Press.

O'Neil, W. (1998). If Ebonics isn't a language, then tell me, what is? In T. Perry & L. Delpit (Eds.), *The real Ebonics debate: Power, language, and the education of African American children* (pp. 38–48). Boston: Beacon Press.

Rickford, John. (1999). *African American vernacular English: Features, evolution, educational implications*. Oxford: Blackwell.

Rickford, J., & Rickford, A. (1995). Dialect readers revisited. *Linguistics and Education, 7(2)*, 107–128.

Rickford, J. R., & Rickford, R. J. (2000). *Spoken soul: The story of Black English*, New York: John Wiley and Sons.

Smitherman, G. (1978). *Talkin' and testifyin': The language of Black America*. Boston: Houghton Mifflin Co.

Smitherman, G. (Ed.). (1981). Black English and the education of black children and youth: *Proceedings of the National Invitational Symposium on the King decision*. Detroit, MI: Wayne State University Press.

Smitherman, G. (2000). *Talkin' that talk: Language, culture, and education in African America*. London: Routledge.

Whiteman, M. F. (1981). Dialect influence in writing. In M. F. Whiteman (Ed.), *Writing: variation in writing: Functional and linguistic-cultural differences*. Hillsdale, NJ: Lawrence Erlbaum Associates.

Williams, R. (1975). *Ebonics: The true language of Black folks*. St. Louis, MO: Robert Williams and Associates.

Wolfram, W. (1969). A *sociolinguistic description of Detroit Negro speech*. Washington, DC: Center for Applied Linguistics.

Wolfram, W. (1994). The phonology of a sociocultural variety: The case of African American Vernacular English. In J. E. Bernthal & N. W. Bankson (Eds.), *Child phonology: Characteristics, assessment, and intervention with special populations* (pp. 227–244). New York: Thieme Medical Publishers.

STUDY GUIDE

1. To whom does the term "students of diverse backgrounds" refer? (Au)
2. What are the characteristics of a constructivist approach to literacy instruction? (Au)
3. How can phonics be most effectively taught to students of diverse backgrounds? Compare and contrast the author's view with that of Louisa Moats in Section III of this book. (Au)
4. How can diverse students' literacy learning be best supported in the classroom? (Au)
5. Public school teachers are now faced with a push to go "back to basics." What options are available to teachers in this highly politicized educational climate? What are the challenges, implications, and consequences of each of these choices? (Au)
6. Who are "linguistically diverse students"? What is unique about these students in comparison to native speakers of English? (Miramontes)
7. What are the educational experiences like for linguistically diverse learners? How typical of linguistically diverse students' is Alfredo's schooling experience? (Miramontes)
8. What are the traditional school assumptions about linguistically diverse students and their families? What are the traditional school assumptions about bilingualism? Are these assumptions tenable in light of what we now know about effective instructional practices for all students? Why has it been difficult to extrapolate our understanding about such best practices to our teaching of linguistically diverse students? (Miramontes)
9. What are the unique challenges facing teachers in promoting linguistically diverse students' social and academic development? How can you adapt instructional strategies that are appropriate for native speakers for effective use with second language speakers? (Miramontes)
10. How can teachers balance the English language learners' needs to learn both language and subject contents at the same time? (Miramontes)
11. Identify and explain the basic principles for guiding the development and implementation of sound literacy programs for linguistically diverse students. (Miramontes)
12. How does the situation of African Americans differ from that of other immigrants in the United States? What are the consequences of these differences for the literacy development of African American students? (Baugh)
13. What are the characteristics of pidgin and creole languages? (Baugh)
14. Does dialect affect one's learning of reading and writing? If so, how? (Baugh)
15. How is African American Vernacular English similar to, and different from, Standard English? (Baugh)
16. What is register switching? How is it different from code switching? (Baugh)
17. Brainstorm about ways in which teachers can adopt a pedagogy that is sensitive to the linguistic barriers experienced by students who speak nonstandard dialects of English that are undervalued in school? (Baugh)
18. What factors have contributed to the comparatively lower literacy and overall academic performance of students from diverse backgrounds? Discuss how these factors can realistically be addressed in the current educational context. (Au; Miramontes; Baugh)
19. What particular knowledge about linguistic and dialect differences do reading teachers need in order to work effectively with students from different ethnic, linguistic, and social communities? (Au; Miramontes; Baugh)

INQUIRY PROJECTS

1. Locate an elementary school with a substantial number of linguistically diverse students. Find out what program (e.g., bilingual, ESOL, none) is currently in place to meet the needs of these students. Interview the principal, teachers, students, and parents about the implementation of the program (or lack thereof). Evaluate the quality of the program based on the 10 basic principles outlined in the Miramontes' article.

2. Follow one nonstandard English dialect speaker (e.g., African American student) and one language-minority student (e.g., native Spanish- or Chinese-speaking student) for one typical school day. Compare and contrast their educational experiences. Discuss the impacts of the schooling experiences on these students' social and academic development.

3. Collect samples of oral and written language from several African American students or English-language learners. Compare the ways in which the grammar of their vernacular or native language differs from that of the school-based language (e.g., standard textbook language). Discuss how you can use the insights gained from such analysis to enhance literacy instruction for these students.

4. Those who believe that African American Vernacular English (AAVE) is radically different from Standard English argue that speakers of AAVE need to be taught using "semi-foreign/second-language" methods. Such a belief seems to be reflected in a 1997 resolution adopted by the Oakland, California, Unified School District's Board of Education that endorses, implicitly or explicitly, the use of Ebonics in classroom instruction. Investigate the soundness, feasibility, effectiveness, and liability of such an approach to literacy instruction for African American students by researching relevant research literature and interviewing teachers and parents.

FURTHER READING

Barbieri, M. (2002). *"Change my life forever": Giving voice to English-language learners.* Portsmouth, NH: Heinemann.

Boutte, G. (2002). *Resounding voices: School experiences of people from diverse ethnic backgrounds.* Boston: Allyn & Bacon.

Boyd, F. B., Brock, C. H., with Rozendal, M. S. (2004). *Multicultural and multilingual literacy and language: Contexts and practices.* New York: Guilford Press.

Delpit, L. (1995). *Other people's children: Cultural conflict in the classroom.* New York: The Free Press.

Fu, D. (2003). *An island of English: Teaching ESL in Chinatown.* Portsmouth, NH: Heinemann.

Gadsen, V. L., & Wagner, D. A. (Eds.) (1995). *Literacy among African-American youth: Issues in learning, teaching, and schooling.* Cresskill, NJ: Hampton Press.

Gersten, R. M., & Jimenez, R. T. (1998). *Promoting learning for culturally and linguistically diverse students: Classroom applications from contemporary research.* Belmont, CA: Wadsworth Publishing Company.

Heath, S. B. (1983). *Ways with words: Language, life, and work in communities and classrooms.* New York: Cambridge University Press.

Helmer, S., & Eddy, C. (2003). *Look at me when I talk to you: ESL learners in non-ESL classrooms.* Toronto, Ontario, Canada: Pippin.

Jimenez, F. (1997). *The circuit: Stories from the life of a migrant child.* Boston: Houghton Mifflin.

Lopez, M. (1999). *When discourses collide: An ethnography of migrant children at home and in school.* New York: Peter Lang.

Nasdijj (2000). *The blood runs like a river through my dreams: A memoir.* Boston: Houghton Mifflin.

Opitz, M. (1998). *Literacy instruction for culturally and linguistically diverse students: A collection of articles and commentaries.* Newark, DE: International Reading Association.

Paley, V. (2000). *White teacher* (2nd ed.). Cambridge, MA: Harvard University Press.

Willis, A., Garcia, G., Barrera, R., & Harris, V. (2003). *Multicultural issues in literacy research and practice.* Mahwah, NJ: Lawrence Erlbaum Associates.

Wolfram, W., Adger, C. T., & Christian, D. (1999). *Dialects in schools and communities.* Mahwah, NJ: Lawrence Erlbaum.

Developing New, Popular, and Critical Literacies

INTRODUCTION

Our conception of literacy shapes and is shaped by social, economic, scientific, and technological development. In a society that is becoming increasingly multimodal, technocratic, and televisual, there is a need to rethink what it means to be literate and how literacy can best be promoted. The three articles in this section address these and related issues.

In the first article, British sociolinguist Brian Street argues against viewing literacy as a single, monolithic state and calls for a broader conceptualization of literacy that recognizes the diverse and complex ways literacy is practiced by different social groups and in different contexts. He argues that to function effectively in a globalized, market-oriented, and technology-reliant economy, one must develop "new literacies," i.e., the ability to design and create meaning by strategically deploying the grammatical and discursive resources of not only language but of other communicative systems such as visual images and gestures. Street suggests that recent literacy reform initiatives, such as the National Literacy Strategy in Britain, are problematic because they fail to take account of the new communicative demands posed by the new work order. He further contends that the so-called "literacy crisis" as portrayed by the media is inaccurate, at best, because it does not recognize the complex, multiple, and changing nature of literacy. The author concludes that a sociocultural, rather than a reductionist, approach to literacy offers an alternative and more powerful explanation of the critical issues and concerns surrounding language and literacy education.

Today's children are immersed in a world that is saturated with TV shows, movies, sports, video games, and rap music. They bring to school diversely rich knowledge about these cultural resources, but such knowledge is often unrecognized, undervalued,

or even dismissed as irrelevant to school work. In the second article, which is based on an ethnographic study of a first-grade classroom in an urban public school, Anne Haas Dyson argues that if we are genuinely serious about making schooling relevant and meaningful to children, we must allow them to bring their out-of-school "funds of knowledge" into the classroom, and we must provide them with opportunities and guidance to explore the symbolic and semantic potential of popular culture in the academic setting. She documents the ways young children use "textual toys" from their everyday lives as tools for entering into, learning about, and engaging with school-based literacy. She demonstrates the mediational power of children's unofficial knowledge of popular culture in their sense-making and learning of the official knowledge of the school curriculum. Like New Zealand early literacy educator Marie Clay, Dyson challenges us to move beyond the single-dimensional, linear view of literacy development to consider multiple pathways to school-based literacy.

As children's textual habitat becomes more multimodal and complex, the need becomes greater for adopting a critical stance toward text. The third article, by American literacy scholars Christine LeLand and Jerome Harste, explores the connection between semiotics and critical literacy. The authors identify a specific text set of children's literature for promoting critical literacy, and they present a taxonomy that categorizes student responses according to the level of thought the responses demonstrate. They also illustrate the four levels of critical thought—taking stock, inquiry, interrogation, and social action—by using language and art samples of responses from both children and adults. LeLand and Harste call on teachers to more actively promote critical literacy in the classroom so that students can attend to issues of social justice and equality.

New Literacies in Theory and Practice: What Are the Implications for Language in Education?

Brian Street
King's College, London

Public Discourses upon Literacy: Contradictions and Alternatives

The idea of "new literacies" is frequently invoked to describe aspects of the complex communication systems of contemporary society: I would like to consider what is meant by this concept as it is used in both popular discussion and academic analysis. I will indicate some recent theoretical approaches to language, literacy and communicative practices more generally and then provide a brief account of current debates about literacy in the media, and of government responses and policies. I shall argue that these dominant discourses are flawed in their account of levels, standards and attainments in literacy, which is too narrowly defined to capture the richness and complexity of real literacy practices in contemporary society. In contrast, I suggest that we need to conceptualize literacy within broader social orders—what is termed the "New Work Order" (Gee et al., 1996; Holland, 1998) and what might analogously be termed a "New Communicative Order" (cf., Kress & van Leeuwen, 1996; Lankshear, 1997). Reviewing these alternative approaches to literacy, the problem to be explained is how it is that research indicates literacy practices to be developing and spreading in more complex ways, whilst educational and government discourse focuses on "falling standards" and lack of literacy skills. An explanation for this gap in perceptions and understanding and a possible bridge between these two positions can be derived from new approaches to language and literacy that treat them as social practices and as resources rather than as a set of rules formally and narrowly defined. I will illustrate these new approaches through an analysis of some concrete examples of texts that might typically be described in terms of new literacies: a water slide from South Africa; a picture of a news stand in New York; and an account of the use of beepers or pagers by American youths. My aim is to suggest some possible implications of such analyses and of the theoretical framework from which they are derived, for Language in Education in particular and for Education more generally.

. . . dominant discourses are flawed in their account of levels, standards and attainments in literacy, which is too narrowly defined to capture the richness and complexity of real literacy practices in contemporary society.

These approaches also provide explanations for other contradictions that lie at the heart of educational debate just now. One phenomenon to be explained is how it is that media and government are so focused upon narrowly defined notions of literacy and concerned to enhance achievement and "standards" in this domain in isolation, whilst employers and adults when questioned see literacy as only a small part of a much larger communicative picture, findings supported by much research in social linguistics and ethnographies of literacy, as I shall discuss below. Second, current educational debate tends to polarize between what might be termed "socio-centric" and "school-centric" explanations for children's success or failure in standard tests of literacy. The socio-centric view tends to privilege home and social background as the major factor in explaining children's achievement at school and to not place much emphasis on "school effect." The school-centric position, on the other hand, tends to ignore social background and to privilege the impact of curriculum, pedagogy, and schooling. The present government's position, as articulated through the speeches of the Secretary of State for Education and as conveyed, in admittedly less overtly political terms by education agencies, such as Ofsted, SEU, DfEE, and TTA is that social explanations have for too long been used as excuses by teachers for their pupils' failings; indeed, stereotypes of children according to background has led to teachers not making much effort with those pupils, whose failure is thereby a self-fulfilling prophecy. In the present state of the debate, any mention of social effects is assumed to fall into this rather crude position and it is difficult to lift the debate to a more reasoned level.

Recently, Mortimore and Whitty (1997) have attempted to refine this discussion by suggesting that, whilst schools clearly make a difference, as their own earlier work had argued, this does not mean one can forget the relationship between poverty, which has been increasing in Britain in recent years, and school achievement, which the government sees as declining (Hilton, 1998). Typically, they have been taken to task in a recent newspaper article for raising again the spectra of social explanations for underachievement, albeit by a particularly anti-intellectual journalist, Melanie Phillips (Phillips, 1998): "Nobody denies the importance of such social problems", she states, "in making teaching difficult. But school failure has been tolerated because poverty has been used as an excuse." She goes on to link this familiar argument with a broader attack on the teaching profession and researchers as a whole for protecting their own interests at the expense of the child's: Mortimore, she suggests, "is attacking the whole notion of holding schools to account." He wants "self assessment rather than 'harsh' inspection, the classic defence of the professional cartel against effective accountability" (Phillips, 1998, p. 19). This attack is indicative of the discourse within which much public educational debate is being conducted and demonstrates the difficulty for researchers of broaching either side of the current polarity without being accused of such partisanship. I would like to suggest that a way out of this impasse can be provided by the social view of language and literacy being put forward here, which offers some explanation for the links between home and school in a way that the partisan debate does not.

Neither of the positions outlined above—the sociocentric and the school-centric positions—offers any close explanation for the *relationship* between school achievement and home conditions. A social literacies perspective claims to offer such an explanation by linking home background to specific linguistic and discursive practices—"ways with words" as Shirley Heath, a major exponent of this view in the USA, eloquently terms it (1983). These ways with words, so researchers in this field suggest, may be different at home and at school. To social linguists this difference is not necessarily a matter of better or worse, although most would recognize the power issues involved in access to standard linguistic and literacy conventions. But what they want to explain is what exactly is it about the "ways with words" of home and school that makes such a difference? Linguistic factors do not in themselves, intrinsically, make for better or worse work or life skills—indeed, as we shall see later, employers implicitly recognize this by putting broad communicative skills above school-based literacy attainments. The answer is in the detail: the micro ways in which people deploy linguistic resources, including especially how they link communicative practices from one domain, such as literacy, with those of another, such as visual images. It is this communicative competence, knowing when and how to use resources from different channels, that affects abilities to operate in different domains. Those from home backgrounds where the mix of oral and literate is different from that of school, may do worse on the school tests, even though they perform successfully in their own social contexts and, importantly for the present debate, may perform as well at work as those trained in schooled discourses. The implications of this for language in education are that we should be attending to the whole spectrum of communicative practices and communicative competence and not restricting ourselves, in teaching or testing or in policy, to one amongst many, thereby ignoring the skills involved in relating them to each other. The reduction of the broad communicative repertoire of everyday life to the single strand of literacy by a narrow communicative focus in schooling may be an explanation for the problems with which the government is concerned, regarding falling standards and access for those from "non-standard" backgrounds: the explanation does not so much lie at either the school end or the home end, but rather in the dynamic of the relationship between them. It is this dynamic and the micro accounts of ways with words in which children engage, that can explain the link between social factors and school success: we would do better not to ignore either but rather to explore the link between the two in terms of communicative practices. It is this dynamic relationship between communicative practices that language in education can address, combining research and pedagogy to provide a fruitful way forward in this rather densely—and tensely—occupied landscape.

Anthropological Poetics and "New Literacies"

I would like to build this argument up in stages and I commence by citing the way in which social science has recently come to place language at the heart of attempts to understand social life. A crucial component of that shift in attention has been the recognition that language is not only a means of representing that social life to ourselves, but more profoundly it is a way of helping to define what constitutes social reality in the first place: language does not just reflect a pre-existing social reality, but helps to constitute that reality. It is, then, within the context of such philosophical, cross-cultural and social linguistic approaches to language that I locate the particular debates about language and literacy in education that are so troubling contemporary society. I begin with a telling quotation about the linguistic turn in the social sciences, taken from a book entitled *Beyond Metaphor* by a group of anthropologists attempting to understand the social uses and meanings of tropes, or figures of speech, in cross-cultural perspective. As we shall see they place this issue at the center of the social scientific project:

> We are living at a very metaphorical moment in the human sciences in the several senses of that assertion. For one thing, there is just now an especially pronounced awareness that what is done in human affairs is not simply to be taken literally, at face value as it were, but that many such doings, like metaphor itself, stand for something else, so that our sober-sided constructions have obligatorily to be deconstructed. For another thing, we are living at a time when the referential value of language, its ability to provide us with an accurate, transparent view through to and mapping of the reality of things—an "immaculate perception," as it is called—is profoundly questioned, and we have become acutely aware of the figurative devices that lie at the very heart of discourse, defining situations and grounding our sense of what is to be taken as real and objective and, therefore, entitled (by means of the figurative entitlements we employ) to have real consequences. As a result and most obviously, we are living at a time when reference to metaphor occurs with ever greater frequency in writings in the social sciences (Fernandez, 1991, pp. 1–2).

In literary studies, the analysis of imaginative texts has long rested on this premise and the deconstruction of what appears at face value has indeed been accomplished through attention to the ways in which language users deploy metaphor, metonymy and other figures of speech. But this has remained an individualistic and subjective activity, firmly separated in the disciplinary boundaries of institutional intellectual life from hard accounts of the reality of things that can be seen for what they are, measured and generally reduced to knowable units. The project of contemporary social science in its linguistic turn is to bridge these two traditions, to apply the nuanced understanding of linguistic processes, and understandings of tropes and metaphors, to real social life, not quite the same as applying the skills of literary criticism to non-fiction as well as to fiction, although that is certainly part of the picture. The anthropologists cited above characterize their part of this larger epistemological turn as a kind of "anthropological poetics":

On the one hand, anthropological poetics challenges the dehumanization that lies in the reductionist tendencies of scientific formalization, while on the other hand, scientific formalization forestalls the excessively extravagant and freewheeling intuitive interpretations that are a tendency in poetic approaches (Fernandex, 1991, p. 13).

As we consider present government attempts to "raise standards" in schools through the imposition of curricula, teacher training, testing and provision of inventories of linguistic terms for teachers and pupils to acquire, we will be reminded of the "dehumanization that lies in the reductionist tendencies of scientific formalization": but at the same time, resistance to these developments, by teacher unions, professional associations and some academics, might well look like the "excessively extravagant and freewheeling intuitive interpretations" that the author critiques here. The bridge that he proposes between these tendencies in intellectual tradition, namely a kind of "anthropological poetics," can also be applied, I suggest, to attempts to bridge the conflicting tendencies in current debates about language and literacy in English public life.

. . . language does not just reflect a pre-existing social reality, but helps to constitute that reality.

What is meant by an "anthropological poetics" may perhaps be further illuminated by reference to Fernandez's comments on the taboo on mixed metaphor. In this debate are linked the literary interpretations of artistic texts and the ethnographic interpretations of social texts. From a philosophic point of view, Fernandez suggests, a metaphoric assertion has been seen as the creation of a new possible world: from a strict philosophical perspective, then, "it is simply fruitless confusion to mix the metaphors upon which philosophical worlds are created." However, from an anthropological perspective, evidence of such mixing in real social contexts is less easily dismissed: revitalization movements in culture, for instance, tend to "be built upon a congeries, a mixing, of metaphors asserted and enacted. Anthropologists, unlike philosophers, find that cultural worlds are brought into being by the performance (enactment) of mixed metaphors" (p. 12). Sometimes, indeed, such mixing is itself a direct challenge to the apparent coherence and unitariness provided by dominant, conventional metaphors: minority groups challenge the dominant discourse by juxtaposing views of the world conventionally separated. Attention to such social contestations over figures of speech and language forms, then links the anthropologist's analysis of real social life and meaning with the literary scholar's analysis of imaginative texts—anthropology and poetics are combined.

It is within this broad epistemological frame that I would now like to examine some of the debates over language and literacy in contemporary Britain and to indicate some of the research that can perhaps illuminate them. Such theory and data, I suggest, can provide new directions for education in general and for the role of language in education in particular. I begin by contextualizing these debates within what have been characterized as the "new work order" and the "new communicative order" and I argue that we can no longer, if we ever could, afford the luxury of debates about language, curriculum and pedagogy that are located only in educational contexts: the wider context of world economic and organizational development impinges at every point, not simply in an economic deterministic sense but in a broader sense of providing the discursive orders to which such debates both respond and, as the authors below suggest, offer some challenge.

The New Work Order

Gee and others, drawing upon the writings of economists and business theorists as well as critical sociologists, have attempted to characterize the new conditions of work associated with globalization of production and distribution, and to consider the implications of these changes for the kinds of language needed in work and in educational contexts. Work, they suggest, is no longer defined and organized along Fordist lines, with mass production on assembly lines and its Taylorist principles of work organization and discipline. "There is now a shift towards forms of production which employ new ways of making goods and commodities, serving more differentiated markets, or niches, through segmented retailing strategies. There is now a great deal more attention paid to the selling environment at every level of production, from design to distribution. So while the old work order stressed issues of costs and revenue, the new work order emphasizes asset building and market share" (Gee et al., pp. vii—viii). Associated with these defining concepts are ideas about proper organizational behavior, including attention to flexibility and adaptation to change. Procedures are put into place to ensure both flexibility on the one hand and uniformity and guarantee of standards on the other. If consumers are perceived, through market research and company predictions, to demand the same jackets or the same tomatoes in shops across their travelling experience, then mechanisms need to be put into place to ensure that wherever these are produced they conform to those standards. This Total Quality Management has been a particular feature of the new work order that has impinged directly on the educational

setting, in providing models for quality control there too and in imposing reductionist and unitized notions of measurement and of quality on educational outputs and "products."

A further organizational change that has been of special significance for education and indeed for language in education has been the notion of team working on projects rather than hierarchical forms of organization that simply pass orders down a chain of command. In the new project-focussed work order, all members of a team combine to design, negotiate and develop "products" for sale and distribution. In order to accomplish this, all members of a team have to be equipped with the discursive skills that such negotiation and development involve, such as ability to present and hear arguments, and to develop material for presentation on communicative devices such as overheads, slide projectors, computer displays, etc. Radical researchers confronted with these changes have particularly focused on the claims often associated with them that suggest a commitment to democracy: words like "collaboration," "participation," "devolution" and "empowerment," all cherished terms of oppositional groups, such as those working in Freirean literacy campaigns, are now used to indicate a partnership between managers and workers. Gee and his colleagues are highly suspicious of these claims and would have us examine them critically, whilst acknowledging that changes are indeed taking place in both the work order and the communicative demands associated with it.

Within education, attention to such discursive practices and the ideology associated with them are not always associated with such a critical stance. They are to be found, for instance, embedded in new oral GCSE exams, with their requirements to present arguments and debates within fairly limited discursive frames; and in the instrumental discourse of the National Literacy Strategy. A couple of examples will have to suffice to indicate the kind of research that could be done to deconstruct the underlying meanings and ideologies in apparently neutral educational texts. The National Literacy Strategy requirements for Year 4, Term 3, for instance, state that for "text level work, pupils should be taught: 21 to assemble and sequence points in order to plan the presentation of a point of view, e.g., on hunting, and school rules; 25 to design an advertisement, such as a poster or radio jingle on paper or screen, e.g., for a school fete or an imaginary product, making use of linguistic and other features learned from reading examples". Whilst there is scope here for an imaginative teacher to bring to bear some of the critical apparatus assumed for fiction texts, the direction indicated by the discourse itself is more instrumental. Whereas fiction is to be analyzed for author's intention and for the ways in which language functions to create meanings, non-fiction is treated as outside such a critical framework, e.g., Year 4, term 1, no. 17: "Pupils should be taught: to identify features of non-fiction texts in print and IT e.g., headings, lists, bullet points, captions which support the reader in gaining information efficiently" (p. 39). The examples here are particularly telling since they represent exactly the discursive style and the underlying ideology of NLS itself, which is mostly written in bullet points with great attention to headings and layout but little concern for analyzing how such features of text may serve to impose and constrain meanings. The view of non-fiction text as conveying information and of reading as being about gaining information efficiently, disguises the extent to which non-fiction, like fiction, is produced by authors, with intentions, using figures of speech and linguistic and semiotic devices to offer preferred readings: in non-fiction as in fiction, things are not as they seem, participants are not always "talking straight." It seems, however, that the new provision for language and literacy in English primary schools fits more with the "immaculate perception" view of language advocated in the new work order than with this critical poetics.

Even were we to accept that the communicative demands of the new work order are more complex and elaborated, if not more critical, than those of the traditional work place, there are still a number of problems with the dominant representation of this change. A number of writers have argued that the account of work organization and its associated discursive practices given in the new work order only refers to a small, elite sector of the contemporary work place. Large tracts of industry and of the new service sector continue to rest upon traditional work hierarchies and, more significantly for our present argument, traditional communicative needs. On the basis of this, writers such as Dankshear (1997) make a distinction between the elite literacies required in the new work order and low level literacies still required in many sectors of employment. Evidence from employers' responses to a Skill Needs Survey conducted for DEET in 1993, however, suggest that such a simple hierarchy does not adequately capture the communicative needs of the workplace. It is not traditional literacy that employers worry about when they are asked to envisage these needs but new literacies: "only 4% of employers felt that their business objectives were being hampered by a lack of numeracy and literacy among their current employees. Further, nearly three times as many employers complained about the lack of management skills, general communication skills (such as motivation) and computer literacy and knowledge of IT, as complained about literacy and numeracy" (Robinson, 1998, p. 147).

Likewise, Levine, reviewing international surveys of adult literacy, cites surveys of employer attitudes and practices that show:

> Only occasionally does a low level of literacy appear to be treated as an absolute bar to employment in the less skilled labor market. Roughly two thirds of Atkinson and Papworth's responding organizations claimed to be willing seriously to consider applicants with reading and writing problems by taking into account counterbalancing strengths such as a good reference. Employers and recruiters appeared willing to accommodate applicants with low literacy in some jobs by making minor alterations in workgroup procedures and organization. In Britain, low literacy is widely regarded as simply one consideration among many others that affect hiring decisions, and that both local labor-market conditions and intra-plant factors may affect how recruiters apply their general predispositions to specific vacancies and applicants (Levine, 1998, p. 57).

Employers' concerns, then, are with communicative skills of a broader kind and with "counterbalancing" social strengths to those indicated by tests of traditional literacy.

Employers' concerns, then, are with communicative skills of a broader kind and with "counterbalancing" social strengths to those indicated by tests of traditional literacy. Robinson's and Levine's evidence shows the problem of focusing narrowly on traditional conceptions of literacy. But, exactly what are these new literacies? The fact that whilst employers acknowledge them because of their everyday experience of literacy in social practice in workplace conditions, the media and government agencies, dealing with proxy measurements and traditional schooling practices do not, indicates the need to conceptualize and study them in their social context. In order to do so, though, we need to develop theoretical and methodological tools that are freed from the traditional models of language being critiqued by anthropological poetics and by new social science, as we saw above. In order to engage with this discussion I need, first, to make brief reference to what may be termed, on analogy with the "new work order," the new communicative order.

The New Communicative Order

A number of writers working in the area of social semiotics and visual design have suggested that the reading and writing practices of literacy are only one part of what people are going to have to learn in order to be "literate" in the future (Kress & van Leeuwen, 1990; Heller & Pomeroy, 1997). They are going to have learn to handle the kinds of icons and the signs evident in such computer displays as the Word for

Windows package with all its combinations of signs, symbols, boundaries, pictures, words, texts, images etc. The extreme version of this position is the notion of "the end of language"—that we are no longer talking about language in its rather traditional notion of grammar, lexicon and semantics, but rather we are now talking about a wider range of semiotic systems that cut across reading, writing, and speech. Kress and van Leeuwen sub-title their book "Reading Images: The Grammar of Visual Design" in order to suggest that this new approach to the semiotic order can apply similar structural and functional analyses as have been applied to language in its more traditional sense. By this they want to indicate not so much a traditional focus on rules, knowledge of which sets the professional apart from the amateur, but rather grammar as meaning the way in which the people, places and things depicted in images "are combined into a meaningful whole" (p. 1). This shifts attention away from the traditional focus in visual semiotics on "lexis," the treatment of images as though they were analogous to vocabulary with denotations and connotations and instead focuses on how they are combined and become "statements" in the same way that grammar in linguistics focuses on how lexical items are put together into larger wholes to create meaning. The authors also, however, want to get away from the formal associations of traditional study of grammar, as though it were simply a set of rules the user had to observe and instead want to emphasize meaning construction, seeing "grammatical forms as resources for encoding interpretations of experience and forms of social (inter)action" (p. 1). I see this as not far away from the initial claims of the Ethnography of Communication tradition in which Del Hymes laid out a schema of the components that went to make up the *social* dimension of language acts (Hymes, 1994). In this case he was challenging the Chomskyan emphasis on linguistic competence and arguing that knowing when and how to use linguistic resources was also a kind of competence—what he came to term communicative competence. Here again the resources of language are only part of a larger set of components, that include attention to gesture, visual images, and the layout of written text as part of what contributes to its meanings and context in its broadest sense. Indeed, Kress and van Leeuwen quote both the Ethnography of Communication tradition and the Systemic Linguistic tradition, the two major influences on the analysis of language in social context, in their own attempt to study semiosis in its social context. From the latter they quote Halliday:

> Grammar goes beyond formal rules of correctness. It is a means of representing patterns of experience . . . It enables human beings to build a mental picture of reality, to make sense of their experience of what goes on around them and inside them (Halliday, 1985, p. 101).

These challenges to dominant formal models of language are echoed by earlier work of the Russian scholar M. Bakhtin, written in the 1920s but now being taken up by social linguists and anthropologists as a way of handling the complexities of modern multiple language experiences and modalities. According to Bakhtin, linguists at that time were concerned with abstract grammatical universalism, with pressures towards a "common unitary language as a system of linguistic norms," pressures which aligned "the same centripetal forces in socio-linguistic and [in] ideological life: the victory of one reigning language over the others, the supplanting of languages, their enslavement, the process of illuminating them with the True Word, the incorporation of barbarians and lower social strata into the unitary language of culture and truth, the canonization of ideological systems" (Bakhtin, 1985, p. 271). Bakhtin, on the other hand, wanted to develop a framework for understanding language that takes account not only of these centripetal forces but also of centrifugal ones:

> Every concrete utterance of a speaking subject serves as a point where centrifugal as well as centripetal forces are brought to bear. The processes of centralization and decentralization, of unification and disunification, intersect in the utterance; the utterance not only answers the requirements of its own language as an individualized embodiment of a speech act, but it answers the requirements of heteroglossia [*raznorecie* "many meanings"] as well; it is in fact an active participant in such speech diversity. And this active participation of every utterance in living heteroglossia determines the linguistic profile and style of the utterance to no less degree than its inclusion in any normative-centralizing system of a unitary language (Bakhtin, 1985, p. 272).

The challenge then for those researching and teaching language is to take account of this heteroglossic character and to acknowledge the centrifugal as well as centripetal forces at work in any utterance or occasion of language use. This has represented a challenge within the field of linguistics itself where at Bakhtin's time, and in some quarters still today, "Linguistics, stylistics and the philosophy of language that were born and shaped by the current of centralizing tendencies in the life of language have ignored this dialogized heteroglossia, in which is embedded the centrifugal forces in the life of language. . . . Real ideologically saturated "language consciousness," one that participates in actual heteroglossia and multi-languagedness, has remained outside its field of vision" (p. 273). Anticipating the references to metaphor with which this paper began,

Bakhtin points out the features of language use that traditional approaches miss: "proper theoretical recognition and illumination could not be found for the specific feel for language and discourse that one gets in stylization, in parodies and in various forms of verbal masquerade, "not talking straight," and in the more complex artistic forms for the organization of contradiction, forms that orchestrate their themes by means of language" (p. 275). This, indeed, is what I take an "anthropological poetics" to be about: The achievement of contemporary scholars such as Hymes, Halliday, Fernandez and Kress has been to apply such views of language not only to explicitly "artistic" forms, as Bakhtin mainly does, but to ordinary everyday utterances in their social context, for there too "not talking straight," not taking utterances literally, at face value, lies at the heart of meaning making and meaning taking.

I have dwelt upon the tradition represented by the work of Bakhtin, Halliday, and Hymes because they offer a different theoretical framework for analyzing, understanding and teaching about language than that which currently dominates public discourse and in particular schooling in the UK. Conceptualizing literacy, for instance, within these traditions and taking account of Kress's point that they refer to other communicative channels than language narrowly conceived, provides a broader and I would suggest more fruitful framework for handling questions of literacy and language in both education and the workplace.

I will provide brief examples of mixed modalities in the new communicative order before returning to the argument about the new work order and "standards" of literacy in Britain. On literacy programs for adults it is a common technique these days to ask learners to take a camera into their immediate environment and to photograph literacy events—activities, signs, and objects in which reading and or writing play a part but which are often so embedded in daily routines that we do not notice them or recognize the communicative work that is going on to make sense of them (cf Hamilton, 1998). In this tradition, I have taken to collecting examples of both photographs of literacy events and graphic objects themselves from different parts of the world and attempting to analyze how they are used in context—in order, as Halliday says, "to build a mental picture of reality." To understand such images and events requires both anthropological interpretation of context, including recognition of the tropes and plays with language that actors engage in, and textual analysis of the kind proposed by Kress and others: a combination of approaches often referred to as "texts and practices". The "Water Quality Slide" depicted in Figure 1 is a classic example of such a text. The slide involves a mix of text and images typical of the "new communicative order," which many people who do not pass standard literacy tests may nevertheless encounter and understand. For research purposes, making sense of such documents calls upon an interdisciplinary array of methods of analysis of the kind I have been describing. The slide is intended to help people in South Africa living near to water sources to recognize when water is safe to drink. From this point of view the slide is typical of a genre of information messages put out by agencies world wide, often with familiar discursive styles and layouts and containing many hidden assumptions about knowledge and meaning. The card uses small drawings of water creatures to indicate what organisms might be found in the water. It also uses a coding system to indicate the

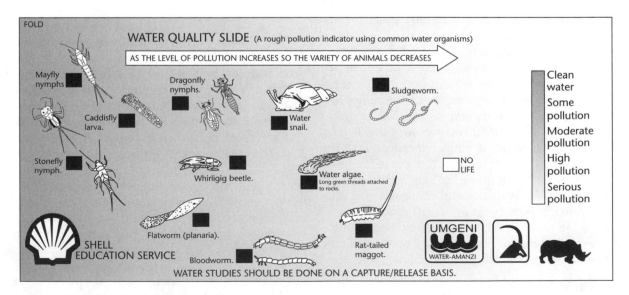

Figure 1   Water slide produced by the Umgeni Trust to promote the use of clean water, South Africa.

relationship between the presence of such creatures and the degree of pollution in water. From left to right the number of creatures reduces so that on the extreme right there are none and this is intended to indicate that pollution has increased on this side. However, this side of the card is lighter than the left, and at first interpretation I took the lightness to represent purity rather than impurity: the left side, with its darker shading, seemed to represent impurity, or pollution.

The mix of images and written text is typical of public documentation in the new communicative order.

Similarly, as someone not accustomed to "seeing" creatures in the water I drink, I assumed that the sector of the card indicating more creatures would be more polluted. The semiotics of the card become more complicated when we realize that there are not only shading, drawing and directionality but also other signs that operate at a different level than the pollution indicators. For instance, on the bottom left is a picture of a shell: this is not, in fact, a real shell of the kind to be found in the water and analogous to the water creatures but is a logo for the oil company whose education service underwrites the slide. Similarly, on the bottom right are a further series of logos: those of Umgeni water itself, indicated by a series of waves in a box; and a rhinoceros, also not to be found in the water but to be interpreted as a logo. The distinction between images indicating real creatures in the water world and images representing the logos of organizations is conveyed through positionality and design features, including the use of boxes, highlighting and drawing style. There is also at the top of the slide an elongated arrow pointing to the right, inside which is written: "As the level of pollution increases so the variety of animals decreases," that is intended to reinforce verbally the message conveyed by the images, shading, etc. The mix of images and written text is typical of public documentation in the new communicative order. But the mix of decoding skills may be less typical of learning environments, especially those where attention is focussed narrowly on literacy at the expense of other semiotic systems and within literacy on phoneme grapheme relations at the expense of the social meanings of literacy or recognition of its significance as a resource in building "mental pictures of reality." For Kress and van Leeuwen, such a text is precisely what they want to focus on in emphasizing the complexity of meaning construction: seeing "grammatical forms as resources for encoding interpretations of experience and forms of social (inter)action," they would address the grammar of such a set of images in ways that move beyond the linguistic code alone. For an ethnographer, attention to the social uses and meanings of such a

text would require observation and discussion of its uses in context. For an educator the slide could provide a source of real materials of the kind advocated by Rogers et al. (1998) in development literacy programs.

One further example will suffice to make the point about the new communicative order. The photograph of a newsstand in New York (Figure 2) works at a number of levels. Firstly, we need to know that it is taken from a letter card sold at shops in New York as part of a genre of reflective images and pictures of the New York environment, and this context is indicated explicitly by a copyright sign and logo *Piece of the Rainbow* © 1997. Again one needs to know how to differentiate meta statements on the text surface, which are about the text itself, from the intended content. On the reverse side from the picture is a meta text of a different kind, indicating not ownership and provenance but a commenting voice directing us to a particular reading of the image: "HOW MUCH STUFF CAN YOU STUFF IN A NEWSSTAND? A LOT OF STUFF! WHAT IS EVEN MORE AMAZING IS THAT THIS GUY KNOWS WHERE EVERYTHING IS." We are, then, as readers, supposed to be amazed, as the exclamation mark reinforces, although our own reading of the text might have been different. For instance, whilst I was dwelling on the issue of how much reading is here laid out, the newsstand owner presumably using semiotic devices such as color, size, shape to provide classification and organization on the stand, my son's attention was drawn to the rows of chocolate bars and the lettering on them. In having this discussion, we switched between seeing the image as a representational resource from which various meanings could be derived, and reading it more literally as though we were observing an actual newsstand in New York. From the latter perspective it seemed to me to tell us that ordinary people walking New York streets would be likely to be surrounded

Figure 2 A New York newsstand. (*Piece of the Rainbow* © 1997)

by a print environment of this complexity and I would hypothesize that even those who could not pass formal literacy tests and might be designated for survey purposes as "illiterate" would actually have considerable acquaintance with such literacy practices and events: their so-called "illiteracy" would be very different from that of someone from a rural area, from South Africa or from India. "Illiteracy," like literacy, is not a single monolithic state, despite the messages of national and international surveys that we will consider below. Again a grammar of the visual layout of such a stand, with its linguistic and non-linguistic signs, could yield a great deal about how meaning is constructed in everyday life and how rich are the resources with which we are surrounded. How this might be taken into account in education is a key theme for exploring the role of language in education.

One final example is particularly indicative of this latter point, the difference between the creativity in using signs as resources evident in everyday life and the often restricted nature of educational approaches to language and sign systems. The example refers to a trend amongst American teenagers to use "beepers" (what are called in the UK "pagers") as communication devices beyond their original remit. An article by Martin Walker (*Guardian*, 22.9.97) describes the ways in which American teenagers have begun to use the sign and sound sequences of the beeper to pass messages to each other that are a mix of Morse code and logographic principles. A sequence of beeps on the digital display that reads 121 is used to mean "I want to talk to you alone." A digital sequence 007, James Bond's number, means "I've got a secret." The relationship between beep signs for numbers and letter inscriptions is also used as a resource in this creative meaning making. You can write 07734 on a digital calculator and then turn the screen upside down to read "Hello" and this tradition has apparently been passed on to beepers. There are historical and cultural associations to draw upon: 66 means "let's hit the road," from the TV series Route 66 and the TV show on Beverly Hills generates 90210 "you are a snob." Plays on digital signs provide; 00010000 "I am really lonely right now," whilst 13579 means "this is really odd." The article ends with a reflective comment by the 30 something author, that the teenage awareness of age has led to the code digits 30 meaning "that's so old, it's history." There are calculated to be more than eight million such beepers owned by teenagers in the USA and an educational debate is proceeding, as with other non-standard variations on linguistic convention: for some it is the equivalent of kids passing notes or whispering in school, a disciplinary issue: for others it is a natural development of teenage slang. From the point of view of the issues raised in this article, the practices

described here indicate the use of semiotic resources in creative and independent ways, the recognition of the communicative possibilities of the sign systems with which we are surrounded, and the ability to cross modalities that Kress and others see as crucial to the new communicative order.

The implications of these examples for the argument outlined above are considerable. Whilst Gee and others were describing the new work order as demanding new high level communicative skills (what Lankshear refers to as "elite literacies"), Levine and Robinson were pointing out that employers seemed unconcerned at the low levels of literacy evident in their work forces. Levine's explanation was that the employers could use other indicators of a potential employee's worth, such as a reference or inferences about job attitudes, to decide whether to employ them, but his data seemed to reinforce the notion that there is a two tier system in employment. I would suggest that the above data and consideration of the new communicative order indicates a different conclusion. If members of contemporary society are all exposed in different ways and different contexts to a variety of communicative practices, of which literacy is only one part often not the most significant, then the skills they bring to the workplace cannot be captured by traditional forms of measurement. Employers realize this and in addition to the social characteristics they infer from observation and from references, they also implicitly or explicitly take into account awareness of the *semiotic range* required in their particular workplace and match that with the semiotic range indicated by applicants. Such matching is a hit and miss affair, although it can be fleshed out by trial periods of work, and by social, class, and ethnic indicators: where employees come from a particular sector or group the skills of one might provide an albeit stereotyped indicator of the skills of another. The evidence from Levine, Robinson and others, along with the analysis of new communicative order skills sketched in above, suggests that taking account of such semiotic range is likely to be a more important indicator of job skills than traditional measures of literacy in the new work order.

This evidence and analysis also suggest that the government's and media's attention to traditional literacy skills is misplaced: even if the development of Literacy Hours, the Literacy framework and intensive teacher training do lead to higher achievements on the traditional scales, these indicators will not tell us much about the actual literacy practices in which people are engaging in everyday life, nor will it be much help, as employers already acknowledge implicitly, in job selection and actual work activity. The task for education, then, is a different one from that currently being set. Re-conceptualizing the role of language in education in terms of this wider framework for language, literacy and communication will become more important as the perceptions outlined above become more widely recognized and as evidence based on this approach accumulates. In the meanwhile, those of us working in this field need to refine the concepts further, provide detailed research to test and develop them and begin to design pilot educational interventions that can indicate a positive direction for future schooling. In the final part of this paper I would like to indicate some example of each of these steps. First, though, I will briefly sketch in the current position regarding dominant discourses regarding literacy and language, as they appear in the media and in government and agency documentation, as they provide the context in which such work must take place.

Conflicts over Literacies for the New Millennium

Newspaper reports on literacy tend to focus on "falling standards" in schools and on "illiteracy" in society at large. This trend has been in place for a very long time—indeed Marshall (1998) shows that HMIs at the turn of the century were making similar comments and Graff reports on inspectors in Canada in the 1880s expressing worries about decline. A headline in the *Independent* (February 7, 1993) shouts "Illiterate England," with pictures of fruit sellers' signs putting extra apostrophes onto their lists of fruit: "Blood Orange's," "Large Fresh Lemon's," as though these were the indicators of "illiteracy." From a linguistic perspective such examples indicate the kind of hypercorrection that occurs precisely when such pressure is brought to bear upon an ambiguous area—and the use of the apostrophe is ambiguous, with analogy less secure as a recourse than in other areas of orthography. In keeping with these general fears of decline, research studies have been commissioned to assess literacy levels and newspaper reports of them reinforce the sense of crisis. A Basic Skills Agency report on school leavers is headlined by the *Guardian* (July 1, 1997) as "Illiteracy spells misery for 2 million." 2 million school leavers were deemed to have a poor grasp of reading and writing and psychologists claimed this might lead to depression and ill health whilst sociologists showed that this category was more likely to be at the bottom of the job hierarchy, suffering low wages and unemployment. Psychologists' studies of reading scores for very young children likewise attract considerable publicity: "Psychologists alarmed by fall in reading standards," whilst some newspapers add to the atmosphere of crisis by designing their own tests and then screaming

about failure as their respondents fail to do well in them: "Nine out of 10 teachers fail spelling test" said the *Sunday Correspondent* on August 6, 1990, referring to a spelling test they gave to delegates at the Professional Association of Teachers involving a number of difficult words such as "allegiance," "abscess," and "occurred". It is hard to avoid the conclusion that government ministers are responding to such superficial media narratives when they "clamp down" on teachers and schools and impose more and more stringent curricula, assessment and inspection of children's reading standards. The newspapers certainly interpret government policy in this way, the *Express* for instance announcing on Sept 10th 1992 "School Blitz on English" as the Minister of Education Chris Patten sent in inspection teams ("hit squads") to failing classrooms. That "English" as a school subject is at the heart of this is clearly signalled by such headlines and by the ways in which successive Government Working Parties have moved from focusing on "Language" to focusing on "English" (Kingman, Cox) and latterly "Literacy" (Literacy Task Force; National Literacy Strategy).

Against such insistent discourse with apparent occasional research support it is difficult to maintain a balanced view of what is happening in everyday uses and meanings of literacy. Nevertheless, occasional reports do attempt a more scholarly view. A British Academy symposium on standards in education reported in the *Times Higher Education Supplement* (October 16, 1998), heard that "the proportion of the population deemed literate has gone steadily up (with a few blips) for 500 years. The proportion gaining qualifications has gone up dramatically this century." And thirdly, issues of comparability that are raised when standards are claimed to "fall," "decline," "plummet" are notoriously hard to define "since acceptable levels of competence change, but it is certain that the criteria have been raised rather than lowered across time: once literacy was measured by ability to sign the marriage register. Now it might be ability to understand a tax assessment form." One can, then, occasionally find newspapers that challenge the dominant media representation. But what does the research literature have to say? Here there is less doubt. Greg Brooks of the National Foundation for Educational Research has investigated the major national surveys of performance conducted in the UK since 1948. His summary of their conclusions makes surprising reading for those only acquainted with newspaper representations:

The main finding is that literacy standards have changed very little in that time. Amongst 8 year olds (children in year 3) in England and Wales, however, standards fell slightly in the late 1980s and then recovered in the early 1990s [possibly due, he suggests, to the introduction of the National Curriculum at that time and the disruption it caused]. Less than one per cent of school-leavers and adults can be described as illiterate, but a significant percentage have limited literacy skills. The British education system has been generally successful in maintaining the standard of achievement in literacy. The international evidence shows that the levels achieved by middling and high performers are comparable to the best in the world. (Brooks, 1997)

In international comparisons, however, there is, a "tail" amongst 9 year olds in Britain, indicating a "trailing edge" of under achievement. These comparisons themselves derive from another set of tests conducted since 1960 across a number of countries. Such tests are notoriously difficult to conduct because of differences in each country's educational system (e.g., whether children start school at age 5, as in the UK, or 6 as in the U.S. and Germany; whether all children are included in classes used for comparison or those "failing" are already excluded; whether the curriculum is nearer to what the tests examine in one country than another e.g., problem solving versus memorization). From the perspective of this paper, deeper differences in the meanings and uses of language and literacy between those societies and methodological problems in comparisons should also make us wary of the claims of which newspapers have made so much. Levine has recently written a powerful critique of the theory, methods and practice of the "International Adult Literacy Survey" (IALS) conducted by OECD (1995). Adults in 7 countries in Europe and North America were given tests to attempt to establish levels and skills of literacy and their variations and the results were used to rank their countries in order of literacy achievements. I have discussed the issues this raises more fully elsewhere (Street, 1996; cf also Goldstein, 1998) so I will just indicate one or two of Levine's arguments that particularly impinge on the position presented in the present paper. Levine describes the procedure whereby respondents are placed in a test situation in their own homes and asked to reply to an array of questions, without the kind of help from peers or other materials that they would call upon in ordinary life. Like me, he sees the test questions and linguistic interactions as:

> a very specific type of discourse with which respondents will be differentially familiar. For example, in relation to a weather chart, a quantitative literacy test question asks how many degrees warmer today's temperature will be in place A than place B (LES. 41–45); but a typical real-world user might well consult the chart to get an overall impression of forthcoming weather—and might do so profitably and accurately, even if he or she were unable to answer correctly a particular test question about specific temperatures. In one document literacy question of the IALS, the test material is a pair of charts illustrating the trend of sales of fireworks and injuries from fireworks (LES, 39). The test question seeks

the year in which there was the lowest number of victims from firework accidents; but a user might fail to get this right while still recognizing, e.g., the upward trend over time in accidents" (Levine, 1997, p. 52).

Levine concludes that such problems might make the test results misleading: "If the test arrangements were experienced by testees as entailing unfamiliar applications of their literacy skills, and if as a result they were stressful and taxing, then the tendency would be for respondents' scores to be depressed in a way that under-estimated their true literacy abilities" (p. 52). Levine's reference here to "true literacy abilities" signals precisely the point that ethnographic approaches to literacy are making: test scores are proxies for what people actually do in the real world and we would do well to begin putting more weight on accounts that are closer to that real world experience. The same point can, of course, be made about the measures of literacy cited above by newspapers and government agencies as evidence of "falling standards" and "under achievement." It may be the measures themselves that are at fault rather than the people and the abilities being measured. Certainly what we know of actual literacy practices from recent ethnographic research suggests that the proxies have missed a great deal that is going on in people's literacy lives (Sheridan et al., 2000; Barton & Hamilton, 1998; Heath, 1983). And, interestingly enough, the respondents in the IALS survey when asked to comment themselves on their literacy skills, do indicate a higher level of satisfaction and accomplishment than the test measures. To the analysts of the IALS this response is further evidence of the problems their survey is uncovering. Levine, on the other hand, sees these responses in the light our approaches above would also indicate, as evidence that "they have been asked to tackle literacy tasks dissimilar to those they habitually encounter at work and in everyday life, and/or that they have been prevented by the nature of the test procedures and situation from exercising skills they habitually employ. . . . The confidence they feel about their literacy in authentic situations is not necessarily misplaced" (p. 53).

The approach to literacy as embedded in other communicative practices and involving a mix of semiotic modes would suggest a further explanation of these discrepancies. Whilst the test procedure focuses upon literacy, because that is what it is designed to do, real life strategies for communication offer a range of substitutes, redundancies and elaborations on the particular literacy skills being addressed. Graff's account of "reading the city" (1991) is a good example from the historical literature of approaches which recognize that people get around cities through a variety of devices, including signs, colors, positions, symbols, smells and shapes. Adult literacy workers in the UK and other countries have been likewise aware of this feature of life for people with low literacy skills (Mace, 1980): it is not just that semiotic modes compensate for poor literacy, it is that they are the communicative channels through which we all operate and that literacy often plays a minor role in everyday activities. From my own experience I will cite just one such example. When I change trains at London Bridge from the Brighton train to the one for Waterloo East I often have very little time in which to find out whether the train I am entering is the correct one. In such circumstances traditional literacy sources of information are unhelpful, both because the display boards are positioned too far away and because they would take too long to read and I would miss the train. Instead I recognize which is the correct train by its color, design and internal layout. Only two kinds of train go from platform 6: one is the Thameslink train to Bedford, and one is the Waterloo East and Charing Cross train. Thameslink trains are dark blue, with patterned seats and recognizable logos. The other trains may be run by a variety of companies, but are recognizable firstly as "not Thameslink" and secondly as having either more commuter-like seating or as having old fashioned carriages with doors to each seating space. When in a hurry I simply glance at the train to establish which type it belongs to, using this variety of coded information of which literacy is a minor part if present at all. Studies of minority communities with numbers of people without a great deal of English show similar processes (Saxena, 1994) in which people catch the right bus because they know the driver, or the bus shape, or simply ask someone else. Faced with a railway timetable in an IALS test neither I nor they would necessarily perform very well, yet we can move about the city perfectly competently. What, then, are the implications of these findings for the current debate about literacy and in particular the role of schooling?

The debate about literacy in contemporary society has been particularly heated with regard to the role of schooling, with government and its agencies representing the same story as evident in the media accounts noted above, namely falling standards both over time and in comparison with other countries. This phenomenon they relate to schooling in terms of teacher training, curriculum and assessment. As a way of "raising standards," the National Literacy Task Force set up by the present government when in opposition, recommended a strategy that has now become the dominant framework for literacy work in schools. The framework sets out teaching objectives for Reception to Year 6, gives guidance on a "literacy hour" in which this teaching is expected to take place every day in almost every primary school in the country and lists the strategies and the knowledge that primary pupils "should" acquire at different stages

of their school progress. The aim of the Secretary of State for Education is that 80% of children should be reading at their reading age by 2001. This will be measured by the SATS already in place which target traditional literacy and numeracy skills and according to which standards are well below this aim. The first reports since the new procedures were put in place have not given the government much relief since maths scores have actually gone down and literacy scores have ceased to rise as quickly as before. Again, as Brooks suggested above for the temporary decline in literacy scores around 1990, this may be because of the disruption caused by a new system. More significant from the point of view of the arguments presented here is whether it matters. Before I examine the arguments that an anthropological poetics would put forward, I will cite evidence from a very different kind of research that throws doubt on the efforts being made around schooling at this point of time.

Robinson surveys a number of reports on what determines levels of attainment in literacy and numeracy, in particular the British Cohort Survey and the National Child Development Study as well as some work by Robertson and Symons from an LSE Unit that analyzed these data. There was indeed one school effect that these studies suggested was significant in pupils' attainment in these areas, namely peer group effect: Mixing with a "good quality" peer group raised performance for poorer pupils (Robinson, 1998, p. 144). For the rest of the conclusions he has a more complex story to tell than we have been hearing:

> However, this was the only measured school variable that was significant in the BCS cohort. The teaching methods employed, homework policy, or whether there was streaming or setting in the primary school had no significant impact on the attainment in numeracy or literacy. In fact, there is no backing in the BCS for many of the features of school organization and curriculum which currently seem fashionable. Schools can make a significant difference to the progress made by their pupils, but overall levels of attainment are heavily determined by social and economic factors. The really important conclusion to be drawn from these analyses is that, if social and economic disadvantage are so dominant in impeding basic skills development, then potentially the most powerful "educational" policy might be one which tackles social and economic disadvantage. A serious program to alleviate child poverty might do far more for boosting attainment in literacy and numeracy than any intervention in schooling (Robinson, 1998, p. 144).

Robinson is, of course, exaggerating the implications of his research for effect and he does concede that "schools can make a significant difference to the progress made by their pupils". But these findings do force us to question the claims about literacy and schooling that dominate current discussion, just as Levine's and Brooks's findings force us to question the claims about falling standards on which such policy appears to be based. Rather than decide between Robinson's social determinism, as it were, and the government's school determinism on the other side, I would like to suggest a different level of explanation for the different achievements in literacy that the various studies indicate. Neither Robinson nor the government really offer any mechanism to explain such differences. A social approach to literacy, on the other hand, does offer some way of understanding why different groups of people handle literacy—and literacy tests and proxies—differently. If we start from a social perspective, then by definition the practices of different groups in different contexts will be different. As Levine noted, the discourse associated with the IALS tests is very different from that of the everyday lives of its respondents. Likewise, the literacy practices of different social groups questioned in the BCS will be very different—at equally deep levels of epistemology, culture and meaning—and we might therefore expect that their responses to questions will be different. In terms of Kress and others' location of literacy within larger communicative practices, one might also expect that people from different mixes of working class, middle class, ethnic and regional groups, for instance, would locate their literacies within different semiotic strategies. As we have seen the tests devised to measure literacy attainment are no more sensitive to these semiotic features of communication than they are to cultural and epistemological differences.

Social Literacies and Language in Education

A social approach to literacy in particular and to communicative practices more generally can, then, suggest the mechanisms that link differential performance to social and economic difference: namely the social and semiotic processes whereby meaning is constructed. As Halliday and Bakhtin would describe it, these processes are integrally derived from a dialogic heteroglossia, in which language is in tension between centripetal forces (currently evident in government prescriptions for literacy) and centrifugal forces (evident in discourse varieties and new communicative practices that elude such centralizing tendencies). Kress would have us analyze these processes by extending the concept of grammar from language traditionally conceived to grammatical forms as "resources for encoding interpretations of experience and forms of social (inter)action," including therefore a grammar of visual design and other

We need to be particularly aware of these often hidden processes at this time of changing work order and changing communicative practices, for it is here . . . that power is manifest.

semiotic modes. According to Halliday it is by these linguistic, semiotic and always social means that reality is not just represented but constituted. I have argued that we need to be particularly aware of these often hidden processes at this time of changing work order and changing communicative practices, for it is here, rather than in a cruder overt exercise of control, that power is manifest. There is a message here for education in general and for language in education in particular, to take on the task of helping new generations to learn how to not take things at face value; to recognize when people are "not talking straight"; to see grammar as a "means of representing patterns of experience" and as helping them "to build a mental picture of reality, to make sense of their experience of what goes on around them and inside them"; to be "aware of the figurative devices that lie at the very heart of discourse"; to recognize the rich variety of tropes, registers and language forms; to deploy to the full the metaphoric potential of language. An anthropological poetics has helped researchers to apply these principles to the meanings and uses of literacy in society and so to see them differently from dominant narrower perceptions. To now apply these principles to schooling, and in particular to language in education, becomes more urgent as centripetal forces and the pressure to take language literally become ever more powerful.[1]

Note

1. Inaugural Professorial Lecture, October 19, 1998.

References

Bakhtin, M. (1981) *The dialogic imagination.* (ed. M. Holquist) Austin: University of Texas Press.

Barton, D., & Hamilton, M. (1998) *Local literacies.* London: Routledge.

Barton, D. (1994) *Literacy: An introduction to the ecology of written language.* Oxford: Blackwell.

Barton, D., & Ivanic, R. (eds.). (1991). *Writing in the community.* London: Sage.

Bhatt, A., & Martin-Jones, M. (1996) *Literacies at work in a multilingual city.* ESRC Report (R-22-1534).

Brooks, G. (1997) "Trends in standards of literacy in the UK 1948–1996." Paper presented at British Educational Research Association.

Bloome, D. (ed.). (1989). *Classrooms and literacy.* Norwood, NJ.: Ablex Publishing.

Fernandez, J. (ed.). (1991) *Beyond metaphor: The theory of tropes in anthropology*. Palo Alto. CA: Stanford University Press.

Freebody, P. (1998) Assessment as communal versus punitive practice: Six new literacy crises. "Virtual Seminar" series. International Applied Linguistics Association (AILA). Special Commission on Literacy (replies by B. Street and C. Kell). [*www.education.Uts.Au/AILA*]

Gee, J. (1991) *Social linguistics: Ideology in discourses*. London: Falmer Press.

Gee, J., Hull, G., & Lankshear, C. (1996) *The new work order: behind the language of the new capitalism*. London: Allen & Unwin.

Goldstein, H. (1998) *Models for reality: new approaches to the understanding of educational processes*. London: Institute of Education.

Gregory, E. (1996) *Making sense of a new world. Learning to read in a second language*. London: P.C.P.

Halliday, M. (1985) *An introduction to functional grammar*. London: Edward Arnold.

Hamilton, M. (1998) Expanding the New Literacy Studies: Using Photographs to explore literacy as Social Practice. In Barton, D., Hamilton, M., & Ivanic, R. (eds.) *Exploring Situated Literacies*. London: Routledge.

Heath, S.B., & Mangiola, L. (1991) *Children of promise: Literate activity in linguistically and culturally diverse classrooms*. Washington, DC: NEA/AERA.

Heath, S.B. (1982) What no bedtime story means: Narrative skills at home and at school. *Language in Society*, 11, 49–76.

_____. (1983) *Ways with words*. Cambridge: Cambridge University Press.

Heller, S., & Pomeroy, K. (1997). *Design literacy: Understanding graphic design*. New York: Allworth Press.

Hilton, M. (1998) Raising literacy standards: The true story. *English in Education*. 32, 3, 4–16.

Holland, C. with Cooke, T., & Frank, F. (1998) *Literacy and the new work order: An international literature review*. London: NIACE.

Hymes, D. (1994) Towards ethnographics of education. In J. Maybin (ed.) *Language and literacy in social practice*. Clevedoo, UK: Multilingual Matters.

Kress, G. (1997) *Before writing: Rethinking the paths to literacy*. London: Routledge.

Kress, G., & van Leeuwen, T. (1996) *Reading images: The grammar of visual design*. London: Routledge.

Lankshear, C. (1997) *Changing literacies*. Buckingham: Open University Press.

Levine, K. (1997) Definitional and methodological problems in the cross-national measurement of adult literacy: The case of the IALS. *Journal of Written Language and Literacy*, 1, 1, 41–61.

Lea, M., & Street, B. (1997) Student writing and faculty feedback in higher education: An academic literacies approach. *Studies in Higher Education*, 23, 2.

MacCabe, C., & Street, B. (1998) Is the box the book's best friend? *Times Educational Supplement*, April.

Marshall, B. (1998) What should they be learning and how should they be taught? *English in Education*, 32, 1, 4–9.

Mortimore, P., & Whitty, G. (1997) *Can school improvement overcome the effects of disadvantage?* London: Institute of Education.

OECD. (1995) Literacy, economy and society: Results of the first international adult literacy survey (IALS). Ottawa: Statistics Canada/OECD.

Phillips, M. (1998) Spare the teachers and spoil the child. *Sunday Times*, October 18, 1998, p. 19.

Prinsloo, M., & Breier, M. (Eds.). (1996) *The social uses of literacy: Case studies from S. Africa*. Amsterdam: John Benjamins.

Robinson, P. (1998) *Literacy, numeracy and economic performance*. London: Centre for Economic Performance, London School of Economics and Political Science/Carfax Publishing Ltd.

Saxena, M. (1994) Literacies among Punjabis in Southall. In M. Hamilton, D. Barton & R. Ivanic (eds.) *Worlds of Literacy*. Philadelphia: Multilingual Matters.

Scribner, S., & Cole, M. (1980) *The psychology of literacy*; Cambridge: Harvard University Press.

Sheridan, D., Street, B., & Bloome, D. (2000) *Writing ourselves: Mass-Observation and literacy practices*. Cresskill, NJ: Hampton Press.

Street, B. (1984) *Literacy in Theory and Practice*. Cambridge: Cambridge University Press.

Street, B. (ed.). (1993) The new literacy studies. *Journal of Research in Reading*, 16, 2.

Street, B. (ed.). (1993) *Cross-cultural approaches to literacy*, Cambridge: Cambridge University Press.

Street, B. (1995) *Social literacies: Critical perspectives on literacy in development*. London: Longman.

_____, (1996) Review of *International Adult Literacy Survey*, in *Literacy across the Curriculum*, Center for Literacy, Montreal vol. 12, no. 3, Winter, p. 8–15.

_____, (1997) The implications of the new literacy studies for literacy education. *English in Education*. 31, 2, 45–54.

Times Higher Education Supplement. (1998) Superb timing as academy leads way on standards. October, 19, p. 14.

Popular Literacies and the "All" Children: Rethinking Literacy Development for Contemporary Childhoods

Anne Haas Dyson
Michigan State University

"I'm mad and I followed the drinking god."
—Denise (age 6, first grade)

Six-year-old Denise is potentially one of those "all" children. Often written with a graphic wink, "all" is sometimes knowingly underlined or righteously capitalized, and it is almost always syntactically linked or semantically associated with that other category, the "different" children—not middle class and not white. In literacy education, these concerns about the "all" children are often undergirded by what might be called the "nothing" assumption— the decision to make no assumption that children have any relevant knowledge. The "all" children are in urgent need, so the argument goes, of a tightly scripted, linear, and step-by-step monitored march through proper language awareness, mastery of letters, control of sound/symbol connections, and on up the literacy ladder.

The assumption that "diverse" children come to school without literacy ignores the resources they bring from popular media texts.

In response, I offer an account of school literacy development for all *children*. This account does not depend on the assumption of "nothing," nor on an idealized, print-centered childhood. Rather, it depends on the assumption that children will always bring relevant resources to school literacy. That is, there will always be local manifestations of true childhood universals—an openness to appealing symbols (sounds, images, ways of talking), and a playfulness with this everyday symbolic stuff.

This account of literacy development is based on an ethnographic study of Denise and her close school friends, all first graders in an urban public school (Dyson, 2003). I studied their childhood culture, documenting their cultural practices—their talk, singing, collaborative play—and the symbolic stuff with which they played. The children had a wealth of *textual* toys, of free symbolic stuff to play with. They found those toys in the words and images of parents, teachers, teenagers, and other kids, as well as on radios, TVs, videos, and other everyday forms of communication. The children not only manipulated or played with their everyday symbolic stuff in the unofficial or peer world, they stretched, reorganized, and remixed this material as they entered into official school literacy.

In this article, I use a metaphoric drinking god to capture the influence that children's nonacademic textual experiences have on their entry into school literacy. That influence may leave us as educators without the proper frame of reference for building on children's efforts. Moreover, any desires we may have for pedagogical uniformity cannot withstand the power of the drinking god. That "god of all learning children" messes up any unitary pathway, renders visible the multiple communicative experiences that may intersect with literacy learning, and bequeaths to each child, in the company of others, the right to enter school literacy grounded in the familiar practices of their own childhoods.

Before explaining this approach for all *children*, I need to do some stage-setting by discussing the "all and nothing" assumption in early literacy pedagogy and its relationship to the desire for uniformity and order. I formally introduce the metaphoric drinking god and briefly describe my study methods. Then I allow the children—and the drinking god—center stage. To clarify my view, I link it to that of Marie Clay, an important scholar who took an early stand against uniformity.

All and Nothing: Putting Childhoods in Pedagogical Order

In my former California locale, districts have been turning to state-approved reading programs designed with the "all" children in mind. The design rests on the assumption that the "all" children bring nothing, as suggested by the following quotes, the first from the program's Grade I Teachers Guide (Adams, Bereiter, Hirshberg, Anderson, & Bernier, 2000):

> As society becomes more and more diverse and classrooms become accessible to more and more children with special needs, instruction must be designed to ensure that *all* [sic] students have access to the best instruction and the highest quality materials and are subject to the same high expectations. . . . Diverse and individual needs are met by varying the time and intensity [but not the means] of instruction. (p. 12F)

The second quote comes from the program's Web site (SRA, 2000, p. 1):

> [The program] is designed such that no assumptions are made about students' prior knowledge; each skill is systematically and explicitly taught in a logical progression, to enable understanding and mastery.

These quotes suggest that the nothing assumption for the "all" children is not about sociocultural variation in children's experiences with literacy, in their ways of communicating with adults and peers, or in the nature of their everyday worlds and, thus, their everyday knowledge (Genishi, 2002; McNaughton, 2003; Nieto, 1999). The nothing assumption rests on a concern that "diverse" children are more apt to come to school without literacy skills.

The nothing assumption recalls the concern in the sixties for the "culturally disadvantaged." In their professional text on "teaching disadvantaged children," Bereiter and Englemann (1966) portray teaching reading skills as a means of overcoming the assumed linguistic barrenness (the nothingness) of children's everyday lives. The potentially unruly disadvantaged children are contrasted with the "culturally privileged" ones. The latter children's assumed language-rich life allows them to come to school, if not with everything, at least with some awareness of words and the alphabetic principle.

This contrast between the ideal children developing literacy and the racialized and classed other children lacking resources has assumed new prominence. Government-backed literacy "science" has made teaching the "all" children a matter of equity (Schemo, 2002). Organize manageable bits of literacy knowledge into a sequenced curriculum and teach it directly to orderly children—and do so as early as possible. No time to waste. Ah, but the rub is the children themselves, whose sociality is among the "worst enemies to what we call teaching" (Ashton-Warner, 1963, p. 103).

School brings many children together in one space. And those children develop social bonds and playful practices linked to, but not controlled by, adults. In other words, children have minds and social agendas of their own. And, as I illustrate below, it is the metaphoric drinking god that wields power over the children and leads them to play "the very devil with orthodox method" (Ashton-Warner, 1963, p. 103).

The Drinking God: The Unruly Spirit of Childhood Learning

I first met the drinking god when he was invoked by Denise as she worked on a task in her first-grade classroom:

> Denise has just participated in a class lesson blending a study of the artist Jacob Lawrence with a study of the underground railroad—that network of pathways and dwellings through which slaves escaped from the southern U.S. to freedom in Canada. The lesson centered on slides of Lawrence's paintings of Harriet Tubman, an escaped slave who led many others to freedom. During the lesson, Rita, the teacher, discussed with the children Lawrence's use of the North Star, which guided the people, and, also the star's location in the constellation called the Drinking Gourd or alternatively, the Big Dipper. Over many days to come, Rita and the children would sing and study the words to Pete Seeger's version of "Follow the Drinking Gourd."
>
> Now that the lesson is over, Denise and her peers are to show what they've learned. And so, sitting side-by-side, Denise and her good friend and "fake sister" Vanessa, both African American, draw their versions of a muscular Harriet Tubman chopping wood, tears streaming down her face. As she draws, Denise becomes Harriet Tubman, writing "Denise That's me" on her drawn image and, then, adding the statement, "I'm mad and I followed the drinking god."

The drinking god. Mmmm. Usually a quiet observer, I intervene and ask Denise if she means the "drinking *gourd*." "It's drinking *god*," she says definitively.

Vanessa agrees. Some people say "god," some say "gourd. *Duh!*" Undaunted, I persist:

Dyson	What does this god do? [very politely]
Denise	He makes the star for them to follow . . .
Dyson	Why did Harriet Tubman follow the drinking god?
Denise	She was a slave.
Vanessa	If she sung a song, her friends would love her. What's that song? [recollecting a tune]

And soon an R & B song learned from the radio arises from Denise and Vanessa's table.

With this vignette, I formally introduce the drinking god factor—the factor that becomes evident when one assumes that children bring, not nothing, but frames of reference (i.e., familiar practices and old symbolic stuff) to make sense of new content, discursive forms, and symbolic tools. As they participate in the official school task of composing "what I learned," Denise and Vanessa blend resources from varied experiences, including those they shared as collaborative child players, churchgoers, participants in popular culture, and attentive young students. They know, for example, that music is a symbol of affiliation, not only for them ("what's that song [we both know]?"), but also for Harriet Tubman and other conductors on the Underground Railroad ("Let my people go"). And they know that people speak different varieties of English—people's voices have different rhythms and rhymes, different ways of drawing out or cutting short sounds; such language variation is an official topic in sound/symbol lessons and in literary ones in *their* room, but not a topic in the first-grade programs for the "all" children, who are to speak in uniform ways.

It is a serious error to assume that any child brings nothing to new experiences. Indeed, all reputable developmental accounts assume that nothing comes from nothing.

Given the power of the drinking god, it is a serious error to assume that any child brings nothing to new experiences. Indeed, all reputable developmental accounts assume that nothing comes from nothing. Any learning must come from something, from some experiential base that supports participation and sensemaking in the designated learning tasks (Piaget & Inhelder, 1969; Vygotsky, 1962).

For Denise and her friends, that base comes from their everyday lives in a complex social landscape like that theorized by Bakhtin (1981, 1986). Their landscape is filled with interrelated communication practices, involving different kinds of symbol systems (e.g., written language, drawing, music), different technologies (e.g., video, radio, animation), and different ideologies or ideas about how the world works. The children experience these practices as kinds of voices (Hanks, 1996)—the voices, say, of radio deejays and stars, sitcom characters, and oft-heard poets, of sports announcers, preachers, teachers, and teenagers, and on and on.

So, in my research project, I studied how children used their experiences participating in all these practices for their own childhood pleasures and for school learning. That is, I studied the recontextualization processes (Bauman & Briggs, 1990; Miller & Goodnow, 1995) through which they borrowed material from these practices, translated it across and reorganized it within childhood play practices, and, also, official school literacy ones.

Studying a Childhood Culture: The Project Data Set

The children's school was an urban elementary school in the East San Francisco Bay. Denise's teacher, Rita, was highly experienced, having begun teaching in the London primary schools of the 60s. Rita's curriculum included both open-ended activities, such as writing workshop, where the children wrote and drew relatively freely, followed by class sharing, and more teacher-directed ones, such as assigned tasks in study units, in which children wrote and drew as part of social studies and science learning.

I spent an academic year in Rita's room studying the childhood culture enacted by a small group of first graders, all African American, who called themselves "the brothers and the sisters"—and they meant that quite literally; they pretended to have a common Mama. The children were Denise, Vanessa, Marcel, Wenona, Noah, and Lakeisha. I observed and audiotaped them on the playground and in the classroom, particularly during composing activities, and I also interviewed their parents.

As the work progressed, I realized how much the popular media informed the children's world. From their experiences with the media, children formed interpretive frames–or understandings of typical voice types or genres. And within those varied kinds of voices, they found much play material, including conceptual content; models of textual structures and elements; and a pool of potential characters, plots, and themes.

Studying how the children used this material in official (or school-governed) as well as unofficial (or child-governed) worlds resulted in this account of literacy development. Because of space constraints, I focus on a key event from Marcel's case, although I allow Denise some time in the spotlight as well.

Literacy Development as Remix

Fittingly enough, as I tried to articulate an account of literacy development grounded in the project's particulars, I turned to a major source of the children's textual toys—hip hop. Hip hop, in fact, is about "making something out of nothing." I heard that explanation more than once from hip hop practitioners, whom I consulted in the course of this project. As they explained, rap was born during a time when public funds for education and for youth programs were slashed and public distrust of youth was heightened. So, informed by cultural traditions that stretch back through time, urban youth took their used cultural stuff and old technologies and transformed them into flexible modes of expression (Yerba Buena Center for the Arts, 2001; Smitherman, 2000). They made a drum out of a turntable, a style of dancing out of karate kicks, a storyteller out of a chanter. They created something, if not out of nothing, at least out of some things that might not originally have been seen as innovative, creative, and generative.

This notion of material that might be seen as "nothing" becoming "something" seemed to capture the essence of my project. I observed the children sampling symbolic material from the communicative practices—the varied kinds of voices—that filled the landscape of their everyday lives. Analogous to rap artists, the children appropriated and adapted this material as they constructed their unofficial and playful practices. Moreover, like producers who remix musical compositions, they adapted that old textual stuff to the new beats required in official literacy spaces.

The children's sampling and remixing—their recontextualization processes—opened up literacy pathways to their resources from diverse communicative practices. I do my own textual sampling to illustrate these processes as enacted in children's unofficial and official worlds.

Sampling Unofficial Textual Play

Like her fake siblings, Denise found many of her textual toys on the Bay Area's leading hip hop radio station. In her recess radio play, she and her fake siblings deconstructed that station into a set of diverse and interrelated kinds of practices, of voices.

The children's sampling and remixing—their recontextualization processes—opened up literacy pathways to their resources from diverse communicative practices.

For example, in radio play, Denise did not simply *sing*. She became a kind of singer—a rapper, a soul singer. Moreover, she could situate singers in relationship to others (e.g., deejays, audience members) and to varied interrelated radio practices (song announcing, radio interviews). She had a sense of the landscape of practices—of voices—upon which she was playing; and she could flexibly manipulate words, phrasing, intonation, even speaking turns as the situation required. Listen to a bit of playground radio play, as Denise interviews herself:

Denise	(assuming a polite, interested tone) Denise. Tell us, why do you like to sing—and your friends?
Denise	(rapping) We want to be a star/In the store/We want to be on stage/For our cage.

For Marcel, sports media was a favored source of textual play materials. He and Wenona and Noah enacted a relational world of coaches, teammates, and rivals. The children had a demanding schedule: their coach was based both in Minnesota (where he had a coed hockey team, the Mighty Ducks, based on a movie of the same name) and in Texas (Dallas, Texas, to be exact, where he coached the Cowboys, a professional football team).

The children's sports play, like radio play, involved a range of interrelated practices that included, first, planning agendas that allowed time for practice sessions, travel to varied destinations (often across state lines), babysitting for relatives, and homework; second, narrating highlights of previous games, featuring themselves; and, third, evaluating the relative merits of teams. And, like professional sports broadcasters, Marcel and his friends made much use of adverbs of time and place. Listen as Marcel and Wenona discuss upcoming events:

Wenona and Marcel are sitting together during a morning work period. They are doing their work in the official world, but they are also doing their "work" in the unofficial world (i.e., planning their upcoming schedule):

Wenona	You know I'm thinking about going over to [a relative's] house today but we gotta play games. I forgot. We playing hockey. Today we playing hockey.
Marcel	Cause we gotta play hockey, [agreeing]
Wenona	In Los Angeles—no—
Marcel	It's in Los Angeles. [affirming]
Wenona	It's in Pittsburgh and Los Angeles.
Marcel	I forgot. We gotta play Pittsburgh.
Wenona	In Pittsburgh.
Marcel	Pittsburgh is real weak.

"*In* Pittsburgh," said Wenona, emphasizing the preposition *in* and, thereby, the distinction between a city location and a city team. In a similar way, the children sometimes played "Minnesota (pause) *in* Minnesota" or "Dallas (pause) *in* Dallas."

In the children's play, Dallas always won, but that was not the case when Marcel engaged in sports chat with other boys. He, Samuel, and Zephenia often repeated football scores to each other after an opening "Did you see the game?" And, in that practice, Dallas could lose. Like Denise, then, Marcel's playful practices evidenced his borrowing and revoicing of symbolic material from a landscape of possibilities. He flexibly manipulated textual material (including scores) in different ways, depending on the social situation he was in.

Official Textual Play

In official school activities, too, children borrowed from their landscape of possibilities. Their remixing processes displayed the drinking god's power—the power of these unexpected frames of reference—to create both order and havoc. On the one hand, these frames guided children's agency, their decision-making about how to manipulate the elements of the written system—its letters, words, syntax—to accomplish some end. On the other hand, they posed very useful symbolic, social, and ideological challenges as they moved across symbol systems and social worlds with different expectations and conventions.

I aim to describe how, energized and guided by the desire for social participation, children use old resources from familiar practices and adapt them to enter into new ones.

Before I illustrate this official remixing with an example from Marcel, I engage in a little textual play of my own. I link this "remix" approach to an earlier nonlinear view of literacy development, that of Marie Clay. In this way, I hope to clarify what the remix view may add to the repertoire of ways of understanding child literacy.

My textual play: Situating Clay's "kaleidoscopic reshuffle." Beginning most notably with *What Did I Write?* in 1975, Clay has detailed a constructivist view of written language development. In this view, children must take control over the written medium, learning to direct and monitor its use in producing and receiving messages. Unlike many other developmental views emerging in the seventies, Clay did not reduce early composing to spelling nor did she posit "stages" of learning. Based on close observation of the ways of writing for children entering New Zealand schools, Clay analyzed how children engage with written language as a complex system, at first "in approximate, specific, and what seem to be primitive ways and later with considerable skill" (p. 19).

Children's first efforts may suggest the idiosyncratic and varied bits of knowledge that they have accumulated from diverse experiences with print in families and communities; among such knowledge may be letter forms, written names, perhaps a sense of how certain kinds of print sound when read. When they respond to school literacy tasks, children orchestrate their knowledge and know-how to construct basic concepts about print—the nature of signs, page arrangement, directionality, voice/print match. Flexibility in child response is important because rigid early learning may keep children from adapting their understandings as new literacy tasks are faced. Clay (1975) notes, "Chance experiences may produce new insights at any time" (p. 7). Hence, her "kaleidoscopic reshuffle"—the reworking of children's understandings of a complex, multilayered system (1998).

I entered the child literacy conversation at a different time and with different conceptual tools—more sociolinguistic, sociocultural, and folkloric than psychological, like Clay's. Given those tools, I aim to situate Clay's cognitive reshuffle within a social notion of communicative practices. That is, I aim to describe how, energized and guided by the desire for social participation, children use old resources from familiar practices and adapt them to enter into new ones. Thus, their pathways into school literacy are found in the converging and diverging trajectories of practices. The ideal developmental outcome of these processes is not only flexibility and adaptability with written conventions but also with symbol systems and with social conventions. To illustrate, I turn to a key event from Marcel's case.

Marcel re-mapping his words and worlds. Marcel is sitting by Lakeisha on one side and a parent volunteer, Cindy, on the other. Lakeisha is his fake sister and understands that he plays for a winning team—Dallas. Indeed, Marcel tells her that he is planning to write about Dallas. Through his text, Marcel will enact a familiar practice—reporting his team's triumphs. His planned text is thus situated at least partially in the childhood world he shares with Lakeisha.

Marcel	(to Lakeisha) I know what I want to write about. "The Dallas Cowboys [beat] Carolina."
Cindy	They [Dallas] lost. Did you watch the game?

The adult Cindy corrects the child Marcel. She is not, after all, a relative; she views Marcel as a little boy who has the facts about Dallas's fate in the football playoffs wrong. She initiates a different practice—a "Did-you-watch-the-game?" practice. Marcel can participate in this practice as well:

Marcel	They're out! Out of the playoffs?
Cindy	They're like the 49ers now.

Marcel changes his plans. He still starts with *The Dallas*, then stops, gets the classroom states map for spelling help, and begins to copy *Minnesota*, whom Dallas had beaten the previous week [see Figure 1].

Marcel	(to the table, generally, as he looks at the map) It's got all the states right here.
	(to himself as he writes Minnesota) Minnesota, Minnesota, Minnesota, Minnesota . . . to the city of dreams. Minnesota, Minnesota, Minnesota, to the city of dreams. (pause) Dallas, Texas. Dallas, Texas. Dallas, Texas.
	(to the table) This has all the states, right here. I have all the states, right over here . . .
	I'm writing "Dallas against Minnesota."

Figure 1   Marcel's sports report.

Marcel then recites "Dallas, Texas" several more times before writing "in Texas."

| Marcel: | It [the score]—it was, 15—no 15 to 48. |
| Marcel: | (to Cindy) This says, "Dallas against Minnesota. In Texas 15 to 48. |

Marcel has recalled the exact score. He does come to school, after all, quite prepared to participate in the "Did-you-watch-the-game?" practice. He simply had not been planning to participate in that one. And, in fact, he now slips back into the fictionalized world of team players and fake siblings that he shares with Lakeisha.

| Marcel: | (to Lakeisha) I be home tomorrow, only me and Wenona will be home late. 'Cause me and Wenona got practice . . . I still got to go to football practice . . . Wenona got cheerleading. |

Marcel and Wenona will both be home with Mama and Lakeisha tomorrow—but they'll be late. The Cowboys may be out of the play-offs, but Marcel's "still got to go to football practice," and Wenona's still got to go to cheerleading.

In this complexly situated event, you can hear Marcel sample from a score-reporting practice of televised sports. And that practice is itself situated within the frame of the children's unofficial sports play. (Dallas won!) That unofficial frame converges with the official one of writing workshop. This converging of different social practices, with their different uses of symbolic media, yields challenges—potential learning and teaching opportunities—including all those discussed by Clay and more.

To begin, you can hear and see the converging of practices when Marcel translates (or remixes) the audiovisual display of sports scores to a paper and pencil display. As Clay might anticipate, Marcel's event reveals how children have to sort out the nature, and allowable flexibility, of different kinds of signs, among them letters, numbers, and images. But Marcel is not grappling with "the" set of written conventions—the conventions of these converging practices differ. In

school, Marcel is expected to write using letter graphics, but, as a sports announcer, Marcel should place team emblems by their names (the Vikings' horn, the Cowboys' star).

Marcel's event also highlights Clay's concepts of directionality and page arrangement. But Marcel's efforts here are not the result of a child engaging solely with print but, again, of a child recontextualizing written language across practices. Marcel does not follow the left-to-right conventions of a prose report; he arranges team names and scores vertically, as on a TV screen.

The converging of different practices is notable too in the complex interplay of what is written and what is read (i.e., voice/print match). To hear that interplay, you have to know that, in the official writing workshop, Rita emphasized that the children should monitor how their spoken and written words match. And you must know too that the sports announcers' practice is to read a more elaborate text than the one visually displayed.

With those practice details as background information, you can hear Marcel as he shifts voices, precariously positioned between practices. He initially writes *The* before he writes *Dallas*, a prose reporting style since he has a sentence planned. "The Dallas Cowboys beat Carolina." After the parent, Cindy, corrects him, Marcel writes a screen-like display of team names and scores to accurately report the previous week's play in which Dallas did beat Minnesota. Between his columns of team names are the words "in Texas," which would not be written on such a display, but which an announcer might read. Marcel himself adopts an announcer voice as he rereads his text to the adult, "Dallas against Minnesota. In Texas. 15 to 48." In so doing, he reads the unwritten "against," but not the written *the*.

Beyond these symbolic and discursive challenges, there are conceptual ones. Marcel grapples with the distinction between cities and states, a distinction *not* made in team names (e.g., the Minnesota Vikings, the Dallas Cowboys). "This [map] has all the states, right here," he announces. Entering into the map-reading practice, Marcel's articulated knowledge emerges as the geographic knowledge embedded in football team names is disrupted and reorganized. In a previous event, Marcel had tried unsuccessfully to find "Oakland" [for the Oakland Raiders] on the states map, which led to a discussion about the map with Rita.

Then, as if all those challenges were not enough, Marcel confronts the situated reality of "truth." What is true in the brothers and sisters' world (that Dallas always wins) is not necessarily true in the real Bay Area world. And, finally, there are the gender ideologies embedded in all football-related events, ideologies that could become salient when they entered the official world through whole-class sharing, as they did when Rita led a class discussion about the truth of a child's assertion that only boys like football.

In sum, when Marcel translated cultural material (e.g., names, informational displays, kinds of texts, text sequencing conventions) across the boundaries of different practices, the symbolic, social, and ideological knowledge embedded in those practices could be disrupted and brought into reflective awareness. Certainly a childhood practice built with the textual toys of media sports shows is not on anyone's list of critical early literacy experiences. But there it was anyway, evidence of the drinking god factor and of Marcel's, and children's, agency in deciding what's relevant to literacy tasks.

Learning to read, or learning anything, for that matter, is actually a process of complex variation.

Similar analyses were done for all the brothers and sisters (Dyson, 2003) whose cases are filled with converging and diverging practices. The practices—the typified voices—of hip hop radio, cartoon shows, and popular films all figured—in unexpected but ultimately productive ways—into the written language trajectories of individual children, brothers and sisters, growing up in these voice-filled times.

Toward Developmental Accounts for All (Unmarked) Children

Institutions serving the "all" children are being urged to reduce literacy to the "basics"—and to reduce early childhoods themselves to a time for reading readiness. And yet, as Anderson-Levitt (1996) comments,

> the premise that learning takes place in stages along a narrow linear path [assumes that . . .] one could learn more only by progressing further along that path instead of by wandering off the track. This is the same flawed idea that Stephen Jay Gould found at the core of intelligence measures. . . . He called it the "fallacy of ranking . . . our propensity for ordering complex variation as a gradual ascending scale" (p. 24).

Learning to read, or learning anything, for that matter, is actually a process of complex variation. "Wandering off the track" was something the brothers and sisters often did without any intention to do so. They simply did what all learners do—they called upon the drinking god, that is, upon familiar frames of reference and well-known materials, to help them enter into new possibilities. The very diversity of organized social spaces within which they lived (e.g., families, schools, media events, not to mention the brothers and sisters' world) mitigated against unilateral control of children's learning by any one institution. And this

was good, as it led to their productive grappling with the symbolic, social, and ideological complexities of written texts and social worlds.

This developmental point of view, with its openness to children's sampling and remixing, should render anemic those views that attempt to fragment written language into a string of skills or to narrowly define the home and community experiences that can contribute to school learning (Reyes & Halcon, 2001). The message for teaching inherent in this view is deceptively straightforward—teachers must be able to recognize children's resources, to see where they are coming from, so that they can establish the common ground necessary to help children differentiate and gain control over a wealth of symbolic tools and communicative practices.

To develop such common ground, teachers like Rita work toward a productive interplay of unofficial and official worlds. For example, through open-ended composing periods, educators can learn about children's textual toys and the themes that appeal to them. And in classroom forums in which children present their work, teachers can help children name and compare how varied kinds of texts look and sound and, moreover, how and why and even if they appeal to all of them as classroom participants (Dyson, 1993, 1997; Marsh & Millard, 2000). As children bring unexpected practices, symbolic materials, and technological tools into the official school world, the curriculum itself should broaden and become more responsive to children's worlds.

But teachers themselves need working conditions that support responsive, interactive teaching, not scripted encounters for the "all" children (Weiner, 2000). Given my constraints and possibilities as an observer of children, I have tried to respond to the current political push for such encounters by bringing word of the drinking god. It is faith in that metaphoric god—in the notion that actions are guided by intentions grounded in experience—that keeps me, and others, from assuming nothing but, rather, staying alert to the resources of all *children* (no winking intended). In other words: Follow the drinking god.

Author's Note

This article is a variant of the full essay entitled "The Drinking God Factor: A Writing Development Remix for 'All' Children" (Dyson, 2002). The research report on which it is based is available in *The Brothers and Sisters Learn to Write: Popular Literacies in Childhood and School Cultures* (Dyson, 2003). The research itself was supported through the generosity of the Spencer Foundation, although the findings and opinions expressed herein are not necessarily shared by that organization. This article was first presented as a talk at The Ohio State University and at the United Kingdom Reading Association International Convention in Chester, UK, July 2002. I thank my hard-working research assistant, Soyoung Lee.

References

Adams, M., Bereiter, C., Hirshberg, J., Anderson, V., & Bernier, S. A. (2000). *Framework for effective teaching: Grade 1 teacher's guide, part A, for Open Court Reading 2000 basal series.* DeSoto, TX: SRA/McGraw-Hill.

Anderson-Levitt, K. M. (1996). Behind schedule: Batch-produced children in French and U.S. classrooms. In B. A. Levinson, D. E. Foley, & D. C. Holland [Eds.], *The cultural production of the educated person: Critical ethnographies of schooling and local practice* (pp. 57–78). Albany: State University of New York Press.

Ashton-Warner, S. (1963). *Teacher.* New York: Simon & Schuster.

Bakhtin, M. (1981). Discourse in the novel. In C. Emerson & M. Holquist (Eds.), *The dialogic imagination: Four essays by M. Bakhtin* (pp. 254–422). Austin: University of Texas Press.

Bakhtin, M. (1986). *Speech genres and other late essays.* Austin: University of Texas Press.

Bauman, R., & Briggs, C. (1990). Poetics and performance as critical perspectives on language and social life. *Anthropological Review, 19,* 59–88.

Bereiter, C., & Engelmann, S. (1966). *Teaching disadvantaged children in the preschool.* Englewood Cliffs, NJ: Prentice Hall.

Clay, M. (1975). *What did I write?* Auckland: Heinemann.

Clay, M. (1998). *By different paths to common outcomes.* York, ME: Stenhouse.

Dyson, A. Haas. (1993). *Social worlds of children learning to write in an urban primary school.* New York: Teachers College Press.

Dyson, A. Haas. (1997). *Writing superheroes: Contemporary childhood, popular culture, and classroom literacy.* New York: Teachers College Press.

Dyson, A. Haas. (2002). The drinking god factor: A writing development remix for "all" children. *Written Communication, 19,* 454–577.

Dyson, A. Haas. (2003). *The brothers and sisters learn to write: Popular literacies in childhood and school cultures.* New York: Teachers College Press.

Genishi, C. (2002). Young English language learners: Resourceful in the classroom. *Young Children, 57*(4). 66–72.

Hanks, W.F. (1996). *Language and communicative practices,* Boulder, CO: Westview.

Marsh, J., & Millard, E. (2000). *Literacy and popular culture.* London: Sage.

McNaughton, S. (2003). *Meeting of minds.* Wellington, New Zealand: Learning Media.

Miller, P., & Goodnow, J. J. (1995). Cultural practices: Toward an integration of culture and development. In J. J. Goodnow, P. J. Miller, & F. Kessel (Eds.), *Cultural practices as contexts for development, No. 67: New directions in child development* (pp. 5–16). San Francisco: Jossey Bass.

Nieto, S. (1999). *The light in their eyes: Creating multicultural learning communities.* New York: Teachers College Press.

Piaget, J., & Inhelder, B. (1969). *The psychology of the child.* New York: Basic Books.

Reyes, M. de la Luz, & Halcon, J. J. (Eds.), (2001). *The best for our children: Critical perspectives on literacy for Latino students.* New York: Teachers College Press.

Schemo, D. J. (2002, January 9). Education bill urges new emphasis on phonics as method for teaching reading. *The New York Times,* p. A-16.

Smitherman, G. (2000). "The chain remain the same": Communicative practices in the hip hop nation. In G. Smitherman, *Talkin' that talk* (pp. 268–286). London: Routledge.

SRA/McGraw Hill. (2000). Open Court reading: Grade levels K–6 (Online). Retrieved August 11, 2003, from *http://www. sra-4kids.com/product_info/ocr*

Vygotsky, L. S. (1962). *Thought and language.* Cambridge, MA: MIT Press.

Weiner, L (2000). Research in the 90s: Implications for urban teacher preparation. *Review of Educational Research, 70,* 369–406.

Yerba Buena Center. (2001). *Hip hop nation: A teacher's guide.* San Francisco: Yerba Buena Center for the Performing Arts.

That's Not Fair! Critical Literacy as Unlimited Semiosis

Christine H. Leland and Jerome C. Harste
Indiana University

Cinder Edna (Jackson, 1994) lived next-door to Cinderella. She also had a wicked stepmother and evil stepsisters, but took a more proactive 'can do' approach to life. While Cinderella moped among the cinders trying to warm herself, Cinder Edna kept warm by hiring out her services to mow lawns and clean parrot cages for the neighbours and by teaching herself to play the accordion. She is described as 'strong and spunky'—someone with a good sense of humour. While Cinderella waited around for a fairy godmother to provide a fancy dress and coach for the ball, Cinder Edna used her cage-cleaning money to put a dress on lay-by and then took the bus to the castle. At the end of the story, Cinderella married the prince (who was as conceited and dull as she was), while Cinder Edna married the prince's dynamic—but definitely not handsome—younger brother. The book ends with the notation that the girl who had once been known as Cinderella ended up living in a big palace where she 'went to endless ceremonies and listened to dozens of speeches' while her husband talked about 'troops, parade formations, and uniform buttons'. The girl who had been known as Cinder Edna, on the other hand, ended up in a small cottage with solar heating where she 'studied waste disposal engineering and cared for orphaned kittens'.

Doesn't Cinder Edna still end up fulfilling the cultural expectation that she will become someone's wife?

When we share this book with our undergraduate trainees, they almost always say that they like it. Many of the women in our classes claim that the book depicts a modern woman who is gutsy enough to do things her own way and who isn't concerned with measuring up to the standard image of what women are supposed to be. But they all get defensive when we wonder aloud about whether the story suggests that a woman can only achieve real happiness by getting married. In spite of all her independent characteristics, we argue, doesn't Cinder Edna still end up fulfilling the cultural expectation that she will become someone's wife? This line of questioning is never popular with our students. They don't want to be pushed out of their comfort zone by an interpretation that interrogates norms they have always taken for granted. While most of them can stretch enough to accept Cinder Edna's decisions to use solar heating and study waste disposal engineering, that's as far as they are willing to go. Even those who display considerable flexibility in other areas are much less flexible when it comes to questioning interpretations that are mediated by cultural norms. Marriage is a sign that comes laden with non-negotiable meaning. Like readers everywhere, our undergraduate students are bringing their own set of meanings to the text rather than making meaning from it. As Daniel Hade (1997) suggests, 'we do not think to get meaning, but rather we use meaning to think' (p. 235).

We do not think to get meaning, but rather we use meaning to think.

C. S. Peirce (1931–1935) described reading in terms of 'signs,' with each sign being composed of three elements: a symbol, a referent and an interpretant. In the case of *Cinder Edna*, the text (what appears on the page) is the symbol. Cinder Edna, herself, is the referent (the object that is represented by the symbol), and the interpretant is the meaning that is brought to the sign. While what Cinder Edna 'means' may vary, individual members within a cultural group share important interpretants. The study of how groups mean is called 'semiotics.' One interpretant, more often than not, triggers another interpretant, resulting in a process called 'unlimited semiosis' (Eco 1980) which extends meaning well beyond whatever triggered the thought in the first place. For example, while many members of our culture will first interpret Cinder Edna as 'gusty', their next thoughts are that 'she is breaking new ground', and then that she might be 'into women's liberation'. At this point, a number of women may decide that they really don't want to be like Cinder Edna

*From "That's Not Fair! Critical Literacy as Unlimited Semiosis," by C.H. Leland and J.C. Harste, 2001, *The Australian Journal of Language and Literacy*, 24(3) 208–219. Copyright 2001 Australian Literacy Educators' Association. Reprinted with permission.

after all, since they perceive that women's liberation is a social movement that they don't necessarily want to join. And we suspect that more than a few of our male students are thinking that this is not exactly the type of woman they had in mind for a wife. The dominant cultural image of the wife as the submissive and subservient partner is seriously challenged by Cinder Edna's non-traditional approach. Further, some students might interpret our interrogation of the assumption that a *wedding equals a happy ending* as a rejection of the institution of marriage, a cornerstone of the current social order. Suddenly the semiotic process seems to be taking many of our students beyond their comfort zones.

Discomfort, however, can be a catalyst for change. As Kress (2000) has suggested, a theory of semiosis needs to go beyond a description of how an existing system of meaning is used and address issues of change and transformation as well. Language is not stable or autonomous, but is continuously transformed by the people who use it. Kress defines an 'adequate theory of semiosis' as one that is 'founded on a recognition of the 'interested action' of socially located, culturally and historically formed individuals, as the remakers, the transformers, and the reshapers of the representational resources available to them' (p. 155). Thus, conversations and attempts to express the meaning of a story through other sign systems (for example, art or drama) can ultimately transform the chain of interpretants and lead to the generation of new perspectives. As the social and individual interests of the participants change, they generate representations that are both new and shaped from the designs of others.

Using Children's Literature to Support Critical Literacy

Semiotics allows us to see reading first and foremost as a process of interpretation, and interpretation as the function of a social group and the dominant discourses that operate within that group. To read semiotically is to read critically, questioning the role of the interpretant in the triad. This approach to reading is not found in any instructional materials that we have seen. As a result, we have been exploring ways to encourage both teachers and children to take a more semiotic stance. One resource we have developed over the past 3 years is a text set of what we call 'critical children's books' (Leland et al. 1999, Harste et al. 2000). These books address tough social issues like violence, racial discrimination and controversial gender issues—topics that are often considered to be inappropriate for children (Leland & Harste 1999). They open up spaces for conversations

that begin to question both the text and different people's interpretation of the text. We introduce our teacher education trainees to this text set and invite them to respond to the books in a variety of ways. *White Wash* (Shange 1997), *White Socks Only* (Coleman 1996) and *Sister Anne's Hands* (Lorbieki 1998) are three critical books that bring our students face-to-face with the issue of racial discrimination and the role it plays in the lives of children.

White Wash (Shange 1997) is the story of Helene-Angel, an African American preschooler who was attacked by a gang of White teenagers as she walked home with Mauricio, her older brother. The gang members beat up Mauricio and painted Helene-Angel's face white. They claimed that they were showing her how to be a 'true American' and 'how to be White'. When Mauricio finally got her home, Helene-Angel was so traumatised that she hid in her room for days. After much urging by her grandmother, she finally gathered up her courage and went out to face the world again. Fortunately, her classmates were waiting to greet her; they promised to stick together so that events like that wouldn't happen again.

White Socks Only (Coleman 1996) is another story about an African American child who experienced racial violence, in this case during the era of legalised segregation in Mississippi. In this story, a young girl saw the 'Whites Only' sign on a public water fountain and interpreted it to mean that one had to be wearing white socks in order to drink there. As a result of this interpretation, she carefully removed her shoes and stepped up to drink from the fountain in her clean white socks. When some of the town's White residents attempted to humiliate and punish the child for drinking from the fountain, a group of African American adults moved in to defend her and take action to get rid of the sign.

In the third story, *Sister Anne's Hands* (Lorbiecki 1998), an African American teaching nun was the target of racial discrimination. In this case, a child was responsible for the message on a paper aeroplane that crashed into the chalkboard in her classroom: 'Roses are red, violets are blue. Don't let Sister Anne get any black on you!' Since she was a skilful teacher, Sister Anne was able to use the incident as a way to help her students learn about history, oppression and the opportunity we all have to make the future different. In the end, when Sister Anne received a new teaching assignment at another school, she left the children with images of multicoloured hands as a metaphor for what we can learn across racial differences. These three books form a kind of mini-text set that the trainees and teachers we work with have used frequently to engage children in conversations about fairness and equity. By studying the responses different people have made to these books, we have begun to see critical literacy as a process of unlimited semiosis.

Understanding Literacy as a Social Semiotic

One of the strategies we have used to introduce these books to both adults and children is 'Sketch to Stretch' (Short et al. 1996). This strategy invites readers to symbolise, through sketching, what a book means to them. Participants often have to be reminded that the goal is not to draw a picture from the book (like their favourite part, a common activity that most have experienced), but to sketch a picture of what they think the book means. This strategy invites abstract thinking and is often difficult at first. Some children (and adults) find it easier to begin by drawing a scene from the book and talking about why they chose that particular scene.

We learn the language of critique by participating in critical conversations.

After collecting numerous examples of responses to these books and others in the critical text set, we developed a taxonomy to categorise the different responses. This taxonomy evolved from our work with children and teacher education trainees as we added a critical literacy perspective to the inquiry approach that we had been developing over an extended period of time. We discovered that the inclusion of a critical perspective led to a deeper understanding of inquiry, power relationships and the possibility for social action. Although the taxonomy is built around four levels of response, we do not see it as developmental in the sense that young children will always be at the level 1 and only more mature individuals can be expected to reach level 4. Instead, we see it as a matter of experience. Participation in discussions about critical issues inducts people (both young and old) into a certain type of discourse. It's not a question of 'age, stage or Piaget' (Harste 1994, p. 1221), but a question of what experiences individuals have had. The more experience they have with this discourse, the more likely they are to begin using it on their own. We learn the language of critique by participating in critical conversations. The four levels were never 'taught' or modelled in any specific sense. However, conversations around books in the critical text set provided opportunities for trainees and children to learn this discourse. Since older children have experienced these conversations for several years, it is not surprising to find that their responses tend to be categorised more often at the higher levels than those of the younger ones. However, we have many examples of very young children operating at levels 3 and 4 when they have had opportunities to participate in conversations about power relationships and social action.

The first level is characterised as 'taking stock'. Sketches at this level show what was actually going on in the story rather than a more a more conceptual representation of the text's overall meaning. Level 1 interpretations suggest that people need to start out by summarising what they know before they can move on to deeper levels of reflection.

The second level, 'inquiry', is characterised by the presence of questions in addition to the 'taking stock' perspective. Inherent in the questions that students pose is an implicit or explicit challenge to one or more systems of meaning that operate in the society in which they live. Through the presence of questions, level 2 interpretations indicate a beginning awareness and understanding of dominant systems of meaning, what Ferguson (1990) has referred to as the 'invisible centre'.

Responses at the third level, 'interrogation', show evidence of the reader's attention to power relationships. Implicit in the response is a new vision of 'what might be'. While, ideally, one would like students to begin to question the roles they have played in maintaining dominant systems of meaning, this rarely happens. Students can often envision a new way of being without acknowledging (or perhaps even recognising) how they have had their 'hand in the cookie jar' (Leland & Harste 2000) in terms of allowing unequal power relationships to flourish.

And at the fourth level, 'social action', there is an articulated effort to effect some kind of change. Responses at this level call for readers to both think and act differently. They not only critique an existing relationship but indicate a willingness to take some sort of action to change it. In addition, their language often changes so that they begin to talk about these issues differently. At level 4, both their talk and their action indicate how they have repositioned themselves differently in the world.

Level 1: Taking Stock

When Kathryn McDaniel read *White Wash* to her first-graders, many of the children's sketches were at the 'taking stock' level. Mieca's drawing (Figure 1A) shows a group of figures and with just one who is not smiling. Her dictated caption reads, 'The girl is on the floor because they were putting paint on her because they didn't like her and they were not her friends'. Similarly, Amy Wackerly's second-and third-grade children produced a number of level 1 responses when she read the books described above and invited them to sketch what they thought the books meant. Tyffani (Figure 1B) responded to *White Socks Only* by showing two separate water fountains marked 'white' and 'coloured' and a building labelled 'Restroom stall white'. Next to this is a tree with the inscription 'Restroom coloured'. Tyffani's drawing, which provided the inspiration for the title of this article, also includes a child who is saying 'That's not fair!' The caption

Figure 1A

Figure 1B

Figure 2A

Figure 2B

reads: 'It's about when they had different water fountains and when the black people couldn't use the same restrooms as white people and they were sad'. We categorised this drawing as a level one example since it shows the learner 'taking stock' and summarising what she understands to be going on in the book.

Level 2: Inquiry

While some of the children's sketches show that they were thinking in terms of 'taking stock', others show that they were also moving forward and asking new questions. Therefore, we categorised these drawings as examples of level 2, 'inquiry'. When Caroline Shockley read the books to her second-graders and invited them to sketch a response, Michael drew a picture (Figure 2A) that was closely tied to the story. His caption, however, suggests that he was thinking beyond what actually happened in the book: 'This is a sign that Sister Anne put up. It has to do with slavery and telling black people to go back to Africa. I have a question—why didn't the slave owners pick their own cotton?' Anyah's picture (Figure 2B), with a large question mark featured prominently in the centre, shows that the book left her with many new inquiries. The picture includes a sad-looking figure,

identified by Anyah as the person telling the story, and lots of hands and feet with different designs on them. The caption for the picture reads, 'The girl is sad because the nun is leaving. I drew the hands because it doesn't matter what colour you are. Should everyone get along?'

Level 3: Interrogation

Some responses go beyond taking stock and asking new questions and begin to interrogate more overtly the power relationships that are implicit in the text. Abby Davis shared the books with fourth- and fifth-graders and offered 'Sketch to Stretch' as one way to respond. Devin's drawing of the yin and yang symbols surrounded by light and dark coloured arms and hands (Figure 3A) suggests that she is thinking beyond what is there and even beyond her own new questions. The caption that accompanies the sketch, 'Just because you are white or black or green, red, purple, or blue, it still does not give you a right to control people or boss them around', begins to interrogate the assumption that power and skin colour should be related. Another example of a level 3 response is the drawing that Caroline Shockley produced as she worked with her students. (We always

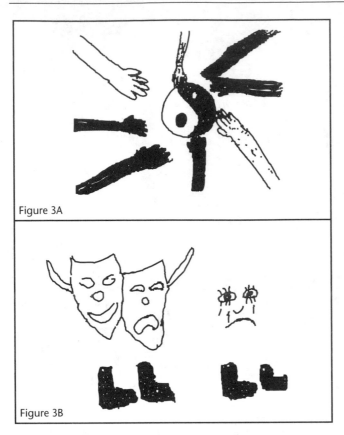

Figure 3A

Figure 3B

encourage teachers to engage in this activity with children and to share their drawings when everyone else does.) Caroline's sketch for *White Socks Only* (Figure 3B) shows the comedy and tragedy symbols, a crying face and a row of socks. Her caption reads: 'There were funny and sad parts in the story. It was funny how the little girl interpreted the sign 'Whites Only'. It was sad when the large man threw her to the side and then whipped her and others. The coloured socks represent the fact that other black people stood up for her, even though they were possibly going to get hit.' The representation of other people's socks lined up to support the cause of ending racial segregation shows attention to issues of power. Caroline envisioned the hypothetical owners of the socks placing themselves in a vulnerable position and risking their own safety to make a 'That's not fair!' statement about equity and justice.

Level 4: Social Action

Occasionally, we find instances where individuals adopt a stance of repositioning and moving on to take some sort of social action. While the format of 'Sketch to Stretch' (drawing) doesn't always lend itself to social action, we have observed that students frequently initiate social action projects after reading and

discussing books in our critical text set. Therefore, we were not surprised when a group of middle school students who were working with Marga Kish at the Center for Inquiry wanted to respond to what they perceived as an unfair editorial in the local newspaper. According to this editorial, 'Phonics, consistency are big IPS [Indianapolis Public Schools] needs' (anon., 2001). After lamenting how many IPS students 'don't read up to standards', the unidentified author flatly stated that 'These kids can't read'. The solution offered was a mandate of intensive, systematic phonics for all IPS students. The editorial went on to endorse Open Court, a commercial phonics-based reading program, as the silver bullet that would solve all of the reading problems in this large urban district.

A number of students were outraged with the editorial's stated claim that IPS kids can't read and with the suggestion that everyone in the district should be forced to use the Open Court reading program. They wrote a response back to the newspaper and argued that many of the claims made in the editorial were 'misleading and wrong'. They suggested that a phonics-based reading program is not the answer for improving test scores since their school always scores high and has never used Open Court or any other phonics-based program. The students proposed that reading books of choice for at least 30 minutes a day and 'having literature studies for an hour and a half each day' was what caused students to do well on tests. They also chastised the editorial writer for singling out the school with the lowest test scores and implied that this kind of bullying was not fair to the students and teachers in that particular school. Their letter ended with a request for the newspaper to correct the misleading statements and to send observers to visit their school so that they could see for themselves how their successful reading program works.

We don't know if this effort will have any long-term effects. It's significant to note that a week after the students' response letter was sent, an associate editor of the newspaper called to make an appointment to visit the school and talk to the students who wrote it. Maybe he will see how articulate and well-read they are and will begin to question his stance on how reading should be taught in schools. But even if the event is brushed off by the newspaper, the more enduring value of the experience might be that the students have learned to take a stand. They now know that newspaper articles don't always tell the truth and that it's up to all of us to read with a critical eye and respond with a critical voice when necessary. We want to argue that this experience positions them as different kinds of consumers and citizens. It's not enough to interrogate systems of power (like the media); it's also necessary to stand up for persecuted minorities (like the students and teachers at the school that ranked lowest in terms of test scores). We can predict that as they mature, their arguments will become more articulate and more sophisticated. They will be able to make the point that somebody always has to come in last when schools are ranked according to test scores and half of any group described by the normal curve has to be below average. Instructional approaches aren't going to change the number of winners and losers when the system of measurement is defined in this way.

'Our social world, with its rules, practices, and assignments of prestige and power, is not fixed; rather, we construct it with words, stories and silence' (Delgado 1995, p. xiv). We agree with Delgado and want to suggest that what can be 'constructed' can also be 'deconstructed' and interrogated. Cultural icons like the Cinderella story and standardised testing can be understood in a new way when readers stop to ask how these texts are trying to position them (Luke & Freebody 1997). Said differently, we are arguing that responses to reading are semiotic in at least three ways. First, an initial response triggers a further response and sets the process of unlimited semiosis in motion. Second, when supported through instructional practices like 'Sketch to Stretch', responses are multimodal and involve more sign systems than just language. Third, sign systems mediate our world and affect the stance that we take to other people and to the issue at hand. It is this social repositioning of self that is at the heart of critical literacy.

. . . it's important to give children and future teachers opportunities to take stock, inquire, interrogate and take action.

Seeing reading as a social semiotic is powerful. Not only do initial interpretations trigger new interpretations, but as the examples in this article demonstrate, the asking of new questions, the interrogation of 'what is', and the exploration of new social action in terms of 'what might be'. In short, a semiotic view of literacy creates space for students to consider the issue of what kind of literate beings they wish to become. For teachers, a semiotic view of literacy creates a window for seeing how our instructional efforts influence the development of our students as certain kinds of literate beings. If we want a society where citizens attend to issues of justice and equity, then it's important to give children and future teachers opportunities to take stock, inquire, interrogate and take action. Reading a book about a marginalised group and concluding 'That's not fair!' is a good way to begin.

References

Anon. 'Phonics, consistency are big IPS needs,' (2001, January). *Indianapolis Star*.

Coleman, E. 1996, *White Socks Only*, Albert Whitman & Co., Morton Grove, Il.

Delgado, R. 1995, *Critical Race Theory: The Cutting Edge*, Temple University, Philadelphia, Pa.

Eco, U. 1980, *A Theory of Semiotics*, Indiana University Press, Bloomington, In.

Ferguson, R. 1990, 'Introduction: Invisible center', in R. Ferguson, M. Grever, T. Minh-ha, & C. West (eds). *Out There: Marginalization and Contemporary Cultures*, MIT Press, Cambridge, Ma.

Hade, D. 1997, 'Reading multiculturally', in V. Harris (ed.), *Using Multiethnic Literature in the K-8 Classroom*, Christopher-Gordon, Norwood, Ma, pp. 233–255.

Harste, J.C. 1994, 'Literacy as curricular conversations about knowledge, inquiry, and morality', in R.B. Ruddell, M.R. Ruddell, & H. Singer (eds), *Theoretical Models and Processes of Reading* (4th edn) International Reading Association, Newark, De, pp. 1220–1242.

Harste, J., Vasquez, V., Lewison, M., Beau, A., Leland, C., & Ociepka, A. 2000, 'Supporting critical conversation in classrooms: A review of more than 50 picture books and young adult novels', in Kathryn Mitchell Pierce (ed.), *Adventuring with Books* (4th edn), NCTE, Urbana, Il.

Jackson, E. 1994, *Cinder Edna*. Lothrop, Lee & Shepard Books, New York.

Kress, G. 2000, 'Design and transformation: New theories of meaning', in B. Cope and M. Kalantzis (eds) for the New London Group, *Multiliteracies: Literacy Learning and the Design of Social Futures*, Melbourne, Australia, Macmillan.

Leland, C. & Harste, J. 1999, 'Is this appropriate for children? Books that bring realistic social issues into the classroom', *Practically Primary*, 4(3), 4–6.

Leland, C., & Harste, J. 2000, 'Critical literacy: Enlarging the space of the possible', *Primary Voices*, 9(2), 3–6.

Leland, C., Harste, J., Ociepka, A., Lewison, M., & Vasquez, V. 1999, 'Exploring critical literacy: You can hear a pin drop', *Language Arts*, 77(1), 70–77.

Lorbiecki, M. 1998, *Sister Anne's Hands*. Dial, New York, NY.

Luke, A., & Freebody, P. 1997, 'Shaping the social practices of reading', in S. Muspratt, A. Luke, & P. Freebody (eds), *Constructing Critical Literacies*, Hampton Press Inc., Cresskill, NJ, pp. 185–225.

Peirce, C. S. (1931–1935). *Collected papers*, Vols. (1–6), in P. Weiss and C. Hartshorne, (eds), Harvard University Press, Cambridge, Ma.

Shange, N. 1997, *White Wash*, illus. M. Sporn, Walker and Company, New York, NY.

Short, K., Harste, J., & Burke, C. 1996, *Creating Classrooms for Authors and Inquirers*, Heinemann, Portsmouth, NH.

STUDY GUIDE

1. What are the "socio-centric" and "school-centric" explanations for children's success and failure in standard tests of literacy? What is the alternative perspective on the relationship between literacy and schooling? (Street)

2. Explain, with examples, what the following statement means: "Language does not just reflect a pre-existing social reality, but helps to constitute that reality." (Street)

3. How is "the new work order" different from "the old work order?" What are the implications of these differences for language and literacy education? (Street)

4. What are the characteristics of "the new communicative order?" Discuss the implications of "the new communicative order" for language and literacy in both education and the workplace. (Street)

5. What are the "new literacies?" What are their social and epistemological bases? (Street)

6. From a "new literacies" perspective, how should we view the current educational standards set by the government and the "literacy crisis" as portrayed by the media? (Street)

7. What would a "new literacies" classroom look like? (Street; Dyson)

8. What does the term "all children" mean? What is the traditional school assumption about these children? What kind of pedagogical intervention was instituted for these children? (Dyson)

9. Identify different ways in which children "remix" their unofficial knowledge of popular culture in their school-based tasks. What is the significance of such unofficial knowledge in children's literacy learning in school? How can teachers encourage and foster a productive interplay between children's unofficial childhood worlds and their official school worlds? (Dyson)

10. How is Dyson's view of literacy development similar to and different from Marie Clay's "kaleidoscopic reshuffle"? How are they different from the traditional view of literacy development? (Dyson)

11. Today's children often incorporate in their writing or literature responses diverse voices and texts from the pop culture that surrounds them. Should teachers censor selections or appropriations that may be deemed "inappropriate" for the classroom, especially in the current high-stakes testing environment in which the set criteria for evaluating writing often devalues pop culture? Explain your answers. (Dyson)

12. How can teachers foster development of multiple literacies in the face of institutional, state, and federal mandates for testing, teaching, and curriculum? (Street; Dyson)

13. What connections can be forged between "new" and "old" literacy? What are the tensions and possibilities between notions of literacy rooted in the new communicative order and those associated with school-based tasks? (Street; Dyson)

14. What is the connection between semiotics and critical literacy? What does the term "unlimited semiosis" mean? (LeLand & Harste)

15. What is critical literacy? Why is it important? How can teachers foster its development? What is its relationship to the basic literacy that so often becomes the focus of school instruction? (LeLand & Harste)

16. What is the role of children's literature in supporting critical literacy development? Could you identify 3–5 text sets that can be used to promote critical literacy? (LeLand & Harste)

17. Identify and describe the four levels of critical literacy responses. What is the relationship among these levels? (LeLand & Harste)

18. In order to function effectively in today's society, one needs not only basic verbal literacies, but visual literacies, cyberliteracies, subject/genre-specific literacies, popular literacies, and critical literacies. It has been suggested that central to the development of these literacies is explicit knowledge of a grammar (or meta-language) that describes how the resources of language, images, and digital devices are deployed, independently or interactively, to construct different kinds of meanings that are appropriate for different contexts. Do you agree? Why or why not? Brainstorm about some possible strategies for developing multiple literacies in the classroom. (Street; Dyson; LeLand & Harste)

INQUIRY PROJECTS

1. The standards-based movement in the United States is not unlike Britain's latest literacy reform initiative as reflected in The National Literacy Strategy. Examine the literacy standards set in your state (e.g., Florida's Sunshine State Standards) and discuss whether these standards reflect the communicative demands of "the new work order." Do the same thing with the "Standards for English Language Arts" set by the International Reading Association (IRA) and the National Council of Teachers of English (NCTE) (accessible through the IRA or NCTE Web sites).

2. Collect excerpts of texts from popular magazines and Web sites, solicitation letters from credit card companies and Publisher's Clearinghouse, TV commercials, science and social studies textbooks, local newspapers, and novels. Examine the way language and images are deployed in these texts and discuss the effects of such deployment on readers' construction of meaning.

3. Collect samples of children's writing or classroom talk. Analyze the ways that children use their unofficial knowledge of popular culture or media to help them make sense of the official knowledge of the school curriculum.

4. Collect diverse (in terms of ethnicity and reading ability) children's oral or written responses to sample pieces of multicultural literature. Compare and contrast children's responses to these books using the taxonomy of critical thoughts created by LeLand and Harste.

FURTHER READING

Cope, B., & Kalantzis, M. (2000). *Multiliteracies: Literacy learning and the design of social futures*. London: Routledge.

Dyson, A. H. (2003). *The brothers and sisters learn to write: Popular literacies in childhood and school cultures*. New York: Teachers College Press.

Goodman, S. (2002). *Teaching youth media: A critical guide to literacy, video production, and social change*. New York: Teachers College Press.

Hull, G., & Schultz, K. (2002). *School's out!: Bridging out-of-school literacies with classroom practice*. New York: Teachers College Press.

Kist, W. (2000). Beginning to create the new literacy classroom: What does the new literacy look like? *Journal of Adolescent and Adult Literacy, 43*(8), 710–718.

Kress, G. (1997). *Before writing: Rethinking the paths to literacy*. London: Routledge.

Kress, G., & van Leeuwen, T. (1996). *Reading images: A grammar of visual design*. London: Routledge.

Muspratt, S., Luke, A., & Freebody, P. (1997). *Constructing critical literacies*. Cresskill, NJ: Hampton Press.

Newkirk, T. (2002). *Misreading masculinity: Boys, literacy, and popular culture*. Portsmouth, NH: Heinemann.

Sloan, G. (2003). *The child as critic: Developing literacy through literature, K–8* (4th ed.). New York: Teachers College Press.

Unsworth, L. (2001). *Teaching multiliteracies across the curriculum: Changing contexts of text and image in classroom practices*. Philadelphia: Open University Press.

Vasquez, V. with Muise, M., Adamson, S., Hoffman, L., Chiola-Nakai, D., & Shear, J. (2003). *Getting beyond "I like the book": Creating space for critical literacy in K–6 classrooms*. Newark, DE: International Reading Association.

Standards, Assessment, and High-Stakes Testing

INTRODUCTION

The passage of the No Child Left Behind Act in 2001, coupled with the proliferation of national and state standards for reading and language arts in the past decade, has ushered in a new era of schooling in the history of American public education. The increased emphasis on standards, testing, and accountability in public schools has led to dramatic expansion of state-level high-stakes testing. This testing mania has had a profound impact on teaching, learning, and our profession. Confusion and debate abound as to what the goals of assessment should be, how student progress can best be measured, what uses can be made of the assessment data, and what can be done to better prepare students for high-stakes tests. The readings in this section address these important issues.

In the first article, Roger Farr examines the complex components of the reading assessment puzzle and proposes a way to solve it. He points out that as the criticism of schools intensifies and the search for alternative assessment continues, more tests are being developed and administered. Meanwhile, because different stakeholders (e.g., the public, school administrators, parents, teachers, students) are interested in different kinds of information from assessment, there have been attempts to make a single test serve the needs of all assessment audiences. As a result, tests have become longer, more expensive, more time-consuming, and more confusing, and the stakes have gotten higher. Teachers are now under immense pressure to boost student performance on high-stakes tests by teaching to the test. One way out of this conundrum, according to Farr, is for education stakeholders to understand and respect each other's needs and to realize that the ultimate goal of assessment is to improve student learning. Farr suggests that good assessment must be congruent with sound reading theory. He acknowledges that norm-referenced tests, while needing improvement, have a place in educational assessment. He advocates the use of criterion-referenced performance assessments because they are more individualized, integrate multiple literacy skills, afford chances for critical thinking, and encourage student self-assessment. Although written a decade ago, this article is still relevant today when the push for standards-based instruction and high-stakes testing is intensifying.

In the second article, John Guthrie offers ideas and advice about how teachers can both prepare students for high-stakes reading tests and avoid watering down the curriculum. He describes the characteristics of high-stakes tests and the reactions of teachers, administrators, and students to such tests. He then discusses what goes into performance on a reading test and describes ways teachers can prepare students for all the requirements of successfully taking reading tests. Finally, he offers caveats about and proposes a framework for planning test preparation. In essence, the author advocates a balanced approach to high-stakes test preparation. He emphasizes that the best test preparation is to build actual reading ability through sound, solid everyday teaching; however, he also acknowledges the importance of familiarizing students with the typical content of a reading test and with test formats such as the types of questions that are included and the expected responses to those questions.

The third article, by Shelby and Kenneth Wolf, shows that it is indeed possible to teach both *true* and *to* the high-stakes writing test. The authors share what they have learned from six elementary/middle school teachers who work within high-stakes accountability systems while remaining honest to sound theory and practice in teaching their students to write. They discuss the limitations of high-stakes assessment, but acknowledge its inescapable reality in the lives of teachers and students. Drawing on their study of writing assessment reforms in Kentucky and Washington, Wolf and Wolf suggest five points that are essential to sound pedagogy both in preparing children to write well and in preparing them to score well on high-stakes assessments. These are: (a) understand established standards and criteria for evaluating student writing, (b) analyze and discuss multiple benchmark models of writing, (c) respond to others' writing, (d) reflect on one's own writing, and (e) simulate test situations. Although the article focuses on two U.S. states, it has implications for teachers in other states who are facing similar challenges and opportunities.

Putting It All Together: Solving the Reading Assessment Puzzle

Roger Farr
Indiana University

Reading assessment has become a genuine puzzle. Confusion and debate continue about what the goals of school assessment of reading should be and about what types of tests and other assessments are needed to achieve those goals. That debate should focus on the purposes for assessment and whether current tests achieve those purposes. Too often, however, the focus of the debate is on the latest testing panacea. In this article, I first examine the complex components of the assessment puzzle. Next I propose a solution to the puzzle that involves linkages among various assessment audiences and approaches. I conclude with a few remarks about how school districts in the United States might pull together all the pieces and solve the assessment puzzle for themselves.

Examining the Pieces of the Assessment Puzzle

The pieces of the puzzle represent many types of assessments, critical attitudes about them, and attempts to challenge or improve them. One of the truly puzzling aspects of reading assessment to many educators is that the amount of testing appears to increase at the same time that criticism of it intensifies (Farr & Carey, 1986; McClellan, 1988; Salganik, 1985; Valencia & Pearson, 1987).

Criticism of Schools Has Led to More Assessment

Public disappointment with student achievement has led to extensive criticism of U.S. schools. This disapproval intensified in the 1950s with a focus on reading. Reading assessment conducted to prove or disprove the criticism has received a great deal of attention ever since. Could Johnny read or not, and how well or how poorly? By the 1960s, and beyond, score declines on tests used to predict how well high schoolers would do in college compounded public concern and criticism (The National Commission on Excellence in Education, 1983).

The conviction that many students were receiving high school diplomas and yet were almost totally illiterate became firmly established in the public's mind (Purves & Niles, 1984). The Peter Doe case in California exemplified that concern (Saretsky, 1973). The case concerned a high school student who sued the school district for graduating him without teaching him to read. As a result of this kind of dissatisfaction with educational outcomes, the use of standardized, norm-referenced assessment intensified, and state minimum competency testing programs proliferated (Madaus, 1985; Salmon-Cox, 1981).

The data to determine whether scores on reading tests were deteriorating over time is sketchy at best and tends not to substantiate dramatic declines in the reading performance of U.S. students over the years (Farr & Fay, 1982; Farr, Fay, Myers, & Ginsberg, 1987; Stedman & Kaestle, 1987). Nonetheless, the public has remained convinced that performance has dropped rather dramatically. Further, the prevalence of minimum competency programs has not significantly altered the conviction of the public and press that student achievement, particularly in reading, continues to deteriorate.

This unabated critical concern was at least partly responsible for the establishment of the National Assessment of Educational Progress (NAEP), an ongoing federally mandated study that now provides some reading performance data over time. Any declines it has depicted are small compared to the public's determined assumptions (Mullis, Owen, & Phillips, 1990). And although careful analyses of the ACT and SAT score declines has cited several reasonable causes other than poor schools, that phenomenon did much to sustain and cement public conviction and the demand for accountability testing (Popham, 1987; Resnick, 1982).

The continuing debate about the quality of U.S. schools has now given rise to a new focus on standards and assessment. At the same time that they reaffirm their conviction that children are not learning in school, critics like Chester Finn (1992) echo the call from the White House "for new American achievement tests" that compare student performance to "world class standards" that would be set as criterion references. President Bush (1991) has called for "voluntary national tests for 4th, 8th, and 12th graders in the five core subjects" to "tell parents and educators, politicians and employers, just how well our schools are doing."

The Search for Alternative Assessments Has Also Led to More Assessment

In addition to dissatisfaction with the schools, there has been a quest for assessments that are closely aligned with more holistic views of language development. Some curriculum theorists concerned with the mismatch between curriculum and assessment have determined that if curriculum is to change, the reading tests must change. This has brought about a proliferation of new assessments—both formal and informal (Brown, 1986; Burstall, 1986; Priestley, 1982; Stiggins, Conklin, & Bridgeford, 1986).

Included in this mix have been modifications of conventional tests with new item formats and the addition of the assessment of behaviors not often included on traditional tests, such as background knowledge, student interests and attitudes, and metacognition. Other assessments in reading have taken an entirely different approach to assessment, relying entirely on student work samples collected in portfolios (Jongsma, 1989; Valencia, 1990; Wolf, 1989). Portfolios have themselves taken many different forms from *show portfolios*, which include only a few carefully selected samples, to *working portfolios*, which include a broad sample of work and which are used to guide and organize daily instruction. In addition, numerous professional publications have published articles calling for the use of a broader range of teacher observations and informal assessment techniques (Cambourne & Turbill, 1990; Goodman, 1991).

Different Audiences Need Different Information

Thus, it seems that the increased amount of testing has resulted from greater accountability demands as well as from attempts to find alternatives to traditional assessments. In order to bring some sense to this proliferation of assessment, we need to understand that tests have only one general purpose: Tests should be considered as nothing more than attempts to systematically gather information. The information is used to help children learn about their own literacy development and to give teachers and others concerned with students' literacy the information they need for curriculum planning. *The bottom line in selecting and using any assessment should be whether it helps students.*

A book that I first authored more than 20 years ago regarding the assessment of reading was entitled *Reading: What Can Be Measured?* (Farr, 1970; Farr & Carey, 1986). I have always felt that the title gave the wrong focus to the review of assessment issues. That book should have been entitled, *Reading: Why Should It Be Measured?* We need to consider who needs information about reading, what kind of information is needed, and when it is needed. Only then can we begin to plan for more sensible assessment.

In order to think more clearly about overall assessment plans, we need to know why we want to test. There are, of course, different groups that need information. Without considering these groups and their information needs, the assessment program in any school system will remain as a set of jumbled puzzle pieces. The general distinctions between audiences are covered in Figure 1.

The public   Members of the general public, who make decisions through their elected officials, including school boards, have a vested interest in the future of children and in their effective and cost-efficient instruction. It is recognized as vital to Americans' and their nation's future that schools produce educated students. Indeed, the most recent federally supported efforts to improve education have been on establishing standards that presumably will result in the development of assessments related to those standards. At the present time, those involved with establishing the standards are moving in the direction of holistic kinds of performance assessment.

Administrators   Ideally school administrators would rely most heavily on performance assessments that are criterion-referenced. These performance measures should compare student performance against a clearly defined curriculum. But since we live in a complex world where mobility and diversity are the reality, administrators also need norm-referenced comparisons of their students' performance.

Parents   While parents share the public's interests, they have a vested interest in their own individual children. In order to monitor their children's progress and to be active in their education, parents want criterion-referenced reports; additionally parents are also typically interested in how their children perform on normed tests in comparison to children from across the United States.

Audiences	The information is needed to:	The information is related to:	Type of information	When information is needed:
General public (and the press)	Judge if schools are accountable and effective	Groups of students	Related to broad goals; norm- & criterion-referenced	Annually
School administrators/staff	Judge effectiveness of curriculum, materials, teachers	Groups of students & individuals	Related to broad goals; criterion- & norm-referenced	Annually or by term/semester
Parents	Monitor progress of child, effectiveness of school	Individual student	Usually related to broader goals; both criterion- & norm-referenced	Periodically; 5 or 6 times a year
Teachers	Plan instruction, strategies, activities	Individual student; small groups	Related to specific goals; primarily criterion-referenced	Daily, or as often as possible
Students	Identify strengths, areas to emphasize	Individual (self)	Related to specific goals; criterion-referenced	Daily, or as often as possible

Figure 1 Assessment audiences.

Teachers   A teacher's primary concern is helping students learn. While teachers are necessarily aware of normed assessment's comparative reports as a kind of bottom-line accountability, they are primarily interested in the kind of information that will support the daily instructional decisions they need to make. This kind of information has been generated by criterion-referenced tests and by other types of assessment that can be utilized more effectively in the classroom as a part of instruction.

Students   Students need to become good self-assessors if they are to improve their literacy skills. They need to select, review, and think about the reading and writing they are doing. They need to be able to revise their own writing and to revise their comprehension as they read. If students understand their own needs, they will improve. Students should, in fact, be the primary assessors of their own literacy development.

The Wall Between Understanding

It is important for each of these audiences to recognize, understand, and respect the needs of the others if we are to pull the assessment puzzle together. Audience needs cluster around those of teachers and students on the one hand and those of other decision-makers on the other.

The assessment needs of these two general groups tend to be dramatically different and even contradictory, and if the users of assessment do not recognize one another's needs, it is because these distinctions create a kind of wall depicted in Figure 2. It is essen-

tial that we breach that wall if we are to get our assessment act together!

Some Tests Attempt to Do It All

No single assessment can serve all the audiences in need of educational performance information. Yet developments in standardized tests have attempted to do so. The tests have added criterion-referenced interpretations, special interpretations for teachers, special reports for parents, individual score reports, and instructional support materials of various kinds. These developments have made the tests longer, more expensive, more time-consuming, and more confusing. Consequently, teachers are expected to justify these investments by making more instructional use of the test results.

No single assessment can serve all the audiences in need of educational performance information.

At the same time, the increased investment in assessment time and money has tended to give these tests even more importance in determining school accountability and in making high-stakes educational decisions. Specifically, four potential problems have arisen.

Teaching to the test   As accountability became more and more of a concern, teachers have felt pressured to place emphasis on what the standardized tests covered, regardless of what the school curriculum

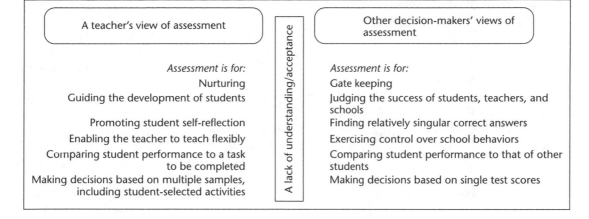

Figure 2 Opposing views of assessment.

called for. Over time, reading curricula have begun to reflect the skill breakdown of many tests, and reading textbooks have tended to emphasize the skills tests cover as well.

Contaminating the evidence   Standardized reading tests used to mean something. They were genuine indications that a student who performed adequately on them could read. This was so because they *sampled* reading behavior. But now that indication is contaminated. If teachers are deliberately stressing the sub-behaviors that they know are on the tests, the assessments are no longer sampling reading behavior—they are, in effect, covering a very limited definition of it. A good score on a standardized reading test no longer indicates that the student can read in general. It means only that the student can do those limited things the test covers.

The reading required on most tests is not much like the reading behavior that our new understanding describes.

Crunching objectives   Attempts to make reading assessment tests more encompassing have tended to make them much longer. Even so, tests are forced to cover the numerous subskills they contain with only a few items each. "What does it mean," a teacher may legitimately ask, "if a student misses one of three items that report on comprehending cause-and-effect?"

The potential for a mismatch   Teachers have long noted that nationally normed tests do not reflect particular emphases in their classrooms. How can a standardized reading test, they have correctly argued, tell them much about a particular curriculum they are following? What can it tell the public about how well the teacher has done using the curriculum?

The more a teacher adheres to instruction related directly to the needs, interests, and backgrounds of his or her particular students, the less assured is the match of that instruction to standardized test content—and the less likely the test's scores will serve that instruction.

Good Reading Theory Recommends Authentic Performance Assessment

Most published tests have not adequately responded to emerging reading theory, which explains reading comprehension as a meaning-constructing process. Any subskills factored out of the process are not discrete; if they actually exist as behaviors, they appear to operate in such an intricate fashion that it is difficult if not impossible to isolate them.

Authentic assessment   Relatively wide acceptance of a constructivist, context-specific definition of reading has promoted a careful analysis of current reading and language arts test content and format to see how authentic the testing experience is. This analysis has led to the conclusion that the reading required on most tests is not much like the reading behavior that our new understanding describes. How valid is the content of a reading test in terms of reader purpose, interests, and background, which we now believe are primary influences on reading behavior?

Performance assessment   Attention to authenticity has accompanied and helped generate the development and use of performance assessment. A student's language behaviors need to be assessed, it is contended, as they are used in real-life situations. Students don't comprehend something read, for example, as a multiple-choice response, and marking those answers has nothing to do with the way reading is actually used, except in taking tests. Reading performance assessment must look at the reading act in process or judge comprehension of a text as it is applied in some realistic way.

Observation Observation is one way to do this and can lead teachers to meaningful insights about the progress and needs of individual students. Yet teachers need to be trained in regard to what they can look for and what those signs suggest. They need to develop useful ways to make discrete notes about observations and to synthesize what they find. Observation generates many details in relatively random order, and they seldom become clearly useful until they are gathered into patterns that can direct instruction.

Portfolios Another highly valuable form of performance assessment is the portfolio. For these collections, students and teachers select numerous samples from drafts and final versions of various kinds of a student's writing. The idea is to demonstrate the student's progress and development in the combined process of reading, thinking, and writing. Thus many of the samples in the portfolio are responses to reading. The portfolio is reviewed and discussed regularly by the teacher and student, who may arrange it for others to examine.

Integrated assessment Assessments in which thinking, reading, and writing are integrated have been developed in recent years. Such assessments have been developed by classroom teachers, school districts, and publishers in an attempt to integrate reading and writing and to assess reading and writing with more realistic activities. These vary widely, but for most of them the student is given a writing task related to a text that is supplied. The task has been deemed to be authentic because it is typical of something the student might do in real life, including the kinds of activities often used for learning in the classroom. It is designed to emphasize the use of information in the reading selection in a realistic and interesting writing task.

For example, one such test asks students to read a nonfiction article that categorically discusses and describes how insect-eating plants lure, capture, and digest their victims. The task is to write a fictional piece telling what a mother bug might say to her children in cautioning them about these plants. Teachers use what the students write to assess students' understanding of the text. They rate other integrated behaviors as well, such as the students' organization and application of the text's content to the task and factors related to writing.

Such reading/writing assessments encourage students to develop a variety of responses based on their interpretation of the reading selection, their background knowledge, and the direction they choose to take in constructing a realistic response. These kinds of performance assessments provide teachers with valuable insights regarding a student's ability to read, write, and construct a meaningful response to an interesting task. Prewriting notes, first drafts, and teacher observation notes all make the assessment a valuable source of information.

In addition, the final drafts can be scored to serve as information that can help determine accountability. The responses can be scored following a "rubric," a list of criteria that describes several levels of performance in each of the categories to be analyzed. Samples of actual student papers ("anchors") that represent each score level described by the rubrics can also be used in scoring. Thus these tests are criterion-referenced. Yet the guides to scoring are somewhat equivalent to normed scores in the sense that the anchor papers were taken from many gathered in field-testing and were judged to be typical of the range of responses described in the rubric.

A Combined Solution to the Assessment Puzzle

None of the preceding types of assessment should be argued to be the single solution to the testing puzzle. Figure 3 depicts how performance assessments can provide direct linkage among the main users of assessment and how the three major types of assessment are linked. The chart is a plan for pulling the pieces of the assessment puzzle together into a solution that can inform all the decision makers involved in a student's development into an effective reader and language user.

Solving the Puzzle Will Require Cooperation

Pulling the assessment puzzle together will require tolerance and compromise on the part of many critics of particular types of assessment. The process would be facilitated if:

- Critics of the schools would become aware that assessment must serve more than school accountability. Ideally, critics will inform their concerns with a better understanding of what schools are trying to accomplish.
- Decision makers would understand that assessment is more than numbers on a test paper. They would begin to understand and use the kinds of assessments that are based on real classroom activities and that represent the types of activities in which students who are effective readers and writers should become proficient.

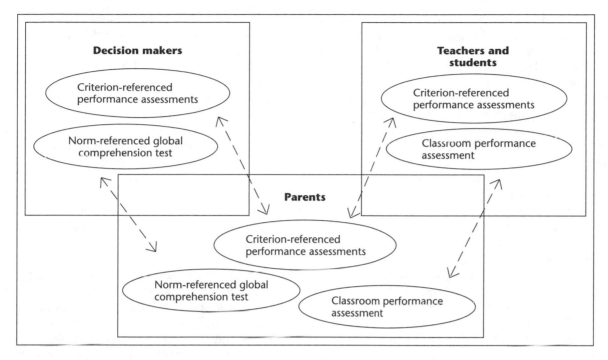

Figure 3   The solution—linkage.

- The most idealistic of the critics of assessment would become more realistic and flexible, tempering their insistence on authentic performance assessment. It seems fruitless, in particular, for some critics to insist that all assessment revolve around observation of activities that are apt not to involve all children and that reveal language use in highly varying degrees.
- Producers of assessments would acknowledge that no one assessment is going to suffice as a school's examination of reading. This would mean that they would no longer promote any of their products as such a test. It would also mean that future revisions of standardized reading tests would undo much of the complexity they now contain.

Pulling the assessment puzzle together will require tolerance and compromise on the part of many critics of particular types of assessment.

None of this is to suggest that critical analysis of reading assessment should stop, nor should attempts to improve tests in response to criticism cease. Efforts to develop and institute the new accountability assessments in Illinois (Pearson & Valencia, 1987), where the assessment allows for multiple correct responses within each multiple-choice item, and in Michigan (Michigan State Board of Education, 1987), where the assessment relies on longer passages followed by more numerous items, have been interesting, if not conclusive, efforts to contribute to a solution

to the assessment puzzle. So have attempts to construct items that will reveal students' awareness of how they are processing texts. Although longer reading test passages, different question formats, etc., will not solve the assessment puzzle, they can certainly shape the parts we pull together for a better fit.

Norm-referenced Tests Need to Change

To solve the assessment puzzle, it will be necessary for teachers and other educators to admit that norm-referenced test results can be of some value to the public and other decision makers, including parents. But these standardized tests should not be of the form that has evolved in response to criticism.

Test authors and publishers should begin to plan assessment *programs* that address the multiple audiences. Teachers and schools will need assistance in developing portfolios, planning performance assessments, and integrating assessment information. What are not needed are large single test batteries that promise to meet all of a school's assessment needs from classroom diagnosis to accountability. That attempt, especially linking accountability assessment and instructional assessment, has led to a narrowing of the curriculum.

For the large-scale assessments, this suggests the elimination of the designation of items by subskills and reporting on those sub-behaviors as if they truly are separable and distinct. More publisher efforts should go into the development of a variety of creative and useful curriculum assessments in which students have to actually perform the behaviors the school is attempting to teach.

What large-scale assessment can and should do is to report a global comprehension score, with no special subtests on traditional focuses like word recognition and vocabulary. Without the time-consuming battery of accompanying tests, reading tests can be shorter while using longer passages of a variety of types. These passages must evoke different purposes for reading that reflect the real reasons students read in and out of school. Thus, the reading test will be more authentic.

Without the burden of reporting on a host of specific reading and thinking subskills, test makers can write items that truly reflect the balance of a passage, the students' probable purpose for reading such a text, and the aspects of the writing that make the text one of quality and worth the students' time.

It should also be remembered that the long-standing primary purpose of large-scale testing has been to provide a general assessment as to how groups of students are progressing in a school district. Such information, if it does not become the focus of instruction, can be one piece of information used to contribute to a broad base of information for planning, supporting, and evaluating school- and system-wide curricula and instruction.

This approach strongly suggests that *matrix sampling* be used for large-scale assessment, thus eliminating the need to administer to all students the same test items or tasks. Testing time can be considerably shorter if carefully selected samples of students take different parts of a test instead of the whole thing. Good sampling should yield results similar to those obtained when all students take the entire test. Nothing is lost in reporting, since individual scores are of little concern. In addition, matrix sampling provides a general indication of the progress of groups of students, not a blueprint for instruction of individual students.

Performance Assessments Can Provide the Key Linkage

Figure 3 illustrates the linkages across three general audience types that will be essential to solving the assessment puzzle. Norm-referenced information provides a link between parents and decision makers other than teachers. However, the key linkage across all three general audiences is criterion-referenced performance assessments. Various approaches to performance assessment are being developed and tried out in school district assessment programs. Such assessments can be designed by teachers themselves. In fact, this has been done in several local school districts around the United States by teachers co-operating and interacting in order to meet their assessment needs. The same procedures are being tried at the state level in Maryland, Arizona, California, and Utah, and other states are sure to move in this direction.

The teachers who have been most successful in using this approach have had the support of administrators who could see over the assessment wall. Their support generated public interest and support. In some school systems, published or teacher-created integrated language performance assessment has already become a primary source of information for judging school accountability.

While teachers can create integrated language performance activities on a classroom basis, using them for accountability will require carefully developed or prepared programs that have been made congruent system-wide. This was done in River Forest, Illinois, where teachers developed their own rubrics, anchor papers, and inservice training. This kind of structuring will be necessary if the public, the press, and administrators are to be expected to value these tests as the key indicators of accountability and sources of direction for key decisions, such as curriculum development.

At the same time, of course, these tests can reflect authentic student performance. Not only are they very closely related to instructional activities and thus of high utility to teachers, they are actually instructional activities in and of themselves so the class time they require is doubly well invested.

The Portfolio Is the Flagship of Performance Assessment

Most developers of integrated language assessment programs highly recommend putting the student products into portfolios, a direct acknowledgement that the roots of language performance assessment lie in a portfolio approach to assessment and instruction. So integral is the portfolio performance assessment in good classrooms today that it is vital to note the qualities that make the portfolio approach a successful one.

A successful portfolio approach to assessment must revolve around regular and frequent attention to the portfolio by the student and the teacher.

A successful portfolio approach to assessment must revolve around regular and frequent attention to the portfolio by the student and the teacher. It does minimal good just to store a student's papers in a big folder and let them gather dust for lengthy periods of time. Papers must be added frequently; others can be weeded out in an ongoing rearrangement and selection process; most importantly, the whole process should involve frequent self-analysis by the student and regular conversations between the teacher and the student.

Too many teachers who contend that they are using portfolios do not do these things. Here are a few requirements if portfolios are to provide good assessment:

- The portfolio *belongs* to the student. It is his or her work and property, not some classroom requirement. Students should have choice about what goes in, and they should be encouraged to decorate and personalize their portfolios in unique ways.
- Portfolios are not primarily a display, although students may help arrange them for their parents and administrators to see. They are a shifting, growing repository of developing processes and ideas—a rather personal melting pot that the student uses to reflect on his or her own literacy development and to discuss interesting reading and writing activities with the teacher.
- The teacher's role in portfolio development is that of a consultant who helps convince the student that the work should show a variety of materials reflecting the reading-writing-thinking process as well as examples of responses to common classroom tasks and the student's favorite creations.
- The portfolio should contain numerous and varied pieces written and revised in response to reading. Reading logs reporting ongoing responses to books and articles make valuable contributions to portfolios.
- Portfolios should be reflective collections, revealing genuinely individual and personal responses to classroom activities and to ideas.
- At an absolute minimum, there should be four one-on-one, teacher/student discussions and analyses each semester of a student's developing portfolio. These sessions should not be short and perfunctory. If this requirement is not met, the assessment potential of the portfolio process is forfeited.
- Keeping the portfolio is an ongoing process. Its real value as an assessment tool materializes as the student can analyze his or her progress and development over time.

New Emphases in Assessment Have Common Qualities

Portfolios are part of a group of classroom performance assessments, some of them quite informal, that link the assessment interests of teachers, students, and parents. Portfolios can also be highly revealing to school specialists and administrators who, with the students' permission, take the time to examine them. All of these emerging strategies are both authentic and involve performance assessment. They are:

- Highly individualized, even though they may take place during activities that involve groups of students.

- A part of classroom activities and instruction designed to match an individual student's interests and needs and to use a student's strengths to develop more incisive and creative use of language.
- Activities that integrate several language behaviors.
- Chances to use critical thinking and to express unique and emerging reactions and responses to ideas encountered in text.
- Models that encourage and develop self-assessment by the student, making him or her aware of the language-related strengths that are developing.

How School Districts Can Begin to Solve the Assessment Puzzle

Too often school district testing programs are nothing more than test-and-file procedures. The tests are administered; when the scores are available, they are reported in some way; and teachers are admonished to peruse and use the test results. Yet many educators across the U.S. already embrace the suggestions made here for solving the assessment puzzle. Administrators are aware that testing programs can and do divide educators.

The assessment puzzle can be solved. The solution, however, is not as simple as identifying a nonexistent test that will do the whole job nor as arbitrary as eliminating most reading assessment.

Superintendents do not want to abandon their accountability responsibilities, yet they want to support effective ongoing classroom assessment that provides teachers with information that is congruent with current knowledge about reading/writing processes. Teachers want to be more involved in developing an assessment program that serves and matches their instructional needs. They all sense that what is needed is an integrated system that is effective in fostering better teaching and learning.

Many of these school districts need help with developing an assessment program that links audiences instead of dividing them—one that supplies broad-based accountability information yet is customized to the particular system, its teachers, and its students. One way for school districts to begin is to discuss the pieces of the assessment puzzle in their system. Representatives of all the audiences with assessment needs should take part. As this process develops, the discussions need to be recorded in some way and synthesized. Out of all this can come other brainstorming sessions and ultimately inservice workshops to help all teachers understand how a broad-based assessment program can be pulled together.

Equally important, many teachers will welcome in-service training on using different types of informal assessments.

These kinds of workshops can be started within school districts right away. For instance, teachers who are exceptionally good observers or use the portfolio approach with great success are almost always easily identified. They could be enlisted and supported by administrators to run workshops that can be conducted while the discussions about broader reading assessment are helping representative groups define the assessment problems and their district's needs.

The assessment puzzle can be solved. The solution, however, is not as simple as identifying a nonexistent test that will do the whole job nor as arbitrary as eliminating most reading assessment. Rather it takes a vision that focuses on what real literacy means and the awareness that various groups have a stake in helping students to develop as literate citizens. Such a vision must not use assessment to isolate. It must respect the complex nature of literacy, it must serve students and help them to become reflective self-assessors, and it must create links that bring instruction and assessment together.

References

Brown, R. (1986). Evaluation and learning. In A.R. Petrosky & D. Bartholomae (Eds.). *The teaching of writing: Eighty-fifth yearbook of the National Society for the Study of Education* (pp. 114–130). Chicago, IL: University of Chicago Press.

Burstall, C. (1986). Innovative forms of assessment: A United Kingdom perspective. *Educational Measurement: Issues and Practice, 5,* 17–22.

Bush, G. (1991). *America 2000: An education strategy.* Washington, DC: U.S. Department of Education.

Cambourne, B., & Turbill, J. (1990). Assessment in whole language classrooms: Theory into practice. *The Elementary School Journal, 90,* 337–349.

Farr, R. (1970). *Reading: What can be measured?* Newark, DE: International Reading Association.

Farr, R., & Carey, R. (1986). *Reading: What can be measured?* (2nd ed.). Newark, DE: International Reading Association.

Farr, R., & Fay, L. (1982). Reading trend data in the United States: A mandate for caveats and caution. In G. Austin & H. Garber (Eds.). *The rise and fall of national test scores* (pp. 83–141). New York: The Academic Press.

Farr, R., Fay, L., Myers, R., & Ginsberg, M. (1987). *Reading achievement in the United States: 1944–45, 1976, and 1986.* Bloomington, IN: Indiana University.

Finn, C.E., Jr. (1992, January 12). Turn on the lights. *The New York Times,* Sect. 4, p. 19.

Goodman, Y. (1991). Evaluating language growth: Informal methods of evaluation. In J. Flood, J. Jensen, D. Lapp, & J. Squire (Eds.). *Handbook of research on teaching the English language arts* (pp. 502–509). New York: Macmillan.

Jongsma, K. (1989). Portfolio assessment. *The Reading Teacher, 43,* 264–265.

Madaus, G.F. (1985). Public policy and the testing profession: You've never had it so good? *Educational Measurement: Issues and Practice, 4,* 5–11.

McClellan, M.C. (1988). Testing and reform. *Phi Delta Kappan, 69,* 766–771.

Michigan State Board of Education. (1987). *Blueprint for the new MEAP reading test.* Lansing, MI: Author.

Mullis, V.S., Owen, E.H., & Phillips, G.W. (1990). *Accelerating academic achievement: A summary of the findings from 20 years of NAEP.* Princeton, NJ: Educational Testing Service.

National Commission on Excellence in Education. (1983). *A nation at risk.* Washington, DC: U.S. Department of Education.

Pearson, P.D., & Valencia, S. (1987). *The Illinois State Board of Education census assessment in reading: An historical reflection.* Springfield, IL: Illinois State Department of Education.

Popham, W.J. (1987). The merits of measurement-driven instruction. *Phi Delta Kappan, 68,* 679–682.

Priestley, M. (1982). *Performance assessment in education and training: Alternate techniques.* Englewood Cliffs, NJ: Educational Technology Publications.

Purves, A., & Niles, O. (1984). The challenge to education to produce literate citizens. In A. Purves & O. Niles (Eds.), *Becoming readers in a complex society: Eighty-third yearbook of the National Society for the Study of Education* (pp. 1–15). Chicago, IL: University of Chicago Press.

Resnick, D. (1982). History of educational testing. In A.K. Wigdor & W.R. Garner (Eds.), *Ability testing: Uses, consequences, and controversies,* Part 2 (pp. 173–194). Washington, DC: National Academy Press.

Salganik, L.H. (1985). Why testing reforms are so popular and how they are changing education. *Phi Delta Kappan, 66,* 628–634.

Salmon-Cox, L. (1981). Teachers and tests: What's really happening? *Phi Delta Kappan, 62,* 631–634.

Saretsky, G. (1973). The strangely significant case of Peter Doe. *Phi Delta Kappan, 54,* 589–592.

Stedman, L.C., & Kaestle, C.F. (1987). Literacy and reading performance in the United States from 1880 to the present. *Reading Research Quarterly, 22,* 8–46.

Stiggins, R.J., Conklin, N.F., & Bridgeford, N.J. (1986). Classroom assessment: A key to effective education. *Educational Measurement: Issues and Practice, 5,* 5–17.

Valencia, S. (1990). A portfolio approach to classroom reading assessment: The whys, whats, and hows. *The Reading Teacher, 43,* 338–339.

Valencia, S., & Pearson, P. (1987). Reading assessment: Time for a change. *The Reading Teacher, 40,* 726–732.

Wolf, D.P. (1989). Portfolio assessment: Sampling student work. *Educational Leadership, 46,* 35–39.

Preparing Students for High-Stakes Test Taking in Reading

John T. Guthrie
University of Maryland at College Park

In the past decade, tests in reading have become a high priority for teachers, administrators, and students. Attempting to improve student achievement, schools and districts have placed an emphasis on accountability. Schools and teachers are expected to show that their students are achieving well on tests in reading, math, and content areas. In this environment of school improvement through accountability, testing is a "high stakes" part of teaching and schooling. In this [article], I discuss how teachers can prepare students to take high-stakes tests in reading. First, I address the issue of what are high-stakes tests. Second, I describe reactions of teachers, administrators, and students to high-stakes testing. Third, I present recommendations for preparing students for high-stakes test taking. Fourth, I discuss hazards in test preparation. Finally, I propose a framework for test preparation planning. Although there are few answers that apply absolutely to everyone, a considerable amount of experience and research sheds light on all these issues.

Characteristics of High-Stakes Tests

A test or testing program is called high stakes when it is used to make important decisions about individual students, teachers, or schools. A recent report by the National Academy of Sciences titled *High Stakes: Testing for Tracking, Promotion, and Graduation* (Heubert & Hauser, 1999) reviews many of these decisions. One prominent decision is promotion and retention of students. When a test is used to decide whether a student has "passed" fourth grade and should move into fifth grade, the decision has many consequences for the learner. The test on which that decision is made is high stakes, because the child's future is affected, the parents are likely to be in-

volved, and teachers will be influenced by it. Across the United States, retention in a grade is a frequent practice. In the 1990s, for children age 6 to 8 years, approximately 18% of the population were retained. For the population age 9 to 12 years, approximately 24% were retained at some point in their school career, and for the population age 15 to 17 years, approximately 30% were retained at least once during their schooling. Whether retention improves achievement cannot be discussed at length here. However, one basis for retention is a high-stakes test, which may be used along with teacher's grades and judgments. Related to retention is graduation from high school. More states are making the granting of high school diplomas contingent on successful test performance. A report from the Board on Testing and Assessment (Feuer, Holland, Green, Bertenthal, & Hemphill, 1999) reviews this practice across all states. In the review, 18% of the states had a high school exit exam, which is a high-stakes event for students and teachers.

The most prominent use of high-stakes tests is improvement of instruction. In 1998, 43% of states in the United States reported using assessment to improve instruction. The tests in these assessment programs may be standardized tests or performance assessments. However, in every case, they are high-stakes events. In some instances, schools scoring low on a high-stakes test are subject to "takeover" by the state department of education. That is, state department staff must approve their curriculum instruction and staffing. The school loses its freedom and flexibility in decision making. When school improvement is the aim of high-stakes testing, publicity often surrounds tests. The press reports test scores in the newspaper that bring high visibility to more successful and less successful schools.

In addition to school improvement, tests may be used for tracking in high school. Students are assigned to academic or general tracks based on a testing event. This event has lifelong consequences, as students rarely shift tracks during their high school experience. In elementary schools, students may be assigned to special resources or special education based on test scores. Such a score is a high-stakes piece of information, because it determines the child's educational experience dramatically.

Tests used for high-stakes purposes vary widely. In some cases, traditional standardized tests are used. Frequently, tests such as the Iowa Test of Basic Skills or comprehensive achievement tests (e.g., Comprehensive Test of Basic Skills [CTBS]) are employed. Often these include a high proportion of multiple-choice items. Traditional items, such as small passages with brief questions and four alternatives, are used. Subtests in the intermediate grades often include vocabulary, word attack skills, and comprehension. Primary grades subtests often assess word recognition, vocabulary, comprehension, and occasionally listening skills. Administrators favor these tests because they are easily administered and can be scored by a machine. This reduces costs and usually increases frequency of test taking. Multiple-choice reading tests have the advantage of high reliability. They are consistent and student performance from one form to the next does not change much. However, many educators question the validity of multiple-choice tests. We rarely confront multiple-choice items in the real world and thus reading experts increasingly prefer the use of "naturalistic" items.

Performance assessments are more popular with reading experts. These assessments include longer passages with full stories, open-ended questions, and constructed responses. Students write their reactions to text and the responses are scored according to a rubric from low to high. Many reading experts consider portfolio assessments even more valid. In this approach, the teacher in the classroom maintains student portfolios. They are coded for reading, writing, and ownership of literacy (Purves, 1993). However, performance assessments and portfolios are less popular with administrators because they are time consuming and expensive. The gain in validity is offset by a high administrative burden. Nevertheless, all three types of assessment approaches in reading are used for high-stakes purposes.

Reactions of Teachers, Administrators, and Students to High-Stakes Testing

Teachers have many reactions to high-stakes tests. One junior high teacher in a study conducted by Haladyna, Nolen, and Hass (1990) stated that "the test raises the anxiety level of everyone. The superintendent likes to use the scores to point out the teachers' weaknesses and create competition between the teachers. He thinks that good scores equal good teaching" (p. 62). In an extensive study of how teachers

react to high-stakes testing programs, Smith (1991) reported five reactions. First, publication of test scores produces feelings of shame, embarrassment, guilt, and anger in teachers. This is most evident in low scoring schools or classrooms, but most teachers feel they could have done better. Consequently, many are disappointed in their level. This leads to the determination to do what is necessary to avoid such feelings in the future. Second, some teachers question the validity of the test and doubt whether a multiple-choice measure of reading, in fact, represents "real reading." Third, many teachers believe that testing has an adverse emotional impact on young children. They think that the testing processes cause inappropriate stress in young students, who worry and feel anxious and incompetent. Fourth, teachers often resent and regret the instructional time required by testing. In some cases, preparing, administering, and recovering tests may cost 100 hours of instructional time. Because the tests are not teaching, students are not learning in this time. Fifth, teachers often adapt to the tests that are high stakes in their school. This adaptation often means narrowing the curriculum and restricting their teaching to specific test-like activities. In reading, this may result in trivialization of the reading process. Because many tests are multiple choice, this leads to a loss of creativity, imagination, and critical thinking in the reading curriculum.

Although teachers may have adverse reactions to high-stakes tests, administrators from the school principal to the state superintendent of education frequently favor them. Administrators expect the tests to guide instruction, hold schools accountable, aid in curriculum planning, and evaluate school programs (Roeber, Bond & Connealy, 1998). Needless to say, administrative emphasis on the results of testing is what makes them "high stakes" for schools and teachers.

Although teachers may have adverse reactions to high-stakes tests, administrators . . . frequently favor them.

Students also react to tests. In the elementary grades, students believe that a test measures how much they have learned, identifying their knowledge and intelligence. According to Paris, Lawton, Turner, and Roth (1991), many students believe that the tests show which teachers are doing the best job in the classroom. They typically indicate that they try fairly hard and are reasonably motivated to succeed on the tests. However, middle and high school students have different views. They are less likely to say, "I gave my best effort on the test we took" than elementary students. Some secondary students believe that the tests serve the school's interest but not their own personal interests. Other students protect their self-esteem because they expect to do poorly and do not wish it to appear that they put forth maximum effort. At the same time, secondary students feel less prepared to take tests than elementary students. They have reported they do not have good strategies for taking the tests and are often anxious about their lack of skills. For secondary students, high and low achievers often react differently. High achievers are likely to report that they do well on reading tests, that the test was easy, and that they reread parts of the passage when needed. They show good strategies and positive self-perceptions. However, low achievers are likely to feel resentment, anxiety, lack of appropriate test-taking strategies, and decreasing motivation. All of these are obstacles to success on high-stakes tests. Consequently, it is important to address students' needs for test preparation.

Preparing Students to Take High-Stakes Reading Tests

In this section, I first discuss what goes into performance on a reading test, and then discuss how teachers can prepare students for all the requirements for successfully taking reading tests. The components of reading test performance are displayed in Figure 1. This pie chart shows that success on a reading test has many dimensions. These components for reading test performance are based on correlation research (Feuer et al., 1999). By looking at how different types of tests correlate to each other and examining performance on different types of items, it appears that all these elements are important. As the pie chart shows, the most important factor was general reading competence and ability. This accounted for 40% of the difference between students. This was based on the fact that if a group of students was given two very different types of tests, such as a simple multiple-choice test and a complex long-term portfolio assessment, their scores were substantially correlated. Students who scored high on the portfolio assessment also scored high on the multiple-choice test. Of course, the agreement is not perfect and there are many exceptions. Also influencing general reading ability is general intelligence. Because a test is a mental activity, it will measure intelligence to some degree. We know this because student scores on reading tests are correlated with their scores on math tests of computation. However, it should be noted that general reading competence is by far the most important single factor for success on a high-stakes test. This has vitally important implications for teachers, which I will discuss later.

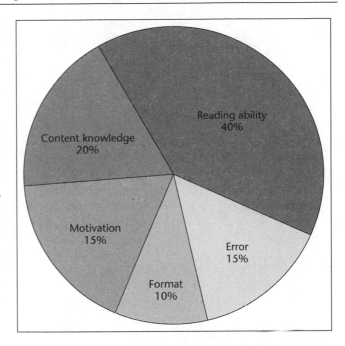

Figure 1 Components of reading test performance.

General reading competence is by far the most important single factor for success on a high-stakes test.

The pie chart also shows that student knowledge of the content of reading passages determines their success on tests. Reading comprehension tests on the same topic were much more highly correlated than reading comprehension tests of the same kind on different topics. If students do not have the content background on volcanoes, deserts, or early colonial history, their performance on a reading test containing such content will be relatively low. Next in importance are the two factors motivation and test-wiseness. Motivation for succeeding in a test is essential. Students who do not care about their success or who are highly anxious will score poorly. They fail to complete items, do not attempt difficult passages, give incomplete answers, and do not concentrate their cognitive energies. Test-wiseness—understanding the format of a test—is likewise important. Strategies for taking an essay-type performance assessment are different from strategies for taking a multiple-choice test. These format factors accounted for no more than 10% of the differences between students, however.

This pie chart was based on research evidence. Studies have shown that when two tests were identical in format and different in content their scores were highly correlated. However, their correlations were only slightly higher than two tests that differed in both format and content. This small increase is due to knowledge of format and test-wiseness of students.

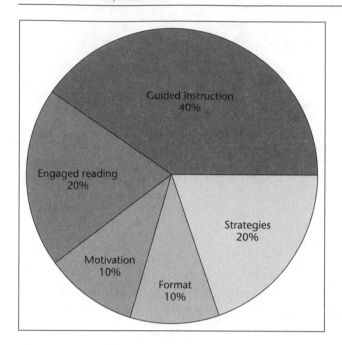

Figure 2 Components of reading test preparation.

These tests look different but they both require general mental activity and intelligence. Finally, it should be noted that no test is perfect. As the chart shows, 15% of the differences between students cannot be traced. These differences are unknown sources of error in the process of measurement.

Preparation for reading tests can be based on requirements for successful test performance. Figure 2 shows the components of successful test preparation. The largest dimension of this test preparation plan is guided instruction in reading and writing for both literary and informational texts. This piece of the pie is 40% of the total. This implies that 40% of specific test preparation should be good instruction in integrated reading-language arts. The second element of test preparation is strategy instruction. This accounts for 20% of the emphasis. The specific strategies needed for reading on the test should be taught explicitly. If the test is designed for grade 4 students and requires comprehension of the plot, character development, and resolution in narratives, these elements of story structure should be taught explicitly. Third, a substantial emphasis should be placed on engaged, independent reading to learn. All reading tests require speed, fluency, and comprehension. This can only be learned in motivated, extended independent reading. The objective of reading to learn during engaged reading is important, as the test situation requires this process. Fourth, practice on the format of the test is valuable. This accounts for 10% of the differences between students in test success. When taking multiple-choice tests, students should understand the strategies for responding to the items, selecting alternatives, and

allocating their time appropriately. Students in performance assessments with extensive writing activities need help with understanding writing prompts and answering completely. Research shows that format practice is beneficial, but evidence also documents that excessive format practice may jeopardize test success (Feuer et al., 1999). Fifth, motivation for reading and test taking should be part of the preparation program. Motivational support can include alleviating students' anxieties, providing meaningful reasons for test success, enabling students to feel self-efficacy toward reading, and most important, fostering extensive amounts of reading throughout the school year.

Research shows that format practice is beneficial, but evidence also documents that excessive format practice may jeopardize test success.

The numbers in the pie chart in Figure 2 are valuable guides. Each number refers to the percentage of time that should be spent in that activity during a 10-week period preceding the test. For example, in the 10-week period preceding an annual high-stakes test of reading, 20% of the time should be spent on strategy instruction. This is related to general strategies in reading required by the test. Approximately 10% of the time should be spent on format practice so the students are familiar with the types of items and questions. The largest time block should be spent on guided instruction in integrated reading-language arts including a healthy array of texts. No less than 40% of the time, teachers should maintain their coherent instruction on fundamental objectives in reading-language arts. This is because test success is only slightly influenced by knowledge of format and slightly influenced by strategies for reading. It is highly influenced by general reading competence gained through substantial time spent in a coherent curriculum that is aligned with the test.

Preparation in Test Formats

When children face a test, the format may be entirely new to them. For example, primary students may face a multiple-choice format that is unfamiliar. Help in understanding the structure of the items is necessary. By providing direct instruction on what is expected in the testing format, teachers enable young primary students to show their true reading competence. For example, many students need to respond to analogies when taking a test of word meaning (e.g., The Woodcock Reading Mastery Test, word comprehension section). They are given one item, such as dog and elephant, and then are given a word such as *stone* and asked to identify the analogous item from the alternatives of *mountain, water, wood*, and *book*. *Mountain* is correct because it is large compared with the stone, as the elephant is large compared with the dog. Helping students understand the meaning of these analogies increases their reading skills as measured by tests with this format (Franklin, 1983).

Actually providing students practice with items from a test has been shown to increase first graders' test achievement scores (Eakins, Green, & Bushell, 1976). First graders who received a unit of instruction, lasting 1 to 2 hours in total time, achieved significantly higher scores than students with no preparation. However, students who received longer test format instruction did not surpass those given the limited 1- to 2-hour intervention. Format instruction is also valuable for high school students. Providing practice on the multiple-choice items in high school physics enabled low-achieving students to increase their test scores (Kirkpatrick, 1934). Test practice is especially beneficial to students with low test-taking skills. These students who are unfamiliar with tests items and lack strategies for reading tests are often found in mildly handicapped or learning disabled populations. More time spent with coaching on the formats of standardized test items has been shown to be beneficial for learning disabled students (Scruggs, Mastropieri, & Tolfa-Veit, 1986). However, it should be noted that the total time spent in format instruction was a 30-minute lesson for each of 5 days.

The phrase "test-wise" is applied to students who seem to have the ability to use the characteristics and format of a test or a test-taking situation to receive a high score. Millman and Bishop (1965) conducted an extensive study of test-wise students who achieved high scores on multiple-choice tests. Their characteristics included the following:

1. Using time effectively by beginning to work rapidly. Test-wise students omitted items that seemed unnecessarily difficult and used their time on items they could get correct.
2. Implementing error avoidance strategies that included paying careful attention to directions, determining the purpose of the task, and checking all their answers after completing the test.
3. Applying a guessing strategy to multiple-choice tests that encouraged guessing when alternatives within an item can be ruled out.
4. Using a deductive reasoning strategy that consisted of eliminating items known to be incorrect and choosing among other options.
5. Adopting an expected level of sophistication. Often multiple-choice items may be partly correct and finding the closest alternative is important.
6. Using cues in the items, such as selecting longer options if they appear to be plausible, avoiding extreme words such as *never*, and considering the relevance of specific details in options.

High test scorers at the middle school and high school levels are more likely to use these strategies than low test scorers. Some minimum time spent discussing and practicing these strategies may increase middle school and high school students' competence and comfort taking high-stakes tests. For example, in performance assessments, students are often expected to construct written responses to a wide array of different types of texts. In these tasks, the criteria for an acceptable response are important to the test taker. Teachers can help students prepare for these performance assessments by discussing the criteria for excellent constructive answers. These criteria are often presented in scoring rubrics that can and should be discussed and taught directly (Mehrens, Popham, & Ryan, 1998). In these open, constructed response items, teachers should foster students' self-evaluation skills. As students read, take notes, write, and perhaps revise, they are continually self-monitoring. This is a complex strategy that can be taught (Garner, 1982). Students need instruction in generalizing these strategies, such as identifying evaluative criteria and self-evaluating with respect to those criteria. Teachers can provide practice on a range of reading and writing tasks in the normal reading instruction program to foster these test-relevant strategies (Mehrens et al., 1998).

Preparation in Reading Strategies

Most reading tests depend heavily on reading comprehension. For many reading theorists, reading and comprehension are the same thing. They believe that students who cannot comprehend cannot read, and students who can comprehend are relatively high achievers. In light of the importance of reading comprehension, good test preparation includes direct instruction in the strategies necessary for effective reading comprehension. However, teaching reading comprehension strategies is a long-term enterprise. Reading comprehension grows constantly during a child's school career. Needless to say, it cannot be accomplished in 1 week prior to the test. Effective test preparation depends on a sustained, long-term plan of providing instruction and opportunities to learn effective comprehension strategies. For effective test preparation, a period of not less than 3 months might be devoted in the school curriculum for teaching reading comprehension strategies that will be required on a high-stakes test.

Strategies needed for success in high-stakes reading comprehension tests are well established. An abundance of research supports the importance of the following: (a) using background knowledge, (b) searching to locate information, (c) summarizing, (d) self-monitoring, (e) self-questioning, (f) concept mapping, and (g) self-explanation. Good readers are known to use these strategies when necessary and poor readers rarely use them. Furthermore, these strategies can be taught and instruction in them will improve high-stakes reading comprehension test performance. For example, Blanton and Wood (1984) suggest that direct instruction in these strategies improves test performance. The direct instruction recommended includes (a) teacher modeling of the strategies, (b) explanation of when and how to use them, (c) repeated opportunities for guided practice, and (d) extended independent reading. Furthermore, primary grade children have been shown to benefit from direct instruction on reading comprehension strategies (Schwartz, 1988).

To help students succeed on tests, long-term strategy instruction on using background knowledge is valuable. Many researchers have documented the benefits of teaching students to use background knowledge and to make inferences between what they already know and new information in the text during reading. For example, Hansen and Pearson (1983) showed that low achievers could improve their reading test scores by learning to use background knowledge and draw inferences as they encountered new text information. In addition, researchers have shown that good readers monitor their comprehension, whereas poor readers are less likely to engage in self-monitoring. For example, Garner (1982) showed that good and poor readers differed in how frequently they used a rereading strategy to improve their understanding. In addition, students who were taught to reread and practiced this strategy frequently improved their tested performance. Self-questioning also has been identified as a powerful strategy for reading comprehension. A large review of intervention studies by Rosenshine and Meister (1994) showed that self-questioning can be taught with a range of texts and it benefits reading comprehension if the instruction is extended over multiple lessons. Self-questioning is frequently used in reciprocal teaching, which is a technique known to increase reading comprehension on standardized tests (Lysynchuk, Pressley, & Vye, 1990).

Many tests require students to locate specific information within a story or informational passage. The processes of searching and locating information can and should be taught as comprehension-relevant strategies. Understanding text structure helps improve search capabilities. By understanding story structure, children can search for particular information about characters or events within stories. By learning the organization of informational text, such as cause-effect or historical sequence patterns, children can learn to locate information needed to answer specific questions. Involving students in inquiry projects is an excellent technique to foster their learning to search and retrieve information. Within inquiry projects, students can be taught concept mapping. With this strategy, they can synthesize information gained from a variety of texts. The strategy of self-explanation also can be included in inquiry projects. As students encounter new text-based information, they can be encouraged to answer the question "Why?" This fosters their integration of new knowledge into old background information. Students who have learned to explain new information to themselves frequently score higher on reading comprehension tests. These strategies are useful for most students in mainstream classrooms, as well as for students with learning disabilities (Hughes & Schumaker, 1991).

It is evident that these strategies are complex. The optimal preparation for tests of reading comprehension that require these strategies begins several months prior to the administration of the test. Incorporating the comprehension strategies needed on a test into the mainstream curriculum planning is the most likely technique for building student confidence and self-confidence for successful test performance.

Test Preparation Through Engaged Reading

One of the most well-established findings in reading research is that reading comprehension is an outgrowth of a wide range of purposeful, motivated reading activities. If we look at standardized test performance in grade 3, 4, 5, or 6, the strongest predictor of achievement is amount of reading. Students who read widely and frequently are high achievers; students who read rarely and narrowly are low achievers (Guthrie, Wigfield, Metsala, & Cox, 1999). Amount of reading is such a strong predictor of reading comprehension that it outweighs intelligence, economic background, and gender. That is, students who are active, engaged readers will be high achievers even if they come from backgrounds with low income or low education in the family. Likewise, students who are infrequent, disengaged readers will be low achievers on standardized tests of reading even if their parents are well educated, their income is substantial, and literary resources are available at home (Reutzel & Hollingsworth, 1991). Different methods of teaching beginning reading and different methods of teaching comprehension strategies are less powerful than the acquisition of engaged active reading. In other words, any method or curricular approach that enables students to become engaged readers will influence standardized reading test performance. However, this is not an overnight process. Engaged reading does not become part of a child's lifestyle in a week or a month. This most important contributor to standardized reading tests achievement requires a long-term commitment from teachers and schools.

Because reading comprehension test scores are more influenced by students' amount of engaged reading than any other single factor, preparation for test taking should include support of engaged reading. A variety of innovative teachers and researchers have shown that long-term engaged reading can be increased with integrated instruction. When students are provided opportunities to connect reading and writing activities to integrated language arts, their engaged reading increases and reading achievement improves (Morrow, Pressley, Smith, & Smith, 1997). Further, when reading and writing are also linked to content learning in social studies and science, engaged reading is likely to be fostered.

Integrated curricula have been reported by Au and Carroll (1997) for the Kamehameha Early Education Program (KEEP), by Gaskins et al. (1994) at the Benchmark School, by Lapp and Flood (1994) in science and language arts, and by Guthrie and colleagues (Guthrie, Anderson, Alao, & Rinehart, 1999) in reading, writing, and science. In all of these instructional designs, students spend 42 to 120 minutes per day actively reading to learn science and social studies. In this process, they use all the strategies described previously and participate actively in writing to express their understanding, including being able to interpret narrative and being able to integrate information from multiple texts (Guthrie et al., 1999).

It is no surprise that the most important ingredient in high-stakes testing is difficult to teach. If reading comprehension were easy to provide for young children, the political controversies, accountability programs, and widespread testing systems would not be as prominent as they are. This implies that success on high-stakes tests is not provided in a quick fix. Rather, it is nurtured over time in integrated curricula that are planned as part of the central instructional objectives of a school.

Preparing Students for Test Taking Through Motivation

Tests are major sources of anxiety and worry for students. As Paris et al. (1991) found in a survey of 1,000 students in four states, many middle school and high school students felt resentment, anxiety, cynicism, and mistrust of standardized achievement tests. They did not feel satisfied with their scores and believed they were not well represented by tests. This increased their anxiety and decreased their motivation for test taking. Elementary school students were less

likely to be anxious, but the ones who did experience anxiety showed low performance. It is increasingly recognized that scores on any test may be low for either cognitive or motivational reasons. Students may lack the reading skills or they may lack the motivation and self-efficacy to put forth maximum effort on the test (Sugrue, 1995; Waid, Kanoy, Blick, & Walker, 1978). Teachers can take steps to alleviate anxiety surrounding high-stakes test taking. Simply allowing students to see a few items and practice the item formats on a test will reduce anxiety and enable students to focus their thinking on a test (Kalechstein, Hocevar, & Kalechstein, 1988). It is likely that providing students specific "test-wise" strategies for handling the formats will enable them to feel prepared for the testing formats and thereby reduce anxiety or increase self-efficacy for test taking (Paris et al., 1991).

It is self-evident that some tests are "high stakes," whereas others are "low stakes." An example of a test that is low stakes for the student is the National Assessment of Educational Progress. Individual scores do not affect the student's life, school prospects, graduation, or other outcomes. Although this test is valuable for the U.S. Congress and the U.S. Department of Education, it is a "low stakes" event for the individual student. However, a standardized test or performance assessment that will be used to determine promotion to the next grade or high school graduation is high stakes for the student. Teachers should discuss the particular uses for the results of a given test. Students are entitled to know how scores will be used. If it is a high-stakes test, students deserve to know the consequences of successful or less successful performance. Having concrete information is likely to be informative and, in some cases, is anxiety reducing.

Although motivation surrounding the particular assessment event is important, more critical is motivation for reading in general. Students who are relatively low achievers, with relatively few good reading comprehension strategies, will not improve their test scores much through mere motivation for the test. However, these students may improve their test scores by becoming more actively engaged readers during the school year. It has been shown that highly motivated students in grade 5 read 30 minutes per day for their own interest, whereas less motivated students read 10 minutes or less for their own interest (Wigfield & Guthrie, 1997). The difference between 30 minutes a day and 10 minutes a day is a large amount of time. It converts to a large number of pages per week, and a large number of books per month. If a fifth grader is facing a high-stakes test in April, the best thing the student can do is begin reading widely and frequently in October. If a teacher will encounter a high-stakes test for her classroom in April, her best preparation is to increase motivation of students for extended, learning-focused, independent reading as early as possible in the academic year. Moving students from 10 minutes of independent reading per day to 30 minutes of learning-oriented reading per day will be the strongest test preparation that can be provided. By fostering students to become engaged readers, the teacher enables them to gain cognitive competence and a sense of self-efficacy. These attributes will shield students against the shocks of unfamiliar and challenging test conditions and foster their ability to demonstrate their level of excellence (Lane, Parke, & Stone, 1998).

Hazards in Preparing Students for High-Stakes Tests

Excessive Format Practice

Earlier, I recommended providing explicit practice on the formats of the multiple-choice test and constructed response formats of the performance assessment. When they encounter a new test, students should not be surprised by the specific tasks in which they will be expected to show their reading skills.

> *When high-stakes tests are heavily emphasized by administration, curricula frequently narrow.*

However, excessive practice in one or two formats can be hazardous for students, because students may "lock in" to a particular format, which is counterproductive. From excessive practice, students will learn particular procedures too well and apply them inappropriately. They will overexpect these formats in one or more tests and be confused if formats change. Although some exposure and some strategy learning is effective, excessive time in format practice is likely to be misleading because the test is measuring general abilities, not specific tasks.

Curriculum Narrowing

When high-stakes tests are heavily emphasized by administration, curricula frequently narrow. For example, if a multiple-choice reading comprehension test in grade 3 is required for promotion of students to the next grade, teachers focus the curriculum on multiple-choice reading activities. They use short passages, brief questions, and recognition responses. Although the narrowed curriculum may have some short-term benefits for some students who need it, the long-term effect is usually negative. In fact, a narrowed curriculum taught for a period of several months leads to decreases rather than increases in

test scores (Yen & Ferrara, 1997). As Smith (1991) reported, when teachers focused instruction on a limited set of specific skills that appeared to be needed by a test, student achievement was likely to decrease in the long term. There is a simple reason for the decrease. A test is a sample of what the student can do. Although one test may sample Skill A with Content 1 in a given format, the next test faced by a student may sample Skill B with Content 2 in a slightly different format. Therefore, excessive practice on any one skill is unlikely to have the breadth needed by students to cope with the possible samples they may be faced with in a testing situation. Maintaining breadth of reading objectives, writing activities, and language arts integrations is the best way to avoid the hazard of a narrowed curriculum.

Incoherent Curriculum

In states that provide performance assessments, such as Maryland, Kentucky, and North Carolina, teachers are often encouraged to give explicit practice on the tasks in the performance assessments to familiarize students with them (Shepard, Flexer, Hiebert, & Marion, 1993). The question to be addressed is, How much task practice is effective? Although the students should understand the formats of the tasks, the formats themselves cannot become the curriculum. Unfortunately, some misguided administrators expect teachers to provide practice on tasks in performance assessments for several weeks or several months. In these cases, the tasks become the curriculum. However, the tasks were designed for testing, not for teaching. Consequently, they do not serve the curriculum well. The curriculum may become disconnected, fragmented, and incoherent. A technique for avoiding an incoherent curriculum is to place extreme limits on task practice and to retain the goals, contents, and procedures of the mainstream curriculum.

Performance Orientation

In the classroom, teachers may be either learning oriented or performance oriented. Learning-oriented teachers emphasize understanding of major content themes. They aim to teach reading skills that can be used widely. In contrast, performance-oriented teachers are concerned with test scores, student achievement, and external evaluations. Researchers have studied the effects of these two orientations. Flink, Boggiano, Main, Barrett, and Katz (1992) asked some teachers to show their students how to understand a problem and to enjoy trying to solve it. These teachers were expected to be learning oriented. The researchers asked a second group of teachers to make sure students scored high on a certain problem-solving test. These were performance-oriented teachers. The teachers were told they would be evaluated based on their students' scores. Teachers in the performance-orientated group were likely to become extremely procedural, showing students specific steps for problem solving. The performance-oriented teachers did not emphasize understanding the problem or being creatively flexible in solving it. Performance-oriented teachers were anxious about their own instruction. The outcome was that students in the performance-oriented group were lower in achievement on the problem-solving test than students in the learning-oriented group. In other words, an emphasis on performance and high scores has a paradoxical effect. In fact, it decreases successful test taking. This principle applies to classrooms as a whole. In middle school science classrooms, Anderman and Young (1994) found that students of teachers who emphasized performance on tests and rewarded students with extrinsic incentives had lower achievement test scores than students of teachers who were learning oriented, emphasizing understanding and encouraging students to be pleased with their comprehension of new ideas. A performance orientation decontextualizes reading and therefore it is likely to decrease the effectiveness of instruction.

Planning Instruction and Curricula in a High-Stakes Testing Environment

Linking Teaching Objectives to Testing

Optimal planning for test preparation begins with a simple step. The objectives of the test should be clearly linked to the objectives of instruction. If one test objective consists of comprehending character development in narratives, then one objective of instruction should consist of comprehending character development in narratives. This objective can be taught with stories or novels. It can be encouraged through reading, writing, and listening. Pursuing this objective for instruction will not result in any of the hazards presented in the previous section. This is a broad objective, not a narrow one, and it can lead to a coherent curriculum, not an incoherent one. Other objectives, such as gaining the main idea from a paragraph or writing to integrate across multiple texts, can be formulated as teaching objectives. When there is an alignment between the objectives of testing and instruction, test preparation is being optimized.

In a previous section, we described the value of practicing item formats. However, we also suggested that this be extremely limited in time and scope. Assessment tasks should not become the curriculum. It is not the format of the test that should be aligned with teaching, but the objectives that should be aligned with teaching.

Time Allocations

As indicated previously, three levels of test preparation are recommended for high-stakes testing in reading. At one level, students are given instruction and practice with test formats. The time allocated to this aspect should be a few days, but never weeks or months. It will be counterproductive if this time allocation is excessive. The second aspect of preparation is strategy instruction for reading strategies needed to perform well on the test, such as gaining the main idea, searching for information, or self-questioning. Time allocated to this portion of the preparation process should be measured in weeks and months. Strategy instruction is a long-term endeavor and strategy learning is time consuming. These strategies are often reflected in the objectives of a test and the objectives of a curriculum and can be incorporated into goals for instruction planned at the beginning of the school year. The third phase of test preparation recommended previously consists of planning for an integrated curriculum that will encourage long-term engaged reading. The time allocated to this phase of preparation should be measured in months and years. The planning across the grade levels within a school and across the months for a given school year should include integrations of reading, writing, and content that will enable students to gain the high-level skills most important on tests. These skills include cognitive strategies, metacognitive awareness, and motivation attributes.

Support for Reading Motivation and Self-Efficacy

Planning for test preparation involves generating ideas for motivational support. Teachers need to address the anxiety students face when they encounter tests. Teachers should help students feel efficacious about their test-taking abilities. However, beyond the immediate test context, teachers can develop students' intrinsic motivation for reading during the months prior to the high-stakes test. Intrinsic motivation will increase students' amount of reading independently and amount of reading in school, both of which will contribute to higher test scores (Guthrie & Alao, 1997).

Conclusion

High-stakes testing is everywhere. From grade 1 to 12, tests are used to decide promotion, graduation,

Building actual reading ability is the best test preparation. Creating balanced instruction with vitality is the best antidote to excessive test-based accountability.

special class placement, and school success. Although many teachers are beleaguered by the increase in testing, schools and teams of teachers can bring balance to the situation. On one hand, specific test preparation in the types of questions, expected responses, and content of a reading test will help students who are totally unfamiliar with the testing formats. On the other hand, too much practice testing can curtail the curriculum. It can do a disservice to children by narrowing their expectations for specific formats. Building actual reading ability is the best test preparation. Creating balanced instruction with vitality is the best antidote to excessive test-based accountability. Teachers should become proactive in fostering this balance.

References

Anderman, E.M., & Young, A.J. (1994). Motivation and strategy use in science: Individual differences and classroom effects. *Journal of Research in Science Teaching, 31*, 811–831.

Au, K.H., & Carroll, J.H. (1997). Improving literacy achievement through a constructivist approach: The KEEP Demonstration Classroom Project. *The Elementary School Journal, 97*, 203–221.

Blanton, W.E., & Wood, K.D. (1984). Direct instruction in reading comprehension test-taking skill. *Reading World, 24*, 10–19.

Fakins, D.J., Green, D.S. & Bushell, D. (1976). The effects of an instructional test-taking unit on achievement test scores. *Journal of Educational Research, 70*, 67–71.

Feuer, M.J., Holland, P.W., Green, B.F., Bertenthal, M.W., & Hemphill, F.C. (1999). *Uncommon measures: Equivalence and linkage among educational tests*. Washington, DC: National Academy Press.

Flink, C., Boggiano, A.K., Main, D.S., Barrett, M., & Katz, P.A. (1992). Children's achievement-related behaviors: The role of extrinsic and intrinsic motivational orientations. In A.K. Boggiano & T.S. Pittman (Eds.), *Achievement and motivation: A social-developmental perspective* (pp. 189–214). New York: Cambridge University Press.

Franklin, M.R. (1983). The effect of practice and instruction on the word comprehension subtest of the Woodcock. *Journal of Psychoeducational Assessment, 1*, 197–200.

Garner, R. (1982). Resolving comprehension failure through text lookbacks: Direct training and practice effects among good and poor comprehenders in grades six and seven. *Reading Psychology, 3*, 221–231.

Gaskins, I., Guthrie, J.T., Satlow, E., Ostertag, F., Six, L., Byrne, J., et al. (1994). Integrating instruction of science, reading, and writing: Goals, teacher development, and assessment. *Journal of Research in Science Teaching, 31*, 1039–1056.

Guthrie, J.T., & Alao, S. (1997). Designing contexts to increase motivations for reading. *Educational Psychologist, 32*, 95–107.

Guthrie, J.T., Anderson, E., Alao, S., & Rinehart, J. (1999). Influences of Concept-Oriented Reading Instruction on strategy use and conceptual learning from text. *The Elementary School Journal, 99*, 343–366.

Guthrie, J.T., Wigfield, A., Metsala, J.L., & Cox, K.E. (1999). Motivational and cognitive predictors of text comprehension and reading amount. *Scientific Studies of Reading, 3*, 231–256.

Haladyna, T.M., Nolen, S.B., & Hass, N.S. (1990). Raising standardized achievement test scores and the origins of test score pollution. *Educational Researcher, 20*, 2–7.

Hansen, J., & Pearson, P.D. (1983). An instructional study: Improving the inferential comprehension of good and poor fourth-grade readers. *Journal of Educational Psychology, 31*, 821–829.

Heubert, J.P., & Hauser, R.M. (Eds.). (1999). *High stakes: Testing for tracking, promotion, and graduation*. Washington, DC: National Academy Press.

Hughes, C.A., & Schumaker, J.B. (1991). Test-taking strategy instruction for adolescents with learning disabilities. *Exceptionality, 2*, 205–221.

Kalechstein, P.B., Hocevar, D., & Kalechstein, M. (1988). Effects of test-wiseness training on test anxiety, locus of control and reading achievement in elementary school children. *Anxiety Research, 1*, 247–261.

Kirkpatrick, J.E. (1934). The motivating effect of a specific type of testing program. *University of Iowa Studies: Studies in Education, 9*, 41–68.

Lane, S., Parke, C.S., & Stone, C.A. (1998). A framework for evaluating the consequences of assessment programs. *Educational Measurement: Issues & Practice, 17*, 24–28.

Lapp, D., & Flood, J. (1994). Integrating the curriculum: First steps. *The Reading Teacher, 47*, 416–419.

Lysynchuk, L.M., Pressley, M., & Vye, N.J. (1990). Reciprocal teaching improves standardized reading-comprehension performance in poor comprehenders. *The Elementary School Journal, 90*, 469–484.

Mehrens, W.A., Popham, W.J., & Ryan, J.M. (1998). How to prepare students for performance assessments. *Educational Measurement: Issues & Practice, 17*, 18–22.

Millman, J., & Bishop, C.H. (1965). An analysis of test-wiseness. *Educational and Psychological Measurement, 25*, 707–717.

Morrow, L.M., Pressley, M., Smith, J.K., & Smith, M. (1997). The effect of a literature-based program integrated into literacy and science instruction with children from diverse backgrounds. *Reading Research Quarterly, 32*, 54–76.

Paris, S.G., Lawton, T., Turner, J., & Roth, J. (1991). A developmental perspective on standardized achievement testing. *Educational Researcher, 20*, 12–20.

Purves, A.C. (1993). Setting standards in the language arts and literature classroom and the implications for portfolio assessment. *Educational Assessment, 1*, 175–199.

Reutzel, D.R., & Hollingsworth, P.M. (1991). Reading time in school: Effect on fourth graders' performance on a criterion-referenced comprehension test. *Journal of Educational Research, 84*, 170–176.

Roeber, E., Bond, L., & Connealy, S. (1998). *Annual survey of state student assessment programs* (Fall 1997). Washington, DC: Council of Chief State School Officers.

Rosenshine, B., & Meister, C. (1994). Reciprocal teaching: A review of the research. *Review of Educational Research, 64*, 479–530.

Schwartz, S. (1988). A comparison of componential and traditional approaches to training reading skills. *Applied Cognitive Psychology, 2*, 189–201.

Scruggs, T.E., Mastropieri, M.A., & Tolfa-Veit, D. (1986). The effects of coaching on the standardized test performance of learning disabled and behaviorally disordered students. *RASE: Remedial & Special Education, 7*, 37–41.

Shepard, L.A., Flexer, R.J., Hiebert, E.H., & Mation, S.F. (1993). Effects of introducing classroom performance assessments on student learning. *Educational Measurement Issues and Practices, 15*, 7–18.

Smith, M.L. (1991). Meanings of test preparation. *American Educational Research Journal, 28*, 521–542.

Sugrue, B. (1995). A theory-based framework for assessing domain-specific problem-solving ability. *Educational Measurement: Issues and Practice, 14*, 29–35.

Waid, L.R., Kanoy, R.C., Blick, K.A., & Walker, W.E. (1978). Relationship of state-trait anxiety and type of practice to reading comprehension. *Journal of Psychology, 98*, 27–36.

Wigfield, A., & Guthrie, J.T. (1997). Relations of children's motivation for reading to the amount and breadth of their reading. *Journal of Educational Psychology, 89*, 420–432.

Yen, W., & Ferrara, S. (1997). The Maryland School Performance Assessment Program: Performance assessment with psychometric quality suitable for high stakes usage. *Journal of Educational and Psychological Measurement, 57*, 60–84.

Teaching *True* and *To* the Test in Writing

Shelby Anne Wolf
University of Colorado—Boulder

Kenneth Paul Wolf
University of Colorado—Denver

In this article, we focus on what we have learned from six exemplary teachers of writing who teach within high-stakes accountability systems in Kentucky and Washington. Based on what we have seen in their classrooms and discussed with them and their students, our response to the reality of high-stakes testing is the need to "Teach *True* and *To* the Test in Writing."

Our first response—*true*—aligns with our interest in how writing teachers help their students prepare for annual tests while remaining committed to effective pedagogy. The six teachers believe that they must be true to sound theory and practice in teaching their children to write. They encourage daily writing in their process classrooms and give many opportunities for topic choice as well as conferencing. They emphasize craft through the study of published models and lessons on voice, developing ideas, organization, and convention. In short, they encourage authentic writing for different audiences and purposes. Nonetheless, the emphasis on teaching *to* the test is an inescapable reality in their classrooms. Thus, they pay attention to the required testing demands, and in many states, including Kentucky and Washington, the demands are high.

We begin this piece with background on writing reform and assessment and then introduce the teachers and schools. Finally, and most important, we address five points that we feel are essential to sound theory and practice in preparing children to write well and score well on assessments: (a) understanding the criteria; (b) analyzing various models; (c) responding to others' writing; (d) reflecting on one's own writing; and (e) rehearsing the performance.

Reform and Assessment in Writing

It was the best of times, it was the worst of times, it was the age of wisdom, it was the age of foolishness, it was the epoch of belief, it was the epoch of incredulity, it was the season of Light, it was the season of Darkness, it was the spring of hope, it was the winter of despair, we had everything before us, we had nothing before us, we were all going direct to Heaven, we were all going direct the other way. (Dickens, 1859/1981, p. 1)

Current issues in writing remind us of the oxymoronic opening of *A Tale of Two Cities*. To contemplate writing reform is to live in the season of Light. The *"conditions* that encourage good writing" (Graves, 1994) are visible in many classrooms, offering children time to write and topic choice as well as opportunities to share their work and to benefit from teachers' demonstrations of writers' craft. In process classrooms, writing is embedded in children's social worlds and allows them to talk with and talk back to others' words and worlds (Dyson, 1997). Literature provides children with exemplary models for discovering new topics and new ways of saying what they want to say (Harwayne, 1992). As Ray (1999) explains, they are learning to "do the sophisticated work of separating *what it's about* from *how it is written*" (p. 10).

On the other hand, to contemplate assessment is to dwell in the season of Darkness. Kohn (2000) suggests that "standardized testing has swelled and mutated, like a creature in one of those old horror movies, to the point that it now threatens to swallow our schools whole" (p. 60). For Newkirk (2000), the monster is no less menacing: "Driven by state testing, teachers are being pulled toward prompt-and-rubric teaching that bypasses the human act of composing and the human gesture of response" (p. 41). He feels that rubric-based assessment is "capitulation" rather than "preparation"—a view that leans on the dark side of Dickens' quote to indicate that under such a system, rather than attaining Heaven, we are "all going direct the other way."

Even the best assessment systems can be distorted when high-stakes accountability is attached.

However, educational measurement expert Lorrie Shepard (1991) takes a more balanced view, explaining that authentic assessments have the potential to measure "complex performances that directly represent the ultimate goals of education. Thus practice on such tasks would lead instruction in a positive direction" (p. 235). Her words align with the view that it is best to "build assessments toward which you want educators to teach" (Resnick & Resnick, 1992, p. 59). Writing assessments that ask students to collect their work in portfolios or to provide written responses to prompts were created to point educators in such a positive direction.

Still, measurement experts are not blind to the potential flaws. Shepard (1997) explains that "even with performance assessments, students may rely on familiar, rote routines and pretend to know" (p. 20). And Linn (2000) believes that even the best assessment systems can be distorted when high-stakes accountability is attached. As Calkins, Montgomery, and Santman with Falk (1998) explain: "Because of the high stakes associated with test scores, far too many educators across the nation are staffing their schools, grouping their children, and designing their curriculum with one goal in mind: to raise test scores" (p. 3). Still, the reality of high-stakes accountability linked to performance assessments has forced individuals who formally kept at a distance from testing to try to "help teachers live thoughtfully in the presence of tests and to do so without selling their souls" (p. 8). In the next section, we introduce six teachers who have learned to do just that.

Exemplary Teachers' Passion for Writing

For the past five years, our team has been researching the assessment reform efforts in Kentucky and Washington through surveys and case studies of exemplary sites. Using exemplary sampling (Heath & McLaughlin, 1993), we located our schools after discussions with state and district leaders as well as site visits with principals and teachers. We were not searching for "no wonder" schools with populations from high socioeconomic communities or magnet schools for the gifted. We didn't want our selections to invite comments like, "Well, *no wonder* they can do it. Look at their population and resources." Instead, we wanted schools and teachers where we would have to look deeper than surface explanations for why good things were happening. Descriptions of the teachers in six of the schools follow. The teacher names are pseudonyms selected by the participants themselves.

We wanted schools and teachers where we would have to look deeper than surface explanations for why good things were happening.

In Kentucky, Ms. Jazz taught fourth grade in a rural Appalachian school where eighty percent of the children qualified for free and reduced lunch. While Ms. Jazz paid close attention to the ongoing as well as the annual assessment requirements, she felt more driven to help her children see writing as a way of thinking. In one of our visits, she told her class. "You're not writing to answer this test question. You're writing to learn for the rest of your life!"

Two hours up the road in a rural school with seventy percent free and reduced lunch, Mr. Bass taught his seventh graders in similar ways. He balanced instruction of genres typically assessed in state prompts with insights into the beauty of other forms. He was a poet who shared his writing with his students: "I really love teaching poetry . . . [and] talking about how to make the senses available to the reader when you're writing poetry."

A fourth-grade teacher, Ms. Olinski seamlessly integrated writing and reading into her daily workshop in a suburban Kentucky school with forty percent free and reduced lunch. She was also a writer who shared her pieces to garner helpful criticism from her students. She considered writing experts mentors from afar and believed that Donald Graves' (1983) "Let the children teach us"—was the impetus for her work. After one observation of her class she told us, "Writing is my passion. I was called to do this."

In the seventh grade, Ms. Morgan's Kentucky middle school had thirty-five percent of its students on free and reduced lunch, and she was notable for her exquisite organizational skills. When she taught a new genre, she provided packets of materials which included benchmark pieces, informational articles, as well as revision and editing checklists. When asked about her goals as a writing teacher, she explained: "You've got to give them the tools to be successful."

Ms. Wright taught fourth grade in a highly diverse elementary school in suburban Washington, where fifteen languages other than English were spoken. Their free and reduced lunch count was at sixty-eight percent. Ms. Wright integrated literacy with social studies, and she placed a special emphasis on genre. She explained: "If you're going to have them write a genre, they have to read it. I know that's common sense, but it makes such a difference. They have to read it so they can write it."

The Washington middle school had twenty-five percent racial and ethnic diversity and twenty-six percent of the students were on free and reduced lunch. As a seventh-grade teacher, Ms. Underwood loved to assemble "bits and pieces" from various resources (e.g., anthologies, writing experts' books) to create original curriculum. She rejected materials that were too prescriptive or too oriented toward the annual test: "My bottom line is responsibility to the kids. Some districts have gone to exclusive (testing) packets. 'You can't do this. You can't do that.' And I couldn't teach that way."

Five Points of Teaching *True* and *To* the Test in Writing

Figure 1 illustrates the key ideas we want to share about the ways the six teachers teach writing. At the center of the figure the notebook image offers some of the forms students learned, and the circle of arrows emphasizes the continual integration of the language arts. Most important, the students did not just write to focus on the test; instead, as Ms. Jazz explained, they wrote "to learn for the rest of their lives." Still, in the high-stakes environment of state testing, these teachers gave their students substantive opportunities to show how well they were learning to write. In consideration of the required performance assessments, the teachers had "developed the understandings necessary to transform their instruction and to make the new kinds of tasks an integral part of it" (Shepard, 1991, p. 237). The points of instruction are the five points of the star, which we explore in the following sections.

Understanding the Criteria

One of the first things the six teachers did was to help students understand the established criteria for evaluating their writing. These criteria included the general goals or standards that a state hopes children will meet, the specific rubrics for scoring children's writing, and the genres students are expected to use (See Table 1). In terms of standards, Washington has the Essential Academic Learning Requirements in Writing (Office of Superintendent of Public Instruction, 2000), while Kentucky sets writing under the first of six Academic Expectations (Kentucky Department of Education, 2000).

These generalized standards are then placed in the context of more specific rubrics for scoring children's writing. In Washington, where children complete two on-demand writing prompts in the annual Washington Assessment of Student Learning (WASL), pieces are scored with a "focused holistic" approach. Kentucky provides two different kinds of

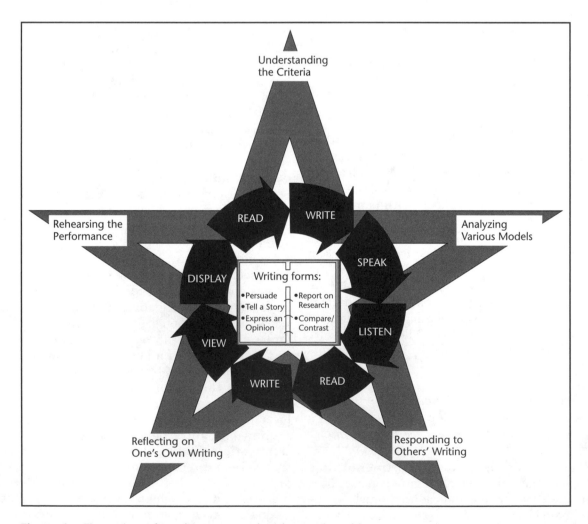

Figure 1 Five points of teaching *true* and *to* the test in writing.

Table 1   Standards, Rubrics, and Genres in Kentucky and Washington

	Washington	Kentucky
Standards	Essential Academic Learning Requirements (EALRs) in Writing • write clearly and effectively, • write in a variety of forms for different audiences and purposes, • understand and use the steps of the writing process, and, • analyze and evaluate the effectiveness of written work.	Academic Expectations (1.11 for Writing) Students write using appropriate forms, conventions, and styles to communicate ideas and information to different audiences for different purposes.
Rubrics	WASL (Washington Assessment of Student Learning) Two on-demand pieces scored with a "focused holistic" approach, • 4 points for content, organization, and style, • 2 points for mechanics.	CATS (Commonwealth Accountability Testing System) Both the portfolio and the on-demand pieces are scored with a "holistic approach" in which readers attend to purpose/audience, idea development, organization, sentences, language, and correctness. • novice • apprentice • proficient • distinguished Open-response questions are scored 0 to 4 depending on the amount of information the child provides.
Genres	WASL On-Demand Prompts Fourth grade: one narrative and one expository piece. Seventh grade: one expository and one persuasive piece.	CATS On-Demand Prompts Students may be asked to narrate, persuade, or respond to text, graphic, or chart. Fourth grade: students are asked to write letters and articles. Seventh grade: students write letters, articles, and editorials. Kentucky Portfolio All portfolios contain a table of contents. Fourth grade: 4 writing areas including (a) reflective writing (letter to the reviewer), (b) personal expressive writing, (c) literary writing, and (d) transactive writing. Seventh grade: 5 writing entries—1 in each category above, plus 1 extra in either personal, literary, or transactive.

scoring criteria. Children's writing portfolios, as well as their on-demand Commonwealth Accountability Testing System (CATS) pieces, are scored with a "holistic" rubric. On the other hand, open-response items are scored with a 0 to 4 rubric that attends to the information the child provides. Open-response items are not an official part of the Kentucky writing assessment, but the exemplary teachers included them as a part of their instruction because students have to read a content area passage (e.g., science, social studies) and answer a question in writing.

The emphasis on *genre* is also critical, and both states are clear about the genres children should produce. Washington fourth graders are asked to complete two prompts, one narrative and one expository, while seventh graders address expository and persuasive prompts. Kentucky children must respond to similar prompts in particular forms, such as a letter, an article, or an editorial. In addition, their portfolios must contain different genres of literary writing and transactive writing which is produced to "get something done" in the real world—such as a persuasive piece.

So how do teachers help children understand the criteria involved in standards, rubrics, and particular genres? First, the six exemplary teachers helped their children think carefully about what they wanted their writing to *express*. What is the purpose of the piece? Who is it for? How can ideas be selected and language chosen to effectively deliver the piece? In short, why is it important to say these things in just this way, and is there a more powerful way to express it? The teachers stressed their state rubrics, providing students with a clear target and guide. And they often asked their children's opinions of the criteria: "What makes a distinguished piece of writing?" and "If you wanted to move this piece from a novice to an apprentice paper, what would you do?" They used the rubrics' technical language, and terms like "purpose," "audience," and "organization" became a part of the children's vocabulary. Still, the focus on rubrics was never allowed to take precedence over the human act of composing.

Indeed, anyone who has used rubrics knows that even the best rubric cannot capture the unique ways in which a piece of writing calls out to its readers. The point is not to wrench a piece in line with standardized rubric criteria, but to meet and then push beyond the boundaries of established rubrics to take the writing to the next level.

The teachers placed strong emphasis on personally understanding their state rubrics through professional development. The Kentucky teachers participated in and led scoring conferences where they discussed the rubrics with other professionals both in and beyond their school sites. Mr. Bass explained: "It's much more effective when you get together with a group of teachers and say, 'Oh, this is why it's apprentice' or 'This is why it's proficient.'"

More important, these discussions of students' writing allowed the teachers opportunities to see beyond the established criteria to acknowledge the unique character development, the careful craft of an argument, or the flash of language that lifted a piece off the page and into the mind and heart of the reader.

With knowledge of the rubrics refined through professional conversations, the teachers were better equipped to do the most difficult task in helping children understand criteria: genre study (Wolf & Gearhart, 1994). They were able to overlay the more generalized rubrics onto specific genres, stretching and fitting them to demonstrate how certain generic principles of writing work within particular forms. For example, "organization" is a principle that looks quite different in a story or a report. Indeed, in terms of understanding criteria, the teachers worked the hardest to explore the specific features of multiple genres with their children.

When teachers felt unsure about a particular genre, they sought advice from writing experts. For instance, Ms. Jazz knew that the nuances of persuasive pieces would be new for her Kentucky fourth graders and

invited her region's writing coordinator to provide a lesson. The coordinator began with sound advice about the genre, explaining that persuasion is to "convince somebody of something we want them to do. And it's hard. Sometimes we want to just whine and cry." She then humorously read a mock piece, with exaggerated moans and multiple "pleases," and the children giggled at the pleading tone. Next, she seriously read a piece with convincing explanations and asked. "Now you tell me which one is the most persuasive." The children unanimously voted for the serious sample. The coordinator's use of sample texts leads us to our next section on the value of analyzing models. While it is important to lay out the criteria for specific genres, the features become clearer with examples.

Analyzing Various Models

Even in Kentucky, where the commitment to professional development is high, having a writing coordinator conduct model lessons is unusual. So how can teachers learn more about the genres they have to teach? Both states provided multiple models, often benchmark papers which teachers could analyze to understand how the rubric criteria would play out in particular pieces of writing. These models were available for discussion in state-organized workshops, assembled in "handbooks" or "assessment samplers," and even obtainable on CD-ROM.

In Kentucky, Ms. Morgan considered benchmark papers to be an essential tool. When her seventh-grade students were working on a portfolio piece in which they were asked to "defend a position," she helped them carefully analyze a distinguished benchmark piece released by the state. With the model on the overhead, she and her students discussed the benchmark's pros and cons. One student noted how the opening "grabbed the reader's attention and had a clear thesis statement." After their discussion, Ms. Morgan reviewed how the student author restated her thesis, gave examples, and then "made a call to action," something she expected of her students. This benchmark piece, as well as other helpful materials, went into their packets, which included a wide range of information that her students could draw on in developing their own papers.

Ms. Olinski used a benchmark entitled "Sore Foot" by "a real fourth-grade writer." She asked her students to read the piece in partners and discuss "Why this is a piece of good writing. Think about the criteria that we know so much about." After the partner discussions, the children talked as a whole class:

Ms. Olinski Tell us why you think it's a pretty good piece of writing.

Ashley It described the way she felt [when she stepped on a nail].

Rick	The ideas flowed together real well.
Maria	"[The blood] looked like cherry Jell-O" was my favorite sentence!
Rick	I think she has good idea development, 'cause it had "thought shots" and it told what she felt.
Ms. Olinski	Focused on a purpose, good organization, and ideas flowed logically. I didn't struggle reading it. I can see the blood dripping off! [The children laugh.]
Nate	But her piece didn't have a conclusion to it.
Ms. Olinski	If the author were here, what would you say?
Nate	I think you should write a stronger conclusion, 'cause it kind of drops off.

In Washington, benchmark pieces were not as available as in Kentucky for two reasons. First, the reform was younger. Kentucky began its current reform in 1990 while Washington began in 1993, making writing tests mandatory in fourth grade in 1998 and in seventh grade in 2000. Second, its testing did not include a portfolio with a representative range of genres; instead, students responded to two on-demand prompts. As a result, the exemplary teachers often made their own models. For example, when teaching her students how to write literary criticism of a poem, Ms. Underwood wrote her own analysis of a poem by John Updike.

Indeed, anyone who has used rubrics knows that even the best rubric cannot capture the unique ways in which a piece of writing calls out to its readers.

In addition, teachers in both states often turned to published pieces of literature and exposition to demonstrate models of writing. Ms. Underwood encouraged her students to analyze the dialogue in S. E. Hinton's (1995) *The Outsiders*, to make their dialogues more effective. Ms. Wright stressed the importance of exaggeration when she taught her students about tall tales. Together they brainstormed their own responses to the opening phrase, "It was so hot . . ."

Alice	. . .that you couldn't spit.
Ryan	. . .their words melted.
John	. . .that I melted into a pool of goo.
Daren	. . .that my plow evaporated!

She then asked her fourth graders to read the story of "Davy Crocket" (Osborne, 1991) and write down the exaggerations they found. The children immediately recognized the improbability implied by constructions like "Davy, who could carry thunder in his fist. . ." One student read the first page, raised his hand, and exclaimed: "Ms. Wright, we'll have to write down the whole story. The whole thing is exaggerations!" Laughing, Ms. Wright told them they could write down the first five they encountered, but the point about exaggeration had been made.

Responding to Others' Writing

Another point that the exemplary teachers consistently made was the need for feedback, especially from teachers and peers. In Washington, one of the four Essential Academic Learning Requirements stressed the need to "analyze and evaluate the effectiveness of written work"; in Kentucky the mantra among teachers and children was "the writing's never done." As Ms. Olinski told her fourth graders:

> You've heard the expression from famous writers who say, "Writing is never finished. You just decide to stop." But we're not stopping yet. I believe the pieces that you've developed show you as awesome writers. But we can get more awesome! This month, we'll take a look at the pieces that we've selected [for our portfolios] and think about the criteria that we use in order to develop our writing. Peer conferencing can help you discover the hidden treasures that you have.

Hidden treasures were often discovered through questioning. Rather than offering direct advice on what an author *should* do, teacher and peer readers formulated questions about an author's choices and expressed their curiosities about aspects of the writing (McIver & Wolf, 1999). In her conferences, Ms. Olinski used questions to show her stance as a curious and analytical reader, and her children took up her stance when they read their peers' work. We watched a peer conference between two girls. One had written a story about a monster lurking under Jessica's new bed—a monster that turned out to be her father's cardigan. After a lengthy discussion, the child offering feedback wrote down her most important queries:

- Could you explain if Jessica was rushing her dad to put the bed together?
- After she found out that the monster was just her dad's old sweater, did she go back to bed?
- Was Jessica still scared?
- Does Jessica like the bed now?

We asked the author if she found these written questions helpful. She nodded and replied, "When I read it again, I understand more 'cause she explained more." She also felt that questions gave her more room to express herself as a writer, referring back to her teacher's emphasis on authorial choice: "Some kids have to write exactly what the teacher tells them to. But I think it's pretty cool that we get to write what we want. We don't have to write about the time in our life when we went canoeing. We can write what we *need* to write."

When students were asked to write in a particular genre, choice and questioning remained essential. In Ms. Wright's fourth-grade classroom, the children were writing research papers on the American West. Ali was writing about Sacajawea. Ms. Wright asked her: "How are you going to lay out your body paragraphs?" Ali replied, "I could go from when she was born to when she died." Ms. Wright nodded, "Is that the way you want to do it? Chronologically?" Later, in a peer conference Ali received two more questions to consider. Dee read her introduction and asked, "Did you tell us why you chose that topic? And [what's] your focus question?" In her next revision, Ali responded: "My focus question is 'Why is Sacajawea important to our history?'"

Conferencing in the elementary classrooms centered on questions—whether voiced orally or written down. The middle school classrooms, however, provided more routines for response. In reviewing their peers' position papers, Ms. Morgan asked her Kentucky seventh graders to highlight supporting arguments in green and underline transition words in blue. She asked them to highlight the introduction in purple "*if* the first paragraph grabs the reader's attention." The specificity required by such tasks demanded that peer reviewers visually justify what the piece contained and what might be missing. Still, the emphasis on needed parts was only a way to get to the meaning of the whole piece. On the Revision Sheet she created to aid effective peer reviews, Ms. Morgan stressed that Making Sense was the most important category and she continually encouraged students to help each other through asking questions.

When students were asked to write in a particular genre, choice and questioning remained essential.

Helping each other was critical to Ms. Underwood's seventh-grade class in Washington as well. She asked students to write a Literary Analysis of a poem, exploring at least two elements (e.g., rhyme and imagery) that they found essential to their selected piece. After drafting, she asked them to seek peer response, explaining: "First of all—and don't you [the author] tell them—can they tell what two elements your paper discusses? Secondly, they're going to tell you what they like about your essay. Finally, they can tell you what they think you need to work on."

One student, Cassie, struggled with an analysis of a poem by Naomi Long Madgett (1994) entitled "Woman with Flower." She knew that she wanted to talk about the use of metaphor in the piece, but she disagreed with the central metaphor. She felt that "flowers *should* be nurtured," and couldn't understand why the author disagreed in the first two lines of the poem: "I wouldn't coax the plant if I were you. Such watchful nurturing may do it harm." Cassie wrote bits and pieces of her analysis and finally turned to a peer who read the poem and responded:

Ron	If a person gets too much nurturing they—
Cassie	Drift away.
Ron	Okay, Cassie, it says "give it the chance to find the sunlight." So if you nurture a person too much they won't want to go out on their own.
Cassie	Too much nurturing? But that's not what I believe. You need to be cared for!
Ron	It says the things we love we have to learn to leave alone, so that's what the going towards the sunlight on their own means.
Cassie	So you can help them grow?
Ron	Yes, but they have to do some of it by themselves.

Ron offered Cassie a new way of thinking about the poem's central metaphor. But he also made room for Cassie's opinion on the necessity of care in learning to thrive. Indeed, Ron's advice could be a metaphor for our next section, for although it is critical for young writers to receive thoughtful teacher and peer feedback, they must also "do some of it by themselves" and learn to be self-reflective about their writing.

Reflecting on One's Own Writing

Being self-reflective about writing is a goal in both states. The Washington Essential Academic Learning Requirements suggest that students learn to evaluate their own work. The emphasis on self-reflection is also clear in Kentucky's portfolio requirement for a "letter to the reviewer" where students reflect on their growth as a writer.

We debated whether to emphasize responding to others' writing or reflecting on one's own writing first. We felt that the students often learned how to be self-reflective from the thoughtful response they received from others about their work. Still, arguing which comes first fails to effectively acknowledge their reciprocal relationship. This was made especially clear in our interview with a fourth grader in Ms. Jazz's Kentucky classroom. We were talking about a mystery story she had written, and she suggested that at one point in creating her piece she had had some trouble:

Tish	I got writer's block after that, and I didn't know what to do.
Shelby	Oh, writer's block. How did you get unstuck?

Tish	Ashley [another student in the class]. She was working on her Nancy Drew thing and she was setting right beside me. I asked her how she was doing hers, and she showed me, and I finally figured out what to do.
Shelby	You know, some people say that all writers need is a quiet room, a place to write. But you seem to need to be able to talk things out. Is that right?
Tish	Yeah. Quiet room and a friend is all I need.

In times of testing, however, children did need opportunities to reconsider and revise their own writing without the help of a friend, even though they resisted the notion.

Students felt disadvantaged by a system that emphasized the importance of response and then denied it during testing time. However, because they were taught to provide and receive feedback and to engage in writing as good readers do, they internalized the processes and could often apply them without assistance when testing time came. As Charles, a Kentucky fourth grader, told us concerning on-demand prompts: "Let's go back to that saying, 'Writing is never over.' I used to think that writing is over once you finish your draft. And then I got into Ms. Olinski's class. She taught us revision, feedback. I bet that's why I'm such a good writer now."

Charles' confidence, however, was not a casual boast. He was able to show us specific places in his portfolio where he had taken the time to reconsider his writing, and this was true of many students. The teachers' daily writing workshops, especially the emphasis on response, became echoes in the ear when children were required to revise alone.

Students felt disadvantaged by a system that emphasized the importance of response and then denied it during testing time.

Teachers made other critical choices in providing support for student self-reflection. One of their most important decisions was to make the elements of sound writing visible and available—posting them on bulletin boards and clipping them to the inside cover of their students' writing portfolios. Ms. Wright in Washington had large posters describing the writing process and various genres for her fourth graders. Ms. Underwood provided evaluative opportunities for each kind of writing her seventh graders were attempting. In preparing their character dialogues, she gave her students a handout with two self-assessment sections. First, they evaluated the communication styles and conventions of their draft dialogues. Second, they analyzed their sentences on a grid to count the number of words in each of their sentences and the verbs they used, which allowed them to look for sentence variety. When we asked if the self-assessment helped, one girl nodded, "It woke me up to what I needed to do."

In Kentucky, visible and available self-assessment ideas were even more pronounced. In addition to commercial posters on the writing process and genre features, teachers displayed helpful acronyms. Ms. Morgan emphasized C.A.R.E. with her seventh graders: "C is for Change, A is for Add, R is for Rearrange, E is for Eliminate—revising is when we take C.A.R.E. of our writing." In the fourth grade, Ms. Olinski had a C.U.P.S. poster that focused on Capitalization, Usage, Punctuation, and Spelling. Again, the emphasis was on questions the children could ask—those for Capitalization were "Have I capitalized: beginning of sentences? proper nouns?"

One final but essential aspect of how exemplary teachers teach true as well as to the test in writing was to offer their children multiple opportunities to rehearse their writing within the test conditions.

Every Kentucky classroom we visited had posted the state rubrics. Official descriptions of novice, apprentice, proficient, and distinguished writing stretched above their chalk boards. In Ms. Jazz's classroom, written reminders of the "four-column method" were laminated and taped to her fourth graders' desks to help students with open-response items, where they had to read a passage and answer a question in writing. Each of the four columns is topped with a heading and a question, and students use the remaining column space for notes:

Know: What do I need to know in order to answer this question?

Do: What is this question asking me to do?

Examples: What examples from the article can I give to answer each part of the question?

Connections: How can I connect some part of my answer to a real-life situation?

Thus, the "four-column method" emphasized student self-reflection through questioning.

When Mr. Bass taught his seventh graders how to use this tool, he used a state-released question as a model. He then created his own hypothetical responses to demonstrate the levels of response according to the state rubric, reminding his students that unlike their portfolio pieces, open-response items were not a time for a lot of personal voice:

Before you answer a question, you must know how to break that question apart, analyze it. You can't just fly by the seat of your pants and do what you want to do.

You have to plan your answer. They [test scorers] are really interested in how you answer the question. Bottom line: Answer the blessed question!

This admonition would come in handy when his students faced the annual test. One final but essential aspect of how exemplary teachers teach true as well as to the test in writing was to offer their children multiple opportunities to rehearse their writing within the test conditions. In short, they practice how to "answer the blessed question."

Rehearsing the Performance

Test practice always comes with its own ironies. Mr. Bass explained the annual conundrum he faced in balancing the completion of his students' Kentucky portfolios with on-demand test practice. In the annual test, students are given two prompts and time to produce a final draft response to one. In helping his students prepare, there were tradeoffs. For Mr. Bass, finding a happy medium meant helping his students meet the portfolio deadline—which was usually two to three weeks earlier than the annual test—and then using those remaining weeks to practice for on-demand prompts as well as open-response questions.

When Mr. Bass's students practiced these forms of testing, he took them to the team room to simulate the testing conditions. Because his writing classroom was typically filled with talk as students conferenced, they needed to feel the quiet of the conditions. They had to understand the moment when they needed peer and/or teacher response and could only rely on themselves.

Still, simulating test conditions demand organization, especially in middle schools where scheduling might not easily allow for larger chunks of time. As Ms. Underwood explained:

> As far as preparing for the on-demand prompts, I did work on structure, especially for both persuasive and expository essays. We wrote an expository essay on the WASL subject from two years ago [explain a good performance—movie, play, concert—to a friend]. They did it in class, but we used more than one day. I couldn't simulate the actual process, because we don't have seventy-five minutes on a regular day to do it.

Scheduling simulations was sometimes supported by the school district. Ms. Morgan's Kentucky district provided "two Continuous Assessment days. This is a mock test that is treated as the real thing. Everything, including special-education modifications and so on, are made. The papers are randomly assessed by the district office, and our teachers grade the rest using our state scoring guide."

Still, Ms. Morgan more typically provided her students with activities that were less simulations than mini and multiple opportunities to practice their performance:

> As a "sponge" activity we work on a prompt every day. Drop everything and write (including the teacher)! It also includes a share time. This works great for middle school children because . . . they need practice in being forced to write on a topic. It also really helps in the development of portfolio entries, because if they like it, they can use it.

In the fourth grade, test rehearsal occurred throughout the year. Washington's Ms. Wright explained. "I give 'WASL-like' prompts to my students according to the genre of writing we are studying. . . . These assessments fit right into my writing program. We studied narrative writing and had many times to practice the writing process and take pieces to final publication. Then I gave the final 'WASL-like' assessment." Ms. Wright also explored the features of prompts that often use keywords to guide young writers toward specific genres. This was important because in an earlier year of the test "there was a problem with a lot of students writing off-mode."

Teachers also set the tone by encouraging their students to do their best on the assessments and to push themselves to reflect on their work in terms of imagery or questions that a reader might have. Once, Mr. Bass was conferencing with a seventh-grade girl about a portfolio piece—a personal narrative describing a time when she had been ill and her mother helped her:

Mr. Bass	I want to see this. I want to see you lying on the couch. I want to feel how you felt. I want to hear what you said to your mama.
Ginny	[Moaning as if she were still on that couch.] Like, "Give me a Tylenol!"
Mr. Bass	[Nodding enthusiastically] Yes. "Give me a Tylenol." Everything like that. Ginny, you gotta be "apprentice." . . . Come through. Work hard!

Rather than see their state's writing assessments as just one more headache, the six teachers saw opportunities for their children to be challenged in their writing. Still, they knew that if they wanted their students to succeed, they had to provide full-fledged simulations as well as multiple, mini-opportunities for test practice.

They also knew that a positive attitude toward the test was essential, and their talk was replace with phrases like "You can do this!" Just before the annual testing each spring, their "can do" attitude was evident when they combined challenge with celebration. Many of the schools provided pep talks and arranged for special ceremonies. In Ms. Wright's elementary school in Washington, the fourth graders were treated to a feast, and they attended a school assembly where several fifth graders (who had taken the WASL the year before) gave enthusiastic speeches to encourage the fourth graders in their upcoming efforts. Still, pizza and inspiring testimonials are only culminating activities and cannot replace the performance rehearsal that the exemplary teachers integrated into their day-to-day practice. Even more important, these ceremonies could not replace the celebrations that took place daily within the context of their writing workshop classrooms as their students learned to express themselves in writing.

Stretching Out in a Limited Space

In one of our final interviews, we spoke with a Washington seventh grader, Natasha, about her performance on a WASL on-demand prompt. She'd been asked to invent an award and pick a person in her school who deserved to win it. Natasha designed a life-achievement award for a teacher who was a cancer survivor. Although she thought she had done a "good job," she was certain she could have done better if she'd been able to talk with the teacher about her experience and have peers or Ms. Underwood respond to her work. And she resisted the silence:

> Can we go ask someone about something? No, you can't. You have to write this here. You have to write it now. It's kind of . . . claustrophobic. But give me my own space. Let me stretch out. With the WASL, it's just like putting you in this little, tiny box. And they'll say you can't come out until you're finished with this, and you want to stretch out.

Rather than see their state's writing assessments as just one more headache, the six teachers saw opportunities for their children to be challenged in their writing.

Still, Natasha and the many other students we observed and interviewed had learned to create their own space for writing in their classrooms. Their teachers helped them prepare for testing without losing sight of the richness of human composition. The students wrote every day, often on topics of their own choice. They had time to devote to their writing and opportunities for peer and teacher response as well as self-reflection. In addition, their teachers helped them understand the standards, rubrics, and genres involved in their day-to-day writing as well as in assessments. And together they analyzed benchmark pieces and published texts to discern the features of quality work.

Rather than despair over the spring test as the onset of a season of Darkness, the six teachers taught their students to believe in themselves and their writing (Wolf, Borko, Elliot, & McIver, 2000). Indeed, in five years of interviewing fourth- and seventh-grade students, we did not meet a single child who felt s/he was a poor writer. Instead, they told us of their successes, showed us places where they'd reconsidered their writing or gotten help from teachers and peers, and they spoke confidently and intelligently about genre, audience, and purpose. While they viewed the annual on-demand test as an activity that couldn't compare to their classroom writing workshops, they felt more prepared to meet the challenge of claustrophobic spaces. Because their teachers taught both *true* and *to* the test in writing, leaning on sound theoretical teachings, varied resources, and creative pedagogy, these students had learned to stretch out and reach beyond the limits of "on-demand" to the very real requirements of writing and learning in the worst as well as the best of times.

Note

Our Center for Research on Evaluation, Standards, and Student Testing (CRESST) team spent five years studying reform efforts of exemplary schools in Kentucky and Washington. The work reported herein was supported under the Educational Research and Development Centers Program, PR/Award Number R305B60002, as administered by the Office of Educational Research and Improvement, U.S. Department of Education. The findings and opinions expressed in this report do not reflect the positions or policies of the National Institute on Student Achievement, Curriculum, and Assessment, the Office of Educational Research and Improvement, or the U.S. Department of Education.

References

Calkins, L., Montgomery, K., & Santman, D., with Falk, B. (1998). *A teacher's guide to standardized reading tests: Knowledge is power*. Portsmouth, NH: Heinemann.

Dickens, C. (1859/1981). *A tale of two cities*. New York: Bantam Doubleday Dell.

Dyson, A. H. (1997). *Writing superheroes: Contemporary childhood, popular culture, and classroom literacy*. New York: Teachers College Press.

Graves, D. H. (1983). *Writing: Teachers & children at work*. Portsmouth, NH: Heinemann.

Graves, D. H. (1994). *A fresh look at writing*. Portsmouth, NH: Heinemann.

Harwayne, S. (1992). *Lasting impressions: Weaving literature into the writing workshop*. Portsmouth, NH: Heinemann.

Heath, S. B., & McLaughlin, M. W. (1993). *Identity and inner-city youth: Beyond ethnicity and gender*. New York: Teachers College Press.

Hinton, S. E. (1995). *The outsiders*. New York: Puffin Books.

Kentucky Department of Education. (October 1, 2000) *Education News*. [On-line]. Available: *http://www.kde.state.ky.us/*.

Kohn, A. (September 27, 2000). Standardized testing and its victims: Inconvenient facts and inequitable consequences. *Education Week, 60*, 46.

Linn, R. L. (2000). Assessments and accountability. *Educational Researcher, 29*(2). 4–14.

Madgett, N. L. (1994). Woman with flower. In S. Blau, P. Elbow, D. Killgalion, R. Caplan, A. Applebee, & J. Langer (Eds.), *The writers craft (red level)* (p. 167). Evanston, IL: McDougal Littell.

McIver, M. C., & Wolf, S. A. (1999). The power of the conference is the power of suggestion. *Language Arts, 77*(1), 54–61.

Newkirk, T. (September 13, 2000). A mania for rubrics: Will the standards movement make satire (and good writing) obsolete? *Education Week, 20*(2), 41.

Office of Superintendent of Public Instruction, State of Washington. (October 1, 2000) *OSPI home.* [On-line] Available: *http://www.k12.wa.us/*.

Osborne, M. P. (1991). *American tall tales.* (M. McCurdy, Illus.). New York: Scholastic.

Ray, K. W. (1999). *Wondrous words: Writers and writing in the elementary classroom.* Urbana, IL: National Council of Teachers of English.

Resnick, L. B., & Resnick, D. P. (1992). Assessing the thinking curriculum: New tools for educational reform. In B. R. Gifford & M. C. O'Connor (Eds.) *Changing assessments: Alternative views of aptitude, achievement and instruction* (p. 37–75). Boston: Kluwer.

Shepard, L. A. (1991, November). Will national tests improve student learning? *Phi Delta Kappan, 73,* 232–238.

Shepard, L. A. (1997). *Measuring achievement: What does it mean to test for robust understanding?* Princeton, NJ: Policy Information Center/Educational Testing Service.

Wolf, S. A., Borko, H., Elliot, R., & McIver, M. (2000). "That dog won't hunt!": Exemplary school change efforts within the Kentucky reform. *American Educational Research Journal, 37*(2), 349–393.

Wolf, S. A., & Gearhart, M. (1994). Writing what you read: Assessment as a learning event. *Language Arts, 71*(6), 425–444.

Wolf, S. A., & McIver, M. (1999, January). When process becomes policy: The paradox of Kentucky state reform for exemplary teachers of writing. *Phi Delta Kappan, 80*(5), 401–406.

STUDY GUIDE

1. Why has assessment multiplied in recent years? What are the consequences of this increase in tests? (Farr)
2. Who are the audiences for assessment? What do they want from assessment? How can their separate needs be reconciled? (Farr)
3. Distinguish the following three terms and give an example of each: criterion-referenced tests, norm-referenced tests, and performance assessment. (Farr)
4. What type of assessment does sound reading theory demand? Name at least three such assessment instruments. What are the characteristics of these assessment tools? (Farr)
5. The idea of using portfolios to document children's progress has gained popularity in the past two decades. What can be done to make sure that portfolios become effective assessment tools? (Farr)
6. What should the ultimate goals of assessment be? What kinds of assessment can be used to achieve these goals? (Farr)
7. What are the common characteristics of high-stakes tests? Give two examples of such tests in your state. (Guthrie)
8. What is the impact of high-stakes testing on teaching, learning, and our profession as a whole? (Farr; Guthrie; Wolf & Wolf)
9. What are the components of reading test performance? How does each of these components relate to the overall test performance? What implications do they have for reading test preparation? (Guthrie)
10. What constitutes poor practice in high-stakes test preparation? What are the consequences of such practices? (Guthrie; Wolf & Wolf)
11. What can teachers do to remain true to sound theory and practice in teaching reading/writing to children within high-stakes accountability systems? (Wolf & Wolf; Guthrie)
12. It has been suggested that by teaching to high-stakes tests, teachers are implicitly supporting the current educational policy, which in effect reinforces injustice and waters down curricula for power and money. What are your thoughts about this issue? What should children know about the business and politics of testing? (Wolf & Wolf; Guthrie; Farr)

INQUIRY PROJECTS

1. In the current educational climate, the issues of what best measures reading progress, how to measure it, and what uses can be made of assessment data are being debated in the public arena with great intensity. Write an editorial for your local newspaper explaining to the public what the reading assessment puzzle really is and how it can best be solved.
2. Interview a principal, teachers, students, and parents on their views of high-stakes testing and its impact on teaching and learning. Share the findings with your class.
3. In the current high-stakes testing environment, the voices of teachers, students, and parents are often silenced. Identify a child who scored low on a high-stakes state test (e.g., FCAT, Florida Writes). Obtain a portfolio of the child's reading/writing over a two-month period. Have the child, his/her teachers, and parents talk about the child's progress using the collection of items in the portfolio. Compare and contrast their views of the child's strengths, needs, and progress. What can conversation with teachers, parents, and children tell us about children's literacy potential that standardized tests cannot reveal? Discuss why it is important to involve all three stakeholders in the assessment process.
4. Identify 3–5 standards for reading/language arts in your state or from professional organizations such as the International Reading Association or the National Council of Teachers of English. Discuss how these general standards can be localized and made more concrete/specific in a particular unit of study for a particular grade level.
5. The media is creating a public perception that schools are doing a poor job of educating children. Is this perception correct? Check out the Web sites of the National Assessment of Educational Progress (*http://nces.ed.gov/nationsreportcard*) to see for yourself how current U.S. students

fare when compared to past students in the country. Also check out the International Association for the Evaluation of Educational Achievement (*http://www.iea.nl/iea/hq/*) to see where U.S. students rank in comparison to their international peers. Based on the information you gain from this search, and on what you have learned about new literacies from the previous section in this book, write an opinion article to your local newspaper challenging the popular perception.

FURTHER READING

Barrentine, S. (1999). *Reading assessment: Principles and practices for elementary teachers.* Newark, DE: International Reading Association.

Calkins, L., Montgomery, K., & Santman, D., with Falk, B. (1998). *A teacher's guide to standardized reading tests: Knowledge is power.* Portsmouth, NH: Heinemann.

Fraser, J. (2002). *Listening to the children: From focused observation to strategic instruction.* Portsmouth, NH: Heinemann.

Graves, D. (2002). *Testing is not teaching: What should count in education.* Portsmouth, NH: Heinemann.

Hillocks, G. (2002). *The testing trap: How state writing assessments control learning.* New York: Teachers College Press.

Heubert, J., & Hauser, P. (1999). *High stakes: Testing for tracking, promotion, and graduation.* Washington, DC: National Academy Press.

Kohn, A. (2000). *The case against standardized testing: Raising the tests, ruining the schools.* Portsmouth, NH: Heinemann.

Murphy, S. (1998). *Fragile evidence: A critique of reading assessments.* Mahwah, NJ: Erlbaum.

Sacks, P. (2000). *Standardized minds: The high price of America's testing culture and what we can do to change it.* Cambridge, MA: Perseus.

Valencia, S. (1998). *Literacy portfolios in action.* New York: Harcourt.

Supporting the Development of Exemplary Teachers

INTRODUCTION

Schools are commonly considered to be the primary site for the development of literacy. To accomplish this mission, schools must provide high quality daily instruction to their pupils. What are the characteristics of high quality instruction? What do classrooms that implement exemplary instructional practices look like? How can teachers develop, implement, and sustain high quality instruction in an educational context plagued by pendulum swings and federal and state mandates? How can we encourage and support the development of outstanding teachers?

The three articles in this section address these and related questions. They demonstrate that teaching is both an art and a science. They argue that the key to providing high quality instruction does not lie in particular methods or programs, but in developing teachers who are knowledgeable, passionate, flexible, reflective, creative, and responsive to student needs. They emphasize the critical importance of establishing an educational environment that supports the development of teachers as informed, independent decision makers and professional experts.

The first article, by Lesley Morrow, Diane Tracey, Deborah Woo, and Michael Pressley, offers a composite portrait of high quality literacy instruction in first-grade classrooms. Based on their study of six exemplary first-grade teachers in New Jersey, the authors found that effective classrooms

a. create a supportive learning community rich in print materials, challenges, choices, social interactions, and home and school connections,

b. offer many types of reading experiences daily, including shared reading, read alouds, guided reading, partner reading, and independent reading,

c. supply opportunity daily for meaningful language experience, journal writing, writing workshop, and reading-writing connections,

d. provide both planned and spontaneous skills instruction that is explicit and that takes advantage of teachable moments,

e. integrate literacy with content areas such as science and social studies, and

f. are well managed.

They conclude that exemplary teaching involves a great deal of knowledge, experience, and expertise, and that it is thoughtful, reflective, and flexible.

In the second article, Gerald Duffy suggests that effective teachers defy rigid adherence to any particular approach, program, or ideology. Instead, they are independent thinkers who creatively adapt and carefully orchestrate multiple methods and materials to meet student needs. In order to be independent decision makers, however, teachers need, according to Duffy, not only professional knowledge, but a vision—a clear, passionate sense of self, commitment, and mission. "Visioning" will, Duffy argues, give teachers the psychological strength to be entrepreneurial and innovative, ultimately enabling them to independently make informed instructional decisions. Duffy contends that developing a vision is especially important in a complex world of teaching where the need to develop multiple forms of literacy for a diverse student population exists alongside mounting public pressures for pedagogical uniformity. Based on his own experience with pre-service and in-service teacher training, Duffy shows that it is possible, albeit not easy, for teachers to develop the psychological strength to be independent thinkers while maintaining a high level of pedagogical competence. He urges teacher educators to rethink traditional ways of teacher preparation in order to address present challenges.

The last article, by Zhihui Fang, Danling Fu, and Linda Lamme, describes a longitudinal professional development project in rural Florida schools that supports the efforts of in-service teachers to make pedagogical transitions from total reliance on prepackaged commercial programs to autonomously making informed decisions about curriculum and pedagogy. The project, which involves a great deal of collaboration among different educational stakeholders, aims at empowering teachers through developing their pedagogical knowledge and skills and their professional wisdom and judgment. It provides a support structure for teachers that includes, among other things, annual summer institutes, regular classroom visits, monthly meetings, and showcase meetings. The authors demonstrate that in order to initiate and sustain qualitative changes in teaching practices, conscious efforts must be made to address a multitude of barriers at the conceptual, pragmatic, attitudinal, and professional levels. They suggest that what is needed in the current standards-based, high-stakes testing environment is an alternative paradigm to the prevailing models of professional development, one that recognizes the complex, multifaceted, and lifelong nature of becoming and being an effective teacher of reading/literacy.

Characteristics of Exemplary First-Grade Literacy Instruction

Lesley Mandel Morrow
Rutgers, The State University of New Jersey

Diane H. Tracey
Kean University

Deborah Gee Woo
Rutgers, The State University of New Jersey

Michael Pressley
Michigan State University

"What does exemplary first-grade literacy instruction look like?" "Who would be chosen if administrators were asked to identify the most outstanding first-grade educators in their districts?" "When observed, what would these teachers do in their classrooms?" "When interviewed, what would these teachers say about their beliefs and practices regarding first-grade literacy instruction?" These questions and others motivated a large-scale investigation of exemplary first-grade literacy instruction. Observations and interviews related to the topic were conducted in five states across the United States; this article presents a description of the research conducted in New Jersey and an analysis of our research findings.

Theoretical Rationale for a Study of Exemplary First-Grade Literacy Instruction

A vast amount of research regarding early literacy instruction currently exists. Often such studies are designed so that a single component of literacy instruction is evaluated, for example, a specific technique designed to improve reading comprehension or students' vocabulary. This type of research, which can also compare one method of literacy instruction with another, provides valuable documentation regarding components of literacy programs or methods that are most likely to facilitate children's literacy growth. By examining specific variables or methods, researchers make recommendations about which individual elements should ideally be included in high-quality literacy education programs.

In contrast to research that examines individual variables or methods and then makes recommendations about how these elements can be integrated into the classroom, studies of exemplary instruction fall into the research category of investigations about expert performance. These studies attempt to capture as many dimensions as possible of expert performances. Studies of expert performances allow us to examine real-life situations in which many variables are already successfully integrated. In this capacity, observations of experts teach us through modeling. Experts also inform us through their own descriptions of their work. Pressley, Rankin, and Yokoi (1996) state,

> Our assumption, consistent with expert theory (Chi, Glaser, & Farr, 1988; Ericsson & Smith, 1991; Hoffmann, 1992), was that effective primary reading teachers would have a privileged understanding of literacy instruction. That is, they would be aware of the elements of their teaching, in part because their teaching is the result of many decisions about what works in their classrooms and what does not. (p. 365)

Surprisingly, however, although studies of experts are a well-used technique in other professions, a review of the literature by Pressley et al. (1996) reported a gap in the literature on early reading instruction from this perspective. This project helps fill that gap.

This project also had a secondary goal embedded within the overall goal of studying exemplary first-grade instruction. This goal was to provide insight from experts about concerns of constructivist, explicit, and balanced instructional approaches that have been discussed for decades. In this project it was believed that studying exemplary teachers' practices and beliefs regarding constructivist models, explicit instructional approaches, and balanced perspectives would meaningfully enhance the reading community's understanding of these issues.

Selection of Exemplary Teachers

We observed six first-grade exemplary teachers from three different school districts in New Jersey. Supervisors and administrators in these districts were asked to choose exemplary teachers using criteria we set forth for them. We asked that supervisors select teachers who were successful in educating large proportions of their students to be readers and writers. We also asked them to check the achievement records, test performances, reading levels, and writing abilities of the students belonging to the nominated teachers over the last 5 years. Furthermore, we asked supervisors to identify teachers who could articulate a sound teaching philosophy that matched their practices in the classroom. Supervisors and administrators were asked to consider student enthusiasm and engagement regarding reading and writing in these classrooms. Finally, we asked that supervisors have firsthand observations of the nominated teachers and that they select individuals who were frequently referred to with positive comments from other teachers, administrators, and parents. Supervisors were asked to rate their own confidence in their evaluations of the teachers by indicating whether they were absolutely certain, highly confident, confident, somewhat confident, or not confident in their opinion.

Procedures Used to Collect and Analyze the Data

We visited each classroom in the study eight times during its language arts block and twice for a full day during the course of an academic school year. Approximately 25 hours of observation were completed in each classroom. During our visits we recorded information about literacy instruction such as the schedule of the language arts block, word analysis instruction, comprehension development, language development, assessment strategies, social interaction during literacy instruction, affective teaching characteristics, student engagement, classroom management, and the physical environment.

We . . . combined the data from the six teachers and created a model of the exemplary practices observed.

During whole-group instruction the entire lesson was recorded. When a small group was meeting as other students worked at centers, the observer would note the variety of activities occurring and then focus on one of them for as long as seemed necessary to understand it. Overall, we attempted to record any information that seemed relevant to understanding

the literacy instruction in the classroom. In addition to observations, teachers were interviewed concerning their philosophies about teaching literacy and practices they chose to implement.

At the beginning of the study each of the four observers coded his or her own data by classifying it into categories that emerged during the observed instruction. After every observer had been in each classroom three times, we compared categories. Together we developed a set of categories that reflected a consensus of the observers about the characteristics of the classrooms. The categories continued to be refined as observations continued. Teacher interviews at the beginning and end of the study were used as data in the coding. The categories that emerged were types of reading and writing, teaching skills, use of teachable moments, content area connections, literacy-rich environments in classrooms, and classroom management.

Teachers were given responsibility for decisions about instruction.

In writing up the study we chose to create a synthesis of what we had observed in the classrooms rather than reporting on each classroom individually. We therefore combined the data from the six teachers and created a model of the exemplary practices observed. Not all of what we describe occurred in all classrooms; nevertheless, this description is based on what occurred in most classrooms.

An Introduction to the Teachers and Their School Districts

Teachers in this study had 9 to 25 years of experience, and all had master's degrees. The districts involved included children from middle to lower middle income families. The school populations were diverse with about 50% of the children being Caucasian, 20% African American, 10% Hispanic, 10% Asian, and 10% from various other backgrounds. The public school districts we chose provided extensive staff development for their teachers, and the principals assumed a major role with instructional issues in the school. Principals tended to visit the classrooms regularly and were respected by the teachers. Teachers were given responsibility for decisions about instruction. In general, a collaborative climate existed among administrators, teachers, and parents in the buildings, thus creating positive and productive atmospheres in the schools.

Interview Data from Teachers

Interviews with the selected teachers about their philosophies and practices used in literacy instruction revealed that they all advocated extended periods of time to develop the language arts. They talked about designing programs around literacy themes, such as the study of poetry, authors, or elements of story structure. They also advocated the integration of a content area unit into their curriculum that also included reading, writing, and math. They believed that skills should be taught within a context and reinforced when opportunities arose. They felt strongly that meeting individual needs required instructing children in small groups based on specific needs. These groups changed often, because student progress was evaluated frequently. They discussed the use of holistic strategies in their teaching, strong programs for skill development, and careful designs for delivering instruction. Teachers recognized the importance of a supportive attitude toward students and a positive atmosphere in their rooms to motivate children to learn. Many also commented on the importance of the home-school connection in supporting children's literacy development. When we observed the teachers we found the ideas they expressed were truly put into practice.

Physical Environment in the Classrooms

The classrooms we observed had literacy-rich environments. Children's desks were grouped to encourage social interaction. The perimeter of the rooms housed learning centers, including several devoted to literacy. The rooms had colorful rugs for group meetings, listening to stories, and minilessons. All rooms had an abundance of materials on the walls including calendars, weather charts, helper charts, rules for the class, other charts with functional information, and many displays of children's work. There was always a special chair where the teacher read to the children and where the children had the opportunity to tell experiences and read stories they had written. This area also had an experience chart easel.

There were tables for guided reading lessons, most often shaped like a half moon. The teacher sat on the inside of the table facing the rest of the class, and the children sat around the other side. In this area the teacher had a pocket chart for sentence strips, individual erasable boards for word analysis work, ability-level reading materials, record-keeping folders, and a stand for writing charts. Children often stored their individual reading materials in resealable plastic bags. These were placed in students' personal corrugated cardboard boxes.

Each of the centers, art, math, social studies, science, and literacy, had materials about the content area and special materials for activities linked to current topics. Reading and writing materials were present at all centers. There were open-faced bookshelves featuring special books about current themes, and books in baskets representing different levels and genres. Bulletin boards where children's work was featured were also present. There were also forms for signing into centers and systems for checking out books to take home. Themes and skills being studied were quite evident through the artwork, written work, artifacts, charts, and posters displayed. Poetry charts were hung in the room and matched either the themes under study or the word analysis skill being taught. All materials were visually and physically accessible for the children.

Types of Reading Experiences

Many types of reading experiences were carried out daily. During the morning meeting children sat on the rug and listened to a shared read-aloud experience for the whole class. The stories read were consistently high-quality children's literature that was tied to the theme being studied by the class. The teacher read sitting in a comfortable chair, facing the children who sat on a rug in front of her. The teacher had a purpose for the reading that was reinforced with discussion before, during, and after the story.

A second type of reading observed in these classrooms was partner reading. Children participated in partner reading independent of the teacher. Sometimes the teachers assigned partners; other times the students were able to select partners themselves. Children then chose stories from a basket that had books related to the authors or themes about which they were learning. The partners took turns reading aloud to each other. They helped each other if needed.

Many types of reading experiences were carried out daily.

Guided reading groups was a third form of reading in the classroom. These groups met daily and were composed of children having similar reading needs. Teachers typically had four to six reading groups in each classroom. Children brought their individual resealable bags containing all of their needed materials to their reading lesson. During the reading groups explicit instruction occurred. Children read a familiar book they had previously read, and then a new book was introduced. The books came most often from a set of ability-level materials. The teachers helped the children read through the books and took notes about their reading performance: "reads slowly, reads word by word, self-corrected errors, used multiple strategies to figure out words," etc. The book was then taken home in the bag with a reading assignment accompanied by a place for a parent's signature. Teachers evaluated students monthly to change their group placements as needed.

Independent reading was supported by elaborate literacy centers in these classrooms. The literacy centers had large collections of children's literature sorted into baskets that were labeled by topics, genre, and levels of reading. This organizational system provided easy access for individual and collaborative reading in school. Colorful rugs, pillows, and stuffed animals attracted students to the area. Simple procedures for borrowing books facilitated reading at home. Storytelling materials accompanied some selections of literature for the students' use and enjoyment. Audiotaped stories, tape recorders, and headsets were also available for the children.

Types of Writing Experiences

Children wrote daily and in many different forms. In interviews, the teachers noted how important and closely connected writing was to the development of reading (e.g., "I can often tell children's reading level when I review their writing. Writing helps them with decoding skills and subsequently with reading").

Children had journals and wrote daily, personal entries. Sometimes they used their journals for spelling words and recording special words. Teachers had writing workshops where children selected and wrote about topics that interested them such as a movie they had seen or a person they admired. Before these writings, teachers carried out mini-lessons about the mechanics of writing, such as punctuation or creating well-formed stories. The lessons were based on the needs of students. Children wrote their stories and had a conference with either another child or the teacher about revisions. When the story was finished it was read to other students for feedback. Children were guided on how to offer constructive criticism, such as, "I like the first part of your story, but you need to explain the second part more clearly." When stories were completed, they were bound and placed in the classroom library for others to read. In addition to journal writing, children participated in story writing, content area writing, and writing with a partner. They also observed their teacher's writing. The following is representative of the amount and kinds of writing activities that happened daily.

The teacher wrote the morning message that was dictated by the children. Her writing provided a fine model of manuscript. Then a story read by the teacher was related to a written assignment for the children to complete at center time with a partner. The partners were encouraged to talk about what they would write. For example, after reading *Swimmy* (Lionni, 1973) during a unit about cooperation, the children were asked to write about when a friend helped them. The teacher checked to see that everyone had an idea as a result of a group discussion. The children talked about what they would write with a partner and then did a first draft of their story. After writing, they read their drafts to their partners, who gave suggestions for revisions. The children did their revisions and then read the pieces to each other for final editing.

Writing was integrated into content areas as well. Records of science experiments were kept in science journals. Math projects often required writing, such as when the students were studying geometric shapes and had to find and list the shapes within objects in their classroom. When studying circles, for instance, Kelly wrote "cookie, clock, and paper plate." Writing was also connected to social studies through a variety of assignments and activities.

Finally, writing was incorporated into guided reading groups. Often students had to write in response to the books that they had read or the activities that had been completed that day.

How Skills Were Taught

Both planned and spontaneous skill development happened during the school day. Early in the day children's language skills were strengthened when they talked about things brought from home. They had to speak clearly in a voice that could be heard, use complete sentences, and pronounce words to the best of their ability. This was a planned activity in which the teacher spontaneously responded to the students.

Both planned and spontaneous skill development happened during the school day.

In a similar mix of planned and spontaneous instruction, teachers printed initial consonants and word chunks for the children to find at the bottom of each morning message. These consonants and word chunks were the skills being emphasized at the time. There were also mini-lessons that featured elements in phonics such as learning about digraphs or vowel sounds. The teachers connected the mini-lesson to the content of a story read. In one observation the class was learning about animals, and the teacher read *Petunia* (Duvoisin, 1950) to promote a discussion about farm animals. She introduced other books about animals, such as *Pet Show* (Keats, 1972), *Pig in the Pond* (Brown, 1973), and *The Tale of Peter Rabbit* (Potter, 1904). She read the titles to the children, and they discussed the animals in the books. She asked the children to study the letters in the titles of the books and asked if they found anything interesting. Several hands went up. Chris noticed that the letter *p* was in all of them. They proceeded to make a list of words that were animals beginning with *p*. They listed *polar bear, panda bears, pigs*, and *ponies*. When they couldn't think of any more the teacher asked for any words that included a *p* and wrote those down.

Much explicit, planned skill development took place during guided reading lessons. The format for the lessons included reviewing words from a story already read, writing in a journal, reading a familiar story already practiced, and building a comprehension strategy into the discussion of the story. After the story was read, children arranged cut up words from the story into sentences and used story sentence strips to sequence and read. They mixed up their words and sentence strips and had to reorganize them to make sense. A word analysis skill taken from the context of the book read was also taught. Each child had his or her own erasable board to work on with words. They worked with sound-symbol relationships and phonemic awareness.

A new book and its new vocabulary were introduced. The book was discussed to build background knowledge, and children took turns reading. Teachers took notes as the children read to document their strengths and needs. Each child wrote new words in his or her journal and a new journal entry. Teachers discussed homework that included reading the familiar book to a family member, practicing word cards associated with the book, and reading the new book. At the end of the reading lesson, teachers wrote notes to each family about the child's progress and explained the homework. Children followed along as the note was written. Parents were asked to sign the homework card and add their own notes.

Planned skill development was also fostered through the study of a "focus child" during guided reading group time. Each day in the guided reading lesson teachers focused attention on one particular child. In this way the teacher was able to assess that particular child's strengths and weaknesses. While all children in the group were observed during the activities, the focus child did more tasks than others and was more closely evaluated by the teacher. Thus, all the children had the advantage of a small-group setting, but once a week each child was the target child and received individualized instruction and evaluation. Teachers often used running records to monitor the focus child's performance.

The teachers had systematic methods for teaching comprehension skills. Comprehension development was embedded in both the reading of storybooks and in guided reading lessons. Many strategies were introduced to students, from engaging them in story retelling, to repeated readings of stories, revisiting the text, making predictions, drawing conclusions, and demonstrating knowledge of structural elements of stories. Students studied styles of authors and illustrators and responded to literature in discussions and writing.

The teachers we observed also had very strong word analysis programs. They introduced vowels, consonants, and word patterns. Whenever we observed, work in some area of word analysis occurred. Phonic skills were taught within mini-lessons and reinforced in independent work and in guided reading lessons. Poems were used to emphasize word patterns, and lists of words demonstrating letter patterns learned were printed on charts. Teachers also had Word Walls on which were listed already taught word families, onsets, and rimes.

We were impressed with the knowledge these teachers had about the teaching of reading skills. In their interviews they supported the idea of a strong emphasis upon skills but stated that the manner in which they were taught was also important. They said they taught skills in contextual settings through the use of children's literature and themes in opportunistic situations and rarely used commercially prepared worksheets. Teachers often created their own sheets for skill development that supported their approach to instruction. They also had manipulative games for skill development.

Taking Advantage of Teachable Moments

In addition to planning their instruction, teachers seized opportunities for teachable moments. For example, on the day the children had talked about the *sh* word chunk, Alida brought in her soccer team shirt because the class was talking about sports in their unit about Healthy Bodies and the importance of exercise. The teacher drew the children's attention to the chart where they had written words that had the *sh* sound to see if the word *shirt* had been included. It wasn't on the chart so they added it. In another example, when reading a story, a word might come up that the teacher sensed was unknown to the group. She or he would begin a discussion about the word, write it on the board, and encourage the children to use it in their writing. In the course of conversation, one would hear these teachers say, "Remember when we were learning about the chunk *ap*? Well, the word *trap* that we just talked about uses that chunk." The teachers used teachable moments whenever possible.

Content Area Connections with Literacy

The teaching we observed included extremely strong cross-curricular connections. The classes were consistently engaged in thematic studies including author, science, social studies, holidays, and special events. The stories that were read in the classrooms were almost exclusively theme related. Books for partner reading and guided reading materials were often related. Topics for writing were connected, and center activities were thematic as well.

One of the first grades, for example, was studying nutrition. The teacher read the story *The Very Hungry Caterpillar* (Carle, 1969), and the children discussed the food the caterpillar ate and why he got sick. The snack for the day was composed of foods the caterpillar had eaten, such as apples, oranges, plums, and pears. The teacher selected a poetry book, *What's on the Menu* (Goldstein, 1992), that was about food and also included a great deal of rhyme. The book was selected to match the nutrition theme and the literary theme of rhyming words. The math center had different fruits in a basket, and the students' task was to ask members of the class which type of fruit each preferred for a snack. The students tallied and graphed the preferences. In the art center students created a collage of pictures of healthy foods from food magazines. A selection of children's literature was available to reinforce the focus on rhyming words, and several were about food. For the guided reading lesson there were predictable books and poems to read about food.

The teaching we observed included extremely strong cross-curricular connections.

The extremely strong presence of themes taught through cross-curricular connections was one of the most extraordinary characteristics of outstanding first-grade literacy instruction. Educators know how difficult it is to pull so many connecting materials and ideas together, but these teachers did it daily, all the time. We were so impressed we asked them about it. They responded: "It was something I learned in college and I believe that it makes learning more interesting and meaningful." "I've worked on this over the years of my teaching. It isn't easy, but I believe it's very important to make skill development purposeful." "Each year I add to my repertoire of stories, songs, poems, art activities, math, science, and social studies for units of study, holidays and other special days. Now it isn't difficult to integrate my curriculum. I have the materials and ideas, but keep adding to them all the time."

Classroom Management

Effective classroom management begins with the physical design of the classroom. These classrooms were rich with accessible materials. Early in the school year, the children were introduced to the design of the classroom and how the different areas were used.

From the first day of school the teachers worked on helping the children become self-directed learners who could think for themselves. The first few weeks of school were used to master the routines that included whole-class lessons, partner reading, guided reading groups, and the use of learning centers. Children learned how to sit on the rug during lessons and how to take turns. Rules were discussed and developed by the class so the children felt a sense of responsibility to carry them out. Children learned how to function with and without the teacher. Teachers were consistent with routines and enforcing rules.

The effective management of learning centers was integral to the success of these classrooms. Initially students had to master the basic system for using the centers, such as how many children could be at a center at any one time, and how many center activities needed to be completed in a single day. Some teachers let the students freely choose which centers they would work at as long as a seat was available; other teachers used a chart to manage group rotation. In all the classrooms, however, children had to account for their work at the centers. In one room, for example, students signed a form after completing activities. In most of the classrooms, children were able to choose free play, computer time, or reading at the literacy center after they had completed their required center activities. Helping students learn how to become independent learners during center time at the beginning of the school year allowed these teachers to devote their attention to small guided reading groups that occurred simultaneously with center time.

Teachers were extremely aware of what was happening in their rooms. They were virtually always in a position where they could see everyone in the room. If involved in reading groups, teachers were in a corner of the room where they could observe all the children working. Similarly, the teachers seemed extremely attuned to intervening *before* a problem escalated in the classroom. Like good parents, these teachers seemed to possess a sixth sense for when things became too noisy, or even too quiet, in an area of the classroom. This high level of *with-it-ness* was a prominent element of the exemplary teachers' classroom management style.

These teachers realized that good planning of interesting activities acted as a preventative measure for misbehavior. The days in their classrooms were highly planned and included a wide variety of activities that took place in whole-group, small-group, paired, and individual settings. Teachers were also thoughtful about the sequencing of their planned activities, ensuring that their young students had opportunities to move around and talk between quieter, more serious, academic activities. All of this careful planning was designed to increase the likelihood that the students would stay engaged and on task during class, ensuring the likelihood of success and a positive classroom climate. One teacher said, "If children are actively involved in interesting experiences that are challenging but can bring success, they are likely to remain engaged in their work."

Students rarely needed discipline because the rules, routine, and a respectful atmosphere created by teachers provided an environment where productive work was accomplished. If problems did occur, however, teachers almost always spoke softly and respectfully about the problem. If possible, the teachers seemed to prefer to talk to the child contributing to the problem in a private conversation. When a child was off task the teacher helped the child redirect his or her energies by setting up contingency rules for continued misbehavior.

Finally, these teachers interacted with their students in a very positive manner. They often gave positive reinforcement and constructive comments when necessary. The positive reinforcement was given for real accomplishment, and constructive comments were given with genuine concern for each child's self-esteem. The teachers had a large vocabulary filled with encouraging and reinforcing phrases, such as "Good job!" "Wow, you really do understand that," "I bet you'll get that right if you try," "Let me give you some clues about that," "I love the way you are doing your work today," and "I think you'll really like this new job I have planned for you." One of the teachers noted, "I treat the children as if they are adults. I never talk down to them. I address them with respect, since I think they appreciate this. In return, I have found that they treat me and each other in the same way."

A Day in These Classrooms

From our observations we have combined elements from all classrooms to create what we believe to be an exemplary first-grade language arts/literacy learning block.

When children enter the room in the morning they take out their journals and begin writing about something of interest to them. After all the children are settled and the school's opening exercises are completed, the students come to the rug for a morning meeting. The day begins by discussing the calendar and weather. The students then count how many days have passed in November and how many days are left. Then, using chart paper, the teacher begins the morning message, which has some news about a guest who will help them with an exercise program, because they are studying about Healthy Bodies and Healthy Minds. Children dictate sentences about healthy food they ate over the weekend and healthy activities they performed. After the message is written and read the teacher asks the class to look for print within the message related to word analysis elements being studied. They notice that the word *healthy* uses the *th* chunk.

Following the morning message several children have the opportunity to share things brought from home that relate to the current theme. Kim has her mom's grocery list, and she reads the healthy foods on it. Keisha has a cookbook and reads a healthy recipe.

After the children's oral sharing the teacher reads a piece of theme-related children's literature. The story, *Grandma's Helper* (Meyer, 1993), is about a Hispanic child and her grandmother who spoke only Spanish. Because the granddaughter could speak English her grandmother would bring her along food shopping. Prior to reading the story the teacher begins a discussion about foods needed to keep our bodies healthy. Then the discussion turns to helping others as a way to make us feel good about ourselves. One child talks about helping her grandma walk because she has to use a cane.

Immediately before reading, the teacher sets a purpose for the children's listening. She asks them to listen to find out in what ways the little girl helped her grandmother. After the story is read, the class talks about how the little girl had helped her grandma. The teacher asks the children how they have helped others. She asks students to write about a time when they helped someone during center activities. As a model for what the children will be doing later, the teacher writes on the chart paper how she had helped her mother prepare Thanksgiving dinner.

At the end of the morning meeting the teacher reviews, and in some cases models, the center activities that the children will be expected to complete later that day. In the math center the task is to "Find a partner, have your partner use a timer, and count how many jumping jacks you can do in one minute. Write it down on the paper provided and do the same for your partner." In the science center there is a figure of a child on a felt board and figures with felt backings of a brain, heart, lungs, and stomach. The children are to place the body organs in the correct part of the body. There is also a sheet with a figure and body parts on which each child is to draw the organs in the correct position. In the art center there are magazines and scissors for children to create healthy food collages. In the language center children are to write all the foods they can think of from A to Z. Working with a partner and using one sheet of paper per letter, children write the food name and draw it as well.

Immediately before the self-directed activities begin the children chant a poem that is on a chart. The teacher asks the children to look for the consonant *t* and the *th* chunk in the words of a chant she wrote.

> We ate toast on Monday
> We ate tomato soup on Tuesday
> We ate tacos on Wednesday
> We ate turnips on Thursday
> We got thirsty on Friday so
> We had ice tea and
> We ate turkey with trimmings on Saturday. Yum Yum!

The self-directed activities begin with students choosing a book to read about nutrition with a partner. The books include *Grandma's Helper* (Meyer, 1993), *Potatoes on Tuesday* (Lillegard, 1993), *Potluck* (Corbitt, 1962), *Cookies* (Pappas, 1980), *This Is the Plate* (Trussell-Cullen, 1995), and *Engelbert's Exercise* (Paxton, 1993). Partners read together, and when finished they start on their writing activity about someone whom they have helped. They continue their partnerships in this writing assignment, from a prewriting discussion to a conference after the first draft. Following these tasks the children complete their center activities.

While the children engage in these self-directed activities, the teacher meets with small groups for guided reading lessons. The day is so well managed and coordinated that when it is snack time, Jonathan, who is in charge, puts on a tape of classical music that signals everyone to set aside what they are doing, take out their healthy snacks, and eat and socialize. After 10 minutes, Jonathan turns the tape off, and the class returns to their independent activities and guided reading groups.

In the reading groups, familiar books are read, some relating to the Healthy Bodies and Healthy Minds theme. The students work with sequencing sentence strips, identifying words from the cut up sentence strips and putting them in order. The story is read and discussed. The initial consonant *t* and the *th* chunk are reviewed. A new book is introduced with background information on the story as well as some phonics skills. The teacher keeps records on the children's performance and sends homework notes home in their bag of materials. Lunch follows these morning activities.

Writing Workshop is in the afternoon. Children work on books about good nutrition, and the teacher leads a minilesson about capital letters at the beginning of sentences and periods at the end. Those who are at the final editing stages with their stories have conferences with the teacher.

In the afternoon there is also a special class activity. It starts with a written recipe for making fruit salad. With the teacher's guidance the students discuss the types and amounts of fruit they need. One student's mother comes in to help make the fruit salad that they eat before going home. The day concludes with a final class meeting. Here the highlights of the day are briefly reviewed, the children are reminded to complete their homework, and the teacher tells them what they can look forward to tomorrow.

Summary

Our goal was to describe characteristics of six teachers identified as exemplary and combine their practices into one story. This observational approach allowed us to answer the question "What is the nature of exemplary early literacy instruction?"

The classrooms we observed were happy, productive places for first-grade children. Teachers built a community for learning that included cooperation, respect, and strong expectations for work and achievement. These characteristics are found in the research on effective teaching. The classrooms were rich with materials for children to have choices, challenges, social interaction, and success. The children completed pencil and paper activities, were exposed to literature, and worked with commercially prepared reading instructional materials. The classrooms had provisions for whole-group, small-group, paired, and one-to-one instruction. The teachers provided varied experiences that were developmentally appropriate and also included an emphasis on skill development. Teaching was explicit, direct, and systematic. It also included experiences designed to foster the construction of meaning, problem solving, and taking advantage of spontaneous teachable moments.

Teachers were consistent in their management techniques, so children knew what was expected of them and consequently carried out work that needed to be done. The day flowed smoothly from one activity to the next, and routines were regular. The activities were varied to keep the children engaged. Furthermore, the affective quality in the rooms was exemplary; teachers were warm and caring. They were concerned about how children were treated. In such an atmosphere, children learned to respect the teacher and one another.

The children in these classrooms experienced literacy in a variety of forms. Shared reading and writing activities, independent reading and writing, social collaborative reading and writing, and guided reading and writing for skill development took place throughout the day. Children took part in oral and silent reading, writing, and mini-lessons modeled by teachers. Content area themes were integrated into the reading and writing experiences to bring meaning to skill development. Children had opportunities to perform or share reading and writing accomplishments. Figure 1 presents the characteristics observed in exemplary first-grade literacy instruction.

The teachers based their classrooms on their philosophies of how children learn. They were consciously aware of their philosophies and could articulate them. Moreover, the teachers worked in schools that supported and expected outstanding performance from them. The atmosphere in their buildings was professional with frequent staff development sessions. Teachers met regularly by grade levels to share and plan, and the principals played an important role in supporting curriculum development.

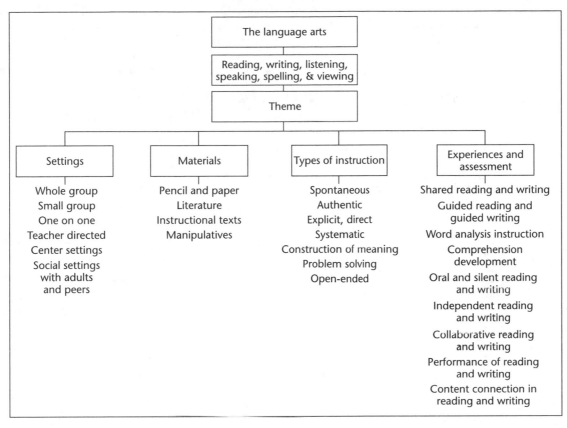

Figure 1 Strategies for first-grade reading instruction.

These teachers took the initiative to expand their knowledge by obtaining graduate degrees in education, attending professional conferences, and reading professional materials.

This study confirms some of what we already know about early literacy instruction and also adds new insights. The descriptions of the teachers in their classrooms and the responses to the questionnaires suggest that teachers use what has been referred to as a balanced perspective for literacy instruction. Children were exposed both to the direct, explicit instruction for skill development associated with traditional literacy instruction and to the experiences that encourage social collaboration and constructive problem solving associated with an integrated language arts approach. The instruction in early literacy that we observed involved explicit skill development taught in the context of authentic literature and integrated with writing and content area connections. All of the language arts instruction was embedded in classrooms with outstanding classroom management systems and positive affective climates. These exemplary teachers used both transmission and constructivist models of learning. Their explicit teaching of skills provided a strong foundation for constructivist activities, and the constructivist activities subsequently permitted the consolidation and elaboration of skills.

Exemplary teaching involves a great deal of knowledge, experience, and expertise.

Exemplary teaching involves a great deal of knowledge, experience, and expertise. The classrooms that we observed occurred as a result of careful thought, planning, and a conscious knowledge of a philosophy of education. These teachers exemplify the best that first-grade literacy instruction can offer. We believe a great deal can be learned from studying their practices, beliefs, enthusiasm, dedication, and very hard work.

Authors' Note

This study was supported by a research grant from the Center on English Learning and Achievement (CELA) at the State University of New York at Albany, USA. Dedicated to improving the teaching and learning of English and the language arts, CELA provides information about how to best develop the literacy skills that will heighten student achievement in the content areas, as well as how achievement in the content areas can strengthen literacy skills. CELA is operated by the State University of New York at Albany in collaboration with the University of Wisconsin—Madison. Additional partners include the Universities of Oklahoma and Washington. The Center is supported by the U.S. Department of Education's Office of

Educational Research and Improvement (Award # R305A 60005). However, the views expressed herein are those of the authors and do not necessarily represent the views of the department.

Children's Books Cited

Brown, R. (1973). *Pig in the pond*. New York: D. McKay.

Carle, E. (1969). *The very hungry caterpillar*. New York: Philomel.

Corbitt, H. (1962). *Potluck*. Boston: Houghton Mifflin.

Duvoisin, R. (1950). *Petunia*. New York: Knopf.

Goldstein, B.S. (1992). *What's on the menu*. New York: Viking.

Keats, E. (1972). *Pet show*. New York: Aladdin.

Lillegard, D. (1993). *Potatoes on Tuesday*. Glenview, lL: Scott, Foresman.

Lionni, L. (1973). *Swimmy*. New York: Random House.

Meyer, L. (1993). *Grandma's helper*. Glenview, IL: Scott, Foresman.

Pappas, L. (1980). *Cookies*. Concord, CA: Nitty Gritty Productions.

Paxton, T. (1993). *Engelbert's exercise*. Glenview, IL: Scott, Foresman.

Potter, B. (1904). *The tale of Peter Rabbit*. New York: Frederick Warner.

Trussell-Cullen, A. (1995). *This is the plate*. Glenview, IL: Goodyear Books.

References

Chi, M.T.H., Glaser, R., & Farr, M.J. (Eds.). (1988). *The nature of expertise*. Hillside, NJ: Erlbaum.

Ericsson, K.A., & Smith, J. (Eds.). (1991). *Toward a general theory of expertise*. Cambridge, England: Cambridge University Press.

Hoffmann, R.R. (1992). *The psychology of expertise: Cognitive research and empirical AI* New York: Springer-Verlag.

Pressley, M., Rankin, J., & Yokoi, L. (1996). A survey of the instructional practices of outstanding primary-level literacy teachers. *Elementary School Journal*, 96, 363–384.

Visioning and the Development of Outstanding Teachers

Gerald G. Duffy
University of North Carolina at Greensboro

In contrast to the reports of educational critics, graduates of America's teacher education institutions maintain an enviable level of success (see, for instance, Anders, Hoffman & Duffy, 1999; Berliner & Biddle, 1996; Bracey, 1997). This is explained, at least in part, by increased pedagogical competence among new teachers. In contrast to former generations of teachers, today's literacy teachers know more about effective teaching behaviors (Brophy & Good, 1986), comprehension instruction (Pearson 1985), strategy instruction (Duffy, Roehler & Sivan, et.al., 1987), assessment (Valencia. 1998), effective classroom practices (Cunningham & Allington, 1999) and exemplary teachers (Pressley et.al., 1998), to name just a few.

Pedagogical knowledge and skill are, of course, crucial. I have recently concluded, however, that pedagogical competence alone is not enough. The complex nature of teaching requires that teachers also be able to independently orchestrate together multiple methods and materials rather than adhering to a single approach or following a particular program (e.g. Duffy & Hoffman, 1999). However, as illustrated by the decades-long paradigm war between whole language and phonics and by the number of restrictive reading programs mandated in our schools, the tendency in reading is to promote a particular ideology, method or set of materials.

The challenges of coming decades demand teachers who are pedagogically competent while also being psychologically strong enough to use professional knowledge in creatively resourceful ways.

Promoting a particular way of teaching is dangerous. It leads teachers to believe that there is only one right way to teach literacy, and that good teaching demands compliance with the tenets of a particular ideology or method or program. They do not learn to do what we know the best teachers do—combine and adapt many methods and materials to fit the situation in which they find themselves. Consequently, this paper argues that the challenges of coming decades demand teachers who are pedagogically competent while also being psychologically strong enough to use professional knowledge in creatively resourceful ways. The question I pose is, "Do we in teacher education develop such strength?"

The Distinguishing Characteristic of Outstanding Literacy Teachers

A school superintendent recently told me, "There's something about literacy teaching that really puzzles me." He then proceeded to describe his observations of two primary grade teachers, one of whom he said was "whole languag-ey" and another who was "very much a direct instruction type." What puzzled him, he said, was that:

> "Method didn't seem to make a difference. I was in both classrooms for three hours, and both sets of kids were getting wonderful instruction. There was lots of whole language stuff in both rooms and those who needed skill help were getting lots of direct instruction in both rooms. And the whole thing was seamless. It was like these teachers were making magic."

His comments struck a responsive chord. I, too, have often marveled at the eclectic characteristics of extraordinary teachers. Their success is not attributable to one method or one theoretical orientation. As Pressley and his colleagues note in recent studies of exemplary teachers (Morrow, Tracey, Woo & Pressley, 1999; Pressley, Rankin & Yokoi, 1996; Wharton-McDonald, Pressley & Hampston, 1998), the best teachers use both transmission and constructivist models simultaneously, going beyond conventional expectations to orchestrate "fluid transitions between the two processes throughout the course of a single lesson" (Wharton-McDonald, Pressley & Hampston, 1998, pp. 122–123). Similarly, and with a note of awe, they point out that the best teachers find multiple ways to integrate content, saying, "Educators know how difficult it is to pull so many connecting materials and ideas together, but these teachers did it daily, all the time" (Morrow, Tracey, Woo & Pressley, 1999, pp. 469).

From "Visioning and the Development of Outstanding Teachers," by G.G. Duffy, 2002, *Reading Research and Instruction*, 41(4), 331–344. Copyright 2002 by the college Reading Association. Reprinted with permission.

Similarly, my colleagues and I were awed by the way the best teachers in a study of teacher explanations modified interventions we provided (Duffy, Roehler & Rackliffe, 1986), spontaneously elaborated in response to students (Duffy & Roehler, 1987), established a common thread of meaning and maintained cohesive networks of relationships across multiple activities (Roehler, Duffy & Warren, 1988), and adapted suggestions from inservice sessions (Duffy, 1994). In short, outstanding teachers possess something more than pedagogical competence.

What they possess, Feldman (1997) suggests, is an ability to "add to a wide set of knowledge" (p. 758). That is, outstanding teachers are distinguished by an ability to take the pedagogical basics learned in teacher education classes and invent instructional modifications appropriate for the situations in which they find themselves.

Outstanding teachers are distinguished by an ability to take the pedagogical basics learned in teacher education classes and invent instructional modifications appropriate for the situations in which they find themselves.

We don't see such instructional creativity as often as we'd like. More typically, researchers report that teachers use "one-size-fits-all recipes" rather than appropriately adjusted instruction (Pajares & Graham, 1998, p. 855), or that new teachers abandon what they learn in teacher education in favor of traditional school practices (Korthagen & Kessel, 1999; Zeichner & Gore. 1990).

We usually explain these disappointing findings by pointing to the complexity of teaching. Because teachers encounter ill-defined and deeply entangled problems (Nespor, 1987), good teaching is not a simple matter of applying theoretical principles (Carter, 1990; Johnston, 1992; Smyth, 1989). As Greene (1991) says:

> . . . when we have our initial experiences with teaching in public schools, . . . we become sharply aware of limits, of structures and arrangements that cannot easily be surpassed. No matter how practical, how grounded our educational courses were, they suddenly appear to be totally irrelevant in the concrete situation where we find ourselves. This is because general principles never fully apply to new and special situations. . . . (p. 7)

All this complexity sometimes causes teacher educators to argue for minimal competency. For instance, Fenstermacher (1993) and Korthagen and Kessel (1999) have recently proposed delaying thoughtful aspects of teaching until after technical and procedural skills have been mastered. But doing so ignores the fact that some teachers do learn to be outstanding. All teachers are not discouraged by the complexity of

the work and all teachers do not conform and comply. To the contrary, some teachers ". . . construct perspectives, choose actions, manage dilemmas, interpret and create curricula, make strategic choices, and to a large extent define their own teaching responsibilities" (Cochran-Smith & Lytle. 1993, p. 100).

Developing teachers who can do this demands an emphasis on independent thinking. Independent thinking, in turn, requires that we free teachers to depend on themselves rather than on us.

Visioning as a Key to Outstanding Teaching

The best teachers are not followers. They evaluate directives from methods course instructors, inservice speakers, teachers guides and other authoritative sources; override such directives when, in their judgment, something else will work better; and revise and invent yet again on the basis of instructional results. In short, they adjust, modify, adapt and invent; they do not emulate.

They can do this because they possess an independent spirit. Educational thinkers describe it in various ways. Greene (1991) calls it "personal reality," by which she means a "particular standpoint, a particular location in space and time" (p. 4); Feiman-Nemser (1990) calls it "personal orientation;" Van Manen (1977) describes it as orientation composed of what a teacher "believes to be true, to be valuable and to be real" (p. 211): Garrison (1997) calls it "practical reasoning:" Rosaen and Schram (1998) call it "the autonomous self" (p. 286): and Schaetti, Watanabe and Ramsey (1999), working in the area of intercultural communication, call it "personal leadership."

I call it *visioning*—a teacher's conscious sense of self, of one's work, and of one's mission. By "vision" I mean a personal stance on teaching that rises from deep within the inner teacher and fuels independent thinking. Hammerness (2001) describes it as "a reach"—a set of images of ideal classroom practice to which teachers strive (p. 143). When teachers have a vision, they assume control over instructional decision-making in order to achieve the mission.

When teachers have a vision, they assume control over instructional decision-making in order to achieve the mission.

Visioning is existential in that it focuses on choice, and on a career-long sense of *becoming*, and it is self-regulatory in that teachers alter their environments and their actions. But, most importantly, visioning is a matter of the heart and the spirit, of personal morality and passion. As Hargreaves (1998) points out, teaching is a moral endeavor; to be fulfilled, each teacher must attain the moral purpose that, consciously or unconsciously, drew him or her to teaching in the first place. Garrison (1997) describes it as "eros"—the passionate desire to attain or do good. Outstanding teachers are not only competent—they are passionate about what they mean by "doing good" as teachers.

Passion is not lacking in teacher education. Many literacy educators passionately promote their favored ideologies or methods or programs. But passion for a particular kind of pedagogy leads teachers to think there is a *silver bullet* and that they must use it. In contrast, the goal of visioning is independent thinking. The intent is to develop teachers who claim the right to make their own decisions consistent with their personal, moral commitment to kids and teaching. A teacher's passion for a personal mission governs decision-making, not a teacher educator's passion for a particular theory, method, or program.

To the extent that literacy educators emphasize their own pedagogical preferences, and do not teach our teachers to claim the right to their own visions, we run the risk of developing followers—teachers who lack the psychological strength to adapt and modify instruction in pursuit of complex forms of literacy. We run that risk when teacher education is based in a technical-rational model, or in a particular ideology or program, or in the charisma of a particular mentor, or in a reverence for research.

In emphasizing a technical-rational model, for instance, ". . . 'best choice' is defined in accordance with the principles of technological progress—economy, efficiency and effectiveness" (Van Manen, 1977, p. 226). Teacher choice is not an option: actions contrary to the technical model are taboo. In emphasizing a single ideology or program, such as whole language or a particular basal text, loyalty to recommended practices is the priority; other actions are taboo (c.f., MacGinitie, 1991; Sfard, 1998). In emphasizing recommendations of a particular mentor, the priority is emulating the mentor, not choosing for one's self. And if we support our recommendations with statements such as "research says" or "as we know from research" without also making clear that educational research findings are tendencies rather than "answers" or "cures," teachers think that research findings should not be adapted to fit unique instructional situations.

In sum, all such emphases, at best, socialize teachers into using only limited theories or methods: at worst, they indoctrinate teachers and subjugate them to a power outside themselves. Visioning, in contrast, helps teachers develop a clearer sense of their purposes for teaching (Hammerness, 2002) and authorizes them to think for themselves. Thus, they can be independent of what a teacher educator or other authority figure might recommend.

One Attempt to Develop Vision

Is it possible to develop the psychological strength to be an independent decision maker while maintaining a high level of pedagogical competence? About a decade ago, I was moved to pursue that question. In studying my own work as a literacy educator, I did not like what I saw. I intended to develop independent decision-makers, but I kept hearing my preservice teachers referring to their fieldwork as "the Duffy project" and as "the Duffy method." In short, they were emulating me; they were not analyzing situations and independently deciding how to adapt or invent instruction to fit the context.

When I examined why my students were not making their own decisions, I discovered that, in my enthusiasm for my favored ways of teaching reading and writing, I was implying that I had the answer, and that my preservice teachers would be well served to follow my lead. All teacher educators are caught in this bind to one extent or another. Yes, we all want empowered teachers—but, deep down, we also want them to do it our way.

Since then, in three different preservice teacher education programs, my colleagues and I have tried to resolve this conflict. We began by emphasizing four characteristics of outstanding teachers. First, of course, we want our teachers to be decision-makers— to invent, adapt, and make "on-the-fly" responses to kids' interests and needs. We call this "entrepreneurial" because the best teachers spontaneously capitalize on opportunities despite the risk (Duffy, 1997). Second, like outstanding teachers, we want our teachers to have a deep, conscious sense of mission and of service, to teach because of a moral commitment to kids and to what they hope their students will become. Third, we want our teachers to use that moral imperative to resist being followers. We want them to figure out how to "do their own thing" despite difficulties. Finally, we want our teachers to be passionate enough about their mission to be able to maintain a sense of joy and renewal despite the frustrations they are certain to encounter.

Concluding that these characteristics were as much a matter of heart and spirit as of mind and cognition, we initiated a student product called a "vision paper." A vision paper is an analytical search of self that was designed to promote two goals articulated by Schaette, Watanabe, and Ramsey (1999). The first is teacher consciousness—of the ambiguity associated with teaching generally and with literacy instruction in particular, of the need for suspending judgment, and of the need to respond appropriately when teaching equilibrium is disrupted. The second is creativity—the propensity, when equilibrium is disrupted, to modify instruction in unique ways in pursuit of a personal mission.

Two discussions designed to eliminate naive misconceptions about a literacy teacher's work precede the first draft of a vision paper. The first focuses on how society is changing, and the implications for literacy (i.e., "functional" literacy of earlier times is no longer sufficient; complex forms of literacy must be the focus). The second focuses on the ambiguous and difficult nature of teaching literacy. Unlike the brain surgeon who operates on a single, sedated patient to correct a purely physical problem using a precise procedure followed in exactly the same way every time, teachers must develop deep meaning rooted in cognitive and affective understandings with twenty-five very active children using methods that do not work in exactly the same way with every kid every day.

With that foundation in place, we ask our teachers to start writing their vision statements by answering questions such as:

- Why did you choose to become a teacher?
- What is your particular gift to your students?
- Do you see your teaching as a mission?
- What is the most important thing you want your students to learn from you?
- When you say you want your students to be "literate," what does that mean?
- If you were to meet your students fifteen years from now, what do you hope they will tell you was the most important thing they learned from you?"

As students begin developing their visions, we introduce the idea that ". . . teachers are inevitably involved in the business of judging and deciding what ought to be done. Whether they are determining ends or means, they cannot escape the commitment to values. . . ." (Codd, 1989, p. 160).

Consequently, as students encounter more and more professional information, we emphasize again and again that the best instructional decisions are based in values as well as in research findings. For instance, we point out how excellent teachers evaluate situations and choose to adapt and modify research-based techniques in light of their respective visions; how they decide in certain situations to combine two or more research-based methods in a single lesson to better achieve a mission; and how they adapt and modify assessment tools to achieve the purposes that drive their work.

As we introduce more and more professional knowledge, we have students revisit and revise their visions again and again in a variety of ways and in a variety of settings. Sometimes they revise it for us to read and sometimes they revise it for sharing with a group of colleagues; sometimes they revise it in light of new professional knowledge about theories, methods or research findings and sometimes they revise it on the basis of experience in the field; sometimes they revise it in cooperative groups and sometimes they revise it individually. But they constantly revise it.

Challenge is also part of the revision process because social psychology research (Petty, 1995) and literacy researchers such as Anders and Richardson (1991) report that attitudes become more stable and durable when subjected to analysis in the crucible of debate. Sometimes challenges take the form of *quickie-writes*, in which students answer questions such as, "How would you convey your vision to students while simultaneously meeting the state's mandates regarding mastery of phonic skills?" At other times teachers having different visions must cooperatively respond to questions such as, "Given what we have learned in this course about individual differences, how do you reconcile your respective visions with the national goal to have all third graders reading at third grade?" When learning about a new method, students are put in simulated situations where the method must be adapted; when discussing informal reading inventories, they are given situations requiring modification of the author's directions; when learning about an instructional technique, they must adapt that technique to a particular situation; when discussing a prescriptive reading program, they must integrate their vision into the mandated program despite apparent restrictions; and when graduation nears, they present their professional visions in mock job interviews. There are no right answers to any of these tasks. Our goal is to prepare teachers ". . . to move outside supposed certainties into the less secure, more tentative and problematic arena of complexities, instability and value conflict" (Smyth, 1989; p. 195), and to use self knowledge as a moral compass when struggling with the inevitable choices faced in the ambiguous environment of classrooms.

Of course, we still teach the expected curriculum of literacy methods courses (i.e., the nature of literacy, instructional methods, techniques of assessment, process writing, etc.), we still promote complex forms of literacy, we still report research findings, and I still make clear my preference for diagnostic, explicit instruction embedded in authentic literacy tasks. But I take pains to point out how my favored methods reflect my particular vision, and we teach other theories and methods with equal vigor. We teach teachers to value research, but not to be enslaved by findings; that they should make decisions thoughtfully and flexibly using research findings in combination with their visions and with their assessment of instructional situations. We repeat over and over, "There is no one way to skin the reading and writing cat. Teaching well means using lots of different methods and techniques." When our students ask us specific "how to" questions, we say, "Here's how I would do it because doing it this way supports my vision for kids and literacy. But you must have the courage of your convictions and make instructional decisions that support your vision for kids and literacy."

But we also emphasize that a vision is not license for "anything goes" teaching. Teachers are public servants; they are not autonomous when paid with taxes to fulfill a duty determined by the citizenry, nor can teachers "self-rule" when working within layers of institutions such as school districts and state education departments, or when subject to legislative oversight. In the complex world of teaching, teachers must be willing to seek common ground, to reconcile apparently conflicting expectations, and to accept what Garrison (1997) calls the "uncertainty, mystery, doubt, and half-knowledge" (p. 85) of teaching while still striving to achieve their visions for their students.

A vision is not license for "anything goes" teaching.

Understandably, most students dislike the visioning process at first. Like students everywhere, they want to get an "A" in the course, and they prefer the task to be simple and straightforward. Negotiating the contradictions between having a vision and being a public servant is just one frustration. Writing the paper itself is also a struggle. Veteran teachers laugh as they recall their reactions to the task. One told me, "I used to think to myself. 'Why doesn't he just tell me what to do? I swear I'll kill him if he doesn't just give me a lesson plan to follow instead of all this vision stuff!'" Another recalled how upset she was when told that she had to revise her vision: "I felt like the first one I wrote was awesome. And you want me to make it better?"

Despite such difficulties, former students now in their third and fourth years of teaching say that visioning has served them well. Consider, for instance, the following self-reports:

- "My vision is still basically the same, and I find that I refer to it in almost everything I do in my classroom."
- "My vision has caused me to keep looking for more ways to connect what I'm teaching to what I said I wanted my kids to do in the real world."
- "What my vision does for me is that it gives me a focus. I've taught different grades and I can take my vision and fit it to different situations and different sets of kids. Even though the job changes, the focus is there."
- "When you get out there, you have to be flexible. There isn't one way to do it, so you have to do what you think is best. That's where your vision comes in."

Veteran teachers particularly emphasize the difference between their professional actions and what they sometimes observe in colleagues:

- "I've noticed that some teachers get worse, instead of better. But I keep changing, I keep doing it differently to get closer to the vision I have for these kids."
- "Teachers who are not independent and who don't think for themselves have done the same things since Day One. And they don't want to try anything different when the situation changes."
- "What I've noticed is that teachers who don't have a vision don't know how to bend, to try new things when things go wrong. But I've found you have to be prepared for everything, you have to be able to try new things."

Those who have not yet begun teaching also acknowledge the strength in having a vision. Consider, for instance, comments from fifth-year students following two consecutive courses emphasizing visioning:

- "Having a vision means that I'm not just going through the motions. Now there's a deliberate reason for everything I do."
- "If you have an idea why you're teaching, you can hold everything up to that. It's your touchstone. You won't allow things that go against that."
- "The vision is my ideal. It's what I'm setting out to accomplish so that despite the politics of the job, I ask myself, 'What's the essence of my being here?'"
- "Vision makes me more reflective. I'm constantly asking myself. 'Is this consistent with my vision? Why am I still standing here talking when my vision is that kids should be the ones to do most of the talking?'"
- "Vision is a feeding of your soul. If what you are doing doesn't feed your soul, get rid of it."
- "Vision provides the wisdom that allows us the serenity to accept the students who come to us, and the courage to change ourselves in response to their needs without losing track of our moral obligation."

The strength and professional dignity embedded in these statements suggest that these teachers go beyond pedagogical competence. They possess a sense of mission that allows them to maintain an independent stance in the face of the pressures to conform and comply.

Conclusion

The visioning process I describe grows out of at least five like-minded efforts. Its immediate antecedent was a study of teachers' knowledge structures (Roehler,

Duffy, Herrmann, et al., 1988) that attempted to link teachers' responsiveness during instruction to their conscious organization of professional knowledge. We drew on Connelly and Clandinin's (1997) work on "teachers' personal practical knowledge" and on studies of teacher narratives and life histories (Collay, 1998) when it became apparent that a teacher's values may be as important as formal teacher education knowledge. We drew heavily on research of teachers' language and discourse, in which writing is seen as a key to transformation and to acquiring new beliefs (Denyer & Florio-Ruane, 1995: Rosaen & Shram, 1998), and on recent research on teacher beliefs, particularly the emphasis on exploring beliefs as a necessary prerequisite to changing practice (Richardson, Anders, Tidwell & Lloyd, 1991) as opposed to earlier attempts to tie beliefs to a preferred model of reading (Duffy & Anderson, 1984; Harste & Burke, 1977). Similarly, we drew on teacher-as-researcher concepts in which teachers learn to "question their assumptions and to be consciously thoughtful about goals, practices, students and contexts" (Richardson, 1994, p. 6). In sum, visioning is part of a widespread teacher education effort to ensure that teachers do not become what Smith (1991) calls "interchangeable technicians."

But despite these commonalties, colleagues do not readily accept visioning. The most frequently raised objection is, "What if a teacher comes up with the wrong vision?" This objection is rooted. I fear, in the assumption that there IS a "right" vision—an infallible ideology or theory or method or program—and that, as literacy educators, we must promote it to the exclusion of others.

Assuming so is a fundamental flaw. It develops followers. However, followers cannot get the job done in the decades ahead when, in order to develop a more complex literacy for a more pluralistic clientele, teachers will have to be more flexible in their use of methods, and materials, more creatively responsive to kids, and less dependent on doing things according to recommended patterns.

Developing such creative and independent teachers requires that teacher educators think differently. Traditionally, we have answered the "what works?" question in terms of theories, methods and programs. But in reality what works is teachers who take risks and change theories, methods and programs when standard practices do not suffice. Developing the strength to do this in the face of pressure to conform is a central task of teacher education.

Such strength comes, I believe, from having a vision—a passionate sense of commitment and mission. But visioning is just a hypothesis. Its validity must be established by research. Consequently, my original intent in writing this paper was to call for such a research agenda.

Upon reflection, however, I am convinced that we cannot do the research without first examining ourselves and our culturally engrained ways of teaching teachers. While all of us like to think we are preparing teachers who are independent thinkers, our traditional role has been to provide answers. If we are to teach teachers to think for themselves, independent of what we recommend, we must carefully examine that tradition and how it affects our interactions with our students.

- To what extent do our courses emphasize freeing teachers to operate independent of us?
- Do our graduates invent instruction that is more complex than what we taught them?
- Do our teachers understand that they are authorized to change what we recommend and to adopt practices we oppose when the need arises?

These questions are at the heart of my premise. They go to our deepest perceptions of ourselves as teacher educators and to our ways of thinking about teacher education. To develop teachers who are thoughtfully independent of us, we must first wrestle with the cultural tradition of teachers looking to us for answers.

Author's Note

The author wishes to thank the following colleagues for valuable suggestions provided in response to earlier drafts of this paper: Dick Allington, Auleen Duffy, Jim Hoffman, Laura Jones, Perry Lanier, Sheild Valencia and Gordon Watanabe. Special thanks also go to the following former students who generously gave time and effort in responding to my questions about their experiences with visioning: Amy Barker, Hillary Davis de Chenquian, Tim Fries, Erika Fromhold, Debbie Hogan, Robin Kaney, Melinda Kenney, Shannon Knight, Jim Meyer, Jennifer Morris, Greg Schroeder, Meredith Sullivan, Lisa Welsh, and Jennifer Yager.

References

Anders, P., Hoffman, J., & Duffy, G. (2000). Teaching teachers to teach reading: Paradigm shifts, persistent problems and challenges. In R. Barr, M. Kamil, P. Mosenthal & P.D. Pearson (Eds.) *Handbook of Reading Research*, 3rd edition (pp. 719–742). Mahwah, NJ: Erlbaum.

Anders, P., & Richardson, V. (1991). Research directions: Staff development that empowers teachers' reflection and enhances instruction. *Language Arts, 68* (4), 316–321.

Berliner, D., & Biddle, B. (1996). *The Manufactured Crisis*. NY: Longman.

Bracey, G. (1997). The seventh Bracey report on the condition of public education. *Phi Delta Kappan, 79,* 120–137.

Brophy, J., & Good, T. (1986). Teacher behavior and student achievement. In M. Wittrock (Ed.) *Handbook of Research on Teaching,* 3rd edition. Riverside, NJ: Macmillan.

Carter, K. (1990). Teachers' knowledge and learning to teach. In R. Houston (Ed.) *Handbook of Research on Teacher Education* (pp. 291–310). NY: Macmillan.

Cochran-Smith, M., & Lytle, S. (1993). *Inside/Outside: Teacher research and teacher knowledge,* NY: Teachers College Press.

Codd, J. (1989). Educational leadership as reflective action. In J. Smyth (Ed.) *Critical Perspectives on Educational Leadership.* (pp. 157–179). London: Falmer.

Collay, M. (1998). Recherche: Teaching our life histories. *Teaching and Teacher Education, 14* (3), 245–255.

Connelly, F., Clandinin D, & He, M. (1997). Teachers' personal practical knowledge on the professional knowledge landscape. *Teaching and Teacher Education, 13* (7), 665–674.

Denyer, J., & Florio-Ruane, S. (1995). Mixed messages and missed opportunities: Moments of transformation in writing conferences and teacher education. *Teaching and Teacher Education, 11* (6), 539–551.

Duffy, G. (1994). Teachers' progress toward becoming expert strategy teachers. *Elementary School Journal, 94* (2), 109–120.

Duffy, G. (1997). Powerful teachers or powerful models? An argument for teacher-as-entrepreneur. In S. Stahl & D. Hayes (Eds.) *Instructional Models in Reading* (pp. 351–366). Mahwah, NJ: Erlbaum.

Duffy, G., & Anderson, L. (1984). Teachers' theoretical orientations and the real classroom. *Reading Psychology, 5* (2), 97–104.

Duffy, G., & Hoffman, J. (1999). In pursuit of an illusion: The flawed search for a perfect method. *The Reading Teacher, 53* (1), 10–16.

Duffy, G., & Roehler, L. (1987). Improving classroom reading instruction through the use of responsive elaboration. *Reading Teacher, 40* (6), 514–521.

Duffy, G., Roehler, L., & Rackliffe, G. (1986). How teachers' instructional talk influences students' understandings of lesson content. *Elementary School Journal, 87* (1), 3–16.

Duffy, G., Roehler, L., Sivan, E., Rackliffe, G., Book, C., Meloth, M., Vavrus, L., Wesselman, R., Putnam, J., & Bassiri, D. (1987). Effects of explaining the reasoning associated with using reading strategies. *Reading Research Quarterly, 22* (3), 347–368.

Feiman-Nemser, S. (1990). Contexts and models of teacher education. In W.R. Houston, M. Huberman, & J. Siula (Eds.) *Handbook of Research on Teacher Education,* NY: Macmillan.

Feldman, A. (1997). Varieties of wisdom in the practice of teachers. *Teaching and Teacher Education. 13* (7), 757–773.

Greene, M. (1991). Teaching: The question of personal reality. In A. Liebeman & L. Miller (Eds.) *Staff Development for Education in the '90s': New Demands, New Realities, New Perspectives* (pp. 3–14). NY: Teachers College Press.

Hammerness, K. (2002). Learning to hope, or hoping to learn? The role of vision in teachers' early professional lives. *Journal of Teacher Education.*

Hammerness, K. (2001). Teachers' visions: The role of personal ideals in school reform. *Journal of Educational Change, 2,* 143–163.

Hargreaves, A. (1998). The emotional practice of teaching. *Teaching and Teacher Education, 14* (8), 835–854.

Harste, J., & Burke, C. (1977). A new hypothesis for reading teacher research: Both teaching and learning are theoretically based. In P.D. Pearson (Ed.) *Reading: Theory research and practice.* 26th Yearbook of the National Reading Conference. Clemson, SC: National Reading Conference.

Johnston, S. (1992). Images: A way of understanding the practical knowledge of student teachers. *Teaching and Teacher Education, 8* (2), 123–136.

Korthagen, F., & Kessel, J. (1999). Linking theory and practice: Changing the pedagogy of teacher education. *Educational Researcher, 28* (4), 417.

MacGinitie, W. (1991). Reading instruction: Plus ca change. *Educational Leadership, 48.* 56.

Morrow, L., Tracey, D., Woo, D., & Pressley, M. (1998). Characteristics of exemplary first-grade literacy instruction. *Reading Teacher, 52* (5), 462–479.

Nespor, J. (1987). The role of beliefs in the practice of teaching. *Journal of Curriculum Studies, 19* (4), 317–328.

Pajares, F. (1996). Self-efficacy beliefs in academic settings. *Review of Educational Research, 66* (4), 543–578.

Pajares, F., & Graham, L. (1998). Formalist thinking and language arts instruction: Teachers' and students' beliefs about truth and caring in the teaching conversation. *Teaching and Teacher Education, 14* (8), 855–870.

Petty, R. (1995). Attitude change. In A. Tesser (Ed.) *Advanced Social Psychology* (pp. 195–256). Boston: McGraw-Hill.

Pressley, M., Rankin, J., & Yokoi, L. (1996). A survey of instructional practices of primary teachers nominated as effective in promoting literacy. *Elementary School Journal, 96* (4), 363–384.

Pressley, M., Wharton-McDonald, R., Allington, R., Block, C., Morrow, L., Tracey, D., Baker, K., Brooks, G., Nelson, E., & Woo, D. (1998). *The nature of effective first-grade literacy instruction.* Report 1007, National Research Center on English Learning and Achievement, University at Albany, Albany, NY.

Richardson, V. (1994). Conducting research on practice. *Educational Researcher, 23* (5), 510.

Richardson, V., Anders, P., Tidwell, D., & Lloyd, C. (1991). The relationship between teachers' beliefs and practices in reading comprehension instruction. *American Educational Research Journal, 28,* 559–586.

Rochler, L., Duffy, G., Herrmann, B., Conley, M., & Johnson, J. (1988). Knowledge structures as evidence of the "Personal": Bridging the gap from thought to practice. *Journal of Curriculum Studies, 20* (2), 159–165.

Roehler, L., Duffy, G., & Warren, S. (1988). Adaptive explanatory actions associated with effective teaching of reading strategies. In J. Readence & R. Baldwin (Eds.). *Dialogues in Literacy Research,* 37th yearbook of the National Reading Conference. Chicago: National Reading Conference.

Rosaen, C., & Schram, P. (1998). Becoming a member of the teaching profession: Learning a language of possibility. *Teaching and Teacher Education, 14* (3), 283–303.

Schaetti, B., Watanabe, G., & Ramsey, S. (1999). *The practice of personal leadership in the SIIC intern program.* Unpublished paper. Spokane: Whitworth College.

Sfard, A. (1998). On two metaphors for learning and the dangers of choosing just one. *Educational Researcher, 27*, 413.

Smith, M. (1991). Put to the test: The effects of external testing on teachers. *Educational Researcher, 20* (5), 8–11.

Smyth, J. (1989). A "pedagogical" and "educative" view of leadership. In J. Smyth (Ed.) *Critical Perspectives on Educational Leadership.* (pp. 179–204). London: Falmer.

Valencia, S. (1998). *Literacy Portfolios in Action.* Fort Worth: Harcourt Brace.

Van Manen, M. (1977). Linking ways of knowing with ways of being practical. *Curriculum Inquiry, 6* (3), 205–228.

Wharton-McDonald, R., Pressley, M. & Hampston, J. (1998). Literacy instruction in nine first grade classrooms: Teacher characteristics and student achievement. *Elementary School Journal, 99* (2), 103–128.

Zeichner, K., & Gore, J. (1990). Teacher socialization. In R. Houston (Ed.) *Handbook on Teacher Education* (pp. 329–343). NY: Macmillan.

From Scripted Instruction to Teacher Empowerment: Supporting Literacy Teachers to Make Pedagogical Transitions

Zhihui Fang, Danling Fu, and Linda Leonard Lamme
University of Florida—Gainesville

I'd taught third grade for nine years. When I became involved with the professional development project, I felt that I was ready for a change. I was ready to give up the teacher-centered classroom. But it was much more difficult than I had anticipated.

The Silver Burdett basal reading series had been the only reading program that I had known. I went story-by-story, used the skill workbooks, following the teachers' edition pretty much the way it was laid out. Each week's schedule was similar, just with different stories. Besides a library book, students did not select what they were to read about. They simply read whatever story was next in the basal. This method was very comfortable to me.

Moving away from the basal . . . was scary. At first, I felt a loss of control, and I wasn't sure that I liked it. But ultimately, reading/writing became a much more challenging and exciting time than in previous years . . .

Our classroom was a home to the basics this year—but much more! Our days consisted of reading, writing and math. Science and social studies were integrated into our reading and writing. Our days were full, but never boring! . . .

I think I took a risk this year, and my teaching will never be the same.

Kim, a third-grade teacher, wrote passionately about her transformation from total reliance on prepackaged commercial curricula to independently making informed pedagogical decisions that are responsive to children's needs and interests. She was one of the teachers from six rural schools in north-

east Florida who were involved in a four-year professional development project. What contributed to Kim's pedagogical transition? How was the project structured to provide the kind of support that sustained her risk-taking? In this article, we deconstruct the support system that undergirded Kim's successful transformation. Before describing the professional development model further, we provide brief background information about the project and its impact on children.

Background

During the past decade federal and state governments have become increasingly involved in legislating what to teach and how to teach in American public schools (Allington, 2002; Garan, 2002). With recent legislation calling for a dramatic expansion of state-wide high-stakes testing, teachers are under immense pressure to comply with the government mandates and to prepare children for such tests. Concomitantly, prepackaged commercial programmes that claim to meet state/federal educational standards and be based on "scientifically-based reading research" have proliferated, particularly within the states of California, Texas and Florida. Many schools are resorting to these programmes for a quick fix. Teachers at these schools are mandated to attend professional development training conducted by commercial publishers. This standards-driven, high-stakes testing climate has had unintended consequences for teachers and students, particularly those in urban and high-poverty schools (Amrein and Berliner, 2003; Hoffman, Assaf and Paris, 2001; Mathison and Freeman, 2003). On one hand, it undermines teacher morale and inhibits their development of professional expertise and wisdom. On the other hand, it increases children's disengagement with school-based tasks and results in less overall learning for them.

It is against this socio-political backdrop that we, three university literacy professors, together with colleagues from the adjacent northeast Florida school districts, began to explore alternative solutions to the current educational dilemma. Together, we developed a model of professional development that fosters a high degree of teacher autonomy and accountability for student learning. The professional development project, funded by the state for four years, was coordinated by the North East Florida Educational Consortium (NEFEC), an educational agency serving northeast Florida school districts. We began in four elementary schools with teacher volunteers whose administrators agreed to create what we called 'professional development classrooms,' or PDCs. In subsequent years, two more elementary schools joined our efforts. The intention of this project was to create classrooms where teachers grow as professionals who design and implement research-based, effective literacy instruction that produces a positive impact on student learning and achievement. Each of the PDCs had a student population comparable to that in other classrooms in terms of gender, ethnicity, socioeconomic status and scholastic aptitude. At least one-third of the students in the PDCs were not reading on grade level at the beginning of the project.

Federal and state governments have become increasingly involved in legislating what to teach and how to teach in American public schools.

According to an independent evaluation of the project commissioned by NEFEC (Florida's Reading Best Practices Center, 2000), the students attending the PDCs significantly outperformed their peers in other classrooms within the same school on standardised measures required by their respective school districts. They also outperformed their peers in sample NEFEC-affiliated school districts whose teachers were involved in other professional development activities. More importantly, the PDC students developed better literacy habits over the years. That is, they became more avid readers and writers and critical thinkers. They not only read many more books and wrote more often both at home and in school than they did in previous years, but they were also more thoughtful and analytical in their responses to texts. The following end-of-year comments by Kim's students and their parents illustrate this point.

- *I'm glad my mom put me in [PDC] because I've read over three hundred books in this program and I love to read. . . . Reading helps me in all my subjects. Reading helps me with everything in life. (student)*
- *My child loves to read this year. He didn't love to read before. Reading was a chore to him. Now serious punishment for him is: sit without a book.*

He doesn't want to do anything but to read. He improved his reading skills greatly. (parent)
- *Writing Workshop has helped me to work toward my dream of becoming an author by helping me to learn about the writing process, and by teaching me that writing good stories takes a lot of time and effort. It is not always easy but it is always rewarding. (student)*
- *My child is knowledgeable about literature. I am impressed by the way he talks about books. He can talk about genres and authors. He is better than my seventh grade child when he talks about literature. (parent)*

The success of these PDCs demonstrates an important point that has been reiterated in recent research on teacher education in reading and literacy: sustained, quality professional development for teachers makes a big difference to student achievement (Anders, Hoffman and Duffy, 2000; Darling-Hammond, 2000). Although more federal and state resources are now available for staff development, school districts often lack the infrastructure, knowledge and experience to plan and implement effective professional development. According to a recent national survey of district directors (Hughes, Cash, Klingner and Ahwee, 2001), "across the country, one-shot professional development experiences continue to be the most common form of delivering information to teachers" (p. 283). Such professional development efforts fail to recognise that the process of becoming and being an expert teacher is a complex, multifaceted and lifelong endeavour. As a result, their impact on improving teacher quality and student learning is understandably limited.

The process of becoming and being an expert teacher is a complex, multifaceted and lifelong endeavour.

How does our professional development model differ from those prevalent in today's education system in the USA? What are the characteristics of such a model? In the rest of this article, we describe our professional development model, focusing on the ways in which it facilitated teachers' transition from consumers of prepackaged commercial programmes to informed, expert curriculum decision-makers and instructional leaders.

Our Professional Development Model: An Overview

Teaching is hard work. Teaching against institutional grains can be even harder. Cognisant of this fact, we developed a support structure for the teachers who were involved in the PDCs. The essential purpose of the support was to empower teachers as professionals through extending knowledge and experience, and through collaborating with other professionals in the field. To ensure this, we first of all requested administrative support at the school and district levels for the participant teachers. This included providing teacher aides as well as giving exemption from textbook adoption and from any pull-out programmes for students with learning difficulties or other special needs.

Our professional development model involved a great deal of collaboration among the classroom teachers, NEFEC staff and university professors. The teachers had applied to be part of the PDCs with the goal of becoming involved in their own professional development and advancement within their school districts. The university professors were eager to have classroom-teacher collaborators in professional development projects. The NEFEC staff facilitated coordination of the programme and communication among different stakeholders. The major delivery mechanisms for the support structure were (a) an annual summer institute, (b) regular classroom visitations by the university faculty, NEFEC staff and fellow teachers, (c) monthly meetings throughout the school year, and (d) the end-of-year showcase meeting. Each of these components is elaborated below.

First, an institute was designed each summer for teachers to extend and refine their knowledge base about literacy teaching, learning and assessment. During the institutes, teachers read professional books and journal articles and viewed video clips to keep themselves abreast of the current trends, issues and techniques in literacy education. They also reflected on, as well as examined, their own literate lives and teaching practices. In addition, they read and discussed award-winning, recently published children's literature. Sandwiched between presentations from the university faculty were sessions in which teachers interacted with each other as readers and writers. They also shared teaching strategies that worked well for them and were congruent with best practices.

Second, as a follow-up to the summer institute, the university faculty and NEFEC staff visited each teacher's classroom at least once a month during the school year. During the visit, we became participant observers, reading to children, holding book discussions, conferencing with individual children, listening to children read, teaching a lesson or observing the teacher do any of the above. At first, teachers were vulnerable and only asked us to observe something that was going well or said "just come in any time", with no educational focus for the visit. In time, the visits became more collaborative, with teacher and observer working together to tackle specific pedagogical

challenges. The visitor conferred with the teacher at the end of each visit. After each visit, the visitor also wrote up a report that identified parts of the lesson that he/she thought were particularly well done, as well as areas of concerns and strategies for addressing those concerns. The teacher often e-mailed her responses to the feedback and sometimes follow-up e-mail discussions ensued. Over time, the classroom teachers also initiated visits to each other's classrooms, sharing insights and ideas about teaching and learning.

Third, in addition to classroom visitations, monthly meetings were held with the teachers, the university faculty and NEFEC staff to provide continuity for further professional development. During these monthly meetings, teachers shared successes and challenges in their daily instruction. Each teacher also brought a packet of information on one child about whom she had concerns. Based on the information provided, the group would, together, discuss what the child could do, what he/she was struggling to do and what could be done to help the child. Lastly, at the monthly meeting, we discussed a recent journal article, a professional book chapter and/or a professional video vignette that we all had read/viewed. Follow-up discussions of these materials often continued via e-mail after each monthly meeting.

Finally, at the end of each year, a showcase meeting was held in one of the participating schools. This was a time when students and teachers displayed their work and shared their thoughts about being involved in the PDCs. Participants at the showcase included representatives from the state education agencies, school and district administrators, parents, and other teachers in the NEFEC-affiliated schools. The occasion allowed us to reflect on what we as a group had accomplished during the year and look forward to what still lay ahead for the forthcoming year(s). In addition, through the showcase we were able to develop a sense of accomplishment and strengthen the bonds among the participants, while at the same time garnering support from the education stakeholders.

Teacher Empowerment Through Monthly Meetings

The monthly meeting provides an example of how teachers were empowered and became equal partners and self-assertive professionals in the project. The evolution of monthly meetings shows how we collaboratively designed and revised our professional development model and how, in the process, the teachers grew to become empowered professionals.

Originally, the monthly meetings were designed to provide time for discussion of teacher concerns and challenges in their implementation of best practices. The idea was that from learning how teachers were implementing best practices in their classrooms, the university professors would provide whatever additional information the teachers needed in order to improve their instruction. At our first few meetings, the teachers tended to show, through video tapes of their instruction or artefacts from their students, what they assumed they were supposed to do: read-alouds, book talks, guided reading, writing conferences, and independent reading and writing. They talked about the concerns and problems in their implementation of best practices. They came to the meeting either to show what they had done or ask if what they had done exemplified what the university professors 'wanted'. They also presented their problems and expected solutions from the ivory-tower professors. It was difficult to give any suggestions or comments by seeing only some excerpts of class teaching, without knowing the whole picture of the teaching (daily or weekly), or reading pieces of students' writing without knowing the history of the students or under what condition those pieces were produced. Much time was wasted listening to general problems, most of which had no immediate solution. Specific students were not mentioned in the discussions.

This format not only did not move us too far, but the worst of all, it put the teachers in a passive stance. They came to the meeting expecting either to be judged or to be helped. We, as a group, decided to change this unequal status and let each teacher assume more control of their own learning, rather than being 'subservient' to the university professors and NEFEC staff. We moved to having each teacher bring to the monthly meeting a packet of information on one child about whom she had concerns. In the packet, which was distributed to all meeting participants, the teacher included a writing sample from early on and a recent writing sample, a written response to literature, and either running records or video clips of the child's book reading. On a cover sheet the teacher provided information to answer the following questions: (a) what is the child's family background and academic history? (b) what can the child do? (c) what is the child currently struggling to do? (d) what have I tried to do to help the child? and (e) what is my goal to achieve in a month for this child?

At the meeting, after participants had reviewed the data, the teacher gave an oral overview of the child, referring to the examples provided in the packet. The group then discussed options for what might be done to help the child move on in literacy learning. The discussion was rich, building one idea upon another until the comprehensive nature of teaching a child with learning challenges became obvious. The written profile on each child provided a whole picture

of the learner: the history of learning (what the child can do), the present challenges (what the child is struggling with), and future goals (what the teacher expects the child to achieve). For the teacher, we learned what she had tried and, together, we—classroom teachers, NEFEC staff and university professors—explored what she could try at this time for this child. Each teacher left the meeting not only with ideas for working with a specific child in her classroom, but also with strategies that might work with many other children. Listening to the discussion and participating in them, we profiled many different children's learning difficulties. The diversity of challenges and the repertoire of possible solutions greatly enhanced the teachers' capacities for dealing with not only at risk children but the general student population.

More important, though, than just 'getting ideas', the teachers changed their perspectives on struggling readers/writers. At the beginning meetings, teachers inevitably talked about children in their classes who were having problems, focusing upon what the children could not do and what was not working. They made statements like, 'Jack has such a short attention span', 'Sam can't read anything', 'Paige doesn't even know her alphabet', or 'Manuel's home life is so bad that he can't concentrate in school'. It was not until the written packet was required that the focus of the discussion fundamentally changed from a deficit model to a developmental one. This philosophical turn signalled a giant leap in a positive tone toward directly meeting the needs of the children who were at risk of failure in their classrooms.

A further benefit of the written protocols becoming a basis for discussion is that our conversation became data-based and, hence, more focused. We no longer based our conversation on impressions, innuendos and opinions. The teachers realised that when discussion becomes data-driven, it is much easier to assess individual students' strengths and needs and accordingly to plan instruction that maximises their learning potential. They agreed that in order to make sound instructional decisions, teachers must systematically collect, analyse, and interpret student data from multiple contexts.

In order to make sound instructional decisions, teachers must systematically collect, analyse, and interpret student data from multiple contexts.

The most significant outcome of these monthly meetings is that the teachers learned to become empowered professionals. They understood and appreciated that instruction should be based on documented student needs, rather than on what is specified in scripted manuals. They learned to look at a child from a positive perspective (what the child can do), from an historical perspective (what the child has learned to do and needs to learn more) and from an individual perspective (where the child is in terms of his/her developmental trajectory). They no longer relied solely on outside 'experts', high stakes tests, commercial programmes, or professional manuals to diagnose and remediate their students. Instead, they learned to trust their own professional wisdom and judgement based on their daily observation of and interaction with students. They became designers of individualised instructional plans, setting goals, selecting materials, deciding on teaching strategies and adjusting instruction for each child. Such a transformation has increased their confidence level, as is evident in the following comments by participant teachers.

- *I am definitely a different teacher now than before. In the past, I just followed the textbooks, now I design my teaching and choose what I want to teach according to what my kids need.*

- *I am a much more confident and informed professional than before. I don't just trust others to tell me how and what to teach, or how my kids are doing. I know how to help my children the best.*

- *I now have multiple ways to assess where a child is in reading and teach according to their needs.*

- *I now know what to look for in determining if a book is authentic and of good quality. I had no idea there were so many good children's books out there.*

Ensuring Success in Professional Development

What are the keys to the success of our professional development model? Throughout the four-year collaborative journey, we made conscious efforts to overcome the "conceptual, pragmatic, attitudinal, and professional barriers" (Welch, 1998) that are known often to impede professional development work. In this section, we highlight three key strategies that contributed to the success of the project. They are (a) forging an equal partnership, (b) making overt connections between professional development and classroom instruction and (c) developing teachers' sense of professionalism.

Forging Equal Partnership

As with any university-school collaborative effort, an important part of professional development involves building a strong partnership among all parties involved, including the public school, the university and other education agencies. Lasley (1992) noted that in order for effective collaboration to occur, there must be shared goals, shared power and shared needs among all people involved, particularly between the university faculty and classroom teachers. Moll made a similar point when he stated:

> *No innovation has a realistic chance of succeeding unless teachers are able to express, define, and address problems as they see them, unless teachers come to see the innovation and change as theirs. The ultimate outcome of the innovation . . . depends on when and how teachers become part of the decision to initiate them. (Moll, 1992, p. 229)*

It appears that a major problem to address in any university-school partnership is the unequal status of the participants. That is, teachers often feel that they have less status than university professors. To overcome this potential problem, we encouraged open dialogue among all parties. In particular, we consciously tried to address the status issue in a number of ways: (a) by setting up specific agenda items for each group during monthly meetings, (b) by placing teachers' voices at the center and letting them share what was working, and (c) by presenting at professional conferences as a team. These allow each member of the project to contribute her/his experience, knowledge and expertise throughout the collaborative journey.

We recognised leadership shifts as the project evolved over the years. Initially the university faculty and NEFEC staff provided leadership at the summer institute, but after the first year, institutes were jointly planned and conducted. Initially the university faculty and NEFEC staff took leadership in classroom visitations, taking on the role of consultants, but gradually teachers assumed leadership by inviting the university faculty and NEFEC staff into their rooms for specific purposes and by visiting each other's classrooms. At times there was equal leadership and collaboration. The classroom teachers collaborated with the university faculty on inquiry projects to explore issues and topics of common concern or interest. For professional conference presentations, there was equal and joint planning and participation. Furthermore, the teachers took leadership of the professional development activities in their own schools. The annual showcase meetings, for example, were designed, organised and conducted by the teachers with minimum involvement of the university faculty or NEFEC staff. In short, different parties assumed leadership at different times in this collaborative model. In effect, collaboration became the impetus for risk-taking for all project participants.

Making Classroom Connections

Another strategy for ensuring the success of our professional development work was to make explicit connections between teachers' professional development and their own practices in the classroom. Providing such a linkage ensures that teachers stay motivated, make sense of their own learning, and ultimately become more effective practitioners. This was done in several ways. First, during monthly meetings, we used students' reading and writing samples and video clips from the teachers' own classrooms to discuss the importance and techniques of 'kid watching' and to brainstorm ideas and strategies that might be helpful to the child reader/writer. This is different from typical professional development workshops where presenters often use artefacts from students about whom teachers have no background knowledge or some remote classroom scenarios with which teachers cannot identify. Our teachers experienced first-hand the usefulness and relevance of these meetings because the children involved in the discussion were real and close to them. Subsequent success in trying out some of the ideas increased their sense of accomplishment and satisfaction. As a result, they were firmly committed to the project year in and year out.

Second, unlike in other staff development workshops where teachers are typically expected to consume the information delivered, and then implement it on their own, we were actively involved in the teachers' classrooms to help them make sense of the information we presented and to address their unique concerns. For example, during classroom visitations, the university faculty sometimes worked with struggling readers and writers while the teacher observed the lesson; other times, the teacher invited the university faculty to give feedback on a lesson in which she tried out newly learned teaching strategies. The post-observation report by the university faculty and subsequent discussion via e-mail and during monthly meetings greatly strengthened the connection between professional development and classroom practices.

Third, throughout the project we emphasized the importance of autobiography in shaping one's own teaching practices (Nieto, 2003) by regularly reminding teachers to bring their own learning experiences to bear upon teaching. Such consciousness-raising allowed teachers to become more aware of and value their own learning experiences and life histories. As a result, they were more active in seeking connections between what they had learned in the professional development project and what they were practising in their classrooms. For example, having read about and seen from videos the benefits of reading and writing workshops during the summer institutes, many teachers were eager to design reading and writing workshops for their students. However, some teachers did not feel that their workshops went as well as they had envisioned. We assisted these teachers to improve their instruction through classroom visitations and monthly meetings. In particular, we asked them to re-read the reflection journals they kept during the summer institutes when they read and wrote nightly and participated in reading and writing workshops. The teachers invariably noted that they had then written about the power of readership and authorship, shared reading and writing experiences and peer critique. Drawing on their learning experience at the summer institutes thus allowed the teachers to notice which key aspects of reading and writing workshops were missing in their own classrooms.

For example, one second-grade teacher who had not been providing regular writing experiences for her students before, latched on to the importance of topic selection and started a daily writing workshop after her first summer institute. Her students would arrive in the morning, get their journals and write in them, knowing that they would get to share with their peers afterwards. While this procedure dramatically increased the amount of writing the children did, it did not set the stage for much progress in writing. The children tended to write the same thing day after day. Furthermore, the children were not learning to revise their writing and improve it because the teacher was more concerned about giving each child an opportunity to share their journals orally. When the teacher voiced her concern to us and asked for suggestions, we pointed out to her the value of revision and asked her to reflect on her own experience with writing at the summer institute. From that point on, the teacher decided to let go of the time-consuming daily share time and to use the journals as a springboard for revising student writing for eventual publication. Instead, she invited parents to her classroom on a monthly basis when student-authored and illustrated books are shared and discussed. As time went on, she conducted frequent explicit lessons on revision, used literature as writing models, and adopted portfolios as a way to assess her students' writing progress.

Developing Professionalism

Our third strategy for ensuring the success of the professional development project was to develop a sense of professionalism among participant teachers. In the first year of the project, the teachers joined professional organisations (e.g., Florida Reading Association, International Reading Association, National Council of Teachers of English) and subscribed to professional journals (e.g., *Florida Reading Quarterly, The Reading Teacher, Language Arts, The New Advocate*). They also attended the annual meeting of the Florida Reading Association in Orlando where they went to a wide variety of sessions and toured exhibits of publishers of current children's literature. In subsequent years, individual teachers initiated classroom inquiry projects with the help of the university faculty and presented their findings at local, state and national professional conferences as well as in professional journals (e.g., Lamme, Fu, Johnson and Savage, 2002). Such inquiry efforts, in time, helped the teachers move away from a transmission model of teaching to a more progressive pedagogy in which they share power and authority with their students (cf. Pappas and Zecker, 2000).

As noted earlier, the teachers and their students organised a conference each spring showcasing their accomplishments. The showcase was held at alternate school sites. Parents, other teachers from the NEFEC school districts, school principals, superintendents and representatives from state education agencies were invited to attend. Students who had previously been identified as at risk of school failure were the focus of this sharing. At this meeting, the teachers shared what they had tried at improving teaching, how they had changed in thinking and practice and how they would further improve. They demonstrated their confidence and professionalism as teacher-researchers and practitioners. On the other hand, parents shared the impact of the PDCs on their children, and the students talked about their progress as learners.

In addition, the participant teachers initiated a faculty reading club within their own schools so that other teachers could learn about best practices, become supportive of the participant teachers and experiment with new ideas in their teaching. They read and discussed professional books and journal articles that were related to their interests and needs. Partly as a result of their involvement in these professional activities, the participant teachers have emerged as instructional leaders within their respective schools and beyond. Some have moved up to become curriculum resource teachers and vice-principals in their own schools; others are providing leadership in a state-wide literacy initiative.

Concluding Thoughts

In the current U.S. educational climate, professional development for teachers is often done haphazardly through training workshops conducted by publishers whose primary interest is in promoting their commercial programmes or by 'experts' who claim to help schools improve student scores in high-stakes testing. These workshops often do not provide the kind of professional knowledge and support that teachers need in order to initiate and sustain qualitative changes of teaching practices. In fact, such run-of-

the-mill professional development activities are not only expensive, but also de-skilling and disempowering. They are likely to further alienate teachers and, in the end, become counter-productive.

Scholars (e.g. Duffy and Hoffman, 1999) have called on teachers to make informed, flexible and creative uses of available instructional resources rather than adhere to a particular programme or dogma. Our experience with the professional development project suggests that effecting pedagogical transitions from total reliance on prepackaged commercial programmes to independently making informed decisions about curriculum and pedagogy can be a challenging undertaking. It requires not only risk-taking on the part of teachers, but also a support structure that scaffolds and facilitates their growth and development. The teachers in our project were provided with ongoing support at the administrative, professional and personal levels. In addition, they were committed to: (a) improving their own literacy through reading clubs and writing workshops; (b) reflecting upon their own teaching and on how it impacts student learning; (c) organising a support group to problem solve in a positive manner the challenges they face; (d) making data-based decisions for the instruction of individual students; (e) initiating inquiry projects to make sense of their own teaching and students' learning; (f) becoming involved in the greater professional community by joining professional organisations, reading educational periodicals/media/books and attending professional conferences; and (g) participating in *long-term* professional development, recognising that the process of becoming and being an expert teacher is a complex, life-long endeavour.

There is no easy or quick fix to the professional development challenges that the education community at large is now facing.

We admit that there is no easy or quick fix to the professional development challenges that the education community at large is now facing. The model we have described in this article represents an alternative to the prevailing paradigm of professional development that exists in today's public schools in America. We are convinced that, however difficult, challenging and time-consuming to implement, a professional development model that empowers teachers will significantly contribute to the development of teacher knowledge, skills and wisdom, and ultimately make a positive, enduring impact on student learning and achievement. Kim's story at the outset of this article is a testimony to the challenges and premises of such a professional development model.

Note

The project reported in this article is made possible by a grant from the Florida Department of Education. The three coauthors contributed equally to the conceptualization and writing of this article. We gratefully acknowledge the contributions of the NEFEC staff and classroom teachers to the development of the professional development model described herein.

References

Allington, R. (2002) *Big Brother and the National Reading Curriculum: How ideology trumped evidence.* Portsmouth, NH: Heinemann.

Amrein, A. and Berliner, D. (2003) The effects of high-stakes testing on student motivation and learning. *Educational Leadership*, 60.5, pp. 32–38.

Anders, P., Hoffman, J. and Duffy, G. (2000) 'Teaching teachers to teach reading: paradigm shifts, persistent problems, and challenges' in M. Kamil, P. Mosenthal, P. D. Pearson and R. Barr (eds.) *Handbook of Reading Research.* vol. 3, pp. 719–742. Mahwah, NJ: Erlbaum.

Darling-Hammond, L. (2000) Teacher quality and student achievement: a review of state policy evidence. *Educational Policy Analysis Archives*, 8.1. Available online at *http://epaa.asu.edu/epaa/v8nl/*.

Duffy, G. and Hoffman, J. (1999) In pursuit of an illusion: the flawed search for a perfect method. *The Reading Teacher*, 53.1, pp. 10–16.

Florida's Reading Best Practices Center (FRBPC) (2000) *Reading Tools for Schools: Building & measuring K-12 reading best practices.* Palatka, Florida: NEFEC.

Garan, E. (2002) *Resisting Reading Mandates: How to triumph with the truth.* Portsmouth, NH: Heinemann.

Hoffman, J., Assaf, L. and Paris, S. (2001) High-stakes testing in reading: today in Texas, tomorrow? *The Reading Teacher*, 54.5, pp. 482–492.

Hughes, M., Cash, M., Klingner, J. and Ahwee, S. (2001) Professional development programs in reading: a national survey of district directors. *National Reading Conference Yearbook*, 50, pp. 275–286.

Lamme, L., Fu, D., Johnson, J. and Savage, D. (2002) Helping kindergarten writers move toward independence. *Early Childhood Education Journal*, 30.2, pp. 74–79.

Lasley, T. (1992) Education's 'Impossible dream': collaboration. *Teacher Education and Practice*, 7.2, pp. 17–22.

Mathison, S. and Freeman, M. (2003) Constraining elementary teachers' work: dilemmas and paradoxes created by state mandated testing. *Educational Policy Analysis Archives*, 11.4. Also available at *http://epaa.asu.edu/epaa/v11n34/*.

Moll, L. (1992) 'Literacy research in community and classroom: a sociocultural approach' in R. Beach, J. Green, M. Kamil and T. Shanahan (eds.) *Multidisciplinary Perspectives on Literacy Research*, pp. 211–244. Urbana, Illinois: National Conference on Research in English and National Council of Teachers of English.

Nieto, S. (2003) *What Keeps Teachers Going.* New York: Teachers College Press.

Pappas, C. and Zecker, L. (2000) *Teacher Inquiries in Literacy Teaching-Learning: Learning to collaborate in elementary urban classrooms.* Mahwah, NJ: Erlbaum.

Welch, M. (1998) Collaboration: staying on the bandwagon. *Journal of Teacher Education*, 49.1, pp. 26–37.

STUDY GUIDE

1. What are the attributes of exemplary literacy teachers? (Morrow, et al.; Duffy; Fang, Fu & Lamme)
2. What do effective literacy classrooms look like physically? What types of reading and writing experiences are provided and how are skills taught in these classrooms? How are these classrooms managed? (Morrow, et al.)
3. What does the study of exemplary teachers tell us about what really matters in ensuring high quality classroom instruction? (Morrow, et al.; Duffy)
4. What steps can beginning or novice teachers take toward becoming exemplary teachers? (Morrow, et al.; Duffy; Fang, Fu & Lamme)
5. In the field of reading education, the pedagogical pendulum swings from one end to the other periodically and teachers are often caught between a rock and a hard place. Discuss ways in which teachers can respond to such a tension. (Duffy; Fang, Fu & Lamme)
6. What is visioning? Why is it important for teachers? How can teacher educators help prospective and in-service teachers develop their visions? (Duffy)
7. What are the characteristics of effective professional development models? (Fang, Fu & Lamme)
8. What can be done to support practicing teachers effectively so that they can become independent, informed instructional decision makers in the current educational climate? (Fang, Fu & Lamme)

INQUIRY PROJECTS

1. Observe an effective and a less effective teacher for one typical day. Compare and contrast their uses of time, text, talk, task, test, and management skills in instruction. Discuss the impact of their instructional practices on student engagement and achievement in class. In addition, interview these teachers about whether and how existing school culture and structure affect their teaching effectiveness.
2. Teachers and teacher education programs are under constant attack by the media for their perceived ineffectiveness in public education and teacher preparation. Find out what the specific accusations are and search for evidence that counters these arguments. Based on your investigation, draft an editorial for your local newspaper that responds to unwarranted attacks and presents a more balanced portrayal of teachers and/or teacher education.
3. Interview one or two reading teachers with at least 20–30 years of teaching experience. Ask them to talk about whether, and how, reading methods and materials have changed over the past few decades. Invite them to share insights into their own growth and development as reading teachers in light of these pendulum swings.
4. Conduct a survey of professional development programs for the past year in a local school. Gather information from teachers and principals on the following aspects:

   a. What were the topics addressed and how were they selected?
   b. What were the funding sources?
   c. Who were the speakers?
   d. What formats were typically used?
   e. What incentives were given to encourage teacher participation?
   f. To what extent did teachers implement what they learned?
   g. How was implementation monitored?
   h. Were teachers satisfied with the existing professional development model?
   i. What, if anything, can be done to enhance teachers' professional development opportunities?

Share your findings with the class and suggest ways in which existing models of professional development can be enhanced.

FURTHER READING

Allington, R., & Johnston, P. (2002). *Reading to learn: Lessons from exemplary fourth grade classrooms*. New York: Guilford Press.

Berlinger, D. (2000). A personal response to those who bash teacher education. *Journal of Teacher Education, 51*(5), 358–371.

Block, C., & Mangieri, J. (2003). *Exemplary literacy teachers: Promoting success for all children in grades K–5*. New York: Guilford Press

Chall, J. (2002). *The academic achievement challenge: What really works in the classroom?* New York: Guilford Press.

Duffy, G., & Hoffman, J. (1999). In pursuit of an illusion: The flawed search for a perfect method. *The Reading Teacher, 53*(1), 10–16.

Hoffman, J., & Pearson, D. (2000). Reading teacher education in the next millennium: What your grandmother's teacher didn't know that your granddaughter's teacher should. *Reading Research Quarterly, 35*(1), 28–44.

Lieberman, T. (2000). *Slanting the story: The forces that shape the news*. New York: The New Press.

Lyons, C., & Pinnell, G. S. (2001). *Systems for change in literacy education: A guide to professional development*. Portsmouth, NH: Heinemann.

Moats, L. (1999). *Teaching reading is rocket science: What expert teachers of reading should know and be able to do*. Washington, DC: American Federation of Teachers.

Morrow, L., Gambrell, L., & Pressley, M. (2003). *Best practices in literacy instruction*. New York: Guilford Press.

Nieto, S. (2003). *What keeps teachers going?* New York: Teachers College Press.

Pressley, M. (2002). *Reading instruction that works: The case for balanced teaching* (2nd ed.). New York: Guilford Press.

Pressley, M. Allington, R., Wharton-McDonald, Block, C., & Morrow, L. (2001). *Learning to read: Lessons from exemplary first grade classrooms*. New York: Guilford Press.

Smith, F. (2003). *Unspeakable acts, unnatural practices: Flaws and fallacies in "scientific" reading instruction*. Portsmouth, NH: Heinemann.

Smith, N. B. (2002). *American reading instruction*. Newark, NJ: International Reading Association.